S0-AAM-113

A Dictionary of Abstract Painting

Translated from the French

Dictionnaire de la Peinture Abstraite

(FERNAND HAZAN ÉDITEUR, PARIS)

by LIONEL IZOD, JOHN MONTAGUE
and FRANCIS SCARFE

First published in 1958

1. 1.

CATALOGUE No. 6007/U

ALL RIGHTS RESERVED S. P. A. D. E. M. AND A. D. A. G. P. PARIS

PRINTED IN FRANCE

A DICTIONARY

of

ABSTRACT PAINTING

preceded by a
History of Abstract Painting

———

MICHEL SEUPHOR

METHUEN AND CO LTD
II NEW FETTER LANE · LONDON E.C. 4

FOREWORD

Although a great deal has been written about abstract painting, there is no one work available which gives a comprehensive historical survey of the subject for all countries in which this new development has manifested itself. The study published by Michel Seuphor some years ago was confined in its historical scope to the first ten years of abstract art and hence gives little indication as to what happened after 1920.

The present work does not pretend to list the name of every abstract painter—obviously an impossible task—nor to make a final critical selection. It will however, we venture to think, provide the general public, students of art and artists themselves with a source of information which has been lacking up to the present time.

This book may be used in three ways: it may be read as a historical work, it may be perused from time to time as an album, or it may be kept at hand as a reference work full of accurate and ample information.

The illustrations have been chosen so as to give the widest possible view of the subject, although this concern has not been allowed to take precedence over such important considerations as the quality of the work illustrated or the proven value of the artist.

The chronological chart given on pages 106 to 113 provides an ever-present guide to the reader who wishes to place a particular development in its historical context as he reads, or to take in at a glance the whole history of abstract art from 1910 to 1956.

THE PUBLISHER

*The Publishers
wish to express their gratitude
to the many Artists, Collectors and
Art Galleries
whose kindness and cooperation
have made it possible to assemble
the material for this book.*

CONTENTS

PART I
History of Abstract Painting

I

PRELIMINARIES. A DEFINITION. THE IMPRESSIONISTS' AWARENESS
OF ABSTRACTION. ABSTRACT ART AND NATURE.
FREEDOM AND DIFFICULTY OF ABSTRACT ART.

It is by no means easy, at this stage, to give a generally acceptable definition of abstract art. From one standpoint it is evident that its authority and range have so widened in recent years that there are few or no young artists, however great or slight their ability, who have no share whatever in its development, at least through some particular aspect of their work. On the other hand we must not overlook the fact that certain artists, and by no means the least important, are suspicious of the term 'abstract' art, if not of the thing itself, and that they try to adopt a non-committal position in order to safeguard their own individualism, seeing present-day 'Abstract' painters as mere offshoots or hangers-on of the earlier abstractionists. Thus critical jargon falls back on terms like *content* and *legibility* or *readability* as if a human work could possibly be devoid of content, and as if a painted work could conform to the same requirements as a written text. But even in literature the readable is not necessarily good, any more than what is unreadable.

But no amount of painting with 'content' or more readable content can save artists from inevitably belonging to their own time. However much they recoil from the term, the painted object which is carried out of their studio shows them to be just as 'abstract' as those whom they denounce as a clique. Their arguments are of no avail, because, in the mid-twentieth century, in matters of art the spirit of the age has firmly lodged itself in abstraction. This is so much the case that we now automatically approach and interpret all works of art, whether ancient or modern, according to abstract data and principles. Faced with some Old Master, the mind of 1955 man tends to interpret in terms of composition, points of technique, psychological details, and we try to penetrate into the character of the man himself by revealing, through a minute analysis of the work of art, the reservations and discoveries, the hesitations and audacities of the painter. Our admiration swings between a synthesis effected on broad schematic lines and an analysis of craftsmanship, while we tend to forget at the same time that the spectator of a few centuries ago was concerned with nothing but the 'subject' in the proper sense of the term, the *what* and not the *how*.

For some of us the *Sistine Madonna* is one of Raphael's finest works because of its outstandingly powerful composition. For the painter's contemporaries this sense of power no doubt lay in the expressive faces of the Virgin and Child. But nowadays we are less attracted by things in themselves than by the way in which they are presented: we find a man's manner of walking more revealing than his objective. The hundreds of little strokes criss-crossed and juxtaposed in bewildering variety on the back of Rembrandt's *Recumbent Negress* afford us more visual pleasure than the woman's back itself, for there are better specimens to be found in albums of photographers' nudes, while we are delighted to find an amplification of Rembrandt's strokes in an abstract by De Staël. This seems to bring an understanding of Rembrandt within the layman's reach and at the same time to demonstrate De Staël's greatness as a draughtsman. In the simplest possible terms, we are looking at art through glasses appropriate to the century we are living in, and not through those we inherit from previous generations. Whether people like it or not these modern 'glasses' exist and are nothing more nor less than *abstraction*. However bitterly the schools and dealers might wrangle over the word's possible meanings, we see all art in terms of its abstract qualities, regardless of its degree of figurativeness or non-figurativeness, representation or non-representation, objectivity or subjectivity.

In any case it is thanks to these squabbles and barrages of apparently futile arguments that abstract art has extended its influence wherever young artists are trained all over the world, as well as penetrating the circles of dealers and amateurs. We need not worry unduly over the historical errors brought about through hasty journalism, nor over half-baked definitions, quibbles over terminology, nor even the bullying and anger that accompanied this change: all this creates a stir and serves to draw the attention of a 'general' public impervious to everything but shouts and posters. After the sandwich-boards comes the show itself, and something positive remains which is gradually sifted and shaped in the mind. It is then time for the historian and the detached interpreter to begin their work.

Let us first try to offer some definition of the material to be dealt with in this book. We shall take as our antinomies figurative painting (or *figuration*) and abstract painting (or *abstraction*) (1).

2

A painting is to be called abstract when it is impossible to recognize in it the slightest trace of that objective reality which makes up the normal background of our everyday existence: in other words, a painting is abstract when the absence of any other form of sensible reality compels us to regard it purely as painting and as nothing else, and to judge it according to values that have nothing to do with representation or with the imitation or reproduction of some other thing. It follows that a transposition of nature, even when it is very far-fetched, remains figurative and is *figuration*; but it also follows that a transposition taken to the point where nothing in the work suggests or evokes some basic naturalistic subject—a transposition, therefore, which to the naked eye does not even imply the act of transposition itself—will rightly be called abstract, *abstraction*.

Thus, even in cases when some representation or transposition of shapes has served as a point of departure, whether in the painter's mind or just on the canvas, the work is to be deemed abstract, providing that no aspect of that point of departure remains recognizable, and so long as the work, *ipso facto,* has nothing to convey to us except the pure elements of composition and colour (2).

Conversely, we shall say that any work of art which, though setting out from abstract principles or processes, either by accident or playfully embodies representational elements, however fantastic or extraordinary they appear, cannot be called abstract (3).

But even if a canvas is strictly abstract—that is to say neither representing, interpreting or transposing any reality from the external world, this cannot prevent our imagination from discerning subjects in it—such as those shapes that people fancy they see in the clouds—that had nothing to do with the painter's own intentions. The abstract painter must do all he can to avoid such representational accidents, though of course he cannot be held responsible for the spectator's whims.

Long before it existed in actual fact, abstraction was "in the air" and painters intuitively tried to grasp it, like the 'frozen syllables' of Mandeville and Rabelais. They were not so lucky as Pantagruel; the words eluded them and the most notorious passwords and incantations failed to make them sing before they were fully matured. Those passwords, however, came as so many unmistakable forewarnings of a new age. We could trot out dozens of quotations from Baudelaire to Cézanne, from Van Gogh to Seurat and Maurice Denis, all centred on the same realisation, that painting is not a matter of subject but of colour, form, sensibility, composition (4). But they felt themselves under no obligation on this account to leave out the theme altogether, and perhaps they were not far wrong, since we all admire the masterpieces they left us. But now that we can look back on it all we cannot help noticing a certain contradiction between their often extreme pronouncements and their actual behaviour as painters. This was because the theory of the abstract in art could only gradually be translated into actual works, and it had to be by a process of evolution rather than revolution. Great discoveries are made slowly, and there is no *eureka* without a long and tedious preparation behind it.

It is true that in 1841 or thereabouts Turner came so close to abstract painting that his works have no parallel in his century. They can be explained only in terms of the 'long preparation' I have mentioned. By the time he was sixty Turner had reached the end of a long evolution in the course of which he had stated the problems of representation and expression on the canvas, with an ever-increasing frankness that enables us to trace the gradual development of his bold yet calm resolve to find a solution to the paradox.

The Impressionists took a long time to catch up with the great English painter. But there are many moments of abstract beauty in some of their works, all arising from the same premonition in the artist. Whether in works that were delicate and mild, or startlingly violent, Impressionism like Fauvism and Cubism later on was a pioneer in abstract painting, and many unpretentious canvases of the period still teem with marvellous lessons for our young abstract painters. I am not thinking only of Cézanne, but of works by Van Gogh (*The wheat-field,* the *Landscape with rooks*), Renoir (*Women in a field*), Claude Monet (*The poppy-field*). In the last of these paintings, in particular, the subtle proportions of red and blue show a craftsmanship fully aware of abstract composition. There is an exquisite delicacy in the *parasol-étoile,* its ultramarine bringing out the redness of the flowers and uttering a kind of gentle exclamation in response to the diffused, soft blue of the sky. But even that is not the finest discovery made in this canvas. To my mind it is to be seen in the discreet stretch of light green just above the line of the horizon, without which the darker green of the belt of trees would be flat or would need stressing,—a solution which would have ruined the general effect which was meant to be calm and soothing. Thus everything in this work is quite simple, as is the case in every really beautiful work, yet there is nothing banal about it.

At this point I can imagine some readers asking "What more can

4

abstract art possibly offer us, than this ? Here we can enjoy non-representation and representation at the same time. What is there wrong in superimposing a real landscape on to pure art ? The truth is that this offers not less, but more than does abstract art." To this I would reply that Monet's first intention was certainly to paint a landscape, and that in order to dispense with subject and paint nothing but *a painting* a certain evolution, or call it if you like a slow revolution, had to be gone through. I would add that art is worth exactly as much as the spectator is able to put into it, and that the spectator at the moment is the man of 1955 and not of 1873.

I think the time has come to assert that abstraction in art does not mean being anti-nature. There is too much of nature in us for it to be other than an intrinsic part of our make-up. There would be no point in trying to rid our inner field of experience of all those visions and perceptions that have impressed themselves on our minds since childhood. It is well known, also, that the most profound visual sensations automatically give rise to symbols which are then nourished by the subconscious, and which cannot but exteriorise themselves in art in a fairly obvious way.

Altogether to exclude nature from our thoughts and works would amount to a harsh form of mental repression, resulting in a kind of narrow mental dictatorship. It cannot be denied, however, that since 1912 the

KLEE. VIBRATION OF SOUTHERN FLORA. WATER-COLOUR, 1927.
Private Collection.

5

most outstanding works and those most calculated to enrich the human mind seem to have been made in the absence of any apparent help from external nature, which incidentally, Cubism tended more and more to reduce to a *still*-life, a nature-*morte*.

Further misunderstanding may be avoided by adding that abstract art does not eliminate nature but expresses it in a different way. The Impressionist used to set up his easel in front of his subject, against the background of the external world; but the abstract painter instals himself, so to speak, in the domain of inwardness, in the inner life, or, to put it another way, he opens up this inner life before the canvas with which he then communes in secret. The mind of man is the greatest of unexplored territories, and it is there that the greatest discoveries are to be made. It is a microcosm in which dream and speculation, idealism and love flourish side by side, and it bears the indelible marks of our experience of material nature. Thus it is not surprising if some unexpected reminiscence of nature occurs in the works of an abstract painter. The artist abhors dogmatism of any kind and to ban any particular thing (black is not a colour !) causes more violent reactions in the field of the arts than elsewhere. It is undeniable that after practising abstract art for some years, certain artists finally returned to representational or figurative art, only to produce threadbare commonplaces and forfeit any claim to our interest. The protection of a few critical mandarins and magazines does nothing to soften their fall, but only makes it the more spectacular. This is because in 1955, as in 1912, the hard way, but the way along which discoveries are to be made, still lies in abstraction.

It is a long and complicated task for any young painter to find his own personal voice and keep it intact and natural. It is a painful triumph over the self, and when it is carried out sincerely and profoundly, in depth, it is bound to be an heroic undertaking.

Even from the outside it looks like a wager, a wild undertaking. Everything seems to have been done already: there are now abstract painters all over the world, every possible form has been invented. For a sensitive person, strict, uncompromising abstraction might well look like a kind of hit or miss. All drawing leads to the ideogram. Everything suggests an image to the fertile imagination: a square is a house, a wavy line a river, a circle the moon, a few dots are the starry sky. If you let the pen doodle on a sheet of paper it is not long before it suggests a human or other figure. Join up a few lines at the foot of the page and you have a tree, a plant, a flame or a fan. Whether you accept these suggestions or dismiss them in

6

KANDINSKY. DRAWING FOR COMPOSITION NO. 2. INDIAN INK, 1910.

your search for something more unusual, you are returning to the figurative world and rediscovering the delights of childhood. The greatest of such enchanters is Paul Klee. He covers a sheet all over with horizontal lines, then adds a few vertical strokes and creates a palace, a village, a fairy-like tower. The towers are turned upside-down and Klee only has to write the word 'rain' under his drawing to suggest cloud-castles slowly pouring down on to the earth. A profound humorist, gifted with a light touch, full of poetic surprises and forever flirting with the absurd, Klee has produced few works that do not contain some allusion to external nature.

The abstract work, on the other hand, is one in which not the slightest suggestion of an image is voluntarily accepted by the artist.

7

2

PERSISTENCE AND VITALITY OF ABSTRACT ART. A UNIVERSAL LANGUAGE. HISTORY AND THE LAW OF CHANGE. AN ART CORRESPONDING TO OUR AGE. THE DISCOVERY OF THE SELF.

Those who have followed the course of abstract art over the past 20 or 30 years will have been struck by its persistence. When the *Cercle et Carré* exhibition was held in April 1930, the Parisian press informed us that such painting was "the mere ghost of an experiment which we thought had died long ago," and that "all this has nothing new to offer." In 1955 the same outbursts of weariness and boredom, if not anger, can be heard at any exhibition of abstract art: "about time the joke was buried. . . same old bag of tricks. . . poor old public. . . "

Maybe. But things become entirely different if we are patient enough to take a closer look. Then we see that abstract art has never stopped adding to its range and means of expression, never faltered in its search for greater depth. If the ABC of this language was firmly established in the 'heroic' phase by Kandinsky, Mondrian, Delaunay and Malevitch, this does not mean that everything has been said in the same language. The critics' ignorance and the public's sophisticated grumbling were unable to prevent it from branching out into the remotest corners of the western world, where it has won over intelligent collectors and gained a hold, even a considerable hold, in civic museums and galleries. Kandinsky and Mondrian, both of whom lived to a good age, thanks to their long working life were able to show their successors what a range of values can be drawn out of such simple elements; Kandinsky stressing inventiveness and Mondrian the importance of increasing depth.

The other movements or schools which sprang up in such great numbers all over the world in the past hundred years all enjoyed a much shorter span of life. At the moment of writing (1955), abstract painting has flourished for forty years and shows no signs of slackening vitality. Those critics who began by encouraging it but who now pull a long face at some geometrical composition by Vasarely or some colour-composition by Riopelle, remind me of Zola when, throwing over his former Impressionist friends in 1896, he voiced his disillusionment in a notorious article in the *Figaro* which does not stand to his credit: "Not a single artist in this

8

KANDINSKY. SKETCH 1912.
Joseph Slifka Collection, New York.

group," wrote the author of *L'Œuvre*, "has succeeded in translating into paint, with the slightest power of finality, the new formula which is to be observed in snippets on their various canvases. . . They are all fore-runners. The genius is yet to be born. . . They are all unequal to the task they have set themselves, they can't talk, they stutter." At the Jeu de Paume Museum (for example) we can now go and see exactly what stuttering meant. No oracle is needed to predict that fifty years hence some other Jeu de Paume will be showing an astonished public those masterpieces of abstract art that are being painted at the present time and which we are treating with contempt.

But those who have been keeping a close watch on art during the past twenty or thirty years will have also noticed that in the twentieth century every form of art has evolved in the direction of abstraction. Thus the term abstract art cannot be used to single out any school, nor any movement however widespread. It is a universal phenomenon, a universal language.

Abstract art has lasted too long for it still to be put down to snobbery, while its styles and its types of expression are too numerous and different

9

for it to be in any danger of being called academic. It would be more accurate as well as simpler to regard it as a fresh departure, setting out from a new principle or datum, to wit *the free expression of the self,* regardless of any laws but those invented by the artist or which his chosen material imposes on him. As for such formulas as "a new basis for a more direct expression of man" or "a healthier foundation for the life of the mind", I am disinclined to speak in terms of 'bases' or 'foundations' in referring to abstract art in general, for such words imply the concept of a plan or theory, and therefore of some system or method. There are twenty different systems or methods of abstract art, and if at times some look more valid than others, that is because the success or otherwise of systems depends entirely on the talents that exploit them at any given moment, or the stature of the genius who thrusts them aside.

Abstract art is art itself, the art of all time, but grasped in its most intimate substance, I mean the apprehension of whatever it is which determines that art is art and not just illustration or education or propaganda or a substitute for literature or religion. It is perhaps a dangerous and certainly a shocking venture. I am not likely to be found saying that abstract art is easy art. There is no abstract art without an awareness, however dim or hard to express in words, of the profound nature of art, or without a secret union between the artist and art integrally itself, to the exclusion of any other alliance. Not a philosophy but a clairvoyance, an insight. And that insight could not possibly express itself in any other way than the very act of creating. From now on man's mind will express itself by the creator's direct action on passive material, without passing, as formerly, through the medium of such external forms as are already generally admitted as being 'beautiful' or 'suitable for pictures'.

A new departure in art, then, but one to which there is no need to presuppose any base or foundation: it strikes out and radiates in every direction, without any particular direction being the dominant one.

This upsets many values which people thought were permanently assured, and that is why abstract art arouses almost as much hostility half way through the century as it did thirty years ago. But its arrival was foretold in the logical progression of the life of art itself. We can be sure that mockery, jibes, violence (cries of 'degenerate art') nor even the shrugged shoulders of the indifferent can never long prevail against the organic evolution of things.

Even within the ranks of these new artists, the various tendencies and their spokesmen are waging a merciless war. Listening to some of them, anyone might take abstract art to be an endless process of destruction, or imagine that nobody has the right to paint unless he is forever in a state of hypnotic trance, or who does not find his daily thrill in a kind of frenzy of painting which is bound to end in some form of aggressiveness. According to others, abstract art, which they assert alone deserves to be called art, cannot be anything but a series of exercises in construction, a matter of clever scaffolding and blueprints put out by somewhat bashful architects. So we must take our stand outside all that and take no part in such squabbles, if we are to see that abstract art is simply the stage that has now been reached in the general evolution of the arts, the multiform style of twentieth-century art.

Life is change.

Like man in the course of his personal existence, societies undergo a transformation of the mind or spirit, as well as of their outward appearance. The universe is a continuous creation, a bearing or 'bringing forth' in Biblical terms, and all its elements are subject, like the world, itself, to the great law of mutation or change. It might be said that history is only an analytical account of the transformation of mankind of which art is the direct and synthetical expression. The essence of successive societies is embodied in the divers forms of art which have been left to us over the centuries. It is an explicit statement, complete in itself and in need of no commentary: for instance the XIIIth century can be read more easily in the statuary of Chartres cathedral than in the most learned history-books. The tedious, futile series of battles and political upheavals seems to have crawled out of the yellow press, when compared with those tangible witnesses we find in works of art. And what other conceivable evidence for the XIIIth century could there be, than those anonymous illustrations of the Scriptures, made by those sculptors and glass-makers who were as humble as they were effective ?

Our century, also, has its own face, its own look, which is reflected in an art made in its own image. It is a century of chain-invention, of short-lived freaks, confused aspirations, violent sensations, accompanied by all the diseases of a society whose institutions are crumbling and in which the very conditions of life are fragile, constantly threatened by a cycle of crises. These features are all to be observed in block letters in the evolutions or revolutions that have occurred in art since the dawn of the century.

There is, however, one dominant idea that permeates the apparent disorder of our time, an idea that determines its spiritual outlook and controls all its reactions whenever they show the slightest hint of seriousness. That is the idea of liberty. I cannot think of a more appropriate word to convey the fundamental characteristic of modern art as a whole. Not only does it define it according to its underlying psychological basis, but the word encloses and sums up all its visible manifestations. There is freedom to say everything, to invent everything, to create a style for its own sake, to prefer discord to harmony, to choose the rule and set limits to it, a freedom from both constraint and licence.

It is the most normal thing in the world for liberty to have its opponents at the best of times, always slandering and failing to understand it. There is a mystery of freedom for every individual, but some are perhaps

ROBERT DELAUNAY. WINDOW NO. 2. 1912.
S. D. Collection, Paris.

12

MONDRIAN. COMPOSITION. 1913
Kröller-Müller Museum, Otterlo.

not mature enough to cleave to it, or else they are inadequately prepared by a misguided education. In any case we know now, after half a century of experiments, that freedom is the best of masters in all that concerns art.

It is a master who by no means condemns the disciplines, easy though that might be to believe. The very opposite is true, for more surely than any other master, liberty teaches restraint and measure through trials and errors of every kind. It alone can enable a personality to discover itself and open out. That is why modern art owes to liberty its discoveries, its infinite variety and freshness.

The same fifty years of experiment has proved that the traditional images—nudes, landscapes, still-lives—have all lost their substance and have nothing essential to offer man to-day. Or, rather, the landscape, fruit-dish or mandoline can only be accepted in so far as they are pretexts for the *real subject*—which however has now come to the forefront—that is to say, painting in itself and for itself.

Thus it has been only logical to take cubism to its natural conclusions, and to cut out the traditional subject and give final expression, in a clear style and in absolute liberty, to the values of pure art as they appear to the artist.

Abstract art came into being when, at almost the same time and in different parts of Europe, there appeared a number of fearless creators who saw, at a glance, both the evidence of an existing problem and evidence of how it could be solved.

This happened between 1910 and 1917. The centres in question were Paris, Munich, Moscow, Florence, Zurich and Amsterdam. The main protagonists were Kandinsky, Larionov, Kupka, Picabia, Mondrian, Delaunay, Malevitch, Magnelli and Arp. Others followed quickly in their wake. A hundred men presented themselves to replace those who practically stopped painting (such as Larionov), or who for varying periods returned to figurative painting (Picabia, Delaunay, Magnelli). It gradually became obvious that there were as many new styles as there were truly creative artists. The greatest of these had their usual band of slavish imitators whose mediocrity did not long pass unnoticed, since an art freed from subject implies and enforces the absolute necessity for creativeness. Thus, under the cheerful finery of 'liberty', obligatory invention has become the new tyrant of art. Henceforward any artist failing to invent himself and become the happy prospector of an autonomous world, was to be condemned out of hand. The object of art became and is now more than ever, to find a personal and inexhaustible mode of expression, the image of our profound inner being.

This put an end to the harlequins, ray-fish, stuffed tomatoes and such-like trifles. Subject in itself only serves to lull the conscience of the uncreative artist, as he basks in sweet oblivion in the arms of short-term art which can offer the amateur nothing but wallowing in shallow enjoyment.

It is in the manifold tendencies of abstract art that modern man, who is equally manifold, can recognise his own being and find once more some substantial nourishment. I mean that he finds in it some response to his own distinct sensibility, the sensibility of the town-dweller involved in the rhythm and technics of present-day life, as well as an answer to his need for harmony and novelty, equilibrium and surprise, the complex and the simple. It is not surprising, then, if abstract art, in spite of all that tries to stand in its way, is finding a world-wide and ever-increasing favour, for it is the only art that really coincides with the age we live in.

Every man is a complete world in himself, full of astonishing poten-tialities; but every man is also a member of a spiritual family whose well-being he shares. The twentieth century is such a 'family'. It has already bequeathed us an infinitely precious legacy, though so many eyes refuse to see and so many ears refuse to hear it.

Once we have learnt to admire the Fauves and the great Cubists, it behoves us to try and understand those who, having learnt from those predecessors and from the canvases they painted in their days of struggle, have each in his own way invented an independent art of painting.

It so happens, by a sort of miracle, that this intensely individualistic art sums up again and again the whole art of painting, whenever it is grafted on to some richly-endowed sensibility which is both honest with itself and capable of giving and communicating itself.

Thus the key to abstract art lies in the discovery of the self and the exploitation, by a suitable technique, of that hidden store of virgin material which we all carry within us, and to which we must find a path—and this is perhaps the hardest aspect of the artist's work—before it can be brought to light.

The next important question is to consider every work in its proper order, watching its apparent tendencies and seeking its autonomous laws. The greatest pleasure for those who care for art is no longer, as it used to be, a matter of penetrating into the represented object by way of a temperament; but to uncover whatever it is in the depths of the artist that dictates the intentions of his work: that is to say, to follow the very process of composition step by step, apprehending it from the inside, much as an orchestra interprets music. The sensitive critic or the informed lover of art can determine where and by virtue of what the artist has remained or failed to remain faithful to himself. And it is precisely at the points where he is unfaithful that we perhaps come closest to the crucial moment of discovery, the enlarging of the self, the shedding of past selves.

3

KANDINSKY AND MONDRIAN.

The immediate forerunners of abstract art, as we know, were Fauvism and Cubism. The influence of the Fauves was decisive in the case of Kandinsky, while Mondrian's formation was completed by that of the Cubists. 1906 and 1912 are two important dates here. The first was not only the year of the death of Cézanne, whose influence on early Cubism has been fully explored; it was also the year when Bergson's *Creative Evolution* appeared, and when Kandinsky spent a long spell in or near Paris. There he sustained the full shock of the Fauves and Gauguin (through the Gauguin retrospective exhibition at the Autumn Salon, showing 227 exhibits). It was after that year's stay in Paris (or rather Sèvres) that Kandinsky emerged from the New Secession style that characterised his previous work, and began to assert an independent personality. (5) As for the year 1912, it found Mondrian in Paris, unreservedly submitting to the influence of Cubism which was to lead him very soon to works that were remarkably mature in their abstraction, and whose originality was at once noticed by Apollinaire.

Both Kandinsky and Mondrian were older in years than the Cubists and Fauves. What the latter discovered—apparently by accident—found a ready soil in the Russian and Dutch painters, both arduously prepared

MONDRIAN. COMPOSITION IN RED, BLUE AND YELLOW. 1930.
Bartos Collection, New York.

16

KANDINSKY. BLACK POINT. 1937.
Jucker Collection, Milan.

by their earlier technical experiments as well as by a certain amount of philosophical speculation. Braque, Picasso, Léger, Delaunay and Matisse were first and foremost painters. Kandinsky and Mondrian were both painters and thinkers, for whom the problems of art could not be approached apart from the other problems facing man. They aimed not only at renewing painting, but thought that man must transform himself and that the whole of mankind is moving towards an age of material and spiritual betterment. The artist appeared to them the person best qualified for preparing and announcing the golden age. That is why the painted work and the painting man must be identical. The evolution of art is unthinkable without a parallel internal development in man himself. Fauves and Cubists are painters and have no intention of being taken for anything else, whereas Kandinsky and Mondrian are prophets.

In Russia, Kandinsky had at first embarked on a career as a scientist. He only turned to painting when he was approaching thirty, impelled by a genuine 'inner necessity' which he had repressed for some years. In his writings on the philosophy of art during his Munich period the term 'inner necessity' constantly recurred, and had an important part to play. It was on this that he based the whole aesthetic justification of his work, after it had already served to justify his career as a painter. After the necessary preliminaries (studies in Munich academies, some instructive travelling) and once he had completed his philosophy of art, (6) Kandinsky flung himself into an orgy of production. A baffling world of forms and colours teemed from his apparently delirious brush. Was it delirium or ecstasy? This dramatic phase in Kandinsky's abstraction still amazes us by its surging overflow, its resonant lyricism, its Wagnerian violence full of clarion-calls. It is the 'Durchbruch', a breaking-through or more precisely a demolition, the battering of the ram on the walls of traditional painting. After a few years this generous strength gradually calmed down. In about 1921 Kandinsky came to accept the geometrical studies of Malevitch and the Russian Constructivists. His painting then progressively changed outwardly but its inventiveness lost nothing of its richness, density and warmth. For a time the presence of Klee could be felt in his work, which began to show touches of humour, and we are not suggesting that this was the least satisfactory part of his output. After 1933 he moved to Neuilly, living in a bright and comfortable flat on the banks of the Seine, where he painted pictures which for the most part are brilliant variations on themes to which he had long been partial. This period has often been called that of the "great synthesis", which is accurate enough so long as it is not taken to include the dramatic period, which finds no echo in it.

Mondrian's period of preparation lasted much longer. Between taking his first art-teaching diploma and his arrival in Paris some twenty-three years slipped by, but they were fruitful years. Rather later than Kandinsky he worked out his own philosophy of art, and the *Stijl* movement was founded on it. At the opposite pole from Kandinsky's, his painting was the pursuit of simplification, of essential measure and economy, at least once Cubism had shown him his way. From Cubism he drew an unexpected lesson, which was that pure rhythm may be reduced to a horizontal-vertical movement. There was only a step from that to the right-angle. He took several years in making that step, painting and meditating, then he laid the first stone of his system, which is that the whole language of painting (and the language of life itself) may be condensed into the dual-

18

ism of the rectangular tension of two straight lines set in a horizontal-vertical relationship. That and that alone makes construction possible. This was the birth of Neo-Plasticism. Till the end of his life, that is to say for another thirty years, Mondrian never diverged from this principle, slowly advancing towards an imaginary perfection which was always within arms'-reach yet always a bit farther on. That was his own expres-

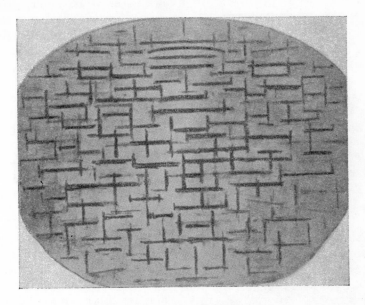

MONDRIAN. THE SEA. DRAWING. 1914.
Bally Collection, Montreux.

sion. "Don't you think, all the same, that it's just a little bit farther on?" he asked a friend as he showed him the latest canvas, which, as ever, must surely be a progress on the one before. Perhaps it was precisely in the last canvas he ever painted, the unfinished *Victory boogie-woogie,* that he came closest to this imaginary perfection. The very least we can say before his work is that we feel ourselves to be in the presence of a wonderful synthesis, fully alive yet denying nothing of the fundamental neo-plastic principle.

Mondrian and Kandinsky represent two different aspects of human genius, crystallised into two archetypes, infinite patience and saintly

19

impatience. According to our temperament we will be drawn towards one or the other, or perhaps towards each in turn. If genius is something like the toil of a bee, the distillation drop by drop of some unique and all-inclusive essence, then we will favour Mondrian. But if intelligence is restless and multiple, if truth progresses in immense leaps, if creation is a crazy sparkling of treasures, the overflow of some unfathomable primal cause, then we will choose Kandinsky and see in him the Ariel of abstract painters. Externally these two great personalities were not unlike, avoiding eccentric manners or dress and preferring the correct turn-out of the professional man to that of the bohemian. But Mondrian's threadbare smartness hid a bleak, lonely existence, while Kandinsky never wanted for money, comfort or recognition. They were both gentlemanly and distinguished-looking and had a certain reserve that hinted at a timid childhood. But they had little in common and met rarely, though politely, in Paris during 1930 and after 1933.

MACDONALD-WRIGHT. SYNCHROMY. 1916.
Earl Stendhal Gallery, Los Angeles.

Kandinsky's merit lay in showing what marvels can be wrung from genuine freedom, and that the limits of the canvas allow of no excess. Mondrian's lay in his lesson of discipline and humility. Reducing his art to the simplest data ever used, he showed how spiritual stature grows with self-denial and how the poorest means are the purest, often the strongest.

20

ROBERT DELAUNAY. SIMULTANEOUS DISC. 1912.
Tremaine Collection, U.S.A.

4

ROBERT AND SONIA DELAUNAY. MORGAN RUSSELL AND MACDONALD-WRIGHT. KUPKA. PICABIA. PARIS AND MUNICH, 1912.

Between Mondrian's strict economy and Kandinsky's ebullience there was room for some restraining, conciliatory element. This place was filled by Robert Delaunay for a short time, just long enough for him to leave a few works of incomparable beauty, by which I mean his *Windows* of 1912.

We are constantly reminded of that exceptional year, 1912. 1912 is increasingly recognized as the peak year of this century's painting, a year of transition in which everything was begun afresh although the old disciplines were neither consciously nor finally cast aside; a year from which the main tendencies of abstract art have radiated and to which we can always turn in our search for origins, for the seed of invention. One of the most valuable and fertile of these was the gay, fresh painting of Delaunay, who

21

named his canvases after an expression of Eugène Chevreul's, *Simultaneous Contrasts*.

Delaunay was born in Paris, in the rue de Chaillot, not far from the present Musée d'Art Moderne. He was the jovial type of Frenchman, or rather a typical Parisian, with a ready tongue and those quick blue eyes which seem to dwell on nothing but look straight through everything. He always spoke his mind without mincing words, while his round, pink face made him the picture of health. For him life meant happiness, a sensual, physical happiness and he approached painting in the same spirit. It was in 1908 or 1909 that he read Eugène Chevreul, the physicist's, theory of simultaneous colours (7) which had already had such an influence on Seurat thirty years earlier. This confirmed the conclusions he had already reached intuitively. In the next few years his natural lyrical gifts found expression through the channel provided by these ideas. His main undertaking was in breaking down the prism and reassembling its elements on the canvas by a discreet though thorough division of surfaces. What Braque and Picasso did with a mandoline, fruit-dish or nude, Delaunay did with light itself, cutting it up and piecing it together again in a new way. This 'new way' implies personal research into the basic laws of painting. Apollinaire had already written "I like contemporary art because I love light more than anything: all men love light more than anything, having invented fire." Delaunay's work between 1911-1914 is a striking illustration of this thought. Like a child with its favorite toy he took the rainbow to pieces and improvised with the separate parts, but without ever going too far or betraying the rainbow's essence. He turned it into the very song of light, both airy and powerful.

Delaunay's works of that period are astonishing achievements. Form and idea are so closely united, the utterance so fused with the style, that in the forty years after him there was no painting capable of conveying such a sensation of physical joy, innocent serenity and strength combined— unless it be the painting of his wife, less candid and spiritually less spontaneous though it is.

In 1910 Delaunay married Sonia Terk, a Russian by birth, who was also a painter, and former wife of the German art-critic Wilhelm Uhde the discoverer of the 'Douanier' Rousseau. She gave him unfailing moral support and I have heard Delaunay say that but for her many a canvas would have remained unfinished. Delaunay was highly-strung, easily discouraged but just as easily stimulated to further effort.

Sonia Delaunay, whom Arthur Cravan so sharply but brillantly attacked in his pamphlet-review *Maintenant* is a remarkably gifted painter. Her large canvas *Electric Prisms,* painted in 1914 is one of the major works of that period. Like her husband she gave up abstract art while living in Portugal during the first World War. It was some years before they returned to pure painting; he in 1930 and she in 1937.

Much as Kandinsky set out from Fauvism and Mondrian from early synthetic Cubism (1912), Delaunay's abstract painting has its roots in Impressionism. The work of all three artists demonstrated well before 1914 that all forms of art are bound to move towards abstraction.

There were two American artists frequenting the same circles as Delaunay in 1911 and 1912. These were Morgan Russell and Stanton Macdonald-Wright, the former being of predominantly French extraction, and the latter, whose real name was Van Vranken, of Dutch parentage. They came to Paris in 1906 and 1907 respectively in order to study painting. Russell, who was the elder of the two, already has a good background as a painter, while Macdonald-Wright, less advanced technically, was trying to train himself through a scientific study of colour and reading—like Delaunay—the works of Eugène Chevreul and other physicists. Shortly after making each other's acquaintance they began to feel sufficiently sure of themselves to launch a movement of their own and founded Synchronism. Synchromism was a departure from the Orphism led by Delaunay. (8) The Synchromists were particularly active in 1913. In this one year they held a large exhibition in Munich, another at Bernheim Jeune's gallery in Paris, as well as sending canvases to the Salon des Indépendants and the Armory Show in New York which were both landmarks in the history of modern painting. But only one of their numerous works shown that year—and it was one of Russell's—can be regarded as abstract in the proper sense of the word: the other canvases are only secondary abstractions of subjects taken from nature, however advanced they might be. It was at this point that Russell's career really began, for at the Salon des Indépendants in the following year he showed his vast *Synchromy in Form* which, over thirty years later, was one of the key items in the exhibition of American abstract art held in the New York Museum of Modern Art in 1951.

Macdonald-Wright was not so quick to develop. The *Synchromatic Piece in Orange-Yellow* of 1915 and the *Synchromy in Red* of 1916 are undeniably abstract works, as was his *Nude or Synchromy in Blue* which was also painted in 1916. The Whitney Museum in New York owns one of his finest canvases, the *Oriental Synchromy in Blue-green* of 1918.

23

Morgan Russell and Macdonald-Wright are the real founders of American abstract art. They made a public and genuine profession of faith in abstract painting in the catalogue of their exhibition at Bernheim jeune's, but unfortunately they both gave up what they had so vigorously defended and returned to figurative art. This is mentioned as a matter of historical fact, and by no means in order to detract from their pioneer achievement.

Although they set out with the same principles these two Synchromist painters both managed to remain highly individual in their expression. The works they turned out during the 'heroic' period of their movement are historically very important for American culture and also show that they had very little influence on each other. Russell was the more temperamental painter of the two. His brushwork is thick and rich and his forms

MORGAN RUSSELL. TO THE LIFE OF MATTER. 1925.
M. S. Collection, Paris.

24

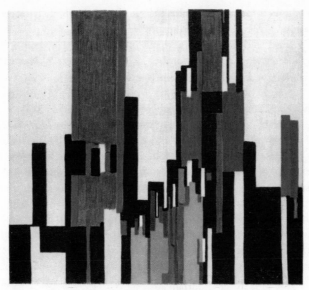

KUPKA. VERTICAL PLANES IN RED AND BLUE. 1913.
Louis Carré Gallery, Paris.

massive and violently set one against the other. His great composition of 1914 (*Synchromy in Form*) has affinities with some of Picabia's works of the previous year, notably the famous *Udnie* and *Edtaonisl* which are of much the same dimensions as Russell's work. But Russell's canvas is more elemental, like some Cyclopean wall.

Macdonald-Wright is a little closer to Delaunay. His canvases are as rich in colour as the Parisian painter's, though far less luminous, while his treatment is less firm. He seeks blurred effects, with submerged outlines, while producing an unusual kind of transparency, with a suggestion of a floating haziness corrected by a few clear, free strokes which impose some kind of order on the composition as a whole. This is in contrast to Russell, who always stresses the underlying skeletal structure, with a characteristic emphasis and a vigour that threatens to overflow the too narrow framework he imposes on it.

At about the same time another American, Patrick Henry Bruce, showed a few works at the Salon des Indépendants which also had some relationship to Delaunay's Orphism and some of Picabia's canvases. I met him much later, in about 1930 in his gloomy flat in the Place de Furstenberg, where he showed me a few coolly coloured pieces which he seemed very worried about. He himself was dispirited and disinclined to talk, and yet his painting radiated happiness and reasonableness. He died a few years later after destroying a large number of his paintings. Nevertheless a number were saved by Henri-Pierre Roché.

Frank Kupka was born in Czecho-Slovakia and came to Paris in 1895, where he made his name as an illustrator (*The Erynnies, Lysistrata, Prometheus*). He also painted portraits and a large *Nude* (1910) which is marvellously bright and fresh in its colouring. In 1911 he suddenly have up representational painting of nature, and in the 1912 Autumn Salon exhibited a *Fugue in two colours* and a *Chromatique chaude* which aroused much comment in the press. At the Salon des Indépendants in the following year he showed his *Vertical Planes, Brown Line Solo,* and at the Salon d'Automne his *Localisations des Mobiles graphiques*. After that he remained faithful to abstraction, except for the illustrations he made for the *Song of Songs* and a few other illustrated works which he published under a pseudonym.

We cannot consider Kupka's production since 1911 without our admiration being tinged with embarrassment, for his work seems to contain something of every style. This painter passes with disconcerting ease from the highly-coloured spherism of his *Newton's Discs* (1912) and their reminiscence of Delaunay, to a rectilinearism expressed in dull tones or a narrow range of colours (*Vertical Planes,* 1912 or 1913). After that he indulges in baroque impressions or nagging reminiscences of the 'Modern style' which made a name for his friend and compatriot Alphonse Mucha, first in Paris in 1900 and afterwards in New York and Chicago. However a very careful selection would show Kupka to have produced a number of works of the first order, which could be classified in two groups: the dionysiac or, rather, orphic, as Apollinaire might have put it, in which the composition is held together by the curved line alone (*Study on a Red Ground,* 1919; *The Fair,* 1921), and secondly those canvases in which only straight lines are used, with a marked preference for verticals, as in *Blue and Red Vertical Planes,* 1913, *Blue in Planes* of 1945, and *Vibrant in Lines,* 1948. In his most simplified works Kupka shows himself to be a romantic in his constant efforts to transcend painting through some literary preoccupation. In a word he is a kind of Gothic artist, either constructing solid but highly imaginative cathedral naves, or pouring out his exaltation in what might be called polyphonic paintings, evoking the lights of stained glass through their obsessional, echoing quality.

Picabia is even more disconcerting, for if Kupka went too far by trying to give everything at once, the Spanish painter has offered us a surfeit of both the worst and the best. In 1912 or 1913 he could be counted among the four or five best painters of his time, after which he blundered into every passing fashion so that the art to which he had contributed some undeniable masterpieces might easily have been misjudged as a phase in his careerism. His outstanding canvases were *Procession in Seville, Udnie, Edtaonisl, Remembrance of my beloved Udnie, New York, The Spring, Dances by the Spring, Star Dancer and her School,* all painted in 1912 or 1913. Picabia cannot be blamed, for after all no man can give more or other than what there is in him to give. It is no secret that he enjoyed the frills and small-talk of social life, but that does not mean that he was not capable of brilliant demonstrations of wit in his painting. His machine-portraits are certainly examples of this, as well as his compositions with anti-aesthetic objects such as combs, sardine-tins and matches, which are in the best Dadaist spirit. His later productions however were not so successful. At Cannes, where he delighted in organizing the festivals, he returned to figurative painting for a number of years, much of it of a disappointing level. It was only in 1945 that Picabia was moved, like many others, by the post-liberation revival and began to paint in the spirit of the age. His natural reaction was to return to abstract art, while still continuing to run it down, producing a series of very personal canvases which were somewhat aggres-sive in colour and in every case full of surprises in their composition (*First seek your Orpheus, Awareness of Misery, Black Eye, The Third Sex,* all of which belong to 1948). Then in 1949 he made a series of pictures consisting of nothing but dots, which are surely among the oddest works that have been produced in abstract art. I admit that I greatly enjoyed them when they were being painted, and was responsible for encouraging Picabia to produce so many of them.

While Delaunay, Kupka, Picabia, Mondrian and others made Paris the capital of abstract art, Kandinsky was working on his own in Munich. Despite his efforts to attract, round his *Blue Horseman,* all the best talents he knew of in the world of art, the fact remains that his own were the only genuinely abstract works in the exhibitions of the famous group in the course of 1912. While Franz Marc and August Macke, his young German colleagues, painted a few completely abstract canvases in 1913 or 1914, they were not recognized until much later, after both these outstanding

PICABIA. LANDSCAPE. 1912.
Simone Collinet Collection, Paris.

representatives of their generation in Germany had lost their lives in the trenches, on the Western Front.

Kandinsky was harshly treated by the critics when he exhibited his first abstract works. Jibes, insults and slander are often the price to be paid for courage and sincerity. But encouragement was not slow to follow. His works were published by Piper; Herwarth Walden took his part in his review *Der Sturm,* while in New York Alfred Stieglitz was attracted by Kandinsky's contributions to the Armory Show and gave the then considerable sum of 800 dollars for one of his canvases. This was the first one to find a buyer in America, and it subsequently caused a sensation at Chicago and paved the way for Kandinsky's success. The Solomon R. Guggenheim Museum in New York now contains the richest collections of Kandinsky's works that is to be found.

5

FUTURIST INFLUENCE. SEVERINI. RUSSIAN 'RAYONISM'.
MALEVITCH. SIMULTANEOUS BEGINNINGS OF ABSTRACT GEOMETRISM.
ARP AND SOPHIE TAÜBER. DADA. THE REVIEW *DE STIJL*.

The most sympathetic are likely to have misgivings about Futurism, for such a mixture of bluff and self-advertisement is hard to reconcile with our lofty conception of the work of art or the artist's mission. But I believe there was something compelling, something that went deeper than it realised, beneath the loud-mouthed huckstering of *futurfascismo*. Indeed a reading of the first Futurist Manifesto of 1909 is enough to make us aware that the bloated rhetoric embodied an idea of genuine value.

Stripped of its trappings, Futurism can be seen to have been inspired by the generous ambition of bringing life into art, of bringing about a

BALLA. AUTOMOBILE IN MOTION. 1915.
Joseph Slifka Collection, New York.

29

closer union between them, while rejecting all dead art in favour of living life itself, the natural creator of new forms. Futurism also has other claims to our gratitude. By making such a noise, such a stir in so many countries and exciting critics and journalists in so many capitals of Europe, it did more than any other single movement to free art from the traditional forms of the past and, as a result, to open the public's mind, all over the world, to a totally new art.

Here again, abstract art was proclaimed in various statements to be found in a number of manifestoes. The painters were demanding *lines of force* and Boccioni wrote "We must assert that the sidewalk can find its way on to the dining-room table, that your head can cross the road all by itself, and that at the same time your own reading-lamp can weave a huge spider's web from one house to another with its chalky beams. We must assert that the whole visible world must make its impact on us, fusing itself with us and creating a harmony dictated by creative intuition alone." He also said "We must open up the figure or shape and fill it full of the environment in which it has its being." But it was Severini rather than Boccioni who was to come closest to abstraction, with his manifesto written in Rome during the winter of 1913-1914. It was never published till now, when it can be read in the *Appendix A* of this book.

Futurism has left few works of any importance by way of giving a plastic justification of its programme. Perhaps its real creativeness lay in its influence on men's minds. However Severini's work prior to 1914 deserves close attention, especially his series of *Dancing-girls* painted in 1913. These are abstract compositions made up of graceful lines and delicate colours, usually applied in the pointilliste manner favoured by the Post-Impressionists. He gave up his abstraction only in order to revert to a kind of academicism which might perhaps be Italian but has nothing modern about it. He returned to abstract art only after 1945, in the same way as Picabia and others. He is now painting compositions in which harsh, abrupt lines are set against flat stretches of skilfully modulated colour. These canvases are also called *Dance* or *Dancing-girls,* though they are very unlike those of the pre-1914 phase.

Among the remaining Futurist painters mention must be made of Balla, who began painting abstracts in 1913, and of a few works by Carlo Carra and De Soffici, and especially of the later canvases by Boccioni, the great hope of Futurist painting and sculpture, who died after falling from a horse in 1916. Later, when Futurism degenerated into 'Aero-painting', the only one to continue on abstract lines was Prampolini.

The many exhibitors at the Blue Horseman included a few Russians, of whom Michael Larionov and Nathalie Gontcharova are worth recalling for their share in the first stirrings of abstract painting in Russia.

In 1909 Larionov, in Moscow, was as close to abstraction (viz, *The Glass*) as Braque and Picasso were to be three or four years later. He gave his first lecture on Rayonism at the A. Kraft Studio in Moscow in 1910. (9) Two Rayonist canvases were exhibited at the same time, namely Larionov's *The Boulevard* which was mainly in greens and yellows, and Gontcharova's *Cats,* mainly yellow and black. In the following year both of them painted a long series of works the dominant characteristic of which was in a large number of straight lines either parallel (Larionov, *The Beach,* 1911), or meeting (Larionov, *Portrait of Gontcharova,* 1912) or else flying off in every direction. These represent the zenith of Rayonism, which was destined to be a short-lived movement. (10)

Larionov was a restless artist, and Goncharova was equally versatile. In Moscow at that time artists were expected to invent a new form of art every 48 hours. Larionov painted soldiers and flowers, and even anecdotal paintings with inscriptions on them, while Goncharova excelled in many different fields, painting cavases covered with numbers, as well as street-scenes that anticipated Dr. Caligari. In 1914 all these Russian experiments were shown in Paris at Paul Guillaume's, a laudatory preface being written for the catalogue by Apollinaire. We are now concerned only with the Rayonist canvases. These are among the very first abstract paintings ever made and for this reason they are of considerable importance. (11) After 1914 Goncharova and Larionov, who were great friends of Diaghilev, did most of their work for the ballet and thus fell outside the main movement in painting. Nevertheless an exhibition of the two painters' Rayonist works was held in Rome in 1917, when an explanatory brochure entitled *Radiantismo* was produced for the occasion. Alfred Barr found an unexpected ancestor of Rayonism, in Leonardo da Vinci. In his remarkable work *Cubism and Abstract Art* he quoted, in this connection, a sentence of Leonardo's: "The air is full of an infinite number of radiating straight lines, which cross and weave together without ever quite coinciding; it is these which represent the true form of every object's essence."

One painter who was to be of considerable importance emerged from the Larionov group, namely Casimir Malevitch.

Nothing could look easier: all you have to do is to take a ruler, draw

31

a square on a sheet of paper and black in its surface area with a pencil. To offer this 'discovery' as a work of art is obviously meant as a joke? By no means: it was an act of faith which was to have unforeseen consequences. It was an end and a beginning, the end of one form of painting and the beginning of a new art.

According to Malevitch art is an additional, extraneous element which thrusts itself into life and thought and evades all dialectical reasoning. This element used to be unconscious and was diffused throughout the world and in man himself, always mingled with many other elements. That is why there was never any pure art. But the time has come for making it visible and independent and ridding it of all its parasites. For half a century this eventuality had been prepared for by Impressionism and

SEVERINI. DANCING-GIRL. 1912.
Estorick Collection, London.

32

LARIONOV. RAYONISM. 1910.
Artist's Collection.

Cubism: all that remained was to learn how to read shapes and how to interpret and analyse them.

The book he wrote with the help of the advance-guard Russian poets and which was published in Moscow in 1915 was nothing more nor less than an attempt to isolate the datum or element of *art* itself. For such an operation to be successful the simplest element had to be found. Malevitch saw that element to be the geometrical square, patiently blacked in with a pencil.

Why the perfect square? Because it is the clearest assertion of man's will, the epitome of his mastery over nature.

Why should it be blacked in with pencil? Because that is the humblest act the sensibility can perform.

Active nature and passive nature thus find themselves brought together and reconciled.

Malevitch gave the name *Suprematism* to this new art and exhibited the first Suprematist drawing, the famous square, at the *Target* exhibition in Moscow in 1913. In the same year he produced a series of other drawings of elemental forms, all in pencil. The first form to emerge from the square was the circle, then came the placing of two rectangular planes in

33

the form of a cross. Progressively more complex compositions were developed in which there appeared the trapezium, the triangle, then the broken line, the curve, and finally the blurred, shaded-off line. This took four years.

Malevitch had to evolve quickly in order to reach that point. He was born at Kiev in 1878, and began painting in the post-Impressionist manner and after that as a Fauve. He soon came under Picasso's influence and became the leader of the Russian Cubists who included Pevsner, Puni, Alexandra Exter, Lyubov Popova and Udalzova. After 1911 cubo-futurist elements were to be seen in his work, which in other respects showed striking affinities to that of Fernand Léger (*The scissors-sharpener, Woman carrying buckets,* both painted in 1912). It was from that stage that he made the leap into Suprematism. When abstract art fell politically into discredit in 1922, Malevitch left Moscow and became Professor at the Academy in Leningrad. He contrived to go to Germany in 1926, and at the Bauhaus made arrangements for the publication of his book *Die Gegenstandslose Welt* (The Objectless World). This remarkable work is the only existing source of information on his art and thought. As it has not yet been translated, extracts from it are given at *Appendix B.*

Although Malevitch was the first painter in the world to use pure geometrical forms, it must be admitted that the Cubists had made everyone vaguely conscious of the idea, even if it was still undefinable. Without having even heard of Malevitch, in 1915 Hans Arp at Zürich and Magnelli in Florence were both making abstract compositions based entirely on geometrical forms.

In the following year Sophie Taüber, also at Zürich, composed a number of smallish works—drawings in coloured crayon—based on a strictly horizontal-vertical movement, thus anticipating Neo-Plasticism.

At the same time, behind the lines in Holland, Mondrian and Van Doesburg came together and began preparing their review, *De Stijl.*

Thus at the very same time, in four different parts of the world which were separated by frontiers that were closed on account of the war, very dissimilar artists who had all heard of Parisian Cubism were reaching exactly similar conclusions.

At Zürich the beautiful experiments of Sophie Taüber and Arp were soon overwhelmed by the Dadaist uproar, which was unlikely to favour such a pure and semi-religious art. Sophie Taüber, who was too retiring and modest to assert or defend herself, carried on working almost in secret until her death in 1943, always leaving the limelight to Hans Arp, whom

34

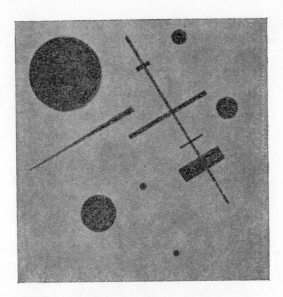

MALEVITCH. SUPREMATIST COMPOSITION. 1913.

she married in 1921. Few people knew or appreciated Sophie Taüber's work during her lifetime. One had to know the Arps well before one was admitted to Sophie's studio, in their house at Meudon where they lived after 1928. She rarely exhibited anywhere, although she took part in *Circle an Square* and helped Arp and Van Doesburg with the decorations for the various rooms in the 'Aubette' in Strasburg, a fine achievement which has since been destroyed. Sophie Taüber's works has grown in prestige since her death, revealing as it does such an inner store of honesty, candour and quiet strength. Her work has an extraordinary variety, but is always sober and full of integrity.

In 1918 and 1919 Arp, together with Sophie Taüber, made some horizontal-vertical *collages* out of paper which they cut with a bookbinder's guillotine. Then he went off in another direction and began exploiting a curved, supple line, that seemed to come as naturally to his hand as the fruit to a tree.

The contribution of Zürich Dadaism to abstract art lies mainly in the 'woods' by Arp which appeared in the review *Dada* or were used as illustrations for books by Hülsenbeck and Tristan Tzara.

35

GONTCHAROVA. THE CATS. 1910.
Artist's Collection.

Marcel Janco made abstract reliefs in a very personal style, most of which are now lost. Finally, Viking Eggeling in 1917 and Hans Richter in the following year produced some drawings which can also be credited to Dadaism. Late in 1918 Richter took Eggeling with him to Germany. It was there, in 1919, that Eggeling composed his famous strip-drawings on simple themes, which he called *Horizontal-Vertical Mass,* followed in 1920 by the strips for his *Diagonal Symphony,* a rather more complex theme of which he made a film in 1921.

Richter's output ran parallel with that of Eggeling who was seven years his senior. In 1919 he made his *Prelude,* the orchestration of a theme which was developed in eleven drawings. In the same year as Eggeling he also produced his first abstract film, *Rhythm 21, screen orchestration in time and space.* Eggeling died in 1925. After that Richter at first turned to more practical activities, and later to Surrealism, his *Dreams that money can buy* (1947) containing some beautiful abstract sequences.

36

It was in Holland, the last of the four great centres of geometrical abstraction, that this form of expression was to find its least compromising and best-reasoned formulation. This is not surprising, since it was in the case of Mondrian that the transition from figurative art to pure geometry took the longest to achieve, lasting from 1912 to 1917. It was only logical that he should be the one to state and explore the problem. Geometrical abstraction achieved its most complete and thorough form in a properly explained and demonstrated use of the horizontal and vertical, with only three primary colours (red, blue and yellow) supported by three 'non-colours', black, white and grey. It was left to Mondrian to work out the system as a whole, and to expound it in a few texts which have become classics thanks to their clarity of exposition. The first number of *De Stijl* was published by Van Doesburg in October 1917. This contained a long article on doctrinal lines by Mondrian, some essential parts of which are worth reproducing (*Appendix C*). This initial statement was followed by many others, notably, two years later, by a long platonic dialogue which is beyond doubt one of the most convincing essays of the 'heroic' period of abstract art. It certainly deserves a place alongside the famous works of Kandinsky and Malevitch. Mondrian continued to write almost as much as he painted for the rest of his life. In French he published *Néo-plasticisme* (Léonce Rosenberg, 1920) as well as contributing to several reviews. After his death an important collection of his English essays was published in New York (*Plastic Art and Pure Plastic Art*, Wittenborn, 1st edn. 1945, 3rd edn. 1951).

But we must not anticipate. To return to Holland in 1917, working with Mondrian and Van Doesburg were the painters Huszar and Van Der Leck (though the latter was not long in leaving the group), the painter and sculptor Vantongerloo, the poet Antonie Kok and a number of architects. Their literary contributions to the review all pointed in the same direction, all upholding the same central idea. But it was Mondrian who produced the most extensive and solidly-constructed writings during the first four years. At the same time Van Doesburg published, alongside his review *De Stijl,* several short but very interesting works which have never been translated from the Dutch. (12) But he was first and foremost a man of action, both quarrelsome and fiendishly energetic. His bustling tempera-ment made him poles apart from Mondrian, but he was one of those indivi-dualists who can serve to complement another individualist, with the result that the two of them made an ideal team, the one slowly ruminating and gathering material which the other wanted to explode like a bomb. That

37

SOPHIE TAÜBER. COMPOSITION IN COLOURED CRAYONS. 1916.
M. S. Collection, Paris.

is how, through the medium of the little Dutch review, geometrical abstraction was to impose itself on a substantial part of the world, in spite of the fact that it was in its narrowest and most meagre form, at first sight the form which seemed most meaningless, in other words Neo-plasticism.

I was already familiar with these ideas and experiments when I happened to pass through Berlin at the end of 1922 and heard Marinetti give a talk at the Futurist Centre there. After a few scathing remarks about Goethe this brilliant mountebank began to expound his ideas on painting and the arts in general. Dynamism and art, he argued, were one and the same thing. Painting means giving life to a plane surface, and the life of a plane surface can never be intense enough, since speed is the only criterion by which any work of art can stand or fall. He wanted art and life to be like the waves of the sea, clashing and struggling together, all with their

38

distinct individuality. In order to understand both life and art, it would be enough to watch the waves unfolding and folding on the beach in a kind of delirious anarchy... In these words I recognized the essence of Futurism, insisting that every man and every day should face a different task. What Marinetti was proposing was the very opposite of Neo-plasticism. That opposition is still going on around us, for everywhere we can see both directed fury and calm organization. Style on the one hand, and a human cry on the other, will no doubt always be the two poles of art.

HANS ARP. STATIC COMPOSITION. 1915.
François Arp Collection, Paris.

39

6

THE SPIRITUAL URGE TO ABSTRACT ART. PAINTERS' MANIFESTOES SHOW THE NEED FOR SPIRITUAL RENEWAL. PARALLEL BETWEEN MONDRIAN AND VAN DOESBURG. THE SPECTATOR'S SHARE IN THE WORK OF ART.

After defining the immediate origins of abstract art as lying in Fauvism and Cubism, and having found one of its incidental causes to be in the change of the social milieu thanks to the growth of mechanisation and science, closer attention must be given to the problem itself in order to see what went on in the minds of its main pioneers at the time when they were passing from figuration to abstraction. One of the ways in which this can be done is through re-reading what they wrote at that time. A surprising fact then comes to light, which is that in most of them the need for abstraction was based on an acute hunger for spiritual values. It looks as though, after a century of materialist philosophy, the artists' own intuition stressed an urgent need to re-charge the spiritual centres. A new humanism then emerged, one which was very different from that of the Renaissance, amounting in this case to a kind of inner humanism, the only form of it that could possibly understand real equality because it brings man face to face with that share of the infinite which he carries within himself, and which seeks its reflection in his fellow-men. Thus a kind of brotherhood of summits is created, for every man is a summit at certain moments and in certain conditions, every man being, when considered in the absolute, the centre and summit of the world.

Spirituality in art, the title Kandinsky gave to his first book, was highly significant. In his conclusion he proclaimed a new era of the spirit, a period of intense spirituality which was to find its direct expression through art.

In Mondrian's unpublished notebooks I found the words "It is the internal life, its strength and joy, which determines form in art." On another page I read "Art has no meaning except in so far as it expresses what is non-material, for it is this that enables man to transcend his own being."

I find the same tendency, though less consciously expressed, in Robert Delaunay's paintings of 1912 and 1913. They contain a semi-mystical exaltation of light. Delaunay remarked to me one day that "Most painters are only peeping-Toms, whereas what they really should aspire to is to be Seers."

It might be asked whether, intellectually, it is just an easy way out to see this unexpected emphasis of spirituality in art, or at least in early abstract art, as an intuitive agreement with Bergson's attempts at revalorizing mind, in the broadest yet deepest sense of the term, after a hundred years of positivism and historical materialism. *Creative Evolution,* the first landmark in this change of values, appeared in 1906. In his remarkable lecture *Consciousness and Life,* published in 1914, I find the following remarks which could perfectly well be applied to the first generation of abstract painters: "Great men of integrity, and more particularly those whose sheer inventive heroism clears new paths for human virtues, serve to reveal metaphysical truth. Though they stand at the highest point of evolution, yet they are closest to the origins of things and make us conscious of that impulse which arises from the very depths." Yes, the impulse rising from the depths and which is nearest to the fundamental truths and to the naked origin of things, surely that is what we expect of art in general and what abstract art appears most fitted to reveal to us, without being hindered by material objects whose presence is no more than an agreable distraction from our main objective, which must be the mind or spirit. (13)

Nobody understood this better than Mondrian, no man ever penetrated it more deeply than he did in the course of a whole lifetime. Yet there seems to be some dichotomy in his thought as regards spiritual values as such, and this needs some brief analysis.

Mondrian was long interested in theosophical speculations. As late as 1916 the portrait of Mme Blavatsky hung on the wall of his studio. Yet in his writings he made no mention of his theosophical sympathies. Even in private conversation he avoided religious topics and closed up at the slightest hint of them. Only in an atmosphere of friendship and trust would he risk the slightest allusion to them, and even then he was more than cautious in his use of words. He usually took up an extreme agnostic position, while praising mechanisation and praising the Futurists for saying that they would prefer a motor-car to the Victory of Samothrace. He also asserted that the day would come when we could leave the job of making works of art to machines, on condition that the machines were controlled by artists. (14)

Vantongerloo came to the same conclusion: "Everything progresses and evolves, and the time is not far off when art and science will unite into a homogeneous whole." This notion was supported by Van Doesburg, who wrote to a friend in Holland, "My final conviction, a conviction arising from the sum-total of all my activities, is that in the future art will develop

41

entirely on a scientific basis. Until now the artist has always been at the mercy of his feelings and has had no means of controlling them. There was nothing to distinguish his methods of work from those of the milliner or pastry-cook, who merely arrange things according to their taste or inclination." (16)

But this scientific outlook was not set up as the enemy of spirituality. On the contrary, in *Classical, Baroque and Modern* the same Van Doesburg wrote "However deep it went, mediaeval art was not a *direct expression* of the religious outlook, because it failed to find in the *means of expression itself* the correlative that was needed for expressing that outlook. It found that correlative in symbolic representation, with the aid of forms borrowed from nature. The expression of the religious outlook was, therefore, not direct but indirect."

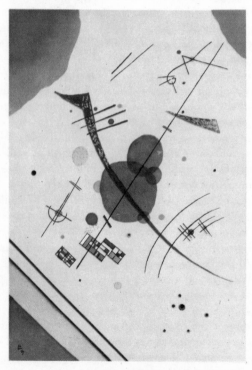

KANDINSKY. WASER-COLOUR. 1923.
M. S. Collection, Paris.

42

At the end of the same treatise, after speaking of a collective style of which he saw a possible fulfilment in Neo-plasticism, the author summed up his views as follows: "A style comes into being when, after achieving a collective consciousness of life, we are able to set up a harmonious relationship between the inner character and the outward appearance of life. A discontinuous development of art is the natural result of the human consciousness's discontinuous development towards truth. Over the centuries, the development of art aimed at giving reality to the aesthetic idea which consists of expressing completely, through the medium of art, this harmonious relationship between the inner life and external appearance of things, between the spirit and nature. . . Modern art's evolution towards the abstract and universal, eliminating all that is external and individual, thanks to a common effort and common idea, has made it possible to bring into existence a collective style which, transcending persons and nations, most definitely and genuinely expresses the highest, deepest and most universal requirements of beauty."

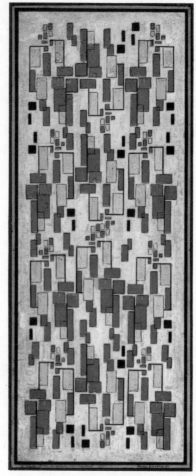

VAN DOESBURG. COMPOSITION VI. 1917.
Private Collection, Meudon.

We can see or read between the lines that for Van Doesburg the terms art, spirituality, abstraction, universality and religion were identical. Neo-plasticism was an effort to bring together again the data and principles which civilisation had divorced from each other in the course of time, but which originally formed a single reality in the mind of man: that is to say, the urge to express his highest aspirations.

43

That, and nothing less, was the aim of the horizontal-vertical style and the "simple distribution of colours". But Van Doesburg gave up the effort in 1924 and it was left to Mondrian to work out and demonstrate the idea. The works he produced in Paris, and perhaps above all those he painted between 1925 and 1932, expressed something absolute in their strict relevance of composition, while never losing their human significance thanks to their colour and some indefinable inner resonance. Every one of his canvases embodies a pure ontology. They are the works of a man capable of expressing in paint the terse aphorisms of, say, some modern Parmenides writing a treatise on *Being as Being*. The rhomboid-shaped canvas of 1931, consisting only of two straight lines of different breadth on a uniform white ground, is in a sense the Vedanta of contemporary painting. After that he had to come down from that rarefied atmosphere and renew his contact with life. (17)

Is it possible to penetrate very far into a painter's work without having known him personally? A man is the living proof of the sum-total of his work, even when it is greater than himself. I am aware that some distinction has to be made between morality and art, but I believe there is some interchange between art and the highest forms of thought. I have observed that every artist contains a hidden mystic, sometimes only too thoroughly hidden. But a shrewd eye can reach the real man on slight evidence. A gesture, a silence, something in the eyes, a tone of voice, set us dreaming of the unique necessity which according to Plotinus is the most important thing in a man. For instance Mondrian's reserve never managed to mask what lay behind it, but rather made it plainer. Knowing the man, what was hidden was seen to be all the more clearly stated in the work.

In spite of his timidness as regards words, everything in Mondrian pointed to the *thing* or essence itself, I mean the mystic that was latent in him. In spite of the cogent things he wrote, Van Doesburg was the very opposite. He radiated violence, destruction, anger, the love of battle for its own sake. He was capable of spreading a seedy atmosphere even over such a noble conception as Neo-plasticism. This detracts nothing from his value as a manager, as an intelligent and energetic purveyor of ideas. However the difference between the the two, as men, goes far to explain the mysterious dissimilarities between their works.

At this point I should like to add a note on the spectator's role. It seems to me that the spectator is required to play a creative part, comparable

44

with that of the artist, in abstract art more than in any other form of art. He is expected to have a well-informed mind and to be generous with it, never shrinking from the efforts that are demanded of him. Eugène Chevreul touched on this in well-chosen terms in a little book published in 1864. After showing (already !) that all the arts are made up of abstract elements, the physicist concluded his argument in these words: "But when I reduce the language of the fine-arts to abstractions, I have to point out that their effects, as abstractions, will be fewer in proportion as the minds to which they are addressed are less civilised or less cultured; for the more civilised or the more cultured people's minds are, the more inclined they will be to associate other ideas with the impressions evoked by these abstractions, —though I would not go so far as to say that they will necessarily be more open to impressions themselves. It is this capacity for grouping thoughts round the impression produced by a masterpiece, which explains the quality and variety of intellectual pleasure that is in reach of a mind that has been broadened by culture without any weakening of sensibility." (18) Thus a work of art is worth exactly what the spectator is worth; that is to say as much as the spectator or lover of art are capable of putting into it.

7

ABSTRACT ART BETWEEN THE WARS. CUBIST AND SURREALIST REACTIONS. THE "ART D'AUJOURD'HUI" EXHIBITION. THE *CERCLE ET CARRÉ* AND *ABSTRACTION-CRÉATION* GROUPS. ADVANCED REVIEWS IN EUROPE. THE BAUHAUS. PUBLIC GALLERIES OPENED TO ABSTRACT ART. DEVELOPMENT AND END OF *STIJL*. SPREAD OF CONSTRUCTIVISM. SOME PAINTERS.

Braque, Picasso and Gris came very close to abstraction in 1914, as can be seen through looking at a few histories of the art of that period. In his *Vision in Motion* Moholy-Nagy set side by side a Braque collage of 1914 and a Malevitch composition of 1921, showing a striking resemblance between the two works. This must have been accidental, since Braque never *intended* to go in for abstraction, while Malevitch had no use for figuration after 1913. For example when Braque said "Let us forget about things,

45

and only consider relationships" (19) he was certainly far from realising how close he was to Mondrian. Words often outstrip thought: did not Picasso once remark about Juan Gris that the disciple often sees things more clearly than his master?

Léger gave much more thought and time to the claims of an integral abstract art, and for a time, between 1913 and 1919, he seems to have been very strongly tempted by it. His admirable series of *Contrasting Forms* of 1913-1914 is not abstract art in the strictest sense of the term, but comes within an ace of it. I have no idea who or what deflected Léger from what would have been his normal evolution. Towards 1924 he interrupted his usual style of painting to produce some mural compositions which were entirely abstract and, indeed, very much in line with Neo-plasticism. Two of them were given prominent places at the *Cercle et Carré* exhibition in 1930.

During the nineteen-twenties, when it was directed by Léger and Ozenfant, the Académie Moderne turned out a large number of young abstract

LÉGER.
CONTRASTING FORMS. 1913.
Musée d'Art Moderne, Paris.

46

PICASSO. THE MAN WITH A GUITAR. 1913.
Private Collection, Paris.

artists. Thanks to their youth they were not slow in pushing Cubism to its logical conclusions, and I know that they were not discouraged by Léger in their pursuit of abstract art. He wrote some years later, "Of all the different directions in which the plastic arts have developed in the past 25 years, abstract art is the most important as well as the most interesting. It is no mere freak of experiment, but an art with its own intrinsic value. It has proved itself and also satisfies a demand, since so many collectors are enthusiastic about it. It is therefore a tendency arising out of life. Maybe future generations will class this form of art as an artificial paradise, but I do not think so. The abstract programme is governed by that desire for perfection and for complete liberty which turns men into saints, heroes or madmen. It is an extreme position in which few artists or their sup-

47

porters can thrive. The very idealism of the abstract programme is its greatest danger. Modern life with all its turmoil and urgency, its dynamism and variety, has no mercy on this fragile, luminous creation rising from chaos. We should respect it and leave it alone, for it had to be done and is done and it will remain." (20) But Léger asserted in the same work that the abstract experiment was already a matter for history and that it "has given all it had to offer."

Whether that is true or not, after 1920 Cubism returned once and for all to figuration. Braque imposed the rhythm while Picasso marked the frontiers of extravagance. Thus Picasso was able to cling to his title as an experimenter while Braque became the classic of the moderns. Gris died prematurely in 1927, having also failed to take the next step into abstraction. This step would have been harder for him than for the others, since he had already chosen the opposite direction, declaring that "Cézanne turned a bottle into a cylinder, but I turn a cylinder into a bottle."

In the same way Fauvism moved rapidly towards abstraction thanks to Matisse. Quite a number of his works of his most productive period —for instance *The Piano-lesson*—were well on the way to abstract painting, but the impulse petered out and Matisse became the most elegant figurative painter in the world.

Purism also stopped on the theshold. Although Ozenfant wanted "the utmost intensity and quality obtainable through the most economical means" he remained fundamentally hostile to abstract art.

Charles-Édouard Jeanneret, better known as Le Corbusier, supported Ozenfant in his Purist programme, but drew much closer to the *Stijl* theories in his architectural works. (21)

The retrogression of the great Cubists, together with the veto from the Purists, held up the popularisation of abstract art, which was still further threatened by Surrealism.

In spite of these strong waves of opposition in Paris itself, abstraction calmly went its own way and from time to time managed to score some minor victories.

In December 1925 the Pole, Poznanski, organized a large exhibition called Art Now (L'art d'aujourd'hui) which was held at the Antiquarians' Syndicate headquarters at 18, rue de La Ville-l'Évêque. The abstract works exhibited included mural compositions by Baumeister, Brunet, Léger, Carlsund; paintings by Jean Crotti, Walter Dexel, Florence Henri; Marcelle Cahn, Francisca Clausen, Kakabadze, Reth, Sevranckx, Poz-

48

nanski himself, as well as the *Simultaneous Colours* by Robert and Sonia Delaunay. Side by side with them were the Rayonists Larionov and Gontcharova; the Dadaists Arp and Janco, and the whole *Stijl* group with Mondrian, Van Doesburg, Huszar, Vantongerloo, Vordemberge-Gildewart and Domela. Futurism was represented by Prampolini and Depero; the Bauhaus by Moholy-Nagy and Klee. Finally there were exhibits by most of the Cubists (Gris, Picasso, Gleizes, Léger, Villon, Laurens, Lipchitz, Marcoussis, Metzinger) and of their sworn enemies the future Surrealists Max Ernst, André Masson, Joseph Sima, Toyen and Styrsky. Almost half of the entire exhibition consisted of abstract works. Some of the artists concerned have not exhibited since.

It was almost five years before another similar effort was made in support of abstract art. In April 1930 the *Cercle et Carré* exhibition was held at 'Galerie 23' (23, rue de La Boétie) with 130 exhibits by 46 artists. Some representational or hardly abstract paintings such as those of Torrès-Garcia and Ozenfant were admitted. The kernel of the group consisted of Mondrian, Kandinsky, Arp, Schwitters, Vantongerloo, Sophie Taüber, Pevsner, Huszar, Van Rees and Vordemberge-Gildewart, supported by a number of newcomers such as Buchheister, Pierre Daura, François Foltyn, Jean Gorin, Hans Welti, Germain Cueto, Eric Olson, Hans Suschny, Henri Stazewski and H. N. Werkman, all of whom sought expression through an integral abstraction. Among the other exhibitors were such artists as Léger, Charchoune, Baumeister, Fillia, Le Corbusier, Sartoris, Prampolini, Russolo, Marcelle Cahn and the American painter Stella, while César Domela, Otto Freundlich, Moholy-Nagy and Jean Xcéron, all members of the group, were absent.

Another noticeable abstention was that of Van Doesburg, who was invited to join the group at the outset—it soon had eighty members— but who curtly refused and decided to make a group of his own. He rallied round him Hélion, Carlsund and Tutundjan and published the one and only number of *Art concret,* a pamphlet whose main interest lies in its title. This is the first appearance of the term concrete art used instead of 'abstract' art which had been undisputed till then. As we know, the new expression was later favoured by Arp and Kandinsky, while the painter and sculptor Max Bill was also to make much of it.

In the following year (after Van Doesburg's death at Davos) Vantongerloo and Herbin got together a new group out of the ruins of *Cercle et Carré.* This group, *Abstraction-Création,* issued the first number of its Journal in 1952, the second in 1933, the fifth and last in 1936. It held its

49

exhibitions in a hall at the back of a courtyard in the Avenue de Wagram, near the Place des Ternes. After the second world war the *Salon des Réalités Nouvelles* was founded on the same lines and at the same premises as *Abstraction-Création,* whose traditions were now carried on by an annual publication of the same format and style as the pre-war ones. I am tempted to smile when I recall that this series of groups and publications—*Cercle et Carré, Abstraction-Création* and *Réalités Nouvelles*—all originated in a visit paid to me at Vanves in 1929 by the Uruguayan painter Torrès-Garcia, which resulted in the founding of *Cercle et Carré*. I claim no particular credit for that, but it was one of those small things which sometimes lead to unexpected results, like those mountain echoes which come back so magnified that they sound like avalanches.

That period from 1920 to 1930 was rich in advance-guard reviews. There was hardly a European country without one and abstract art often had a prominent place in them. They were all in contact with each other and they exchanged contributors, so that a kind of International of abstract art came into being. Political developments snapped all these valuable links that stretched across the frontiers, and the network was never restored.

Here are the titles of some of those reviews, all memorable for their courage and independence: *De Stijl, Mecano* and *The next call,* in Holland;

BRAQUE. HOMAGE TO J.-S. BACH. 1912.
H.-P. Roché Collection, Paris.

50

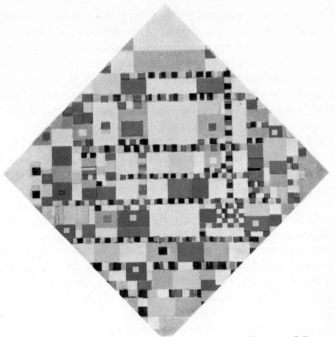

MONDRIAN. VICTORY BOOGIE-WOOGIE. 1943-1944. *Tremaine Collection, U.S.A.*

Het Overzicht and *Ça ira* at Antwerp; *Anthologie* at Liège; *Sept Arts* and *l'Art libre* at Brussels; *La vie des lettres et des arts, L'esprit nouveau, Les feuilles libres, Orbes, L'œuf dur, Cercle et Carré*, 391, *Le Bulletin de l'Effort moderne* and *le Mouvement accéléré*, all in Paris; *Manomètre* at Lyons; *Zenith* at Belgrade; *Contemporanul* and *Punkt* at Bucarest; *Zwrotnica* and *Bloc* at Warsaw; *Ma* at Vienna; *Merz* at Hanover; *Pasmo, Disc* and *Stavba* in Czecho-Slovakia; *Der Sturm* and *G (Gestaltung)* in Berlin; *A.B.C.* at Zürich.

Paris was the hub of all this activity, the centre in Paris itself being Montparnasse. It was a lively time, when on the same day, in front of the Dôme café you could meet Marinetti on a lightning visit to the capital, Gabo fresh from Berlin, Cendrars just back from America, Delaunay out for a spree, Arp trying to find somebody, Tzara and Ehrenburg sitting there with inscrutable faces; you could risk a few words with Hans Richter or argue with Van Doesburg of Kiesler, or listen to the international speechifiers making themselves drunk with their own eloquence, or you could even manage to be bored by it all.

51

At the *Sacre du Printemps,* an art-gallery which has now disappeared but which was at 5, Rue du Cherche-Midi, Paul Dermée and I used to hold exhibitions of abstract art and literary meetings in 1927. Marinetti, Walden, Kassak, Schwitters and many others had their turn at holding forth with recitations and speeches accompanied by catcalls or applause. Canvases by Werkman, Huszar, Vantongerloo, Mondrian, Arp, Sophie Taüber and others who are now forgotten were shown and eagerly discussed there. All this fertile activity, carried on in the face of hostility from the established critics of the day, was brought to an end on the eve of the second world war, though not before it had been strengthened for a time by the effects of Nazism as it emptied Germany of ther intellectuals.

One of the most important undertakings between the wars was the Bauhaus in Germany, a kind of university of pure construction and applied art which was founded by Walter Gropius at Weimar in 1919.

There has been much discussion of Van Doesburg's influence on the Bauhaus two years after its foundation (23). There is no doubt that the ideas of the *Stijl* group made themselves strongly felt in the Bauhaus, as well as those of the Russian Constructivists which were introduced by Lissitzky. From the Bauhaus these two movements spread through Germany across the whole of central Europe. But the Bauhaus was less a training-ground for abstract painters than a centre for the revival of taste, through the study of matter for its own sake, in spite of the presence of such eminent teachers as Klee, Kandinsky, Feininger, Moholy-Nagy, Albers and Schlemmer. This study and research at the Bauhaus were founded on a new vision of things, a vision purified of prejudices and conventional ideas, so that its teaching prepared the way in a high degree for an understanding of abstract art. The student as well as the general public were also enabled to share the thoughts of the Bauhaus leaders through the *Bauhausbücher,* a famous series of works published by the institution. Those dealing with painting or with art in general were written by Malevitch, Mondrian, Van Doesburg, Kandinsky and Moholy-Nagy (vide Bibliography). The Bauhaus was obliged to leave Weimar in 1925 and was set up again in the open country not far from Dessau. The new buildings, designed by Gropius, were officially opened in December 1926. The premises were beyond doubt the most rational and scrupulously functional work that the world had so far seen. I remember my amazement when I visited the Bauhaus in 1928, and my impression that I was standing before the ideas of *De Stijl,* boldly exemplified and fulfilled in an awe-inspiring

EL LISSITZKY. STORY OF TWO SQUARES. 1920.

block of buildings. The main façade was entirely of glass. The Bauhaus was closed down by the Nazis in 1933. It was certainly thanks to the Bauhaus, which had prepared the public's mind for it, that the first room or gallery was set aside in a public museum, permanently open to viewers, at Hanover in 1925. It was also the first time that any of Mondrian's works found their way into a national collection. This famous "abstract gallery", with its interior strikingly designed by Lissitzky himself, was destroyed by the Nazis in 1937.

1926 saw the first of the travelling exhibitions of abstract art which were sent on tour round the United States by the "Société Anonyme". This Society, founded in 1920 by Miss Katherine Dreier, Marcel Duchamp and Man Ray, had an outstanding influence on the teaching of art. In 1927, also in America, the A. E. Gallatin collection was thrown open to the public under the title of the Museum of Living Art; but in this case the Cubists were most strongly represented, the pure abstractionists only being introduced much later, after 1935.

To be historically exact, the second official museum to open permanent shows of abstract painting was the gallery at Lodz, in Poland. This collection was created entirely out of gifts or bequests which were mainly drawn from or arranged in Paris. I myself contributed to some extent with canvases by Baumeister, Huszar, Vordemberge and Werkman which were then my property. Arp, Sophie Taüber, Charchoune, Calder, Sonia Delaunay, Van Doesburg, Foltyn, Gleizes, Gorin, Vantongerloo, Hélion, Herbin, Schwitters and others not so well known, also gave it their support. An illustrated catalogue was issued in March 1932. The abstract rooms in the Lodz gallery are now closed to the public, but the collection itself appears to have remained intact.

In 1937 the Museum of Non-objective Painting (now the Solomon R. Guggenheim Museum) was founded in New York. Finally, in 1939, also in New York, the Museum of Modern Art opened its new premises, destined to become the most important centre in the world for the study of abstract art, thanks to its exhibitions, its well-stocked library and its own publications.

This period could be surveyed in another way, by giving an account of the main personalities involved. But let us first see what happened to the *Stijl* movement.

After being deflected from its original course by Van Doesburg himself in 1924, the famous review (*De Stijl*) was carried on without Mondrian, but with the addition of some younger artists (Domela, Vordemberge, and the scenario-writers Eggeling and Richter). It closed down in 1928, but a posthumous number was published by Mme Van Doesburg in 1932.

After Van Doesburg's death in March 1931, Mondrian's influence increased in both depth and breadth through his work in the studio. He had fervent supporters in every country in Europe, but more especially in Germany and Switzerland. In 1934 he was visited by a very young American, Harry Holtzman, who was to be his first direct disciple in the States. (24)   In the same year Ben Nicholson, a painter of experience, came to see him and once again the studio in the Rue du Départ left an indelible memory.   As a result Nicholson became the recognized leader of abstract painting in Great Britain.

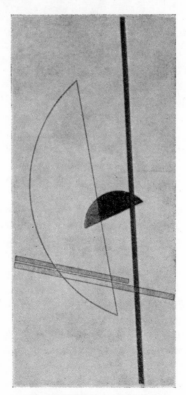

MOHOLY-NAGY. CONSTRUCTION.
LITHOGRAPH. 1923.

55

BAUMEISTER. COMPOSITION. C. 1936.
Jeanne Bucher Gallery, Paris.

George Vantongerloo, who had settled in France in 1919 (first at Menton, then in Paris) embarked on a series of fascinating mathematical calculations, all tending to prove by dint of figures and formulas that Mondrian's works—and of course his own—were infallibly correct. He gave up this enterprise later to seek refuge, no less infallibly, in the curved line and what he called "the indeterminate".

Of the rest of the *Stijl* team only the painters Vilmos Huszar and Bart van der Leck remained in Holland. The latter gave up abstraction almost as soon as he tried it. As for Huszar, in 1921 (three years before Van Doesburg) he made use of the diagonal line in compositions whose theme was often based on or intended for stage-sets, and he gradually brought in representational elements. A flower-composition (*Fleurs,* admittedly geometrical) was shown at the Anonymous Society exhibition in the Brooklyn Museum in 1926.

56

In Holland there was an outsider, the attractive printer and painter Henry Nicolas Werkman, of Groeningen. He painted, wrote, drew and printed. Like Kurt Schwitters in Hanover, he published his own review, *The next call*. This he printed with his own hands, and often in an unusual way. One y the numbers could be unfolded so as to make a kind of poster on which the words *plattegrond van de kunst en omstreken* (a plan of art and its surroundings) were blocked out in rectangles of different colours. For a few years Werkman showed an unusual virtuosity in his creation of large monotypes in brilliant colours. The most interesting are those he painted between 1923 and 1929. After 1935 he returned to occasional suggestions of naturalism, and in the end to figuration. Werkman was very active in the Dutch resistance during the war and

SCHWITTERS. COLLAGE. 1927.
Mme Van Doesburg Collection, Meudon.

57

was shot by the Nazis on the night before their retreat from Groeningen. A considerable part of his work was lost in the fire.

As we have seen, the other important geometrical abstract stream came from Russia. There it went under such different names as Suprematism (Malevitch), Constructivism (Tatlin), Non-Objectivism (Rotchenko) and *Proun* (Lissitzky). When the Soviet leaders began to look unfavourably on abstraction in 1921, Lissitzky, Gabo, Pevsner and Kandinsky left Russia and went to different parts of Europe. Kandinsky went to Weimar, Pevsner to Paris, and Gabo and Lissitzky settled in Berlin. Lissitzky in particular had considerable influence in Germany. Two of his close friends were the Hungarians Laszlo Moholy-Nagy, whom he had already met at Düsseldorf in 1920, and Laszlo Peri who had spent some months as an architect in Russia. The first of these in due course achieved fame in Europe and America thanks to his manifold activities as an artist, teacher and writer; but the second is less well-known. Peri kept in the background and produced little, and as far as I know there is only one of his canvases in a public collection. Peri's constructivism is more austere and reserved than Lissitzky's, and more concentrated than Moholy's which is characterised by a lyrical handling of the medium and experiment in new techniques.

I would suggest however that the Constructivist stream found its richest fulfilment in the copious body of work so patiently and quietly produced by Sophie Taüber in Zürich and Paris over a period of thirty years.

Mention must be made of two painters in the *Stijl* tradition, the Polish artists Henry Stazewski and Ladislas Strzeminski, who painted works of exceptional purity during the 'thirties. The first of these in particular impressed me with his white canvases on which the handling of the paint alone contrived to present an extremely simple design of planes arranged in a strictly horizontal-vertical relationship. Both of them were members of the *Cercle et Carré* group in 1930. Another Pole, Henri Berlewi had already composed abstract works before them, which he called *mechanofaktur* and which aimed at a kind of alphabet of simple plastic forms.

In Germany there were also Domela (Berlin), Vordemberge (Osnabrück), Baumeister (Stuttgart) and Schwitters (Hanover). The first two of these worked at first according to orthodox *Stijl* principles, but later developed towards a more varied form of expression.

Domela settled in Paris in 1933. He is now best known for his 'objectpaintings' in which the curve is most prominent and into which he introduces all kinds of themes and substances which he combines or sets off against each other with unequalled craftsmanship.

Vordemberge fled from Germany just before the war and went to live in Amsterdam. He is now teaching art at Ulm and paints very sober Neo-constructivist compositions in delicate pastel-like tones.

Baumeister attracted attention as far back as 1921 by some mural compositions of a very personal quality in which the curve is exploited in harmony with the straight line and the circle with the square. On one occasion (1922) he produced a mural relief consisting entirely of horizontals and verticals.

As for Kurt Schwitters, he is undoubtedly one of the most outstanding personalities of that period. His varied activities, full of surprises, and the unusual disinterestedness of his work and thought, have already made him something of a legend. Among his plastic productions are a large number of collages (*Papiers collés*) which can only be described as being beyond description. Everything he does has the same decisive and genuine candidness.

In Paris the fluid Hélion, as elusive as quicksilver, first flirted a little with Neo-plasticism, then invented a strong and sensitive style of his own, after which he proceeded to run wild.

In about 1930 Herbin began painting abstracts full of curves, from which basis he gradually evolved his own alphabet of geometrical features for which he is now famous.

Sergei Charchoune, a thorough romantic who is often capable of subtlety and is sometimes obscure and disturbing, composed some sober canvases between 1925 and 1935 which were painted in an ochre, maroon or olive monochrome and which he unfortunately baptised "ornamental cubism". There is nothing ornamental about them but they are moving in their gentleness, having a kind of repressed sentimentality which none the less, thanks to their transparent honesty, manages to show through their hazy indecision.

Albert Gleizes's intellectualised Cubism helped him to discover personal forms of abstraction which range from the extremely simple to the extremely sophisticated. His study of art-history afterwards led him away from that initial manner until he settled down to the interpretation or schematisation of a kind of religious painting based on the Romanesque style. Gleizes will also be remembered for restoring Robert Delaunay's faith in himself by his praise of Delaunay's intuitive work in 1912-13, and for having brought him back to abstract painting in 1930 or thereabouts.

59

FREUNDLICH. COMPOSITION. 1930.
Private Collection, Paris.

Alfred Reth, one of the 'forgotten children' of Cubism along with Van Rees, Tour Donas and others, found himself driven by some inner necessity to all sorts of unrewarding experiments in new materials and themes. The results he achieved in this way were often surprising but often disappointing. It was only after 1945 that he found himself, in a monumental style which leaves no further doubt that he has a genuinely creative personality.

Henri Nouveau began as a musician, then took up plastic art in 1920 when he produced some abstract collages of miniature proportions. He led and is still leading a very secluded life, still keeping an eye on the outside world, an essentially humorous eye, like Klee's, though he almost always avoids the slightest hint of figuration. His painting is immensely amusing, full of discoveries and arrangements which are often comical and always discreet and rhythmical.

Finally, another outstanding personality was Otto Freundlich, a painter, sculptor and poet who began as a member of the German Expressionist school. After he came to Paris he began to paint in primary colours, laid on in flat tints. It was 1919 before he broke away from representation. In the twenty years that followed Freundlich painted a series of large canvases composed of rectangles of unequal size painted in lively hues, in which the darker areas were balanced with lighter areas. His works are impressive in their concentrated strength and there is something exhilarating in their controlled lyricism.

MAGNELLI. PAINTING NO. 0530. 1915.
Artist's Collection.

61

8

ABSTRACT PAINTING IN FRANCE SINCE KANDINSKY'S DEATH. MAGNELLI. THE 'FOUNDERS OF ABSTRACT ART' EXHIBITION AT THE MAEGHT GALLERY. 'LES RÉALITÉS NOUVELLES'. THE MAY SALON. HARTUNG, DE STAËL AND WOLS. SOME OUTSTANDING PAINTERS. 'TACHISME' AND 'UNIFORMISME'. WOMEN PAINTERS.

We are now coming to the present time, when the works to be discussed are so recent that some errors of assessment are bound to occur. I shall do my best to be generous, as understanding is out of the question unless one keeps an open mind. However it is hard to be generous in the 'jungle' of art, in which we sometimes meet people who put us on the defensive instead of arousing our admiration.

The second world war, in which millions lost their lives, also thinned the ranks of artists of all kinds. It was not survived by Delaunay, Freundlich, Mondrian and Kandinsky. Delaunay died in 1941; Freundlich in a concentration-camp in 1943; both Mondrian and Kandinsky in 1944, the first in New York at the beginning of that year, the second in Paris three months after the liberation. The war and the German occupation sent art underground in France. Fear was the dominant factor. But as soon as 'degenerate' art was able to come into the open it was seen that the artists had carried on their work in secret. At the first important exhibition of abstract art after the war—it was called Concrete Art (*Art concret*) and was held at the Drouin gallery in the Place Vendôme in June 1945— works painted during the war by Kandinsky, Herbin, Magnelli, Gorin, Pevsner, Freundlich, and Domela were shown together with pre-war canvases by Robert and Sonia Delaunay, Arp, Sophie Taüber, Mondrian and Van Doesburg.

The most important event immediately after the war was the immediate success of Alberto Magnelli. Thanks to him Italy was able to make up lost ground in abstract art, in which her painters had so far made only a mediocre showing. As is well known Alberto Magnelli had painted a few geometrical abstracts in Florence in 1915 after a short stay in Paris. After those first attempts he returned to figuration, and for about ten years produced mainly artificially-constructed landscapes and monochrome seascapes. He returned to Paris in 1933, where he painted broken pieces of rock and thus made his way back towards abstraction. During the war

62

Magnelli fled to Grasse in the south of France where he met Arp, Sophie Taüber and Sonia Delaunay. The four of them worked together as a team, producing drawings and designing lithographs which were later published in Paris. (25) Magnelli's fame grew by leaps and bounds after the war, and he was soon the most important abstract painter in Paris. With the strong support of the critics in Paris, Switzerland and Italy (who called him 'Kandinsky's disciple of genius') he held an unforgettable exhibition at the Drouin Gallery in 1947. He is a hard worker with great reserves of strength. He is, of course, a disciple of Kandinsky, but is more robust and massive than the Russian painter. You can feel behind his work the background of the sturdy Florentine palaces of his native city, and it has sometimes the sober green and white lyricism of the famous Baptistery near which he was born. Magnelli has tirelessly strengthened and refined his style. One of his most successful discoveries is the multi-coloured line which acts like a kind of transparent skin, surrounding or even sectioning his forms and subtly changing whatever area it penetrates while respecting the values it finds there.

While the return to liberty in France was marked by the death of Kandinsky and the sudden rise of Magnelli, perhaps the main contribution of the immediate post-war period lay in the sudden inrush of a host of new painters who brought every kind of talent to the service of abstract art. The crowd of young artists who spontaneously turned to abstractions as though it represented the main tradition of art fully justified the founding of a separate Salon which would be devoted exclusively to the various forms the new plastic language has taken. That is how *Réalités Nouvelles* came to be founded by Fredo Sidès, though oddly enough he was an antique-dealer. (26)

Altan, Boumeester, Bryen, Chesnay, Coulon, Dewasne, Deyrolle, Engel-Pak, Folmer, Gorin, Hartung, Kosnick-Kloss, Lardeur, Leppien, Malespine, Ney, Piaubert, Poliakoff, Quentin, Marie Raymond, Schneider, Villeri, Vajda, Warb, Wendt, Wols, Léo Breuer, Jeanne Coppel, Duthoo, Fleischmann, Gœtz, Loubchansky, Lhotellier, Mathieu, Evelyn Marc, Néjad, Soulages, Smadja, Vasarely, Vulliamy, Davring, Del Marle, Dufour, Gœbel, Germain, Maria Manton, Nina Negri, Pillet, Pons, Bott, Closon, Dumitresco, Istrati, Koskas, Montlaur, Hella Guth, Fahr-el-Nissa Zeid, Neuberth, Marcelle Cahn, Nemours, Staritsky, Tsingos, Lapoujade—the above is a list of only a few of the painters, and to name them all would be impossible, who represented the French contingent at the *Réalités Nouvelles* shows. The same Gallery also did good work in showing exhibitions

63

by foreign artists, some of which were of great interest, such as the Swiss and Swedish sections in 1948.

At the same time the other Salons became increasingly willing to make room for abstract art. The May Salon in particular drew some of its best contributors from Réalités Nouvelles in 1949. The same May Salon brought together the widely different abstract talents of Lanskoy, Estève, Palazuelo, Singier, Manessier, Le Moal, Bazaine, Hosiasson, Tal Coat, Gischia, de Staël, Riopelle, Lutka Pink, Chastel, Diaz, Lapicque, Lombard, Messagier, Pallut, Springer, Szobel, Rezvani, Léon Zack, Vieira da Silva, Geer van Velde, Ubac, Szenès and many others. Details of all these painters will be found in the Dictionary section of this book.

It was also in 1949, in April, that my book 'Abstract Art, its origins and founders' was published, while at the same time the accompanying exhibition of 'Founders of Abstract Art' was held at the Maeght gallery from April to June.

Then André Bloc brought out the first number of the review *Art d'aujourd'hui* (June 1949-December 1954) which served to amplify the book and exhibition already mentioned, and which was the first review in the world entirely given to a defence of abstract art. It contained important studies of the principal abstract painters, and special numbers appeared on America, Italy, Germany, and the Scandinavian countries. The complete collection of thirty-six parts, notwithstanding occasional errors, provides a unique documentation of abstract art in France and indeed all over the world.

Among the numerous painters mentioned above there are a few who stand out and deserve closer attention. First of these are Hartung, de Staël and Wols.

These three are all intuitive painters. The line together with spots or patches of paint make up Hartung's medium, while most often de Staël uses only the patch and Wols the line. The latter's painting is a display of spasms. His work gives off a sort of mental electricity, full of involuntary references and unconscious perversity. Wols died in 1951, leaving behind him an enormous number of strange scrawls which provided a nervous outlet for a somewhat indolent character, as well as some large canvases in which his over-cerebral intellectual dream is directly expressed through the act of painting in itself, without the slightest interpretation or process being allowed to come between him and the work.

De Staël, on the other hand was a completely conscious, deliberate painter. His first aim was to bring the canvas to life, and this he did with the energy of a virile temperament. He used to give everything he had to the canvas, coming back to it again and again till he achieved the finish and subtlety he wanted. Often enough he would wring the neck of his own painting, as Verlaine talked of wringing the neck of eloquence, and this gave de Staël's work its intimate warmth, its own personal accent, its eloquence. The painter ended his life by hurling himself from his studio window at Antibes in March 1955.

The eldest of the three, Hartung, is also the richest. His work as it stands at present is the most restrained and yet there is no stiffness about it, nor are there any signs of a wilful self-discipline. Hartung's apparent ease is a discipline in itself. He anticipates the very gesture of

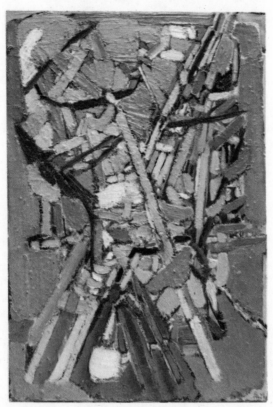

DE STAËL. COMPOSITION: HARMONY IN GREY, BEIGE, RED PATCHES. 1940. *Private Collection, Paris.*

65

WOLS. PEN AND INK DRAWING. 1949.

painting, breaks it up into its natural parts and renews it at the level of direct action, with a studied slow sincerity which heeds only a few faint echoes of what was decided in advance and has already joined the deep reserves of the unconscious mind. Painting thus becomes a religious act, an act of faith. And religion implies revolution, though in his case, however deep it may be, the revolution is bloodless like those of Beethoven or Gabriel Fauré.

Schneider, Soulages and Hosiasson will, I trust, not object if I count them among the spiritual family of Hartung. This is not to suggest that they are in any way his followers, but that there is a certain affinity between them.

Gérard Schneider's style is much less smooth than Hartung's. He has a liking for black shapes, which are stretched and roughly hacked out, looming threateningly from their lighter ground. There is more sorrow than joy in his work, in which an obvious anguish seems to be furtively craving for elegance.

Soulages has the gift of a simple and natural strength. His dark canvases, with pale wisps of colour that seem to lurk or survive in the half-light, are successful dramatic works. His strength is in the kind of discoveries he makes, in the way the amplified structure or framework is enough to make the whole composition. He gives this something like a soul, and out of a terse gesture of the brush he evokes a monument or a temple. No other contemporary painter has such a calm, reliable strength.

Hosiasson works in mud—but there are no work or mud equal to his, which strive after and achieve the pure quality of tonal harmony with an underlying wave-like movement. The wave springs from the obscure depths of the consciousness, and loses nothing of its immensity even in his smallest works.

Mathieu owes some of his symbols to Hartung, as well as something of his private apprenticeship to freedom, but otherwise the resemblance goes no further than a few external features. Their technique is just as different as their minds. Mathieu takes refuge in himself, his passion is deliberately intense and short-lived, and perhaps its impulse lies in contempt. He shows no signs of remorse: the harm is done and is better left as it is. He is a painter who has no scruples about squeezing a whole tube of bright red over a surface of twenty square centimetres, or brushing over an enormous canvas in two hours.

Manessier, Singier and Le Moal, the worthy trinity of the Galerie de France are much more serious painters. They are close friends and have

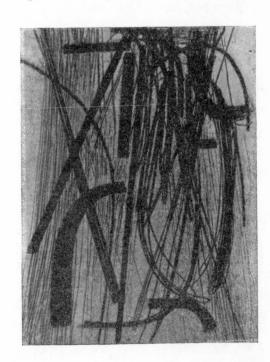

HANS HARTUNG.
ENGRAVING. 1953.

67

obviously influenced one another, though there are marked differences between them. Manessier is as grave as Le Moal is fresh and lively, while Singier holds the balance as a scholarly and sometimes precious painter. The work of all three is typically French, with its love of order and restraint and unadorned gracefulness. They have created an abstract art of their own, related to the tradition that goes back to the stained glass of Chartres and the Arras tapestries.

The same French lyrical use of colour which found its great champion in Delaunay, has new exponents in Bazaine, Estève, Lombard, and Germain, while it is also noticeable in the work of such oriental artists as Néjad and Rezvani. The most popular is Bazaine, who writes as well as paints. Rezvani is from Persia and produces work as rich and urbane as a Persian carpet. Néjad's characteristically broken shapes can be disturbing and often irritating, but they spring from a genuine painter's temperament in that they have no use for grace and facility alone. His mother is Princess Fahr-el-Nissa-Zeid, well known for her very large compositions executed in bright colours, again something like oriental carpets and redolent of the pungent perfumes of Asia Minor.

BEN NICHOLSON. PAINTED RELIEF. 1939.
Museum of Modern Art, New York.

68

Let us turn now to geometrical abstracts. The first names to suggest themselves are Vasarely, Dewasne and Pillet. Vasarely prefers a refinement of forms which is enhanced by his sober colour. Dewasne on the contrary is more concerned with colour for its own sake and the interplaying contrasts he can get out of it. He is at his best in ambitious mural compositions in which he seems more at home than with the easel. Pillet's often linear compositions are governed by his pursuit of subtle inflections of colour.

Davring and Leppien are two painters of German origin who have been settled for a long time in the south of France. They both have a very linear style which reconciles the straight and curved line. Leppien is the more light-hearted of the two and perhaps the more consistent, but although Davring is occasionally disappointing he is much more resourceful. Davring was at one time the youngest of the German Expressionists, and went under the name of Davringhausen.

Jean Piaubert is another geometrical painter who is known for his very severe canvases and for the remarkable lithographs he made for Jean Cassou's *33 Sonnets*. Sergei Poliakoff's geometrical designs have something unpolished about them which is not without admirers, and sometimes his touches of awkwardness are successful in their effect.

Geer van Velde is of Dutch origin and is a painter of exceptional crafstmanship. He was slow in his approach to abstraction and has shown no haste in his exploration of it since. Every one of his work has behind it the weight of a painter's training and experience, and the brush offers us a selection of his rich powers which are painstakingly conveyed on the canvas. His canvases are worked up slowly in a polished economical style in which the colour is always discreet. His restrained undertones are modulated in a polytonality in which the ryhthm is marked by a rectilinear stress which never degenerates into stiffness.

Geer's brother Bram van Velde has an engaging temperament which nevertheless is full of smouldering revolt and denial. His few canvases seem to be painfully drawn from an undecided personality, fluid and frameless, which together with their cold lucidity makes them all the more expressive.

Much has been said in Paris in the last year or two about *Tachisme*. This term is used to describe a movement which runs parallel with abstract Neo-Expressionism, originating in America. Its immediate ancestors are Henri Michaux (whose works are always closer to figuration than to abstraction because they are full of literary allusions) and Hans Hartung, whose painting has been strictly abstract over the past twenty years. Its more distant origins lie in the work Kandinsky produced in his so-called dramatic period of 1910-1912. The real *tachistes* are Bryen, Mathieu, Greta Sauer, Lee Hersch, Bogard, Riopelle and a number of others. Under Riopelle's influence there has developed a certain uniformity which enables painters to avoid the slightest problem of composition and to reduce the act of painting to a physical gesture. The American, Pollock, prepared the way for this in 1950. In Paris, Chelimsky and Sam Francis have taken this up, and more recently Wendt, Istrati and Nallard.

Meanwhile a number of painters who rely on pure colour-sensibility are going their own way between all these extremes, though they do no go so far as to cut out all content from their 'dialogue' with the canvas. They are thus continuing a tradition of finesse and adaptability which is always a pleasure to the eye. These painters include Vulliamy, Kolos Vary, Lagage, Debré, Van Haardt, Bott and Szenès.

Women painters have made a contribution to the phenomenology of abstract art which must not be underestimated. Berthe Morisot and Mary Cassatt were the only female Impressionists, while Marie Laurencin, Maria Blanchard and Tour Donas were the only women of note among the Cubists. After Sonia Delaunay and Sophie Taüber there has been no lack of women painting on abstract lines. It might be asked whether they are less creative than the man, whether they are inferior in strength or invention, or whether they show less restraint. My own sincere opinion is that this is not so. It cannot be denied that the greatest painters are men, and the same goes for the other arts. But such men are few and can be counted on one hand. If we carry on counting on the other hand the women find their place as equals with the men. Some of them, such as Evelyn Marc and Christine Boumeester paint with more delicacy than the men; others such as Jeanne Coppel, Marcelle Cahn, Nathalia Dumitresco and Aurélie Nemours are their equals in restraint and discipline; some are in no way inferior in their creative improvisation, such as Vieira da Silva, Karskaya and Staritsky, while others equal the men in their energy, for instance Sonia Delaunay and Nina Tryggvadottir. The part women have to play is not always easy. Their work is examined with the same aggressive suspicion by feminists and anti-feminists alike, the former expecting them to prove more than they are capable of and the latter pouncing on the slightest pretext for running them down. There is no such thing as sex where sensibility is concerned, and I know many a highly-regarded canvas which would meet with derision if it were signed with a woman's name.

9

ABSTRACT ART IN OTHER COUNTRIES.

The first artist to turn to abstract art in Belgium was Victor Servranckx. His works are made up either of rounded shapes like fragmentary worlds (*Éventration,* 1919) or sometimes of more orthogonal, rectangular features. The latter are related to the aesthetics of the machine of which the Futurists made so much (*Le règne de l'acier poli* or Polished steel kingdom, 1923). Servranckx later abandoned abstraction but gradually returned to it after 1946. In 1920 a painter from Antwerp, Joseph Peeters, began working in the abstract geometrical style. At the end of the following year he held an exhibition which attracted some notice and he was then asked to become co-editor of the advance-guard review *Het Overzicht*. In it he published several articles on his idea of 'community art' in which he took a stand against the views of *De Stijl* which he thought were too narrow. Apart from works by Delaunay, Juan Gris, Kandinsky, Moholy-Nagy, Huszar,

JOSEPH PEETERS. LINO-CUT. 1920.

71

Larionov and others, *Het Overzicht* reproduced abstract works by such Belgian artists as Peeters, Servranckx, Karel Maes, Edmond van Dooren, Prosper de Troyer, Jos Leonard and Paul Joostens. Within a few years they had all returned to figurative painting or, as in the case of Peeters and de Maes stopped painting altogether by 1926. During the next twenty years abstract art was almost totally neglected in Belgium. On the other hand a number of Belgian painters have been making abstracts in France for some years now, particularly Engel-Pak, Closon, Lempereur-Haut, Orix, Alechinsky. In Belgium itself at the present time the abstract group consists mainly of Delahaut, Bury, Jan Saverys, Van Lint, Anne Bonnet, Kurt Lewy, Meerbergen, Mendelsohn and Gaston Bertrand.

Almost the same thing happened in Holland as in Belgium: the *Stijl* group was left without successors. The young painters emigrated and became known, much later, as advance-guard artists of repute in their country of adoption. There were, of course, a few isolated exceptions such as Werkman who has already been discussed and who was the only abstract artist in Holland between 1925 and 1930, and a little before him but for a very short period A. C. Willinck. This is another case in which abstract art came to the fore after the country was liberated. The principal abstract painters now working in Holland are Sinemus, Van der Vossen, Willy Boers, Rooskens, Frieda Hunziker, Ouborg, Will, and Alkema.

In Germany abstract art has never been very lucky. Its two best representatives Franz Marc and August Macke both lost their lives in the first world war. Not long after his rise to power Hitler condemned and forbade all advance-guard art. Many artists and intellectuals left the country. Baumeister was one of the few who remained behind, but he had often combined figuration and abstraction and could hardly be considered as a pure abstractionist. Now there are quite a number of abstract painters in Germany, of whom the most outstanding are Ernst W. Nay, Theodor Werner, Fritz Winter, Julius Bissier, Karl Otto Götz, G. K. Schmelzeisen. Worth mentioning among the younger generation are Schultze, Sonderborg, Schilling and Fath Winter.

In Scandinavia the Swedish painter Carlsund and the Dane Francisca Clausen introduced abstract art in about 1930. However in Sweden at present I can see no more than two painters who seem genuinely drawn towards abstraction: these are Ollé Baertling, a disciple of Herbin, and

Ollé Bonnier, a much freer painter but one who has come under various influences.

There is a group of abstract painters in Iceland, notably Thorvaldur Skülarson, Svavar Gudnason, Valtyr Petersun and Sverrir Haraldson. One of the most powerful of them, Nina Tryggvadottir, has been working in Paris for some years now.

England has Ben Nicholson, who has already been mentioned, and a few painters who work with or near him at Saint Ives in Cornwall. A fairly large group has gradually gathered in London, among whom Victor Pasmore is definitely the most significant. This painter has a completely personal style in which a Celtic, linear element comes to terms with rectangular geometrical features. The same group contains Anthony Hill, Terry Frost, Adrian Heath, Kenneth Martin, Roger Hilton and Sven Blomberg. The two women painters Marlow Moss and Paule Vézelay belong to the preceding generation. For many years the former of these was a keen disciple of Mondrian, in Paris, and she has a definite talent which she puts at the service of that doctrine of extreme caution. Paule Vézelay clearly owes most to Hans Arp, yet she has her own manner. She can express great tenderness and gentle shyness through the medium of her neutral greys and fragile, graceful shapes.

In Italy, as we have already noted, the Futurism of Boccioni, Carrà and Soffici often approached abstraction. But Balla and Magnelli are the only painters since then to have produced works of a radical and deliberate abstraction. Before 1914 Severini painted a few abstract works in Paris. A large number of abstractionists have appeared in Italy since the war, including Vedova, Corpora, Bertini, Burri, Guerrini, Bozzolini, Savelli, di Salvatore, Capograssi, Prampolini, Soldati, Dorazio, Righetti, Reggiani, Santomaso. Some of these are well known in Paris and New York. Pettoruti, who was for many years keeper of the Museum of Fine Arts in Buenos-Ayres and who is known in America for his Cubist works which are sometimes similar to those of Gris, returned to abstraction in 1953, having already tried it in Italy when he was a young man.

As for Switzerland, having had the benefit during the 1914-18 war of the presence of many foreign intellectuals, then of the beginnings of Dadaism, none the less it remained more or less indifferent to advance-guard art of every kind, so that there were no immediate developments there. It was not until 1936 that a public exhibition (at the Zürich Kunsthaus) drew attention to an abstractionist who was both of Swiss nationality and resident in Switzerland. He was Max Bill. Apart from that, Switzerland did much to make up lost ground after Léo Leuppi founded the *Die Allianz* group. This led to important exhibitions being held in Zürich, Basel (1938), the publication of a throughly documented guide or yearbook in 1940, then further exhibitions at Basel in 1944 and Zürich in 1947. The last of these had a particularly large number of exhibitors. Apart from Bill and Leuppi mention should be made of Eble, Eichmann, Lili Erzinger, Graeser, Lhose, Spiller, Tiravanti, Fischli, Bodmer, Vreni Lœwensberg, Hinterreiter.

After the *Cercle et Carré* venture, Torrès-Garcia returned home to Uruguay, where he ran an art-school in Montevideo until his death in 1949. This school had a large number of students and spread its influence all over Buenos-Ayres. However, what Torrès-Garcia was teaching in the same of abstract art was in reality a form of figurative art which had deep roots in the native primitive art of South America. This led to some misunderstanding, and it is not hard to see why the first really abstract painters in Argentine preferred the term "concrete art" which had been favoured by Max Bill.

There are quite a number of abstract painters in Argentina. To name a few of these: Hlito, Ocampo and Villalba are all related to Vordemberge and the Swiss painter Eichmann; Mele produced Neo-constructivist paintings with an element of relief in them; Vardanega has made some interesting experiments, using glass; Maldonado often comes close to pure Neo-plasticism. But Argentina also has an indigenous tendency which has been called *Madi,* and which is led by Arden-Quin, Rothfuss and Kosice. This movement became known in Paris through its frequent contributions to the *Réalités Nouvelles* salon. Among its innovations are the use of a non-orthogonal frame, pictures composed of several separate or detachable parts, and suchlike. Arden-Quin lived in Paris from 1948 till 1953, where his art became more refined. A Parisian *Madi* group soon gathered round him which included Sallaz, Roïtman, Marcelle Saint-Omer, Alexandre and Neyrat. In Argentina itself the Madi movement runs a profusely illustrated review edited by Kosice. Madi art also has a follower in Cuba, namely Sandu Darie who was born in Rumania. Darie is the simplest and most level-headed of the Madi artists. His works are strictly geometrical, create a very pleasant effect and are marked by a certain coolness.

74

GAKUI OSAWA. CALLIGRAPHIC PAINTING.

There is a school of abstract painting in Brazil, at the Flexor studio in Sao Paulo.

Mexico is socially hostile to abstract art, but it has a young painter whose canvases, full of crystalline shapes and strange effects of light, are certainly impressive. He is Gunther Gerzso.

The abstract painters are working in isolation in Australia (Grace Crowley and Ralph Bason) and in South Africa (Nel Erasmus).

There is a considerable group of abstractionists in Jugoslavia, the nucleus of which is formed by Picelj, Kristl and Rasica.

Spain has had a group, for some time now, which exhibits in Madrid at the Galeria Fernando Fé. Some of these are Canogar, Delgado, Feito, Luque, Rodriguez Zambrana and Luiz de la Orden.

Many Japanese artists have reached abstraction through calligraphic art. (27) The reviews *Bokubi* and *Bokuzin* edited by Siryu Morita give generous space to Parisian and New York artists who have influenced such calligraphic painters as Yoshimichi Sekiya, Toko Shinoda, Futoshi Tsuji, Bokushi Nakamura, Gakiu Osawa, Youichi Inoue, Sogen Eguchi and above all the monumental manner of Siryu Morita himself. Exhibitions of Japanese calligraphy held in New York, Amsterdam, Brussels, Basel and Paris show parallels between Eastern and Weestern experiments. Tobey, Kline, Tomlin, Alcopley in America; Hartung, Soulages, Schneider, Mathieu and Alechinsky in France; Götz and Bisser in Germany are calligraphers in the modern oriental sense. The same expressiveness and liberty of style are achieved in colour in the West—except for Kline—and in black and white in the East.

75

IO

ABSTRACT ART IN THE UNITED STATES.

The United States' contribution to abstract art is now almost as large as that of France, and this means that in the past few years Paris has begun to share with New York the supremacy she had in the advanced arts. New York has become an important centre for manifestations of abstract art through the shows held at the Museum of Modern Art, the Whitney Museum and the Salon of American Abstract Artists. Numerous galleries (Janis, Kootz, Fried, Willard, Parsons, etc.) have either allowed or invited American abstractionists to show their work and made them known to the public.

Some outstanding exhibitions of European abstract art have been held in the States, following the one organised by Katherine Dreier at the Brooklyn Museum in 1926. However the first official recognition of American abstractionist painting came in the form of a show at the Museum of Modern Art in New York in January 1951, which coincided with the publication of Andrew Ritchie's book *Abstract painting and sculpture in America*. A few days after the varnishing the same Museum held a series of talks in the form of a symposium, in which statements were made by the five best qualified representatives of American abstract art, Morris, de Kooning, Calder, Glarner and Motherwell. Nervous and uneasy, de Kooning was mainly negative in his opinions, and left the impression that he was fundamentally hostile to both Neo-plasticism and any form of purely geometrical art. On the other hand Glarner gave a short and quiet demonstration of what he calls "relational painting", meaning by that a painting of relationships or a relative painting. I happened to be present at that meeting. When Glarner was asked a question about Mondrian, in the course of the discussion which followed his talk, he answered simply "He was my friend and my master." Glarner is generally considered, on the other side of the Atlantic, as the only successor to Neo-plasticism worth taking seriously. This summary judgment implies some injustice towards painters of such quality as Diller, Kelly, Charmion von Wiegand, Cavallon and Bolotowsky. Yet there is no doubt that the supporters of Neo-expressionism outnumber the Neo-plastic artists and are better known in America. The leaders are Hofmann, Pollock, de Kooning, Kline, Clifford Still and Rothko, others being Tworkow, Stamos and Newman.

Somewhere between the two movements I have already mentioned (Neo-plasticism and Neo-expressionism) come two others, one abstract stream deriving from Cubism and represented by Davis, Morris and Gallatin, and the other originating in Surrealism (Gorky, Motherwell and Baziotes).

A central position among all four tendencies should be given to a fifth class of painters who are fairly numerous and whose work points to a new type of experiment, whether rhythmical or arhythmical, which sometimes reaches the monumental. Tobey and Tomlin are characteristic of this movement.

Mondrian's presence in New York in the last three years of his life was very important for America and for art in general. He arrived there in October 1940 and died on the first of February 1944. In those last years he painted some of his most remarkable works, of which the most famous are the two *Boogie-woogie* canvases. He also took part in numerous art events, publishing essays and holding two exhibitions at the Valentine Gallery. After spending his life almost as a recluse in Paris, followed by two years of obscurity in London, Mondrian was at last able to lead a happy and almost brilliant existence. He found himself surrounded by friends and everywhere held in the highest respect, even by those whom he had formerly believed to be his enemies: he had some pleasant meetings with Max Ernst and André Breton. However financial success only came after his death. Overnight he was praised and publicised in the newspapers and magazines which had hitherto been most scornful of abstract art, and he became rich when he lay in his grave. Designers made 'Neo-plastic' dresses, art-dealers scoured the world in search of his works, his life became a legend and his name a symbol, he was credited with hundreds of witty sayings and all the schools in America started explaining what Neo-plasticism really meant.

The exaggeration was such that some reaction was bound to take place sooner or later. A handful of artists went to the opposite extreme and founded the Abstract-Expressionist movement, with Pollock and de Kooning at its head. American critics tend to regard this as being an authentically American movement and regard the continuation of Neo-plasticism as being no more than a second-hand form of European art. I would suggest that those who assert this have forgotten about Kandinsky: no more is needed than to visit the Solomon R. Guggenheim Museum and see a dozen canvases painted by Kandinsky between 1912 and 1918, to grasp the fact that Abstract Expressionism was and is just as European, since it was born in Munich.

American abstract art undoubtedly has its roots in Europe. This is not my personal wish or decision: it is history's. But whatever the roots, a tree can be grafted and yield extraordinary flowers.

Two strong personalities in the States are Arshile Gorky and Marc Tobey. Gorky was born in Armenia at the beginning of the century and

BOLOTOWSKY. BLACK AND WHITE. PAINTING. 1948.

emigrated to America in 1920. His life was full of surprises. After certain tragic accidents and disappointments in his private life, he committed suicide in 1948 at the very time when he was achieving fame. Gorky was influenced for a long time by various European painters. A considerable part of his work shows a striking parallel with the experiments of Picasso and Miró, as well as, for a time, those of Léger. His abstract compositions painted in 1933 and the years immediately after were still very close to Picasso. After all these adventures and trials and errors Gorky was destined to find his own genius at last, and this happened in about 1940. The works of his last years are of the highest standard and full of meaning. Almost at once he found a personal style in which a fluid use of line gave perfect expression to a refined, erotic sensuality. This style has left a mark on Matta and de Kooning, though in different ways.

Marc Tobey has had an even longer evolution than Gorky, and was born ten years earlier than he. After travelling about in Europe and Asia he went to live in Seattle near the Pacific coast. At Seattle during the last

78

ten years he has produced a body of work, for the most part abstract, which owes some of its unusual rhythmic qualities to a study of Chinese calligraphy. One of his earliest abstract paintings, *Broadway norm,* dating from 1935, consists of a network of white lines on a neutral ground. But it was only after 1943 that he began painting abstract compositions to which he gave all his personality. His rhythm is abrupt yet continuous and he spreads an equal intensity of vision over the whole surface of the canvas: these two characteristics have had a quiet but deep influence on other artists. Nobody can deny that he laid the foundations for Pollock and Tomlin and many others. Large mural panels of 'direct writing' are now a common feature in America, but there has been no finer 'writing' than Tobey's.

Clifford Still, who was for many years a teacher of art in California and who still has a great influence there, became the centre of the idea on

FRANZ KLINE. HIGH STREET. PAINTING. 1950.

which the "Pacific School" or "West Coast School" is based. Much has been said and written about this in recent years, but quite recently the American critic Hubert Crehan did much to this rather pretentious bubble. (28) None the less, Still is an astonishing painter. Late in 1950 I saw an exhibition of his work in New York which leaves me no doubt as to this painter's personality, which is out of the common. He is a kind

79

of cartographer or map-maker who works on large black surfaces cut into unequal sections, strangely animated and dramatised by means of a single trail or drag of bright red, or which he contrasts with ochres and greys.

There are also a number of women painters whose personality cannot be denied. To mention only a few, attention should be given to the paintings on glass by Pereira, the free compositions of Buffie Johnson, Edda Sterne and Suzy Freilinghuysen, or the rhythmical canvases of Ronnie Elliott, the collages of Hilda Rebay and Beate Hulbeck, as well as Alice T. Mason's and Charmion von Wiegand's geometrical experiments and the luminous, hazy effects of Pearl Fine.

Now as always, Paris has quite a large contingent of American painters. Among the abstractionists there are Pfriem, one of Gorky's followers; Sam Francis who, with a deliberate monotony, works in little spots or patches placed side by side; Alcopley, a master of calligraphic improvisation; Jenkins, subtly poetic with his mysterious glimpses of light; finally Chelimsky, Levée, Childs and Malina.

Perhaps I might also count among the Americans the Austrian-born but naturalised Mexican, Wolfgang Paalen. This painter at first gravitated among the surrealist group, but after seeking further experience in his research into ancient Mexican art, discovered an art of his own which is powerfully expressive and has an exhilarating sense of colour. In 1951 Paalen organised an exhibition at the San Francisco Museum of Modern Art in which, apart from his own work, he introduced some abstracts by Lee Mullican and Gordon Onslow-Ford, two exceptionally lyrical painters. The first of these is obsessed by the theme of the sun which gives his canvases a dynamic, expansive movement, while the second is calmer and is enamoured of the glittering effects to be obtained from juxtaposing little spots of colour or vertical lines, producing some interesting optical impressions.

This rapid accumulation of names will no doubt leave the reader somewhat confused. I have tried to keep to the main lines of my inquiry in order to avoid further bewilderment, but this has more than once obliged me to over-simplify and make a rather arbitrary choice among the numerous artists concerned. Present-day art is so rich and varied that it might well seem a glory-hole in which treasures and baubles become indistinguishable. Time will perhaps give greater stature to what at first sight looks commonplace. Like mountains, paintings are more beautiful when seen from a distance.

11

CONCLUSION

Taking a bird's-eye view in an attempt to summarise all the activity that has been described so far, it might be said that the field of abstract art is at present divided into two camps, into geometry and algebra, or, to put it another way, into style and emotional outcry. In some countries such as Germany, the United States and Japan the algebraists are in command, while in others such as Italy, England, the Scandinavian countries, Belgium and Argentina the power is in control of the geometricians. Paris becomes a kind of arena in which the two sides are in combat and where the odds are fairly even. Points are marked up for each side from day to day. Each side has its artists of unquestionable value, great painters who are small-minded and small painters who have a certain greatness in them. Let us not, however, forget the no-man's-land lying between them, the domain of pure sensibility in which style and cry come together and sometimes produce something like ecstasy.

If contemporary abstract art is rich in every kind of experiment, it is still as alive and as tensed.towards the future as it was thirty or forty years ago. We still see every artist at grips with his own conception of the world and of man, and with all the problems that accompany the laws and means of self-expression. This daily drama, this cool struggle for the conquest of truth or of plastic purity represent the essence of the artist's vocation. These problems only became acute in our century, and were hardly noticeable before the advent of abstract art.

Abstract art's function has been and is to reflect the face and being of our century. I wrote at the beginning of this book that living is change, and it is thanks to change that we become what we are. Through the evolution and constant changes of art mankind is able to discover, however slowly, its most profound concern and its truest unchanging quality, which is the tireless inquiry of the human mind, the advance of mind towards self-knowledge despite the apparent frivolity of every style and every love.

All art is metaphysical.

Whether we consider the time-worn works of prehistory, Greco-Egyptian sculptures, Byzantine mosaics, Romanesque painting, Gothic sculpture or even the superb pagan outburst of the Renaissance, every art points to a religion, every art is full to running over with ideals and admi-

81

rations. Surely any active admiration is already a form of adoration? There is no difficulty in pointing out a religious tropism in the shadows of a Rembrandt, or the razor-edge of ascesis in El Greco. But on the other hand did not Raphael and Michelangelo bring a naturally mystical mind to rest, the former by virtue of a kind of supernatural tenderness, the latter through a cosmological anguish, a Maelstrom which draws us inwards towards art like a great whirlpool of hidden loves?

None the less it has been through a long abandonment of the religious theme in the proper sense of the term that abstract art, in our time, came to reveal the metaphysical nature of all art. Not that the support of naturalism strips art so that nothing is left but pure spiritual adoration, or that the artist effaces himself before some evidence or other of the absolute. In that case we could no longer speak of art as such, for it is the nature of all art to love itself with a carnal affection, so fanatical and exclusive that very often the artist becomes numb to other kinds of beauty, or even regards it and them as spurious imitations of the one true beauty, which is beauty as created by himself.

But it is precisely this absolutism of art, it is precisely this power of total love which proves that man is now brought face to face with realities that are beyond his understanding. After thousands of years of being a meditation on the ineffable, and regarding the support of man's intellect as a sign of intellect itself, in our century art has become a meditation on itself, that is to say a meditation on the relativity of the "ineffable". Thanks to abstract art, every artist finds himself faced with the problem of terms of expression, which implies a technique, and secondly with the problem of his own inner life, which implies a dialectic. All the creative artists who have advanced abstract art since it first began have demonstrated that success and undeniable originality depend on a perfect harmony between a developed technique and a state of mind. Perhaps it is that harmony itself, even in a latent state, which brings the artist to raise his hand towards the paint or the canvas, and which determines the embodiment of his thought or his will in a work of art.

If to live is to change, it is also to feel oneself being, to feel that one exists in spite of all changes within or without. There again, it seems to me that art brings fresh succour to the consciousness, an irrefutable test or ordeal which determines a universal constant by means of as many soundings as there are valid works. Thus every artist becomes a unique witness of the life of the mind, the life of the spirit. And oddly enough, the more exceptional or unique he appears, and the more odd or unusual the work

82

itself, the greater will be the number of people who recognise themselves in it. It is as though what is most rare is fundamentally the most universal. Thus it is that if I may illustrate my argument through a commercial image, the most unsellable picture is precisely the one that becomes most 'quoted' or sought after.

Abstract art is the *style* of our century in the same way as, generally speaking, Naturalism was the style of the Nineteenth. Naturalism takes about twenty forms, and in the same way there are some twenty branches of abstract art.

If the two terms now seem to be at opposite poles from one another, it is not for any lack of long and painful discrimination as regards naturalism even in the very first phases of abstraction. The transition stages which ran from the later works of Cézanne up to synthetic Cubism in 1914, rank among the finest manifestations in the whole history of art. Periods of transition, not only in the lives of individuals but in history as a whole, are often charged with greater sensibility because of the uneasiness that goes with breaking things down, as well as the hesitations in creating new things and the effort to establish novelty. This sensitive instability, however, has no meaning except when we relate it to the higher significance of the classicism we are always aspiring towards, in which all struggles come to an end in peaceful contemplation.

Thus the history of art, like the history of every man, is an endless movement between two opposite poles, the uneasy desire for rest and then rest itself which prepares some fresh creation. If living is to feel oneself being, the most profound identity of being is no doubt a perpetual state of birth and beginning. In the artist, who is perhaps the acutest though even then not fully conscious witness of his age, this state of birth expresses itself directly in his work. In the best of cases, it is undistinguishable, because it has no intermediary, from creation itself. But this 'best of cases' is, precisely, given every help by abstract art, because, as it puts an end to the tyranny of naturalistic representation, it allows of a direct communication of a certain inner density or intensity, without any parasitical medium intervening. Once the instrument has become familiar and prepared for its task, the expression of successive states of birth becomes as simple and as fluent as writing, or at least just as unified or concerted. Like handwriting it can be stable or changeable, clear or obscure, orderly or irregular. But the work of art, like writing, will always be a direct grasping and effusion of the self, with no intervening substance to pervert it. There is no closer relationship than that between the artist and his

83

work, and no union is more jealous, more entire and exacting or capable of being blinder to all that lies beyond possession.

If it is true that there is no substance without energy, there is no mind without rest. The body seeks its development and continuity in time, but the mind begins by a pause. To live spiritually means contemplating and finding pleasure in the self, welcoming what comes from without and rejoicing in what lies within. To live physically is to swarm like bees: matter must conquer, but spirit must bide its time.

Art, then, is a spiritual act committing body and spirit together. It is man expressing himself at his highest but most fragile level where matter and the unknown unite. In art the striving of substance and the concentration of the spirit are inseparable. The words 'spiritual act' imply an insoluble contradiction in terms, showing what a mystery underlies art, why it refuses all philosophical analysis. Any dialectical approach to art is blocked by paradox.

Art is the only moment when mind, without ceasing to be mind, is converted into physical expansion, and when matter submits to the mind's transcendence and is converted into speculation, non-contingency.

If this is so, we can understand how art withers away beneath social compulsion, why it eschews social power. Pure disinterestedness, it leads man away from wordly success.

By means of a pure expression of the mind through the submission of matter, the human being makes himself a place or finds himself in a world which is not the everyday world of weights and measures, a world of complete gratuity or disinterestedness which can be called mystical.

The result of this complete gratuitousness is that the work of art is not often recognisable when it is newly born: by definition it eludes all conventional ideas of what it ought to be.

Art is a creation which offers no guarantees. The artist is a man walking into space, and we cannot know by what miracle the solid earth rises up to support his feet.

All that an artist makes or does has the power of law, however upsetting this might appear. Almost as upsetting is the fact that those who follow him along his newly-made path appear more or less insignificant: they are coiners, forgers. The first alone is a creator, and those who follow him have nothing to say or do. Art is elsewhere, where others are travelling onwards, losing the way, losing themselves.

NOTES

(1) There is also a dispute over terminology which has caused much ink to be wasted. Van Doesburg was always starting hares or looking for trouble, and began it in 1930 when he suggested *concrete,* instead of *abstract* which until then had been considered satisfactory. For a while Hans Arp also preferred the term *concrete,* and Kandinsky came out in its favour in 1938. Max Bill became its greatest advocate and through his influence it was adopted in South America and Italy.

Some years ago in New York Miss Hilla Rebay somewhat fanatically insisted on the expression *non-objectivism.* This inevitably caused some confusion in the outlook of some of the young American painters, especially as some American critics apply the term abstract to works which are not so (see Thomas B. Hess, *Abstract Painting*).

Even in Paris there are painters who make a specious distinction between the words *abstract* and *non-figurative.*

We have no intention of being caught up in these quibbles. On the authority of the first abstract painters we have adopted the simplest and most generally accepted term.

(2) In making this distinction no attention should be paid to the title given by a painter to his work. An obvious still-life can easily be called *composition* or even *abstraction* without the title making it any less figurative, while an abstract canvas can be called *Joie de vivre* or *Trafalgar Square* without containing the slightest hint of a story or a landscape. A boy can be baptised *Marie* without being turned into a girl.

(3) This is true of Klee, Miró and often Picasso. Sometimes Picasso will add to his abstract forms—rather casually, according to all accounts—a few brush-strokes which suggest a face or figure. We know that for Picasso "there is no abstract art". He ought to say or perhaps means "there ought not to be any abstract art".

(4) Baudelaire in *L'Art romantique:* "There is no line or colour in nature. It is man who creates line and colour. They are two abstractions whose dignity comes from a common origin... Line and colour both make us think and dream; the pleasures resulting from them are of a different nature, though equal to ordinary nature, and absolutely independent of the picture's subject."

Flaubert, *Correspondance,* 1852: "Perhaps beauty will become a sentiment for which mankind has no further use, and art will be something half-way between algebra and music."

(5) I have been told that in his research into abstraction Kandinsky was influenced by a Lithuanian painter, M. K. Ciurlionis, who died in 1911. This painter composed, from 1904 onwards, abstract paintings which are often characterised by arabesques being used together with geometrical shapes. He also painted some dream-landscapes or dreamscapes, full of symbolic references, which have certain affinities to Kandinsky's more romantic works. A substantial exhibition of Ciurlionis' paintings was held in Moscow in the year of his death. In 1916 W. Ivanov published a book in Russian about Ciurlionis, published by Mussaget, Moscow. Mme Charmion von Wiegand regards Ciurlionis as the first abstract painter (*Encyclopaedia of Art,* New York 1946).

85

(6) *Uber das Geistige in der Kunst* (Spirituality in Art) was published in Munich in 1912, thanks to Franz Marc's intervention with Piper's firm. The work was written in 1910 but was rejected by several publishers.

(7) Michel-Eugène Chevreul: *De la loi du contraste simultané des couleurs* (The law of simultaneous colour-contrast), Paris 1839, and *Des couleurs et de leurs applications aux arts industriels à l'aide des cercles chromatiques* (Colours and their application in the industrial arts with the help of chromatic circles), Paris 1864. Chevreul's theories have found their fulfilment outside the scientific field, thanks to their influence on two great painters. The germ of an idea can have astonishing results in domains for which it was not intended, nor, at first sight, appropriate.

(8) It is well known that Apollinaire gave the name *Orphism* to a group of painters whose free-expression and lively colour had nothing to do with what the Cubists were aiming at. The three main painters of the group were Delaunay, Kupka and Picabia. In this connection he also spoke of 'cubisme écartelé' (quartered or dispersed Cubism). His definition of Orphic Cubism was as follows: "the art of painting new unified compositions (ensembles nouveaux) the elements of which are not drawn from visible reality but are entirely created by the artist, who endows them with powerful reality."

(9) At the same Studio, Larionov also demonstrated what could be done with shades of the same colour and the effects produced by varied handling of the same colour: 1) white upon white—imposing on a polished, glossy white surface, a particular shape in rough, lustreless white: 2) black upon black—imposing on a black porous surface, a particular shape in polished, shiny black: 3) similar combinations with other colours laid on in different ways. These details were provided by M. Larionov.

(10) A Rayonist Manifesto was drawn up by Larionov in June 1912 and appeared in Moscow in the following year (*Luchism,* pubd. by C. A. Munter, Moscow 1913). But by then Rayonism seems to have been already given up by its two inventors.

(11) Much has been said about the influence of Futurism on the work of Larionov and Gontcharova. The two painters deny this and claim that their work was completely independent. The allegation is that Marinetti went on a propaganda mission to Russia in 1910 and exerted considerable influence there. Some critics have denied that the visit was ever made, and I have made inquiries which so far have yielded only negative results. If the journey did take place it seems to have left no trace whatever in the Russian press, whereas Marinetti's visit to Russia in the winter of 1913-1914 certainly did.

(12) *De nieuwe beweging in de schilderkunst (The new movement in painting)* published at Delft in 1917, and *Drie voordrachten over de nieuwe beeldende kunst* (Three lectures on recent plastic art), published at Amsterdam in 1919. These two short books are abundantly illustrated: the illustrations of the second work are accompanied by commentaries which are often very much to the point. These were excellent introductory works for the general reader, written in a lively and enthusiastic style.

(13) The aim was "to raise art into those impersonal, disinterested regions beyond time, place and space, where mathematics, poetry, and the higher arts, all come together with all that is purest and freest in man's mind and heart." (Ozenfant and Jeanneret, *Modern Painting,* p. 164). We find everywhere the same desire to create in art a kind of new quadrivium or union of the liberal arts.

86

(14) This brings to mind the 1918 *collages* of Arp and Sophie Taüber, which they made out of bits of paper, all cut the same size with a bookbinder's guillotine. Arp gave further information about this in *Jalons* in 1950: "Our researches into the static arose from essentially different aims from those of most of the Constructivists. We were hoping for pictures to provoke meditations,—mandalas, guide-posts. Our rods of light, like surveyors' poles, were intended to show paths into space, depth, into the infinite."

(15) Georges Vantongerloo: *L'Art et son avenir* (Art and its future), Antwerp, 1924.

(16) From a letter to Paul Citroën (in Dutch), February 1930.

(17) Van Doesburg wrote on 13 July 1930, six months before he died, "The modern painter's studio should have a mountain atmosphere of three thousand metres above sea-level, with everlasting snow; height kills off microbes." (*De Stijl,* posthumous number).

(18) M. E. Chevreul: *De l'abstraction considérée relativement aux beaux-arts et à la littérature* (Abstraction considered in its relationship to the fine arts and literature), Dijon, 1864, p. 35.

(19) *XXᵉ siècle,* No. 3, Paris 1952.

(20) In *Fernand Léger, la forme humaine dans l'espace* (*Fernand Léger, the Human Form in Space*), Montreal 1945, pp. 73-74.

(21) In *New World of Space,* New York 1948. Le Corbusier called Mondrian "an heroic pilgrim", whose "tragic destiny" was to show the younger generation the right direction in architecture.

In his numerous writings Le Corbusier has often found some impressive literary approaches to Neo-plasticism. For example: "I am in Brittany. That pure line in the distance is the limit of the ocean and the sky: a vast horizontal plane stretches towards me. This sovereign repose fills me with a voluptuous pleasure. . . There are a few rocks on the right. The undulating sandy beaches enchant me with their most gentle modulation on the horizontal plane. Suddenly I stop walking. A sensational event has taken place between the horizon and the eye: a vertical rock, a slab of granite is standing erect like a menhir, its verticality making a right-angle with the sea's horizon. It crystallises and fixes the whole area. This is the place where a man must stop, because there is a total symphony, there are wonderful relationships, nobility. The vertical fixes the sense and direction of the horizontal. The one comes to life because of the other. Here are synthetic powers. I pause to reflect: why am I so disturbed? Why has the same emotion occurred in my life in other circumstances and in other forms? I visualise the Parthenon, its sublime entablature with all its overwhelming power. I think, by way of contrast or comparison, of other works full of sensibility but which are so to speak aborted, unfulfilled, such as the Butter Tower at Rouen, or flamboyant arches in which so much thinly-spread genius was sacrificed without achieving brilliance, for instance the brilliance of the bronze pendentives of the Parthenon on the Acropolis. Then, with nothing but two strokes I draw this *place of all measurements* and say to myself 'There, that's enough: such poverty, such want of means, and yet what sublime limits they are. Everything is there, the keys to poems of architecture. Nothing but distance and height, and they are all that is needed.' " (*Cercle et Carré,* No. 3, 30 June 1930).

(22) *Abstraction-Création* at one time had over 400 members, half of whom were in Paris.

87

(23) "In 1919, through Feininger, the influence of the Dutch *Stijl* group began to permeate through the Bauhaus. Two years later Doesburg, the leader of the *Stijl,* began to divide his time between Weimar and Berlin. His presence at Weimar brought about a veritable revolution: from the mysticism and transcendentalism of the Expressionists the Bauhaus turned towards clarity, discipline and the desire for a consciously developed style in architecture and the allied arts which the Dutch movement had already initiated.

Within a few months, Gropius, who had been engaged in designing a picturesque wooden block house with Cubist decorations, remodelled the theatre at Jena under the influence of the *Stijl* and sent to the Chicago Tribune competition a skyscraper project of extreme simplicity." (Alfred H. Barr jr.: *Cubism and Abstract art,* p. 156.)

(24) For a few years Mondrian already had two other direct disciples in Europe: the Englishwoman Miss Marlow Moss and the French artist Jean Gorin. An important date in Mondrian's life was when Miss Katherine Dreier visited him early in 1926. It was thanks to her that his work was introduced to America. In the same year Miss Dreier wrote in the illustrated catalogue of the 'Société Anonyme', "Holland has produced three great painters who, although they were a logical expression of their country, managed to rise above it by their strength of personality. The first was Rembrandt, the second Van Gogh, the third is Mondrian. We can realise Rembrandt's powerful personality by comparing him with other men of his time, with men as great as Franz Hals. In the same way Van Gogh stands out in strong contrasts to Mauve, Israëls and other quite good painters of his epoch. And now we have Mondrian, starting off from a strongly individualistic expression and achieving a clarity which was never reached before him."

(25) *Album de dix lithographies originales en couleurs,* edited by Jacques Goldschmidt, Paris 1950.

(26) A previous exhibition entitled *Réalités Nouvelles* had already been held in 1939, at the Charpentier gallery in Paris. This was organised by Mme Van Doesburg and Fredo Sidès.

(27) Of course writing, in China and Japan, has always been regarded as one of the fine arts. In the 11th century Kuo Hsi stated categorically that there is no difference between the study of writing and that of painting. It is generally thought in China that the art of painting subjects from nature was invented by Wang Hsichih, who is regarded as the greatest of calligraphers. (See S. Macdonald-Wright, *Magazine of Art,* New York, Oct. 1919.)

(28) *Is there a California School?* in "Art News", New York, January 1956.

Appendices

APPENDIX A.

Among his papers Severini has kept the manuscript copy of the following manifesto, written during the winter of 1913-1914 and originally intended for publication in the review *Lacerba*. It is here printed for the first time and clearly shows how close Futurism, as indeed was also the Cubist movement of the same period, then was to a purely abstract conception of art: *Objects no longer exist...* *The important thing is not to represent the speeding motor-car, but to represent the speed of the motor-car.*

NEO-FUTURIST PLASTIC ART

Analogies.

In achieving that higher type of Impressionism summed up in the expression : object + atmosphere, Futurist painting and sculpture have brought the illustrious wheel of Impressionism full circle.

A plastic art that is both quantitative and qualitative should succeed an art that is qualitative only, and hence completely dynamic.

THE WHOLE UNIVERSE MUST BE CONTAINED WITHIN THE WORK OF ART. OBJECTS NO LONGER EXIST.

We must forget external reality and our knowledge of its integral values, in order to CREATE those new dimensions whose order and extent in the universe are to be determined by our regenerate sensitivity.

We shall thus be able to express not only those plastic emotive responses which are relative to an EMOTIVE ATMOSPHERE, but also those which are bound up with the whole universe, since reality considered as a TOTAL

FORCE (or a dynamic absolute) encloses the universe within an infinite circle ranging from affinities, analogies and resemblances to opposites and specific differences.

Thus, the sensation produced in us by a reality which we recognise as being square in shape and blue in colour may be expressed plastically by its complementary shapes and colours, in other words by rounded shapes and shades of blue.

For henceforth, external reality and our perception of it no longer determine plastic expression. As for the action of memory on our sensory faculties, only the memory of the feeling subsists and not that of the cause which engendered it.

The effect of MEMORY in the work of art will thus be not only that of an AGENT OF PLASTIC INTENSIFICATION but also that of a DIRECT EMOTIVE CAUSE independent of any *unity of time and place*.

(Since 1911, in my painting "Souvenirs de Voyage"—the first Futurist composition in Paris, February 1912—I have envisaged the possibility of widening the horizon of plastic sensitivity to the infinite by totally destroying the unity of time and place with a painting of memory which embraced in a single plastic entity realities perceived in Tuscany, on the Alps, in Paris, etc.).

But it should not be thought that memory, either as an agent of plastic intensification or as a direct emotive cause, should be a morbid and sentimental exaltation of things far off in time and space. All these old nostalgic trappings we leave to the literature enamoured of the past, and go on to consider MEMORY from the point of view of PHYSICAL AND EMOTIVE SENSATION.

In any case it would be impossible to separate emotion from memory without arresting the fleeting continuity of matter.

Since both living beings and things by equal right go to make up universal motion, it is impossible to envisage any reality as separate from its wider dynamic implications which are perpetuated precisely by the memories, affinities and contrasts that it arouses SIMULTANEOUSLY within us.

These memories, affinities and contrasts are so many analogical realities or qualitative continuities directing our sensory awareness towards the universal dynamic totality of the reality in question.

Thus the spiral forms and contrasts of yellow and blue that our intuition may have discovered one evening as we felt ourselves carried away by the movements of a dancer, may be rediscovered later, either by affinity or by contrast, in the spiral flight of an aeroplane or the glinting reflections of the sea.

In the same way, certain shapes and colours which express the sensations of sound, smell, light, heat, speed, etc., relative, for example, to the reality: "transatlantic liner" may also express by plastic analogy the same sensations aroused in us by the far-removed reality: "Galeries Lafayette".

The reality "transatlantic liner" is thus linked to the reality "Galeries Lafayette" (and each reality linked to its *specific difference*) by its qualitative continuities which travel throughout the Universe on the wireless waves of our sensibility.

Here then is a complex realism which TOTALLY does away with the integrality of matter—the latter is now considered SOLELY at its MAXIMUM vitality and may be expressed thus : dancer = aeroplane = sea; or Galeries Lafayette = transatlantic liner, etc.

This system of complementary images which I intend to use is not designed to result in the "metaphor", i.e. the designation of one thing by comparison with or opposition to another thing. My intention is to create a new reality: out of the DANCER and the AEROPLANE is engendered the SEA.

To arrive at a desired reality through the comparison or contrast of two other realities is one of the techniques proper to poetry; in the same way, through the use of *two complementary colours,* a third colour—the colour desired—may be obtained.

In music also, fifths, fourths and thirds are simply juxtapositions of notes designed to produce a given chord or harmony.

Through this purely qualitative and universal approach to reality, and by these "appropriate means", both matter itself and its volition may be simultaneously expressed at the maximum of their intensive and expansive activity.

This, moreover, brings the plastic emotive response back to its physical and spontaneous origin: LIFE, from which any intellectual consideration as such would tend to separate it.

In this interpenetration of planes and simultaneous representation of atmosphere as used in Futurist plastic art, we have shown the reciprocal influence of objects and the vitality-atmosphere of matter (intensity and expansiveness of the object-atmosphere). With qualitative Neo-Futurist art I extend to the infinite the field of these influences, continuities, volitions and contrasts of which the SINGLE FORM, CREATED by my sensibility, is the expression of the absolute vitality of matter or of universal dynamism.

It is difficult to establish laws for the various means of expression relative to the individuality of each artist. Nevertheless, these are the technical bases, already partially employed by us, but intensified and developed in relation to the UNIVERSAL PLASTIC SENSIBILITY OF NEO-FUTURIST ART.

With Regard to Form.

1. Simultaneous contrast of lines, planes and volumes. Contrasts by groups of analogous forms arranged in spherical expansion. Constructive interpenetration.

2. Rhythmic arabesque-type construction, consciously ordered so as to point to a new qualitative architecture, composed exclusively of quantitative qualities.

3. Dynamic composition open towards space in all directions, vertically, or of rectangular, square or spherical form.

4. Rejection of the straight line, which is static and dead unless it is duly vitalised by contrasts. Rejection of parallel lines.

With Regard to Colour.

1. Exclusive use of pure prismatic colours in simultaneously contrasting zones, or in groups of analogous colours, either separately or in sequence.

(The system of complementaries in general, and the divisionist use of analogous colours, constitute the colour analogy technique. Through these analogies is obtained the *maximum intensity of light, heat, musicality and constructive and optical dynamism*).

2. The use, as means of *realistic intensification,* of onomatopoeic signs, of unattached verbal expressions and of all possible kinds of matter.

My need for absolute realism has led me to model shapes in relief on my pictures and to colour my plastic compositions with all the colours of the prism arranged in spherical expansion.

All sensations, when they take on plastic form, are expressed concretely in the sensation *light*—they can therefore be expressed only by *all the colours of the prism.*

To paint forms other than with all the colours of the spectrum would mean that one of the most important motions of matter, that of *irradiation,* would be arrested.

The coloured expression of the sensation *light,* within the context of spherical expansion in Futurist painting, can only be centrifugal or centripetal in relation to the organic construction of the work. Thus, for example, the plastic entity: Dancer = Sea, would for preference be expressed with light irradiation (forms and colours, and light) moving outwards from the centre towards the surrounding space (centrifugal irradiation).

This is also relative according to the plastic sensibility of each individual artist, but it is of essential importance to destroy the principle of using light, localised tones and shadow to show the action of light on natural objects—a principle which belonged to the relativity of momentary and accidental light phenomena.

I have given to this new plastic expression of light the name: SPHERICAL EXPANSION OF LIGHT IN SPACE.

The spherical expansion of colour may thus be obtained, in perfect harmony with the spherical expansion of forms.

For example, if the centre of a group of forms is *yellow,* the colours will follow outwards in sequence (in spherical expansion), from colour analogy to colour analogy, until the complementary colour *blue,* or even if necessary, until *black* (absence of light) is reached, or vice versa.

Obviously it is possible to have, in the one picture or plastic entity, several centrifugal and centripetal groups in simultaneous and dynamic competition with one another.

One of the most important scientific advances which have contributed to the transformation of our sensibility and its canalisation towards our Futurist conclusions is no doubt that which has given rise to the conception of SPEED.

Speed has given us a new notion of *space* and *time,* and consequently of *life* itself. The plastic art of our time must therefore be *characterised* by a STYLISATION OF SPEED, which is the most immediate and most expressive manifestation of our modern way of living.

Naturally, what we have said with regard to *motion* in general, is equally true with regard to *speed;* in other words, the important thing is not to represent the *speeding motor-car,* but the *speed* of the motor-car.

In the interests of identifying the work of art to the greatest possible extent with modern life, I consider it desirable that, just as we rejected the nude in our first manifesto of Futurist painting, the HUMAN BODY, STILL LIFE SUBJECTS and RURAL SCENES should be rejected AS CENTRES OF EMOTIVE INTEREST.

For it is my opinion that a complex of realistic and dynamic elements such as: aeroplane in flight + man + landscape; speeding tramcar or motor-car + boulevard + travellers; or underground railway carriage + station-posters-lights + crowd, etc. and all their qualitative prolongations and specific differences, constitute infinitely vaster and more interesting sources of emotion and plastic lyricism.

But, in addition, the age-old and academic distinctions of pictorial form and sculptural form must also be done away with.

Plastic dynamism, the *absolute vitality of matter,* can only be expressed by *form-colour entities* at a *maximum degree* of relief, depth, intensity and light irradiation, that is, by painting and sculpture united in a single plastic creation.

I therefore predict the *end of the picture and the statue.* These art forms, even employed in the most genuine innovating spirit, limit the creative freedom of the artist. They have within themselves their own destinies: museums and collectors' galleries, in other words, cemeteries.

THE PLASTIC CREATIONS OF THE NEO-FUTURISTS WILL LIVE AND WILL COMPLEMENT ONE ANOTHER IN ARCHITECTURAL ENTITIES, AND ALONG WITH THESE THEY WILL TAKE PART IN THE COOPERATIVE ACTIVITY OF THE EXTERNAL WORLD OF WHICH THEY REPRESENT THE SPECIFIC ESSENTIAL.

GINO SEVERINI,
Rome, 1913-1914.

APPENDIX B.

THE NON-REPRESENTATIONAL WORLD

By "Suprematism" I mean the supremacy of pure sensibility in art.

From the point of view of the Suprematists, the external appearances of nature are of no interest whatever; the essential thing is the artist's sensibility as such, regardless of the surroundings which brought it into being.

The so-called "concretisation" of sensibility signifies, in actual fact, the "concretisation" *of the reflection* of a particular sensibility by a natural representation. A representation of this sort is of no value in Suprematist art, and not only in Suprematist art but in any form of art; for the lasting and authentic value of a work of art (to whatever "school" it owes allegiance) lies solely in its expression of sensibility.

Academic naturalism, the naturalism of the Impressionists, "Cézannism", Cubism, etc.—all these approaches are to a certain extent only a variety of dialectic methods which, in themselves, have no determining influence whatever on the real value of the work of art.

The representation of an object (that is, the object regarded as the raison d'être of the representation) is something which, as such, has nothing at all to do with art. The use of an object in a work of art, however, may not preclude that work from having a high artistic value.

Nevertheless, for the Suprematist, the means of expression will always be that given element which makes it possible for the sensibility to express

97

itself as sensibility in all its fullness, without any reference to conventional representationalism. For him, the object in itself means nothing.

Sensibility is the only thing that counts, and it is by this means that art, in Suprematism, arrives at pure expression without representation.

All that has gone to make up the representative structure of life and art—ideas, notions, images—has been rejected by the artist so that he may give his undivided attention to pure sensibility.

The art of the past which, at least judging by its outward appearance, owed it allegiance to Church and State, must awaken to the pure (non-applied) art of Suprematism to find a new life and to build a new world, the world of sensibility.

When, in 1913, I made my desperate attempt to deliver art of the dead weight of the object, I sought refuge in the shape of a square and I exhibited a picture which showed nothing else but a black square on a white ground. The critics, and with them the public, burst into lamentations, crying: "All that we loved is lost—we are in a desert, faced with a black square on a white ground!"

They tried to find destructive words to blot out the symbol of the *desert* and to see in the "dead square" the loved image of representative reality and sentiment.

The perfect square seemed to both critics and public incomprehensible and dangerous. What else could one expect?

The ascent to the summit of non-figurative art is difficult and full of torment—yet it is satisfying just the same. Accustomed things fall away gradually, and at every step objects fade further and further into the distance, until finally the world of pre-conceived notions—all that we loved and all that we depended on for life—completely disappears from sight.

No more images of reality, no more idealised representations—nothing but a desert!

But this desert is full of the spirit of non-objective sensibility pervading all.

I too was filled with a kind of timidity and I held back to the point of anguish when the time came to leave "the world of will and representation" in which I had lived and created—when the time came to leave the authenticity in which I had believed.

But the feeling of satisfaction which I experienced as a result of my liberation from the object drew me further and further on into the desert to the point where there was no other authenticity but that of sensibility alone—and so it was that sensibility came to be the very substance of my life.

The square that I had exhibited was not an empty square—it was the sensibility of the absence of any object.

I realised that the object and the representation of it had been held as identical with sensibility and I understood the falsehood of the world of will and representation.

Could the milk-bottle be the symbol of the milk?

Suprematism is the rediscovery of pure art which, in the course of time, had become hidden by the accumulation of objects.

It seems to me that the painting of Raphael and Rubens and Rembrandt, etc., is no longer, for contemporary critics and contemporary society, more than the "concretisation" of the innumerable objects which hide its value real, i.e. its causal sensibility. People admire in these works only the virtuosity of the figurative accomplishment. If it were possible to abstract from the works of the great masters the sensibility expressed therein—i.e. their true artistic value—and to conceal it completely, society (including the critics and the connoisseurs) would not even be aware of its absence.

It is thus not surprising that my square seemed empty to such a society.

When a person claims that a work of art may be judged according to the virtuosity of the figurative accomplishment—or according to the accuracy of the illusion—and when he believes that the symbol of the causal sensibility is to be seen in the object represented, that person will never be able to partake of the truly beneficent content of the work.

Society as a whole thus remains convinced that art is bound to disappear once it turns its back on the representation of that so dearly loved reality. And it is with a presentiment of disaster that society watches the widening assertion of that execrated *element of pure sensibility,* that is, of the principle of abstraction.

Art is no longer content to be the servant of Church and State, it is no longer content to be the illustrator of customs and costumes, it is no longer willing to have anything to do with objects as such, and it believes that it is capable of existing of itself and for itself independently of the object, independently of " that source of life which has so long stood the test of time".

Casimir MALEVITCH.

(From *Die Gegenstandslose Welt.* Albert Langen Verlag, Munich, 1927, pp. 65-72).

APPENDIX C.

THE NEW PLASTIC APPROACH TO PAINTING

(*Note.*—This introduction gives only a brief outline of several ideas which I hope to deal with later and in more detailed fashion in a series of articles.   P. M.)

The life of a cultivated man in our time is gradually being divorced from natural objects and is becoming more and more an abstract existence.

Since natural (external) phenomena are becoming more and more automatic, the vital attention turns increasingly to the things of the inner life.   The life of the truly modern man is neither purely materialistic nor purely sentimental; it appears rather as a more autonomous existence of the human mind in the process of achieving a greater degree of consciousness of itself.

Modern man—although one in body, mind and soul—shows a change in consciousness: all the expressions of life appear in a new light, a more positively abstract light.

The same is true in the world of art.   Art is to become the product of another duality in man: the product of a cultivated exteriority and of a more conscious and deepened interiority.   As a pure representation of the human spirit, art will express itself in a purified aesthetic form, i.e. in an abstract form.

The truly modern artist is consciously aware of the abstractness of a feeling for beauty; he consciously recognises that a feeling for beauty is cosmic and universal. The inevitable corollary of this conscious recognition is the adoption of an abstract plastic approach—man clinging solely to that which is universal.

This new plastic approach cannot therefore take the form of natural or concrete representation, although it must be admitted that this type of representation does always show, or at least conceal within it, some indication of the universal. The new plastic approach cannot appear clothed in those things which are characteristic of particularisation, that is, in natural form and colour. It should, on the contrary, find its expression in the abstraction of all form and colour, in other words in the straight line and clearly defined primary colours.

These universal means of expression were discovered in modern painting by the gradual and logical development of the abstraction of form and colour. Once the solution was found, there appeared, as if spontaneously, the exact representation of pure relationships, and in these relationships the essential, fundamental factor of all plastic feeling for beauty.

The new plastic approach is thus an aesthetic relationship perfectly represented. The artist of today constructs this plastic approach, in painting, as a logical consequence of all the plastic theories of the past—and I say in painting advisedly because painting is the art form least tied up with contingent factors. The whole of modern life, as it becomes increasingly profound, may find its true reflection in the picture. In painting—painting that creates a picture, and not decorative painting—the naturalistic plastic approach itself, and also its means of expression, are "interiorised" by their adoption of the trend towards abstraction. Decorative painting, however, has never been able to achieve more than a generalisation of natural form and colour.

Thus, through creative painting, the sensitive quality of the aesthetic plastic appreciation of relationships finds its lucid expression.

In this art of painting—which embraces within itself existing decorative art, or rather, which becomes the true decorative art—the free expression of relationships will no doubt still remain relative and limited. However unique and at one with itself the real nature of all art may be, however clearly the sensibility of the aesthetic plastic appreciation of relationships may be expressed in all the arts, not all the branches of the arts can express this clear relationship with equal effectiveness.

For, though the content of all the arts is one and the same, the possibilities of expression in each art are different. These possibilities of expression should be found in each branch of the arts within the specific context of that branch and should remain one with that context.

Each art has its own particular accent and its own means of expression, and it is in this that the existence of the different branches of art finds its justification. The particular accent of painting may be defined as the most logical and most rational expression of pure relationships. For it is the peculiar privilege of painting to be able to express these relationships *freely*. This means that these means of expression (as the outcome of their own inherent logic) make it possible for the extreme "one" and the extreme "other" to be made explicit by their positional relationship alone, without adopting any form or any semblance of enclosed form, as is seen in architecture.

In painting, the duality of the relationship may be expressed by isolated positions, which is not possible in architecture or in sculpture. And it is for this reason that painting may be said to be perhaps the purest of the plastic arts.

The untrammelled autonomy of the means of expression is the particular privilege of painting. The liberty of the sister arts, sculpture and architecture, is more restricted. The other branches of art are even less at liberty to exercise a predetermining influence on the means of expression.

Painting, without going beyond the limitations of the means of expression proper to it, is still capable of determining clearly, and even of interiorising these means of expression.

Despite all this, the new plastic approach still remains strictly within the realm of pure painting—its means of expression still remain form and colour, although these are completely interiorised; the straight line and flat colour are still purely pictorial means of expression.

Whatever its method of expression, each art tends to become, through the gradual cultivation of the human mind, an exact representation of balanced relationships. For the balanced relationship is, in fact, the purest representation of that universality, that harmony and that unity which are the essential qualities of the mind.

If then we concentrate all our attention on the balanced relationship, we shall be able to *see* the unity which exists in natural objects. This unity is not however obviously apparent. But even if no exact expression can ever be given of this unity, all representation can at least be reduced to its terms. Thus the exact representation of unity can be expressed; it must be expressed since it is not visible in concrete reality.

In external nature it can be observed that all relationships are subservient to a single primordial relationship: that of the *extreme one* vis-à-vis the *extreme other*. The abstract plastic approach to these relationships represents the primordial relationship specifically by the positional duality which constitutes the right angle. This positional relationship is the most balanced of all since it provides a perfectly harmonious expression of the relationship of the extreme one and the extreme other, and at the same time incorporates within itself all the other relationships.

If we conceive of these two extremes as being the manifestation of interiority and exteriority, we shall see that in the new plastic approach the link between spirit and life is unbroken; thus, far from considering this approach as a negation of the essential vitality of life, we shall see in it the reconciliation of the duality between matter and spirit.

If, through contemplation, we come to the realisation that the existence of any one thing is aesthetically defined for us by a series of equivalences, this is possible because the idea of this manifestation of unity is already potentially present in our consciousness. And our individual consciousness is simply a particularised aspect of universal consciousness, which is one.

If the consciousness of man is moving away from the indeterminate towards what is positive and determined, the sense of unity in man will also be moving towards what is positive and determined.

If unity is contemplated in a precise and determinate manner, the attention will be drawn solely towards the universal, with the result that the particular in art will disappear—as has already been shown in painting. For the universal can only be expressed purely when the particular is no longer present to obstruct it. It is only then that universal consciousness (i.e. intuition), which is the basis of all art, can be rendered directly, giving birth to a purified type of artistic expression.

This expression, however, cannot be expected to come into being before its time. For it is the consciousness of the time which determines the nature of artistic expression which, in turn, reflects the consciousness of the time. The only truly living art form of the present time is that which gives expression to the consciousness of the present—or of the future.

The new means of expression (employed in pure plastic art) bear witness to a new vision. Though it may be said that the aim of all the arts is the plastic appreciation of relationships, it is only now that, through a more conscious vision, we have been able to attain to a clearer expression of this aim, and it is precisely because of the new attitude to the plastic means at our disposal that this has become possible.

The plastic means of expression should be in complete harmony with what they have to express. If they are called upon to be a direct expression of the universal, they themselves cannot be any other than universal, that is, abstract.

In composition, the artist has complete liberty, for as long a time as may be necessary, so that his subjective consciousness may express itself in a certain measure.

The rhythm of the relationships between colours and measures brings out what is absolute in the relativity of time and space.

Thus the new plastic approach is dualistic in composition. By virtue of its exact plastic appreciation of cosmic relationships it is a direct expression of the universal. By virtue of the rhythm and the material reality of its plastic technique it is an expression of the subjective consciousness of the artist as an individual.

It is thus a revelation of universal beauty, without however implying any negation of the general human element.

Piet MONDRIAN.

(*De Stijl,* No. 1, October, 1917. From the French translation of the original Dutch by M. S.)

Chronological table of abstract art

	FRANCE	RUSSIA	GERMANY
1910	Analytical Cubism.		Kandinsky's first abstract water colour. *Der Sturm* founded by Walden.
1911	Delaunay's first *Windows*.	"Rayonnisme" (Larionov and Gontcharova).	Friendship of Franz Marc an Kandinsky. *Der Blaue Reiter*.
1912	Mondrian in Paris. Delaunay: Simultaneous Rhythms. Kupka's works at the Salon des Indépendants.	Cubo-Futurism (Malevitch).	Kandinsky: *Uber das Geistige der Kunst*. Arp's visit to Kandinsky.
1913	Notable abstract works by Picabia. The American Synchromists. Léger—Contrasting Shapes.	Advent of Suprematism (Malevitch) and of Constructivism (Tatlin). Lecture tour by Marinetti.	Kandinsky: *Rückblicke*. *Herbstsalon* of "Der Sturm".
1914	Synthetic Cubism. Larionov and Gontcharova Exhibition.	Return of Kandinsky to Moscow.	Death of Macke on the Wester Front.
1915		Suprematist manifesto.	
1916			Death of Franz Marc on the Wes ern Front.
1917		Return of Gabo and Pevsner to Moscow.	
1918	Death of Apollinaire.		
1919	Freundlich's first abstract works Return of Mondrian to Paris.	Lissitzky: *Proun*. Kandinsky teaching at the Moscow Academy.	Founding of the Bauhaus at We mar. Dada demonstrations in Cologn and Berlin.

SWITZERLAND	HOLLAND	U. S. A.	
rp in Weggis.	Mondrian working in Zealand—exhibition in Amsterdam with Sluyters.		1910
	Mondrian—departure for Paris in late December.		1911
			1912
		Armory Show. Picabia and Marcel Duchamp in New York.	1913
	Return of Mondrian to Holland in July.	Publication of *291*.	1914
rp in Zurich—first abstract works.	Mondrian—large abstract drawings; meeting with van Doesburg.	W. H. Wright: *Modern Painting, Its Tendency and Meaning.*	1915
dvent of Dadaism. ophie Taeuber—first abstract works.	Mondrian—meetings with van der Leck in the village of Laren. First abstract works of Huszar and van Doesburg.		1916
Dada publications. anco—polychromatic reliefs.	October: first number of *De Stijl* published. First abstract works of Vantongerloo.	MacDonald-Wright—exhibition at Stieglitz gallery.	1917
Arp and Sophie Taeuber—jointly executed "collages". Zara—lecture on abstract art at the Kunsthaus, Zurich.	Abstract works of Mondrian in the Kröller collection at The Hague.		1918
Picabia in Zurich. Dada demonstration in the Kaufleuten, Zurich.	Mondrian—essays in *De Stijl*. Van Doesburg—essays printed by various Dutch publishers.		1919

	FRANCE	RUSSIA	GERMANY
1920	*L'Esprit Nouveau* founded by Paul Dermée. *Néo-Plasticisme* published by Mondrian. Arp and Tzara in Paris.	Cabo and Pevsner: *Realist Manifesto*.	Klee teaching at the Bauhaus. Publication of Marc's letters a drawings.
1921	Dadaist demonstrations in Paris.	Constructivist exhibition. Abstract art discredited. Exodus of artists.	Van Doesburg at the Bauhaus. First abstract works of Moho Nagy. Abstract films of Egg ling and Richter.
1922			Kandinsky teaching at the Ba haus. Marinetti in Berlin.
1923	Pevsner in Paris. *De Stijl* exhibition shown by Léonce Rosenberg.		Schwitters—publication of t periodical *Merz*. *G* (Gestaltung) published by Ric ter and Lissitzky.
1925	"L'Art d'Aujourd'hui" exhibition. Katherine Dreier—visit to Mondrian.		Mondrian: "*Neue Gestaltung*" Opening of abstract art secti at the Hanover Museum.
1926	"Cahiers d'Art" founded. Arp in Paris. *La Chatte* produced by Diaghilev.		Bauhaus moved to Dessau. Kandinsky: *Punkt und Linie Fläche*.
1927	Vantongerloo in Paris. Dermée and Seuphor: *Documents Internationaux de l'Esprit Nouveau*.		Malevitch: *Die Gegenstandslo Welt*.
1928	Completion of the "Aubette" in Strasbourg (Arp, van Doesburg and Sophie Taeuber).	Return of Lissitzky to Moscow.	
1930	Seuphor and Torrès-Garcia: *Cercle et Carré*. Van Doesburg: *Art Concret*. Kandinsky exhibition.		
1931	Delaunay—new abstract rhythms. Cahiers d'Art: *De l'Art Abstrait*.		Kandinsky exhibition in Berlin.
1932	First album of *Abstraction-Création* Group.		
1933	Kandinsky and Domela take up residence in Paris.		Bauhaus closed. Abstract art in disfavour ("deger erate" art). Exodus of artist

SWITZERLAND	HOLLAND	U. S. A.	
		Société Anonyme founded by Katherine Dreier, with Duchamp and Man Ray.	**1920**
	Van Doesburg: *Classique, Baroque, Moderne.*		**1921**
	Schwitters in Holland. *Mecano* published by van Doesburg.		**1922**
		W. H. Wright: *The Future of Painting.*	**1923**
Arp and Lissitzky: *Les Ismes de l'Art.*	"Élémentarisme" (Van Doesburg). Withdrawal of Mondrian from *De Stijl.*		**1925**
"Die Neue Welt" published in "*Das Werk*".	*The Next Call* published and abstract monotypes composed by the painter-typographer H. N. Werkman.	Exhibition of abstract art at Brooklyn Museum.	**1926**
	The periodical *I 10* published by Müller-Lehning.	*Gallery of Living Art* (Gallatin Collection) opened to the public at New York University.	**1927**
			1928
			1930
Death of van Doesburg at Davos.			**1931**
			1932
		Hélion: *The Evolution of Abstract Art* (Gallatin).	**1933**

	FRANCE	RUSSIA	GERMANY
1935	Delaunay: *Les Rythmes Sans Fin.* Reth Exhibition.	Death of Malevitch in Leningrad.	
1936	Magnelli—return to abstract art.		
1937	Periodical *Plastique* published by Arp and Sophie Taeuber.		
1938	Freundlich Exhibition. Departure of Mondrian for London. Zervos: *Histoire de l'Art Contemporain.*		
1940			
1941	Death of Delaunay.	Death of Lissitzky in Moscow.	
1942			
1943			
1944	Death of Kandinsky.		
1945	*Art concret* Exhibition.		
1946	Salon des Réalités Nouvelles inaugurated.		
1947	Magnelli Exhibition. Retrospective exhibition of Delaunay's works shown by Carré.		Domnick: *Abstrakte Malerei.* Baumeister: *Das Unbekannte in der Kunst.*

SWITZERLAND	HOLLAND	U. S. A.	
	Bendien: *Richtingen in de Hedendaagsche Schilderkunst.*	Whitney Museum: American Abstract Art.	1935
...ie *Allianz* Exhibition.		Alfred Barr: *Cubism and Abstract Art.*—American Abstract Artists Foundation (First Exhibition in 1937).	1936
...ordemberge-Gildewart in Zurich. ...onstruktivisten Exhibition in Basle.		School of drawing founded by Moholy-Nagy in Chicago. Beginnings of the Guggenheim Foundation.	1937
...ie *Allianz* Exhibition in Basle.	*Abstracte Kunst* Exhibition at the Stedelijk Museum, Amsterdam.		1938
...ie *Allianz* illustrated almanach.	Vordemberge-Gildewart — residence in Amsterdam.	Arrival of Mondrian in New York. New York Museum of Modern Art moved to present premises.	1940
			1941
		Peggy Guggenheim: *Art of This Century.* Helena Rubinstein: *Masters of Abstract Art.*	1942
...eath of Sophie Taeuber in Zurich.		Mondrian Exhibition at the Valentine Gallery (Dudensing).	1943
...onkrete *Kunst* Exhibition at the Kunsthalle, Basle.		Death of Mondrian. Janis: *Abstract and Surrealist Art in America.*	1944
		Mondrian—retrospective exhibition at the New York Museum of Modern Art. Mondrian: Essays (Wittenborn).	1945
...Max Bill Exhibition in Zurich.	Mondrian—large retrospective exhibition in Amsterdam.	Death of Moholy-Nagy. Kandinsky Exhibition at the Carnegie Institute.	1946
...Mondrian—retrospective exhibition in Basle. ...ie *Allianz* at the Kunsthaus, Zurich.		Moholy-Nagy: *Vision in Motion* (published posthumously).	1947

	FRANCE	RUSSIA	GERMANY
1948	Abstract art exhibitions at the Galerie des Deux Iles (Rayonnisme, Éloquence de la Ligne, Picabia, Black and White).		Travelling exhibition of Fren abstract painting. Albers, Arp and Bill Exhibition
1949	Seuphor: *L'Art Abstrait.—Les Premiers Maîtres de l'Art Abstrait* Exhibition, Galerie Maeght. Founding of "Art d'Aujourd'hui".		*Blaue Reiter* retrospective exhition. Travelling exhibition of Swi abstract art (*Konkrete Kunst*)
1950	Numerous abstract art exhibitions (Galerie Denise René, Galerie Colette Allendy).		Franz Marc retrospective exhition. Monograph on Hans Hartu (Domnick). "Kunstwerk": *Abstrakte Maler*
1951	Tapié: *Véhémences Confrontées*. Death of Wols. "Art d'Aujourd'hui": *La Peinture en U.S.A*. Founding of the *Espace* Group.		Fritz Winter travelling exhibitio
1952	"Art d'Aujourd'hui": *Témoignages pour l'Art Abstrait*. American abstract artists at the Galerie de France. Glarner Exhibition (Carré).		Fleischmann Exhibition in Stut gart. Numerous other exhibitions abstract painters.
1953	Galerie Craven: *Jeunes Américains de Paris* Exhibition. Galerie Bing: Sonia Delaunay. Death of Picabia.		
1954	Espace Group—open-air exhibition at Biot. "Informal Art" exhibitions organised by Tapié at the Galerie Rive Droite.		Baumeister—large retrospecti exhibition in Stuttgart. Arp-Sophie Taeuber Exhibitio in Hanover.
1955	Ben Nicholson at the Musée d'Art Moderne, Paris. Tobey at the Galerie Jeanne Bucher. "Collages" by Schwitters at the Galerie Berggruen. Death of De Staël.		Hochschule für Gestaltung (ne Bauhaus) opened at Ulm. Death of Baumeister in Stuttga
1956	Japanese calligraphers at the Musée Cernuschi. Hartung and Soulages at the Galerie de France. Seuphor: *Piet Mondrian, Sa Vie, Son Œuvre*.	Several young painters secretly painting abstract works photographed by visitors to Russia.	Vasarely Exhibition in Cologn Exhibition of "Poem-pictures" Wupperthal.

SWITZERLAND	HOLLAND	U. S. A.	
...onograph on Sophie Taeuber (Basle).	Travelling exhibition of Kandinsky's works. *Vrij Beelden* published by a group of young painters.	Death of Arshile Gorky. Hitchcock: *Painting Toward Architecture*. Arp: *On My Way*.	1948
...vsner, Bill, Vantongerloo Exhibition in Zurich.		Leepa: *The Challenge of Modern Art*. Arp in New York.	1949
	Section devoted to Mondrian opened at the Municipal Museum of The Hague.	Exhibition of French abstract painting at the Galerie Carré in New York.	1950
	Retrospective exhibition of *De Stijl* in Amsterdam.	Ritchie: *Abstract Painting and Sculpture in America*. Hess: *Abstract Painting*.	1951
		Death of Gallatin. *Modern Artists in America* published by Wittenborn.	1952
		Death of Morgan Russell. Death of Tomlin.	1953
...ench abstract painters at the Musée de Berne. ...phie Taeuber retrospective exhibition.	Eight Argentine abstract painters at the Amsterdam Museum.	J. J. Sweeney—exhibitions of European and American abstract art at the Guggenheim Museum. Return of MacDonald-Wright to abstract art.	1954
...ondrian retrospective exhibition in Zurich.	Retrospective exhibition of Mondrian's works at the Hague Museum. Five American abstract artists at the Amsterdam Museum.	Retrospective exhibition of Robert Delaunay's works at the Guggenheim Museum. Sonia Delaunay at the Rose Fried Gallery.	1955
...p and Schwitters at the Kunsthalle, Berne.	A new group, *Nieuw Beelden*, working in close cooperation with architects in Amsterdam.	Death of Pollock. American Abstract Artists Group preparing an album to celebrate its twentieth anniversary.	1956

PART II
Dictionary of Abstract Painting

A

ABNER Raymond (b. Cairo, 1924). Educated in Cairo. Works exhibited at Cairo Salons of 1941 and 1942. Private exhibition, Aladin gallery, 1948. Worked in London in 1945 and Paris in 1946. Began studies at the Beaux-Arts but left, on the advice of Matisse, to study under Othon Friesz and Fernand Léger. Took up abstract art in 1952. Works shown in various Salons in Paris, and also in Yugoslavia and Venezuela. Private exhibition, Galerie Denise René, Paris, 1956. Believes himself to be the only non-figurative Egyptian painter. Lives in Paris.

ACCARDI Carla (b. Trapani, Italy, 1924). Took part in group exhibitions in Florence and Milan, and also at the Biennale in Venice in 1948. Private exhibition, Galerie Stadler, Paris, 1956. Graphic signs inscribed direct on black ground. Now living in Rome.

ACHT René-Charles (b. Basle, 1920). Studies at Basle Academy. First private exhibition Galerie Moos, Geneva, 1947. Lived in Scandinavia 1947-1950. Visited France, Italy, Holland. Abstract works since 1948. Took part in Salon des Réalités Nouvelles, Paris, 1951 and 1952. Work exhibited Basle (1940), Helsinki (1947), Copenhagen (1951), Zurich (1951) and Milan (1952). Now living in Basle.

ACKERMAN Paul (b. Jassy, Roumania, 1908). Came to France at the age of 4 years. Studies, Faculté des Lettres, Faculté de Droit (Uni-

versity of Paris). Doctor of Laws. Began painting at Fernand Léger's Académie Moderne. Encouraged by Bonnard. Several private exhibitions at the Galerie Creuze, Paris, since 1947. Series of abstract works painted in 1944 but never exhibited. New phase of abstract art (large polychromatic fantasies) in 1955. Private exhibition, Galeria dell' Grattacielo, Milan, 1956. Lives in Paris. In giving his talent full rein after a long apprenticeship, Paul Ackerman has proved himself to be a painter of astonish-

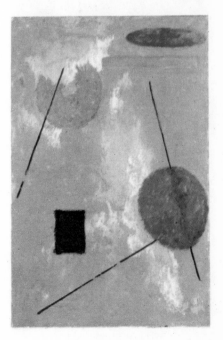

ABNER. ESCAPE. 1955.

117

ingly fertile inspiration. One is frequently reminded of the more unusual compositions of Klee. Has succeeded in combining graphic line (reminiscent of Chinese calligraphy) and plastic texture.

ACKERMANN Max (b. Berlin, 1887). Studied under Henri van de Velde at Weimar. Further studies at the Academies of Dresden and Munich, and under Adolf Hölzel at Stuttgart. In Paris and Normandy in 1926. Professor at Stuttgart in 1930. Debarred from exhibiting and (in 1936) from teaching under the Nazi regime. Numerous exhibitions in Germany after 1945. Now living in Stuttgart. Ackermann calls his art "absolute painting".

AFRO. GOUACHE. 1955.
Private Collection.

Is a very cultivated painter and seems to wish to found a personal style on the laws of music; is haunted by the ideas of theme, counterpoint, movement, melody and accompaniment. "The beginning and the end of Ackermann's painting is the quest for laws which make possible the composition of colours within order and ordered movement" (Kurt Leonhard). — *Bibl.* Dominck: *Abstrakte Malerei* (Stuttgart 1947).

AFRO Basadella (b. Udine, Italy, 1912). First exhibition, "Il Milione" gallery, Milan, in 1920. First influenced by Cubism. Gradually turned to abstract art which he now practises with a vigorous feeling for colour and a suppleness of form typical of the cultivated painter. Visited New York in 1950 and exhibited at the Viviano Gallery. Now living in Rome.

AGAM Jacob Gipstein (b. Israel, 1928). Son of a country Rabbi. Studied at "Bezabeel" Art School, Jerusalem, and later (in 1951) at the Atelier d'Art Abstrait in Paris. Visited Italy, Holland, Belgium, Switzerland. Private exhibition, Galerie Craven, Paris, 1953, with pictures with movable sections. Took part in the "Mouvement" exhibition at the Galerie Denise René, Paris, 1955. During the same year he produced a number of experimental abstract films. A further exhibition of his work was held in 1956, at the Galerie Denise René. He is now living in Paris. Agam is at the same time artist and inventor—his works with sliding or pivoting sections are remarkable both for their ingenuity and freshness of colour. The shapes used are geometrical but extremely varied. He also produces paintings on wood with triangular facets which change colour (and warmth of tone) as they are viewed from left, right or centre. All these experiments (or divertissements) might be used to good effect in architecture.

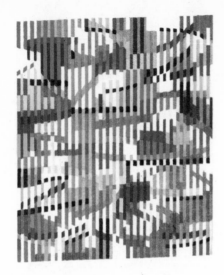

AGAM. PICTURE WITH ADJUSTABLE
MOVEMENT. 1954.
Galerie Denise René, Paris.

AGUAYO (b. Sotillo de la Ribera, Spain, 1926). Has been painting since 1945. Arrived in Paris in 1952. Exhibition Galerie Jeanne Bucher (Paris) 1955, with heavily impasted abstract works. Now living in Paris.

ALBERS Josef (b. Bottrop, Westphalia, 1888). Berlin Academy 1913-1915, then in Essen and Munich. Student at Bauhaus, Weimar, then professor at Bauhaus when transferred to Dessau (1925-1933). From 1933 to 1950 professor at Black Mountain College, N. Carolina, U.S.A. Since 1955 professor at Yale University, New Haven. Has stayed long periods in South America and Mexico. Numerous exhibitions in the United States. Now living in New Haven, U.S.A. The dominant feature of Albers' art is his surprise effects gained with the use of the most pure and tranquil means. Demonstrates the infinite variety of motifs which can be obtained from rectilinear geometry. — Bibl. *American Abstract Artists* (New York, 1946); *Collection of the Société Anonyme* (New Haven, 1950); "*Spirale 5*" (Berne, 1955).

ALCOPLEY Name adopted by Dr. Alfred L. Copley (b. Dresden, 1910). Went to the United States in 1937. Became American citizen. Numerous exhibitions in New York, Germany, Switzerland, Holland. In Paris since 1952. Took part in the Salon des Réalités Nouvelles, 1953-1955. Exhibitions of drawings at the Rose Fried Gallery (New York) in 1955, in company with Sebro Hasegawa and Michel Seuphor. Work shown in Amsterdam (Stedelijk Museum), Brussels (Palais des Beaux-Arts) and Paris (Galerie Bing). Alcopley's work belongs to the great calli-

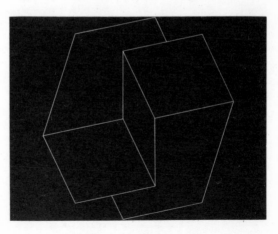

ALBERS. COMPOSITION. 1955.
Max Bill Collection, Zurich.

graphic movement which originated in the East but which counts among its exponents such American artists as Tobey, Kline and Tomlin. His drawings, often of very small format, have a graphic quality that is at the same time substantial and delicate and of undeniable charm. — Bibl. *Bokubi* No 16, Sept. 1952 (Kyôtô, Japan); Seuphor: *Écritures, Dessins d'Alcopley*, "Les Nourritures Terrestres" (Paris 1954); Seuphor: *Deux Peintres Américains*, Galerie Bing (Paris 1956).

ALCOPLEY. PAINTING WITH COLLAGE. 1955.

ALECHINSKY Pierre (b. Brussels, 1927). Studied at the School of Architecture and Decorative Arts, Brussels. Took part several times in a group exhibition at the Galerie Maeght, Paris. Founder of the "Cobra" movement and the review of the same name in Brussels. Worked with S. W. Hayter at *Atelier 17*. Private exhibitions at Amsterdam, Paris (Galerie Nina Dausset, 1954) and Brussels (Palais des Beaux-Arts, 1955). Visited Japan in 1955. Now living in Paris. Alechinsky's best canvases are surfaces covered with a compact conglomeration of abstract signs packed one against the other, all of equal force and giving an overall effect of discipline without excessive severity.

ALECHINSKY. SWIMMING. 1955.
Colette Allendy Collection, Paris.

ALVA (b. Berlin, 1901). Studied music at the Berlin Conservatorium. Worked for some time as a typographer. Began painting while on his first visit to Paris in 1928. Took part in the Salon d'Automne, 1932. Visited Palestine and gave his first individual exhi-

120

bition in 1934. First abstract work *(Dynamic Composition)* in 1945. Exhibitions in London (Leicester Gallery), New York (Meltzer Gallery), Jerusalem (Artists' House) and Brussels (Palais des Beaux-Arts). Lived in England from 1935 to 1955, then moved to Paris. Since 1935 has produced ideogrammes, sometimes abstract, sometimes figurative, always reduced to only a few lines. Colours used are evidence of a constant search for extremely refined harmonies. — *Bibl.* Herbert Read and Maurice Collis: Alva, *Recent Paintings and Drawings* (London, 1951); R. van Gindertael: *Alva* (Paris, 1955).

ALVAREZ Manuel (b. Buenos Aires, 1923). Began painting in 1942. Turned from figurative to abstract art in 1951, finally developing, two years later, a pure geometrical abstract style. Numerous exhibitions in Buenos Aires since 1949. Work shown at the Galerie La Roue (Paris) in 1954-1955

ANNENKOV Georges (b. Petropavlovsk, Kamchatka, 1894). Son of an exiled politician. In St Petersburg in 1898. Was in Paris in 1911, remaining till autumn 1913 in which year he exhibited at the Salon des Indépendants. Returned to Russia and joined the Cubo-Futurist movement of Tatlin and Malevitch. Work shown at the Dobytchina Salon and the Union of Youth. In 1918 he illustrated Alexander Blok's poem *The Twelve*. Was responsible for the open-air settings for the

Spectacles de Masses in Petrograd in 1920. The following year in the same town, he published his famous manifesto "Le Théâtre jusqu'au Bout" (which was reproduced under this title by the review *Cimaise,* January 1955, Paris). He then exhibited, at the Institute of Pictorial Culture in Petrograd, large non-figurative group compositions with various metals, some of which were polychromatic. These works remained in Russia and it is not known what has become of them. Returned to Paris in 1925 as a representative of the U.S.S.R. at an International Congress on Drawing. After the Congress he settled in France and exhibited figurative works at various Salons. Returned to abstract principles in 1946 with a series of large compositions executed in an impetuous manner, for which he used supplementary thicknesses and

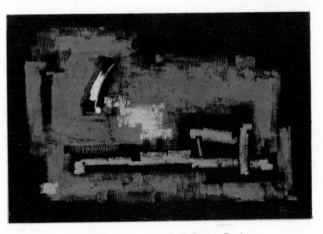

ALVA. DUO. 1955. *M. S. Collection, Paris.*

various materials (string, etc.) in relief. Now living in Paris.

APPLEBY Theodore (b. New Jersey, U.S.A., 1923). Studied with John Corneal 1938-1939. Became acquainted with Japanese engraving in Yokohama, 1945-1946. Frequently at Fernand Léger's studio in Paris, from 1950 to 1953. Took part in group exhibitions at Paris, New York, and in Portugal, and also in the Salon des Réalités Nouvelles (1950 and 1951). Now living in Paris.

ARCAY Wifredo (b. Havana, 1925). Studied painting and sculpture at the Havana Academy of Fine Arts (1943-1945). Came to Paris in 1949. Associated with Dewasne and Pillet's studio of abstract art (1950-1952). Work shown at several Salons and group exhibitions. Private exhibition at the Galerie Arnaud, Paris, 1952. Numerous serigraphy reproductions of the works of masters of abstract art executed in his studio, including those in the two albums published by *Art d'Aujourd'hui* in 1953 and 1954. Now living in Paris.

ARDEN QUIN Carmelo (b. Rivera, Uruguay, 1913). Studied under Marist brothers in Brazil. In 1930 travelled in the virgin forests of Brazil and Argentina. In Montevideo in 1935 first heard of abstract art at the lectures given by Torres-Garcia on his return from Europe. In Buenos Aires in 1938. While travelling to Rio de Janeiro in 1941, made the acquaintance of Vieira da Silva and her husband, Arpad Szenes. In January 1944 he published the sole number of the review *Arturo* and a manifesto setting in embryo all the ideas of the Madi movement. Acquainted at this time with Vincent Huidobro, Torres-Garcia, Rothfuss, Maldonado and Kosice. First exhibition of "Irregularly framed" works in 1945. In 1946, with several friends, launched the Madi movement at the Buenos Aires Institut des Études Françaises, and published several declarations of the principles of the movement. In 1948, exhibition of *Arte Madi* in the studio of the painter Martin Blaszko. Came to Paris in 1948 and in 1950 founded a scientific

Madist movement. Exhibitions in various galleries (Colette Allendy, Suzanne Michel) and regularly took part in the Salon des Réalités Nouvelles In South America from 1953 to 1956. Now living in Paris.

Arte Madi, of which Arden-Quin is one of the leading exponents, seeks to emphasise the mobile quality of art, hence the practice of presenting pictures in irregularly shaped frames, and sometimes even in several pieces. But this is not the movement's only preoccupation—Arden-Quin writes: "Until my arrival in Paris I understood neither Mondrian nor Malevitch, least of all the Malevitch exponent of *white on white*. It was the work of Vantongerloo which made me conscious of this problem for the first time. Now, with the creation of scientific Madism, I consider white as the plastic basis of this new experiment. For me, white is not a relationship as it is for Mondrian, nor is it a void as it 'is for Vantongerloo—it is the plastic essence, light and space, function and creation".

ARNAL François (b. La Valette, France, 1924). Educated at the Lycée de Toulon and the Faculty of Law at Aix-en-Provence. Began painting in 1944 and took it up as a full-time activity. Has lived in Paris since 1948. Exhibitions at the Galerie Drouant-David (1950), Galerie Craven (1953). Designed immense abstract tapestries for a public building in Sarrebrück.

ARP Jean or Hans (b. Strasbourg, 1887). Immediately attracted by modern painting when he saw examples in Paris in 1904. Academy of Weimar in 1907. Académie Julian, Paris, 1908. In 1909 settled in Weggis (Switzerland), where he met Klee. In contact with Kandinsky in 1912, and joined the Blue Rider group, Munich, 1912-1913. In Paris in 1914. In December 1915 showed his first abstract works at the Galerie Tanner in Zurich. Experiments in "papier collé" with Sophie

Taeuber. In 1916, with Tzara, Ball, Hülsenbeck, Janco, founded the Dada movement. With Max Ernst in Cologne in 1920. Married Sophie Taeuber in 1921. Settled at Meudon in 1926 and became a member of the Surrealist group (1926-1930). Decorations for the "Aubette" café (Strasbourg), with Sophie Taeuber and Theo van Doesburg (1928). Member of the "Circle and Square" group in 1930, and of the "Abstraction-Creation" group (1932-1934). Worked with Sonia Delaunay and Magnelli, at Grasse, during the Second World War. His wife killed in an accident in Switzerland in 1943. Visited America in 1949 and 1950, Greece in 1952 and 1954. Large retrospective exhibition (with Schwitters) in Berne, 1956. Now lives part of the time in Meudon, part of the time in Basle. Arp is more sculptor than painter but some of his best work has been done in "papier collé" and wood engraving. His influence, since the beginnings of Dadaism, has been immense. But his personality is so simple that it remains inimitable—inimitable and inexplicable—like the art of children. The development of his work shows how, under an artist's hand, an elementary shape can become richer and progressively more profound without losing its elementary quality.

Bibl. Arp and Lissitzky: *Les Ismes de l'Art* (1925); Arp: *On my Way,* Poems and Essays (New York 1948); Seuphor: *L'Art Abstrait, ses Origines, ses Premiers Maîtres* (Paris 1949); *Collection of the Société Anonyme* (New Haven 1950); Seuphor: *Arcadie d'Arp,* La Hune (Paris 1950); *Derrière le Miroir,* No. 33, Galerie Maeght (Paris 1950); *Témoignages pour l'Art Abstrait* (Paris 1950); *Dada Painters and Poets* (New York 1951); Seuphor: *Arp,* "Sidney Janis Gallery" (New York 1949); *Onze Peintres vus par Arp* (Zurich 1949); Arp: *Dreams and Projects,* "Kurt Valentin" (New York 1952); Seuphor: *Mission Spirituelle de l'Art,* Galerie Berggruen (Paris 1953); *Dictionary of Modern Painting* (Methuen, London 1956); Marcel Jan: *Jalons d'Arp,* "Les Lettres Nouvelles" (Paris, February 1956). Arp has illustrated with abstract wood engravings, a number of collections of poems by his friends, including:—Hülsenbeck: *Phantastische Gebete* (1916), *Die Newyorker Kantaten* (1952); Tzara: *Vingt-cinq Poèmes* (1918), *Cinéma Calendrier du Cœur Abstrait* (1920), *De Nos Oiseaux* (1923); Bryen: *Temps Troué* (1952); Frey: *Kleine Menagerie* (1955).

ATLAN Jean (b. Constantine, Algeria, 1913). "I am of Judeo-Berber stock, like most of the folk in those parts, in that town, old as Jugurtha, which was once the capital of Numidia and which is *built* of rocks and ravines, eagles' nests and cactus. Despite all that, the pictures that hang in the museum of the town where I was born were scarcely any incentive to me to discover painting in my youth. So, one fine day I arrived in Paris to take a degree in philosophy at the Sorbonne. And my vocation as a painter? I think it was

ARP. WOODCUT. 1948.

123

ATLAN. PAINTING. 1951. *M. S. Collection, Paris.*

the Galerie Maeght and participation in numerous exhibitions in France and other countries. My work is represented in several French and foreign museums and in private collections. Michel Ragon has written an original study of me and my work: *L'Architecte et le Magicien.*" (Atlan). Now living in Paris.

"Like Chagall, Atlan has the gift of using successfully certain impossible colour tones. His orange shades are as strange as Chagall's purples—as pathetic, as heart-rending, and as sentimental. Like Soutine his expression frequently comes through a kind of formal violence, distorting lines and planes; he loves colours and delights in sombre incandescent effects." (Léon Degand).

a direct result of the fact that my studio was in the Rue de la Grande-Chaumière... I would rather not talk much about the war years (my wife and family were imprisoned by the Nazis, my brother killed as a commando, myself in prison in one place and another, including Sainte-Anne's, the lunatic asylum). In 1944, first exhibition in a little gallery in the Rue de Sèvres, shortly afterwards a new pictures shown at the Salon des Surindépendants (canvases now in the Gertrude Stein collection) and an exhibition at the Galerie Denise René. In 1945 I worked in Mourlot's studios on black and white lithographs, to illustrate Kafka's *Description of a Battle.* In 1947 one-man show at

AUGEREAU Claude (b. Chartres, 1927). Studied in Chartres and then for three years at the École des Arts Appliqués in Paris. Spent a year at the Académie Frochot under the direction of Metzinger and Audebès. Later influenced by Magnelli and Vasarely. Has exhibited at several Paris Salons and group exhibitions. Now living in Paris.

124

B

BÆRTLING Olle (b. Halmstad, Sweden, 1911). Began as an Expressionist and then became a portraitist under the influence of Matisse. Visited Paris frequently and travelled widely in Europe. Studied under André Lhote in 1948 and then under Fernand Léger. Influenced by the latter and by the work of Mondrian, he began to make his way as an abstract painter. His work has been exhibited in Stockholm, Copenhagen and Paris. Bærtling's painting, which is frequently characterised by large surfaces of black, reaches an extreme degree of simplification and of power. Now living in Stockholm. — *Bibl.* Tage Nilson: *Olle Bærtling* (Stockholm 1951); Eugen Wretholm: *Olle Bærtling*, Den Unga Konsten (Stockholm 1951); *Bærtling, Jacobsen, Mortensen*, Liljevalchs Konsthall (Stockholm 1956).

BALLA Giacomo (b. Turin, 1871). One of the five painters—the others were Boccioni, Severini, Carra and Russolo—who signed the Futurist Manifesto of 1910. He had come to Paris at the beginning of the century and had later been the teacher of Boccioni and Severini whom he instructed in the Divisionist technique as practised by the Neo-Impressionists. Considering that his work was not yet ready, he did not take part (despite the fact that his name figured in the catalogue) in the exhibitions of Futurist painting held in Paris in 1912. It was in 1912 however that he painted a number of typically Futurist works (*Dog on the Leash, Swallows in Flight and Interpenetration of the Eaves*). A little later he painted *Abstract Speed, Plasticity of Light*

and Speed and *Atmospheric Thicknesses*—all of which, apart from the titles, are incontestably abstract works. The basic structure of linear design is a dominant feature of these works. However in 1914 he showed a marked preference for massive scrolls which recreate the illusion of depth and give a sense of lofty grandiloquence in space. At the same time he painted what might be described as cosmogonic visions (*Mercury Passing in Front of the Sun,* is an example). Balla is beyond doubt the most resolutely

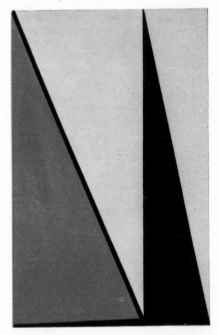

BÆRTLING. RED, YELLOW, BLACK AND WHITE TRIANGLES. 1955. *Lars Holmberg Coll., Sweden.*

125

BALLA. RHYTHM OF THE VIOLINIST. 1914. *Collection Estorick, London.*

a deeper philosophy of abstract art. The only great influence on me has been Mondrian. I believe him to have been the only really abstract painter. Recently I have been interested in the works of certain painters in New York and in their colourist technique which seems to open up infinite possibilities for abstract art. I believe that painting should penetrate deeper and deeper into the mystery and rhythm of the spectral, which means digging into existence itself." Ralph Balson is now living in Sydney.

abstract of all the Futurist painters. He is moreover the only one who has remained faithful to abstract art. It is true that later he also painted some figurative subjects, apparently under some external compulsion. He is now living in Rome. The work reproduced here is typical of the 1912 period and shows the characteristic Futurist endeavour to express bodily movements—a type of expression in which both Balla and Russolo particularly distinguished themselves in works which are now classics of their kind. — *Bibl.* Carrieri: *Pittura e scultura d'avanguardia in Italia* (Milan 1950); *Dictionary of Modern Painting* (Methuen, London 1956); Seuphor: *Le Futurisme... Hier,* " L'Œil " (Paris, February 1956).

BALSON Ralph (b. England, 1890). In Australia in 1913. Did not begin painting till about 1922. Studied at the Sydney Art School. Through his reading and associating with artists who had been abroad he got to know modern art. An exhibition of his work was held in Sydney in 1940—the first exhibition of abstract art in Australia. "Since then", he said, "I have kept on in the same way trying to work out

BARTA. PRAYER. MOSAIC. 1945.

126

BANDEIRA Antonio (b. Fortoleza in the northwest of Brazil, 1922). His first work was done in common with a group of young painters in his native province. In Rio de Janeiro in 1945, he was offered a bursary by the French cultural attaché to study in Paris. Studied drawing, painting and engraving at the Beaux-Arts and at the Académie de la Grande-Chaumière. Friendship with Wols and Bryen. Exhibited with them at the Galerie des Deux-Iles in 1940. Took part in the Venice and Sao Paulo Biennales and also in the Salon des Réalités Nouvelles in 1953 and 1954. Exhibitions of his works have been held in Rio de Janeiro, Sao Paulo, Paris (Galerie du Siècle) and London (Obelisk Gallery). Now living in Paris.

BARNS-GRAHAM Wilhelmina (b. St. Andrews, Scotland, 1912). Studied at the Edinburgh College of Art (1931-1936). Work exhibited in London in 1948 and 1952. Took part in an exhibition of English abstract art in New York in 1951. Now living at Leeds.

BARRÉ Martin (b. Nantes, 1924). Studied at Nantes. Came to Paris in 1943. Abstract painter since 1950. One man exhibition at the Galerie La Roue, Paris, 1955. Has taken part in the Salon des Réalités Nouvelles and the Menton Biennale. Now living in Paris. His paintings are of monochromatic shapes on a light ground with very simple straight-line variations.

BARTA Lazlo (b. Nagykoros, Hungary, 1902). Studied at the Budapest School of Fine Arts. Has been in France since 1926. Illustrated numerous books and had his work shown at the Salon d'Automne. Turned to abstract art in 1948. After learning directly from the craftsmen at Ravenna, he became a mosaicist. Showed some remarkable examples of mosaic work at the Galerie Arnaud in Paris in 1954. Now living at Saint-Tropez.

BARRÉ. PAINTING. 1955.
Michel Ragon Collection, Paris.

BAUDINIÈRE Robert (b. Cluny, Saône-et-Loire, 1919). After working at a number of different occupations, took up painting in 1942. Took part in the exhibition held at the Galerie Maeght ("Les Mains Éblouies") in 1947. Received official awards in 1950 and 1951. Is a convinced but intelligent disciple of Albert Gleizes. Now living at Saint-Tropez.

BAUER Rudolf (b. Lindenwald, Poland, 1889; d. U.S.A., 1954). Studied in Berlin. Began as a caricaturist, then became member of the "Sturm" group. In

127

1929 founded "Das Geistreich", a private museum of Abstract Art, in Berlin. In 1939 went to America where his work had already been introduced some years earlier by the Société Anonyme and the Guggenheim Foundation. Died near New York in 1954. — Bibl. *Art of Tomorrow*, S. R. Guggenheim Collection (New York 1939).

BAUMEISTER Willi (1889-1955). Born in Stuttgart. Was apprenticed to a house painter at the age of sixteen, but worked at the time as an independent student at the Stuttgart School of Fine Arts. Made his first visit to Paris in 1912 and exhibited in Zurich in the same year. The following year took part in the first German Autumn Exhibition (Herbstsalon) in "Der Sturm" Gallery in Berlin. Spent some time with Oscar Schlemmer in Paris in 1914. After being influenced by Lautrec, Gauguin and Cézanne, Baumeister gradually developed from 1919 to 1931 a highly personal style of his own embracing both Cubist and Constructivist elements.

Made frequent visits to Paris where he showed his work a number of times and mixed with the leading figures in the world of art. Appointed professor at the School of Fine Arts in Frankfort in 1928. In 1930 was a member of the "Cercle et Carré" group and exhibited with them. Belonged to the "Abstraction-Creation" group in 1932. Dismissed from the Frankfort School of Fine Arts by the Nazis in 1933, and officially disqualified as an artist. All his canvases were withdrawn from German museums and galleries. Continued painting clandestinely while working for a printing firm. In 1938 sent some sixty paintings to Switzerland for safety. Among the thousand "degenerate" works of art burnt in Berlin were a number of Baumeister's pictures. During the Second World War he was obliged to work in a paint and varnish factory. Unable to continue painting, he produced drawings to illustrate several Biblical books and Shakespeare's "The Tempest". Once the war was over he returned to Stuttgart and took up his former activities again. Has now a very great influence on the younger generation, and it is largely thanks to his example that art in Germany has so quickly been set back on the road to complete freedom of expression. In 1946 began teaching at the Stuttgart School of Fine Arts. Numerous exhibitions of his work in Germany. Published *Das Unbekannte in der Kunst (The Unknown in Art)* in 1947. Several exhibitions at the Galerie Jeanne Bucher in Paris. A very full retrospective exhibition of his work was held in Stuttgart in 1954.

Since 1930 the development of Baumeister's art has been marked by the

BAUMEISTER. SAFER WITH PIPE. 1953. *Galerie J. Bucher, Paris.*

128

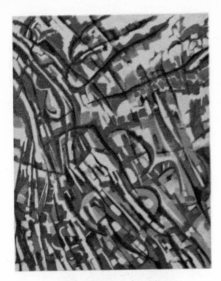

BAZAINE. THE CLEARING. 1949.
Cavellini Collection, Brescia.

presence of two apparently divergent trends which however occasionally combine to produce a curious mixture of themes—one, rough and almost bristling, is an attempt to give formal order to certain amorphous and intuitive perceptions, the other is a continuation of his earlier geometrical tendency, crystal-clear and precise. Typical of his work are the *Afrikanische Bilder (African Pictures)* series and the brightly-coloured *Montaru* and *Montari* series. — Bibl. *Sélection*, special number on Baumeister, with articles by Will Grohmann, Waldemar George, Arp, Zervos, Le Corbusier, Seuphor and others (Antwerp 1931); Domnick: *Abstrakte Malerei* (1947); Grohmann: *Willi Baumeister* (Stuttgart 1952); *Dictionary of Modern Painting* (Methuen, London 1956); Roh: *Willi Baumeister* (Baden-Baden 1954); Seuphor: *Exit Baumeister,* "Aujourd'hui" No. 5 (Paris 1955).

BAYER Herbert (b. Haag, Austria, 1900). Studied architecture at Linz. At the Bauhaus (Weimar) in 1921 where he was in Kandinsky's painting class. Taught typography at the Bauhaus from 1925 to 1928. Paintings exhibited in several centres in Europe, including London and Paris, between 1929 and 1937. Was in New York in 1938. Now living at Aspen (Colorado). — *Bibl.* Alexander Dorner: *The Way Beyond Art—The Work of Herbert Bayer* (New York 1947).

BAZAINE Jean (b. Paris, 1904). Studied sculpture at the École des Beaux-Arts. Graduated Licencié-ès-Lettres. Exhibition at the Galerie Jeanne Bucher in 1941. Works exhibited at the Galerie Carré and various foreign museums and galleries from 1942 to 1948. Took part in the Venice Biennale in 1948 and 1952. Stained-glass windows for church at Assy in 1950. Large ceramic mural for church façade at Audincourt (Doubs) in 1951. Published *Notes sur la Peinture d'Aujourd'hui* (Publ. Floury, Paris 1948). One-man exhibitions at the Gallery Maeght in 1949 and 1954. Took part in the "Four Walls" exhibition at the same gallery in 1951, along with Braque, Chagall, Léger, Matisse, Miró, Picasso and Rouault. Visited the United States in 1952. Now living in Paris.

"Each time I begin a new canvas, it is as if I had never painted before, and there is a kind of inescapable logic in the way the shapes and colours develop—in the way certain colours and certain shapes literally impose themselves on me at certain periods. It is never the result of clear deliberate calculation, it is an inner obligation from which I cannot escape, and it is often against all my inclinations, against my mood, my taste and my considered opinion. As Braque says, the canvas must kill the idea" (Bazaine). Bazaine's works are calm, harmonious compositions embracing the whole canvas with an equal delight in painting, an equal intensity of feeling and an equal continuity in colour. — *Bibl.* P. Courthion: *Peintres d'Aujourd'hui* (Geneva 1952); *Jean Bazaine,* Galerie Maeght (Paris 1953).

129

BAZIOTES William (b. Pittsburgh, Pennsylvania, 1912). Studied at the National Academy, New York, till 1936. Work developed slowly, becoming entirely abstract about 1940. His first ona-man exhibition was organised by "Art of this Century" (New York) in 1944. Numerous exhibitions of his work at the Kootz Gallery (New York) from 1944 to 1955. Took part in an exhibition at the Galerie Maeght in Paris in 1947. Is now a professor at New York University. Lives in New York. The highly unusual, though simple, shapes he invents tend to create a feeling of hallucination which often comes chose to Surrealism. — *Bibl.* Hess: *Abstract Painting* (New York 1951).

BELLEGARDE Claude (b. Paris 1927). Studied drawing and sculpture at a private studio, then began working independently. Has taken part in group exhibitions since 1946, in Paris, Buenos Aires, Madrid, Dusseldorf and elsewhere. Special exhibitions devoted to his work have been held in Paris at the Centre Saint-Jacques (1953), Galerie Arnaud (1954) and the Studio Facchetti (1955). Now living in Paris.

BENNER Gerrit (b. Leeuwarden, Holland, 1897). Is a self-taught artist. Since 1945 his work has been shown in Indonesia, the United States, Copenhagen, Berlin and Milan. He has also taken part in the Sao Paolo Biennale. Now living in Amsterdam.

BÉRARD Marius Honoré (b. Salindres, Gard, France, 1896). Studied at Alès. Has been experimenting with painting of musical inspiration since 1921. In 1927 left his position in the postal administration. Exhibited at Cannes, Paris and Boulogne-sur-Mer. In 1946 became a member of the organising committee of the Salon des Réalités Nouvelles. From 1950 onwards has travelled and exhibited in South

BERGMAN. PAINTING NO. 6. 1955.

America — among these an exhibition of French religious art. Bérard's abstract compositions usually originate from a musical theme. Greatly influenced by the music of Claude Debussy and J. S. Bach.

BERGMAN Anna-Eva (b. Stockholm, 1909). Studied in Oslo and Vienna. Abstract painter since 1947. Numerous exhibitions in Scandinavia, Germany and at the Galerie Ariel in Paris. Married to the painter Hans Hartung and living in Paris. Her paintings are characterised by large solid blocks of a single colour often isolated in the middle of the canvas. They are almost hypnotic in their effect. Has produced many engravings all marked by this same individual style. — Bibl. *Art d'Aujourd'hui* (Paris, February 1954).

BERKE Hubert (b. Buer, Germany, 1908). Studied history of art and philosophy at Königsberg and Münster. Pupil of Paul Klee in Düsseldorf (1932-1933). Exhibitions at Cologne, Duisburg, Bochum, Berne, Zurich, Basle, Paris and Brooklyn. Has had work shown at the Salon des Réalités Nouvelles in Paris. Is a member of the "Zen" group. Now living at Alfter, near Bonn.

BERLEWI Henri (b. Warsaw, 1894). Studied at the Warsaw School of Fine Arts, and later at the Beaux-Arts in Antwerp (1909-1910) and Paris (1911-1912). After a period during which he underwent various influences, mostly in the manner of Cézanne, he met Lissitzky, van Doesburg, Eggeling and Richter in Berlin in 1922. Exhibited with the Novembergruppe. In 1924, influenced by the Russian Constructivists and the Dutch Neo-Plastic school, he developed a type of abstract painting which he called *Mechanofaktur* and which he wished to bring as close as possible to the processes of machinery. Also in 1924, he published a manifesto in Warsaw under this same title, and held an exhibition of his works (Mechano - Faktur Gestaltungen) at "Der Sturm" Gallery in Berlin. In 1926, however, he returned to figurative painting. He now lives in Paris. — *Bibl.* Berlewi: *Mechano - Factur*, "Der Sturm", Drittes Vierteljahrheft, Berlin 1924.

BERTHOLLE Jean (born Dijon, 1909). Studied at the Écoles des Beaux-Arts at Saint-Étienne and Lyons. Work shown at various Salons in Paris and at the Galerie Jeanne Bucher. Now living in Paris. "Life must no doubt be lived in the context of what exists at a given time, and Bertholle is fully conscious of the existence, only recently recognised, of paintings as objective phenomena in themselves. But one must also be conscious of those forces which subsist from other times and still have their echoes in our time, and Bertholle has elected to be with all those for whom painting is a magical means of discovering the world, of going beyond outward appearances to reach the essence and the heart of things. He has a feeling for the delicate plastic properties of paint, a taste for such colours as blue and black, which call up deep emotional responses, and for sequences of subtle beauty" (Jean-Jacques Lerrant). — *Bibl.* Descargues: *Bertholle,* Presses Littéraires de France (Paris 1952).

BERTINI Gianni (b. Pisa, 1922). Specialised studies in mathematics. Since 1947 many exhibitions in Italy and at the Galerie Arnaud in Paris. His *Epilogo per un' Arte Attuale,* with wood engravings, was published in Venice in 1951. Lives in Paris.

BERTHOLLE. COMPOSITION. 1955. *Musée d'Art Moderne, Paris.*

131

BERTRAND Gaston (b. in the village of Wonck in Belgian Limburg, 1910). Began the study of classics in Brussels but was obliged to interrupt his studies to earn his living. Worked as carpenter, clerk, mechanic, and at the same time attended evening classes in drawing. Enrolled at the Brussels Académie des Beaux-Arts in 1933. Spent a short time in Paris in 1938. First exhibition devoted entirely to his work held at the Galerie Dietrich (Brussels) in 1942. Work characterised by a predilection for odd truculent figures (1947). Shortly afterwards moved towards an entirely abstract form of art, highly individual and remarkable for its extremely refined geometrical style. Exhibitions in Brussels,

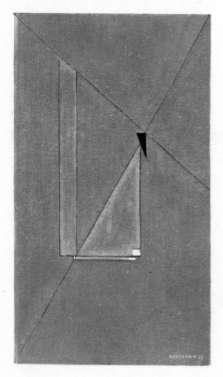

G. BERTRAND. YELLOW LANDSCAPE. 1955.

Antwerp, Liège, New York (Stable Gallery) and Milan (Il Milione Gallery). Has often exhibited in Europe with the " Jeune Peinture Belge" group. One-man exhibition at the Galerie Colette Allendy, Paris, in 1956. Lives in Brussels. — *Bibl.* R. L. Delevoy: *Gaston Bertrand,* De Sikkel (Antwerp 1953). Same author: *Gaston Bertrand,* Brient (Paris 1955).

BERTRAND Huguette (b. Écouen, Seine-et-Oise, France, 1925). First exhibition in Prague, 1946. Has taken part in group exhibitions at the Galerie Maeght and at various Salons in Paris. Several individual exhibitions at the Galerie Arnaud (Paris). Showed work in New York in 1956. Now lives in Paris. "My aim is to dismember and at the same time to reconstitute space, to render it, paradoxically, cut up into pieces, set in motion by a linear process which though it wrenches at the form is not a negation of form itself, thus making it possible, in a sense, to go into and out of the canvas freely in a back-and-forth movement — in short, the canvas becomes a choreographic argument".

BIEDERMAN Charles (b. Cleveland, Ohio, 1906). Of Czech parentage. Studied at the Art Institute, Chicago (1926-1929). Attempted, without success, to work in Czechoslovakia in 1932. Returned to Chicago and began painting in the Fauve manner. Then underwent the influence of Cubism and gradually moved towards abstract art. In Paris in 1936-37 he unconsciously began painting in the Neo-Plastic manner, though his original intention had been simply to use the Neo-Plastic technique as a means of experimenting with relief effects. In New York in 1938 he made a close study of the work of Mondrian which proved to be the starting point of a voluminous work published ten years later—*Art as the Evolution of Visual Knowledge.* Two exhibitions of his abstract works in Chicago in 1941. Now living at Red Wing, Minnesota.

H. BERTRAND. COMPOSITION. 1954.
Galerie Arnaud, Paris.

in 1951. In the following year he was appointed Rector of the "Hochschule für Gestaltung", at Ulm (Germany), a kind of university of plastic techniques which tended to fill the position formerly occupied by the Bauhaus. This school was officially opened in 1955. Max Bill resigned his rectorship the following year. He now lives in Ulm and Zurich. He has had a marked influence on many young painters both in Argentina and Italy and has been responsible for the founding of various "Concrete Art" groups in these two countries. He is a firm admirer and defender of Mondrian and Kan-

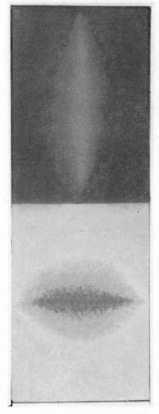

MAX BILL. TWO ACCENTS. 1949.

BILL Max (b. Winterthur, Switzerland, 1908). Studied at the Zurich School of Arts and Crafts and at the Bauhaus in Dessau. From 1929 onwards a variety of occupations as painter, sculptor, architect and publicity artist. His opposition to the concept of "abstract art" and his advocacy of the cause of "concrete art" (as propounded by van Doesburg in 1930) dates from 1935. From 1928 he took part in numerous exhibitions throughout Europe and also in North and South America. Was the organiser of the international exhibition of "Konkrete Kunst" (Concrete Art) at the Kunsthalle in Basle in 1944. Took part in an exhibition at Stuttgart in 1948, in company with Arp and Albers. In 1949 he showed more than fifty of his works at the Zurich Museum along with Vantongerloo and Pevsner. In the same year he organised the "Zürcher Konkrete Kunst" exhibition which travelled throughout Germany. A retrospective exhibition surveying the whole of his work was held at the Sao Paulo Museum in Brazil

dinsky. His main source of inspiration is mathematics. — *Bibl*. Maldonado: *Max Bill* (with comprehensive bibliography on the work of the artist, Buenos Aires 1955).

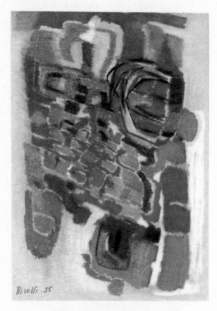

BIROLLI. GOUACHE. 1955.
Private Collection.

BIROLLI Renato (b. Verona, 1906). His work was influenced first by Ensor and van Gogh. Well known as an anti-Fascist, he was persecuted by that régime and suffered imprisonment. After the war he first followed the lead given by Pignon and Picasso but gradually turned away to an entirely free Expressionism. His work, which has been abstract since 1952, sometimes shows affinities with that of Bazaine. Now living in Milan.

BISSIER Julius (b. Freiburg-im-Breisgau, 1893). Studied at the University and Academy of Karlsruhe. Turned to abstract art in 1929. Friendship with Baumeister and Schlemmer. Has lived in retirement at Hagnau, Lake Constance, since 1939. — *Bibl*. Kurt Leonhard: *Julius Bissier* (Stuttgart 1948); *Das Kunstwerk,* Baden-Baden, Heft 8-9, 1950.

BISSIÈRE Roger (b. Villeréal, Lot-et-Garonne, France, 1888). "When I came to Paris about 1910, I did all kinds of jobs to earn a living. Up to the outbreak of war in 1914 I was attached to the staff of several newspapers. Towards the end of the war I made the acquaintance of Lhote and Favory and exhibited my work in company with them at the Salon d'Automne and the Salon des Indépendants up till 1918. My meeting with Braque in 1922 was the beginning of a long friendship. After a brief excursion into Cubism, I turned away from it, feeling that it was already outdated. From 1925 to 1938 I taught at the Academie Ranson, which for me was a somewhat unexpected departure as I have always been convinced that nothing can be taught. In fact, I used to persuade any pupils that really interested me to leave the Académie since I felt that the only effect it would have on them would be to get them into disastrous habits. In 1939 I left Paris to live in the country and settled down in the Lot country in the house where I had lived as a boy. For five years I did absolutely no painting whatever. Then I took it up again and had an exhibition at the Galerie Drouin in 1946. I showed quite a number of paintings and some tapestries made from little pieces of material sewn together. After this exhibition I went back to the country and began to work for myself, at first without any idea of exhibiting. It was then that I came to know Jaeger (manager of the Galerie Jeanne Bucher) and it is to his friendship and understanding that I owe my return to the land of the living." — *Bibl. Dictionary of Modern Painting* (Methuen, London 1956); Max-Pol Foucher: *Bissière,* Le Musée de Poche (Paris 1955); Lassaigne: *Bissière,* Galerie Jeanne Bucher (Paris 1956).

134

BITRAN Albert (b. Turkey, 1929). Came to Paris 1949 to study architecture. In 1950 suddenly took up painting on Constructivist lines. Since then he has often changed his style but without abandoning pure abstract art. Has exhibited at the Salon des Réalités Nouvelles, at the Galerie Arnaud and at the Galerie Denise René. Now lives in Paris.

BISSIÈRE. PAINTING. 1955. *Galerie Jeanne Bucher, Paris.*

BLASZKO Martin (b. Berlin, 1920). Of Polish - Jewish parentage. Was in Paris in 1939 and then went to Argentina. In 1945 he made the acquaintance of Arden Quin from whom he took lessons. In the following year he joined the Madi movement and took part in all the "Arte Madi" exhibitions at Buenos Aires where he now lives.

BLOCH Pierrette (b. Paris 1928). Her work has been exhibited in various Salons since 1949. Individual exhibition at the Galerie Mai in 1951, after which she visited New York and exhibited there. Her work has a vigorous individual style and also a marked dramatic tendency which owes much to the influence of Soulages. Is now living in Paris.

BLOW Sandra (b. 1925). Studied at St. Martin's School and the Royal Academy Schools, London, and in Italy in 1947, in Spain in 1949 and France in 1950. Has held one-man exhibitions in London in 1952 and 1954.

BOCCIONI Umberto (b. Reggio, Calabria, Italy, 1882; d. 1916). Was in Rome in 1901 where he met Severini and Balla who encouraged him to take up painting. In 1909 in company with them he founded the Futurist movement and

BISSIER. VARIATION. INDIAN INK. 1947.

135

published the famous Manifesto in the following year. Visited Paris in 1911 and 1912 at the time of the important Futurist exhibition. Later turned to a more dynamic style of painting which opened the way to abstract art. Work on similar problems in sculpture. Ardent "Interventionist" from the beginning of the first world war. He died in 1916 when he fell from his horse during artillery exercises near Verona. — *Bibl.* Carrieri: *Pittura e Scultura d'Avanguardia in Italia* (Milan 1950); *A Dictionary of Modern Painting* (Methuen, London 1956); Seuphor: *Le Futurisme... Hier,* "L'Œil" (Paris, February 1956).

BODMER Walter (b. Basle, 1903). Studied in Basle, Paris and in Spain. Was a member of the "Allianz" and in the exhibitions of this group exhibited abstract paintings, and more particularly, wire reliefs. Is now living in Basle.

BOCCIONI. ELASTICITY. 1912.
Private Collection, Milan.

BOGART Bram (b. Delft, Holland, 1921). Work shown for the first time at the Bennewitz Gallery at the Hague in 1940. Took part in group exhibitions at the Hague, Amsterdam, Rotterdam, London and Paris. Individual exhibitions of this work were held at the Galerie Creuze in Paris in 1954 and 1955. Is now living in Paris. Bogart paints in the Neo-Expressionist manner but with a subdued range of colours.

BOLOTOWSKY Ilya (b. St. Petersburg, 1907). Studied at Bakou in the Caucasus and then at a French school in Constantinople. First visited the United States in 1923. Was at the New York National Academy from 1924 to 1930. Travelled through Europe, visiting France, Italy, Germany, Scandinavia and England, in 1932. Adopted an abstract style of painting in 1933. Has exhibited various murals in the United States. Was a member and co-founder of the "American Abstract Artists" group (1936). Taught at Black Mountain College 1946 to 1948 and then at the University of Wyoming. Numerous one-man exhibitions of his work have been held in America since 1930, mainly at the New Art Circle in New York. Now living at Laramie, Wyoming.

BONNET Anne (b. Brussels, 1908) of Walloon parents. Studied at the Academies of Brussels and Saint-Josseten-Noode, and founded the group under the name of "La Route Libre" in 1939 in company with Louis van Lint and Gaston Bertrand. In 1941 was a foundation exhibitor at the "Apport" Salon. In 1945

136

BONNET. ASTRAL INFLUENCES. 1954.
Fr. Delcoigne Collection, Italy.

was one of the founders of the Jeune Peinture group in Belgium. Her work has been shown many times since 1941 at the Palais des Beaux-Arts, Brussels, and at other centres in Belgium. The Galerie de Verneuil (Paris) has exhibited her paintings along with those of Louis van Lint. Exhibition also at the Springer Gallery in Berlin. Took part in the Venice Biennale in 1948 and 1956 and in the Biennale in Sao Paulo in 1954. Is living in Brussels. Anne Bonnet's first abstract works date from 1950. Since then she has developed a thematic plastic manner, both substantial and sensitive, which has earned for her the reputation of being one of the best of the Belgian artists painting at the present time. — *Bibl.* Walravens: *Anne Bonnet en de Abstracte Schilderkunst,* Bulletin des Musées Royaux (Brussels 1953); Davay: *Anne Bonnet,* De Sikkel (Antwerp 1954).

BONNIER Olle (b. Los Angeles, 1925). His family is of French origin. Went to Sweden in 1930. Studied at technical college and art school from 1940 to 1946. Travelled extensively in Europe and in Africa from 1946 to 1951. Since

1947 he has taken part in many exhibitions in Sweden, in Copenhagen and Paris, and in the United States. His first abstract works were produced in 1943. Has shown a Constructivist tendency since 1947. Is now living at Storangen, near Stockholm.

BOTT Francis (b. Frankfort-on-the-Main, 1904). Started out as a kind of European vagabond and later became a journalist. Began painting in 1936 following the advice of Kokoschka. Came to Paris in 1937 where he joined the Surrealist movement and gradually developed towards completely abstract art. Exhibitions of his work have been held in Paris and in Germany and Switzerland. In 1953 he was responsible for the remarkable stained glass windows in the chapel of the Château de

BOTT. COMPOSITION IN RED. 1955.

137

BREER. COMPOSITION IN BLUE AND RED. 1955.

Reux, Calvados. Is now living in Paris. Bott works with a combination of plane shapes and sharply angled lines thus obtaining a restless topographical effect on which the composition as a whole exercises a pacifying influence, frequently with obvious success. — *Bibl.* Seuphor: *Francis Bott,* "Kunsthaus" (Zurich 1955).

BOTTENBURG Hendrik van (b. Amsterdam, 1911). His first exhibition was held in Amsterdam in 1948. Visited France for the first time in 1934. After receiving a grant to study, came for a second time in 1956. Paints in an energetic style and also works as a fabric designer.

BOUMEESTER Christine (b. Batavia, Java, 1904). In Holland in 1921. Graduated as teacher of drawing in 1925. Arrived in Paris in 1935 and married the painter Henri Goetz in the same year. Numerous exhibitions of her work have been held in Paris, in Holland and in Switzerland. Is a regular exhibitor at the principle abstract Salons in Paris. Has illustrated many books. Lives in Paris.

BOZZOLINI Silvano (b. Fiesole, near Florence, 1911). Studied at the School of Fine Arts in Florence. First abstract paintings in 1947. Produced a number of woodcuts both in Switzerland and in Copenhagen. His work has been exhibited in Paris, Sofia, Milan, and Lausanne. Is now living in Paris. His paintings are geometrical compositions of shapes in motion with cleverly devised gradations of colour. — Bibl. *Témoignages pour l'Art Abstrait* (Paris 1952).

BRAZZOLA Donato (b. Lausanne, 1905). Studied philosophy. Art studies at the Académie des Beaux-Arts, Lyons, and later at Lausanne. Has exhibited his work in Berne, Basle and Lausanne. Has also taken part in the Salon des Réalités Nouvelles in Paris. Lives both in Paris and Lausanne.

BREER Robert C. (b. Detroit, 1926). Studied at Stanford University, California, Came to Paris in 1949. Has exhibited at the Salon des Réalités Nouvelles and at the Galerie Denise René. Has also taken part in exhibitions in Stockholm and in Cuba. Has produced abstract films. Now living in Paris.

BREETVELT Adolf (b. Delft, 1892). Studied at the School of Fine Arts at the Hague. From 1920 to 1937 was a teacher in Indonesia. His work developed from Expressionism to a new type of Realism and then from 1945 onwards turned to abstract art but with the colours of his earlier manner. Now living in Holland.

138

BRENSON Theodore (b. Riga, Latvia, 1893). Studied architecture in Riga. Later lived in Rome and in Paris. Went to the United States in 1941 and became an American citizen. Many individual exhibitions of his work have been held in America, in Paris, Italy and Switzerland. Now living in New York.

BREUER Léo (b. Bonn, 1893). Studied at art schools in Cologne and Kassel. His work has been shown in many towns in Germany. Lives in France since 1940. Is a regular exhibitor at the Salon des Réalités Nouvelles. Now living in Paris.

BREUIL Georges, real name Adrien Dubreuil (b. Quevillon, near Rouen, 1904). Began painting in a prison camp in Germany during the years 1940 to 1945. Individual exhibition of his work in 1954 at the Galerie Colette Allendy. Now living in Rouen.

BRIELLE Roger (b. Malicorne, Sarthe, 1899). Spent his childhood in Paris. Education at the Collège Chaptal. Up to 1930 wrote art criticisms for many papers and reviews. At the same time published poetic and literary essays. Then began painting in a style not unlike Surrealism. Joined the Surrealist movement in 1947 and took part in several group exhibitions in Paris, Prague, Rio de Janeiro and Brussels. Later turned to abstract art, and his works in this style display a spirit of fantasy comparable to that of Paul Klee. Took part in the Salon des Réalités Nouvelles in 1955 and in the same year exhibited at the Galerie Michel Warren in Paris. Now lives at Blois.

BROOKS James (b. St. Louis, Missouri, 1906). Studied at the Southern Methodist University, and at the Art Students' League, New York. Individual exhibitions at the Peridot Gallery, New York, in 1950 and 1951. Now living in New York.

BRUCE Patrick Henry (b. Virginia, 1880; d. New York, 1937). Of Scottish parentage. Studied in New York with Robert Henry. Came to Paris in 1907. Worked in Matisse's studio, and exhibited at the Salon d'Automne. Later joined up with the Orphist movement led by Robert Delaunay. Exhibited at the Armory Show in 1913. Showed abstract works at

BRUCE. COMPOSITION. *c.* 1933. *H.-P. Roché Collection, Paris.*

the Salon des Indépendants in 1914. From 1920 onwards was invited by Miss Katherine Dreier to take part in the exhibitions of the "Société Anonyme". In a fit of melancholia in Paris in 1933 he destroyed the greater part of his paintings. Those remaining have been collected by Henri-Pierre Roché. "His constant endeavour was to create works which, by reason of their structural qualities, could be looked at from four sides. The absence of these qualities in the works of other modern painters was, rightly or wrongly, a constant source of anguish to him. For several years he exhibited at the Salon des Indépendants, but later gave up because no one understood the problem with which he was grappling and because people considered his works simply as pleasantly coloured decorative panels." (Henri-Pierre Roché). — *Bibl.* Wright: *Modern Painting* (New York 1915); Dreier: *Western Art and the New Era* (New York 1928); *Collection of the Société Anonyme* (New Haven 1950); Seuphor: *La Peinture aux Etats-Unis,* "Art d'Aujourd'hui" (Paris, June 1951); Ritchie: *Abstract Painting and Sculpture in America,* Museum of Modern Art (New York 1951).

BRYEN Camille (b. Nantes, 1907). Has written poetry and produced drawings and paintings. Is very active in the artistic coteries of St.-Germain-des-Prés and Montparnasse. Has exhibited his work in Paris since 1932. Took part in the first three Salons des Réalités Nouvelles. Exhibited in company with Arp in Basle in 1946 and in Zurich in 1950. Individual exhibitions of his work have been held at the Galerie Pierre and at the Galerie Colette Allendy. Has also taken part in numerous exhibitions of 'informal' art. Is now living in Paris. "Painting is the expression of the inner life, and its nature is that of a cosmic function. Far from being a simple product of sensory excitation, it should, in its proper capacity, act like a magical phenomenon making itself felt not only through the optical, but also through the para-optical per-

BRYEN. APOCALYPSE. 1953.
Galerie Colette Allendy, Paris.

ception, not only through the dimensions of shapes and colours present, but also through what is not present, through memory and the ambivalences of the physical and psychical personality". (Bryen).

BUCHHEISTER Karl (b. Hanover, 1890). Studied at Hanover and Berlin. After the first world war, in company with Kurt Schwitters, founded an association of Abstract painters in Hanover. Member of the "Sturm" group and the "Novembergruppe". Took part in the "Cercle et Carré" exhibition in Paris in 1930. Was also a member of the "Abstraction-Création" group. Work exhibited at the Galerie Creuze in Paris in 1954. Since 1945 has been a professor at the Hanover Academy. Lives in Hanover.

BUCHHOLZ Erich (b. Bromberg, Germany, 1891). Son of an illiterate shepherd. Despite the poverty of his youth he became a school teacher, but gave up this calling in 1917 to become a painter. Was a member of the "November-gruppe" after the first world war. His first abstract works, which showed a geometrical tendency, were produced about 1919. Paintings exhibited at the Sturm Gallery in Berlin in 1921. Was a friend of Lissitzky. His career as an artist was interrupted by the Nazi régime but he returned to painting after the second world war. Retrospective exhibition at the Rose Fried Gallery, New York, in 1956. Now living in Berlin. "Buchholz's affinity with the Suprematists and with Mondrian is obvious in his relief paintings produced during the 1920s. These severely geometrical works with white, black, red and gold might be described as twentieth century icons". (R. Hülsenbeck).

BURRI Alberto (b. Citta di Castello, Italy, 1915). Studied medicine at Citta Perugia. Began painting in 1944 while a prisoner of war in Texas. From 1945 onwards has lived in Rome and concentrated entirely on painting. Individual exhibitions of his work have been held in many centres in Italy and also in Chicago.

Took part in the Venice Biennale and the New Decade exhibition at the New York Museum of Modern Art in 1955. Now living in Rome. Burri's works are composed of pieces of cloth sewn together and of oil colours—their unity is due to the characteristic climate created by the artist himself who has the gift of combining an apparent awkwardness of manner with absolute perfection of taste. — Bibl. *Art News* (New York, Dec. 1954).

BURSSENS Jan (b. Malines, Belgium, 1925). Studied at the Ghent Academy. Travelled in England, Holland, Italy and France. His work has been shown in various centres in Belgium and also in London and in Norway. Is now living at Mariakerke near Ghent.

BURY Pol (b. Haine-Saint-Pierre, Belgium, 1922). Studied at the Beaux-Arts in Mons. From 1947 exhibited with the "Jeune Peinture Belge" group, and in 1955 took part in the Mouvement exhibition at the Galerie Denise René, Paris. Is now living at Haine-Saint-Paul, Belgium.

BUCHHEISTER. BLACK AND WHITE. 1932.
Yale University, U.S.A.

141

C

CADORET Michel (b. Paris, 1912). Studied at the École des Beaux-Arts, Paris, and the School of Decorative Arts, Dusseldorf. Visited America and Egypt. Was mobilised in September 1939 and taken prisoner in June 1940. Escaped from France and joined the army again at Casablanca. Took part in the Normandy campaign and then served in Germany. From 1947 onwards he illustrated books and took part in various exhibitions, including the exhibition "France Comes to You" which travelled through the United States. Spent three years in Mexico where he worked in the village of Erongaricuaro, Micheacan. Individual exhibitions in New York in 1953 and 1954, and at the Galerie Furstenberg in Paris in 1955. Lives either in New York or in Paris.

CAGLI Corrado (b. Ancona, Italy, 1910). First worked on large-scale mural painting. Spent some time in the United States continuing his training and then took up abstract art. Has exhibited in the main centres in Italy and also in Paris, Zurich, New York and San Francisco. Now living in Rome.

CAHN Marcelle (b. Strasbourg, 1895). Early training in Strasbourg. Was in Berlin during the first world war and associated with the artists of the Sturm group. Came to Paris in 1919. Met Munch a number of times in Zurich in 1922. Was associated with the studio of Fernand Léger in 1925, and took part in the "Art d'Aujourd'hui" exhibition. Exhibited at the 1926 exhibition of the Société Anonyme at the

CADORET. THE JOYOUS CITY. 1955. *Galerie Furstenberg, Paris.*

142

CALLIYANNIS. BLACK AND WHITE. 1954.
Galerie Mouradian-Vallotton, Paris.

Africa he returned to Paris and in 1955 his work was shown at the Studio Facchetti. Exhibition also held at the Martha Jackson Gallery in New York. His painting owes a great deal to the influence of Pollock and Rothko. His latest works show the maturing of his personality. P. Restany wrote: "It was in Paris that Calcagno found his true personal style which he worked out from the chaotic tyranny of over-exacting natural vigour".

Brookland Museum. In 1930 was a member of the "Cercle et Carré" group and made the acquaintance of Mondrian and Arp. A regular exhibitor at the Salon des Réalités Nouvelles. Now living in Paris. Her works are subdued in manner with little variation of colour and generally of simple geometric design.

CALLIYANNIS Manolis (b. Lesbos, Greece, 1926). Served in the R.A.F. during the war. Began painting at the age of 15 and at the same time continued his architectural studies which he completed in 1947 at the University of Johannesburg, South Africa. Came to Paris in 1948. Has exhibited at the Galerie

CALCAGNO Laurence (b. San Francisco, 1916). Self-taught artist. Travelled in the East and in Mexico. Individual exhibitions in New Orleans in 1945, San Francisco in 1948, and Florence in 1950 and 1952. Spent some time in Paris in 1952 and 1953 when he took part in several group exhibitions. After visiting North

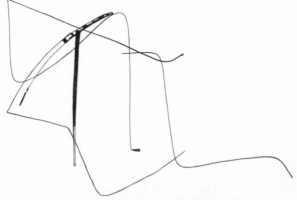

MARCELLE CAHN. INK DRAWNING. 1952.

143

Arnaud in Paris, at Gimpel's in London, and also in Belgium and at Amsterdam. His palette is sober, but he skilfully organises his rich material in solid compositions. Now living in Paris.

CARLSTEDT. COMPOSITION. 1955.

CALMIS Charlotte (b. Aleppo, Syria, 1918). Came to Paris at the age of 17 and frequently visited the studios of Lhote, Gromaire, Lurçat. Was advised by her friend Jacques Villon. Took part in the "Les Mains Éblouies" exhibition at the Galerie Maeght in 1947. Individual exhibition at the Galerie Arnaud in 1953. Visited Cairo and showed her work their in 1956. Now living at Saint Tropez. Effusive style of painting with violent colours which in 1955 became more disciplined without, however, losing its warmth.

CAPOGROSSI Giuseppe (b. Rome, 1900). Completed his studies in law before devoting himself to painting. Lived in Paris from 1927 to 1932. Founded the "Gruppo Romano" in Rome in company with the painters Cagli and Cavalli, and then the "Origine" group to which he belonged up to 1951. Has taken part in the Venice Biennales since 1928. His work has been shown in numerous exhibitions in Paris, Vienna, Prague, Budapest, Warsaw, New York, Buenos Aires, London, Berne and Berlin. Now living in Rome. Capogrossi's abstract work is an endless variation on a single theme, a kind of claw or trident on which he effects the most extraordinary transformations. — *Bibl.* Seuphor: *Capogrossi,* Cavallino (Venice 1954).

CARLSTEDT Birger Jarl (b. Helsinki, 1907). Travelled and studied in France, Italy and Germany. First individual exhibition of his experimental abstract works at the Konsthallen in Helsinki in 1930. From 1936 to 1938 was special correspondent of a Helsinki newspaper in various European countries. Took part in numerous group exhibitions in Paris, Berlin, Rome, Oslo, Copenhagen and Stockholm, and also at the Salon des Réalités Nouvelles in Paris in 1951 and 1952. Now living in Helsinki.

CARLSUND Otto Gustaf (b. St. Petersburg, 1897; d. Stockholm 1948). Was brought up in Sweden. Attended the Dresden Academy from 1921 to 1922, and the Oslo Academy from 1922 to 1923. Came to Paris in 1924 to study Cubist mural painting. Entered Léger's studio and became one of his favourite pupils. Frequent contacts with Mondrian in 1927. Gradually adopted and used Neo-Plastic ideas. Met van Doesburg in 1929. Was co-founder of the "Art Concret" group in 1930 with van Doesburg and Helion. In the following year organised a notable exhibition of Cubist and abstract art in Stockholm. Discouraged by the lack of success of this exhibition he abandoned painting for some time. Became an art critic in 1931. After the death of Mondrian in 1944 Carlsund decided to take up painting again. Was elected president of the Artists' Club in 1947. Died the following year. — *Bibl.* Oscar Reutersvard: *Carlsund och Neoplasticismen*, Konsthistorisk Tidskrift (Stockholm 1949); *Hommage à Otto G. Carlsund,* Galerie Artek (Helsinki 1950).

CAPOGROSSI. GOUACHE. *Private Collection, Italy.*

CARO Anita de (b. New York, 1909). Studied drawing and painting at the Art Students League in New York with Max Weber and Hans Hofmann. First visited Europe in 1930. Travelled in France, Germany, Austria, Spain, England and Italy. Lived in Zurich from 1935 to 1938 where her first individual exhibition was held. Then came to Paris where she studied engraving with S. W. Hayter at the "Atelier 17". Work shown at the Galerie des Quatre Chemins. In 1939 married the engraver Roger Vieillard. After the war her painting became gradually more abstract. Exhibited paintings at the Galerie Jeanne Bucher, Paris, in 1950, at the Hanover Gallery, London, 1953, and at the Galerie Marcel Évrard in Lille in 1954. Has exhibited at the Salon de Mai since 1948. Now living in Paris. Intuitive type of painting, in which colour maintains a constant and delicately modulated dialogue with itself.

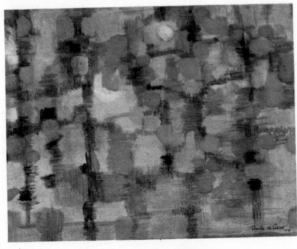

ANITA DE CARO. GOUACHE. 1954.

145

CARRADE Michel (b. Albi, France, 1923). Has taken part in several provincial Salons and then in the Salon de Mai and the Salon d'Octobre in Paris. Individual exhibitions at the Galerie Arnaud in Paris in 1952 and 1953, and at the Galerie Granier, Castres, in 1955. Work shown in group exhibitions in Turin, Milan, Florence, Mannheim and Offenbach (Germany) and in Vienna. Now living in Paris.

CARREY Georges (b. Paris, 1902; d. Knokke, Belgium, 1953). Studied for a short time at the École des Arts Décoratifs, Paris, then worked individually doing caricatures, posters, commercial drawings and stage settings. Settled in Brussels in 1922. Began portrait painting in 1925. His first abstract works were produced in 1946. Returned to Paris in 1948. Individual exhibition at the Galerie de Beaune in 1950. Works also shown at the Galerie Arnaud, the Salon de Mai and the Salon d'Octobre in 1952.

CAVAEL Rolf (b. Königsberg, 1898). Studied at the School of Fine Arts in Frankfort. His first exhibition, in company with Albers, was held at Braunschweig in 1933, but was suppressed by the Nazi régime. Spent two years in concentration camp in Dachau. Then lived in isolation at Garmisch-Partenkirchen, forbidden to continue painting. Since 1947 has exhibited at Basle, Cologne, Munich, New York, Paris, etc. Now living in Munich.

CAVALLON Giorgio (b. Italy, 1904). Went to America at an early age. Studied with Charles Hawthorne and Hans Hofmann. Has exhibited with the "American Abstract Artists" group since 1936. Took part in an exhibition at the Sidney Janis Gallery, New York in 1950, and in an exhibition of American abstract and at the New York Museum of Modern Art in 1951. Visited Paris and Italy in 1953. Now living in New York. Painting characterised by expanses of invitingly warm colours. — *Bibl.* Ritchie: *Abstract Painting and Sculpture in America,* Museum of Modern Art (New York 1951).

CAZIEL Casimir Zielenkiewicz (b. Poland, 1906). Studied at the College of Lodz and then at the Warsaw Academy of Art. Came to France in 1939. Has taken part in the Salon de Mai and the Salon des Surindépendants on several occasions. Now living in Paris.

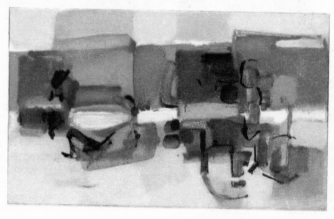

CARRADE. PAINTING. 1955. *Pierre Wurth Collection, Paris.*

146

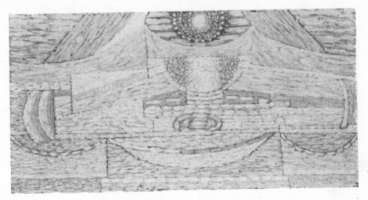

CHARCHOUNE. THE FLUTE. 1954.

CHAPOVAL Jules (b. Kiev, 1919; d. Paris 1951). Educated in Paris where he studied medicine. At the École des Beaux-Arts of Marseilles and Toulouse during the war (1939-1945). Returned to Paris after the Liberation. Individual exhibition at the Galerie Jeanne Bucher. Took part in a number of group exhibitions and also in the main abstract Salons. Was one of the most promising of the young abstract painters when he died at an early age. — Bibl. *Témoignages pour l'Art Abstrait* (Paris 1952).

CHARCHOUNE Serge (b. Bougourouslan, Russia, 1888). Refused entry to the School of Fine Arts in Kazan. Worked for several months in various Academies in Moscow. Arrived in Paris in 1912 and was associated with several independent Academies. Exhibited for the first time at the Salon des Indépendants in 1913. Spent the years 1914 to 1917 in Spain. His first individual exhibition was held in a bookshop in the Rue Dauphine in Paris in 1920. Between 1921 and 1924 he contributed to a number of reviews of the Dada movement. Work shown at the Sturm Gallery in Berlin in 1922. Has also exhibited in Barcelona, Stockholm, Brussels, New York and Prague. Several individual exhibitions at the Galerie Creuze in Paris (1947 to 1956). Now living in Paris.

The major part of Charchoune's work is abstract, but he does not hesitate to make occasional and sometimes startling excursions into figurative painting. Some of his best canvases owe their inspiration to the music of Bach or Beethoven, although this fact adds nothing to their obvious plastic qualities. It must be admitted that in his sentimental or mystical compositions Charchoune is disappointing. He is more at his ease in his Symbolist fantasy pieces. His work reaches unequalled heights of delicacy in modulations of single colour. These pictures, which are a kind of spiritual exercise for the eye, must be numbered among the best examples of pure painting. — *Bibl.* Autobiographical sketch in *L'Art Abstrait, ses Origines, ses Premiers Maîtres* (Paris 1949); *Collection of the Société Anonyme* (New Haven 1950).

CHASTEL Roger (b. Paris, 1897). Studied at the École des Beaux-Arts (Atelier Cormon) then at the Académie Julian and the Académie Ranson. Drawings and caricatures for exclusive magazines. Numerous exhibitions from 1926 onwards. Took part in the Venice and Sao Paulo Biennales. Did the illustrations for Paul

Éluard's *Bestiaire*. Drew sketches for Gobelins Tapestries in Paris. Has taken part in the Salon de Mai since its inauguration in 1948. His work is sometimes abstract but more often tending towards figurative art. Now living at Saint-Germain-en-Laye, near Paris. "The faculty of abstraction is peculiar to man, it is the specific quality of the creator... My practical objective is to attain complete abstraction, rejecting preconceived technical solutions. As the work progresses the original visual emotion, whether objective or subjective, suggests new relationships between colours and shapes which become more and more abstract as they take their place within the pattern of an inward illumination". (Chastel).

CHELIMSKY Oscar (b. New York, 1923). Studied at the Art Students League with Hans Hofmann (1946-1947). Came to Paris in 1948. Individual exhibition held at the Galerie Jeanne Bucher, Paris, 1953. Has taken part in many group exhibitions in Paris, Madrid, Minneapolis, Amsterdam, and also in a number of Salons in Paris where he is now living. Chelimsky's painting is in a kind of calligraphic style—delicate and warm. His colours seem to float on the surface of the canvas as if reluctant to penetrate its texture. This abstract flora appears to be rippled as if by a soft breeze which, however, does not destroy its order. The artist's style changed in 1955 when he abandoned the use of mat-finish synthetic paint, and he began experimenting with shiny oils and thick mixes.

CHERMAYEFF Serge Ivan (b. Russia, 1900). Studied in London from 1910 to 1917, and then in Germany. Was appointed professor of architecture at Brooklyn College, United States, in 1952. From 1946 to 1951 was director of the Institute of Design in Chicago. Became an American citizen in 1946. Has taken part in many exhibitions in America and an individual showing of his work was held in Chicago in 1950. Now living in Chicago. His painting is rich in colour and skilful colour contrasts. His compositions are classical and frequently erudite.

CHESNAY Denise (b. Versailles, 1923). Educated in Algiers. Came to Paris in 1944. After first having experienced the influence of the earlier Cubists, then of the young abstract painters she developed a purely sensitive form of abstract art for herself. Has taken part in many group exhibitions and various Salons in Paris.

CHASTEL. DOOR TO A DREAM. 1954

148

CHILDS Bernard (b. New York, 1910). Studied at Pennsylvania University then worked with Kimon Nicolaides (1932) and with Amédée Ozenfant (1947). Individual exhibitions at the "Obelisco" in Rome in 1951, at the Galerie Breteau in Paris in 1953, and the Zimmergalerie in Frankfort in 1955. Has also taken part in many group exhibitions in Paris and in the Salon des Réalités Nouvelles in 1954. Now living in Paris. After first painting canvases in diffused colour sequences full of poetic fantasy, Childs adopted a more calligraphic style using a pizzicato effect of small black or grey strokes converging or dispersing.

CITRON Minna (b. Newark, New Jersey, 1896). Studied in New York. Travelled in Europe. Many exhibitions in America. Has taken part in the Salon des Réalités Nouvelles since 1947. Work shown at the Galerie Creuze, Paris, 1951. Travelling exhibition in South America in 1952. Now living in New York. — Bibl. *Minna Citron, Paintings and Graphics,* articles by Jean Cassou and others (New York 1952).

CLARK Edward (b. New Orleans, 1927). Studied for five years at the Chicago Art Institute. Began painting in 1946. Came to Paris in 1952 and took up abstract art in 1953. Has taken part in several group exhibitions. Individual exhibition at the Galerie Creuze, Paris, in 1955. His compositions are tall improvisations of very vivid colours. Now living in Paris.

CLAUSEN Fransiska (b. Denmark, 1899). Studied in Denmark and later in Berlin where she took lessons from Moholy-Nagy and Archipenko (1922). Abstract "collages" of geometrical shapes showing a marked influence of the Russian Constructivists. Worked in Paris from 1924 to 1933, first as a pupil of Léger and then independently. In 1926 she took part in Miss Dreier's International Exhibition of the Société Anonyme in Brooklyn. In 1929 she made the acquaintance of Mondrian, Arp and Seuphor, and joined the "Cercle et Carré" group with whom she exhibited in 1930. After her return to Denmark she gradually abandoned abstract art and took up portrait painting. Now living in retirement in Denmark. — Bibl. *The Société Anonyme,* Brooklyn Museum (Brooklyn 1926); *Art d'Aujourd'hui* (Paris, Oct. 1953).

CLOSON Henri J. (b. Liège, Belgium, 1888). Unsettled youth. Came to Paris after the 1914-1918 war and met Claude Monet, Mondrian and Béothy.

CHELIMSKY. PAINTING. 1955. *Galerie Jeanne Bucher, Paris.*

149

His studies of the reflection of colours in moving water gradually brought him to abstract art. Has regularly taken part in the Salon des Réalités Nouvelles. Now living in Paris.

COGGESHALL Calvert (b. New Utica, U.S.A., 1907). Studied art and architecture at Pennsylvania University and the Art Students League. Worked in Europe in 1937 and 1938. Individual exhibition at the Betty Parsons Gallery in New York in 1951, and in the same year his work was shown in the Abstract Painting and Sculpture in America exhibition organised by the Museum of Modern Art in New York. Now living at North Stonington, Connecticut.

COHEN Harold (b. 1928). Studied at the Slade School London, and held his first one-man shows at Oxford in 1951 and London in 1954. In 1956 was appointed Fellow in Fine Arts at Nottingham University.

COLLIGNON George (b. Liège, Belgium, 1923). Studied at the Académie des Beaux-Arts in Liège. Has produced abstract paintings since 1949. Took part in the "Les Mains Éblouies" exhibition at the Galerie Maeght in 1950 and 1951, and also in the Salon de Mai in Paris. Individual exhibitions in Liège (A.P.I.A.W.), Brussels (Galerie Apollo). Frankfort (Zimmergalerie), and Paris (Galerie Arnaud). Now living in Paris.

COMPARD Émile (b. Paris, 1900). Naturalist painter encouraged by Félix Fénéon and also by Bonnard who exchanged canvases with him. From 1946 onwards he turned towards figurative art and showed no works for almost ten years. Individual exhibition of abstract paintings at the Galerie Ariel, Paris 1955. Now lives in Paris.

CONGDON William (b. Providence, Rhode Island, 1912). Studied at Yale (New Haven), then worked with George Demetrios in Boston. Visited Italy in 1948. Individual exhibitions at the Betty Parsons Gallery, New York, in 1949, 1950 and 1952. Now lives either in New York or in Venice.

CONOVER Robert (b. Philadelphia, 1920). Studied in Philadelphia, in New York (Art Students League) and at the Brooklyn Museum School. His first individual exhibition was held at the Laurel Gallery in New York in 1950. Now lives in New York.

JEANNE COPPEL. COMPOSITION. 1955.

150

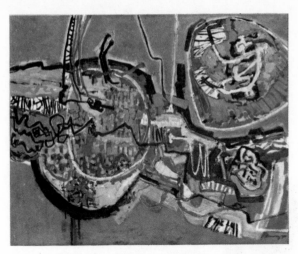

CORNEILLE. THE FLAMING SUMMER. 1955.
Galerie Craven, Paris.

CONSAGRA Pietro (b. Mozzara del Vallo, Italy, 1920). Individual exhibitions in Rome and Venice. Was one of the organisers of the Abstract Art in Italy Exhibition in Rome in 1948. Now lives in Rome.

CONTE Michelangelo (b. Spalato, Dalmatia, 1913). Formal studies in classics, but is a self-taught artist. Gradual development towards abstract art. His work has been shown in exhibitions in Naples, Rome, Venice, Berne, Vienna and Sao Paulo. Now lives in Rome.

COPPEL Jeanne (b. Galatz, Roumania, 1896). Childhood and youth spent mainly in Switzerland and Germany. Came into contact with the Sturm movement in Berlin in 1913. First abstract compositions in 1918 and 1919. Produced abstract "collages" about the same time. Settled in Paris in 1919 and worked at the Atelier Ranson with Sérusier, Vuillard, and Maurice Denis. Returned to abstract art in 1947, and has exhibited at the Salon des Réalités

Nouvelles since 1948. Individual exhibitions at the Galerie Colette Allendy (1950), and the Galerie Arnaud (1955). Lives in Paris. Jeanne Coppel's work has the same serious quality as that of Braque, the same serenity, the same discretion and the same measured tranquillity. She has a preference for mat tones and subdued colour combinations. At times she adds a vivid touch which is designed not so much to startle as to draw attention, by this apparent levity, to the underlying and hidden power in the work. — *Bibl.* Herta Wescher: *Jeanne Coppel,* Cimaise No. 5, Paris 1955.

CORBETT Edward (b. Chicago, 1919). Son of a Merchant Marine officer. Studied art in San Francisco from 1938 to 1940. In the Merchant Marine himself from 1942-1944. In New York from 1944-1946, and taught in various art schools in California from 1947-1950. Has taken part in several group exhibitions: New York 1947 ("American Abstract Artists"); Art Institute of Chicago in 1947; Henry Art Gallery, Seattle 1950; Museum of Modern Art, New York 1952 ("15 Americans"). Now living at Taos, New Mexico.

CORNEILLE Cornelis van Beverloo (b. Liège, Belgium, 1922). Of Dutch parentage. Attended classes in drawing at Amsterdam Academy from 1940 to 1943. In company with Appel and Constant founded the Dutch Experimental Group in 1948. Was co-founder of *Cobra* in Paris also in 1948. Individual exhibitions

151

in Amsterdam (1951 and 1954), Rotterdam (1952), Budapest (1947), Copenhagen (1950), Antwerp (1953), and Paris (1953 and 1954). Has taken part in numerous group exhibitions at the Galerie Maeght, the Galerie Pierre, the Salon de Mai, and elsewhere in Paris. Now living in Paris. Painting characterised by the use of powerful arched structural motifs. Its expressive qualities are obtained by graphic effects either in black or colour, employed with both sensitivity and firmness.

CORPORA. GOUACHE. 1955.
Private Collection.

CORPORA Antonio (b. Tunis, 1909). Studied at the École des Beaux-Arts in Tunis. At the age of 20 went to Florence. Studied the Masters in the Uffizzi Gallery. Later came to Paris where his work was noticed by Modigliani's friend Zborowsky. Spent the years from 1930 to 1937 either in Paris or Tunis. His work was shown at the Milione Gallery in Milan in 1939. Has taken an active part both as a writer and lecturer in the controversy about abstract art. His main preoccupation is to combat the ideas of the "Novecento" group. Has taken part in many exhibitions in Tunis, in Italy and in Paris. Lives in Rome. — *Bibl.* Zervos: *Antonio Corpora* (Publ. Centre d'Art Italien, Paris 1952).

CORSI Carlo (b. Nice, 1879). Studied at the University of Bologna and Albertina Academy, Turin. Has taken part in the Venice Biennale since 1912 and also in many other Salons. Showed some very remarkable abstract "collages" in a group exhibition at the Palais des Beaux-Arts in Brussels. Now lives in Bologna.

COULON Jean-Michel (b. Bordeaux 1920). Studied history in Paris. Visited Picasso in 1943. Has produced abstract works since 1939. Held an exhibition of gouaches in various centres in South America in 1949. First individual exhibition at the Galerie Jeanne Bucher, Paris, in 1950. Spent a considerable time in Amsterdam. Took part in a group exhibition at the Sidney Janis Gallery, New York, in 1950. Visited Spain in 1952. Now lives in Paris.

COVERT John (b. Pittsburgh, Pennsylvania, 1882). Studied in Munich 1908-1912. Worked in Paris from 1912 to 1914. Visited England. Took part in various exhibitions in the United States. Gave up painting to go into business in 1923. Most of his work is in the collection of the Société Anonyme, New Haven. Lives in Pittsburgh. Covert was one of the first American abstract artists, and is still regarded as one of the most original figures in American painting of the period immediately following the first world war. — Bibl. *Collection of the Société Anonyme* (New Haven 1950); Ritchie: *Abstract Painting and Sculpture in America* (New York 1951).

CRAWFORD Ralston (b. Sainte Catherine, Canada, 1906). Abandoned his career as a sailor to study art in Los Angeles and Philadelphia (1927-1933). Was in Europe in 1932 and 1933. Taught at the Cincinnati Academy in 1940 and 1941, and then at Buffalo and the Brooklyn School of Art (1948-1949). First individual exhibition in Philadelphia in 1937. Now living in New York.

CORSI. CASTLE ON THE SEA. PAPIER COLLÉ. 1954.

CRIPPA Roberto (b. Monza, Italy, 1921). Studied at the Milan Academy. Many exhibitions in Italy (since 1947) and in the United States (since 1951). Has regularly taken part in the Venice Biennale since 1948. He has developed a very calligraphic style with maze-like curved line patterns. Now lives in Milan.

CRIPPA. COMPOSITION. 1952.
Private Collection, Paris.

CROWLEY Grace (b. Australia, 1895). Studied at Sydney Art School. Spent some years in France (1927-1931). Studied under André Lhote and was influenced by Albert Gleizes. Took part in various exhibitions in Paris, but it was only after her return to Australia that she gradually gave up representational painting to become (with Ralph Balson) one of the few representatives of abstract art in Australia. Lives at Mittagong, Australia.

D

DAMIAN Horia (b. Bucharest, Rumania, 1922). Arrived in Paris in 1946. Studied under Lhote, then under Léger. Came to abstract painting in 1949. Met Herbin, and discovered neo-plasticism in 1951. Exhibited at the Salon des Réalités Nouvelles and in various group-shows, especially at the Galerie Arnaud. Lives in Paris.

DARIE Sandu (b. in Rumania, 1908). Educated in France. In Havana since 1941; a naturalized Cuban. One-man shows in Havana (The Lyceum) in 1949 and 1950. Included in exhibitions in New York and Japan. Since 1946, his work has been abstract. Sandu Darie uses panels of a simple geometrical design presented in frameless compositions. His favourite figure appears to be a triangle within which the neo-plastic elements, horizontal and vertical, are lightly and elegantly inscribed.

DAVIE Alan (b. Grangemouth, Scotland, 1920). Studied at the College of Art in Edinburgh and at the Royal Scottish Academy. Travelled and studied in France, Switzerland, Italy, and Spain. First exhibition in Edinburgh, 1946. Exhibited in Florence and Venice in 1948, in London in 1950 and 1952. Included in the *Jeunes Peintres* exhibition organized by the Congress for Cultural Freedom in Rome and in Paris in 1955, and also in an exhibition at the Galerie Bignou in 1956. Lives in London. Agonised abstractions derived, sometimes, from expressionism.

DAVIS Stuart (b. Philadelphia, 1894). Studied in New York. Exhibited five water-colours at the 'Armory Show' (1913). First one-man show in 1917. A cartographer in the army in 1918. In Paris, 1928-1929. Taught at the Art Students League, New York, 1931. Government post from 1933 to 1940. Then taught at the New School for Social Research, New York. Retrospective exhibition at the Museum of Modern Art, New York (1945).

STUART DAVIS. SALT-CELLAR. 1931.
Museum of Modern Art, New York.

154

Lives in New York. Among American painters, Stuart Davis is the one whose training was most influenced by cubism. From that point, his work slowly developed towards abstraction, more especially since 1938. Davis's style is generally forceful, but because of the very fresh colours, never harsh; there is always something of a joyous circus atmosphere. — *Bibl.* Hitchcock: *Painting toward Architecture* (New York 1948); Ritchie: *Abstract Painting and Sculpture in America* (New York 1951); *Art d'Aujourd'hui* (Paris, June 1951); *Art News* (New York, summer 1953); *50 Ans d'art aux États-Unis,* Musée d'Art Moderne (Paris 1955).

DEBRÉ. STILL LIFE. 1954.

DAVRING Henri (b. Aachen, 1900). Studied at Dusseldorf Academy and then under the painter Eckstein. He was famous in Germany under his real name, Davringhausen, having precociously exhibited at Flechtheim's, Dusseldorf, and been a member of the 'Novembergruppe' in Berlin. Took part in numerous exhibitions in Germany up to 1933. Emigrated when Hitler came to power. His work was included in the 'Degenerate Art' exhibition. Spent a few years in Spain and in Switzerland, came finally to France. One-man shows at the Galerie des Deux-Iles, Paris, 1949 and 1950, the Galerie Verneuil, Paris, 1955. Lives in Cagnes-sur-Mer (Alpes-Maritimes, France). Almost all of Davring's canvases are variations on a simple theme : two or three straight lines intersected by one or two curves. This movement details the opposition of two principles, their fusion in a composition being celebrated variously, in delicate or crude colours, according to the mood of the painter. The theme develops in a complete calm with no hint of tragedy, like a cloudless sky.

DEBRÉ Olivier (b. Paris, 1920). After matriculation, he travelled in Italy and studied architecture for a year at the École des Beaux-Arts, Paris. Spent a year as a student in England (1939). Became more and more interested in painting. Met Othon Friesz, Segonzac, and Picasso (1941). Took part in the Salon des Surindépendants and the Salon d'Automne. One-man show at the Galerie Bing, Paris, 1949. Visited Holland, 1950. Included in various group-shows in New York and Paris. Exhibited with Germain at the Galerie Warren, Paris 1957. Lives in Paris. He composes with planes of dulled colours very cleverly combined. He makes one think of the best of De Staël, whom he seems to have already excelled.

DELAHAUT. ASTRAL. 1953.

timentality, anchored to the pedestrian conclusions of sensual perception, was not done in a day. But now it is an accomplished fact, and Degottex, at the helm, can guard the spoils" (André Breton).

DEGOTTEX Jean (b. Sathonay, Ain, France, 1918). Self-educated. Came to Paris in 1933. His first paintings, done during a stay in Tunisia (1938-41), were in the Fauve manner. On his return to Paris, took part in various exhibitions. His first non-representational canvases exhibited at the Galerie Denise René in 1949 and 1952. Included in the Salon de Mai and the Salon d'Octobre. Took part in the exhibition 'Tendances', Galerie Maeght, Paris, 1952; in many exhibitions at the Galerie Kléber, Paris, 1954 and 1955, and also in the 'Younger European Painters' exhibition at the Solomon R. Guggenheim Museum, New York, 1953-4. One-man show at Étoile Scellée, Paris, 1955. Lives in Paris. Through his exploration of the possibilities of a highly coloured line, Degottex developed, about 1955, a powerful style; the projection of a self-sufficient personal vision which seeks to reveal itself spontaneously in every work. "In art, this quest for eternal verity, necessarily at odds with immediacy, has, during the last three-quarters of a century, become more and more urgent. To loosen the bonds which hold us, by habit as much as by sen-

DELAHAUT Jo (b. Liège, Belgium, 1911). Studied at the Académie des Beaux-Arts, Liège. Doctorate in Archaeology and Art History (1939). Made his debut in 1940 under the Fauve banner. First abstract paintings in 1944. Exhibited every year at the Salon des Réalités Nouvelles. Organised, 1952, the Belgian 'Art Abstrait' group, of which the first members were Bury, Collignon, Plomteux, Saverys, Burssens, Carrey, Milo. After submitting to the influences of Pignon and Gischia, Delahaut turned toward mathematical abstraction and became friendly with Herbin. One-man show at the Galerie Arnaud, Paris, 1952. Taught design at the Athénée of Shaerbeek. In 1956, exhibited in Brussels 'plastic mobiles' and 'spatial reliefs'. Lives in Brussels. His painting is restrained and geometric, in swathes of undiluted colours. — *Bibl.* Séaux: *Delahaut*, De Sikkel (Antwerp 1955).

DELAUNAY Robert (b. Paris, 1885; d. Montpellier, 1941). At 17, worked in a scene-designer's in Belleville. Began painting in Brittany during holidays, under the influence of the Pont-Aven School. Devoted himself entirely to painting in 1905; neo-impressionism. Friendly with Metzinger, then with Douanier Rousseau.

156

Romantic painting (*Église de Laon, Intérieur de Saint-Séverin*) in 1909. In 1910, began the lyrical series of the *Tour Eiffel*, the *Villes*, the *Fenêtres*. Included in the "Blaue Reiter" exhibition in Munich, 1912. Friendship with Apollinaire and Albert Gleizes. Travelled to Berlin with Apollinaire in 1913, when his one-man show was being held at the Der Sturm Gallery. Met de Macke in Bonn. Was travelling in Spain in 1914, when the war broke out. Stayed for some time in Lisbon. Met Diaghilev for whom he designed the decors of the ballet *Cleopatra*. Returned to Paris 1921. Retrospective exhibition at the Galerie Paul Guillaume, 1922. His house became a favourite meeting-ground for the poets of the avant-garde. In 1930, incited by Gleizes, he returned to

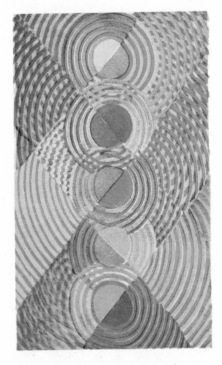

R. DELAUNAY. RHYTHM. 1936.

abstract themes abandoned in 1912 and began the series of the *Rythmes sans Fin* and paintings in relief. Met Kandinsky in 1938. Included in the "Réalités Nouvelles" exhibition at the Galerie Charpentier, Paris, 1939. During the 1940 invasion of France, he took refuge in Auvergne, then in Mougins, near Cannes. Died in Montpellier.

To Delaunay fell the task of maintaining the continuity of the French contribution to pure abstraction, never breaking with the lyrical tradition and rationality representative of the Paris School. In estimating the evolution of painting since 1911, his merit cannot be overstressed. Without departing radically from recent tradition, he was instinctively more influenced by his senses than by his reason, although finally always holding the senses within limits: he thus revealed a highly individual approach, never tired of trying new resonances of colours, of experimenting with new rhythms, which always, as though spontaneously, blended into an absolute harmony. The man himself was disarmingly frank, and if he sometimes dreamt of the impossible with excessive fervour, he can be forgiven for his art; one can nowhere find the slightest hint of exasperated revolt, of a too brutal solution of continuity. Delaunay's art is exalting, and yet not boundlessly so. He is the most eminent French representative in the emerging movement of abstract art. This is why he should be ranked with the great pioneers of abstract art, Mondrian, Kandinsky, Malevitch; neither beneath them nor apart from them in reputation. The work of Delaunay from 1912 to 1913 is as rich and pregnant as theirs. Important retrospective exhibition of Delaunay's work in Paris at the Musée d'Art Moderne in 1957. — *Bibl.* Jean Cassou: préface pour l'exposition à la Galerie Carré (Paris 1946); Seuphor: *L'Art Abstrait, ses Origines, ses Premiers Maîtres* (Paris 1949); Gille de la Tourette: *Robert Delaunay* (Paris 1950); "Art d'Aujourd'hui" (Paris, October 1951; studies by Degand and Seuphor; March 1950: article on *Orphisme,* by Seuphor);

157

SONIA DELAUNAY. COMPOSITION. 1955.

designing and decoration. For a number of years, she held a very lively salon, Boulevard Malesherbes, in which she tried to renew the trends of fashion, or better to give fashion a new spark by challenging it with the plastic arts. She published printed materials, which she exhibited in a famous stand at the Arts Décoratifs exhibition in Paris. Took part in the 'Réalités Nouvelles' exhibition, Ga-

A Dictionary of Modern Painting (Methuen, London 1956); George L. K. Morris: *Dialogues with Delaunay*. Art News (New York, January 1955). Catalogue of the Musée d'Art Moderne exhibition; Degand: *Robert Delaunay*, "Aujourd'hui", nº 12, Paris 1957; *Art Abstrait, les premières générations*, Musée de St. Étienne, 1957.

DELAUNAY Sonia Terk (b. Ukraine, 1885). Studied in St. Petersburg, then in Germany. Travels to Paris and Finland in 1905. Settled permanently in Paris the following years. First married to the German critic Wilhelm Uhde, in whose gallery she exhibited in 1907. Then married Robert Delaunay in 1910. In 1913, she illuminated Cendrars's *La Prose du Transsibérien* and painted large abstract canvases (Simultaneous Rhythms), which represent a serious contribution to the evolution of abstract art. Her stimulating presence played an important role in the development of her husband's art. Lived in Spain and Portugal, 1914-1919. Back in Paris in 1920, she devoted herself mainly to fashion-

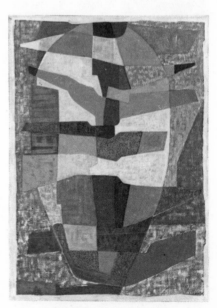

DEYROLLE. SULTANAH. 1955.
Private Collection, Brussels.

158

lerie Charpentier, 1939, and helped to organize the 'Art Concret' exhibition, Galerie Drouin, 1945. Since 1946, exhibited at the Salon des Réalités Nouvelles. Took part in exhibitions in London, Vienna, Belgium and South America, as well as in *Premiers maîtres de l'Art abstrait,* Galerie Maeght, Paris 1949. These last years, Sonia Delaunay has resumed her painting with brilliant results. Her art, which at the beginning, inclined more towards the Fauves and Gauguin, than Cézanne and Cubism, has retained its warmth and an exuberant lyricism befitting the "orphic" powers of the Delaunays. One-man show in Paris, Galerie Bing, 1954, in New York, Rose Fried Gallery, and Liège (A.P.I.A.W.) in 1955. Took part with her husband in the exhibition *Art Abstrait, les premières générations,* Musée de St. Étienne, 1957. Lives in Paris. — *Bibl.* Seuphor: *L'Art Abstrait, ses Origines, ses Premiers Maîtres* (Paris 1949); *Témoignages pour l'Art abstrait* (Paris 1952); *A Dictionary of Modern Painting* (Methuen, London 1956).

DEWASNE. BADIA. 1954.

DEWASNE Jean (b. Hellemmes-Lille, 1921). Began to paint at the age of 12, whenever he could find time free from school and music lessons. After matriculation, studied architecture for two years, but only to prepare himself better for painting. He sketched every morning for five years, from still and life models. Performed many kinds of manual labour, often more out of curiosity than necessity. Then, in turn, professor of perspective, assistant in films, journalist. Abstract painting since 1943. A member of the Galerie Denise René group, from its formation (1945) up to 1956. Directed the Academy of Abstract Art with Pillet (1950-2). One-man show at the Galerie Denise René. Was included in the great abstract Salons in Paris and in numerous group-shows in the main European countries. Lives in Paris. Dewasne excels in great mural compositions. In his easel works, the striking colours in vehement opposition seem sometimes to leap out from the frame, despite the solid structure of the composition. — *Bibl.* Pierre Descargues: *J. Dewasne* (Paris 1952); *Témoignages pour l'Art abstrait* (Paris 1952); Léon Degand: *Dewasne,* 'Art d'Aujourd'hui' (Paris, December 1953).

DEYROLLE Jean (b. Nogent.s.Marne, 1911). Childhood in Brittany. Studied advertising in Paris, then began painting, without instruction. Travelled in Morocco and in Spain from 1932 to 1937. Returned to Brittany in 1938. Influenced by Sérusier and then by Braque. Came to Paris in 1942. Increasingly influenced by the cubists until he met Domela who launched him into abstraction. Jeanne Bucher bought his first non-representational canvases. In 1948, met Wilhelm Uhde who encouraged his work. A number of stays in Denmark (where he drew two albums of lithographs) and in Germany. Exhibited regularly in the Galerie Denise René from 1946 on. Took part in a number of group-shows and in the abstract Salons of Paris. Lives in Paris. Deyrolle composes free structures in shaded tones, sometimes discreet and sometimes subtle. His work seems dominated by a patient and wise analysis of values. "To touch many levels of meaning, square, bird, warmth, friendship, through multiplicity and formal combinations, is that what I am looking for? How can I know? When vision becomes so multiple, one naturally ceases to attach importance to the so-called object. Besides it is only when the painting is completed that one can discuss colours, forms, dynamism. But during the work, reason is not called upon constantly, everything seems intuitive. One should not be overmuch concerned about theory: most painters play fast and loose with theirs. This is no irony, even less a criticism. For me, this cheating is a phenomenon of permanent inventiveness; it is, in the end, this very cheating which nurtures the evolution of the artist and keeps the art from sclerosis". (From conversations of Deyrolle, noted by Julien Alvard). — Bibl. *Témoignages pour l'Art abstrait* (Paris 1952).

DIAS Cicero (b. in Pernambuco, Brazil, 1908). School of Architecture in Rio de Janeiro. First exhibition in Brazil in 1928. Taught drawing and painting in Pernambuco. 1937, moved permanently to Paris. 1938, shows at the galleries Jeanne Castel and Caputo. 1943, exhibitions in Lisbon and London. Painted his first abs-

DIAS. COMPOSITION. 1954.

tract compositions the same year. Included in exhibitions at Denise René's and the Galerie Drouin. Biennale of Venice in 1950 and 1952. An attaché at the Brazilian Embassy in Paris. — *Bibl.* 'Art d'Aujourd'hui' (Paris, Sept. 1954).

DIEBENKORN Richard (b. Portland, U.S., 1922). Studied at Stanford and the University of California (1940-3), then at the California School of Fine Arts (1946). Many one-man shows in California since 1948. Included in the *Younger American Painters* exhibition at the Solomon R. Guggenheim Museum in New York, 1954, and in the *Jeunes Peintres* exhibition at the Museum of Modern Art, Paris, 1955. Was a professor at the University of Illinois. Lives in Berkeley, California. Diebenkorn's work is a supple plastic universe which can be placed in the tradition of Motherwell and Hans Hofman. He seems one of the most assured young talents in American painting.

DILLER Burgoyne (b. New York, 1906). Began to paint at the age of fourteen and studied for many years in various academies. Held various practical jobs related to the fine arts; was a professor of industrial design. After being successively interested in expressionism and impressionism, he turned to Cézanne and cubism, and then, logically launched into neo-plasticism. He has been a disciple of Mondrian (1934) longer than anyone in the United States. He was intimate with Harry Holtzmann, who travelled to Paris for the sole purpose of meeting Mondrian. One-man shows at the Rose Fried Gallery in New York in 1946, 1949, 1951. Exhibited with the "American Abstract Artists". Included in the "Abstract Painting and Sculpture in America" show at the Museum of Modern Art, New York, 1951. Lives in New York. Diller is the only American painter to apply in a thorough way the principles of pure neo-plasticism: horizontal-vertical composition and primary colours. Although the influence of Mondrian is obvious, the painting does not lack a distinctive character, springing from the personal vision of the painter. "Diller is one of the most imaginative of the neo-plastic painters. It is impossible te realize the richness and possibilities of this form of art unless one has seen the hundreds of studies which Diller has made in pencil, crayon, pastel and watercolor on white paper." (Kath. S. Dreier). — Bibl. *Collection of the Société Anonyme* (New Haven 1950); Ritchie: *Abstract Painting and Sculpture in America* (New York 1951); *Diller paints a picture*, Art News, New York, October 1952.

DMITRIENKO Pierre (b. Paris 1925). Studied architecture at the same time as painting. Has devoted himself completely to painting since 1947. Took part in various exhibitions in a number of important galleries in Paris, and in exhibitions of French Art in Madrid, Edinburgh, as well as at the Salon de Mai. One-man show at the Galerie Lucien Durant, Paris 1953 and 1954. Lives in Paris.

DOESBURG Theo van (b. Utrecht, Holland, 1883; d. Davos 1931). His real name was Küpper. He wrote also under the pen-names of I. K. Bonset and Aldo Camini. Studied in Holland. First thought of becoming an actor. First paintings in 1899. First exhibition in The Hague, 1908. Published articles and a collection of poems (1913). Met Mondrian in 1915 and planned the review *De Stijl* with him. The first issue of it appeared in October 1917. Collaborated with the Dutch

DMITRIENKO. DIVES-SUR-MER. 1955. *Galerie L. Durand. Paris.*

161

architects Oud and Wils from 1916 on; painted his first abstract canvases the same year. Went on a propaganda tour around Europe in 1920-1921, to publicize the ideas of *De Stijl*. Introduced dadaism in Holland in 1922 and published the *Mecano* review. Friendship with Kurt Schwitters who accompanied him on a 'dadaist tour' of Holland. 1923, invited by Léonce Rosenberg to organize a *De Stijl* group-exhibition at the Galerie de l'Effort Moderne, Paris. Collaborated with the Dutch architect van Eesteren. Abandoned neo-plasticism in 1925 and published the 'Elementarist' manifesto (*De Stijl* no. 75-76). Decorated the 'Aubette' *café-dansant* in Strasbourg in collaboration with Arp and Sophie Taeuber (completed in 1928). In Paris 1929-1930. Published *Art Concret* with Hélion, Carlsund and Tutundjian.

Principal works of Theo van Doesburg: *De Nieuwe beweging in de schilderkunst* (Delft 1917); *Drie voordrachten over de nieuwe beeldende kunst* (Amsterdam 1919); *Grundbegriffe der neuen gestaltenden Kunst* (Munich 1924); *Classique, baroque, moderne* (Paris 1921); *Wat is dada?* (The Hague 1923); *L'Architecture Vivante* (Paris 1925). — Bibl. *Prisma der kunsten*, Zeist (Holland, May 1936); Barr: *Cubism and abstract art* (New York 1936); *Art of this Century* (New York 1942); *Painting toward Architecture* (New York 1948); Seuphor: *L'Art abstrait, ses Origines, ses Premiers Maîtres* (Paris 1949); *Collection of the Société Anonyme* (New Haven 1950); Raynal: *De Picasso au Surréalisme* (Geneva and Paris, 1950); Catalogue of the *De Stijl* exhibition (Amsterdam 1951); *The dada painters and poets* (New York 1952); 'Art d'Aujourd'hui' (Paris, Dec. 1953); *A Dictionary of Modern Painting* (Methuen, London 1956).

DOMELA Cesar (b. Amsterdam, 1900). Began to paint at the age of 19. Lived in Switzerland from 1922 to 1923. Abstract paintings included in the 'Novembergruppe' exhibition in Berlin, 1923. Friendship with Mondrian, Paris, 1924; he joined the *De Stijl* movement. Exhibition in The Hague in 1924. In Berlin from 1927 to 1933. Then settled in Paris. One-man show at the Galerie Pierre in 1934. Co-publisher of the review *Plastique* with Arp and Sophie Taeuber in 1937.

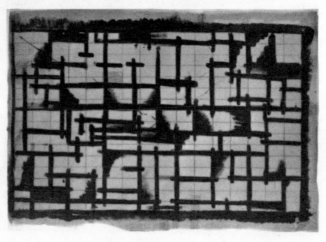

VAN DOESBURG. DESIGN. 1916.

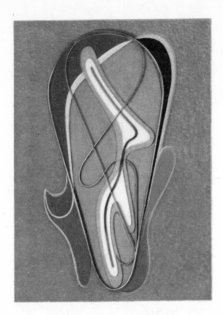

DOMELA. COMPOSITION. 1955.

Included in the "Réalités Nouvelles" exhibition, Galerie Charpentier, 1939. Founded the 'Centre de Recherche' group in 1946. One-man show at Denise René's, Paris 1947, and the Galerie Colette Allendy in 1949 and 1951. Took part in the great abstract Salons in Paris as well as in exhibitions in London, Amsterdam, Stockholm, etc. Travel to Brazil and an exhibition there in 1954. Since 1928, Domela constructs "tableaux-objets", paintings which are also things, composed of various materials. He lives in Paris. "I feel certain that meditation, before and after work, will play an immense part with the majority of abstract artists. Before beginning their painting, they already have, as a result of this meditation, a more or less precise foresight of their composition. The fact that a painting should be an organization and not an arrangement, obliges them to know their theme thoroughly in order to attain full resonance. In abstract art, com-

pletely liberated from all narration, there remains only one link with the other arts: rhythm. Since the sanskrit root for *charm* is the same as *to pray* and *to paint*, couldn't one conclude, that a painting, especially an abstraction, is the crystallization of a painted prayer ? Couldn't a painting be the basis for a meditation, a sort of yantra for the western soul ?" (Domela). — Bibl. *Art of this Century* (New York 1942); *Französische Abstrakte Malerei* (Stuttgart 1948); *Témoignages pour l'Art Abstrait* (Paris 1952); *Domela*: Six reproductions in colour, préface by Kandinsky (Paris, no date); Brion, Sibert: *Domela*, Museo de arte moderna (Rio de Janeiro 1954).

DONATI Enrico (b. Milan, 1909). In Paris from 1934 to 1940, and then in the U.S. Friendly with Breton and the Surrealist group. Numerous one-man shows in New York, Paris, Milan, Venice, Rome. Took part in the Venice and Sao Paolo Biennales. Lives in New York. For some time past, Donati's art has developed toward the analysis of the material *per se,* which causes him to lose the taste for complexity and leads him to simple values which are impressive in their austere nudity. — Bibl. *Donati,* Ed. el Milione (Milan 1954); *Donati* (Cavallino, Venice 1954).

DORAZIO Piero (b. Rome, 1927). Studies in Rome and Paris. Since 1947, one of the exponents of abstract art in Rome. Travelled to the U.S. in 1954; one-man show at the Rose Fried Gallery. Other individual exhibitions : Galleria Apollinaire, Milan 1955, Galleria del Cavallino, Venice 1956, Galleria La Tartaruga, Rome 1957. Has taken part in many group exhibitions, in Italy, Switzerland, France and the Scandinavian countries. Occasional contributor to the leading Italian art reviews. Lives in Rome, where he published in 1954 *la Fan-*

163

tasia dell'arte nella vita moderna (Ed. Polverani e Quinti).

DORFLES Gillo (b. Trieste, 1910). Co-founder with Munari and Monnet of the Milanese 'Arte Concreta' group. Included in the first exhibition of Italian abstract art, in Milan, 1945. One-man shows since 1949. Included in many group-shows. Dorfles is also an art critic. He has published a number of articles on abstract art in specialized reviews in France and in Italy. Lives in Milan.

DOUCET Jacques (b. Boulogne.s.Seine 1924). Friendly with Max Jacob who encouraged him to paint. Influenced by Picasso's 'Blue Period'. After the Liberation, he discovered colour through the work of Matisse; stark plasticism through the work of Miro and Klee. Various one-man shows at the Galerie Colette Allendy, Paris, since 1948. Takes part in the "Les Mains Éblouies" exhibition, Galerie Maeght, 1949. Travels, accompanied by exhibitions, in Central Europe, Italy and Switzerland. One-man show at the Galerie Ariel, Paris, 1954. Lives in Paris.

DOUCHEZ Jacques (b. Mâcon, 1921). Academic mission in Brazil. Studied abstract painting under Flexor, in Sao Paolo, from 1948 on. Took part in the Abstraction Workshop in Brazil. Included in the Sao Paolo Biennales. One-man show at the Museum of Modern Art of Sao Paolo in 1955. Lives in Sao Paolo.

DOVA Gianni (b. Rome, 1925). Studied at the Brera Academy in Milan. One-man shows in Milan, Venice, Rome. Included in a number of group-shows in Paris, more especially at the Galeries Craven and Rive Droite (1954). Lives in Rome.

DOVE Arthur G. (b. Canandaigua, U.S.A., 1880; d. Huntington, U.S.A., 1946). Began to study art at the age of nine. Worked as a book-illustrator, then, about 1908, travelled in France and in Italy. First exhibition at the 'Stieglitz Gallery 291' in 1910. As early as 1912, starting from naturalistic subjects, he developed towards abstraction. — Bibl. *Collection of the Société Anonyme* (New Haven 1950); Ritchie: *Abstract painting and sculpture in America* (New York 1951).

DOWNING Joseph Dudley (b. Kentucky, 1925). Studied at the Art Institute of Chicago. After a one-

DOUCET. PAINTING. 1955.
Prince J. Troubetzkoy Collection, Paris.

164

man show in Chicago, he came to Paris where he took part in a number of group-shows, his painting developing all the while towards a completely abstract art, finally attained in a one-man show at the Studio Fachetti, in 1955. "The artist expresses himself like a medium communicating to us the secrets revealed to him. Sometimes we are summoned to bright feasts, sometimes we hear gentle lays." (Herta Wescher).

DOWNING. KAYFER QUEENISH. 1955.

DREIER Katherine S. (b. New York, 1877; d. Milford, Conn., 1952). Studied art privately and at the Art Students League. Came to Paris in 1907. Periods in London, Munich and Holland. Returned to New York in 1913. Took part in the "Armory Show". Founded, in 1920, with the direct collaboration of Marcel Duchamp and Man Ray, the Société Anonyme. In China, 1921-1922. Met Mondrian in Paris, 1925. Bought one of his paintings for the Société Anonyme, the first Mondrian in America. A member of "Abstraction-Création". Marcel Duchamp's famous *Nude descending the staircase*, which was the sensation of the 'Armory Show' in New York, 1913, opened her eyes to the merits of creative abstraction. But her work as a painter is much less important than her influence as an *animateur*. The travelling exhibitions across the States, containing the works of Malevitch, Mondrian, Brancusi, Kandinsky, Schwitters, and many others, which she organized to publicize the new art, cleared the way for the full development of abstract art in the United States. Her *Portrait de Marcel Duchamp* (1918) is at the Museum of Modern Art, New York. — Bibl. *Katherine S. Dreier,* Academy of Allied Arts (New York 1933); *Collection of the Société Anonyme* (New Haven 1950).

DUFOUR Bernard (b. Paris, 1922). Intended to be a Forestry Inspector, but was sent on compulsory duty

in German factories in 1943. It was there he discovered modern painting through reproductions. Came back to France in 1945. Agricultural Engineer in 1946. At the same time, he frequented the studios of Montparnasse and the École des Beaux-Arts. Exhibited in various salons from 1949 on, at the Galerie Jeanne Bucher and at the Galerie Pierre. Lives in Paris. "I notice in my study of nature, that completely different landscapes often provoke almost identical feelings, and I wonder then what can be this special, secret language, of which I perceive fragments almost accidentally. Seeing nature in that light, I sense that there must exist a series of constants which I perceive through their reflections in my soul, reflections constantly identical, in so far as a sensitive instrument like the soul can respond in the same way under all circumstances. It seems possible therefore, that from natural events, from the subjective and the objective, one may one day deduce something like an intimate and fundamental law." (Dufour).

DUMITRESCO. PAINTING. 1954.
Pierre Wurth Collection, Paris.

DUMITRESCO Natalia (b. Bucharest, Rumania, 1915). Matriculated in 1934. Degree in Fine Arts in 1939. Included in various group-shows and official Salons in Bucharest. Came to Paris in 1947. Travelled in Holland and Italy in 1948, in Spain in 1953. Took part in many Paris exhibitions, as well as in the Salon des Réalités Nouvelles. After a number of years working in black and white, she prudently tackled the problem of colours, showing undoubted originality and a great freshness of colours in her recent compositions. Married to the painter Istrati. Lives in Paris.

DUSTIR Wilma (b. Baku, Russia, 1914). Abstract painting since 1948. Has taken part in group-shows in Buenos Aires where she lives.

166

E

EGGELING Wiking (b. Lund, Sweden, 1880; d. Berlin, 1925). From 1900 to 1908, travelled and studied in Switzerland and in Italy. Paris in 1911. Met Modigliani and Arp. Back in Switzerland again in 1915, where he met Tristan Tzara. Composed abstract drawings in 1917, becoming a member of the dada movement in Zurich. Became friendly with Hans Richter in 1918; accompanied him to Germany, in Klein-Koelzig. Created in Berlin, 1919, the famous *rouleau* he called *Messe Horizontale-Verticale* and, in 1920, the *Symphonie Diagonale* rouleau, which he filmed the following year. — *Bibl.* 'Plastique no 2' (Paris 1937); Seuphor: *L'Art abstrait, ses Origines, ses Premiers Maîtres* (Paris 1949); *Wiking Eggeling*, National-museum (Stockholm 1950); *The Dada Painters and Poets* (New York 1951).

EGUCHI Sogen (b. Japan, 1919). Exhibited at the Japanese Institute of Calligraphy as an Art-form (1949-1951). A member of the Bokusin-Kai School since 1952. Contributed to the Japanese reviews of abstract calligraphy *Bokubi* and *Bokuzin*. Included in exhibitions in Osaka and in Tokyo, as well as in the two exhibitions of Japanese abstract calligraphy at the Museum of Modern Art, New York (1954); at the Galerie Colette Allendy, Paris, 1955; at the Stedelijk Museum in Amsterdam; at the Kunsthalle in Basel; and at the Musée Cernuschi in Paris (1956). Lives in Japan. — *Bibl.* Seuphor: *La Calligraphie Japo-*

naise, 'Art d'Aujourd'hui' (Paris, Dec. 1954); Catalogue de l'exposition au Musée Cernuschi (Paris 1956).

EICHMANN Heinrich (b. Fluhi, Switzerland, 1915). Included in group-shows in Zurich and Paris since 1944. A member of the 'Die Allianz' Association. Lives in Zurich.

ELLIOTT Ronnie (b. New York, 1916). First influenced by the Impressionists and Cézanne. Attracted by surrealism in 1937. Then veered towards

EGUCHI. BLACK AND WHITE. 1954.

167

the art of Kandinsky and Mondrian. Since 1945, her work is completely abstract. A number of exhibitions in America since 1933. Took part in the Salon des Réalités Nouvelles, Paris, from 1948 on. One-man shows at the Galerie Creuze, Paris, 1948, and Galerie Colette Allendy in 1952. Lives in New York. In her most recent work, Ronnie Elliott moves towards an abstract impressionism with a textural quality akin to Monet.

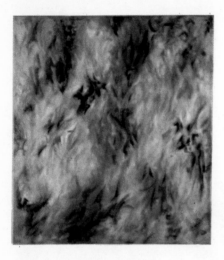

ELLIOTT. PAINTING. 1953.

ÉNARD André (b. Le Mans, Sarthe, 1926). Came to Paris in 1944. École des Beaux-Arts. Worked in the studios of Lhote and Léger. Influenced by Herbin and neo-plasticism in 1950. One-man show at the Galerie Arnaud, Paris, 1952. Lives in Paris.

ENGEL-PAK (b. Spa, Belgium, 1885). Also known under the name of Engel-Rozier. A chequered career as a young man. First exhibition at the Galerie Vignol, Paris, 1926. In 1927, after a long connection with Torrès-Garcia, he

came by stages to abstraction. Lengthy stay near Toulon. Included in an abstract group-show in Paris after the Liberation and exhibited many times at the Salon des Réalités Nouvelles. Has illustrated with coloured lithographs Paul Éluard's *Objet des mots et des images* (Paris 1947). One-man show at Colette Allendy's in 1952. Lives in Southern France. Stains of bright colours almost life-like in their vividness, on a monochromatic background.

ERASMUS Nel (b. Bethal, Transvaal, 1928). Dutch ancestry. Studied Fine Arts at the Witwatersrand University in Johannesburg. Worked as a label- and letter-designer in a factory and then as a teacher. Travelled to London in 1953. In Paris (1953-1955), attended classes at the École des Beaux-Arts and the Académie Ranson. Included in group-shows and in the Salon des Réalités Nouvelles. Lives in Transvaal.

ERNST Jimmy (born Cologne, 1920). Son of Max Ernst. Studied at the Lindenthal Real Gymnasium, Cologne, and the School of Applied Arts in Altona. Came to New York, 1938. Has taught in Brooklyn College since 1951. Numerous one-man shows in the United States. Included in the 'Abstract Painting and Sculpture in America' exhibition at the Museum of Modern Art, New York, 1951, and in 'Younger American Painters', at the Solomon R. Guggenheim Museum, New York 1954. Lives in Rowayton (Connecticut). Compositions in very clear plastic language: lines predominate; frank lines and forms without ambiguity.

ERZINGER Lili (b. Zurich, 1908). Studied in Switzerland and in Paris. Worked under Lhote, Bissière, Severini, Léger, Arp (1936-1937). Taught painting for some time in the United States. Lives in Neuchâtel (Switzerland).

ESTÈVE Maurice (b. Culan, Cher, 1904). Studied at various Paris Academies. Spent a year in Spain and directed a workshop of design for a textile factory in Barcelona. Then worked until 1927 at the Académie Colarossi, Paris, and since 1928 has exhibited in the main Paris Salons. One-man shows: Galerie Yvangot (1930); Galerie Carré (1948); Galerie Galanis (1955 and 1956). Took part in a number of group-shows in Prague, Stockholm, Copenhagen, Amsterdam, etc. Collaborated with Robert Delaunay in the decoration of the Railway and Aviation Pavilions at the Exposition Universelle, Paris 1937. Lives and works in isolation in his Montmartre studio. Likes to brave colours at their most naked and exciting, showing a particular fondness for red which he can make vibrate with masculine ecstasy. "Esteve is one of those painters in whom one can best see, reduced to scale, the harmonious organization of aspects, emotions, suggestions, thoughts, even illusions, excited by contact with a theme which is at first vague, and which yet gradually attracts and centres the artist's sensations, both vivid and quiescent." (Pierre Courthion, *Peintres d'Aujourd'hui,* Geneva 1952).

EVANS Merlyn (b. 1910). Born of Welsh parentage in Cardiff. Studied at Glasgow School of Art, and at the Royal College of Art, London. In 1936 met Ozenfant, Mondrian, Kandinsky, Hé-

ESTÈVE. WATER-COLOUR. 1955.
Galerie S. Heller, Paris.

lion, Hayter and other leaders of abstract art, and began to study engraving. In 1939 went to Durban (South Africa) where he held his first exhibition. His first London exhibition was held in 1949; a large retrospective exhibition was held at Whitechapel in 1956.

F

FALCHI Ettore (b. Rome, 1913). Began as a music-hall performer. At one time was world-famous as a variety-show athlete. Began to paint in 1939. Studied at non-institutional Academies. Studied Egyptian art and the Italian primitives. First abstract painting in 1946. Exhibited in New York (1947), Paris (1948), Copenhagen (1950), Lausanne (1954); took part in the Salon des Réalités Nouvelles and in displays of the 'Espace' group. Great geometrical compositions with reliefs. Lives in Paris.

FASSBENDER Josef (b. Cologne, 1903). Studied at the Fine Arts School in Cologne. His works are in a number of museums and private collections. Took part in the German non-representational exhibition at the Cercle Volney, Paris, 1955. Lives in Cologne.

FATHWINTER (F. A. Th. Winter) (b. Mainz-Castel, Germany, 1906). At first a factory-hand. Self-educated. From 1926 to 1928, travelled through Belgium, Holland and Poland. First exhibition in 1931. From 1933 on, being under a Nazi ban, worked in seclusion in Krefeld. 1945, many exhibitions, particularly in Munich, Cologne, Hanover and Wuppertal. Stayed a few months in Paris on a French government grant. Included in the Salon des Réalités Nouvelles in 1954 and 1955. Lives in Dusseldorf.

FAUTRIER Jean (born Paris, 1898 of parents from Béarn). Educated in London. Recalled to France by the 1914 war. Campaigned for three years; was both wounded and gassed. Exhibited ten canvases in a Paris garage in 1921. For a few years, starting from 1925, Paul Guillaume encouraged him. At

FATHWINTER. ACCENT IN GREY. 1954.

170

the time, Fautrier kept a hotel in the Alps and gave skiing lessons. After the Second World War, exhibited at the Galerie Drouin, Place Vendôme, Paris. Fautrier paints in thick masses, using a very limited palette, grey for preference. His is pure painting, if ever there was; the titles change nothing: *fruits, nus, otages, objets* are all interchangeable. He had one-man shows at the Galerie Rive

FEITO. COMPOSITION. 1954. *John Koenig Collection, Paris.*

Droite, Paris, in 1955 and 1956. Lives in Châtenay-Malabry, near Paris. — *Bibl.* Paulhan: *Les objets de Fautrier,* Galerie Rive Droite (Paris 1955); Tapié: *Fautrier paints a picture,* 'Art News' (New York, Dec. 1955); Ponge: *Paroles à propos des nus de Fautrier,* Galerie Rive Droite (Paris 1956).

FEITO (b. Madrid, 1929). San Fernando School of Fine Arts in Madrid. After a number of group-shows, one-man shows at the Gallery Buchholz and the Gallery Fernando Fe (Madrid 1954) followed by a one-man show at the Galerie Arnaud (Paris 1955). Lives in Madrid.

FÉLY-MOUTTET (b. Collobrières, Var, France, 1893; d. Toulon, 1953). Attended the École des Beaux-Arts (Atelier Cormon) and the School of Decorative Arts in Paris. Later became the director of the École des Beaux-Arts in Toulon. Exhibited in numerous Salons, then turned to abstraction and became one

of the mainstays of the Salon des Réalités Nouvelles. Organized an important exhibition of Abstract Art at the Museum of Toulon (1952). A retrospective exhibition of his work was held in the Salon des Réalités Nouvelles, Paris, in 1954.

FERREN John (b. Pendleton, Ore., 1905). Studied in California. Self-educated. Worked first as a sculptor and a craftsman in San Francisco. Began painting in 1930. In Paris (1931-1938) he frequented S. W. Hayter's famous 'Studio 17'. Composed a series of engravings printed on plaster. Exhibitions at the Galerie Pierre and the Galerie de l'Effort Moderne. Returned to America in 1938. A number of exhibitions in the U.S., particularly at the Galerie Pierre Matisse, New York (1936, 1937, 1938); Willard Gallery (1942); Santa Barbara Museum of Art, California (1952). Lives in New York. An experimental painter whose work has passed through many stages before attaining an extreme refinement of colour and form. He writes : "Sworn enemies as they have always been, all artists never-theless tell the same story, the same few rare things, in so far as they can make themselves und-erstood at all." — *Bibl.* Ritchie: *Abstract Painting and Sculpture in America* (New York 1951); 'ArtNews' (New York, Feb. 1954); Leepa: *The Challenge of Modern Art* (New York 1949).

FICHET. PAINTING. 1955. *Galerie Arnaud, Paris.*

FICHET Pierre (b. Paris, 1927). Self-taught in matters of art. First abstract works in 1947, followed by a re-presentational period. Return to abstraction in 1951. One-man shows at the Galerie Arnaud, Paris 1954 and 1955. Took part in the Salon des Réalités Nouvelles and a number of group-displays, especially in Stockholm and in Germany. Lives in Paris.

FIETZ Gerhard (b. Breslau 1910). Studied at the Breslau Academy and the Schlemmer Studio (1930-1932), then in Dusseldorf and Berlin. Drafted in the East German Army. Took part in the Salon des Réalités Nouvelles, Paris, 1948, and the Venice Biennale, 1950. Included in the exhibition of German abstract painters, Cercle Volney, Paris 1955. A member of the German 'Zen' group. Lives in Buch-bei-Illertissen (Wurtemberg).

FINE Perle (b. Boston, 1908). Numerous one-man shows in America. A member of the 'American Abstract Artists' group. Took part a number of times

in the Salon des Réalités Nouvelles, Paris, and in a few important group-shows in the United States. Lives in New York or Provincetown (Mass.) Starting from compositions with geometrical elements, Miss Fine has slowly progressed towards a more supple art, characterized, these last years, by a cloudy monochrome. Perle Fine is also known for her erudite interpretation of Mondrian's *Victory boogie-woogie* in twelve analytical charts. — *Bibl.* Hitchcock: *Painting towards Architecture* (New York 1948).

FINK Don (b. Duluth, Minn., 1923). Studied at the Walker Art Institute, Minneapolis, and at the Art Students League, New York. In Paris 1953-1954; one-man show at the Galerie Craven. After spending some time in the United States, returned to Paris in 1955 and took part in art competitions. A calligraphy of fine black lines coiled, after the manner of Pollock, against a background of monochrome.

FITZSIMMONS James (b. Shanghai, China, 1919). Educated in Switzerland, England, and New York

(Columbia University). At first a commercial photographer in New York (1938-1944). After 1945, he investigated the possibilities of photolithography and discovered a new way of making coloured monotypes out of photographical elements. From 1947 to 1950, exhibited his researches at the San Francisco Museum of Art, the Art Institute in Chicago, and the Pinacotheca in New York. At the same time, he developed a geometrical style of painting and exhibited at the Rose Fried Gallery, New York, 1951. A well-known critic, he has contributed to many American reviews. He is at present director of the magazine "European Art this Month" in Zurich. — Bibl. *Collection of the Société Anonyme* (New Haven, Conn., 1950).

FLEISCHMANN Adolf Richard (b. Esslingen, Germany, 1892). Attended the Academy of Fine Arts, Stuttgart, then worked in advertising. Severely wounded in the war, 1917. During his convalescence in Switzerland, was a castmaker at the University of Zurich Hospital. In 1922, first participation in the 'Neue Secession' exhibition in Munich. 1930-1933, was in Ascona (Tessin); 1933-1936 in Spain; 1936-1938 in Italy. Settled then in France where he took part in a number of exhibitions, especially at the Salon des Réalités Nouvelles. One-man shows at the Galerie Creuze (1948); the Galerie Colette Allendy (1951); the Gallery Lutz und Meyer, Stuttgart (1952). Left for the United States in 1952. One-man show at the Rose Fried Gallery, New York, in 1955. A member of the "American Abstract Artists" group with whom he exhibits regularly. Lives in New York.

Fleischmann has gradually passed from curves to straight lines; from undulating to rectilinear calmness. For a number of years, he has like Mondrian only used horizontal and vertical positions. He brings to the neo-plastic principles infinitely rich scales

of tones and a great suppleness in the interplay of shades. He is one of the few disciples of Mondrian to-day who can infuse neo-plasticism with a personal vision. "Fleischmann is the Juan Gris of our time." (Will Grohmann). — Bibl. *Témoignages pour l'Art Abstrait* (Paris 1952); Dario Suro: *Fleischmann,* El Caribe, 26 de Junio 1955.

DON FINK.
RED AND BLACK COMPOSITION. 1955.

173

FLEXOR Sanson (b. Rumania, 1907). His father was an agricultural officer. Came to Paris 1924. Frequented the École des Beaux-Arts and the Académies Ranson and Grande Chaumière. Became a naturalized French citizen in 1929. Exhibited in a number of Salons and executed decorations in churches. Since 1948, when he left for Brazil, has tended toward abstract art, encouraged by the critic Léon Degand. Founded the Abstraction workshop in Sao Paolo. A number of group-shows in Brazil. Took part in the Venice and Sao Paolo Biennales. One-man shows at the Museum of Modern Art, Sao Paolo (1954) and Rio de Janeiro (1955). Lives in Sao Paolo.

FOLMER Georges (b. Nancy, France, 1899). First abstract work in 1935. Took part every year in the Salon des Réalités Nouvelles with works inclining sometimes towards a relatively simple geometrical style which seems close to neoplasticism. Numerous one-man shows at the Galerie Colette Allendy. Lives in Paris.

FONTENÉ Robert (b. Paris, 1892). Attended the École des Beaux-Arts, Paris, and a number of Academies in Montparnasse, but worked mainly in isolation. One-man show Galerie Heller, Paris 1955. Took part in a number of important Salons, and since its foundation, in the Salon des Réalités Nouvelles, of which he was elected President in 1956. Lives in Paris.

FRANCIS Sam (b. San Mateo, California, 1923). Studied Medicine and Psychology at the University of California. Abstract painting since 1947. Settled in Paris in 1950. Took part in various exhibitions in California and in France. One-man shows in Paris, Galerie Nina Dausset (1952) and Galerie Rive Droite (1955). Lives in

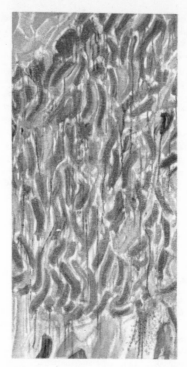

SAM FRANCIS. RED AND YELLOW. 1955.

Paris. "I believe the value of an action (painting) lies in the realm of the unintentional. For the intended necessarily has a surface which betrays us, for it conceals nearly the all. I feel the work must put one in a position of doubt." (Francis). — *Bibl.* Read: *An Art of internal Necessity.* "Quadrum" Nº 1 (Brussels 1956); Duthuit: *Préface à l'exposition Sam Francis,* Galerie Rive droite (Paris 1955).

FREIST Greta (b. Vienna, 1914). Came to Paris 1957; her early paintings tended toward Surrealism. Ventured upon abstract art in 1949. Took part in many Salons, especially the Salon des Réalités Nou-

174

velles where she sent, from 1954 to 1955, large compositions in dulled colours. Lives in Paris.

FRELINGHUYSEN Suzy (b. in New Jersey, U. S. A., 1912). Started realistic painting on her own. Lived later in New York where she became known as an opera-singer; at the same time she kept on painting. Since 1936 her work has been abstract. Exhibited regularly with the 'American Abstract Artists' group. Took part in the Salon des Réalités Nouvelles, Paris, as well as in group-shows in Rome and Amsterdam. Married to the painter George L. K. Morris. Lives in New York and Lenox (Mass.).

FREUNDLICH Otto (b. Stolp, Pomerania, 1878; d. Poland, 1943). At first a shop-apprentice, then an assistant. Later on he studied Art History in Munich and Florence. Began painting and sculpting at the age of 27. Specialized from 1908 in constructive painting with swathes of pure colours. Came to Paris 1909; had a studio at the 'Bateau Lavoir', Place Ravignan, where he became friendly with Picasso. Exhibited with the cubists in Paris, Amsterdam, Cologne. Executed mosaics and stained-glass windows. Composed his first entirely abstract paintings in 1919. A member of the 'Cercle et Carré' group in 1930, then of 'Abstraction-Création'. Hitler classed him among the 'degenerate artists'; he was deported as a Jew to the concentration camp of Lublin - Maidanech (Poland) where he died in 1943. Retrospective exhibition at the Galerie Rive Droite, Paris 1954.

"The artist is a barometer of transformations. He senses them in his acts and his thoughts before they are realized in the world. When he detaches himself gradually from the generally admitted forms and truths, he is executing the edicts of a new reality. All artistic realisations have an inclination: a narrow inclination when it is the safeguard of the artist, a large one when the artist renounces himself and his work opens mental frontiers. A forcing of barriers—social, political, spiritual—begins every great historical period. Ours will for the first time accomplish the union of man with the whole earth and will thus change nostalgia and desire for far-away things into something else, certainly much greater, although everywhere within our reach." (Freundlich in *Cercle et Carré*, nº 2). — *Bibl*. Seuphor: *L'Art Abstrait, ses Origines, ses premiers Maîtres* (Paris 1949).

FREUNDLICH. COMPOSITION. 1930.

175

FROST Terry (b. Leamington, England, 1917). Began painting when a war-prisoner in Germany. Then studied in London and was greatly influenced by Victor Pasmore who had just turned to abstraction. One-man show in London, 1952. Lives in St. Ives (Cornwall).

FRUHTRUNK Günter (b. Munich, 1923). After five years of war-service, studied painting at a non-institutional Academy, and then under Fernand Léger (1952). One-man show at Ueberlingen, Germany, 1948. Lives in Paris since 1954 and takes part in a number of Salons.

G

GABRIELLI Louis (b. Corte, Corsica, 1901). Studied Law in Aix-en-Provence. Settled in Paris 1928. Began modelling clay and painting, 1930. One-man shows of abstract paintings entitled 'informals' at the Galerie Creuze, Paris 1949 and 1955. At the Galerie Colette Allendy, 1952, exhibited monochromatic paintings where movement and shape depend on the thickness of the paint alone. In his recent work, disintegrating forms seem to float in the air or slowly swim through a clouded atmosphere. Lives in Paris.

GALLATIN A. E. (b. Villanova, Pa., 1882; d. New York, 1952). Studied Law in New York. Began painting without instruction. Each year, from 1921 to 1938, he spent a few months in Paris where he became acquainted with the world of painters, sculptors, and collectors. It was during those years he formed his famous avant-garde collection known as the Gallery of Living Art. It contains works of the great cubists as well as of Miro, Arp, and Mondrian. This collection is now at the Museum of Philadelphia. As a painter, Gallatin progressed from the influence of Léger to an abstract art half-way between cubism and constructivism. Numerous one-man shows in New York since 1938. Took part in art-shows in the main cities of America and Europe.

GARBELL Alexandre (b. Riga, Latvia, 1903). Came to Paris in 1923 and worked at the Académie Ranson under Bissière. One-man and group-shows, since 1928, in Paris, Copenhagen, Lausanne. Lives in Paris. Garbell came to abstraction a few years ago, with a rich palette and a great elegance of expression. His untrammelled compositions suggest a painter expert in colours. They keep, even at their most lyrical, a lovely inner balance. — *Bibl.* Courthion: *Peintres d'Aujourd'hui* (Geneva 1952).

176

GAUTHIER Oscar (b. Fours, Nièvre, France, 1921). Studied in Paris, under Othon Friesz at the Académie de la Grande Chaumière. Travelled to the United States, 1946-1947, and to Mexico, from which he brought back expressionistic canvases. Abstract painting since 1948. One-man shows at the Galerie Colette Allendy (1950 and 1951) and Galerie Arnaud (every year since 1952). Took part in a number of group-shows. Lives in Paris.

GEAR William (b. Fife, Scotland, 1915). Studied in Edinburgh, 1932-1937. Travelled through Europe. Worked in Paris, 1947-1950. One-man shows in Paris, New York, Hamburg, Florence, and London. Took part in the Salon des Réalités Nouvelles in 1949 and 1950 as well as in exhibitions of British art on the continent. Lives in Buckinghamshire.

"Art is a living thing; the real artist contributes to the evolutionary process, expanding by his work the scope of human vision and delight. The artist like the research scientist is concerned with the discovery of new truths in nature. I regard my work not as a denial of nature, but rather as an extension of it." (Gear).

GEIGER Rupprecht (b. Munich, 1908). Studied architecture, but was largely self-taught as a painter. Travelled to Greece and Spain. Has exhibited since 1950. Member and founder of the 'Zen' group. Took part in the Salon des Réalités Nouvelles, Paris. One-man shows in 1953, Munich (Gallery Stangl) and Cologne (Gallery Der Spiegel). Took part, 1955, in an exhibition of German abstract painters, Cercle Volney, Paris. Lives in Munich. Compositions in large planes, somewhat sombre, sometimes even black, made more dramatic still by single tracks of red or blue light.

GAUTHIER. THE GRENADIER. 1954.
Private Collection, Paris.

GEORGES Claude (b. Fumay, Ardennes, France, 1929). Worked on a degree in physics. Travelled to Italy, Holland, Sweden. One-man show at the Galerie Drouin, Paris 1955. An anguished sensibility expressing itself in turbulent canvases. Inorganic nature in violent gestation. — Bibl. *Claude Georges*, Galerie Drouin (Paris 1955).

GERMAIN Jacques (b. Paris, 1915). A student of Fernand Léger at the Académie Moderne, 1931. Attended the Bauhaus (Dessau), 1932. Exhibited at the Surindépendants, 1947 and 1948. One-man show at the Galerie des Deux-Iles in

177

1949. Took part in the Salon de Mai in 1951 and 1952, and in a group-show at the Galerie Maeght. One-man show at the Galerie Warren, Paris 1955. Lives in Paris. To judge by his recent work, Germain seems the direct successor of Cézanne in the domain of the abstract. Richly varied greens predominate. With great subtlety, a suggestion of red, yellow, or ochre flicked on this universal green sets everything off.

GILLET. PAINTING. 1954.
Galerie Jeanne Bucher, Paris.

GERRITS Ger (b. Nieuwer-Amstel, Holland, 1893). At first a lithographer and an advertising-designer. Has painted in many styles since 1930. Exhibited in Antwerp, Chicago, Venice, Vienna, Prague, Berlin, Hamburg, Copenhagen, Stockholm, Cincinnati, Monaco, San Francisco, and took part in the Salon des Réalités Nouvelles, Paris, 1949 and 1950. Rectilinear geometry very soberly conceived. Lives in Amsterdam.

GILBERT Stephen (b. Scotland, 1910). The grandson of Alfred Gilbert, the English sculptor who was a friend of Rodin's. Spent his youth in Ireland. Was in Paris 1938-1939; in Ireland 1940-1945. Had a number of exhibitions in Dublin. Short abstract period in 1942, followed by seven years of expressionism. Took part in many exhibitions of the Dutch 'Cobra' group. Went to Denmark, 1949. Left 'Cobra' and started on a second abstract period (1950). Has since taken part regularly in the Salon des Réalités Nouvelles and, in 1952, in the Salon d'Octobre. Lives in Paris.

GILLET Roger Edgar (b. Paris, 1924). Studied at the École Boulle and the School of Decorative Arts. Took part in a number of exhibitions of 'informal' art since 1952. One-man show at the Galerie Craven, Paris 1953. Took part in the Salon de Mai, Paris 1955. Lives in Paris. Lyrical painting contained within a limited chromatic range. A whirlwind projection of ideas with powerful effects from reds, blacks, whites, in an ochre ensemble.

GISCHIA Léon (b. Dax, Landes, France, 1903). Studied Literature, Art History, Archaeology. Devoted himself to painting from 1923 on. Studied under Othon Friesz and Fernand Léger. Made a number of trips to Spain and Italy. Lived in the United States from 1927 to 1930. Stopped painting from 1927 to 1937. Included in exhibitions of contemporary French art circulating through South America, the United States, Sweden, Switzerland. Exhibited mainly at the Galerie de France, Paris. A member of the Salon de Mai committee. The author of *La Sculpture en France depuis Rodin* (in collab. with N. Védrès). Launched into abstraction about 1948, but does not mind returning occasionally to representational art. Swathes of frank colours, side by side, without blending.

GLARNER Fritz (b. Zurich, 1899). Attended the Academy of Naples, 1915-1918. In Rome and Milan, 1918-1923; then came to Paris. Took part in a number of Salons. At first influenced by impressionism, he slowly turned to abstraction. A member of 'Abstraction-Création' in 1933. In Zurich in 1935. Settled in New York, 1936 and became an American citizen. Struck up a friendship with Mondrian, New York, 1943. One-man shows: in New York, Kootz Gallery, 1945; Rose Fried Gallery 1949, 1951; in Paris, at the Galerie Carré, 1952 and 1955. Since Mondrian's death, Garner, who calls his work *relational painting*, has modified pure neo-plasticism by the introduction of the *slanted* line, which is always to be found between two perpendiculars. Thus his basic form is never a rectangle, as in Mondrian, but a trapeze-rectangle. He has composed a number of circular canvases (*tondo*) and handles greys with great virtuosity.

"It was fortunate for the art world that Mondrian came to New York, and that dur-ing the few years that Mondrian lived here he was able to introduce the philosophy underlying his work to both Diller and Glarner. There were others who were fascinated by Mondrian's approach to art, but they never seemed to have absorbed his philosophy, and without the philosophy there is no continuity of thought and work. However, Diller and Glarner have absorbed Mondrian's philosophy without becoming imitators, but have instead retained their own individuality". (Kath. S. Dreier). — Bibl. *Collection de la Société Anonyme* (New Haven 1950); Ritchie: *Abstract Painting and Sculpture in America* (New York 1951); 'Art d'Aujourd'hui' (Paris, juin 1951); *What abstract art means to me* (New York 1951).

GLEIZES Albert (b. Paris, 1881; d. Avignon, 1953). Trained in his father's workshop of industrial design. At first influenced by impressionism. Exhibited in 1911, in the famous Room 41 of the Salon des Indépendants, the room where cubism started. With Jean Metzinger, a theoretician of the Movement. A friend of Robert Delaunay and Jacques Villon. Wrote a number of works where he interprets the History of Art through his own doctrines. His theories had a great influence on young painters from 1930 on; one can indeed say that the impetus for a good deal of the abstract art movement sprang from his books and his numerous lectures. Gleizes's influence brought Robert Delaunay back to abstraction in 1930. He himself painted a number of abstract canvases, though their titles indicate that symbolism is not too far off.

Principal works of Albert Gleizes: *Du Cubisme* in collaboration with Jean Metzinger (Figuière, Paris 1912); *Du Cubisme et des moyens de le comprendre* (La Cible, Paris 1920); *La Peinture et ses lois, ce qui devait sortir du cubisme* (Paris 1924); *La Forme et l'Histoire* (Povolozky, Paris 1932). — Bibl. *Collection of the Société Anonyme* (Yale University 1950);

GLEIZES. COMPOSITION. 1915.
Galerie Henri Benezit, Paris.

179

Raynal: *De Picasso au Surréalisme* (Skira, Paris and Geneva 1950); *A Dictionary of Modern Painting* (Methuen, London 1956); *Art Abstrait, les Premières Générations* (Musée de Saint-Étienne, 1957).

GOEBEL Gottfried (b. Vienna, 1906). Attended the School of Fine Arts, Vienna. Travelled for a time. Settled in Paris, 1936. Was at first influenced by Delaunay's orphic cubism. Turned to abstraction in 1946. Took part in numerous group-shows in France, Austria, Germany, Italy, America, as well as in the Salon des Réalités Nouvelles. First one-man show at the Galerie Colette Allendy, 1951, followed by a number of exhibitions at the Galerie Arnaud. Exhibits at Salon des Réalités Nouvelles and with Austrian abstracts, Galerie Arnaud, 1957. Goebel's painting has changed often and suddenly. His recent abstract manner consists of pure geometrical forms filled in with delicate atmospheric nuances in the impressionistic manner. Lives in Paris. — *Bibl.* Neuwirth: *L'Abstraction* (Paris 1956).

GONTCHAROVA. ELECTRICITY. 1910-1911.

confusions of surrealism; but it gradually became more positive, using the delicacies of colour without sacrificing its original dreaminess of atmosphere. — *Bibl.* Lorsky: *Henri Goetz* (Paris 1952).

GOETZ Henri (b. New York, 1909). Studied at the Mass. Institute of Technology, Harvard, and Grand Central Art School. Came to Paris, 1930. Painted portraits. Married Christine Boumeester, 1935. Abstract painting since 1936. A naturalized French citizen. One-man shows in a number of Paris galleries since 1937 and participation in the main abstract art Salons. Illustrated books, published albums of etchings. Gave weekly lectures on painting over the French radio network, 1945. Professor at the Académie Ranson 1951, at the Académie de la Grande Chaumière, 1955. One-man show, Galerie Ariel, Paris, 1954. Lives in Paris. Henri Goetz has slowly progressed from surrealism to abstraction. His abstract work remained for some time vague and undefined, as though lost in the

GONTCHAROVA Nathalie (b. Toula, Russia, 1881). Studied in Moscow. Began exhibiting in 1900. Travelled to England, Spain, Switzerland, Italy, Greece, etc. As early as 1910 she launched with Larionov into the rayonist venture. Designed many stage-decors and ballet costumes. Settled in Paris with Larionov, 1914. Formed a friendship with Diaghilev. Exhibited her rayonist and other work together with Larionov, at the Galerie Paul Guillaume, 1914 (preface to the exhibition by Guillaume Apollinaire). Practically gave up painting in order to devote herself to the ballet. Retrospective exhibition at the Galerie des Deux-Iles, Paris 1948. Included in 1952, in the 'L'Œuvre du xxᵉ siècle' exhibition at the Museum of Modern

Art, Paris. She returned to painting in 1956 and exhibited about fifty of her works, dated 1907 to 1956, at the Galerie de l'Institut, Paris, the same year. Lives in Paris. — *Bibl.* Barr: *Cubism and Abstract Art* (New York 1936); Seuphor: *L'Art Abstrait, ses Origines, ses Premiers Maîtres* (Paris 1949).

GOODNOUGH Robert (b. Cortland, U.S., 1917). Attended the University of Syracuse. Then studied in New York under Hofmann. Was for a time assistant-professor in the Department of Painting, New York University. Exhibited with the 'American Abstract Artists' group. Included in the 'Aspects de la Peinture Américaine' show, Galerie de France, Paris, 1952. One-man show at the Tibor de Nagy Gallery, New York 1952. Lives in New York. Little touches of bright colour (commas) on a white background.

GORIN Jean (b. Saint-Émilien-Blain, Loire-Inférieure, France, 1899). Studied at the Académie de la Grande Chaumière, then at the Ecole des Beaux-Arts in Nantes. Settled in Nortsur-Erdre (Loire-Inférieure), 1932. Influenced by Cézanne, Van Gogh, Matisse. Gleizes's books on cubism hastened his development. After a flirtation with purism (Ozenfant), he struck out into neo-plasticism as early as 1926. First contacts with Mondrian in 1927. Included in the 'Cercle et Carré' exhibition 1930. Exhibited at the Salon des

Réalités Nouvelles since its foundation. After a lengthy stay in Nice, he settled in Le Perreux, near Paris, in 1955. His long friendship with Mondrian left a strong imprint of neo-plasticism; he must be considered as one of the most typical and gifted of Europeans working in that tradition. He does not hesitate, however, to infringe the severe dogmas of neo-plasticism by using diagonals and circles, particularly in reliefs, works which yet testify to high spiritual nobility. — *Bibl.* Biederman: *Art as the evolution of visual knowledge,* Redwing (Minn. 1948); *Témoignages pour l'art abstrait* (Paris 1952).

GORKY Arshile (b. Armenia, 1904; d. New York, 1948). Studied at the Polytechnical Institute in Tiflis (Georgia). Came to the United States, 1920. Studied engineering at Brown University and painted in his spare time. In New York, 1925. Was expelled from three academies successively. Moved towards abstract art from 1929 on, being influenced in turn by Picasso, Léger, and Miro. Mastered a highly personal style of organic abs-

GORKY. THE PLOUGH AND THE SONG. 1947.

181

traction in 1940. Met André Breton, Calder, Matta, and Max Ernst. A fire in his studio, in 1946, destroyed thirty paintings and a number of drawings. Committed suicide after having been operated upon for cancer and having had a car accident. Important retrospective exhibition at the Whitney Museum, New York, 1950.

"Arshile Gorky's productive artistic life comprised little more than sixteen years, but within that short time he achieved a fulfillment which cannot be without effect upon future American art. Gorky's examination of nature and conquest of space were visually achieved in the fullest terms of modern experience. It is possible that this art, as much as any other individual manifestation, offers us the image of our times in one of those rare moments when art triumphs over the tragedy of living." (Hamilton) — *Bibl.* Breton: *Le Surréalisme et la Peinture* (New York 1945); Janis: *Abstract and Surrealist Art in America* (New York 1944); *Fourteen Americans* (New York 1946); *Collection of the Société Anonyme* (New Haven 1950); Ritchie: *Abstract painting and sculpture in America* (New York 1951); Hess: *Abstract Painting* (New York 1951); *Arshile Gorky Memorial Exhibition* (New York 1951).

GOTTLIEB Adolph (b. New York, 1903). Studied in Europe, 1921-1922. Carried out many decorative works, notably for the Post Office of Yerrington (Nevada) and for the Synagogue of Millburn (New Jersey). One-man shows in New York from 1930 on, especially at the Kootz Gallery. President of the United States Modern Painters and Sculptors Federation (1944-1945). His works are to be found in a number of American museums. Lives in New York. "With his friend Mark Rothko, Gottlieb has searched for the point where Mondrian and Soutine join, and Picasso can be left behind." (Hess). — *Bibl.* Hess: *Abstract Painting* (New York 1951).

GÖTZ Karl Otto (b. Aachen, Germany, 1914). 1931-1932, worked at the School of Decorative Art and became acquainted with the Bauhaus theories. After the war, had numerous exhibitions in Germany. Took part in the 'Art en Allemagne 1930-1949' exhibition in Zurich, 1949. Included in the 'Cobra' exhibition in Amsterdam and Liège. One-man shows: Galerie Creuze, Paris; Dusanne Gallery (Seattle, U.S.A.); Werthmüller Gallery, Basel; Colibry Gallery, Malmoë (Sweden); and 'Nordisk Kunsthandel', Copenhagen. Included in the 'Phases' exhibition, Salle Balzac, Paris, 1955, and in the German abstract painting show at the Cercle Volney, Paris. Lives in Frankfurt-am-Main. After a painting of symbols and themes with variations revealing the marked influence, now of Arp, and again of Willi Baumeister, Götz has progressed towards a more exuberant lyricism. His calligraphic improvisations in monochrome have the suppleness of a whirlwind filmed in slow motion.

GRAESER Camille (b. Geneva, 1892). An architect and interior-decorator. Studied at the School of Applied Arts in Stuttgart and under Adolf Hölzel. A member of the 'Sturm' and 'Deutscher Werkbund' groups. Exhibited since 1919 in various German cities and in Switzerland. A member of the Swiss 'Die Allianz' association. Lives in Zurich. Pure geometrical abstraction. — Bibl. *Almanach neuer Kunst in der Schweiz* (Zurich 1940); *Allianz* (Zurich 1954).

GREENE Balcomb (b. Niagara Falls, New York, 1904). Studied in New York, Paris, and Vienna. Self-taught in matters of art. Exhibited with the 'American Abstract Artists', 1937-1945. Took part in group-shows in Paris and in the great American museums, especially the Museum of Modern Art, New York, 1951.

182

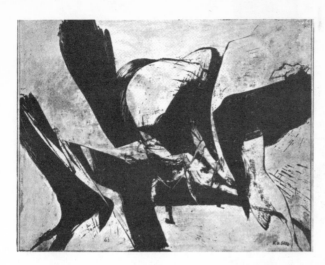

GÖTZ. COMPOSITION. 1955. *Private Collection, Paris.*

After a period of abstract art tending markedly toward the geometric, Greene swung to representational art. His recent works are mainly studies in the decomposition of the object by light: he has therefore, returned to abstraction, though from a very different angle. — *Bibl.* Ritchie: *Abstract Painting and Sculpture in America* (New York 1951); Hess: *Abstract Painting* (New York 1951).

GREIS Otto (b. Frankfurt-am-Main, 1913). Studied engineering. Devoted himself to painting in 1933. Studied painting in Frankfurt, under Bunk and Höhl, until 1938. Met E. W. Nay in 1945. Took part since 1948 in group-shows throughout Germany. Travelled to Switzerland, France, Italy, Belgium. Contributed to the Salon des Indépendants, Paris 1952. Lives in Bad Soden, near Frankfurt.

GUDNASON Zvavar (b. Iceland, 1909). Studied at the Academy of Copenhagen, then in Paris under Fernand Léger. Took part in a number of exhibitions throughout Scandinavia. Included in the Salon des Surindépendants, Paris, 1950. Travelled to Rome, 1955. Lives in Reykjavik (Iceland).

GUERRERO José (b. Granada, Spain, 1914) Studied at the School of Fine Arts of Granada, then Madrid. Studied fresco-painting at the École des Beaux-Arts, Paris (1945-1946). Travels and exhibitions in Rome, Brussels, Paris, London, and Switzerland (1947). In New York, 1950; an American citizen since 1952. Took part in the exhibitions of contemporary Spanish painting, Schaeffer Galleries, New York, 1953. Exhibited with Miro at the Art Club, Chicago. Was included in the 'Younger American Painters' exhibition, Solomon R. Guggenheim Museum, New York, 1954. One-man show at the Betty Parsons Gallery, New York, 1954. Lives in New York or Paris. Strong contrasts of black forms compacted against light backgrounds. Guerrero has also composed murals in bricks and cement. He uses the same symbols, making massive blues and reds vibrate against grey backgrounds.

GUERRINI Mino (b. Rome, 1927). A co-signer of the abstract art manifesto *Forma I,* Rome, 1947. Took part in a number of group-shows in the main cities of Italy. His painting has a geometrical tendency. Guerrini is also a poet and an art-critic. Lives in Rome.

183

GUTH. MYSTERY FOUR. 1955.

GUEVARA Luis (b. Valencia, Venezuela, 1926). Studied at the School of Fine Arts in Caracas. A number of exhibitions in Venezuela until 1949. Then settled in Paris; was included in the Salon des Réalités Nouvelles in 1951 and 1952, as well as in numerous group-shows in various Paris galleries. A member of the 'Madi' group founded by Arden-Quin. Lives in Paris.

GUITET James (b. Nantes, France, 1925). Attended the the École des Beaux-Arts in Nantes. Taught drawing in Angers. Exhibition at the Galerie Arnaud, Paris 1954. Took part in the Salon des Réalités Nouvelles and the Menton Biennale. Lives in Angers. Free-styled compositions subtly shaded, showing an affinity with Geer van Velde's work.

GUSTON Philip (b. Montreal, 1913). Studied at the Art Institute, Los Angeles, 1930. First exhibition at Midtown Galleries, New York, 1945. Began to paint abstract canvases in 1948. Was included in the 'Cinquante ans d'art moderne aux États-Unis' exhibition, Museum of Modern Art, Paris, 1955 and in 'Twelve Americans', Museum of Modern Art, New York, 1956. Lives in New York.

GUTH Hella (b. near Carlsbad, Bohemia, 1912). Studied at the School of Applied Arts in Vienna and the Academy of Prague. Came to London, 1939. Her early painting tended towards surrealism. Exhibited at the Czech Institute, London (1943). Has travelled to Italy a number of times since 1947. Came to Paris, 1951. Gradually abandoned representational art. Exhibited at the Galerie Arnaud and took part in the Salon des Réalités Nouvelles, 1954. Lives in Paris. Acquired British nationality in 1947. Exhibits at the Galerie Colette Allendy, Réalités Nouvelles since 1954.

184

H

HAARDT Georges van (b. Poznan, Poland, 1907). Bachelor in Law. Doctor in Philosophy of the University of Poznan. A magistrate from 1933 to 1939. His surname is Jerzy Brodnicki. So that his painting should not be regarded as a distraction from his official duties, he exhibited under the name of his wife, Egga van Haardt, who, until her death in 1944, was thought to be the author of his paintings. Exhibited in Poland and many other countries. Left Poland for Italy (1939), then Greece and Turkey where he volunteered in the Polish Brigade. Settled then in Palestine and worked as a painter in Jerusalem; the museum there contains paintings of his from various periods (1940-1948). Worked in Paris from 1950 on. One-man show at the Galerie Nina Dausset, 1951, and at the Studio Facchetti in 1952. Travelled and exhibited in Germany, 1954. Took part in the Salon des Réalités Nouvelles. Lives in Paris. Visited and exhibited in London in 1947.

"Painting is not a pretext. It exists in itself and does not represent anything. It presents, proposes. It is not to be understood: it is to be taken, accepted or rejected. But one has to perceive first, in order to reject. The values and the tones of the colours are co-equal. Yellow does not mean jealousy or a note of music affecting or shrill. Painting penetrates noiselessly. It is thus ridiculous to measure the temperature of colours or shades. For colours are neither warm nor cold, but simply different, as colours. The painter is not an optician. This is why it is useless to invoke the laws of complementary colours from a discipline that has nothing to do with painting. Red can be married as effectively with green, brown, grey, or red as with any other colour, according to the free choice and responsibility of the creator. The luminosity of colour in painting remains a myth" (van Haardt). After a period deeply influenced by graphism, a type of writing biting deeply into the mass of the paint, van Haardt has become more of a colorist and his work has gained in lightness, in invention, without ceasing to be a sort of writing.

VAN HAARDT. INK DRAWING. 1953.
M. S. Collection, Paris.

185

HAMOUDI Jamil (b. Baghdad, 1924). Studied at the Art Institute in Baghdad. Was sent to Paris in 1947 to study the art situation on behalf of the government of Iraq. Took part in a number of exhibitions in Baghdad and in Paris. One-man show at the Galerie Colette Allendy, 1952. Lives in Paris.

HARTLEY Marsden (b. Lewiston, 1877; d. Ellsworth, Maine, 1943). Studied in New York. In Paris, 1912-1913; made contacts with the cubists. Took part in the 'Blaue Reiter' show in Munich and in the first German Salon d'Automne, in Berlin, 1913. Included in the 'Armory Show' in New York, the same year. Abstract painting in Germany, 1914-1916. One-man show in Berlin. Returned to the United States in 1916 and took part in various exhibitions. Returned to representational art after 1918. — Bibl. *Collection of the Société Anonyme* (New Haven 1950); Ritchie: *Abstract Painting and Sculpture in America* (New York 1951).

HARTUNG Hans (b. Leipzig, 1904). In Basel 1912-1914, then in Dresden until 1932. Began to paint at an early age, first under the influence of Rembrandt, then Kokoschka, Nolde, and Franz Marc. Abstract drawings and water-colours as early as 1922. Met Kandinsky in 1925. His father forced him to take classes at the Academies of Leipzig, Dresden, and Munich from 1924 to 1928. Representational paintings during that period. At the same time he studied art history and philosophy. Travelled and studied in France, Italy, Holland and Belgium. First exhibition in Dresden, 1931. In Spain, 1933 and 1934. He returned then to Berlin where he got into trouble with the Gestapo. He left Germany in autumn 1935 with the help of the critic Grohman and of Christian Zervos, and settled in Paris. In 1939, volunteered into the French Foreign Legion. In 1943, was in North Africa with General de Gaulle's forces. Wounded in Belfort in November 1944; his right leg had to be amputated. Naturalized French citizen in 1945. During the following years, Hartung took part in a number of exhibitions in Paris, in Germany, and in New York. He has become one of the most famous exponents of French abstract art. His art is both sensitive and wilful, supple and well-defined. Lives in Paris. "The more we enter within ourselves, the clearer and the more imperative the image of inner sedimentations that we can reproduce, and the more universal our expression." (Hartung). — Bibl. *Französische abstrakte Malerei* (Stuttgart 1948); Seuphor: *L'Art Abstrait, ses Origines, ses Premiers Maîtres* (Paris 1949); Madeleine Rousseau: *Hans Hartung* (Stuttgart 1950); 'Art

HARTUNG. PAINTING. 1954.
Private Collection, Paris.

HAYTER. JUNGLE. 1954.

d'Aujourd'hui' (Paris, March 1951); Seuphor: *Hans Hartung,* 'Art Digest' (New York, 1st March 1955); René de Solier: *Hans Hartung,* 'Quadrum' (Brussels 1956).

HAYTER Stanley William (b. London, 1901). Studied at King's College, London. Worked in the chemistry laboratories of the Anglo-Iranian Oil Company, Abadan (1922-1925). Studied art with his father who was a professional painter, and at the Académie Julian, in Paris. Founded the *Atelier 17* which specialized in the technical aspects of engraving, Paris, 1927. A member of the surrealist group, 1934-1940. In New York 1940-1950. Returned to Paris in 1950, re-opened his *Atelier* and resumed his researches. Published *New Ways of Gravure* (New York 1949), a major work on the technique of engraving. One-man shows, particularly at the San Francisco Museum of Art (1940 and 1948), in Paris (Galerie Carré, 1951; Galerie Denise René, 1955) as well as in London, New York,

Chicago, Brussels, etc. Lives in Paris. Painting and engraving are kindred in Hayter's work: if the line is always present in the canvases, planes of colour are often the background of the engraved work. The human figure, sketched traditionally for a long time, has little by little given way to free lines where the spectator can read what he wants. Hayter's line, with its strong inner tension, is not without influence, especially on the work of the Chilean painter Matta.

HEATH Adrian (b. in Burma, 1920). England 1925. Began to paint, 1938. Studied at the Slade School. Volunteered in the R.A.F. in 1940. Was a prisoner of war from 1942 to 1945. Returned to the Slade School, 1945-1947. Then spent one year in Carcassonne, Southern France, where he painted landscapes and portraits. Returned to London in 1948 and rapidly progressed towards abstraction through his interest in the works of Seurat, Villon, Gris, and Mondrian, successively. Exhibited abstract paintings in a group-show, 1948. Included in the 'English Abstract Art' show at the Galerie Gimpel Fils, 1951. Lives in London. — *Bibl.* Alloway: *Nine abstract artists* (London 1954).

HÉLION Jean (b. Couterne, Orne, France, 1904). Studied engineering in Lille, and architecture in Paris. In 1926, met Torrès-Garcia, who introduced him to cubism. Met van Doesburg in 1930, and collaborated in 'Art Concret'. Went to Russia, 1931. A member of 'Abstraction-Création' from 1932 to 1934. Then, in America until the war. He volunteered in the French army, was made a prisoner; he escaped and published in America an account of his adventures. After having been under the influence of Mondrian (1930), from whom he developed an undeniably personal style (1936), Hélion has returned to representational painting. Lives in Paris.

187

HERBIN Auguste (b. Quiévy, near Cambrai, Northern France, 1882). Attended the École des Beaux-Arts in Lille 1900-1901. In Paris, 1903; worked in isolation. Struck up a friendship with Wilhelm Uhde. Exhibited in Léonce Rosenberg's Galerie de l'Effort Moderne, from 1917 on. In 1923, he painted landscapes in brownish tones, following a period of simplified cubism where pure geometrical elements were sometimes introduced. Abstract painting since 1926. Co-founder with Vantongerloo of the 'Abstraction-Création' group in 1931. The inventor of a system of abstract painting analysed in his *Art non-figuratif et non-objectif* (Galerie Lydia Conti, Paris 1949): it borrows very much from Goethe's theory of colours. Herbin exercised a great influence upon young abstract painters, in France and elsewhere. He exhibits regularly at the Salon des Réalités Nouvelles (of which he was a director until 1955) and at the Galerie Denise René. Lives in Paris. — *Bibl.* Jakovski: *Herbin* (Paris 1933); 'Art d'Aujourd'hui' (Paris November 1949 and December 1951); *Témoignages pour l'Art Abstrait* (Paris 1952); Massat: *Auguste Herbin,* Collection Prisme (Paris 1953).

HERSCH Lee (b. Cleveland, Ohio, 1896; d. Madrid, 1953). Studied at the Cleveland School of Art and the National Academy of Design (New York). A member of the expeditionary corps in France, 1918. Numerous one-man shows in the United States. Abstract painting from 1943 on. Included in group-shows at the Whitney Museum and the Solomon R. Guggenheim Museum (New York) as well as in the Salon des Réalités Nouvelles (Paris). Retrospective exhibition at the Studio Facchetti, Paris. One room was devoted to his work in the Salon des Réalités Nouvelles in 1953. His works calmly exude generous colours. — *Bibl.* Seuphor: *Lee Hersch* (Paris 1954).

HEURTAUX André (b. Paris, 1898). Painting after Nature, 1921. First imaginative paintings, 1930; progressed towards neo-plasticism at the end of 1933. Exhibited at the Salon des Indépendants from 1925 to 1930, at the Surindépendants from 1931 on. Took part in abstract art exhibitions in Lille, Cannes and South America. Lives in Paris. Geometrical compositions with large, delicately shaded surfaces.

HILL Anthony (b. London, 1930). The son of an academic painter. Was at first interested in science. Took classes at the Central School of Arts and Crafts. Took part in 1951 in the first post-war exhibition of English abstract art. Travelled to Paris where he met Vantongerloo, Sonia Delaunay, Picabia, Seuphor. Lives in London. — *Bibl.* Alloway: *Nine Abstract Artists* (London 1954).

HERBIN. LUCK. 1953.

188

HOFMANN. UNDULATING EXPANSE. 1955.

HILTON Roger (b. Northwood, England, 1911). Studied at the Slade School, London, and the Académie Ranson, Paris (under Bissière). Exhibited at Gimpel Fils's, London 1952, and took part the same year in an exhibition of modern English painting at the Galerie de France, Paris. Lives in London.

HINDER Frank (b. Sydney, Australia, 1906). Studied in Sydney, Chicago, New York, New Mexico. Toured Europe in 1927. A professor at the National Art School, Sydney. One of the few exponents of abstract art in Australia. Lives in Sydney.

HLITO Alfredo (b. Buenos Aires, 1923). Studied at the Academy of Buenos Aires. Expressionistic paintings in 1943. First abstract works in 1944. A member and founder of the 'Arte Concreto' group. First one-man show, 1952. Lives in Buenos Aires. A painting emphasising planes and lines, traced with subtlety: an art stripped to the bone. — Bibl. *Grupo de artistas modernos de la Argentina* (Buenos Aires, 1952); *Acht argentijnse abstracten,* Stedelijk Museum (Amsterdam, no date).

HÖCH Hannah (b. Gotha, Thuringia, 1889). Studied in Berlin. Took part in the dada movement from 1917 to 1921. Was a member of the 'Novembergruppe'. Friendly with Schwitters, Raoul Hausmann, Van Doesburg, Moholy-Nagy, Arp. Was in Holland from 1926 to 1929. Returned to Berlin. Took part in numerous exhibitions in Holland, Germany, and New York (Sidney Janis Gallery). Both abstract and representational work. She also composed a number of photo-montages. Lives in Berlin.

HOFMANN Hans (b. Weissenburg, Germany, 1880). Studied in Germany and in France. After having followed the secessionist movement in Germany, he founded a School of Modern Art in Munich (1915) and taught in the Bavarian mountains, in Italy, and in France, successively. In 1930, he left for America to teach at the University of California, then at the Art Students League, New York. Became an American citizen and founded the Hofmann School in New York, in 1934. He has trained a number of American artists and his influence is still spreading. One-man shows: Paul Cassirer gallery, Berlin, 1910; Betty Parsons Gallery, New York,

189

1947; Galerie Maeght, Paris, 1949, and every year since 1947 at the Kootz Gallery (New York). Lives in New York.

Hofmann's work is densely expressionist, but sound, full of vigour and delight. It is a perpetual feast where order has but recently prevailed, and is gaining more and more room. "Art is for me the glorification of the human spirit and as such, it is the cultural documentation of its time. The deepest purpose of art is, clearly, to keep the spirit of man lastingly young in a world constantly fluctuating. Art must counterbalance the banal weight of everyday life, it must give us the constant aesthetic joy we need." (Hofmann). — *Bibl*. Janis: *Abstract and Surrealist Art in America* (New York 1944); *Derrière le Miroir* (Paris, January 1949); Hess: *Abstract Painting* (New York 1951).

HOLTY Carl (b. Freiburg, Germany, 1900). Came to the United States as a child. Studied at the Art Institute in Chicago, then in Munich under Hans Hofmann. In Europe, 1925 to 1933. First one-man show at the Nierendorf Gallery, New York, 1938. Included in the "American Abstract Artists" shows from 1937 to 1946. Friendship with Mondrian in New York. Lives in New York.

HOLTZMAN Harry (b. New York, 1912). Studied at the Art Students League (New York) from 1928 to 1933. Came to Paris in 1934 to meet Mondrian and had a number of interviews with him. Returned to America and participated in the foundation of the 'American Abstract Artists' group. It was thanks to his insistence and his financial help that Mondrian was able to go to New York in 1940. Was the sole beneficiary of Mondrian when the latter died (1944). He gave up painting almost completely then, in order to devote himself to the study of semantics and to teaching. The publisher of the review *Transformation* since 1950. Lives in

New York. — Bibl. *Collection of the Société Anonyme* (New Haven 1950).

HOSIASSON Philippe (b. Odessa, 1898). Studied law and travelled frequently in Switzerland, Austria, Germany, Sweden. Was in Italy for some

HOSIASSON. PAINTING. 1955.
Galerie Stadler, Paris.

time at the end of the First World War. First one-man show in Rome. In Berlin, 1922. Exhibited at Flechtheim's and worked as a designer for the Romantic Ballet. Settled in Paris, 1924. Was a founder of the Salon des Surindépendants where he exhibited until 1939. A number of one-man shows in France, Italy, Belgium. His painting went through many phases before reaching non-representational art in 1947. Took part in the Salon de Mai from 1948 on. Exhibited at the Galerie du Haut-Pavé, Paris 1955, and Galerie Stadler, Paris 1956. Lives in Paris.

Hossiason's work proceeds by monochromatic series. The painter lets himself

190

be enchanted by a wave of blue, then green, then black. It is a painting of sudden eruptions, but long years of training, of spiritual decantation precede the sudden and violent impulses of creation. This art disconcerts some by its brutal and unanswerable frankness, but it persuades others by its deep humanity. "M. S. has found a formula I love: *art is anything, but with a certain style*. I think that general circumstances, in our time, have brought painting to complete autonomy through the progressive discarding of representation. But the heart of the matter remains unchanged, because nonrepresentational paintings, as well, must be accomplished *with a certain style* to accede to the rank of art." (Hossiason).

HULBECK Charles R. (b. in Germany, 1892). Known under the name of Richard Hülsenbeck as one of the leading members of the dada movement in Zurich (1916), then in Berlin. After an eventful career, finally arrived in New York where he became a psychiatrist and took the name of Hulbeck. For some years now he has managed to paint vigorous abstract works in the intervals between interviews. His wife, Beate Hulbeck, born in Berlin in 1903, has also done some abstract painting but has mostly specialized in collages. A member of the 'American Abstract Artists' group. One-man shows: Paris, 1950 (Galerie des Deux-Iles), and Berlin, 1956 (Kunstantiquariat Wasmuth). Lives in New York.

HULL James (b. 1921). First one-man show in London, 1949. Then exhibited at the Gallery Gimpel Fils, London, 1951 and 1953, and took part in the exhibition of modern English painting at the Galerie de France, Paris, 1952. Exhibited at the Passedoit Gallery, New York, 1953. Lives in London.

HUNDERTWASSER Fritz (b. Vienna, 1928). Attended the Academy of Fine Arts in Vienna. Travelled in Africa and South West Europe. One-man shows in Vienna since 1952, as well as in Italy and Paris (Studio Facchetti). Took part in a number of group-shows in Paris and elsewhere. Lives in Vienna. An obsessive art, akin to the more bizarre and morbid aspects of surrealism. It has gained in strength in becoming abstract.

HUNZIKER Frieda (b. Amsterdam, 1908). Studied at the Institute of Design. Came to abstraction about 1945. Travelled to Curaçao, 1951 and 1952. Lyrical forms and colours influenced by her travels in the tropics. Exhibited in Amsterdam, The Hague, Paris, Antwerp, Curaçao and Indonesia. Lives in Holland.

HURTADO Angel (b. Venezuela, 1927). School of Fine Arts in Caracas. Travels in Spain and in France. Took part in a number of exhibitions in South America and in Paris. First abstract works in 1948. Lives in Paris.

HUSZAR Vilmos (b. Hungary, 1884), Settled in Holland in 1905. A friend of van Doesburg and a co-founder of the 'De Stijl' group, 1917. Composed abstract stained-glass windows and neoplastic interiors. A lecturer and an essaywriter. Attempted to bring the 'De Stijl' principles into the theatre; to that end he produced a series of remarkable sketches (1922) which are also works of art. He then returned to representational painting. Lives in Hierden (Holland). — *Bibl.* The works of van Doesburg and the complete files of the review *De Stijl*.

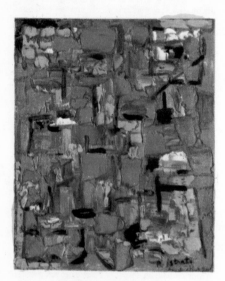

ISTRATI. PAINTING. 1954.
Galerie Craven, Paris.

IDOUX Claude (b. Lyons, 1915). École des Beaux-Arts, in Lyons. Mostly interested in fresco-painting. Renews with Lenormand the great and inspired traditions of this discipline. Took part in a number of international exhibitions: Germany, Sweden, Denmark, North America, and Sao Paolo. One-man show at the Galerie Mai, Paris, 1951. Lives in Paris.

IONESCO Nicolas (b. Bucharest, 1919). School of Fine Arts in Bucharest. Took part in a number of exhibitions there. Came to Paris in 1946; studied under Lhote and Léger. Turned to abstraction in 1949 and studied in the Dewasne and Pillet Studio. Met Herbin. Took part in the Salon des Réalités Nouvelles. One-man show at the Galerie Arnaud in 1952. Lives in Paris.

ISTRATI Alexandre (b. Dorohai, Rumania, 1915). Bachelor in Law. Studied at the same time at the School of Fine Arts, where he eventually stayed as an assistant professor for nine years. Came to Paris in 1947 on a grant from the French Institute in Bucharest. Worked at the École des Beaux-Arts, under Lhote, and then on his own. One-man show at the Galerie Colette Allendy in 1952. Took part in a number of group-shows, particularly at the Galerie Denise René and the main abstract Salons in Paris. One-man show at the Galerie Craven, Paris, 1956. Lives in Paris.

"I have investigated colour a long time: it has always attracted me and my craving to seek further brought me to abstraction. It is colour, considered not only in terms of its chromatic relations but as an *inner* resonance, that guided me toward form. I sensed form through colour." (Istrati). His recent works are usually great monochromatic panels voluptuously laden with paint, the colour feeding upon itself and yet vibrating through the subtlety of its tones or the presence of some thinly suggested complementary. — Bibl. *Premier Bilan de l'Art Actuel* (Paris 1953); Gindertael: *Istrati,* 'Cimaise' (Paris, Dec. 1953); Gindertael: *Propos sur la peinture actuelle* (Paris 1955).

J

JANCO Marcel (b. Bucharest, 1895). Studied architecture at the Polytechnic school in Zurich (1915-1916). Took an active part in the reunions at the famous 'cabaret Voltaire', the cradle of dadaism, with Arp, Tzara, Hugo Ball, Hülsenbeck and a few others. He drew and composed costumes and masks for dadaist sessions. Made painted reliefs and abstract sculptures from 1917 to 1919. He foresaw the close relationship between abstract art and architecture. In 1919, created the "Peintres Radicaux" group expressing his confidence in a social structure where art would be an integral part of life and architecture. Took part in exhibitions with Klee, Richter, Arp, Sophie Taeuber and other pioneers of abstract art. In 1920, founded a new group in Switzerland, "Das Neue Leben" (New Life), then left for Paris where he met Picabia, Ernst, Dali. After quarrelling a few times with Tzara, returned to Rumania where he created the movement and the review *Contimporanul* (1922-1940). Emigrated to Israel in 1940 where he took part in the cultural movement of the country. Since Dadaism, Janco's painting has passed through many stages. One can often sense in his work a certain pressure of anguish. His most noteworthy compositions remain the polychromatic reliefs as well as the drawings and the water-colours of his dada period. Lives in Tel-Aviv. — Bibl. *Dada Painters and Poets* (New York 1951).

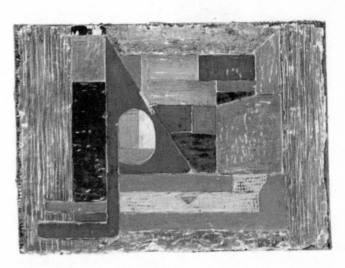

MARCEL JANCO. SUN BRIGHT GARDEN. PAINTED RELIEF. 1918.

193

JAREMA Josef (b. in Poland, 1900). Studied at the Academy of Cracow, in Paris and in Egypt. Took part in exhibitions in Paris, Poland, Italy and the Near-East. President and founder of the Italian Art Club in Rome. The friendship and influence of Prampolini, Reggiani and Soldati converted him to abstraction in 1948. Settled in Nice in 1951 and made friends with Jean Gorin, one of the first disciples of Mondrian in France. His work then approached toward a very simple geometry without however becoming neo-plastic. Was in Paris, 1955. Took part in a number of art Salons in Paris as well as in a group-show at the Museum of Rouen (1955). Jarema is still working ardently towards art principles that would substitute universalism for individualism. Exhibits tapestries at the Galerie Mai, Paris 1956.

JEAN Marcel (b. La Charité-sur-Loire, France, 1900). Attended the School of Decorative Arts, Paris (1919-1921). Various activities until 1924. Spent a year in the United States where he made a living as an industrial designer. Exhibited at the Salon d'Automne, 1930. Then took part in the surrealist movement with which he exhibited regularly. Was in Hungary 1938-1945: published there an illustrated essay *Mnésiques*. Essays on the pre-surrealist poets. Exhibited at the Salons des Sur-indépendants and other shows, abstract canvases where nothing remains of the literary painting dear to his fellow-surrealists. Lives in Paris.

JENKINS Paul (b. Kansas City, 1923). Studied in Kansas City and Struthers (Ohio). Was in the Armed forces, 1944-1946. Studied at the Art Students League, New York (1948-1952). Travelled to Spain and to Sicily. In Paris, 1953. One-man shows: Studio Facchetti, Paris; Zimmergalerie, Frankfurt; Zoe Dusanne Gallery, Seattle. Lives in Paris or New York. A painter full of charm and mystery. The half-colours and the flickering light of night time. "That which has been left in silence rounds off the statement and renders the unknown perceptible and clear." (Jenkins).

JOBIN Arthur (b. Yverdon, Switzerland, 1927). School of Applied Arts in Lausanne. Abstract painting since 1949. Numerous visits to Paris. Has progressed in the neo-plastic direction since 1953. One-man shows in Lausanne, 1952 and 1954. Lives in Lausanne.

JOHNSON Buffie (b. New York, 1912). Studied in New York and in Los Angeles, later at the Art Students League. Lengthy stays in Paris. Exhib-itions in Paris and in America. Took part

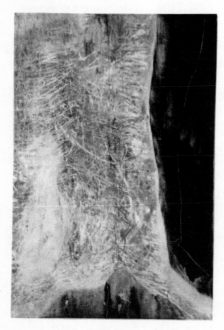

JENKINS. SOLSTICE. 1955.

194

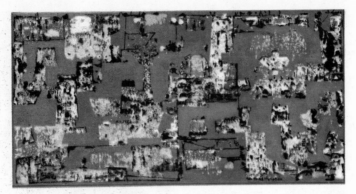

BUFFIE JOHNSON. THE GARDEN III. 1954.

in the Salon des Réalités Nouvelles in 1949. A number of exhibitions at the Betty Parsons Gallery, New York. Lives in New York and Paris. Buffie Johnson's painting is full of the the delicacies of impressionism. On a background of colour, usually monochrome, fragments of calligraphy merge and emerge. The French poet Pierre Emmanuel has written an appreciation of this painter comparing her with Mozart. — *Bibl.* Seuphor: *Buffie Johnson et Alcopley*, Galerie Bing (Paris 1956).

JOHNSON Ray (b. 1927, Detroit, Michigan). Studied at Black Mountain College under Albers. A member of the "American Abstract Artists" group. Lives in New York.

K

KAKABADZE David (b. Georgia, 1890). Professor of Natural Sciences in Moscow. Settled later in Paris where he published a manifesto, about 1925. Exhibited regularly at the Salon des Indépendants from 1920 on. His works are partly in the National Museum in Tiflis and partly in the collection of the Société Anonyme (U. S. A.). Whereabouts unknown.

KALINOWSKI Horst Egon (b. Dusseldorf, 1924). Academy of Dusseldorf (1945-1948). After some time in Italy, settled in Paris (1950). Attended the Abstract Art workshop of Dewasne and Pillet (1950-1952). Took part in a number of group-shows. Two one-man shows at the Galerie Arnaud, Paris. Lives in Paris. After industriously painting abstract works with precise forms and colours, so trenchant that they offended many critical susceptibilities, Kalinoswki followed the general movement towards more feeling and warmth in painting. A dramatic atmosphere now prevails, but the development of his work is certainly not yet closed.

KALLOS Paul (b. Hernadnemeti, Hungary, 1928). Spent a year in a concentration camp in Germany (1944-1945), before he had even matriculated at Kiskunhalas. Attended the School of Fine Arts in Budapest (1946-1949). In Paris, 1950; first abstract paintings the same year. One-man show at the Galerie Pierre, Paris, 1956. Lives in Paris.

KANDINSKY Wassili (b. Moscow, 1866; d. Paris, 1944.) Studied in Odessa, then at the University of Moscow (law and political economy). Was sent in 1889 on an ethnographic mission in the North of Russia. Travelled a number of times to Paris before he was appointed artistic director of a Moscow printing-press. Went to Munich in 1896 to study painting; it was there he met Jawlensky. First exhibition in Munich, 1901. Travelled to Holland and again to Paris in 1902. Was in Tunisia and Italy 1903-1904; in Dresden, 1905. Then, again in Paris 1906-1907, where he contributed wood-cuts to the review *Tendances Nouvelles*. Returned to Munich where he met Franz Marc (1910), then Macke and Klee (1911). Published *Ueber das Geistige in der Kunst* (Concerning the Spiritual in Art) and painted his first abstract works. Was a co-founder with Franz Marc of the 'Der Blaue Reiter' group and compiled with him a famous year-book under the same insignia. In 1913, *Der Sturm* published his 'Rückblicke' (Glimpses of the Past), an autobiographical essay where he carefully described his progress toward abstraction. When the war broke out, he moved to Switzerland, and then returned

KALINOWSKI. PAGAN IKON. 1955.

to Russia through Italy and the Balkans. From 1896 to 1914, he had spent a few weeks in Russia each year. In 1916, went to Stockholm; in 1917, to Finland : he had at one and the same time an exhibition in Helsinski and Saint-Petersburg. Was appointed professor of the Fine Arts Academy in Moscow, 1918. In 1919, reorganized the Russian museums and founded the Museum of Pictorial Culture. Met Pevsner, Gabo, and Chagall. A professor at the University of Moscow in 1920: a one-man show organized by the government was held the same year in Moscow. Left Moscow at the end of 1921, and the following year, was appointed professor at the Bauhaus (Weimar), of which he soon became vice-president. In 1925, followed the Bauhaus to Dessau and formed a class of free-style painting. In 1926, he published *Punkt und Linie zu Fläche* (Point and Line to Surface) and marked his sixtieth birthday by a number of large exhibitions. Did a good deal of travelling from 1927 to 1932.

196

The Bauhaus having been closed by order of the Nazi government, Kandinsky left for Paris where he settled permanently, remaining in Neuilly, until his death. In 1937, about fifty of his works were confiscated by the Nazi government and classed as 'Degenerate Art'. Exhibited in London in 1938, then in Paris and in New York. He died in Paris in December 1944 as he was working on the sets of a ballet. Many retrospective exhibitions have taken place since his death, at the Galerie Drouin and the Galerie Maeght, Paris.

In his abstract work of the "Blaue Reiter" period, Kandinsky is the precursor of the 'effusionist', lyrical, and neo-expressionist styles which play a large part in abstract painting today. Later on, in 1921, he introduced into his work the geometrical elements of Malevitch. Then, probably under the influence of Paul Klee, also a professor at the Bauhaus, a new element of poetry and fantasy appears in his work. The last period of his life is characterized by balanced compositions, in sober tones, sometimes delicate. But the imaginative variety of his forms always astonishes. No artist in this century has left us as rich and varied a work testifying, once for all, to the infinite resources of abstract art. — *Bibl.* Grohmann: *Kandinsky* (Paris 1931); *Selection,* n° 14, texts by Grohmann, Zervos, Baumeister, Seuphor, Sartoris (Antwerp 1933); *Kandinsky memorial* (New York 1945); Debrunner: *Wir entdecken Kandinsky* (Zurich 1947); Seuphor: *l'Art abstrait,*

ses Origines, ses Premiers Maîtres (Paris 1949); Raynal: *De Picasso au Surréalisme* (Paris-Geneva 1950), *The Collection of the Société Anonyme* (New Haven 1950); 'Art d'Aujourd'hui' (Paris, January 1950); Max Bill, Magnelli, Arp, Estienne: *Kandinsky,* published by Galery Maeght (Paris 1951); Barr: *Masters of Modern Art* (New York 1954); *Kandinsky, œuvre gravée,* Galerie Berggruen (Paris 1954).

KARSKAYA Ida (b. Bender, Southern Russia, 1905). "I came to France at the age of 18 to study medicine. After I married Serge Karsky, who was at that time a painter, I became tired of sitting for him, and I launched out into painting on my own. I never had any instructor, I have never attended any school. I carefully examined the vision and the technique of all the painters who influenced me, both good and bad; I had no help other than the exacting criticism of my husband and of Soutine." One-man shows at the Galerie Breteau (1949), Galerie Calligrammes (1950), Galerie Colette Allendy (1954), in Paris.

KANDINSKY. FIRST ABSTRACT WATER-COLOUR. 1910.

197

Took part in a number of group-shows, contributing mostly collages. To an exhibition Coppel-Karskaya-Koenig, Galerie Arnaud, Paris 1956, she contributed a number of collages, some which she called *Lettres sans Réponse,* composed solely with the bark of trees. Lives in Paris. — Bibl. *XXᵉ siècle,* nᵒ 6 (Paris 1956).

KAUFFMANN Louis (b. in Switzerland, 1923). Began to paint in 1942 and came to non-representational art in 1945. Took part in the Salon des Réalités Nouvelles from 1949 to 1951. One-man show at the Galerie Arnaud, Paris 1951. Lives in Bienne (Switzerland).

KAYLER Richard (b. Paris, 1927). Began to paint in 1946, abstract compositions since 1952. One-man show at the Galerie de Beaune, Paris 1954. Took part in two group exhibitions at the Galerie Creuze, Paris 1957. Geometrical compositions of great sobriety, usually confined to two or three colours seeking their harmony in an elementary form. Lives in Paris.

KELLY Ellsworth (b. Newburgh, U.S.A., 1923). Studied in Englewood (New Jersey) and in Brooklyn. Then studied two years in Boston with Carl Zerbe. Came to Paris in 1948, where he at first studied Byzantine art. Then changed his manner completely and turned toward geometrical abstraction. In 1950, met Arp, Vantongerloo, Seuphor. Took part in the Salon des Réalités Nouvelles in 1950 and 1951. One-man show of paintings and polychromatic reliefs at the Galerie Arnaud, in 1951. Was twice represented in group-shows at the Galerie Maeght (1951 and 1952) by paintings with large orthogonal planes of unabashed colour. Kelly is one of the purest followers of Mondrian's neo-plasticism. Returned to the United States in 1954; exhibited at the Betty Parsons Gallery, 1956.

KENNEDY Jack (b. Otterbein, Indiana, 1922). Studied in Chicago. Began to paint in 1942. Came to Paris in 1949. Travelled throughout Europe. One-man shows at the Esquire Gallery, Chicago, 1949, and Galerie Creuze, Paris 1951. Started then on a manner of painting he calls *Formessence* on flat non-orthogonal frames. He has, therefore, in an unexpected way, an affiliation with the Argentine school of 'madism'. Kennedy's forms, generally rounded off, make one also think of Arp. Lives in the United States.

KARSKAYA. LETTER WITH NO ANSWER. GOUACHE. 1955.

198

KINLEY Peter (b. 1926). Studied at St. Martin's School of Art, London (1949-1953). Took part in exhibitions in London since 1951. One-man show at Gimpel's, London 1954. Lives in London.

KLEE Paul (b. Münchenbuchsee, near Bern, 1879; d. Muralto-Locarno, Tessin, 1940). Educated in Bern. Studied art in Munich (1898 to 1901). Travelled to Italy and France. Exhibited with the Secession group, in Munich and Berlin, 1908. Met Kandinsky, Marc, Macke, Arp, in 1911. Took part in the second "Blaue Reiter" exhibition (1912) as well as in the "Sturm" Herbstsalon, Berlin 1913. Went to Tunisia with Macke and Moilliet

KLEE. AIR-TSU-DNI. INK DRAWING. 1927.

(1914). He brought back landscapes from this trip, that were almost abstract works. A professor at the Bauhaus, in Weimar, then in Dessau (1921 to 1931). Travelled to Sicily, Corsica, Brittany, Egypt. Exhibited at Flechtheim's, Berlin 1929, and at the Museum of Modern Art, New York (1930). Taught at the Academy of Dusseldorf, 1931. Under a Nazi ban in 1933; went to live in Switzerland. Retrospective exhibition in Bern, 1935. Seventeen of his works were included in the "Degenerate Art" exhibition in Munich, and a hundred and two others were seized by the Nazi authorities. Many retrospective exhibitions of Klee's work have been held since the last war, notably in Paris, Brussels, London, Amsterdam, New York, and in Switzerland, Germany and Italy.

All the lands of the spirit lie open to Klee. The free spirit transfigures everything in a ceaseless act of creation achieved through the tip of the pen, the bristles of a paint-

brush. No inner call goes unanswered, no single solicitation, however strange or outlandish, remains unobeyed. Klee is incredible, stupefying. And yet he is true. He reaches more truth with a touch of his hand, than any other painter with the most strenuous efforts. This is because he does not follow Nature, but acts as she does, acts through her. His act is Nature herself, as much Nature as the blooming of a flower, the rippling of a river, the hoot of an owl. His is not an intelligence which dominates and exploits, which considers and explains, but a sensibility which mingles, submitting to the inner laws of creation, less acting than acted upon. "Art," says Klee, "does not render the visible, but renders visible". He inserts himself into nature, steeps in it, and then expresses what he feels, what he sees through this second sight, a sort of *post-mortem*, from a vantage-point where all things are equal, a pin as large as a

199

KOENIG. DEPARTURE FROM WEISWAMPACH.
1955. Private Collection, Montreal.

mountain, good and evil without significance other than movement, variety, measures and usages. — *Bibl.* Klee: *Pädagogisches Skizzenbuch* (Munich 1945); Klee: *Ueber die Moderne Kunst* (Bern 1945); *Paul Klee,* Museum of Modern Art (New York 1946); Geist: *Paul Klee* (Hamburg 1948); Read: *Paul Klee on Modern Art* (London 1948); *Paul Klee,* 'Kunst museum' (Basel 1950); Giedion-Welcker: *Paul Klee* (Stuttgart 1954); Grohmann: *Paul Klee* (Stuttgart 1954); Seuphor: *Paul Klee ou la création ininterrompue,* 'Preuves' (Paris, March 1955). Klee: *Tagebücher 1898-1918,* Du Mont Schauberg (Cologne 1956).

KLINE Franz (b. Wilkes-Barre, Pennsylvania, 1910). Studied at Boston University, then at Heatherly's Art School, London. Returned to New York in 1938. One-man shows at the Egan Gallery from 1950 on. Took part in a number of exhibitions in America as well as in an exhibition of American painting at the Galerie de France, Paris 1952. Taught at Black Mountain College and at the Pratt Institute, Brooklyn. Lives in New York. Powerful linear work. Striking tension between black, white, and grey. A large-scale calligraphy; the richness and the texture of the paint testify to the authenticity of the painter's talent. — *Bibl.* Hess: *Abstract Painting* (New York 1951); *Cinquante Ans d'Art aux États-Unis,* Musée d'Art Moderne (Paris 1955).

KOENIG John Franklin (b. Seattle, United States, 1924). After having fought in Europe during the war, he attended classes of painting and drawing at the American University in Biarritz, created for the G.I.'s. Returned to America

DE KOONING. PAINTING. 1948.
Museum of Modern Art, New York

200

in 1946. Travelled in Mexico; studied decoration, drawing and architecture at the University of Washington. Exhibited in Bellevue (Wash.). Returned to Paris in 1948. First abstract works in 1951. One-man shows at the Galerie Arnaud, Paris, 1952 and 1955. Took part in a number of group-shows and in the Salon des Réalités Nouvelles. Co-director of the Galerie-Librairie Arnaud, and editor of the review *Cimaise*. Lives in Paris. Highly sophisticated collages with scraps of paper. Monochromatic works in the abstract impressionist manner. Extreme delicacy of the colour, both in the collages and the oil-paintings.

KOLOS-VARY Sigismond (or Kolos-Vari, b. Banffyhunyad, Hungary, 1899). Attended the School of Applied Arts in Budapest. Settled in Paris (1926), where he continued his studies and became a naturalized French citizen. Travelled and studied in Italy. Exhibited in Paris, New York, Geneva, Bern, Basel, Antwerp, Amsterdam, Brussels, Milan, Tokyo. Took part regularly in the Salon de Mai. Lives in Paris. Kolos-Vary came to abstraction through long and patient examination of the possibilities of his favorite themes and the both firm and delicate character of his palette. — Bibl. *Sigismond Kolos-Vari*, 'Documents' n° 14 (Geneva 1955); R. van Gindertael: *Propos sur la Peinture Actuelle* (Paris 1955).

KOONING Willem de (b. Rotterdam, 1904). Left school at the age of twelve to be apprenticed to a house-painter. Took night-classes at the Fine Arts Academy in Rotterdam, at the same time. One of his professors introduced him to the *Stijl* principles. Spent a year in Brussels where he saw the Flemish expressionist paintings which left him with a very deep impression. Came to the United States in 1926. Worked for some time as a house-painter. First abstract works in

1934. First one-man show at the Egan Gallery, New York, 1948. Took part in the 'Abstract Painting and Sculpture in America' show at the Museum of Modern Art, New York, 1951, as well as in 'Regards sur la Peinture américaine', Galerie de France Paris, 1952. Although he had reverted in recent years to a representational painting much influenced by expressionism, an exhibition at the Sidney Janis Gallery, New York 1956, showed a further return to an abstract manner. Lives in New York. — *Bibl.* Ritchie: *Abstract Painting and Sculpture in America* (New York 1950); *What abstract art means to me* (New York 1951); 'Art d'Aujourd'hui' (Paris, June 1951).

KOLOS-VARY. COMPOSITION. 1955.

KOSICE Gyula (b. on the Czech-Hungarian border, in 1924). A naturalized citizen of Argentine. Studied in the non-institutional Academies of Buenos Aires. Took part with Arden Quin in the creation of e 'Madi' movement,

(1946). Since 1947, the director of the review *Arte Madi*. A number of exhibitions in Buenos Aires with various abstract groups. Took part in the Salon des Réalités Nouvelles, Paris, 1948 and 1950. Lives in Buenos Aires.

KOSKAS Georges (b. Tunisia, 1926). Came to Paris, 1946. Attended Fernand Léger's studio. In 1949, turned toward abstraction and was included in the 'Mains Éblouies' exhibition at the Galerie Maeght. One-man show at the Galerie Arnaud, 1951, and at the Galerie Colette Allendy, 1952. Spent some time in New York in 1955 and had a one-man show at the Rose Fried Gallery. Lives in Paris.

KOSNICK-KLOSS Jeanne (b. Glogau, Silesia, 1892). Studied in Cologne and Geneva. Married the

KOSNICK-KLOSS.
CRYSTALLINE ARCHITECTURAL COMPOSITION. 1929.

pianist and writer Henri Kosnick in Berlin. Came to Paris in 1925, and started painting the following year. Exhibition at the Galerie Billet, Paris 1927. Mett Otto Freundlich in 1929: she became his companion and collaborator. She composed with him a number of mosaics. After Freundlich's death in a concentration camp (1943), she kept on working on her own and took part in many exhibitions in Paris. Jeanne Kosnick-Kloss has created abstract tapestries dense with movement and colour. She freely lends young abstract painters Freundlich's studio for their work. Lives in Paris.

KUPKA Frank (b. Opocno, Czechoslovakia). Entered the School of Fine Arts in Prague at the age of 17. Came to Vienna 1892; studied at the Fine Arts School and exhibited portraits and landscapes at the Kuntsverein. In Paris, 1895. Illustrated books and exhibited at the Société des Beaux-Arts. A member of the Salon d'Automne in 1906. Great fame as an illustrator of rare books and as neo-impressionist painter. In 1911, suddenly turned to abstraction. Exhibited abstract canvases for the first time at the Salon d'Automne, 1912: *Fugue à deux Couleurs* and *Chromatique Chaude*. It is in connection with his works (and those of Delaunay and Picabia) that Apollinaire spoke of *orphic* painting. In 1913, contributed to the Salon des Indépendants *Plans Verticaux* and *Solo d'un trait brun,* and the same year, to the Salon d'Automne: *Localisation des mobiles graphiques*. One-man shows: Galerie Povolotsky, Paris 1921 and Galerie La Boétie, Paris 1924. There was a major retrospective exhibition of his work at the Museum of Prague in 1946, and

KUPKA. THE DECISION. 1921.

another at the Galerie Carré, New York, in 1951. Honorary president of the Salon des Réalités Nouvelles to which he contributes every year. Lives in Puteaux, near Paris.

"Almost fifty years ago, Kupka gave a memorable reception on New Year's Day in his studio on the rue Caulaincourt. Shortly afterwards, he began to *see* abstract, as one says nowadays. For, in those happy days, the word was not yet in the dictionary. Apollinaire used the word *orphism* when he spoke of these things. . . and now all the would-be fathers are tracing their rights of paternity, for none of them would admit of the polypaternity of this gigantic child." (Marchel Duchamp). — *Bibl.* Gremilly: *Kupka* (Paris 1922); Seuphor: *L'Art abstrait, ses origines, ses premiers maîtres* (Paris 1949); *Catalogue Illustré de l'exposition Kupka,* Galerie Carré (New York 1951); *Art d'Aujourd'hui* (Paris, March 1952); *A Dictionary of Modern Painting* (Methuen, London 1956).

L

LACASSE Joseph (b. Tournai, Belgium, 1894). An ordinary workman, he attended night-classes in drawing and painted in his spare time. His friends made fun of his free-style paintings and nicknamed him 'mosaic-er'. Then attended the School of Fine Arts in Tournai, and from 1919 to 1920 the Fine Arts Academy in Brussels. Travelled in Italy in 1921. Settled in Paris in 1924. He made himself a reputation, for a few years, as a painter of great religious compositions (1927-1936). Then came to abstraction. Numerous one-man shows in Belgium and in Paris. Took part in the main Belgian Salons and in the Sao Paolo Biennale. One-man show at the Rose Fried Gallery, New York 1955. Lives in Paris. "In art, the more simple the means the more powerful the form. Every true artist is always fascinated by the undefinable beauty of light. He constantly and unwittingly eliminates the visual object that bars him from the universal principle of life." (Lacasse). — *Bibl.* Bordier: *Il faut maintenant connaître Lacasse,* 'Art d'Aujourd'hui' (Paris, Nov. 1954).

LAGAGE Pierre César (b. Croix, Northern France, 1911). Studied at the School of Fine Arts in Roubaix; he attended classes in drawing, wood-cuts, and etching. Worked at painting on his own; influenced by the Flemish primitives. First exhibitions in Paris and Lille, 1932. Exhibited in a number of Polish towns, 1936-1937, then in Brussels. Settled in Paris, 1937. His work, geared at that time towards experiment in style and colour, progressed, after the Liberation, in the direction of a more mural conception of painting, and finally came to abstraction in 1950. Many exhibitions in Sweden and in Paris (Galerie Drouant-David, 1949, Galerie de Beaune, 1952). He exhibited also in Zurich and

in Los Angeles. Lives in Paris. In Lagage, the harmonies of tones are, in a sense, the real subject of the canvases. His range of reds, or yellows, or greys, underlined by a touch of ultramarine are modulated with a rare technical adroitness. It is a balanced art where nothing is left to chance. Few painters possess in such measure the art of charming by lyrical nuances of colour.

LAGO Antonio Lago Rivera (b. La Coruña, Spain, 1916). Studied art in La Coruña and in Madrid, then at the École des Beaux-Arts, Paris (1945-1946). Professor of drawing at the French *lycée* in Madrid. Came to Paris, 1951. Abstract paintings since 1952. Numerous one-man shows in Spain since 1941, particularly at the Buchholz gallery in Madrid (1945). One-man shows in Paris: Galerie Altarriba (1946), Galerie Breteau (1953), Galerie Arnaud (1954 and 1955). Took part in the Venice, Sao Paolo, and Menton Biennales, as well as in the Salon des Réalités Nouvelles. Lives in Paris.

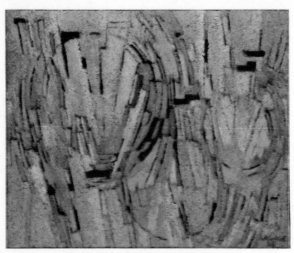

LAGAGE. COMPOSITION. 1955.
M. S. Collection, Paris.

LANSKOY André (b. Moscow, 1902). His youth was spent in Saint-Petersburg, Kiev and in the Crimea. Came to Paris, 1921. Worked at the Académie de la Grande Chaumière; studied under Soudeikine. First exhibition in a group-show, Galerie La Licorne, 1923. One-man show, Galerie Bing 1925. Travelling exhibition in Holland, 1938. First abstract gouaches, 1939. First abstract paintings, 1944. Formed a connection with the Galerie Carré (1944), where, in 1948, he exhibited works dated 1944 to 1948. Numerous exhibitions in a number of European countries from 1948 to 1952 (Brussels, London, New York, Lausanne, Zurich, Berlin, etc. . .). Took part regularly in the Salon de Mai. Composed cartoons for large tapestries. Lives in Paris.

One of the richest temperaments among contemporary Paris painters; his colours are generally warm and his touch is deft, sometimes akin to a fluent handwriting, He has some affinities in disposition with his compatriot De Staël : there is the same disquiet in both men, the same romanticism seeking to surpass itself in each mastered style. But whereas De Staël reaches a dead end of funereal greys, Lanskoy bypasses the stage of anguish and achieves liberation in a painting of pure lyricism (with reds and yellows predominating from 1954 and 1955) where joy appears exuberantly victorious.

"Painting was always abstract, but one did not notice it. When one no longer looks for apples, trees, or young girls in a picture the word *abstract* will become redundant. It is not what enters the painter's eye which enriches a picture, but what springs from his brush. There is no progress in religion or art. But in order to remain the same man, one must develop: thus, if there were only one painter for all the periods, and he were still alive, his message would remain always the same, although worded differently. Let us paint; we shall always die alone." (Lanskoy). — *Bibl.*

Gindertael: *Lanskoy,* 'Art d'Aujourd'hui' (Paris, October 1951); *Témoignages pour l'Art Abstrait* (Paris 1952); Ashton: *Lanskoy,* 'Arts' (New York, March 1956); Grenier: *Lanskoy,* 'L'Œil' (Paris, May 1956).

LANYON Peter (b. St. Ives, Cornwall, 1918). Studied at the Art School in Penzance and at the Euston Road School in London. Worked under Ben Nicholson and Naum Gabo. Exhibited in London, 1949, and in New York, 1953. Travelled in Italy. A retrospective exhibition of his work was held in Plymouth and in Nottingham, 1955. Co-principal of St Peter's Loft Art School in St. Ives. A professor at the Bath Academy of Art in Corsham. Lives in St. Ives.

LAPICQUE Charles (b. Theizé, Rhône, France, 1898). Studied the sciences as well as art. Devoted himself totally to painting from 1943 on. A friend of Bazaine, Manessier, and Jacques Villon.

LANSKOY. GOUACHE. 1954.
Galerie Jacques Dubourg, Paris.

205

One-man shows in Paris: Galerie Jeanne Bucher (1929 and 1941), Galerie Carré (1946), Galerie Denise René (1949 and 1951), Galerie Galanis (1953 and 1956). After some very successful abstract works (the *Régates* series), strong in colour and audaciously drawn, Lapicque has turned toward a more narrative style akin to Dufy. Lives in Paris. — *Bibl.* 'Documents' n° 38 (Geneva 1956); Lescure: *Lapicque* (Paris 1956).

LAPOUJADE Robert (b. Montauban, France, 1921). At first held various jobs, notably that of butcher's boy. Lived alone for one year in a cave in the Alps (1941). First exhibition, Galerie Jeanne Castel, Paris, 1947. In 1949, exhibited portraits of literary celebrities. The following year, he turned to abstraction and published a book analysing the problem of form *Le Mal à Voir*. In 1952, one-man shows at the Galerie de Babylone and the Galerie Arnaud, Paris. He gave a number of lectures on painting the same year, and took part in the Salon de Mai and the Salon des Réalités Nouvelles. Travelled and exhibited in Italy and Germany, 1953. In 1955, published a new theoretical work *Les Mécanismes de la Fascination* (Éditions du Seuil, Paris). Lives in Paris.

LARIONOV Michel (b. Tiraspol, near Odessa, 1881). Attended the School of Painting, Sculpture, and Architecture in Moscow. Took an active part in the artistic events in Moscow as early as 1898. In 1909, exhibited an almost abstract composition which he called *The Glass* at the Society of the Free Aesthetic. He launched the *rayonist (luchism* in Russian) movement the following year. Published the rayonist manifesto in Moscow in 1913. Was a friend of Malevitch and the instructor of Tatlin, the founder of constructivism. In Paris, 1914. Exhibited at Paul Guillaume's, the same year, with his wife Na-

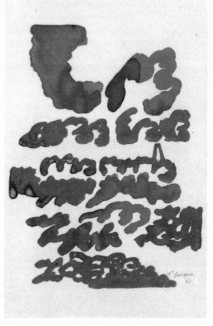

LAPICQUE. THE SEA. WATER-COLOUR. 1951.

thalie Gontcharova (cf. that name): Apollinaire prefaced the exhibition. Then he began to work for Diaghilev's Ballets Russes and almost completely gave up painting. Retrospective exhibitions of rayonism were held in Rome (1917), and in Paris (Galerie des Deux-Iles, 1948). Some of Larionov's works were included in the 'Premiers Maîtres de l'Art Abstrait' exhibition, Galerie Maeght, Paris 1949, and 'L'Œuvre du xxe Siècle' at the Museum of Modern Art, Paris 1952. Also, about forty of Larionov's canvases, dated 1903 to 1915, were gathered at the Galerie de l'Institut, Paris, in 1956. Lives in Paris. — *Bibl.* Barr: *Cubism and Abstract Art* (New York 1936); Seuphor: *L'Art abstrait, ses origines, ses premiers maîtres* (Paris 1949); 'Art d'Aujourd'hui' (Paris, Nov. 1950); *A Dictionary of Modern Painting* (Methuen, London 1956).

206

LATASTER Gerard (b. Schaesberg, Holland, 1920). Attended the School of Industrial Art in Maestricht and the Academy of Fine Arts in Amsterdam. Took part in exhibitions in Paris, Rome, Brussels, Berlin, Stuttgart, and in the United States. Brief smears of paint freely combined with graphisms. Lives in Holland.

LAUBIÈS René (b. Cholonville, Indo-China, 1922). Has lived in Indo-China, Morocco and England. Took part in a number of group-shows in Paris, Nice, Brussels. One-man show at the Studio Facchetti, Paris 1953. Supple lines of calligraphy dissolving into subtle backgrounds.

LAUTREC Lucien (b. Nîmes, France, 1909). Attended the School of Fine Arts in Nîmes. Taught in various schools in Paris. After many different stages, his recent work tends toward lyrical abstraction, taking its departure in landscape. Took part in the Salon de Mai. Lives in Paris.

LAVIOLLE Gaston (b. Marseilles, 1906). Received a classical education. A professor of drawing from 1944 on. Took part in a number of group-shows, particularly in the Salon des Réalités Nouvelles (1953 and 1954) One-man show at the Galerie Suzanne Michel, Paris 1954. Lives in Paris.

LAZZARI Pietro (b. Rome, 1898). Educated in Rome. Drafted in the Italian Infantry during the First World War. Then came to France (on foot from Marseilles to Paris). Went to America, 1925. Painted in Greenwich Village: no affiliations. Became an American citizen. Did some large mural painting in Florida. These last few years, his inspiration seems close to the expressionist vigour of certain works of Hans Hofmann. Lives in the United States.

LECK Bart van der (b. Utrecht, Holland, 1876). Studied at the Academy of Amsterdam. He progressed slowly towards painting in swathes (1916). Met Mondrian many times in 1917. The same year, he transposed his representational works into geometrical compositions employing only the three fundamental colours. Mondrian and van der Leck have greatly influenced each other, more especially through their long theoretical discussions in Blaricum, in 1917. Worked on the first issue of *De*

LARIONOV. RAYONNISME. 1912.

207

Stijl but immediately quarrelled with van Doesburg. As early as 1918 he went back to representational painting; he only reverts to abstraction in decorative works (carpets, interior decoration), and more recently, in ceramics. Lives in Blaricum (Holland). — Bibl. *Catalogue de l'Exposition rétrospective van der Leck,* Stedelijk Museum (Amsterdam 1949); Seuphor: *Le Peintre Bart van der Leck,* 'Werk' (Zurich, Nov. 1951).

LEEPA Allan (b. New York 1919). Studied at the American Artists School, then at Hans Hofmann's Academy. Published *The Challenge of Modern Art* in 1949. In Paris, 1950 to 1951. Numerous exhibitions in America. A professor at Michigan State College, East Lansing (Mich.).

LEGRAND René (b. Nantes, France, 1923). Attended the School of Decorative Arts in Paris, 1941-1942. Worked at the Académie de la Grande Chaumière in 1943. He was encouraged by Manessier and the Argentine sculptor Vitullo who introduced him to the splendours of modern art. Took part in the Salon de Mai since 1949. One-man show at the Galerie Arnaud, Paris 1953. Lives in Paris.

LE MOAL Jean (b. Authon-du-Perche, France, 1909). Attended the School of Fine Arts in Lyons, then the Académie Ranson in Paris, where he met Bissière. Worked with a group of friends: Manessier, Bertholle, Martin. Exhibitions in Lyons and Paris. Composed many murals from 1937 on. Generally exhibited with Singier and Manessier at the Galerie de France, Paris. Designed the sets for a number of stage productions. One-man show at the Galerie de France, 1956. Lives in Paris. Le Moal's painting seems to have

basic affinities with that of Bazaine on the one hand, and Manessier on the other. The diversity of the titles (*Prairie, Barques, Midi sur le Port, Floraison*) does not prevent a certain uniformity of plastic inspiration: linear tracings, mainly vertical, with dashes of bright colour regularly spaced between. — *Bibl.* Bourniquel: *Trois Peintres (Le Moal, Manessier, Singier),* Drouin (Paris 1946); Jacques Lassaigne: *Le Moal,* 'xxᵉ siècle' nᵒ 6 (Paris 1956).

LEPPIEN Jean (b. Luneburg, Germany, 1910). Studied under Kandinsky at the Bauhaus of Dessau (1929-1930). In Berlin, 1930-1933. Worked in Moholy-Nagy's studio. In Paris, 1933 to 1939. Volunteered for the army at the declaration of war. Was deported in Germany, 1944. All his work prior to 1944 was destroyed by the Nazis. Settled on the Riviera in 1945. Took part in the Salon des Réalités Nouvelles and the Salon de Mai.

LE MOAL. VERDURE. 1956.

208

One-man shows at the Galerie Colette Allendy, 1949 and 1951. Lives in Roquebrune, near Menton. Thematic compositions of geometric elements reduced to the essential. A series of canvases with criss-crossing curves and straight lines; another series of multiple and separate rectangles. — *Bibl.* Sibert: *Jean Leppien,* 'Art d'Aujourd'hui' (Paris, Feb. 1954).

LEVÉE. OCTOBER III. 1955. *Private Collection, Paris.*

LEUPPI Léo (b. Zurich 1893). Founder and President of the 'Die Allianz' society, which assembles the principal contemporary Swiss painters. Took part in numerous exhibitions in Switzerland, Italy, Paris, South America, etc. Lives in Zurich. Swathes of paint in combined transparent planes.

LEVÉE John H. (b. Los Angeles, 1924). Studied at the Art Center School, New York, then at the Académie Julian, Paris. Took part in the Salon de Mai from 1954 on. Travelling exhibition in Germany: 'Amerikanische Künstler in Frankreich'. Exhibited at the Stedelijk Museum, Amsterdam 1955, with the American painters Alcopley, Chelimsky, Fontaine, and Parker. One-man show at Gimpel's, London, in 1955. Took part in a group-show, Galerie de France, Paris 1956. Lives in Paris. After passing through a period of black and heavy graphism somewhat like Soulages, Levée found a more personal style, a brilliantly improvised painting of dull colours, which yet retains the same wilful emphasis.

LEWIS Norman (b. New York, 1909). Self-educated in art matters. Began painting in 1935. Exhibited at the Willard Gallery, New York, and took part in the 'Abstract Painting and Sculpture in America' show at the Museum of Modern Art, New York 1951, as well as in 'Le Dessin aux États-Unis' at the Museum of Modern Art, Paris 1954. Delicate compositions which seem as frail as mesh or lace.

LEWY Kurt (b. Essen, Germany, 1898). Studied at the Volkswangschule in Essen and the Staatliche Hochschule für Bildende Künste, Berlin (1919-1923). In 1924, apprentice in enamel-work in Pforzheim (Bade). Then worked in Essen (painting, enamel, graphic arts), where he taught at the Volkswangschule until 1933. In 1935, settled in Belgium. Naturalized Belgian citizen in 1951. A number of exhibitions of abstract paintings and enamels in Germany, England, Italy, notably at the Volkwang-Museum, Essen 1925, at Brussels 1952, and at Ghent 1955. Long matured geometrical fantasies suggesting nobility and inner calm. Lives in Brussels.

209

VAN LINT. WHITE AND BLUE. 1955.

LHOTELIER Henry (b. Calais, 1908). Received a classical education. Attended at the same time classes of painting at the School of Decorative and Industrial Arts in Calais. Took a degree in Law at the University of Lille. Abandoned a legal career in 1935 in order to devote himself to the study of stained glass at Boulogne-sur-Mer. Composed (1938) twenty four small abstract stained glass windows for the Pavillon de l'Artois at the exhibition of Social Progress in Lille-Roubaix, and (1951) nineteen abstract stained glass windows for the Little Seminary of Boulogne-sur-Mer. The following year, he constructed a 130-foot-square abstract in stained glass as a partition in an apartment house in Hardelot (Pas-de-Calais). Takes part regularly in the Salon des Réalités Nouvelles. Lives in Boulogne-sur-Mer. "The multiplicity of appearances disguises the void, but completeness of perfection dwells in stark simplicity". (Lhotellier).

LINT Louis van (b. Brussels, 1909, of a Flemish father and a French mother). Attended the Academy of Saint-Josse-ten-Noode (1924-1937). In 1939, founded the *la Route libre* club with Anne Bonnet and Gaston Bertrand. First one-man show at the Palais des Beaux-Arts, Brussels, 1941. One of the leading members of the 'Jeune Peinture' Belgian group, founded in 1945. Designed the sets for *L'Histoire du Soldat* (Stravinsky) and took part in numerous exhibitions in Belgium, Holland, Switzerland, Italy as well as in the United States and in Paris. Abstract works since 1951. Has been a long time under the influence of Bazaine. Lives in Brussels. — *Bibl*. Sosset: *Van Lint*, De Sikkel (Antwerp 1953).

LISSITZKY Eliezer (El) Markovitch (b. in the district of Smolensk, Russia, 1890; d. Moscow, 1941). Studied engineering in Darmstadt, 1909-1914. Then returned to Russia. Joined the constructivist movement of Rodchenko and Tatlin in 1919, and began, the same year, the famous series of drawings for which he invented the name *Proun*. Was a professor in Moscow, 1921. The hostility of the Russian government towards modern art forced him to leave for Berlin, where he contributed to various reviews with van Doesburg and Moholy-Nagy. In Switzerland from 1923 to 1925. There, he organized the 'ABC' group and partly directed its periodical. In 1925, published with Arp *The Isms of Art*. From 1925 to 1928, was in Hanover as the guest of the Kestnergesellschaft. It was then he composed the interior decoration of the famous abstract room in the Landesmuseum, later destroyed by

210

the Nazis. After a short stay in Berlin, 1928, he returned to Moscow, where he specialized mainly in visual education. — *Bibl.* Kallai: *El Lissitzky,* Jahrbuch der jungen Kunst (Leipzig 1924); Barr: *Cubism and Abstract Art* (New York 1936); Dorner: *Art of this Century* (New York 1942); *The way beyond art* (New York 1947); *Collection of the Société Anonyme* (New Haven, 1950).

LOHSE Richard Paul (b. Zurich, 1902). Educated in Zurich. Travelled in Italy, France, Germany. Took part in many exhibitions in Switzerland from 1936 on. A member of the 'Die Allianz' society. Lives in Zurich. Rhythmical studies in vertical and horizontal lines, very exactly traced, in the neo-plastic tradition.

LOLO Dolorès Soldevilla (b. Pinar del Rio, 1911). First devoted herself to trade-unions activities. Then began to paint and sculpt. Exhibited at the Salon d'Automne and at the Indépendants, in Paris. Travelled and studied in Italy, Spain, Belgium, England, Switzerland, Czechoslovakia. One-man shows of paintings, objects, and collages at the Galerie Arnaud (1945) and the Galerie La Roue, Paris 1955. As the Cultural delegate of the Cuban Republic in Europe, she organized an exhibition of contemporary Cuban painting at the Museum of Modern Art, Paris, 1951, and an exhibition of Parisian abstraction in Havana, 1956. Collages and paintings starting from very simple elements and recalling the work of Sophie Taeuber or the suprematism of Malevitch.

LOMBARD Jean (b. Dijon, France, 1895). Attended the École des Beaux-Arts in Lyons and Paris. Impatient with academic teaching, he left to work on his own. Exhibited in the various major Salons from 1922 on. After 1943, he abandoned working from the model; his desire to give the plastic full play slowly brought him to abstraction. The director, since 1942, of an Academy of Painting the students and alumni of which form the "Vert-Bois" group. Lombard's canvases are scholarly transcriptions of landscapes into pure painting. The initial subject is entirely sacrificed to the composition and the lyricism. Lives in Paris.

LONGOBARDI Xavier (b. Algiers, 1923). A volunteer in the war (1942-1945). Studied literature and philosophy in Paris and took a degree in classics. Studied in various Academies. One-man shows Galerie de Beaune, Paris 1953, and Galerie Arnaud, Paris 1954 and 1955. Composed representational tapestries (commissioned by the Government). Abs-

LOMBARD. PAINTING. 1954. *Adam-Teissier Collection, Paris*

211

tract collages and paintings: an exceptional density of overlapping forms and colours. Lives in Paris.

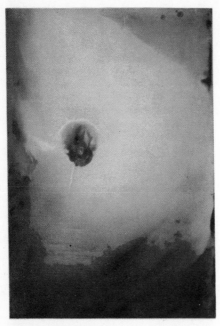

LOUBCHANSKY. GRAIN OF AMBER. 1955.
Galerie Kléber, Paris.

LOPUSZNIAK (b. Tarnopol, Poland, 1904). Studied at the Fine Arts School in Cracow. Exhibited in Cracow and Warsaw since 1930. In Paris, 1938. Was first influenced by Bonnard, then by surrealism. Came to abstraction in 1946. One-man shows: Galerie Arnaud and Galerie Colette Allendy, Paris. Lives in Paris and in Southern France (La Turbie) where he has built his own house. Painting with large rectilinear and geometrical forms.

LOUBCHANSKY Marcelle (b. Paris, 1917). Began to paint after the Liberation of Paris (1944). Took part in various group-shows, particularly 'Younger European Painters', New York 1954. One-man shows at the Galerie de Beaune, Paris 1950, and the Galerie Kléber, Paris 1956. After a painting characterized by melting and viscous forms, rather melancholy in effect, she tackled the problem of colour, showing a predilection for bright red. She has recently launched into multicoloured cosmogony, and joined, on a larger scale, the studies of Malespine.

M

MACDONALD-WRIGHT Stanton (b. Charlottesville, Virginia, 1890). Of Dutch origin: his real name was van Vranken. In Paris, 1907. Attended the Academy of Fine Arts, the Académie Julian, and the Sorbonne. Met Morgan Russel in 1912, and founded with him the *synchromist* movement, akin to Delaunay's *orphism*. Exhibited at the Salon des Indépendants the following year. Synchromist exhibitions in Munich and in Paris (Galerie Bernheim Jeune, 1913). Took part in the 'Armory' show, New York. Returned to the United States in 1916. One-man show at the Stieglitz Gallery 291, in 1917. About 1919, he came back to representational painting. Travelled in Japan in 1937, and spent some time there in 1952-1953. Restrospective exhibition, together with Morgan Russel and Bruce, at the Rose Fried Gallery, New York 1950. Reverted to abstraction in 1954. Important retrospective exhibition in Los Angeles (County Museum), 1956. Lives in Santa Monica (Calif.) The recent works of Macdonald-Wright show a lyricism which is both brilliant and refined. — *Bibl.* W. H. Wright: *Modern Painting, its tendency and meaning* (New York 1915); Seuphor: *L'Art abstrait, ses origines, ses premiers maîtres* (Paris 1949); Ritchie: *Abstract Painting and Sculpture in America* (New York 1951); Catalogue of the Los Angeles Exhibition, 1956.

MACKE August (b. Meschede, Ruhr, 1887; d. Perthes, France, 1914). Studied in Cologne, Bonn, Dusseldorf. Travelled in Italy, Holland, Belgium, France, etc. In 1910, met Franz Marc, then Kandinsky and Jawlensky. Took part in the 'Blaue Reiter' group. In 1912, travelled to Paris with Franz Marc. They met Delaunay and Le Fauconnier. In April 1914, travelled to Tunis with Moilliet and Paul Klee. Drafted in 1914, he was killed on the front. Only a few of Macke's works can be considered abstract. He died too early to have found his own style. Letters to Franz Marc, as yet unpublished, indicate violent reaction against some of Kandinsky's abstractions. — *Bibl.* Seuphor: *L'Art Abstrait, ses origines, ses premiers maîtres* (Paris 1949).

MACDONALD-WRIGHT. TASK OF SISYPHUS. SLEEP IV. 1955.

213

MAC NEIL George (b. New York, 1909). Studied at the Art Students League, then under Hans Hofmann. Exhibited with the 'American Abstract Artists' group from 1937 on. Took part in the 'Abstract Painting and Sculpture in America' show, Museum of Modern Art, New York, 1951. Lives in New York.

MACRIS Constantin G. (b. Cairo, 1919, of Greek parents). Studied academic painting under an instructor who belonged to the Munich School. Exhibited regularly in Cairo. Was drafted in the Greek air force during the war. In Paris, 1948. Studied drawing in Léger's studio. Then worked on his own. His paintings, large abstract works the surfaces of which are covered with closely placed smears of paint, give the impression of walls, and show a definite affinity with the chequered compositions of Mondrian. Lives in Paris.

MAGNELLI. COMPOSITION. 1944.
Jucker Collection, Milan.

MAGNELLI Alberto (b. Florence, 1888). Self-educated in matters of art. Travelled many times to Paris. Frequented the futurists, in 1913, without, however, taking part in their movement. Another trip to Paris, 1914. Met Apollinaire, Max Jacob, Picasso, Léger, Gris. Representational compositions in swathes. Returned to Italy at the time of the declaration of war. In 1915, while in Florence, painted a series of abstract canvases in bright and effective colours. Reverted then to representational painting, for a period of almost twenty years. Returned to Paris in 1933, painted compositions he called *pierres éclatées* (shattered rocks), and soon was drawn back to abstraction. Numerous one-man and group-shows. Took part in the main Abstract Salons in Paris. Important one-man shows : Paris, Galerie Drouin, 1947; Brussels, Palais des Beaux-Arts, 1954; Eindhoven, Van Abbe Museum, 1954; Museum of Antibes, 1955. Lives in Paris.

"It is very easy to draw parallel or curved lines, or to draw visual or imaginary forms. But it is difficult to make them glow with fire, to make them expressive." (Magnelli). "In the years of unreal darkness 1941-1942, the reality of beauty was the sole consolation of our small group in Grasse. Sonia Delaunay, Sophie Taeuber, Susi Magnelli, Alberto Magnelli and myself were part of that group. During these years, Magnelli was rich in ideas which he now carries through with mastery. This careful work links him to the popular art of the great periods. The black, brown, blue, of Magnelli's paintings recall the colours in frescoes of the first Cretan periods. His works could well balance these august and serene decorations. They are natural ornaments, neither blatant nor exceptional." (Arp). — *Bibl.* Arp: *Magnelli*, 'Galerie Drouin' (Paris 1947); Seuphor: *L'Art abstrait, ses origines, ses premiers maîtres* (Paris 1949); *XXe Siècle*, no 1 (Paris 1951); *Témoignages pour l'Art abstrait* (Paris 1952); *A Dictionary of Modern Painting* (Methuen, London 1956).

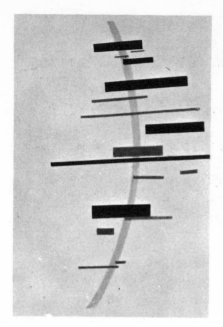

CASIMIR MALEVITCH.
SUPREMATIST COMPOSITION. 1916.

MALDONADO Tomas (b. Buenos Aires, 1922). Academy of Fine Arts in 1938. A member and founder of the 'Arte Concreto' group. Met Max Bill and Vantongerloo. First abstract paintings in 1944. Travelled to Europe in 1948. Editor of the review *Nueva Vision* (Buenos Aires). In 1955, a professor at the Hochschule für Gestaltung (Ulm, Germany). Lives in Ulm.

MALESPINE Émile (b. Lyons, 1892; d. Paris, 1952). From 1922 to 1928, published the avant-garde review *Manomètre* in Lyons. Took a degree in Science and qualified as an M.D. In 1925, founded the 'Donjon' theatrical company; has written number of plays. In Paris, 1929. In 1944, discovered a new style of abstract painting on paper. He then exhibited in the main Abstract Salons in Paris and in a number of galleries.

Malespine's plastic work is very spectacular: a fusion of worlds, a turmoil of virgin matter, a seething of potentialities. Cloud-gardens where fancy can fashion what it will. One penetrates to the heart of whirl-winds, one assists at the birth of elements. Nothing human yet, but suggestions, vague presentiments of emotion everywhere in the air. — *Bibl*. Malespine: *Peinture intégrale*, 'Cahiers d'Art' (Paris 1947).

MALEVITCH Casimir (b. Kiev, 1878; d. Leningrad, 1935). At first influenced by the impressionists and the fauves. A member of the 'Jack of Diamonds' group in Moscow, 1911. Became the leader of the cubist school in Russia, after a trip to Paris (1912). Exhibited the first elements of suprematism, notably a perfect black square on a white background, in a small art gallery 'La Cible', 1913 (testimony of George Annenkow who was present). Two years later, published his *From Cubism to Suprematism* manifesto in Moscow. A professor at the Fine Arts School in Moscow, 1919, in Leningrad after 1921. Took part in an exhibition of Russian art in Berlin, 1922. Was granted the permission to go to Germany, 1926, to prepare the publication of his book *Die gegenstandslose Welt* (The world without objects). Then returned to Russia, leaving about sixty of his works to a friend who still has them today (Feb. 1956). He died completely destitute. He asked his friends to bury him with arms extended in the form of a cross. According to dependable witnesses, Malevitch must have been imprisoned after he came back from Germany, but released when his health began to fail.

Malevitch's suprematism originated in futurist and cubist influences, both of which worked powerfully on the young Russian artists of the time (the dynamic Marinetti had made a momentous lecture-tour in Russia). One knows, on the other hand, that the great collectors Stchoukine and Morosov introduced the cubist works of Braque and Picasso in Moscow, before the paint was dry on the canvases. Whatever the reasons, however, no one had proposed as radical a solution as Malevitch did with his suprematism, in 1913: works composed solely with squares, circles, triangles, and

MANESSIER. THORNS. 1955. *Galerie de France, Paris.*

crosses. Later on, he introduced other simple elements, zigzags and ovals. But presently he returned to straight lines and in 1919 painted his double white square on a white background (now at the Museum of Modern Art, New York). After 1921, when the Moscow government relegated Malevitch to Leningrad, he finished up by making applied art, exactly like his colleagues Rodchenko and Tatlin. But the compositions he painted on delf cups and beakers remain perfectly recognizable suprematist works. — *Bibl.* Barr: *Cubism and Abstract Art* (New York 1936); *Circle, international Survey of Constructive Art* (London 1937); *Art of this Century* (New York 1942); Janis: *Abstract and Surrealist Art in America* (New York 1944); Biederman: *Art as the Evolution of visual Knowledge* (Red Wing 1948); Moholy-Nagy: *Vision in Motion* (Chicago 1947); Seuphor: *L'art abstrait, ses origines, ses premiers maîtres* (Paris 1949); *Collection of the Société Anonyme* (New Haven 1950); 'Art d'Aujourd'hui' (Paris, June 1952); Barr, *Masters of Modern Art* (New York 1954); *A Dictionary of Modern Painting* (Methuen, London 1956); Seuphor: *Au temps de l'avant-garde,* 'L'Œil'

(Paris, Nov. 1955); Brion: *Art Abstrait* (Paris 1956).

MALINA Frank Joseph (b. Brenham, Texas, 1912). Studied mechanics and technology in Texas and in California (1934-1940). Carried on research work in interplanetary fuses and rockets. A professor at the Institute of Technology, Pasadena (Calif.). Composes paintings on trellis work with effects of transparency, and paintings of transformations with the aid of interior lighting. One-man shows Galerie Arnaud (1954) and Galerie Colette Allendy (1955). Took part in the Salon des Réalités Nouvelles. Lives in Paris.

MANESSIER Alfred (b. Saint-Ouen, Somme, 1911). Attended the lycée and the School of Fine Arts at Amiens. In Paris, 1931. Studied architecture at the École des Beaux-Arts. Attended at the same time classes at the Louvre and at various Academies of Montparnasse. Met Bissière at the Académie Ranson in

1935. A group was then formed around Bissière, with the painters Le Moal and Bertholle and the sculptor Martin. Numerous one-man and group-shows from 1937 on. Took part in the Salons from 1933 on. Since 1945, has been included in many exhibitions of young French painters abroad. Composed cartoons of abstract stained glass windows for a number of churches, including Bréseux (Jura), Saint-Pierre de Trinquetaille (Arles), the Chapel of Hem (near Roubaix) and the Church of All Souls (Basel). Manessier lives in Paris.

Some critics question the purely abstract quality of Mannessier's works, because the young artist gave his paintings such titles as *La Couronne d'Épines, Portement de la Croix,* which, they contend, confer a superfluous literary connotation. One should nevertheless realise that the mystical atmosphere which permeates Manessier's work expresses itself mainly in completely abstract plastic terms. No artist has done more, by the simple eloquence of his work, to introduce abstract art to large ecclesiastical circles. "Non-representational art", writes Manessier, "seems to me to give the modern painter the best chance of reaching his personal reality,

of becoming aware again of what is essential in him. Only by starting from an understanding of this point can an artist eventually regain balance and revitalize even the exterior reality of the world. If man is indeed a hierarchy of values, then his outward appearance is merely a transparent envelope, if void of spiritual content." Manessier has published many coloured lithographs. — *Bibl.* Bourniquel: *Trois Peintres (Le Moal, Manessier, Singier),* Drouin (Paris 1946); Dorival: *Alfred Manessier, artisan religieux,* 'L'Œil' (Paris, Oct. 1955); Howe: *Alfred Manessier,* 'Apollo' (London, June 1957).

MANSOUROV Paul (b. Saint-Petersburg, 1896). A friend of Malevitch and Tatlin. Exhibited with them from 1917 on. Lives in Paris since 1929. A study in very simple motifs, usually painted on lengths of plank.

MANTON Maria (b. Blida, Algeria, 1915). Studied at the School of Fine Arts in Algiers. Met Nallard in 1941. In Tunisia from 1943 to 1945. Settled in Paris 1947. Took part regularly in the Salon des Réalités Nouvelles from 1947 on. Oneman shows Galerie Lydia Conti, Galerie des Deux-Iles, Galerie Colette Allendy and Galerie Arnaud, Paris. Took part in exhibitions in Italy, Germany, Switzerland, Belgium, and New York. Travelled in Italy and Yugoslavia in 1952. Lives in Paris. A painting often monochromatic and restrained in effect. Perfect poise in the

MARIA MANTON. COMPOSITION. 1954.

EVELYN MARC. INK DRAWING. 1955.

1910. They organised the 'Blaue Reiter' exhibitions together and published the famous 'Blaue Reiter' almanac. Third trip to Paris with Macke in 1912. Met Delaunay who greatly influenced him. Abstract works in 1913. Drafted in 1914, he was killed in front of Verdun, in 1916, leaving behind letters and a famous album of abstract sketches.

composition: simplicity and clarity. A rigor that is never hard.

MARC Evelyn (b. Angers, France, 1915). Her parents, Willy Eisenschitz and Claire Bertrand are both painters and disciples of Cézanne and Van Gogh. She spent a year in an American University (1935-6) and then attended a few Paris Academies. Dazzled by her first contact with abstract painting and surrealism. "There is a deep separation between what really impresses me and what I can learn in the schools." Exhibited many times, in Marseilles and in Paris, together with her parents who remained attached to figurative art. Took part in the Salon des Réalités Nouvelles. Blurred, melting colours and forms, sometimes fervent in feeling.

MARC Franz (b. Munich, 1880; d. Verdun, 1916). Was the son of the painter Wilhelm Marc. Studied at the University of Munich and then at the Academy of Munich. Came to Paris in 1903, travelled in Greece, 1906. Second trip to Paris in 1907. Made friends with Kandinsky in

Marc played a very important role in the compilation of the famous 'Blaue Reiter' almanac. The idea came from Kandinsky, but Marc found the publisher and helped Kandinsky along during the whole enterprise, both with the exhibitions and the publications. All Marc's force of conviction expresses itself in the words: "Traditions are beautiful, but only when one creates them, not when one lives on them." Through the representation of animals in natural life, Marc developed a style which slowly withdrew him from the object, until he attained pure abstraction in a few works painted in 1913 and 1914. (*Formes en lutte, Formes cassées, Petites compositions,* etc...) Retrospective exhibitions of Franz Marc's work have taken place in Germany, Holland, Belgium, and Switzerland. — *Bibl.* Dreier: *Modern Art* (New York 1926); Barr: *Cubism and Abstract Art* (New York 1936); Seuphor: *L'Art abstrait, ses origines, ses premiers maîtres* (Paris 1949); *Collection of the Société Anonyme* (New Haven, 1950); *Catalogue of the retrospective exhibition 'Der Blaue Reiter'* (Munich 1949); *Catalogue of the Franz Marc exhibition* (Munich 1950); Raynal: *De Picasso au Surréalisme* (Paris and Geneva 1950); *A Dictionary of Modern Painting* (Methuen, London 1956).

218

MARCUS Gert (b. Hamburg, 1914). A painter and a worker in mosaic. Exhibited a series of works called *la Croix d'espace* at the Franco-Swedish gallery, in Stockholm (1952) and contributed geometrical compositions to a group-show at the Norrköping Museum, Sweden, 1956. One-man exhibition at the Galerie Colette Allendy, Paris 1956. Lives in Stockholm.

MARELLI Giulio (b. Velletri, Italy, 1907). Took a diploma at the J. Romani Art School (1928). Took part, as a sculptor, in various exhibitions in Italy and elsewhere. From 1947 on, devoted himself completely to abstract painting. Included in the 'Arte astratta e concreta in Italia' show, Rome, 1951. Lives in Rome.

MARGO Boris (b. in Russia, 1902). Studied at the Analytical Art Institute in Leningrad, under Filonov. In the United States, 1930. Many exhibitions in America from 1939 on, particularly at the Betty Parsons Gallery, New York. Lives in New York. Abstract paintings reminiscent of surrealism; one recognizes also the characteristic forms of Max Ernst and Tanguy. But these forms are achieved through the projection of 'cellocut' against the surface of the canvas, a technique akin to that of Dubuffet's works in plastic. — *Bibl.* Janis: *Abstract and Surrealist Art in America* (New York 1944); *Catalogue of the Boris Margo exhibition,* Betty Parsons Gallery (New York 1955).

MARLE Felix del (b. Pont-sur-Sambre, France, 1889; d. Paris, 1952). Studied painting in Brussels and in Paris. Friendship with Kupka in 1920 and with Mondrian in 1925. For a short time, took over the plastic direction of the review *Vouloir,* in Lille. Painted in the futurist and in the neo-plastic manners. Reverted to realism for a few years. After the Liberation, the emphasis in his compositions was on architecture and colour in space. General Secretary of the Salon des Réalités Nouvelles since 1946. One-man show at the Galerie Colette Allendy, 1949. Founded with André Bloc the group 'Espace' (1950).

MARTIN Kenneth (b. Sheffield, England, 1905). Studied at the Royal College of Art, London. Taught painting in a number of London schools. In 1951, published with Victor Pasmore *Broadsheet nº 1* completely devoted to abstract art in England. Organized an exhibition of abstract art at the A.I.G. Gallery, London, with Robert Adams,

FRANZ MARC. ABSTRACT DESIGN. 1914.

Adrian Heath, Anthony Hill and Victor Pasmore. Lives in London. — Bibl. *Nine Abstract Artists* (London 1954).

MASON Alice Trumbull (b. Litchfield, Connecticut, 1904). One-man shows at the Museum of Living Art, New York 1942, and at the Rose Fried Gallery, New York 1948. Included in group-shows in France and in the United States. A member of the "American Abstract Artists" association. Lives in New York.

MATHIEU Georges (b. Boulogne-sur-Mer, 1921). Studied law and philosophy. Took a degree in English literature. Began to paint in 1942. Settled in Paris in 1947. Exhibited at the Salon des Réalités Nouvelles and the Salon des Sur-indépendants. Organized with Bryen and others, various exhibitions of an abstract art claiming to be 'lyric', 'psychic' and 'in a spirit of reaction against abstract formalism'. In close sympathy with the ideals of the American neo-expressionist painters. One-man show at the Galerie Drouin in 1950. Took part in many group-shows. Exhibited at the Kootz Gallery, New York, 1954. Wrote a manifesto addressed to the American avant-garde painters. One-man show at the Galerie Rive-Droite, Paris 1954 and 1956. — Bibl. *Art News* (New York, Feb. 1955).

MAUKE Rudolph (b. Magdeburg-on-the-Elbe, 1924). Studied at the Fine Arts School in Berlin from 1949 on. One-man shows in Berlin 1954 and 1955. Included in the German abstract painting exhibition at the Cercle Volney, Paris, 1955. A great simplicity of planes and lines, soft colours. Lives in Berlin.

MAUSSION Charles (b. Nantes, France, 1923). Settled in Paris, 1946. Studied at the Institute of Art and Archaeology. Attended the studio of Lhote, and then of Léger. Abstract painting since 1949. Worked at the Dewasne-Pillet academy the same year. Included in the

MATHIEU. CAPETAN ENTELECHY. 1954.
D. H. Clark Collection, New York.

220

Salon des Réalités Nouvelles in 1951, 1952, and 1953. One-man show at the Galerie Arnaud in 1952. Lives in Paris. Supple geometrical abstraction; very precise stains and lines on a white background, combined like a piece of music consisting of clear rhythms.

MENDELSON. RECITATIVE. 1954. *A. Niels Collection, Brussels.*

MEERBERGEN Rudolf (b. Antwerp, 1908). Studied at the Fine Arts School in Antwerp (1926-1930). Stayed in Paris and in the South of France, 1932. Then visited Germany, Holland, Spain, and Italy. Many one-man shows in Belgium. Launched into abstraction in 1951. Sober compositions with large and stripped forms. Lives in Antwerp.

MEISTERMANN Georg (b. Solingen, Germany, 1911). Studied at the Academy of Dusseldorf. Devoted himself for a few years to painting on glass. Reverted to free-style painting after 1943 and came progressively to abstraction. Many exhibitions in Europe, India, New Zealand, Japan, America. A professor at the School of Fine Arts in Frankfurt since 1953. Included in the German abstract painting exhibition at the Cercle Volney, Paris 1955. Lives in Frankfurt-am-Main.

MELE Juan N. (b. Buenos Aires, 1923). Attended the Fine Arts Academy in Buenos Aires. Tackled abstract art in 1945, and the following year, exhibited with the 'Arte Concreto' group. Travelled to Europe 1948-1949. In Paris, met Vantongerloo, Pevsner, Domela, Herbin, Seuphor. Made the acquaintance of Max Bill and of the Italian abstract painters. When he returned to the Argentine, figurative compositions reappeared in his work. But he reverted to pure abstraction in 1952. Retrospective exhibition of his works at the Meeba gallery, Buenos Aires, 1952. Lives in Buenos Aires.

MENDELSON Marc (b. London, 1915 of an English mother and a Belgian father). The founder of the Belgian group 'Jeune Peinture Belge'. Numerous exhibitions in Belgium and other countries. Composed large abstract decorations for a restaurant in Brussels and for the Kursaal in Ostend. One-man show at the Palais des Beaux-Arts, Brussels 1955. Took part in the Venice Biennale with about ten canvases (1956). Each year Mendelson spends a few months in Palamos (Spain), where he has a studio, but generally lives in Brussels. — *Bibl.* Séaux: *Marc Mendelson* (Antwerp 1954).

MILO. SIKU ZOTE III. 1954.
Van Geluwe Collection, Brussels.

and North Africa. One-man show of collages and small pictures at the Galerie du Haut Pavé, Paris, 1956. Lives in Paris. Michel's collages are in the best tradition of Klee and Schwitters. They are held to be among the most refined in this genre.

MILO Jean (Émile van Gindertael) b. Brussels, 1906. Attended the Academy of Fine Arts in Brussels. Spent some time with the Etikhove group of Flemish painters, who took their name from the village they settled in. Travelled to Paris, London, Holland, and the Belgian Congo. A member of the 'Jeune Peinture Belge' group. Changed over to abstraction in 1950. Included in the Salon des Réalités Nouvelles in 1952. Numerous one-man shows in Paris and Brussels. He is the brother of the Parisian critic R. van Gindertael. Lives in Brussels. — *Bibl.* R. V. Gindertael: *Jean Milo,* Éditions 'Signe' (Paris 1953); Luc Haesaerts: *Jean Milo,* De Sikkel (Antwerp 1954).

MESSAGIER Jean (b. Paris, 1920). Attended the National School of Decorative Arts in Paris, 1942. Included in the Salon d'Automne since 1947 and the Salon de Mai since 1948. Took part in a number of group-shows in Paris and in the main European countries. Travelled and studied in Algeria (1946) and in Italy (1948). His plastic works have affinities with those of the American painter Rothko. Lives in Paris. "Starting from nature, to re-group the various emotions, preserving all the while the utmost detachment. To waste none of the energy of a rage or passion. To pinpoint the great rhythms and then marshall them." (Messagier).

MICHEL (Michel Wulff) (b. Stettin, Germany, 1924). Studied typography at the School of Fine Arts in Hamburg (1946-1949) and worked for some time as a sub-editor in a printing-press. Came to Paris 1951. Took part a number of times in the Salon des Réalités Nouvelles and in other group-shows. Travelled throughout Europe as well as Asia Minor

MIOTTE Jean (b. Paris 1926). Studied in the non-institutional studios of Montparnasse. First abstract canvases in 1948. Travelled in Italy, Spain, England, and Algeria. Took part in the Salon des Réalités Nouvelles from 1953 on. Compositions high in colour and well articulated in design: they hang extraordinarily well.

MITCHELL Fred (b. Meridan, United States, 1923). Studied at the Carnegie Institute of Technology (1942-

1943) and the Cranbrook Academy of Art (1946-1948). Completed his studies in various schools in Rome (1948-1950). Taught in a number of colleges and academies, contributed to *Pictures on Exhibit,* exhibited in Pittsburgh, Rome, Minneapolis and New York (Tanager Gallery, Stable Gallery, Solomon R. Guggenheim Museum). Teaches at the Cranbrook Academy (Michigan).

MITCHELL Joan (b. Chicago, 1926). Studied at the Art Institute in Chicago. Was in France 1948-1949, then in New York where she had a number of one-man shows (New Gallery 1953; Stable Gallery 1953 and 1955). Returned to Paris in 1955. Friendship with Riopelle. Abstract-expressionist painting, roughly similar to that of Tworkow and Esteban Vicente.

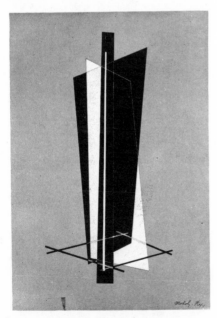

MOHOLY-NAGY. CONSTRUCTION. 1922-1923. *Jeanne Coppel Collection, Paris.*

MOHOLY-NAGY Lazslo (b. Bacsbarsod, Hungary, 1895; d. Chicago, 1946), Studied law in Budapest. Was wounded in the First World War: during his convalescence, began to draw portraits. When the war was over, was attracted by Russian avant-garde art. In 1922, published *Buch Neuer Künstler,* the first anthology of world avant-garde art, with the Hungarian poet Kassak, in Vienna. From 1920 on, his work was completely abstract. Met Walter Gropius who appointed him a professor at the Bauhaus: from 1922 to 1928, he played an important role in the publications of the school as well as in its research work in new materials to be used in the applied arts. In Amsterdam, 1934. In London, 1935: he published a few books of documentary photographs and started on the paintings-sculptures he called *space modulators.* Was in the United States, 1937. When the new Chicago Bauhaus, of which he had become the director, had to fold up for financial reasons, he founded his own school (School of Design) which proved very successful. Published *The New Vision* in New York, 1946. There have been a number of retrospective exhibitions of his works in America. One of his books was published posthumously: *Vision in Motion,* Chicago 1947. His wife wrote a number of essays about him as well as a biography. — *Bibl.* Barr: *Cubism and Abstract Art* (New York, 1936); S. Giedion: *L. Moholy-Nagy* (Zurich 1937); Hitchcock: *Painting towards Architecture* (New York 1948); *Collection of the Société Anonyme* (New Haven 1947); 'Art d'Aujourd'hui' (Paris, Oct. 1951); *A Dictionary of Modern Painting* (Methuen, London 1956).

MOISSET Raymond (b. Paris, 1906). Attended the school of Applied Arts. Devoted himself to painting from 1954 on. Took part in the Salon de Mai every year since its creation (1945). One-man show at the Galerie Simone Heller,

Paris, 1956. Came to pure abstraction slowly, taking his departure always in a landscape theme. Lives in Paris.

MONDRIAN Piet (b. Amersfoort, 1872; d. New York, 1944.) Since his father wanted him to be a teacher, he obtained the two degrees needed to teach design in state schools. Entered the Academy of Amsterdam in 1892, and attended all its classes very regularly. Painted in the open air around Amsterdam. In order to make a living, gave drawing lessons, copied paintings in the museums, worked as an industrial designer. Friendship with the Dutch painter Jan Sluyters, then with Simon Maris whom he accompanied on a short trip to Spain (1901). Painted a whole year in the Dutch Brabant (1903-1904). Became a member of the main painters' associations in Amsterdam. In 1908, first stay in Domburg (Zeeland) where he met the painter Toorop, then very famous and the leader of an important group of painters. In Zeeland, painted in the divisionist manner, as a fauve, and as a disciple of Van Gogh, all in turn. In 1911, became a member of the Directing Committee of the Modern Art Club in Amsterdam: the club organized a number of important exhibitions, showing for the first time in Holland fauve and cubist painters. Was in Paris, 1912 to 1914. Exhibited at the Salon des Indépendants works influenced by cubism and yet almost completely abstract. Came to abstraction through an embellishment of his favourite themes: a tree, scaffoldings, the wall of a cathedral. First complete abstract paintings in 1913. Was on a visit to Holland when the war broke out: he remained there until 1919, kept on working, and after having met Van Doesburg, contributed to the creation of the 'De Stijl' movement. From 1917 to 1924, was one of the principal collaborators to its review. Returned to Paris and published *le Néo-Plasticisme,* a summary of his doctrine, at the Galerie de l'Effort

Moderne, 1920. During the following years, contributed a variety of articles to many Paris avant-garde reviews, while, in Germany, the Bauhaus published *Neue Gestaltung* (1925). Took part in many large international exhibitions of abstract art in Paris and in America. A member of the 'Cercle et Carré', then of the 'Abstraction-Création' groups. In London, 1938-1940. The bombings of London made him leave for New York. One-man show at the Valentine Gallery, New York 1942. His last exhibition, together with the Brazilian sculptor Maria Martins, was held at the same gallery in 1943.

The purely neo-plastic work of Mondrian is a kind of metaphysics of painting. One must approach it as one approaches icons which seek to express an immutable truth: that truth which, for the artist, is embodied in the dualism of horizontal and vertical, and glides towards us on black rails. These stark works, especially the square canvases of the 1929-1932 period, demand intellectual rather than visual contemplation. Later on, after the experience of New York, an unexpected lyricism pierces through the work (the *Boogie-Woogie* series). The rails fly up in splinters, black is banished as the last vestige of the 'tragic', a touch of exhilaration appears without, however, banishing the neo-plastic. Thus, a new abundance of inspiration is heralded (the *Victory Boogie-Woogie* remains unfinished), when death surprises the painter.

Retrospective exhibitions of his works were held at the Museum of Modern Art, New York (1945), at the Stedelijk Museum, Amsterdam (1946), the Kunsthalle, Bern (1947), the Municipal Museum, The Hague (1955), the Kunsthaus, Zurich (1955), the Whitechapel Gallery, London (1955), the Venice Biennale (1956) as well as in Rome and Milan (1956). — *Bibl.* Dreier: *Modern Art* (New York 1926); Barr: *Cubism and Abstract Art* (New York 1936); *Art of this Century* (New York 1942); Sweeney: *Mondrian* (New York 1948); *Catalogue of the* retrospective exhibition in Amsterdam (1946); Seuphor: *L'art abstrait, ses origines, ses premiers maîtres* (Paris 1949); Hitchcock: *Painting towards Architecture* (New York 1948); *Collection of the Société Anonyme* (New Haven 1950); 'Art d'Aujourd'hui' (Paris, Dec. 1949); *Catalogue of the Mondrian exhibition,* Sidney Janis Gallery (New York 1951); *Retrospective exhibition of the 'Stijl'* (Amsterdam 1951); *Magazine of Art* (New York, May 1952); Raynal: *From Picasso to Surrealism* (Paris-Geneva 1950); 'Art d'Aujourd'hui' (Paris, Feb. 1954); *A Dictionary of Modern Painting* (Methuen, London 1956); *XXᵉ Siècle*, nᵒ 4 (Paris 1954); Zevi: *Poetica dell'architettura neoplastica* (Milan 1953); *Catalogue of the retrospective exhibition in The Hague* (1955); Seuphor: *Humanisme de Mondrian*, 'Aujourd'hui', nᵒ 2 (Paris 1955); Catalogues of the retrospective exhibitions in Zurich and London (1955); Jaffé: *De Stijl, 1917-1931* (Amsterdam 1956); Seuphor:

De Stijl, 'L'Œil' (Paris, Oct. 1956); Seuphor, *Piet Mondrian*, Dumont-Schauberg (Köln), Abrams (New York) and Flammarion (Paris), 1956.

MONNET Gianni (b. Turin, 1912). Cofounder, with Murani and Dorfles, of the 'Movement for Concrete Art', Milan 1949. Included in the 'Arte Astratta e Concreta in Italia' exhibition, Museum of Modern Art, Rome, 1951. Monnet is also an architect and an artcritic. Lives in Milan.

MONNINI Alvaro (b. Florence, 1922). Attended the Fine Arts Academy in Florence. One of the founders of the 'Arte d'Oggi' group. Took part in various exhibitions in Italy and in other countries of Europe and America. Lives in Florence.

MONDRIAN. COMPOSITION NO. 7. 1913.
Guggenheim Museum, New York.

MONTE M. G. dal (b. Italy, 1907). Was in Berlin, 1931. Contributed to the *Der Sturm* review. Then pursued his plastic researches in Paris, Prague, Geneva. Lives in Italy.

MONTHEILLET Pierre (b. Lyons, 1923). Studied Classics at the University of Lyons. Then devoted himself to painting. Exhibited in various Salons from 1939 on. Took part in all the displays of the 'Jeune Peinture Lyonnaise' group as well as in the Salon des Réalités Nouvelles and the Salon de Mai. Lives in Lyons.

G. L. K. MORRIS. SPACE-RECESSION. 1954.

MORENI Mattia (b. Pavie, 1920). Was educated in Turin. Included in various group-shows in a number of European countries. One-man shows in Turin (1946) and Milan (1947-1949). Lives in Bologna.

MORITA Shiryu (b. in Japan, 1912). Active since 1938 in the movement based on calligraphy considered as a plastic art form. Exhibited at the Institute of Calligraphy Shodo-Geijitsu in 1949. A member of the Bokuzin-Kai School in 1952. Included then in numerous exhibitions of calligraphy in the main Japanese cities, as well as in New York (Museum of Modern Art, 1954) and in Paris (Galerie Colette Allendy, 1955). Director of the *Bo-*

kubi and *Bokuzin* reviews, in which great space is devoted to American and European abstract artists. There are issues given over to Alcopley's drawings, to Bryen, to Tryggvadottir, to Seuphor. Morita is one of the artists who have worked most towards a rapprochement and mutual comprehension between Japanese and occidental artists in the field of abstraction. In his own works, he attempts to achieve significance through black patches, spread widely on the paper, having an interior vibration and a powerful tension of volume. — *Bibl.* 'Art Sacré' issue devoted to Japan (Paris 1954); Seuphor: *la Calligraphie japonaise,* 'Art d'Aujourd'hui' (Paris, Dec. 1954); Alechinsky: *Au delà de l'écriture,* 'Phases', nº 2 (Paris 1955).

MORRIS George L. K. (b. New York, 1906). Studied at Yale. While still in college, began to paint in the academic tradition. First contact with abstract art in Paris, 1930. While studying at Léger's studio, met Arp, Hélion, Mondrian. Round the world tour 1933. Contributed to *Par-*

MORITA. BREAK FOR CONSTANT CREATION. 1954.

226

tisan Review in New York and the review *Plastique* in Paris. President of the 'American Abstract Artists' association until 1951. Numerous one-man and group-shows in New York and Paris. The most recent ones were held at the Downtown Gallery New York. Married to Suzy Frelinghuysen (cf. that name). Took part in the 'Abstract Painting and Sculpture in America' show, Museum of Modern Art, New York 1951. Lecture tour for UNESCO in Europe and Asia Minor, 1952. Lives in New York. — Bibl. *American Abstract Artists* (New York 1946); Ritchie: *Abstract Painting and Sculpture in America* (New York 1951); *What abstract art means to me* (Museum of Modern Art, New York, 1951); 'Art d'Aujourd'hui' (Paris, June 1951).

MORRIS Kyle (b. Des Moines, U.S.A., 1918). Studied at the Art Institute in Chicago (1935-1939). Then taught in a number of universities and colleges in the United States. Exhibited at the Walker Art Center (Minneapolis), the Whitney Museum (New York) and in the 'Younger American Painters' show at the Solomon R. Guggenheim Museum, New York, 1954. Lives in New York.

MORTENSEN Richard (b. Copenhagen, 1910). Worked for two years in an Academy in Copenhagen and then on his own. Contact with Kandinsky's work during a trip in Germany made him forcibly aware of his own approach. First abstract works in 1933. In Paris, 1937. Organised an exhibition of the abstract works of Paris painters in Copenhagen. Returned to Paris, 1947. A member of the Galerie Denise René group, with whom he exhibited regularly. In 1956, he assembled there a group of very large compositions simple in line and vivid in colour, one of which, *Opus Normandie,* was at least twenty-eight foot long. Lives in

Paris. "The power of Mortensen's painting is not immediately apparent, because of its great and perhaps cloaking refinement; refinement of articulation; refinement of spirit; the refinement, even, of restraint. The brilliance of this painting is almost always most vivid, but never brutal. The

MORTENSEN. JARGEAU. 1953.
Dr. Aronovitch Collection, Stockholm.

grasp is steel, not cast-iron" (Léon Degand). — *Bibl.* 'Art d'Aujourd'hui' (Paris, Dec. 1951); *Témoignages pour l'Art Abstrait* (Paris 1952); Catalogue of the Mortensen exhibition, Galerie Denise René (Paris 1956).

MOSER Wilfrid (b. Zurich 1914). Travelled extensively before he settled in Paris, 1945. Painted his first abstract works the same year. Exhibitions: Stockholm: 'Six Young Painters of Paris' (1951); Zurich: 'Dix Artistes de Paris' (1951); Paris, Galerie Jeanne Bucher, together with the painter Nallard (1952). One-man show in Zurich 1953. Lives in Paris.

MOSS Marlow (b. Richmond, Great Britain, 1890). Studied in London and in Paris. She was the first and purest disciple of Mondrian in Paris, about 1925. A member of the 'Abstraction-Création' group. Took part in group-shows in Paris, London, Holland, Switzerland, as well as in the Salon des Réalités Nouvelles. One-man show at the Hanover Gallery, London 1953. Is presently engaged in sculpture. Lives in Penzance (Cornwall).

MOTHERWELL Robert (b. Aberdeen, U.S.A., 1915). Studied in the Philosophy department at Harvard. University of Grenoble in 1938.

MOSER. PAINTING. 1955.
Galerie Jeanne Bucher, Paris.

School of Art and Achaeology at Columbia, New York. Travelled many times to British Columbia (1932, 1934, 1937), France, England (1938-1939) and Mexico (1941, 1943). Self-educated in matters of art; then studied engraving with Kurt Seligmann and S. W. Hayter. Taught at Hunter College, New York, 1951. Eleven one-man shows from 1944 to 1952 in American galleries and museums. At Wittenborn and Co.'s, New York, directed the *Documents of Modern Art* collection. A lecturer and essay-writer. Took part in the 'Abstract Painting and Sculpture in America' show at the Museum of Modern Art, New York, 1951. Numerous exhibitions at the Kootz Gallery, New York. Included in the 'Cinquante ans d'art aux États-Unis' exhibition at the Museum of Modern Art, Paris 1955. "One is to know that art is not national, that to be merely an American or a French artist is to be nothing; to fail to overcome one's initial environment is never to reach the human." — Bibl. *Fourteen Americans* (New York 1946); Ritchie: *Abstract Painting and Sculpture in America* (New York 1951); *What abstract art means to me,* Museum of Modern Art (New York 1951); 'Art d'Aujourd'hui' (Paris, June 1951); Hess: *Abstract Painting* (New York, 1951).

MULLICAN Lee (b. Chickasha, Oklahoma, 1919). Studied at the Oklahoma Art School and the Art Institute in Kansas City. One-man shows in a number of American cities and at the Willard Gallery, New York. Included, in 1951, in the 'Dynaton' exhibition, organized by Wolfgang Paalen at the San Francisco Museum of Art. — Bibl. *Dynaton 1951,* San Francisco Museum of Art; *Art News* (New York, Oct. 1953).

MUNARI Bruno (b. Milan, 1907). Took part in the futurist movement. A painter, an essaywriter and constructor

228

of mobiles. Co-founder of the Milanese 'Arte Concreta' group, 1949. Included in many exhibitions in Italy, especially 'Arte Astratta e Concreta in Italia', at the Museum of Modern Art, Rome, 1951. Lives in Milan.

MURO José Antonio Fernandez (b. Madrid, 1920). Studied art in Buenos Aires. A naturalized Argentine citizen. First one-man show in 1942. Included in 1948 in the exhibition of Latin American Painting organized by the UNESCO in Paris. Abstract painting since 1943. Included in the 'Eight Argentine Abstracts' show at the Municipal Museum, Amsterdam, 1953. Husband of the abstract painter

MOTHERWELL. GRENADE. 1949.
Nelson A. Rockefeller Collection, Washington.

Sarah Grilo. Lives in Buenos Aires. Journey to Paris in 1957.

N

NAKAMURA Bokushi (b. in Japan, 1916). Took part in many exhibitions of abstract calligraphy in Japan and in other countries, particularly at the Museum of Modern Art, New York (1954), the Galerie Colette Allendy, Paris (1955) and the Musée Cernuschi, Paris (1956). Lives in Japan.

NALLARD Louis (b. Algiers, 1918). Educated in Algiers. Began to exhibit in Algiers at an early age. First exhibition of abstract painting in 1945. Settled in Paris, 1947. Travelled in Holland and in Spain. Took part in numerous exhibitions in Paris and abroad. One-man show at the Galerie Jeanne Bucher, Paris,

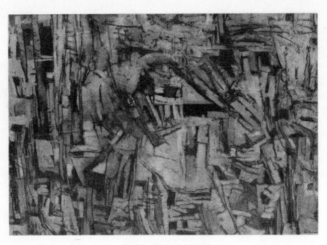

NALLARD. PAINTING. 1955.
Henri Perrenoud Collection, Paris.

1953. Took part regularly in the Salon de Mai. He often exhibited together with his wife, the painter Maria Manton. Lives in Paris. Supple variations of graphism within a restricted gamut of colours, sometimes limited to brown-ochres.

NATIVI Gualtiero (b. Pistoia, 1921). Studied Classics at the University of Florence. Devoted himself to painting at the same time. Was a co-founder of the 'Arte d'oggi' group, and signed the *Manifesto dell'Astrattismo,* Florence 1950. Took part in numerous exhibitions in Italy and in the other European countries. Lives in Florence. Compositions in rectilinear geometrical forms.

NAVARRO Pascal (b. in Venezuela, 1923). Studied painting and engraving at the Fine Arts Academy in Caracas (1938-1944). Was in Paris in 1947. Free-lance studies and travels in Italy, Spain, England, Belgium. Launched into abstraction as a result of the 'Premiers Maîtres de l'Art Abstrait' show at the Galerie Maeght, Paris 1949. Worked in the Abstract Art workshop of Dewasne and Pillet (1950-1952) and took part in the Salon des Réalités Nouvelles. One-man show at the Galerie Arnaud, Paris 1952. Lives in Paris and Caracas.

NAY Ernst Wilhelm (b. Berlin, 1902). Attended the School of Fine Arts in Berlin (1925-1928). Travelled to Paris, 1928. Spent 1931-1932 in Rome. Kept on painting clandestinely under the Nazi regime. Was a student of Carl Hofer (1936-1937). Visited Edward Munch in Norway. Travelled abroad extensively. After having started from expressionism and neo-realism, he slowly progressed towards abstraction, which he attained about 1948. One-man shows in Munich, 1950 and 1952. Took part in numerous exhibitions in Germany and other countries, particularly "Peintures et Sculptures non-figuratives en Allemagne d'Aujourd'hui", at the Cercle Volney, Paris 1955. A member of the German group 'Zent' with whom he exhibited in Munich,

1955. Lives in Cologne. Nay's painting is often ebullient, but never beyond measure. This painter has retained from expressionism a love of vivid colours and striking oppositions. — Bibl. *Das Kunstwerk*, nº 8-9 (Baden-Baden 1950).

NEBEL Otto (b. Berlin, 1892). Studied architecture. Travelled extensively in Europe. After the First World War, he studied painting under Kandinsky. First one-man show in 1921. First abstract paintings in 1924: he called them 'architectures of light'. Contributed to the *Sturm*. Spent some time in Switzerland and in France. After further travels through Europe, he composed an album of caricatures (1931). Lives in Bern. Geometrical fantasies, rectilinear or curved, on a white background. A kind of game in space, reminding one now of Klee, now of Kandinsky. A text or title affixed to the bottom of the canvas, after the manner of Klee, always adds a poetical touch. — *Bibl.* Liebmann: *Der Malerdichter Otto Nebel* (Zurich 1935); *Almanach neuer Kunst in der Schweiz* (Zurich 1940); *Collection of the Société Anonyme* (New Haven 1950); Otto Nebel: *Worte zu Bildern* (Berne 1954).

NEGRI Nina (b. Argentine, 1909). Studied in France, Argentine, England, and Belgium. Travelled many times in Europe, Africa, South America. Took part in the Salon des Indépendants, the Salon des Réalités Nouvelles, and the Salon de Mai. One-man shows at the gallery 'Il Milione' (Milan) and the gallery 'Circle and Square' (New York). Took part in numerous group-shows in Paris. Lives in Paris. An experienced painter and engraver in whose works one can observe a fair proportion of science and mastery. The manner and the message fuse where the strictness of the composition yields to sudden discovery. The psychological intention of such an art is confident self-expression while keeping alert for the secret murmurs one must decode.

NEJAD Mehmed D. (b. Istanbul, 1923). Attended the Academy of Fine Arts in Istanbul, and was a student of the French landscape-painter Léopold-Lévy. Then studied the byzantine mosaics of Saint Sophia, arabic calligraphy, and Islamic abstract art. Was in Paris in 1945. His manner then altered completely. Travelled and studied in the main European countries. Nejad is the son of Princess Fahr-el-Nissa Zeid (cf. that name). One-man shows at the Galerie Lydia Conti (1950), Galerie de Beaune (1951), Studio Facchetti (1953) and

NEBEL. THE SONG OF THE PILOT II. 1951.
Galerie Simone Heller, Paris.

231

Galerie M. C. Coard (1956), Paris. Took also part in the Salon des Réalités Nouvelles and the Salon de Mai, as well as in group-shows. Lives in Paris. "In painting, I throw the whole of the work into question every time I take up my brush. One must break down, destroy, to the point of seeming insane. But that which seems madness is, at the very moment of creation, only the logic of the work of art, expanding into life like a plant, without our aid." (Nejad). In Nejad's works, whether black or coloured, sensibility and a despotic will come into violent conflict, sometimes fusing in a sudden and exceptional euphoria. — Bibl. Boudaille and Lassaigne: Nejad, Coll. 'Artistes de ce temps', Paris 1955.

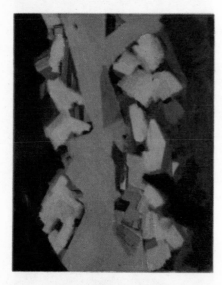

NEJAD. ALTITUDES I. 1955.

NEMOURS Aurélie (b. Paris, 1910). Studied in turn under Paul Colin, André Lhote, and Fernand Léger. Took part in a number of Salons since 1944. Published poems and contributed to the *Mercure de France*. Slowly progressed towards total abstraction and took part in the Salon des Réalités Nouvelles in 1953. One-man shows at the Galerie Colette Allendy (1953), Galerie de Beaune (1954), both in Paris, and in the Galerie Saint-Laurent (Brussels) in 1955. Lives in Paris. Aurélie Nemours' work aspires to a 'primary geometry' which attains the very basis of simplicity, like that of Mondrian, Sophie Taeuber, and Klee. In her charcoal sketches of modulated blacks and greys, this voluntary paucity of rhythm seems, in her own words 'inseminated to the point of tears'.

"Having to face his own vision, each man is eternally Adam; a lifetime gives him ground to walk on, but he must beget himself again and experience the whole trying process through his own flesh. Only then does he become humble and virile. Only then does painting become art, and art consciousness." (Aurélie Nemours).

NESCH Rolf (b. Oberesslingen, Germany, 1893). Studied under Ludwig Kirchner and Edward Munch. Later on developed towards abstraction, using a very personal technique of impression on paper. Took part in many group-shows, particularly at the Petit Palais (1954) and the Cercle Volney (1955), both in Paris. Lives in Aal (Norway).

NEUBERTH Jean (b. Paris, 1915). Was first an aviator and and took part in various aviation meetings as an acrobatic parachutist. Then met the painter Closon who introduced him to painting. Began to take part in exhibitions of abstract art in 1937, while still a military pilot. Then turned toward the theatre. In 1941, he took up again his studies under Closon. A member of a symphony orchestra in 1942. Played the piano in an American night-club, was a nightwatchman and a speaker on the Montpellier radio network. Devoted himself totally to painting

NEMOURS. PASTEL. 1955.
M. S. Collection, Paris.

from 1942 on. Was an organizer, together with Francis Bott and Michel Seuphor, of an exhibition of abstract art at the Museum of Nîmes (1949). Retrospective exhibition of his works held in Montpellier, 1950. Included in the Salon des Réalités Nouvelles. Lives in Montpellier.

NEWMAN Barnett (b. New York, 1905). Studied at the Art Students League. Published South American magazines and taught painting and drawing in various schools. Organised exhibitions of Pre-Columbian and Indian art. Included in numerous exhibitions in the United States. Lives in New York.

NEY Lancelot (b. Budapest, 1900). After secondary school, attended the School of Fine Arts in Budapest. Travelled

in Germany in 1922. Met Kurt Schwitters and Moholy-Nagy. Settled in Paris, 1923. Spent 1928 in the South of France. Became friendly with Michel Seuphor who introduced him to Mondrian a little later. During the following years, oscillated constantly between representation and abstraction, choosing now one and then the other. Numerous one-man shows in Paris. Took part in the Salon des Réalités Nouvelles. Lives in Paris. "When things seen achieve a certain density in memory, transparencies, colours, and reflections detach themselves from the objects which first bore them and compose themselves, no longer as a representation or a figuration, but solely according to the intrinsic and unformulated laws of pure painting." (Lancelot Ney).

NICHOLSON Ben (b. 1894 near Uxbridge, England), the son of the painters William and Mabel Nicholson. Studied at the Slade School, London. Was later influenced by cubism.

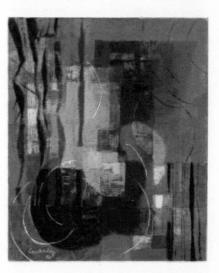

NEY. COMPOSITION. 1955.

233

Travelled many times to Paris. Composed abstract geometric reliefs as early as 1934. Visited Mondrian the same year. Included in many exhibitions in England and in America. A member of the 'Abstraction-Création' group, and then of the English 'Axis' group. During two years (1938-1940) was Mondrian's next door neighbour in Hampstead. After the Second World War, a whole group of young painters formed around him in Saint Ives, Cornwall. Exhibitions showing his complete work in Venice, Paris, Brussels, Zurich, Amsterdam. Lives in Saint-Ives.

In a now published letter to a friend, Nicholson relates how astonished he was by the atmosphere of Mondrian's studio when he visited the painter for the first time, in 1934. The English painter was then forty, the Dutch, sixty-two. One had already harvested the fruits of maturity, the other had gained enough assurance of personality not to be destroyed by the powerful example of his senior. There is indeed no work of Nicholson that is not totally his own. In his panels, both large and small, the nearest to neo-plasticism in his work, there is always a kind of lighthearted jauntiness which remains his characteristic imprint. "I think that so far from being a limited expression, understood by a few, abstract art is a powerful, unlimited, and universal language." (Nicholson). — *Bibl.* Barr : *Cubism and Abstract Art* (New York 1936); Nicholson and Gabo: *Circle* (London 1938); Summerson: *Ben Nicholson,* Penguin Books (London 1948); Read: *Ben Nicholson* (London 1948); Hitchcock: *Painting toward Architecture* (New York 1948); *A Dictionary of Modern Painting* (Me-

thuen, London 1956); 'Aujourd'hui', n° 1 (Paris 1955); *Ben Nicholson,* Museum of Modern Art (Paris 1955); Seuphor: *Léger and Nicholson,* 'Art Digest' (New York, April 1955).

NIGRO Mario (b. Pistoia, Italy, 1917). Took a diploma in mathematics. Self-educated in matters of art. Took part in numerous exhibitions in Italy. One-man show at the Salto Bookshop, Milan. Included in the 'Arte astratta e concreta in Italia' at the Museum of Modern Art, Rome 1951. Lives in Leghorn.

NOUVEAU Henri (b. Brasov, Transylvania, 1901). Studied music in Berlin. Was in contact with the *Sturm* group. Under the name of Neugeboren, composed abstract drawings as early as 1923. Settled in Paris in 1925 and composed abstract collages. Met Klee at the Bauhaus in 1928. Had his chamber music compositions produced in Paris, from 1928 to 1938. Took part at the same time in exhibitions in Zurich, Stockholm, and Berlin. After the second world war, he became friends with Picabia and took part in the Salon des Réalités Nouvelles. One-man show at the Galerie Colette Allendy in 1950. Travelling exhibition in Germany together with Francis Bott, in 1951. Lives in Paris. Henri Nouveau contributes to the great current of plastic fantasy inaugurated by Klee and Kandinsky. He is an inventor of rhythms and counterpoints which never lack a subtle and discreet humour.

234

O

OCAMPO Miguel (b. Buenos Aires, 1922). Began to paint in 1944. Travelled to Europe in 1948. One-man show in Paris and participation in the "Salon des Jeunes Peintres". Numerous one-man shows in Buenos Aires. Took part in the 'Eight Argentine Abstract Painters' at the Municipal Museum of Amsterdam, 1953. Lives in Buenos Aires.

OLIVE-TAMARI (b. La Seyne, Southern France, 1898). The General Secretary of the Salon des Réalités Nouvelles until 1954. Took part in numerous abstract art displays in Paris, the provinces, and the main European countries. Was appointed Director of the Fine Arts School of Toulon in 1955.

OMCIKUS Pierre (b. Rijeka, Yugoslavia, 1926). Attended the School of Applied Arts (1940-1944) then the School of Fine Arts (1944-1947) in Belgrade. Exhibited representational paintings in Belgrade, from 1949 to 1951. Slowly progressed towards abstraction. Was in Paris, 1952. Travelled to and exhibited in London. Included in the Salon de Mai, Paris 1955. The same year, exhibited abstract gouaches at the Galerie Arnaud. Lives in Paris.

ONGENAE Jozef Jan Marie (b. Antwerp, Belgium, 1921). Self-educated. Travelled in the United States, the Belgian Congo, Norway, and Asia. In 1945, worked in the Flemish expressionist manner, but the following year, came to

OMCIKUS. COMPOSITION. 1954.

235

abstraction. Later on, he launched into pure neo-plasticism. Exhibited in the main cities of Belgium and Holland. He executed mural paintings for the Municipal Museum in Amsterdam. Lives in Amsterdam.

ORIX. MINDSCAPE. 1955.
Sir Dinshaw Petit Collection.

ONSLOW-FORD Gordon Max (b. Wendover, England, 1912). After ten years in the Royal Navy, came to Paris and devoted himself to painting. Spent a short time in the studios of Lhote and Léger, in 1937. A member of the surrealist group in 1938. Organized an exhibition of surrealist art in London, 1940. Lectures in New York from 1940 to 1941. Retreated to an isolated village in Mexico (1941-1947). One-man show in San Francisco, 1948. There, also took part in an important exhibition organized by Wolfgang Paalen in 1951. His painting then lost all connection with surrealism. He is currently moving towards a kind of lyric plasticism both sparkling and profound.

Lives in Mill Valley (Calif.) — Bibl. *Dynaton 1951,* The San Francisco Museum of Art (U.S.A.).

ORIX Guillaume Hoorickx (b. Antwerp, 1900). Studied Medicine in Antwerp. A volunteer in the 1914-1918 war. Was attracted by painting about 1940. A member of the Resistance in Belgium, 1940 to 1942. Was deported by the Germans to the concentration camp of Mauthausen. After his return, he painted scenes of concentration camp life. Launched into abstraction in 1949. Took part in the Salon des Réalités Nouvelles from 1950 on, and was included in a number of group-shows in the South of France. He calls his paintings *ideograms* and *mindscapes.* One-man shows in Brussels, 1952, and London, 1955. Lives in Nice and in Paris.

OSAWA Gakiu (b. in Japan, 1890; d. in Japan, 1953). At first an elementary-school teacher, a poet, a novelist. Devoted himself to calligraphy from 1933 on. Studied under Tenrai Hidai (1872-1939), the precursor of the modern school of calligraphy. All his works prior to 1945 were destroyed in the bombings of Tokyo. But he started working again and took part in an exhibition of Japanese calligraphy at the Museum of Modern Art, New York, in 1954. "Perhaps because of his extreme freedom and a certain humour which he knew how to inject even into his most dramatic compositions, he ended his life after seeing one of his major works refused by the National Salon of Tokyo. In the middle of academism, dying and being born, it was the greatest honour that could have been conferred on him." (Pierre Alechinsky).

OSVER Arthur (b. Chicago, 1912). Studied at the Chicago Art Institute. Travelled in France and in Italy. Numerous one-man shows in New York. Took part in an exhibition of American painting at the Galerie Jeanne Bucher, Paris 1953. Lives in New York.

OTANO Juan Andres (b. Buenos Aires, 1914). A painter and a sculptor. Abstract works since 1948. One-man shows in Buenos Aires. Composed mural paintings in collaboration with his wife, the painter Dustir. Lives in Buenos Aires.

OUBORG P. (b. Dordrecht, Holland, 1893; d. 1956). For many years, taught drawing in the Dutch West Indies. Returned to Holland in 1931. Abstract paintings since 1947. General exhibition of his work at the Municipal Museum, Amsterdam, 1954. A member of the 'Vrij Beelden' group in Amsterdam. — *Bibl*. Catalogue of the Amsterdam exhibition, 1954; Oudshoorn: *P. Ouborg,* 'Museum-journaal' (Groningen, Sept. 1956).

P

PAALEN Wolfgang (b. Vienna, 1907). Studied in France, Germany, Italy. Travelled extensively in Europe and in America. Lived in Paris until 1939, and then in Mexico. Became a Mexican citizen in 1945. One-man shows in various galleries in Paris, London, New York, and Mexico City. After having belonged to the 'Abstraction-Création' group (1932-1935), he became a member of the surrealist group (1936-1940). Organized an international exhibition of surrealism, together with André Breton, Mexico City, 1940. Left the surrealist movement in 1941, and founded the review *Dyn,* in Mexico City. In 1945, published *Form and Sense* (Wittenborn and Co.) in New York. In 1951, together with Gordon Onslow-Ford and Lee Mullican, organized the *Dynaton* exhibition at the San Francisco Museum of Art. The same year, returned to Paris. One-man show at the Galerie Pierre, 1952, and at the Galerie Galanis, 1954. Lives in Paris and Mexico City.

"It is the painting which, in turn, examines

PAALEN. BEATRICE LOST. 1953.
Private Collection, Paris.

237

and interrogates the spectator: what do *you* represent? Painting is not a trade, but a way of meditating on the world which makes and unmakes us." (Paalen). — *Bibl.* Regler: *Wolfgang Paalen* (New York 1946); *Illustrated catalogue of the Dynaton exhibition* (San Francisco 1951); *Cahiers d'Art* (Paris 1952).

PAJAK Jacques (b. Strasbourg, 1930). Attended the School of Architecture. First exhibitions of abstract paintings in Strasbourg, 1951. Then turned to applied arts. Exhibitions of drawings at the Galerie de Beaune, Paris 1955. Elegant and supple graphism, in black or in colour. Lives in Paris and Strasbourg.

PALAZUELO Pablo (b. Madrid, 1916). Began painting in 1940. Settled in Paris in 1948. Took part in the Salon de Mai and a number of group-shows. Exhibited in Lausanne, Zurich, Liège, and Toronto. Included in 'Tendance' at the Galerie Maeght, 1951 and 1952. One-man show at the same gallery, 1955. Lives in Paris. An artist's greatest hindrance may be his own abundance of talent. The conquest of personality begins by rejection of nearly everything in order to find the essential. Sobriety and restraint are the trump-cards of an artist like Palazuelo. A true harmonist suppresses everything of his internal struggle except the final victory. Behold, here are

lines and planes: music for two hands. Reduced to a few notes it will but serve better for the articulation of the rare.

PANTALEONI Ideo (b. Legnago, Italy, 1904). Took part in the Salon des Réalités Nouvelles from 1949 on. Was also included in 'Arte Astratta e Concreta in Italia' Museum of Modern Art, Rome, 1951. A number of trips to Paris. Abstract forms in supple compositions evidently influenced by Magnelli. Lives in Milan.

PARISOT Adriano (b. Turin, 1912). Attended the Academy of Fine Arts in Turin. One-man shows in Milan, Turin, and Paris. Since 1948, took part in numerous group-shows in Italy and in other European countries. The director-editor of *I 4 Soli,* Turin, a review welcoming all the trends of abstract art. Travelled many times to Paris. Abstract works with brisk dabs of colour assembled by instinct into a harmonious graphism. Lives in Turin.

PARISOT. SPACE, CONTINUITY, TIME. 1955.

238

PASMORE Victor (b. Chelsham, England, 1908). Spent his childhood in the country. London, 1927. Working as an employee of the London County Council until 1937. Painted in his spare time and attended night classes in drawing. At first attracted by the impressionists, then by the cubists. After a period of pure painting, returned to the study of Cézanne, Seurat, and Van Gogh. From there came back to his first sallies in abstraction in 1947-1948. Has since developed a very individual abstract style, where lines and planes are interwoven, sometimes with the addition of collages. Took part in a number of group-shows in England. One-man show at the Institute of Contemporary Arts, London 1954. Taught at the University of Durham. He is at present mainly concerned with reliefs and mobiles. Lives in London.— Pasmore is, after Ben Nicholson and Paule Vézelay, the first English artist to tackle the problems of abstract art resolutely. After having shown definite talent in impressionist painting, talent which would certainly have brought him success in Great Britain, Pasmore chose the less easy way and became the undisputed leader of the London abstract group. — Bibl. *Victor Pasmore,* 'Penguin Books' (London 1945); Sylvester: *Victor Pasmore,* 'Britain to-day' (London, Dec. 1950); Alloway: *Nine Abstract Artists* (London 1954).

PEETERS Jozef (b. Antwerp 1895). Attended the Academy of Fine Arts in Antwerp. Progressed rapidly towards geometric abstraction, which he attained in 1921. The same year, one-man show in Antwerp. Actively contributed to a Congress of Modern Art, in Antwerp, 1921, and in Bruges, 1922. In 1922, Seuphor asked him to take part in the direction of the review *Het Overzicht* in which he published pithy articles about a 'community' art. Visited Paris the same year and called on Mondrian. Travelled to Berlin with Seuphor at the end

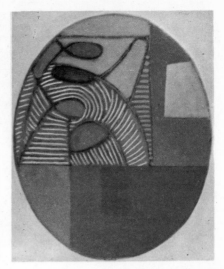

VICTOR PASMORE. OVAL MOTIF IN OCHRE, BROWN AND PINK. 1951.

of 1922. Met Walden, Gabo, Marinetti, Moholy-Nagy, and Prampolini. Took part in a number of abstract art displays in Belgium and gave up painting for about twenty years. Lives in Antwerp.

PEREIRA Rice (b. Boston, 1907). Studied at the Art Students League, New York. Then worked in Paris, Italy, North Africa, England. Since 1933, one-man shows in many museums and art galleries throughout the United States. Retrospective exhibition at the Whitney Museum, New York, 1953. Pereira has taught in various schools in New York from 1935 to 1943. Lives in New York.

"I employ the abstract idiom in painting, rather than more traditional forms of expression, because it offers me a wider range for experimentation. In these pictures I have endeavored to explore the formal possibilities of painting, with special emphasis

239

on constructional ways of expressing space and on experimenting with new use of materials such as glass and parchment, and new pigments. The paintings on glass are executed in a number of planes in spatial opposition. In these I have tried to produce an integrated picture using actual light as part of the painting." (Rice Pereira). — Bibl. *Fourteen Americans*, Museum of Modern Art (New York 1946);

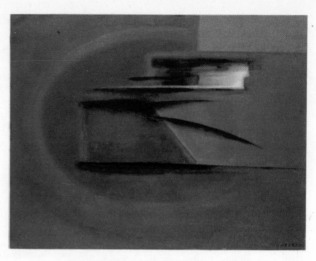

PIAUBERT. VORACIOUS BLUE. 1955.

Hitchcock: *Painting toward Architecture* (New York 1948); Ritchie: *Abstract Painting and Sculpture in America* (New York 1951); Rice Pereira: *Light and the New Reality*, 'The Palette' (New York 1952).

PERI Laszlo (b. Budapest, 1889). At first a brick-layer in Budapest. Composed expressionist drawings from 1918 to 1920. After 1921, joined the constructivist movement in Berlin, together with his compatriot Moholy-Nagy. From 1924 to 1928 worked as an architect for the Berlin City Council. During this period, he contributed reproductions of abstract art, mostly in black and white, to almost all the avant-garde reviews of Central Europe. His work, a very sober constructivism, achieved a monumental quality through surprisingly simple means. Peri abandoned abstract painting in 1928. He emigrated to London in 1933. "Peri called his compositions of 1920-28 *Space Constructions*. The credo of the Constructivists to whom he then belonged was to see the world through the prism of tech-

nique. The Constructivists do not want to give an illusion by means of color on canvas, but work indirectly in iron, glass and related media." (Alexandre Dorner). — Bibl. *Het Overzicht*, nº 17 (Antwerp 1923); *Jahrbuch der jungen Kunst* (Leipzig 1924); Arp and Lissitzky: *Les Ismes de l'Art* (Zurich 1925); *Collection of the Société Anonyme* (New Haven 1950).

PERILLI Achille (b. Rome, 1927). Took part in many exhibitions of Italian abstract art, particularly 'Arte Astratta e Concreta in Italia' at the Museum of Modern Art, Rome 1951. A predilection for contrasting dynamic and static forms in space. Lives in Turin.

PETURSSON Valtyr (b. Iceland, 1919). Studied under the painter H. Bloom in Boston. Spent a long time in Florence and in Paris. Included in the Salon de Mai, Paris, in 1950 and in 1951; included as well in numerous exhibitions in France and Scandinavia.

240

PFRIEM Bernard (b. Cleveland, Ohio, 1916). Studied in Cleveland. Painted first in the academic manner. Was in Mexico from 1940 to 1942. In the armed forces 1942-1946. Gave lectures at the Museum of Modern Art, New York. Contributed articles on art to the American review *Interiors*. Settled in Paris in 1951. Many group-shows in America. One-man show at the Hugo Gallery, New York, 1951. Sensual and subtle work at times very much indebted to Gorky's influence (cf. that name).

PIAUBERT Jean (b. Pian, South-West France, 1900). Attended the School of Fine Arts in Bordeaux. Came to Paris in 1922. Designed materials and stage-costumes for the 'couturier' Paul Poiret. First one-man show in 1932; was included for a few years in the Salon des Tuileries. Slowly moved away from representation from 1940 onwards. One-man shows in Paris: 1932, 1946, 1947, 1951. In 1950, he published Jean Cassou's *XXXIII Sonnets* illustrated with thirty-three large lithographs where he proved brilliantly the potentialities of black and white (Librairie La Hune, Paris). Took part regularly in the Salon de Mai and numerous exhibitions in Paris and abroad. One-man show of paintings and tapestries, Paris, 1955. Lives in Paris.

"Piaubert is one of those chosen from birth for the task of creating style or symbol. Among contemporary painters, he is the one who, to my mind, has broken with all compromise and created the plastic world closest to the idea governing contemporary thought. Space is no longer defined as a volume with three dimensions, but is conjugated with a fourth: time. Thus, in Piaubert, the object becomes thought, thought movement, and movement a characteristic of space." (H. Bing-Bodmer). — *Bibl.* Cassou: *Piaubert* (Paris 1951). Elgar: *L'univers prophétique de Piaubert* (Copenhagen 1957).

PICABIA Francis (b. Paris, 1879; d. Paris, 1953). Attended the École des Beaux-Arts and the School of Decorative Arts. Composed impressionist works from 1903 to 1908. Travelled extensively in Spain before he visited America (Feb-April, 1913) to take part in the 'Armory Show'. Returned to America in 1915. Collaborated in the *291* review with Marcel Duchamp. Went to Barcelona in 1916; published the first number of the review *391* which he sustained the same year in New York, again with Marcel Duchamp. In Lausanne, 1918, was introduced to the Zurich dada group. After a short stay in Zurich, he returned to Paris, kept on working on *391* and organized a great dada festival (1920). He published *Jésus-Christ rastaquouère*, composed the ballet *Relâche*, contributed to the surrealist reviews. After composing remarkable abstract works from 1912 to 1913 and inventing the series of the *ironic machines*, Picabia reverted to represen-

PICABIA. COMPOSITION. 1948.
M. S. Collection, Paris.

241

tational art for more than twenty years. He lived mostly in Cannes at the time. When he came back to Paris in 1945, he tackled abstraction again. Retrospective exhibition at the Galerie Drouin, Paris, in 1949. On this occasion, he published a single issue of a *491* review. The same year, at the Galerie des Deux-Iles, he exhibited a series of paintings solely composed of points. A retrospective exhibition of his work was held at the Galerie Furstemberg, Paris, 1956.

"Life for an artist should lie in working for himself without considering the results of his work in the eyes of merchants, critics, amateurs, only the joy that accomplishment gives. A marvellous curiosity about oneself, never quite satisfied, and every day renewed. . ." (Picabia). "Francis Picabia is a Christopher Columbus of art. No one has his detached philosophic indifference, his creative abundance, his assured craftsmanship. He journeys without compass." (Arp). — *Bibl.* Barr: *Cubism and abstract art* (New York 1936); *Art of this Century* (New York 1942); Seuphor: *L'Art abstrait, ses origines, ses premiers maîtres* (Paris 1949); *Collection of the Société Anonyme* (New Haven 1950); Raynal: *De Picasso au Surréalisme* (Paris-Geneva, 1950); *The Dada Painters and Poets* (New York 1952); Seuphor: *Épitaphe à Picabia,* 'Preuves' (Jan. 1954).

PICELJ Ivan (b. Okucani, Yugoslavia, 1924). Attended the Academy of Fine Arts in Zagreb, 1943-1946. In 1948, together with the architect V. Richter and the painter A. Srnec, formed a committee for the organisation of art exhibitions in Yugoslavia and abroad. Launched out into abstraction in 1951; the same year, together with the architects Bernardi, Bregovac, Radic, Rasica, Richter, Zarahovix and the painter Srnec, founded the 'Exat 51' group (experimental workshop 51). Included in the Salon des Réalités Nouvelles, Paris 1952 and in the 'Exat 51' group-shows in Zagreb

and Belgrade, 1953, as well as in the Salon 54 (exhibition of contemporary Yugoslavian art in Rijeka). Travelled and studied in Stockholm, Vienna, New York, Chicago, Venice, and Paris. Lives in Zagreb.

PICHETTE James (b. Châteauroux, France, 1920). Self-educated in matters of art. Was wounded in the war, 1940. Painted in a representational manner until 1945. Took part in the Salon des Réalités Nouvelles in 1950 and 1951. One-man shows in Paris: Galerie de Beaune (1951), Galerie Dina Vierni (1955). Travelled and exhibited in Italy, Switzerland, Belgium, Holland. Lives in Paris. Compositions of curves and straight lines among coloured planes of great clarity. Certain poetic elements in Pichette's recent work suggest a movement back towards representation.

PILLET Edgar (b. Saint-Christoly-de-Médoc, South West France, 1912). Was at first a sculptor. Attended the Fine Arts School in Bordeaux, then in Paris. Spent seven years in Algeria. Returned to Paris in 1945 and contributed to the *Gazette des Lettres.* Was the chief editor of the review *Art d'Aujourd'hui* (1949-1954). One-man show at the Galerie Denise René, Paris 1951. Took part in numerous group-shows in Paris and in Scandinavia. Directed, with Dewasne (cf. that name), the Abstract Art Workshop (1950-1952). Produced films on Magnelli and Laurens. Executed large mural decorations in a printing-press in Tours (1952). Spent some time in Finland the same year. Produced an abstract film called *Genèse.* A number of one-man shows at the Galerie Arnaud, Paris. Travelled and exhibited in Switzerland, Belgium, and Italy. Was in the United States, 1955-1956. Lives in Paris.

Together with Dewasne, Pillet greatly influenced the young painters who attended

EDGAR PILLET. GOUACHE. 1953.

ble rather fanciful gardens: a whole alphabet of symbols in colour constituting a total effect now harmonious, now disparate.

PLOMTEUX Léopold (b. Belgium, 1920). Attended the Academy of Fine Arts in Liège (1940-1946). Took part in numerous Salons and group-shows in Belgium since 1945. A member of the 'Art Abstrait' group. Lives in Liège.

the Abstract Art Workshop, from 1950 to 1952. His own work shows exact technique and brilliant colour. Sometimes planes are interwoven or smoothly overlap, sometimes a heavy linear display composes a calligraphic symbol of a voluntary simplicity. — *Bibl.* Alvard: *Edgar Pillet* (Paris 1952); Pillet: *Idéogrammes,* préface by Seuphor (Paris 1954).

PINK Lutka (b. Warsaw, 1916). Attended the Academy of Fine Arts in Warsaw, 1930-1937, then the Academy of Cracow. Travelled in Italy. Was in Paris, 1939. The work she did in Poland was completely destroyed by the Nazis. Took part in a number of group-shows in Paris. One-man shows at the Galerie Jeanne Castel in 1952 and the Galerie Arnaud in 1954. Was in the United States 1952-1953. Lives in Paris. After having undergone the influence of Bonnard and Vuillard, Lutka Pink deduced from her masters the abstract lesson contained implicitly as well as explicitly in their works. She has never ceased to progress towards an always increasing subtlety. Her more recent paintings resem-

POLIAKOFF Serge (b. Moscow, 1906). Studied in Moscow and travelled extensively in Russia before the revolution. Stayed in Constantinople, Sofia, Belgrade, Berlin. Was in Paris, 1924. Studied painting in autonomous academies. Attended the Slade School in London from 1935 to 1937. Returned to Paris, exhibited in a number of galleries and slowly progressed towards abstract art. In 1938, met Kandinsky, Delaunay, and Freundlich. From 1938 to 1945, exhibited every year at the Salon des Indépendants and once at the Salon d'Automne. From 1946 on, he took part in the Salon des Réalités Nouvelles and the Salon de Mai. One man exhibition at the Galerie Denise René, Paris 1947 and 1949. Showed at Copenhagen in 1948 and took part in many group exhibitions in different countries. One-man show at the Galerie Bing, Paris 1956. Lives in Paris.

A certain rudimentary series of forms, usually geometric, form the basis of Poliakoff's abstract work. At the same time, the manner almost always retains some

POLIAKOFF. COMPOSITION. 1953.
Pierre Brach^e Collection, Paris.

primitive boisterousness which provokes the spectator to an almost physical appreciation of the substance of the painting. A warm inwardness plays in the relationship of colours; one sometimes detects naive discordances. This painting remains voluntarily rough against a background of well assimilated western culture. When the formal conflicts are reduced by the harmonies of dull colours, Poliakoff's painting can achieve strikingly spontaneous successes. A spontaneity full of secret and unexplored intelligences. "In a certain way, Poliakoff could be regarded as a painter of the same family as Juan Gris. They have nothing in common in matters of form, but they show the same concern for starkness, they exercise the same economy of means, they are both emotive in spite of the character of their paintings." (Michel Ragon). — *Bibl.* 'Art d'Aujourd'hui' (Paris, Dec. 1951); *Témoignages pour l'Art Abstrait* (Paris 1952);

Premier bilan de l'art actuel (Paris 1953); Ragon: *L'Aventure de l'Art abstrait* (Paris 1956).

POLLOCK Jackson (b. Wyoming, U.S.A., 1912; d. Southampton, New York, 1956). Spent his childhood in Arizona and North California. Came to New York about 1929. Studied at the Art Students League. Travelled a number of times throughout the States in order to draw landscapes. Tackled abstract art about 1940. First one-man show 'Art of this Century', New York 1944, followed by a number of others in America and in Europe: Betty Parsons Gallery, New York, 1948 and 1951; Studio Facchetti, Paris 1952; Sidney Janis Gallery, New York 1952 and 1955. "My painting does not come from the easel. I hardly ever stretch my canvas before painting. I prefer to tack the unstretched canvas to the hard wall or the floor. I need the resistance of hard surface. On the floor I am more at ease. I feel nearer, more a part of the painting, since this way I can walk around it, work from the four sides and literally be *in* the painting. This is akin to the method of the Indian sand painters of the West. I continue to get further away from the usual painter's tools such as easel, palette, brushes, etc. I prefer sticks, trowels, knives and dripping fluid paint or a heavy impasto with sand, broken glass, other foreign matter added." (Pollock).

But the violence of Pollock's work is mostly exterior. In reality this aggressive painting is very slowly and seriously executed. I see no provocation in this painter, but a real need to do what he does, as he does it; in a word an intimate union between the man and the work. It is pleasant to stress the fact that this painting now, so influential in the United States, is diametrically opposed to the precise and balanced art of Mondrian, which has been no less influential in the same country. "Compared to Pollock, Picasso, the little gentleman who troubles the sleep of his colleagues with the eternal nightmare of his destructive enterprises, becomes a placid conformist, a painter of the past." (Bruno Alfieri). — *Bibl.* Janis: *Abstract and Surrealist Art in America* (New York 1944); *Possibilities I* (New York 1947); Ritchie: *Abstract Painting and Sculpture in America* (New York 1951); *Catalogue of the '15 Americans' exhibition,* Museum of Modern Art (New York 1952); *Catalogue of the Pollock exhibition,* Studio Facchetti (Paris 1952); Seuphor: *La Peinture aux États-Unis,* 'Art d'Aujourd'hui' (Paris June 1951); Catalogue of the *'15 years of Jackson Pollock'* exhibition, Sidney Janis Gallery (New York 1955).

PONS Jean (b. Paris, 1913). Studied at the École Estienne. First exhibited at the Salon d'Automne, Paris 1940-1944, then in the major abstract Salons. One-man shows in Paris: Galerie Suzanne Michel (1954) and Galerie Colette Allendy (1955). Lives in Paris.

POUSSETTE-DART Richard (b. Saint-Paul, Minn. 1916). Self-educated in matters of art. Lived a long time in New York where he had a number of one-man shows since 1939. Lives at present in Eagle Valley (New York).

PRAMPOLINI Enrico (b. Modena, 1896; d. Rome, 1956). Studied at the Academy of Rome. Joined the futurist movement very early. Took part in the running of the *Casa futurista* in Berlin in 1922. Great friend of Marinetti, accompanying him on several journeys in Europe. Was a co-signer of many futurist manifestoes, particularly *l'Art mécanique* (1923). Took an active part in the Futurist Congress in Milan (1924) for which he drew the abstract insignia borne by each different regional delegation. Was in Paris from 1925

to 1937. During that time, contributed to various avant-garde reviews, designed stage-decors, took part in exhibitions. A member of the 'Cercle et Carré' group (1930), then of the 'Abstraction-Création' group (1932). Had already been a member of the 'Novembergruppe' in Berlin, 1913. Worked very seriously on the futurist review *Noi*. In Paris, Prampolini made friends with Dermée, Mondrian, Vantongerloo, Seuphor. Once back in Rome, like the other futurists, he followed the politics of fascism and his relations with Paris were broken off. Since the war, Prampolini has once more taken part in all the important exhibitions of Italian abstract art and published many essays on modern art. Prampolini's painting only finally broke away from representation in his last years. The works of his final phase

POLLOCK. SEARCH. 1955.
Sidney Janis Gallery, New York.

245

PRASSINOS. THE RED STONES. 1954. *Galerie de France, Paris.*

plastic improvisations in which the emotion of the visual impact subsists, integrated in the composition. Lives in Paris.

PRATI Lidy (b. Resistencia, Argentine, 1921). Studied art in Buenos Aires. In 1944 took part in the avant-garde movement centred around the review *Arturo*. Exhibited regularly with the Argentine group 'Arte Concreto', since 1946. Has been married to Maldonado. Lives in Buenos Aires.

are from a pure painting point of view the best of his output. — *Bibl.* Carmelich: *L'art de Prampolini*, 'L'Effort Moderne', Paris, March 1926; Sartoris: *Esaltazione di Prampolini*, 'Origini', Rome, July 1939; Pfister *Enrico Prampolini*, 'Arte moderna italiana', nº 34, Milan 1940.

PRASSINOS Mario (b. Constantinople, 1916). Greek by birth. Volunteered in the 1939-1940 campaign and became a naturalized French citizen. Numerous exhibitions of paintings and engravings in Paris, New York, Brussels, Antwerp, Turin, Amsterdam. Exhibited regularly at the Galerie de France and contributed every year to the Salon de Mai, Paris. Has illustrated numerous literary works, particularly Sartre's *Le Mur,* the *Bestiaire* of Apollinaire, the *Journal d'un Fou* of Gogol, and Poe's *Corbeau*. He designed decors and costumes for a number of ballets, notably for Paul Claudel's *Toby et Sara*. Came gradually to abstraction through the way in which his painting transcended its basis of natural impressions. A herd of bulls or a forest-fire become the themes of purely

PRÉAUX Raymond (b. Paris, 1916). Studied in the free academies of Montparnasse. Then, worked on his own. First abstract works, in the constructivist manner, 1947. Took part in the Salon des Réalités Nouvelles since 1948. After 1953, progressed towards a more supple style of painting, where spontaneous sensibility is reintegrated. Lives in Sartrouville, near Paris.

PROBST Joseph (b. Vianden, Luxembourg, 1911). Studied in Luxembourg, Brussels, and Vienna. Composed various mural paintings. At first influenced by Matisse and Léger. Progressed towards abstraction from 1948 on and accepted it fully in 1951. Took part in numerous group-shows in Paris, Lyons, Luxembourg, Liège, Menton, Amsterdam, as well as in the Sao Paolo Biennale, 1953. Lives in Junglister, Luxembourg.

246

PUNI Ivan (better known under the name of Jean Pougny; b. in Finland, not far from Saint-Petersburg, in 1894; d. Paris, Dec. 1956). Was in Paris, 1912-1913. Exhibited abstract works with the constructivist and suprematist painters in Saint-Petersburg, in 1915 and the years following. Left Russia for Berlin in 1921 and exhibited at the *Der Sturm* gallery. Then settled in Paris; he returned to representational art and became a sophisticated successor of Vuillard in paintings usually small in size. — Bibl. Umanskij: *Neue Kunst in Russland* (Potsdam 1920); *Collection of the Société Anonyme* (New Haven 1950); *A Dictionary of Modern Painting* (Methuen, London 1956).

Q

QUENTIN Bernard (b. Somme, Northern France, 1923). Attended the School of Decorative Arts for four years. Travelled in Switzerland, Belgium, Sweden, Germany, Italy, Spain, England. Took part in many exhibitions at the Galerie Maeght, Paris, from 1947 on. Included in the Salon de Mai and Salon d'Automne in 1951 as well as in the "Nouvelle École de Paris" show in 1952. His first abstract canvas is dated 1947. "In order to reach this point, I underwent the influence of Klee, whose work I discovered in Switzerland. It was mainly architecture, however, that gave me feeling for proportions and structure: from arabic design, I derived inspiration for the graphic side of my work." (Quentin).

Later on, progressed toward a more lyrical painting. Lives in Paris.

QUENTIN. COMPOSITION. 1955.

247

R

RADICE Mario (b. Como, 1900). Self-educated in matters of art. One of the first promoters of abstract painting in Italy (1930). Worked with many architects and contributed to Italian art reviews. Took part in exhibitions of abstract art in Italy and in Scandinavia. Lives in Milan.

RADOU Othello (b. Monte Carlo, 1910). Prepared the entrance examinations for the École Polytechnique and the École des Mines, then studied painting and drawing under various instructors, particularly Jean Lombard. Took part in the major Parisian Salons from 1943 on. Exhibited his first abstract canvas at the Salon de Mai in 1946. Modulations of supple lines and planes. Radou lives in Paris and takes part every year in the Salon des Réalités Nouvelles.

RAY Man (b. Philadelphia, 1890). Dropped his studies of architecture and engineering in order to devote himself to painting (1907). First one-man show in 1912. The 'Armory Show' in 1913 sharpened his interest in abstract art. Together with Marcel Duchamp and Picabia, founded the New York dada group. In 1920, the co-organiser of the 'Société Anonyme' with Katherine S. Dreier and Marcel Duchamp. Came to Paris in 1920. In the following years was very much involved with the dada group, then the surrealist group. Contributed to *Sturm* (Berlin) and *De Stijl* (Holland). About 1922, he developed a new technique of photography and became one of the leading composers of photograms and a producer of surrealist films. Was in Hollywood from 1940 to 1951. He then returned to Paris where he is still living.

Although it belongs mainly to surrealism, Man Ray's work can be considered on the

MAN RAY. THE TIGHT-ROPE DANCER ACCOMPANIES HERSELF WITH HER SHADOWS. 1916. *Museum of Modern Art, New York.*

limits of abstraction in a certain number of compositions where no identifiable representation remains. With his works painted in 1915 and 1916, he became one of the first abstract painters in his country, a creator of strange and highly individual forms. — Bibl. *Art of this Century* (New York 1942); *Collection of the Société Anonyme* (New Haven 1950); Ritchie: *Abstract Painting and Sculpture in America* (New York 1952).

RAYMO Leopold (b. Botucatu, Brazil, 1912). A doctor in Sao Paolo. Began painting on his own and without previous art education, in the cubist manner. In 1950, attended the Abstraction Workshop of the painter Flexor, and has remained a member of the Sao Paolo abstract group with which he still exhibits. Lives in Sao Paolo.

RAYMOND Marie (b. La Colle-sur-Loup, in the Alps, 1908). Studied in autonomous academies in Nice and in Paris. Representational painting (portraits and landscapes) until 1938. Without knowing the works of Klee, Kandinsky, and Mondrian, she came to abstraction through the revelation of freedom she found in the works of Picasso. Settled in Paris in 1943. Took part in the Salon des Réalités Nouvelles, the Salon de Mai, and various group-shows. One-man shows at the Galerie de Beaune, Paris, 1950 and 1951. Included in exhibitions in Holland, Italy, Germany, Switzerland, Japan, and Brazil. The wife of the Dutch painter Klein, Marie Raymond has been for some years the Paris correspondent of the Dutch review *Kunst en Kultuur*. Lives in Paris. "Colour, the symbol of life, must attain the maximum of expression and through its harmonies constitute in some fashion the image of a whole to which thought can cling." (Marie Raymond). — *Bibl.* 'Art d'Aujourd'hui' (Paris, Dec. 1951); *Témoignages pour l'Art Abstrait* (Paris 1952).

REBAY Hilla (b. Strasbourg, 1890). Studied in Dusseldorf, Paris, Munich. Took part in the 'Secession' in Munich, 1914-1915. A member of the 'Novembergruppe' in 1918. Exhibited at the Salon des Indépendants, the Salon des Tuileries, and the Salon d'Automne. Through expressionism and cubism, her work slowly worked toward abstraction. Her canvases are often aggressively lyrical. Her collages, the best part of her work, have a highly individual imprint. Thin strips of coloured paper shape a fluid and delicate style. Madame Rebay has taken an active part in the foundation (1937) and the direction of the Museum of Non-Objective Painting, New York, which is mostly devoted to the works of Bauer and Kandinsky (it is now the Solomon R. Guggenheim Museum). Has taken part several times in the Salon des Réalités Nouvelles in Paris. Lives near New York. — Bibl. *Art of Tomorrow* (New York 1939); Catalogue of her exhibition at the Museum of Non-Objective Painting (New York 1948); Catalogue of the *Bauer-Kandinsky-Rebay* exhibition at Lakeland (Florida) 1955.

REGGIANI Mauro (b. Modena, Italy, 1897). Educated in Florence. The co-signer, with Bogliardi and Ghiringhelli, of the first Italian abstract art manifesto, Milan 1934. One-man show, with a preface by Alberto Sartoris, at the Galleria del Milione, Milan 1936. Took part in many exhibitions throughout Italy. Lives in Milan. Highly whimsical geometries, vigorously conceived and composed in swathes. Bright colours. — *Bibl.* Nello Ponente: *Mauro Reggiani*, 'I 4 Soli' (Turin, Nov. 1955).

REICHEL Hans (b. Wurzburg, 1892). Met Klee in 1919, Kandinsky in 1924. Was in Paris 1928. Numerous one-man shows, particularly at the Galerie Jeanne Bucher (after 1930). Lives in Paris.

249

Reichel's work is the creation of an imaginary world, like Klee's, but emphasizing tenderness more. He is only abstract, properly speaking, in a minute fraction of his work. "I do not believe that the nightingale, after having sung, says, at night: I have worked. Neither can my little watercolours properly be called *works*. They are rather songs, prayers, little tunes in colour which have given joy to many, no more, no less." (Reichel). — *Bibl.* Bissière et Morlet: *Reichel* (Paris 1953).

REICHEL. WATER-COLOUR. 1954.
Galerie Jeanne Bucher, Paris.

REINHARDT Ad (b. Buffalo, New York, 1913). Studied at Columbia (New York). Self-educated in matters of painting. Exhibited with the 'American Abstract Artists' group from 1939 to 1946. First one-man show in New York, 1945. Numerous shows at the Betty Pars-

ons Gallery, New York. Travelled in Europe in 1952 and 1954. Famous in the United States for his cartoons on the history and the present situation of art in his country. These last years, his painting has progressed towards the horizontal-vertical principle and dull harmonies. Lives in New York. — *Bibl.* Ritchie: *Abstract Painting and Sculpture in America* (New York 1951); Hess: *Abstract Painting* (New York 1951); *Modern Artists in America,* Wittenborn (New York 1951).

RENDON Manuel (b. Paris, 1894). He was the son of an Ambassador of Ecuador in Paris. First exhibition at Zborowsky's, Modigliani's friend (Paris 1925). In 1927, entered the Galerie de l'Effort Moderne (Léonce Rosenberg) and contributed to its review. Exhibitions in Guayaquil and Quito, in Ecuador. Then, again in Paris: Galerie d'Art du Faubourg (1949), Galerie Ariel (1951). Adopted completely the abstract manner which he had been approaching for a number of years and exhibited in Washington (Pan American Union) and in Paris (Galerie de Berri) in 1955 and 1956. Lives in Guayaquil.

RESSE Guy (b. Châtillon-sur-Indre, France, 1921). A painter and a ceramist. Studied at the School of Fine Arts in Tours and Lyons, then at the School of Decorative Arts in Paris. One-man shows in Paris: Galerie Saint-Placide (1947) and Galerie La Roue (1954). First abstract work in 1949. The director of the Galerie La Roue. Lives in Paris.

RETH Alfred (b. Budapest, 1884). After some time in Italy, settled in Paris in 1905 and worked in various autonomous Academies. From 1908 to 1910, his work was marked by Hindu influences. Took part in the Salon d'Automne and the Salon des Indépendants in 1910. In 1913, completely engaged in cubist painting; exhibited at the Galerie Berthe Weill, Paris, with Metzinger, and at the Gallery Der Sturm, Berlin. In 1926, in a retrospective exhibition of cubists anterior to 1914, he was represented by about ten canvases. Then exhibited in numerous Paris galleries, his paintings always testifying to new studies. A member of the 'Abstraction-Création' group in 1932. Took part in the Salon des Réalités Nouvelles from 1946 on. Was in Sweden 1952. Retrospective exhibition at the Galerie de l'Institut, Paris 1955. Lives in Paris. Reth has for a long time devoted himself to the study of materials (sand, pebbles, coal, ground brick, egg-shells, cement, etc. . .) which he incorporates in his compositions with perfect mastery. No one has investigated the possibilities of new techniques more thoroughly. — *Bibl.* Seuphor: *L'Art abstrait, ses origines, ses premiers maîtres* (Paris 1949); *Témoignages pour l'Art Abstrait* (Paris 1952); Waldemar George: *Alfred Reth* (Paris 1955).

RENDON. THE DAWN. 1954.

RETH. COMPOSITION. 1955.

RETS Jean (b. Paris, 1910). A member of many modern art groups in Belgium. Numerous exhibitions in Liège. Attained complete abstraction and exhibited his works at the Galerie Ex-Libris, Brussels, 1953. Lives in Liège.

REVOL Jean (b. Lyons, 1929). Took part in a number of group-shows in Lyons and Paris. One-man shows at the Galerie Creuze, Paris, 1952 and 1955. Neo-expressionist abstract paintings, with twisted symbols violently interwoven. Lives in Paris.

251

REZVANI Serge (b. Teheran, 1928). Came to France as a child. Attended the Académie de la Grande Chaumière. First exhibited at the age of seventeen. First abstract canvases in 1947. Included in group-shows at the Galerie Maeght. One-man shows in Paris: Galerie Arnaud (1950) and Galerie Berggruen (1953). Took part in the Salon de Mai and the Salon des Réalités Nouvelles. Lives in Paris. Highly coloured work, completely oriental in its warmth, but bathed in a sensibility born of the atmosphere of Paris, such as can be found also in Delaunay's *Fenêtres*.

RICHTER Hans (b. Berlin, 1888). First became acquainted with modern painting through the *Blaue Reiter*, 1912. Then influenced by Cézanne and cubism. First one-man show in Munich, 1916, where he exhibited works 'created in a vegetative manner'. The review *Die*

RICHTER. COMPOSITION. 1952.

Aktion devoted one whole issue to him. In 1916, Richter also joined the dada group just formed in Zurich. First abstract works (in black and white) in 1917. In 1918, met Eggeling, and the following year, composed on a large *rouleau* (reel or roll) a series of abstract designs developed like a musical theme. Met van Doesburg and contributed to *De Stijl*. First abstract film in 1921: *Rythme 21,* now a classic of avant-garde moving-pictures in the same way as Eggeling's films of the same period. From 1923 to 1926, the co-editor of the German review *G* (Gestaltung). Went to America in 1941. Appointed professor at New York City College and Director of the Film Institute. Produced a film *Dreams that money can buy* containing many abstract sequences in colour. In 1950, one-man show of paintings and abstract *rouleaux* at the Galerie des Deux-Iles, Paris, and the Galerie Feigl, Basel. Other one-man shows at the Galerie Mai, Paris, and the Municipal Museum, Amsterdam, in 1952. Lives in New York.

The blacks and whites of Richter, Arp, and Janco are the most typical plastic works of the Zurich period of the Dada movement. Later, Richter tried to apply in films the horizontal-vertical principle so much advocated by the *Stijl* painters. But his most remarkable works are probably the large *rouleaux* he composed during and after the war. They are rather like gigantic papyri composed of conflicting forces; among the disturbance and the swirls, unexpected delicacies appear. They testify to an enthusiastic temperament, both lyric and violent.

RIGHETTI Renato (b. Rome, 1916). First exhibition in 1934. First abstract works in 1937. Numerous one-man shows. Takes part every year in the Salon des Réalités Nouvelles. Lives in Paris. The work of Righetti is imbued with great freshness. His colours are vivid and his compositions charm by their almost child-like simplicity.

Most painters desire to be a force of nature integrated into nature, and to lose control in order to gain a certain explosive vigour, a constant source of masterpieces. The memory of Van Gogh haunts them. But no one can choose his rightful drama, nor decide his own spiritual density. — *Bibl.* Duthuit: Preface to the exhibition at the Galerie Rive-Droite (Paris 1954); Pierre Schneider: *Riopelle*, 'L'Œil' (Paris, June 1956).

RIOPELLE. COMPOSITION. 1955. *Jean Larcade Collection, Paris.*

RIOPELLE Jean-Paul (b. Montreal, 1924). One-man shows in Paris ever since 1947, particularly at the Galerie Creuze (1949), the Studio Facchetti and the Galerie Pierre (1952), the Galerie Rive-Droite (1954), and the Galerie Jacques Dubourg (1956). Exhibits regularly at the Salon de Mai; lives in Paris. Riopelle paints large monochromatic or polychromatic symphonies. The colour fizzles, sparks, splutters, spangles, radiates, falls into place, breaks loose again, surrenders. A kind of aerial impressionism, extremely fickle, adapting its fury to the capacity of the executor, and ruling it in powerful rhythms.

RITSCHL Otto (b. Erfurt, Germany, 1885). Self-educated in matters of painting. At first a writer, he turned to painting about 1919: he then burnt all his books and manuscripts. Worked until 1922 in the manner of Kokoschka and of the

RITSCHL. COMPOSITION 54/53. 1954.

253

'Brücke'. Was in Paris, 1928. Very much under the influence of French painting (Cézanne, Matisse, and cubism), he slowly progressed towards abstraction. Great retrospective exhibition at the Museum of Wiesbaden in 1955. Ritschl's work does not pay allegiance to the abstract neo-expressionism so characteristic of modern German art. His work of recent years shows him to be much closer in spirit to certain Paris painters, like Dewasne and Vasarely. He is an isolated figure in his own country, although widely esteemed. Lives in Wiesbaden. "Ritschl has suppressed the object not merely aesthetically through a play with forms, but rather ethically, through a philosophical by-passing of the objective world, which is to be considered as fiction." (Kurt Leonhard). — Bibl. Domnick: *Abstrakte Malerei* (Stuttgart 1947); Catalogue of the retrospective Ritschl exhibition at the Museum of Wiesbaden, **1955.**

RODCHENKO Alexandre (b. Saint Petersburg, 1891). Attended the Academy of Kazan. First abstract works made with a pair of compasses in 1914. The founder of the non-objectivist movement in Moscow, 1915, a movement akin to, although at first competing with, Malevitch's suprematism. Exhibited with Malevitch and Tatlin from 1917 to 1922. The three movements were then generally grouped under the same name of constructivism. After 1922, Rodchenko devoted himself entirely to the applied arts. Lives in Moscow. — *Bibl*. Barr: *Cubism and Abstract art* (New York 1936); Seuphor: *L'Art abstrait, ses origines, ses premiers maitres* (Paris 1949).

ROITMAN Wolf (b. Montevideo, 1930). Was in Buenos Aires in 1936. Was forced into studying architecture. Published poems and contributed to the review *Poesia Buenos Aires*. Was in Paris, 1951. Became friendly with Arden Quin whom he joined in the Madi movement. Since 1952 has taken part in all the Madi displays in Paris. One-man show at the Galerie de Beaune in 1955. Lives in Paris.

ROTHFUSS Rid (b. Montevideo, Uruguay, 1920). A professor of drawing and painting at the Industrial School and the Teachers College of Uruguay. Co-signer of the *Madi* manifesto in 1947. Took an active part in all the 'Arte Madi' shows in Buenos Aires and contributed to the Madi review. Numerous exhibitions in Montevideo and Buenos Aires. Sent paintings to the Salon des Réalités Nouvelles, Paris, in 1948. Lives in Montevideo.

ROTHKO Mark (b. Dvinsk, Russia, 1903). Emigrated to America in 1913. Studied under Max Weber at the Arts Students League. One-man shows from 1933 on, especially at the Betty Parsons Gallery, New York. Painted in an expressionist representational manner until 1939. First abstract works in 1945. Included in 1951, in the 'Abstract Painting and Sculpture in America' show at the Museum of Modern Art, New York. Included also in 'Cinquante Ans d'art aux États-Unis' at the Museum of Modern Art, Paris, in 1955. Lives in New York.

Ashy colours, a dulled pink, an ochred yellow spread and melt away and vibrate through the mere fact of their existence, of their unexpected expanse. A more orange yellow makes a splash or some blue is less generously laid on: there is the relation—or harmony—which is the whole object of the composition. A soft wind breathes over this desert. It is the innocence of art. — Bibl. *Possibilities I* (New York 1947); 'Art d'Aujourd'hui' (Paris, June 1951); Ritchie: *Abstract Painting and Sculpture in America* (New York 1951); Hess: *Abstract Painting* (New York 1951); *Art news annual* (New York 1951).

ROTHKO. NUMBER 10. 1950.
Museum of Modern Art, New York.

RUDULPH Rella (b. Livingston, Alabama, 1906). Attended the Chapelle School of Art in Denver, 1928. Was in New York, 1933. Studied at the Art Students League. Travelled in Peru, Ecuador, Chile, Mexico. One-man shows in Birmingham (Ala.), 1940; in New York, 1941; in Los Angeles, 1945. Was in Paris, 1948. First non-representational works in 1949. She feels an artistic affinity with Soldati. One-man show at the Galerie La Roue, Paris 1955: large geometrical compositions on aluminium. Lives in Paris.

RUSSELL Morgan (b. New York, 1886; d. Broomall, Penn., 1953). Studied painting under Robert Henri and Henri Matisse. Founded the synchromist movement with MacDonald-Wright (cf. that name) in Paris, 1912. Included in the Salon des Indépendants in 1912 and 1913. Exhibited in Munich with MacDonald-Wright and sent some paintings to the 'Armory Show' in New York. Exhibited his 'synchromies' with MacDonald-Wright in Paris, 1913, and New York, 1916. A little later he reverted to representational painting (still life and portrait). Lived a long time in isolation in the French provinces. Returned to America in 1946. Retrospective exhibition of his abstract work at the Rose Fried Gallery, 1950. Included in the 'Abstract Painting and Sculpture in America' show at the Museum of Modern Art, New York (1951), with major works from the years 1913 and 1914. "Color is form; and in my attainment of abstract form I use those colors which optically correspond to the spatial extension of the forms desired." (Morgan Russell). Russell's 'synchromies' are distinguished from those of MacDonald-Wright by their more precise forms, and a certain quest for mass, akin to the cubist preoccupation, but in a quite different register of colours. — *Bibl.* W. H. Wright: *Modern painting, its tendency and meaning* (New York, 1915); Seuphor: *L'Art abstrait, ses origines, ses premiers maîtres* (Paris 1949); 'Art d'Aujourd'hui' (Paris, June 1951); Ritchie: *Abstract painting and sculpture in America* (New York 1951).

RUVOLO Felix (b. New York, 1912). Spent his childhood in Sicily. Was in Chicago from 1926 to 1948: studied at the Art Institute. First exhibition in 1947. Then exhibited in numerous galleries and academies throughout America. Composed a number of mural decorations in Chicago. Lives in Walnut Creek (Calif.).

255

S

SANTOMASO. COMPOSITION. 1955.

SALVATORE Nino di (b. Verbania Pallanza, Italy, 1924). One-man shows in Italy since 1944. The director of the School of Fine Arts in Domodossola since 1949. Took part in the Salon des Réalités Nouvelles in 1951, and in numerous exhibitions of Italian abstract art. Lives in Domodossola. A combination of curves and straight lines forming coloured planes.

SANDIG Armin (b. Hof-an-der-Saale, Germany, 1929). Studied naturalist painting. Was in Munich, 1949-1950. Took part in numerous group-shows. One-man show in 1951. Lives in Hamburg.

SANFILIPPO Antonio (b. Partenne, Italy, 1923). Studied at the Academy of Fine Arts in Florence. Co-signer of the *Forma I* manifesto in 1947 and contributor to the *Forma I* review. Took part in the main abstract art displays in Italy, as well as in the Venice Biennale. Also included in group-shows abroad. Lives in Rome.

SANS Klaas (b. Sappemeer, Netherlands. 1927). Educated in Groningen, Travelled to Canada and Paris, where he frequented the Académie Ranson. Took part in group-shows in Holland and in Paris. Started by painting portraits and landscapes. Discovered modern painting in the museums of New York and Chicago. Sans leads a wandering life, but spends most of his time in Paris. Abstract works at the Galerie Olga Bogroff, Paris, and the Salon des Réalités Nouvelles in 1955. Lives in Paris and in Holland.

SANTOMASO Giuseppe (b. Venice, 1907). Attended the Academy of Fine Arts in Venice. Began to exhibit in 1928. After some time spent in Holland and in Paris, he tried to 'mature personal experience on the universal level'. Since 1940, numerous one-man shows in Italy as well as in Paris (Galerie Rive Gauche) and London (The Hanover Gallery). Has illustrated Éluard's *Grand Air* with

256

twenty-seven original drawings (Galeria Santa Radegonda, Milan 1945). About 1952, his painting attained abstraction without completely abandoning the natural visual pretexts which pure painting integrates and transforms in its autonomous themes. It is a supple art, of great poetical charm. Santomaso lives in Venice. "His personality is best expressed—writes Giuseppe Marchiori—in the invention of a coloured atmosphere in which each form strives towards a visual incantation, a harmony where painting and music truly blend." — *Bibl.* Venturi: *Otto pittori italiani*, De Luca editore (Rome 1952); Read: *Santomaso*, The Hanover Gallery (London 1953); Marchiori: *Santomaso*, Alfieri (Venice 1954); Venturi: *Santomaso*, De Luca editore (Rome 1955).

SAUER Greta (b. Bregens, Austria, 1909). Attended University in Germany. Emigrated to France (Paris) in 1937. Abstract gouaches and collages since 1939. Included in group-shows in Paris, Marseilles, Copenhagen, San Francisco, and Turin. One-man shows in Paris: Galerie du Montparnasse (1947); Galerie de Beaune (1950); Galerie Arnaud (1951 and 1952). Lives in Paris. Direct projections of a wild, restless mind. There is a refined delicacy in the nuances of the collages.

SAVELLI Angelo (b. Pizzo-di-Calabria, Italy, 1911). Took part in various exhibitions of Italian abstract art. Studies in simple rhythms and great contrasts in colour. Lives in Rome.

SAVERYS Jan (b. Petegem, Belgium, 1924). The son of the painter Albert Saverys. Attended the Academy of Fine Arts in Ghent (1943-1946), then non-institutional academies in Paris (1946-1948). First abstract paintings in 1949. Calligraphic works of ordered elegance. A member of the Belgian 'Art Abstrait' group. Included in group-shows in Brussels, Knokke, Antwerp, Charleroi, (Belgium), in Bergen (Norway), and in Edinburgh. Lives in Petegem.

SCHANKER Louis (b. New York, 1903). Studied in various art-schools in New York. Lived in France and in Spain, 1931-1933. First one-man show in New York, in 1934. In 1944, published an album of wood-cuts in colour (Wittenborn). Since 1943, teaches the technique of wood-engraving at the New School for Social Research, in New York. Numerous one-man shows at the Willard Gallery New York, since 1944 (paintings and engravings). Lives in New York.

SAUER. COLLAGE. 1955.

257

SCHATZ Bezalel (b. Jerusalem, 1912). The son of Professor Boris Schatz, the founder of the first Fine Arts Academy in Israel. Studied in Paris and New York. Took part in exhibitions in the United States, London, Paris, and Israel. Abstract compositions in a free-style calligraphy influenced by his numerous contacts with modern Western artists.

SCHILLING Albrecht (b. Bremen, Germany, 1929). Began to paint on his own in 1946. After a cubist period, he came to pure abstraction about 1950. Travelled and studied in Italy and Switzerland (1951). Was in Paris in 1952. Lives in Bremen.

SCHMELZEISEN Gustav Klemens (b. Dusseldorf, 1900). Studied under von Wessel. A doctor in Law and professor of the history of German law. Came to abstraction in recent years. Lives in Hechingen (Germany).

SCHMIDT Gerhard Michael (b. Lesten, Silesia, 1922). An office worker in Berlin. Began to paint at the end of the war. Attended the Fine Arts school in Hamburg (1948-1952), under Willi Breest. Took part in numerous group-shows in Germany from 1952 on. Spent some time in Paris in 1952 and 1955. Together with Dieter Benecke and Jutta Benecke-Eberle, exhibited abstract works at the Librairie Didier, Paris, 1955. Lives in Hamburg.

SCHNEIDER Gérard (b. Sainte-Croix, Switzerland, 1896). Spent his childhood in Neuchâtel. Was in Paris in 1916. Attended the School of Decorative Arts, then the École des Beaux-Arts (under Cormon). When his studies were completed, returned to Switzerland where he took part in numerous exhibitions after 1920. Came back to Paris in 1924; by putting into practice his knowledge in matters of decoration he made a living restoring paintings. Starting from various subjects (figures and imaginary landscapes) he painted his first abstract canvas in 1944. Took part in the Salon d'Automne and the Salon des Surindépendants. After 1946, exhibited at the Salon des Réalités Nouvelles and the Salon de Mai (of which he is a co-organizer). One-man shows in Paris: Galerie Lydia Conti (1947); Galerie Galanis (1955). Sent some works to the Venice Biennale in 1948. Took part in group-shows at the

SCHNEIDER. CÉRAK. 1955. *Raymond Mindlin Collection, New York.*

Galerie Carré (Paris and New York) in 1950 and 1951 as well as in important displays in America, Germany, Scandinavia, Italy, Belgium, Japan, etc. One-man show at the Kootz Gallery, New York, in 1956. Lives in Paris.

His paintings looks as if they had been shaped by thrusts of a sickle, volatile in appearance, but perfectly conceived and composed. Among European abstract painters, Schneider is probably the closest to Japanese abstract calligraphy. Brief and deliberate symbols of a graphism where the significant spirit of the whole surpasses the effect of each letter. "There has not really been a brutal break between representational and non-representational art, but rather a logical development, a continuous enrichment since impressionism, which was the first move towards abstraction of the motif on behalf of a sensual impact based solely upon atmospheric relations. The cubists also worked toward abstraction when they imagined *a priori* forms, structures, and new relations between objects. We find abstraction again in the Fauvist tendency to draw clear orchestral harmony from the motif, with the help of intense colours. So many attempts to liberate painting from servile reproduction of the object broke the ground for an independent art, for an autonomous painting existing only for and in itself." (Schneider). — *Bibl.* 'Art d'Aujourd'hui' (Paris, June 1951); *Propos de Schneider sur l'Art Abstrait,* 'Les Amis de l'Art' (Paris, Jan. 1952); Brion: *Schneider,* 'I 4 Soli' (Turin, Jan. 1955). Schneider has also illustrated Ganzo's *Langage* with twelve abstract lithographs, ed. Lydia Conti (Paris 1948).

SCHWITTERS. COLLAGE IN BLUE AND WHITE. 1926. *Private Collection, Paris.*

SCHULZE Bernard (b. Schneidemühl, 1915). Attended the School of Fine Arts in Berlin and Dusseldorf. Travelled in France in 1945 and 1953. Took part in exhibitions in Paris, London, and the United States. 'Informal' painting striving toward confused and ambiguous states. Lives in Frankfurt-am-Main.

SCHWITTERS Kurt (b. Hanover, Germany, 1887; d. Ambleside, England, 1948). At first an academic painter. Studied six years at the Academy of Dresden: painted portraits. During a stay in Munich was influenced by Franz Marc and Kandinsky. About 1918, his work was in the line of Picasso's cubism. Returned to Hanover in 1919 and founded his own sector of the Dada movement: *Merz,* and for a number of years published a review of that name. Met van Doesburg in 1922 and accompanied him on a 'dada' tour in Holland. About the same time, composed his famous verbal symphony *Lautsonate.* Contributed regularly to the review *Der Sturm.*

For years he 'constructed' the interior of his house with abstract compositions, into which he incorporated hundreds of various objects, sometimes even picked up in the street. A member of the 'Cercle et Carré' group in Paris 1930, and then of 'Abstraction-Création', 1932. In 1933, left Germany for Norway. Settled in England in 1941. In Ambleside, started on a new *Merz* construction inside a farmhouse. He died before he could complete the work (1948).

"Emerging from dada, Schwitters' paintings and his *Merz* constructions are among the most evident achievements of modern art. He collates accidental scraps of everyday life into compositions of great plastic beauty, thus affirming the superiority of spirit over matter. Through his humility a new purity is born. Schwitters' collages are as mystical and delicate as Taoist paintings." (Charmion von Wiegand). — *Bibl.* Arp and Lissitzky: *Les Ismes de l'Art* (Zurich 1925); Dreier: *Modern Art* (New York 1926); Barr: *Cubism and abstract Art* (New York 1936); *Art of this Century* (New York 1942); Moholy-Nagy: *Vision in Motion* (Chicago 1947); an article by Edith Thomas in *L'Art Abstrait, ses origines, ses premiers maîtres* (Seuphor, Paris 1949); *Collection of the Société Anonyme* (New York 1950); Hitchcock: *Painting toward Architecture* (New York 1948); *The Dada Painters and Poets* (New York 1951); *Catalogue-Album of the Schwitters exhibition,* Galerie Berggruen (Paris 1954).

SCOTT William (b. Greenock, Scotland, 1913). Studied in Belfast and in various Royal Academies. From 1937 to 1939, travelled in France and in Italy. One-man shows in London in 1942, 1948, 1950. Lives in London. — *Bibl.* Alloway: *Nine abstract artists* (Tiranti) London 1954).

SEKIYA Yoshimichi (b. in Japan, 1920). Studied at the Teachers College in Gifu. Exhibited at the Institute of

SEKIYA. CALLIGRAPHY. 1954.

calligraphy considered as an art-form (Shodo-Geijitsu-In) and the Japanese Academy of Fine Arts (Nitten) from 1949 to 1951. A member of the Bokusin-Kai School from 1952 on. Included in the exhibition of 'Present-day Fine Arts' (Kobe, 1953); in the Modern Art Fair (Osaka); in the exhibition of Japanese calligraphy at the Museum of Modern Art, New York; as well as in the Bokusin-Kai show in Tokyo, Kyoto, and Kobe, in 1954. Lives in Japan.

SEKULA Sonia (b. Lucerne, Switzerland, 1918). Was in the United States in 1934. A naturalized American citizen. Studied under Kurt Roesch and Morris Kantor. First exhibition at the 'Art of this Century' show, New York, 1946. She exhibits regularly at the Betty Parsons Gallery, and takes part in numerous art-displays throughout America. Lives in New York.

SERPAN Iaroslav (b. Prague, 1922). Was in France, 1929. Began to paint about 1940. At first a member of the surrealist group, with which he exhibited at the Galerie Maeght, Paris, in 1947. Then worked towards 'the realisation of a dynamic pictorial space', and took part in numerous group-shows, in Paris, Vienna, Berlin, Prague, London, and Rome. Published also theoretical and critical essays in various reviews, particularly in Italy. Lives in Paris. A graphism in brief slight strokes, commas or squiggles, gathered in compact masses or scattered across the canvas in galaxies. Serpan's works are highly strung in aspect.

SERVRANCKX Victor (b. Dieghem, near Brussels, in 1897). Attended the Academy in Brussels from 1912 to 1917. First one-man show in Brussels, 1917. Since 1932, a professor at the School of Industrial and Decorative Arts in Ixelles. He was the first Belgian painter to launch into abstraction. After the First World War, was a member of the 'Effort Moderne' group (Léonce Rosenberg) in Paris. Numerous one-man shows in Bel-

gium, in Paris, and in the main European countries. His work was first introduced in America by the 'Collection Anonyme' in 1926. Important retrospective exhibition at the Palais des Beaux-Arts, Brussels, in 1947. Takes part regularly in the Salon des Réalités Nouvelles; lives in Brussels.

The first part of Servranckx's work shared the aesthetic of the machine advocated by the futurists, but in a very individual and entirely abstract way. Then the painter progressed toward studies in imitation of substances, more akin to the ambiguous conceptions of surrealism. His recent work clearly indicates a return to compositions in simple elements, sometimes very close to neo-plasticism. — Bibl. *Het Overzicht,* n° 21 (Antwerp 1924); *Catalogue of the retrospective exhibition* (Brussels 1927); Seuphor: *L'Art abstrait, ses origines, ses premiers maîtres* (Paris 1949); *Collection of the Société Anonyme* (New Haven 1950).

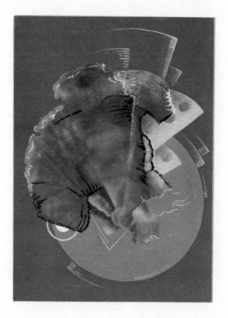

SERVRANCKX. PAINTING. 1920.

261

SEVERINI Gino (b. Cortona, Italy, 1883). Came to Rome in 1901 to study painting. Met Balla and Boccioni about 1904. In Paris, 1906. Had a studio in Impasse Guelma where Utrillo, Braque, and Dufy also had theirs. Met Modigliani and Max Jacob. Co-signer of the first futurist manifesto in 1910. In 1912, took part in the momentous futurist exhibitions in Paris, London, Berlin, etc. Married the daughter of the poet Paul Fort in 1913. His futurist work of the time bears the imprint of cubism as well as of the impressionism of Seurat. A series of paintings dated 1913 and 1914 (*Danseuses*) can be considered as pure abstractions. Severini reverted then to representational, and even academic, art for many years. In Italy after 1933. In Rome during the Second World War. Composed numerous mosaics and frescoes for churches in Switzerland and in

SEVERINI. THE MODISTE. 1911.
Joseph Slifka Coll., New York.

Italy. In 1946, published the first volume of his memoirs *Tutta la vita di un pittore* (Garzanti, Rome). In recent years, Severini has sporadically returned to abstraction. Exhibition of mosaics at the Galerie des Cahiers d'Art, Paris 1952. Retrospective at the Galerie Berggruen, Paris 1956. Severini has regularly contributed to the principal art Salons in Paris, and also showed some of his works at the exhibition "Art Abstrait, les Premières Générations", which was held at the Musée de Saint-Étienne in 1957. Lives in Paris where he directs a school of mosaics in the ancient Ravenna technique. — *Bibl.* Carrieri: *Pittura e scultura d'avanguardia in Italia* (Milan 1950); *A Dictionary of Modern Painting* (Methuen, London 1956); Seuphor: *Le futurisme . . . hier,* 'L'Œil' (Paris, Feb. 1956). Catalogue-Album of the Berggruen Exhibition (Paris 1956); Catalogue of the Saint-Étienne Exhibition (1957).

SHINODA. TRISTESSE. 1954.

SHAW Charles G. (b. New York, 1892). Studied in London, Paris, and the Art Students League, New York. First one-man show at the Valentine Gallery, New York 1934. Exhibited with the 'American Abstract Artists' from 1937 on. Lives in New York.

SHINODA Toko (b. in Japan, 1912). A member of the 'Institute of calligraphy considered as an art-form' since 1950. Took part in exhibitions of Japanese calligraphy at the Stedelijk Museum in Amsterdam, the Kunsthalle in Basel, the Musée Cernuschi in Paris, in 1955 and 1956. The author of a book: *How to learn the new calligraphy in twelve months*. Lives in Tokyo. Supple and velvety designs with delicate shading of greys.

SINEMUS Wilhelmus Friedrich (b. Amsterdam in 1903). Attended the School of Fine Arts in The Hague. Worked in France from 1928 to 1944. Devoted himself to abstract art since 1937. A member of the Dutch group 'Vrij Beelden'. Lives in The Hague.

SINGIER Gustave (b. Warneton, Belgium, 1909). Came to Paris in 1919 and was naturalized a French citizen. Until 1936, worked as a designer-decorator (installations of shops and apartments). During this period, he painted from Nature. Met Charles Walch, who advised and encouraged him and introduced him to pure painting. Included in the Salon des Indépendants, the Salon d'Automne, the Salon des Tuileries, and since 1945, in the Salon de Mai, of which he is a co-founder. Exhibition at the Galerie Drouin, Paris 1946, together with Le Moal and Manessier, followed by one-man shows at the Galerie Billet-Caputo (1949 and 1950) and the Galerie de France (1952 and 1955). Lives in Paris.

Sometimes close to that of Manessier, Singier's painting is yet lighter in appearance, and often decorative. Outstanding successes in the harmony of blues. His ready gift could easily tend to make this painter somewhat precious; but he strives to break away from such charm in large canvases where the tension of forms can be more amply realised. — *Bibl.* Bourniquel: *Trois Peintres (Le Moal, Manessier, Singier),* (Paris 1946); Marester: *Singier et la sérénité,* 'XXe Siècle' (Paris 1952).

SKULASON Thorvaldur (b. Bordeyri, Iceland, 1906). Studied at the School of Fine Arts in Oslo. Travelled in Italy, Switzerland, Belgium, Netherlands, England. Was in Paris from 1931

SINGIER. ESTUARY. 1955
Galerie de France, Paris.

263

to 1933 and from 1938 to 1940. First abstract works (rectilinear geometry) in 1938. Took part in numerous exhibitions in Scandinavia, as well as in Brussels, New York, and Rome. One of the first exponents of abstract art in Iceland. Lives in Reyjavik.

SMADJA Alex (b. Mostaganem, Algeria, 1897). Exhibited at the Salon d'Automne ever since 1929. After the Liberation, his work became completely abstract; one-man show at the Galerie Breteau, Paris 1948. He took part in the Salon des Réalités Nouvelles, the Salon de Mai, and exhibited in Copenhagen. Lives in Paris. Smadja's recent works are very rhythmical compositions in supple lines, mostly in foggy greys, with light and joyful stresses of colour.

SMITH Leon Polk (b. in Ada, Oklahoma, 1906). Studied at Oklahoma State College and in New York. Taught in Oklahoma high schools from 1934 to 1939. Travelled in Europe in 1939. Then taught in various colleges in the United States. Was in New York from 1945 to 1949. One-man shows in a number of American cities since 1940. A professor in Winter Park, Florida. Compositions of a great geometrical precision, akin to Mondrian's neo-plasticism.

SOLDATI Atanasio (b. 1887 and d. 1953 in Parma, Italy). Took a Diploma in Architecture in 1920;

then turned to painting. His first one-man show was held in Parma, 1922. Slowly, through a number of influences, particularly Klee's and Kandinsky's, Soldati progressed toward total abstraction, which he attained in 1949. One-man shows in all the main cities of Italy. Took part in group-shows in Italy, in Switzerland, and in Paris. A clear architecture in joyful, almost naive, colours was always Soldati's main concern. In recent years (1951-1953), his works are more simple and more powerful. — *Bibl*. Dorfles: *Soldati*, 'Arti visive' (Rome, Dec. 1952); Venturi: *Soldati*, Galleria Bergamini (Milan 1954).

SONDERBORG K. R. H. (b. in Sonderborg, Alsen Island, Denmark, in 1923). At first a shop-assistant in Hamburg. Interned in the Fuhlsbüttel concentration camp (1941-1942). Attended the Fine Arts School in Hamburg from 1947 to 1949. Travelled in Italy and spent some time on Stromboli Island. Worked under Hayter in Paris, 1953. A member of the group 'Zen 49'. Took part

SONDERBORG. 3-XI-54—11.5 a.m. to 12.10 p.m.
André V. Naggar Collection, Paris.

264

in many exhibitions of German abstract art, particularly in Amsterdam (1954) and in Paris (1955). Lives in Hamburg.

SOTO Jesus Raphael (b. in Ciudad Bolivar, Venezuela, 1923). Studied at the School of Plastic Arts in Caracas (1942-1947). Was then appointed director of the School of Plastic Arts in Maracaibo. Was in Paris in 1950. Took part every year in the Salon des Réalités Nouvelles. Was also included in a number of shows at the Galerie Denise René. At the same time, exhibited his abstract works in Venezuela, particularly in Caracas (1951) and in Valencia (1955). Lives in Paris. Soto composes 'cinetic structures' with elements close to suprematism and neo-plasticism.

SOULAGES Pierre (b. Rodez, South-West France, in 1919). While attending school in his home-town, he began to paint, completely unaware of any modern painting, but greatly attracted by prehistoric and romanesque art, of which there are numerous remains in that part of France. During a few months in Paris, in 1938, he got acquainted with the younger school of painting. Then, he worked on his own in Rodez. Settled in Paris in 1946, and the following year, exhibited for the first time at the Salon des Surindépendants. After that, he exhibited many times in Paris, in Germany, in Belgium, in Denmark, etc. Has taken part in the Salon de Mai since 1949. Costume and set-designer for a number of plays, including Vaillant's *Héloïse et Abélard* at the Théâtre des Mathurins, Paris 1949, and Graham Greene's *The Power and the Glory* at the Athénée, Paris 1951. Exhibitions at the Kootz Gallery, New York, 1954 and 1955, and at the Galerie de France, Paris 1956. Lives in Paris.

Black painting, in heavy lines, where an essential symbol summarizes the graphism. A certain gradation of greys or the clear

SOULAGES. PAINTING. 1954.

tints of the background produce by contrast a powerful dramatic effect. The sobriety of the forms, the reduction of colours to only black chords, attain their utmost significance through cleverly distributed lighting. Soulages' best canvases testify to an accomplished knowledge of *chiaroscuro*. The symbol rules, but it is conceived as a structure and the structure tries to become a force. — Bibl. *Premier Bilan de l'Art actuel* (Paris 1943); 'La Table Ronde', nº 77 (Paris, May 1954); Ragon: *Soulages*, 'Cimaise' (Paris, January 1956).

SPENCER Vera (b. Prague, 1926). Came to England in 1936. Took English nationality. After a period of expressionist painting (under the direction of Kokoschka), she studied for three years at the Slade School, London. First abstract paintings in 1950. One-man show at the Galerie Arnaud, Paris, 1952. Contributed collages to group-shows in England, in France, and in New York. Lives in London.

SPILLER Jurg (b. Basel, 1913). Lived in England, in France, and in Germany while attending university and studying painting. His first paintings were expressionist. Later on, the French influence became noticeable in Spiller's tendency towards a constructive realism. Before the Second World War, he exhibited in London and in Berlin, then in Basel, Zurich, Paris, and Copenhagen. Travelling exhibition in Germany, in 1950. Spent some time in Mexico (1951-1952). In company with the Swiss artist Bodmer, at the Galleria del Milione, Milan, 1949, exhibited abstract works often marked by a search for horizontal-vertical rhythms but always with a lyrical quality reminiscent of Paul Klee (Entre Jour et Nuit, 1947). Lives in Basel.

SPRINGER Ferdinand (b. in Berlin, 1907). Studied philosophy and art history at the University of Zurich.

Came to Paris in 1928. Worked at the Académie Ranson under Bissière (cf. that name), then at S. W. Hayter's 'Atelier 17'. One-man shows in Paris, Basel, and New York, from 1935 to 1937. Drafted in the French army in 1939, he retreated to Switzerland when the Germans invaded Southern France (1942); lived in forced residence in a village near Bern, in the Oberland, until 1945. Then settled in Grasse. Illustrated numerous books with engravings testifying to an exceptional gift for adopting various styles: one can quote *The Symposium of Socrates* (London 1937), *Eupalinos* by Valéry (Paris 1947); *le Mythe de la Caverne* (Paris 1948). He came to abstraction with seventeen etchings for the *Tao-te-King*; afterwards the French Government commissioned four tapestries. Took part in various Paris Salons. His painted or engraved works have been exhibited in the United States, in Great Britain, in Germany, and in Switzerland. Lives in Paris and in Grasse.
— Bibl. *Das Kunstwerk*, heft 8-9 (Baden-Baden 1950); Springer: *Der Kupferstich ein Technik der Gegenwart*, 'Werk' (Winterthur, Jan. 1950).

STAËL Nicolas de (b. Saint-Petersburg, 1914; d. Antibes, 1955). Studied classics and attended the School of Fine Arts in Brussels. Travelled in Holland in 1930. In Paris, 1932, he made a living as a decor-painter. Travelled in Spain in 1935. The following years, he spent some time in Italy and North Africa. Returned to Paris in 1940. Met and became friendly with Braque. One-man show at the Galerie Jeanne

SPRINGER. PERSIAN THEME. 1954.

266

Bucher, Paris, 1945. After 1950, he exhibited mainly at the Galerie Jacques Dubourg, Paris, and took part regularly in the Salon de Mai. He had a number of exhibitions in New York. " The brush, and more often the trowel, organizes the surface in light panels with few nuances. The palette welcomes flashy reds, quiet blues, golden ochres, and amethysts; Staël can even make black luminous by charging it more and more heavily." (R. Van Gindertael). He reverted imperceptibly to representation from 1953 on and found himself in a cul-de-sac. He committed suicide by throwing himself from the window of his studio in Antibes. Staël's lyrical and brilliant painting had a marked influence over many young Paris painters about 1950. A generous and ardent nature, with a tendency to exaggeration, Staël seems to have been defeated—during the last two years of his life—by apparently insoluble problems. His tragic end remains as mysterious as that of Van Gogh, with whom he had evident affinities in character. One of his last canvases (les Mouettes, 1955) recalls irresistibly Paysage aux Corbeaux. His most beautiful works, both powerful and harmonious, are still those he painted between 1950 and 1952 : the abstract composition built up in large planes and free architecture Grands Footballeurs will probably remain as a masterpiece of modern art. Then, this fire, a token of a great wisdom, settled down little by little until it flickered out completely in representational works in grey. Did Staël burn himself out with the too violent ardour of his temperament ? Did the return to traditional painting seem to him too heavy

DE STAËL. THE FOOTBALLERS. 1952. *Estorick Collection, London.*

a load to carry ? We shall never know the real cause of his fatal flaw. A large retrospective exhibition of his work was held at the Museum of Modern Art, Paris, 1956. — *Bibl.* Duthuit: *Nicolas de Staël* (Paris, 1950); Gindertael: *Nicolas de Staël* (Paris 1951); Courthion: *Peintres d'aujourd'hui* (Geneva 1952); *Cimaise*, nº 7 (Paris, June 1955); Catalogue of the retrospective exhibition at the Museum of Modern Art (Paris 1956).

STAMOS Theodoros (b. New York, 1922). Began as a sculptor. Spent three years at the Stuyvesant High School, New York. Then, turned to painting and took up many trades in order to live. First one-man show in 1943. Has exhibited regularly at the Betty Parsons Gallery, New York, since 1947. Took part in the 'Jeunes Peintres' show as well as in 'Cinquante ans d'Art aux États-Unis', both at the Museum of Modern Art, Paris, 1955. Lives in New York. — Bibl. *Contemporary American Painting*, San Fransisco 1950; Ritchie: *Abstract Painting and Sculpture in America*, Museum of Modern Art, New York 1951.

267

STILL. PAINTING. 1951.
Museum of Modern Art, New York.

STARITSKY Anna (b. Poltava, Ukraine, 1911). In Moscow, attended classes of drawing taught by Tolstoy's daughter. Studied at the School of Fine Arts in Sofia, Bulgaria. Was in Brussels from 1932 to 1947. Worked as a designer in a printing-press. One-man shows in Brussels, Antwerp, Paris, Nice, etc. Has taken part in the Salon des Réalités Nouvelles since 1951. She is married to the painter Orix (cf. that name). Lives in Paris and in Nice. Paintings of pure effusion, very rich in substance.

STARK Gustl (b. Mainz, Germany, 1917). Educated

in Wurtzburg and Nuremberg. Studied in Sylt and in Paris, where he spent some time. Took part in numerous group-shows in the main cities of Germany as well as in the Salon des Réalités Nouvelles. Combinations of elementary graphism and coloured planes. Lives in Mainz.

STERNE Hedda (b. in Rumania, 1915). Came to America in 1941, after having studied in Paris, Bucharest, and Vienna. Exhibited at the Betty Parsons Gallery, New York, since 1947. Took part in numerous group-shows in the United States. Is married to the American cartoonist Steinberg. Lives in New York.

STILL Clyfford (b. Grandin, North Dakota, 1904). Educated in Alberta (Canada); worked his way through Spokane University (Washington) by working on a farm during vacations. Taught at Washington State College (1933-1941) and at the California School of Fine Arts (1946-1950). One-man shows: San

STARITSKY. COMPOSITION. 1955.

268

Francisco Museum of Art (1941); 'Art in this Century' (1946), Betty Parsons Gallery, New York (1947, 1950, 1951). Took part in the exhibition 'Cinquante ans d'Art aux États-Unis' at the Museum of Modern Art, Paris, 1955. Taught at Hunter College, New York, and Brooklyn College, New York. Lives in New York.

"From the most ancient times the artist has been expected to perpetuate the values of his contemporaries. The record is mainly one of frustration, sadism, superstition, and the will to power. The anxious find comfort in the confusion of those artists who would walk beside them. The values involved, however, permit no peace, and mutual resentment is deep when it is discovered that salvation cannot be bought. We are now committed to an unqualified act, not illustrating outworn myths or contemporary alibis. The artist must accept total responsibility for what he executes. And the measure of his greatness will be in the depth of his insight and his courage in realizing his own vision." (Still). Large monochromatic surfaces of shredded forms. Often a red smear scorches the broadly spread black, a thick living black peculiar to Still. He must be considered among the American painters who have created an autonomous style owing little to the European tendencies of the last fifty years.— Bibl. *Fifteen Americans,* Museum of Modern Art (New York 1952); Greenberg: *American-type painting,* 'Partisan review', n° 2 (New York 1955).

STRZEMINSKI Wladislas (b. 1893 and d. 1952 in Poland). One of the leading Polish painters of the school of pure abstraction; took a very active part in the review *Blok,* founded in Warsaw in 1924. He was a close friend of Henri Stazewski who was included in the 'Cercle et Carré' exhibition in Paris, 1930, and whose whereabouts are now unknown. In the same Polish group were Berlewi,

Zarnowerowna, Szezuka, Kobro, Krynski. It seems that they were all very much influenced by Malevitch when he came to lecture on suprematism in Warsaw, in 1924. Moreover, Berlewi introduced in the group the neo-plastic conceptions which van Doesburg had directly imparted to him in Berlin, 1922.

SUGAÏ Kumi (b. in Kobe, Japan, 1919). He came from a family of classical musicians. Attended the School of Fine Arts in Osaka (1927-1932). Had a studio

SUGAÏ. CRACKER. 1954.
Galerie Craven, Paris.

in Kobe until 1951. Was a poster-designer. Was in Paris in 1952. One-man show at the Galerie Craven, Paris 1953. Took part in group-shows in Brussels, New York,

London, and Pittsburgh. He is attached to the concepts of Zen buddhism. Abstract compositions where oriental refinement fuses with a western sense of order. A very quiet and restrained emotion corrects the rigour of the integrated rule.

SZENÈS Arpad (b. in Budapest, 1900). Came to Paris in 1925 and worked under Lhote, Léger, Bissière. Exhibited at the Salon des Surindépendants from 1932 to 1938. As early as 1932, his work was very close to abstraction. Lived in Brazil from 1939 to 1947 with his wife Viera da Silva. One-man shows in Lisbon, Rio de Janeiro, and, a number of times, at the Galerie Jeanne Bucher, Paris. Took part in the Salon de Mai. Lives in Paris. Szenès was for a time on the borders of surrealism. His recent and abstract work is quite an individual phenomenon: a snowy world which reveals its story in melting white expanses. This affirmed paleness, these hardly perceptible tracks in the white are the vocabulary of a painter very sure of his meaning, but who whispers it and cares little about being heard. Besides, he thinks, one only speaks to those who already know and who can take a hint.

SZENÈS. COMPOSITION. 1955. *Galerie Jeanne Bucher, Paris.*

270

T

TABUCHI Yasse (b. in Japan, 1921). Attended the University of Tokyo. Took part in exhibitions in Tokyo from 1947 to 1950. Settled in Paris in 1951 and took part in numerous abstract art displays. One-man show at the Palais des Beaux-Arts, Brussels, in 1955. "The mainspring of Tabuchi's art is probably not the antagonism of the elements—real or imaginary—but their secret complicity under the vigilant control of man, who is not for all his special position, however, allowed to mislead." (Édouard Jaguer).

TAEUBER-ARP Sophie (b. in Davos, Switzerland, in 1889; d. in Zurich, 1943). Educated in Switzerland, in Munich, and in Hamburg. From 1916 to 1929 was a professor at the School of Arts and Crafts in Zurich. Entered the dada movement in Zurich with Arp whom she married in 1921. Composed mural paintings and stained glass windows in Strasbourg. In Strasbourg also, in 1928, she worked together with Arp and Theo van Doesburg on the remarkable interior decoration of the 'Aubette' *café dansant* (the decorations have since been destroyed). Settled in Meudon, near Paris, with Arp, from 1927 to 1940. Was a member of "Cercle et Carré' and then of 'Abstraction-Création'. Also a member of the Swiss group 'Die Allianz'. In Meudon, from 1937 to 1939, directed the review *Plastique*. Was in Grasse from 1941 to 1943. There she composed lithographs in collaboration with Sonia Delaunay, Arp, and Magnelli. She died accidentally in Zurich.

"Sophie Taeuber belongs already to the second generation of abstract artists: her

ARP AND SOPHIE TAEUBER-ARP.
COMPOSITION. 1942.

first works, dated 1916, water-colours and coloured crayon drawings composed of rectangles, no longer have the experimental and haphazard characteristics of the works of the preceding generation, 1900-1912. One can no longer discern the least trace of the troubled struggle for victory over the object. With logical calm, Sophie Taeuber already combines in her first works the rectangular form or rhythmical element derived from cubism, with pure colour or the melodic element, established by Delaunay. The fusion of formal rhythm and coloured melody—with an evident predominance of

271

rhythm — characterises all the work of Sophie Taeuber. The progress of her work was but the development of the same themes, untroubled and continually enriched." (Georg Schmidt). — *Bibl.* Schmidt and others: *Sophie Taeuber-Arp* (a monograph, Basel 1948); Seuphor: *L'Art abstrait, ses origines, ses premiers maîtres* (Paris 1949); Arp: *On my way* (New York 1948); *Onze peintres vus par Arp* (Zurich 1949); Arp: *Jalons,* chez l'Auteur (Meudon 1951); *Catalogue of the Sophie Taeuber-Arp exhibition,* Sidney Janis Gallery (New York 1950); 'Art d'Aujourd'hui' (Paris, May-June 1950; December 1951; December 1953); Seuphor: *Mission spirituelle de l'art* (Paris 1953); *A Dictionary of Modern Painting* (Methuen, London 1956).

TAL COAT. SIGN AND RETURN. 1952.
Galerie Maeght, Paris.

TAL COAT Pierre (b. Clohars-Carnoët, Brittany, 1905). His parents were fishermen. Under the influence of the French and foreign painters who frequented the fishing-village where he was born, his vocation was awakened early. Worked in a pottery factory in Quimper. Came to Paris at the age of nineteen. Spent some time in Burgundy and in Provence. Had a number of one-man shows at the Galerie de France, after 1943; at the Galerie Maeght in 1954. Lives in Paris or in Aix-en-Provence. Tal Coat has many times revealed undeniable affinities with Picasso. In recent works, he has drawn the best of his inspiration from Cézanne. Glistening lines, voluntarily hesitant, furtive, seeking only to skim lightly but surely, seeking not to ring out but to sharpen hearing by a whisper of such quality that it will last. — Bibl. *Derrière le Miroir,* Galerie Maeght (Paris, April 1954).

TANAKA Shu (b. Tokyo, 1908). Attended the École Normale Supérieure. Then, travelled in England, Belgium, China, Egypt, Italy, and Holland. Took part in exhibitions in Japan and in Paris. Lives in Paris.

TANCREDI (b. Feltre, Italy). Academic schooling in Italy. For some time he practised the 'automatic' painting advocated by the surrealists. One-man show in Venice, at the Gallery Sandri. A member of the Italian 'Pittori spaziali' group. Lives in Venice.

TAPIES Antonio (b. Barcelona, 1923). Broke up his law studies in order to devote himself to painting. In 1948, a co-founder of the review and the group *Dau al set,* in Barcelona. Was in Paris in 1950 and 1951 and travelled in Belgium and in Holland. Spent a short time in New York in 1953, while his works were exhibited at the Martha Jackson Gallery. Numerous one-man shows in Spain. First Paris one-man show at the Galerie Stadler,

272

1956. Lives in Barcelona. From various influences more or less absorbed (Miro, Dubuffet) Tapies has been able to evolve an intense and deeply dramatic art, incantatory in effect. — *Bibl.* Michel Tapié: *Antonio Tapies et l'œuvre complète*, Galerie Stadler (Paris 1956).

TATAFIORE Guido (b. Naples, 1919). Attended the Art Institute in Naples. Many one-man shows in Naples. Included in the 'Arte Astratta e Concreta in Italia' exhibition, at the Museum of Modern Art, Rome 1951. Lives in Naples.

TESTA Clorindo (b. Naples 1923). He emigrated to Argentine at an early age. First travelled and studied in Europe from 1949 to 1951. First one-man show in 1951, in Buenos Aires, followed by many others in the main cities of Argentine. Included in 1953 in the 'Eight Argentine Abstract Painters' show at the Municipal Museum in Amsterdam. Lives in Buenos Aires.

THIELER Fred (b. Königsberg, East Prussia, in 1916). Studied medicine (1937-1941) and began to paint. Attended the School of Fine Arts in Munich (1946-1948). Was in Paris in 1951 and 1952. One-man shows in Amsterdam, Galerie Le Canard (1951); in Paris, Galerie Suzanne Michel (1953); in Munich, Ophir Gallery (1953); in Oslo, Gallery of Modern Art (1954). A member of the 'Zen 49' group. Included in the exhibition 'Peintures et Sculptures non-figuratives en Allemagne d'Aujourd'hui' at the Cercle Volney, Paris, 1955. Lives in Munich. Abstract neo-expressionism expressed in turbulent visions of a universe in violent disintegration. "Thieler is one of the few post-war artists to have attained a substantial place in the artistic life of modern Germany." (J. A. Thwaites).

TINGUELY Jean (b. in Basel, 1925). Attended the School of Fine Arts in Basel (1940-1944). At first a painter, but from 1944 on, devoted himself to the study of movement in space. One-man show of mobiles, Galerie Arnaud, Paris 1954. Took part the same year in the Salon des Réalités Nouvelles. A member of the group 'Espace'. Was extensively represented in the exhibition 'Le Mouvement' at the Galerie Denise René, Paris 1955. Lives in Paris.

TOBEY Mark (b. in Centerville, Wisconsin, 1890). A self-educated painter. Came to New York in 1911: spent half his time in New York and half in Chicago. Was in Seattle in 1923: taught two years at the Cornish School. Then travelled

TOBEY. COMPOSITION. 1955.
Galerie Rive Droite, Paris.

273

to Europe and the Near East. Returned to Seattle in 1927. Was in England from 1931 to 1938. Travelled throughout Europe, in Mexico, in Asia. Studied chinese calligraphy in China. Between all these travels, his fixed residence was in England. In 1939, he returned again to Seattle where he is still living today. First exhibition at the Knoedler Gallery, New York, in 1917. Since 1944, he exhibited regularly at the Willard Gallery, New York. In 1951, took part in the 'Abstract Painting and Sculpture in America' exhibition at the Museum of Modern Art, New York. The same year, a retrospective exhibition of his works was held at the Whitney Museum, New York. Was in Europe in 1954 and 1955. Took part in various exhibitions, particularly at the Galerie Rive Droite and the Museum of Modern Art, Paris. One-man shows in London and Paris (Galerie Jeanne Bucher, 1955).

One may wonder why some works of small format — gouaches, water-colours, drawings—of Klee or Tobey, seem much

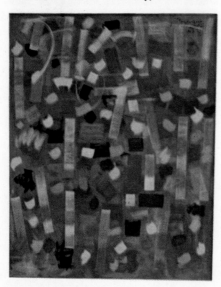

TOMLIN. NUMBER. 4. 1952.

more convincing to us than the vast compositions of Riopelle, Mathieu, Pollock, or Sam Francis. It must be because inflated language overreaches its goal and lacks zest. The spectacle of animal power, even magnificently endowed physically, always leaves us with a nostalgia for perfume, for inwardness, in spite of the spell of pure size. The restraint of Tobey or Klee touches us more because true eloquence comes from the heart, and the heart is a seed slow to mature.

"Our ground today is not so much the national or the regional ground as it is the understanding of this single earth. The earth has been round for some time now, but not in man's relations to man nor in the understanding of the arts of each as a part of that roundness. As usual we have occupied ourselves too much with the outer, the objective, at the expense of the inner world wherein the true roundness lies. America more than any other country is placed geographically to lead in this understanding, and if from past methods of behavior she has constantly looked toward Europe, today she must assume her position, Janus-faced, toward Asia, for in not too long a time the waves of the Orient shall wash heavily upon her shores. All this is deeply related with her growth in the arts, particularly upon the Pacific slopes. Of this I am aware. Naturally my work will reflect such a condition and so it is not surprising to me when an Oriental responds to a painting of mine as well as an American or a European." (Tobey).— *Bibl.* Janis : *Abstract and Surrealist Art in America* (New York 1944); *Fourteen Americans* (New York 1946); Hitchcock: *Painting towards Architecture* (New York 1948); *40 American Painters, 1904-1950* (U. of Minnesota, 1951); Ritchie: *Abstract Painting and Sculpture in America* (New York 1951); Catalogue of the Tobey exhibition at the Whitney Museum (New York 1951); Hess: *Abstract Painting* (New York 1951); Barr: *Masters of Modern Art* (New York 1954); Alvard: *Tobey*, 'Cimaise'

(Paris, May 1955); Flanner: *Tobey, mystique errant,* 'L'Œil' (Paris, June 1955).

TOMLIN Bradley-Walker (b. Syracuse, New York, 1899; d. New York, 1953). Attended the University of Syracuse. Spent some years in Europe after 1921. Taught for about ten years in a New York college (1932-1941). One-man shows since 1924, particularly at the Rehn Gallery and the Betty Parsons Gallery, New York. After having painted a long time in the cubist manner, Tomlin turned toward the calligraphic style characteristic of his work about 1946. The work he left, which is very close in spirit to Tobey's, although somewhat less *intimate,* somewhat less restrained, will always remain very significant. The surfaces covered with dancing signs, both precise and supple, are feasts of the free spirit which, plastically, vocalizes, alliterates, invents, associates, organizes. — *Bibl.* Ritchie: *Abstract Painting and Sculpture in America* (New York 1951); Hess: *Abstract Painting* (New York 1951); *Fifteen Americans* (New York 1952); Barr: *Masters of Modern Art* (New York 1954); *50 ans d'art aux États-Unis,* Museum of Modern Art (Paris 1955).

TRIER Hann (b. Dusseldorf, 1915). Attended the School of Fine Arts in Dusseldorf (1934-1938). The brother of the art-critic Edouard Trier. Travelled in France, Holland, Italy, Switzerland, Spain, Colombia. A member of the German group 'Zen 49'. Took part in numerous art displays in Germany. Lives in Cologne. "Sceptical, but very open and eager for new experiences, Hann Trier is by no means an artist who paints according to set rules. The contours vibrate and each form is pregnant with unexpected possibilities. This instability in composition may reflect the spiritual situation of our time, where objects and concepts change every day; for us, indeed, reality is no longer constant, but a dynamic process." (Gert Schiff).

TROKES Heinz (b. Hamborn, on the Rhine, 1913). Worked under Johannes Itten and Georg Muche at the Bauhaus of Dessau. One-man shows in Amsterdam, Zurich, Paris, Brussels, Berlin. Lives in the Balearic Islands.

TRYGGVADOTTIR. PAINTING. 1955.

TRYGGVADOTTIR Nina (b. in Seydisfjordur, Iceland, 1913). Attended the Royal Academy in Copenhagen (1935-1939), and spent some time in Paris. Returned to Iceland and took part in a number of exhibitions in Reykjavik. Was in New York in 1943 in order to complete her art studies. She worked under Fernand Léger and Hans Hofmann. First one-man show at the New Art Circle, New York, 1945. Married the American painter Alcopley (cf. that name) in 1949. Was in Paris in 1952. One-man show at the Galerie Colette Allendy, Paris 1954, in Brussels (Palais des Beaux-Arts), and in Copenhagen. Took part in the Salon des Réalités Nouvelles and in numerous other group-shows. Lives now in Paris. Nina Tryggvadottir's art is sober and powerful. She composes cyclopean walls, from which the weight melts into colour; from which even, occasionally, the stones themselves escape into the sky. One also knows her collages, with their multiple and strong black veins, which could be cartoons for unexpectedly archaic stained glass windows. She is without question the most striking personality of her country in the field of plastic arts.

TSINGOS Thanos (b. Eleusis, Greece, 1914). Began to paint at the age of seventeen. In 1936, received a diploma in architecture and engineering from the Polytechnical School in Athens. Was an architect in Greece up to the war. From 1939 to 1946, fought in the Greek army. Joined the allied Armies on the El Alamein front. After the war, he settled in Paris and took up painting again. One-man show in Paris, Studio Facchetti, 1952. He took part in the Salon des Réalités Nouvelles and numerous other group-shows. Lives in Paris. A black lyricism, lineary effusions cut deep in the mass of fresh paint. In his recent work, Tsingos shows a desire for clarity and organization.

TSUJI Futoshi (b. Gifu, Japan, 1925). Exhibited at the "Institute of Calligraphy considered as an art-form" in 1950 and with the Kei-Sei-Kai school in 1952. A member of the Bokubi and Bokusin group of modern calligraphies (Shiryu Morita).

Took part in all the exhibitions organised by the group in various Museums of Europe (Amsterdam, Basel, Paris) and at the Museum of Modern Art, New York. Lives in Japan.

TURAN Selim (b. Istanbul, 1915). Attended the Academy of Fine Arts in Istanbul. Travelled in Germany, France, England, Greece, Italy, Turkey. One-man show at the Galerie Breteau, Paris, 1950. First non-representational canvas in 1945. Took part in the Salon des Réalités Nouvelles since 1947. Lives in Paris.

TURCATO Giulio (b. Mantua, Italy, 1912). Was a member of the 'Forma I' group and took part in numerous group-shows in Italy and various other countries. Lives in Rome.

TWORKOV Jack (b. Biala, Poland, 1900). Came to the United States in 1913. Attended Columbia University 1920-1923. Spent some time at the Art Students League and the National Academy of Design. Exhibited at the Dudensing Gallery, New York, from 1931 to 1935, at the Egan Gallery, New York, since 1947. Took part in numerous group-shows throughout America. Taught at various colleges since 1948. Lives in New York. Abstract impressionism in a harsh and sometimes very violent style. — *Bibl.* Hess: *Abstract Painting* (New York 1951); *Art News* (New York, May 1953).

U

UBAC Rodolphe Raoul (b. Malmédy, Belgium, 1910). At first wanted to become a Forestry Inspector. Came to Paris in 1929, entered the Classics Department at the Sorbonne, but soon deserted the University in order to attend the Grande Chaumière in Montparnasse. Travelled extensively in Europe. Practised surrealistic photography for some time. A member of the surrealist group in 1934; but about 1942, abandoned surrealism and photography, and devoted himself exclusively to painting and drawing, progressing more and more towards abstract art. From then on, one of his favourite materials was cut and engraved slate. One-man shows at the Galerie Maeght, Paris 1950 and 1955. Lives in Paris. — *Bibl.* Frenaud: *Une peinture tragique,* 'Derrière le Miroir', nº 34 (Paris 1950); *Premier bilan de l'art actuel* (Paris 1953); *Raoul Ubac,* 'Derrière le Miroir', nº 74-75-76 (Paris 1955); Frenaud: *La peinture tragique de Raoul Ubac,* 'XXᵉ Siècle' (Paris, June 1956).

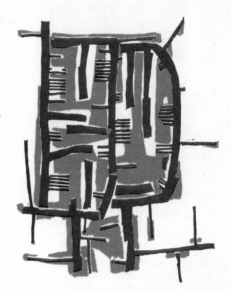

UBAC. WOODCUT. 1956.

V

VAÏTO Agathe (b. Hungary, 1928). Attended the School of Fine Arts in Budapest. Came to Paris in 1949. Took part in the Salon des Surindépendants (1951 and 1952), in the Salon de Mai and the Salon d'Octobre (1954), as well as in a group-show at the Galerie de France, in 1956. Lives in Paris.

VALENSI Henry (b. Algiers, 1883). The founder and the director since 1932 of the 'Association des Artistes Musicalistes', in Paris. Travelled extensively in Europe and Africa. Included in the Salon des Indépendants since 1907. Organized twenty-three Salons of 'Musicalist painting' in Paris, in the provinces, and

VALMIER. THE FIVE SENSES. 1931.
Galerie Saint-Augustin, Paris.

were painted between 1919 and 1923 and most of them have musical titles (*Fugue, Scherzo, Improvisation*).

VANBER Albert (b. Lestre, France, 1905). Studied at the School of Fine Arts in Paris, under Cormon and Pierre Laurens. One-man show of abstract works at the Galerie Suzanne Michel, Paris 1953. Took part in the Salon des Réalités Nouvelles the same year. Lives in Paris.

VANNI Sam (b. Viborg, Finland, 1908). Attended the School of Fine Arts in Helsinki (1927-1928). Studied under the sculptor W. Aaltonen in 1930. Travelled many times in France and in Italy. Numerous one-man shows in Finland. Abstract painting since 1948. Took part in group-shows in Paris, Rome, Stockholm, Oslo, Copenhagen, and Reykjavik. Lives in Helsinki.

abroad. He is the Vice-President of the Salon des Réalités Nouvelles. Lives in Paris. Allegorical compositions in bright colours.

VALMIER Georges (b. Angoulême, France, 1885; d. Paris, 1937). Attended the École des Beaux-Arts in Paris in 1905. Afterwards worked on his own. Was drafted in the 1914-1918 war. Exhibited in Paris in 1921. Designed a number of decors for Marinetti's futurist plays. An excellent musician, he made a living as a choir-master. His last works were decorations for the Exposition Universelle, Paris 1937. Starting from cubism, and henceforth from objective reality, Valmier's work is often transposed as far as abstraction. Among his best compositions one must count those now at the Solomon R. Guggenheim Museum in New York. They

VANTONGERLOO Georges (b. Antwerp, 1886). Attended the Academies of Antwerp and Brussels. At first a sculptor. Was drafted in the Belgian army in 1914, and imprisoned in Holland after the fall of Antwerp. Met Theo van Doesburg in 1916. Co-signer of the *De Stijl* manifesto and a contributor to the *De Stijl* review during the first years of its publication (1917-1920). Was in Menton from 1919 to 1927, then settled in Paris. Friendships with Mondrian and Seuphor, later with Max Bill and Pevsner. Took part in the 'Cercle et Carré' exhibition in 1930. The founder with Herbin of the 'Abstraction-Création' group (1931). After having for a long time followed—as well in his painting as in his sculpture—the fundamental horizontal-vertical principle of *De Stijl,* Vantongerloo adopted the curve about 1935, and from there turned to the

278

study of the 'indeterminate'. Nevertheless the basis of his works remains almost always mathematical, sometimes elaborately so. More than sixty of his works were exhibited in 1949 at the Kunsthaus of Zurich together with works by Pevsner and Max Bill. Lives in Paris. — *Bibl.* Vantongerloo: *L'art et son avenir* (Antwerp 1924); Barr: *Cubism and Abstract Art* (New York 1936); Vantongerloo: *Paintings, Sculptures, Reflexions* (New York 1948); Seuphor: *L'Art abstrait, ses origines, ses premiers maîtres* (Paris 1949); Catalogue of the Zurich exhibition (1949); Catalogue of the retrospective *De Stijl* exhibition (Amsterdam 1951).

VARAUD Serge (b. near Lyons in 1925; d. in Toulon, 1956). First abstract works in 1948. Exhibited in Toulon in 1948 and in Paris in 1949. He founded a group of abstract painters in Toulon and organised exhibitions in his own studio to encourage them. "To the calm of the horizontal, to the spirituality of the vertical, join the two sources of life: the curve with its feminine gentleness and the diagonal with its masculine purpose. Out of the coloured life of harmonies, contrasts, and dissonances, create a work where feeling expression can gain completeness with a minimum of constraint." (Varaud).

VARDANEGA G. (b. Possagno, near Venice, 1923). Attended the School of Fine Arts in Buenos Aires. In 1946, became a mem-

ber of the Argentine group 'Arte Concreto-Invencion'. Travelled in Europe 1948-1949. Spent a year in Paris and returned to Buenos Aires where he continues to investigate painting on glass and construction in space. Lives in Buenos Aires.

VASARELY Victor (b. Pecs, Hungary, 1908). Was enrolled at the School of Medecine in Budapest but classes in anatomy of the nude, at the Podolini-Volkman Academy, attracted him more. In 1929 he entered the Bauhaus of Budapest: the 'Mühely' of Bortnyik. He attended lectures by Moholy-Nagy and was introduced to the works of Malevitch, Mondrian, Gropius, Kandinsky, Le Corbusier. Settled in Paris at the end of 1930. A member of the Galerie Denise René group since its foundation in 1944. Took part in the Salon des Surindépendants, the Salon des Réalités Nouvelles, the Salon de Mai. One-man shows in Budapest (1930, 1933), in Copenhagen (1950), in Stockholm (1952),

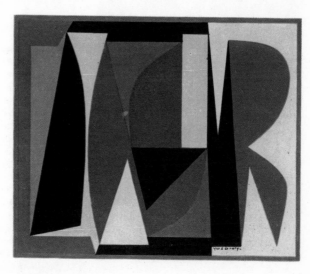

VASARELY. YELLAN. 1950. *Galerie Denise René, Paris.*

279

in Brussels (1954), and at the Galerie Denise René, Paris (1944, 1946, 1949, 1952, 1955).

"The ways of abstract painting are not easy ones. One does not create a new universe overnight without abandoning tender sentimental habits: I mean, without regret for a representational training. One has to harden oneself, learn a way of life for which there exists no tradition, foster affections between unknown forms, invent a world of emotions without previous example, and never, never lose grip. This is the climate in which Vasarely casts off his old self, with that brilliant austerity which endows his compositions with a characteristic note of heroism." (Léon Degand). — Bibl. *Témoignages pour l'art abstrait* (Paris 1952); Dewasne: *Vasarely*, Presses Littéraires de France (Paris 1952); Catalogue exposition Galerie Denise René, 1955.

BRAM VAN VELDE. COMPOSITION. 1955.

VEDOVA Emilio (b. Venice, 1919). Self-educated. Began to exhibit in 1936. His painting passed through periods of cubism and expressionism before it attained abstraction. He travelled across Italy, living among the workers and the poor. Hostile to Fascism, he took part in the battles of the Liberation. Was the promoter in Venice of the New Front of the Arts (1946). One-man shows in all the main cities of Italy as well as in New York (Viviano Gallery) and in Munich (Gallery Günther Franke). Took part in the Venice Biennales and numerous other Salons in Italy, in France, in Germany, in South America. He travelled to Paris, Brazil, Vienna, Germany. Lives in Venice.

"For Vedova, painting is a conception of the world, the very image of the eternal conflict between being and non-being, good and evil. It is not the primary forces of the cosmos which fuse and explode in his paintings, but the deep impulses of the human soul." (Giulio Carlo Argan). — *Bibl.* Mazzariol: *Appunti sulla poetica di Emilio Vedova*, 'I 4 Soli' (Turin, Nov. 1955).

VELDE Bram van (b. Zonderwonde, Holland, 1895). A very difficult early life in Leyden and The Hague. A house painter, then a decorator in a luxury-shop. His employer helped him to get to Paris (about 1924) so as to study painting. Spent some time in the Balearic Islands. Returned to Paris in 1936. Included in the Salon des Indépendants and the Salon des Surindépendants. One-man shows at the Galerie Mai (1946), the Galerie Maeght (1952), and the Galerie Warren (1955). Lives in Paris. Supple forms integrated into each other; a sinuous line (baroque) but without anguish. The colour is light (blues, greens, whites) and seems to float in a timeless, limpid, atmosphere, deeply fraught with human sensibility. — Bibl. *Derrière le Miroir,* n° 11-12 and 43 (Paris 1948 and 1952).

280

VEDOVA. SKETCH FOR "RÉVOLTE". GOUACHE. 1951. *Private Collection.*

VERONESI Luigi (b. Milan, 1908). In 1934, a member of the 'Abstraction-Création' group in Paris. One-man shows in Milan and Paris in 1939. Produced abstract films. Took part in various abstract art displays in Italy, particularly at the Galleria del Milione (as early as 1935). Lives in Milan.

VELDE Geer van (b. Lisse, Holland, 1898). Brother of the preceding painter. Came to Paris in 1925. Exhibited at the Salon des Indépendants in 1926 and 1930. First one-man show in London, Gallery Guggenheim Jr., in 1938. From 1939 to 1945, was in Cagnes-sur-Mer. One-man shows at the Galerie Maeght, Paris 1946 and 1952. Took part in the Salon d'Automne, the Salon des Tuileries and the Salon de Mai. Exhibited at the Kootz Gallery, New York, together with his brother, in 1948. He has had and still has a great influence upon younger painters. Lives in Paris. Playfully rigorous compositions, the principal element of which is a sure knowledge of the harmony of nuances. "Van Velde's gay colours and Impressionist taste for gentle diffused tones often recall the painting of Villon" (Frank Elgar). — Bibl. *Derrière le Miroir,* nº 11-12 and 51 (Paris); *Premier Bilan de l'art actuel,* Paris 1953.

VEZELAY Paule (b. Southern England, 1893). Educated in London. At first illustrated books for English publishers. First exhibition in 1921, at the Gallery Dorian Leigh, London. Was in Paris from 1923 to 1939; first abstract paint-

GEER VAN VELDE. COMPOSITION. 1953.

281

ing in 1928. A member of 'Abstraction-Création' in 1934. Included in the Salon des Surindépendants from 1929 to 1939 and in numerous exhibitions of abstract art. On the committee of the Salon des Réalités Nouvelles. Main one-man shows: Galerie Jeanne Bucher, Paris 1928, 1932, 1934, 1937, 1946; Galerie Lefevre, London, 1936, 1942; Galerie Colette Allendy, Paris 1950; Gimpel fils Gallery, London 1950. Lives in London. Few artists illustrate as well as Paule Vézelay the many-sidedness of art. She has practised painting, sculpture, collages, compositions with stretched strings, drawing, engraving. Her work has a discreet charm, a childish and yet very elegant purity. — *Bibl*. 'Art d'Aujourd'hui', Paris, December 1954.

VICENTE Esteban (b. Spain, 1906). From 1928 to 1935, exhibited in Madrid, Barcelona, Paris, London. First exhibition in New York, 1937, at the Kleeman Galleries. Took part in numerous group-shows in various New York galleries, as well as in 'Aspects de la Peinture Américaine', Galerie de France, Paris 1952. Lives in New York. Surfaces freely organized by a lyricism of colour. The improvisation is only on the surface; there is a true discipline in the combination of lines, forms, and colours. Vicente has composed collages possessing a surprising density of forms and colours. — *Bibl*. Hess: *Abstract Painting* (New York 1951).

VIEIRA DA SILVA Maria Elena (b. Lisbon, 1908). Came to Paris at the age of nineteen to study sculpture under Bourdelle and Despiau. Then attended the studios of Friesz and Léger, and Hayter's engraving workshop. In 1930, she married the Hungarian painter Arpad Szenès. Travelled extensively in Europe. Was in South America during the Second World War. Came back to Paris in 1947. One-man shows at the Galerie Jeanne Bucher since 1933, at the Galerie Pierre since 1949. Numerous exhibitions in London. She

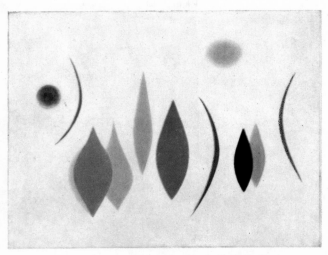

VÉZELAY. COMPOSITION. 1954. *M. S. Collection Paris.*

takes part regularly in the Salon de Ma. Lives in Paris.

Little by little, through embellishment of her familiar theme, Vieira da Silva has created an exceptional art, a rare type of painting. Something is there that was never expressed before: a space without dimensions, both limited and boundless, a hallucinating mosaic where each element is endowed with an inner power transcending its own matrix. Each touch of paint is charged with restrained dynamism, but the whole canvas reveals potency. The art of Mondrian was pure style, that of Van Gogh pure anguish. In Vieira da Silva, style and the cry of the heart are simultaneously present in each work, closely involved in each minute of it. It is a hymn of restraint and invention: rigour and freedom in an exalting marriage. — *Bibl.* Descargues: *Vieira da Silva* (Paris 1949); Seuphor: *Promenade autour de Vieira da Silva*, 'Cahiers d'Art', nº 2 (Paris 1949); Grenier: *Vieira da Silva*, 'L'Œil' (Paris, Feb. 1956); Guéguen: *Vieira da Silva*, 'XXᵉ Siècle' (Paris, June 1950).

VILLALBA V. (b. Canary Islands, 1925). Attended the Academy of Fine Arts in Buenos Aires. Has taken part in the group-shows of 'Arte Concreto-Invencion' since 1946. Lives in Buenos Aires.

VILLERI Jean (b. Oneglia, Italy, 1898). Came to France in 1906. At first an impressionist painter in the South of France. A member of the 'Abstraction-Création' group in 1932. Took part in the Salon des Tuileries, the Salon des Réalités Nouvelles, the Salon de Mai. One-man show at the Galerie Maeght in 1948. Included in a number of group-shows in Germany, Belgium, Brazil, and the United States. Lives in Cagnes-sur-Mer (on the Riviera) and travels frequently to Paris. Villeri is a painter of great culture. His work, like that of most painters, is torn in the constant contradiction between improvisation and the desire for structure. His most successful canvases are those where the struggle remains visible.

VIEIRA DA SILVA. SPACE ASLEEP. 1954. *Galerie J. Bucher, Paris.*

283

VILLON. RACEHORSE. 1922. *Galerie Louis Carré, Paris.*

VILLON Jacques (b. Damville, Normandy, in 1875). His real name is Gaston Duchamp; he is the brother of the sculptor Raymond Duchamp-Villon, and of Marcel Duchamp. Attended the École des Beaux-Arts and studied under Cormon about 1894. For a long time he contributed cartoons to the comic papers of the period. A member of the Salon d'Automne. First exhibited with Duchamp-Villon in Rouen, 1905. Joined the cubist movement in 1911. It was in his studio in Puteaux that the group 'Section d'Or' assembled: the principal members were Léger, Picabia, La Fresnaye, Metzinger, and Gleizes. Was mobilised during the First World War. First abstract paintings in 1919, Included in the exhibitions of the Société Anonyme, in New York, from 1922 on. From 1921 to 1930, to make a living, he engraved a series of coloured reproductions of modern paintings, often very remarkable. New period of abstract painting from 1931 to 1933. In the United States in 1935. Took part in the 'Réalités Nouvelles' exhibition at the Galerie Charpentier, Paris 1939. Since the Liberation, he has exhibited regularly at the Galerie Carré, Paris. Lives in Puteaux, near Paris.

As with Klee, only a fraction of Villon's work belongs to abstract art, but more than Klee's, each of Villon's works is on the way to abstraction. He has written: "Modern painting is a painting of creation, a painting of rhythms and volumes. In order to satisfy the exigencies of this painting, one must extract rhythms and volumes from the subject, as one extracts a diamond from its matrix." Villon's painting may seem light, puny, superficial. But the quick look is more mistaken than ever: here is a compact and measured world of which the painter has counted all the riches, probed all the dimensions, without overlooking the most secret. A world both solid and supple, like a tree—as vibrant and dense as a tree. — *Bibl.* Barr: *Cubism and Abstract Art* (New York 1936); *Art of this Century* (New York 1942); Paul Éluard et René Jean: *Jacques Villon ou l'Art Glorieux* (Paris 1948); 'Art d'Aujourd'hui' (Paris, Dec. 1949); *Collection of the Société Anonyme* (New York 1950); Raynal: *De Picasso au Surréalisme* (Paris-Geneva 1950); *A Dictionary of Modern Painting* (Methuen, London 1956); Seuphor: *Klee et Villon* 'Preuves' (Paris, June 1955). Catalogue of the exhibition at the Musée de Saint-Étienne, 1957.

284

VISEUX Claude (b. Paris 1927). Studied architecture at the École des Beaux-Arts in Paris. First non-representational paintings in 1950. Took part in numerous Salons and group-shows in Paris and abroad. Lives in Paris. "I envisaged a kind of landscape-portrait, like a crowd where everyone shouts at the top of his voice; an infinite paroxysm, blinding the very one who thought he could see." (Viseux, in an interview with Julien Alvard).

VORDEMBERGE-GILDEWART Friedrich (b. Osnabrück, Germany, in 1899). Studied architecture and sculpture in Hanover. Was a constructivist painter from the beginning (1919). Since 1924, a member of the 'Sturm' (Berlin) and the 'Stijl' (Holland). Was in Paris 1925-1926. Returned to Paris in 1929 and had a one-man show at the Galerie Povolotsky. Took part in the exhibition 'Cercle et Carré', Paris 1930. A member of 'Abstraction-Création' (1932). Was in Berlin 1936-1937; in Zurich the following year, then in Amsterdam. Became a Dutch citizen. Included in numerous avant-garde exhibitions in Europe and the United States, and in the 'Premiers Maîtres de l'Art abstrait' show at the Galerie Maeght, Paris 1949. One-man shows in Cologne and Ulm (1955), in Zurich and Rio de Janeiro (1956). Since 1955, a professor at the Hochschule für Gestaltung in Ulm.

Lives in Ulm. He has written many books, particularly an album on Kandinsky (published by Duwaer, Amsterdam).

VOSSEN André van der (b. Haarlem, Holland, 1893). First studied lithography. Attended a school of Industrial Art in Haarlem. Began to paint in 1928. At first an impressionist, then progressively came to abstraction. His work is non-representational since 1946. Took part in numerous group-shows in Amsterdam, The Hague, Brussels, in the Salon des Réalités Nouvelles (Paris). Lives in Overveen, near Haarlem.

VULLIAMY Gérard (b. Paris, 1909, of Swiss parents). Studied advertising, decoration, stage-designing, engraving. Began to paint in 1928 (landscape and still life). Spent three years at the Academy Lhote. Launched into abstraction in 1932 and joined the 'Abstraction-Création' group. First one-man show at

VORDEMBERGE-GILDEWART. COMPOSITION NO. 180. 1950.
Th. Bally Collection, Montreux.

285

VULLIAMY. PAINTING. 1953. *Galerie Benador, Geneva.*

the Galerie Pierre, Paris 1953; abstract canvases the technique of which recalls that of fresco-painting. Then attracted by surrealism. He left the movement in 1937. "I think then that there is no real opening for painting in surrealism; only poetry and liter-

ature can have their say in that mode." Joined the Swiss group 'Die Allianz'. One-man show at the Galerie Jeanne Bucher, Paris 1948. Reverted to a fresco-technique while studying graphic and spatial movement. Took part in the Salon des Réalités Nouvelles and the Salon de Mai. Exhibited in Bern and in Basel (1949) together with Gérard Schneider. One-man show at the Galerie Roque, Paris, 1952. Lives in Paris. Very luminous abstract impressionism: the colours vibrate in space, yellow often predominating like a rioting sun. Vulliamy eschews black, even sombre colours. — *Bibl.* Gindertaël: *Propos sur la peinture actuelle* (Paris 1955).

WARB Nicolaas (b. Amsterdam, 1906). Her actual name is Sophie Warburg. Studied at the Academy of Amsterdam. In Paris in 1928. Frequented various academies in Montparnasse. For some time, she was very much under the influence of Vantongerloo. She moved away from it and progressed toward a constructivism to which she added elements of her own invention which gave it sometimes a poetic and spontaneous touch. Took part in the Salon des Réalités Nouvelles since 1946. One-man shows at the Galerie Creuze (1947) and the Galerie Colette Allendy (1954). Took part in numerous exhibitions of abstract art in France, Holland, and other countries. Lives in Paris. — *Bibl.* Warb: *Aperçus et pensées sur la peinture abstraite* (Paris 1942).

286

WEBB Marie (b. Sydney, 1901). Attended a non-institutional school of painting in Sydney, about 1930. Took part in various exhibitions in Australia from 1936 on. First one-man show in Sidney, 1945. Was in London in 1947. In Paris, 1949, she launched out into abstraction. One-man shows at the Galerie Colette Allendy (1950) and the Galerie Suzanne Michel (1953). Exhibited many times at the Salon des Réalités Nouvelles as well as in various Parisian displays. Lives in Paris.

WEBER Hugo (b. Basel, 1918). Studied in Basel and in Paris: painting and sculpture. Moholy-Nagy appointed him a professor at the Institute of Design in Chicago (1946). Afterwards, a professor at the Illinois Institute of Technology. Numerous exhibitions in the United States, Canada, France, Switzerland, Norway, Lebanon. Lives in Chicago. "I like to call my approach to painting 'energetic'. I work fast in a semi-automatic manner, with a feeling for the total expanse of the flat area. I attempt a balance of physical and psychic sensation, like a dancer might do. The results are open forms, fluid spatial structures; vision in flux." (Weber).

WEBER Max (b. Bialystok, Russia, 1881). Came to the United States in 1891. Attended the Pratt Institute from 1898 to 1901. Studied in various Paris academies from 1905 to 1908. He studied under Henri Matisse, together with Bruce and A. B. Frost, about 1907. Included in the Salon des Indépendants and the Salon d'Automne. Returned to the United States in 1908. First one-man show at the Haas Gallery, New York, in 1909. Greatly influenced by cubism, Max Weber attained complete abstraction in a series of paintings dated 1915, the inspiration of which comes from the landscapes and the atmosphere of New York. After 1918, he reverted to representational painting. Lives in New York. — *Bibl.* Cahill: *Max Weber* (New York 1930); *Collection of the Société anonyme* (Yale University 1950).

WARB. MYSELF SECRET. 1955. *Mills Collection, Paris.*

WELLS John (b. Penzance, Cornwall, 1909). Studied medicine. Was a doctor until 1946. Then, devoted himself exclusively to painting. Was greatly influenced by the sculptor Gabo, while the latter lived in England. One-man shows in London (1948) and in New York (1952). Lives in Saint Ives (Cornwall).

WERKMAN. TYPOGRAPHICAL COMPOSITION. 1928.

WENDT François Willi (b. Berlin, 1909). Studied philosophy and art history at college from 1928 to 1934. First non-representational paintings in 1932. In Paris since 1937. Studied six months in Léger's studio, took part in a group-show and met Kandinsky, Delaunay, Freundlich, Hartung, Poliakoff. Included in the Salon des Surindépendants, the Salon des Réalités Nouvelles, the Salon d'Octobre, and in numerous other group-shows. One-man show at the Galerie Colette

Allendy in 1951. Lives in Paris. Wendt's work is varied, but always marked by a concern for balance and quiet distinction. There is more discipline than effusion, more style than anguish. The colours are generally light, but not aggressively so. The light is diffuse, more interior than dazzling. — *Bibl.* Gindertaël: *Propos sur la peinture actuelle* (Paris 1955).

WERKMAN Hendrik Nicolaas (b. Leens, 1882; d. Groningen, 1945, in Holland). At first a journalist, then a printer in Groningen, Werkman began to paint at the age of thirty five. About 1923, he began using typographical material in printed abstract compositions. At first, he composed his works on large sheets of paper, with blacks and greys. Then, after 1925, he began to use the larger typographical characters (wooden poster characters) as abstract motifs in multicoloured compositions. An exhibition of these works was held at the Galerie Sacre du Printemps, Paris, 1927. At the same period, Werkman published a review of dadaist inspiration,

WENDT. PAINTING. 1955.

288

The next Call, which he printed himself. He reverted to representational art after 1938. He was shot by the Nazis a few days before the Liberation of Groningen (April 1944).

Werkman was one of the most enterprising minds in Holland between the two wars. His monotypes are those of an artist who does not shrink from adventure, shirks no encounter and always remains receptive. A constructivist influence can be recognized in his first impressions and a certain impressionism softens his later work; but the accent remains highly individual and the spirit uncompromising. — *Bibl.* Catalogue of the H. N. Werkman retrospective exhibition at the Municipal Museum of Amsterdam (Dec. 1945); 'Art d'Aujourd'hui' (Paris, February-March 1952); Catalogue de l'Exposition à la Librairie La Hune (Paris 1952).

WERNER Lambert (b. Stockholm, 1900). Educated in Paris and Berlin. Took part in the Salon des Surindépendants, Paris. One-man shows in Stockholm (Gallery Farg och Form); Paris (Galerie Creuze); Basel (Gallery of Modern Art); Berlin (Gallery Bremer); Brussels (Galerie Apollo); Lucerne (Galerie d'Art National). Lives in Stockholm.

WERNER Theodor (b. near Tübingen, Germany, 1886). Attended the Academy of Stuttgart (1908-1909), travelled extensively, and spent some time in Paris every year. Settled in Paris from 1930 to 1935, then in Potsdam. Werner is one of the most active and most pure exponents of abstract painting in Germany since 1945. Numerous one-man shows in Germany, and in Paris (Galerie des Cahiers d'Art, 1950). A member of the German group 'Zen 49'. Woty Werner, his wife, attended non-institutional academies and studios in Berlin, Munich, and Paris. She is mostly known for the remarkable abstract designs on printed material which she ex-

hibited in Germany and in Paris. Both Theodor and Woty Werner were included in the 'Peinture et Sculpture non-figurative en Allemagne d'Aujourd'hui' exhibition at the Cercle Volney, Paris 1955. They live in Berlin-Charlottenburg. — *Bibl.* 'Art d'Aujourd'hui' (Paris, August 1953); catalogue of the exhibition at the Cercle Volney (Paris 1955).

WESTPFAHL Conrad (b. Berlin, 1891). Studied in Berlin under Orlick (1910-1912), then at the Academy in

THEODOR WERNER. INK DRAWING. 1949.
Private Collection, Paris.

Munich. Stayed extensively in Paris, in Italy, North Africa, and in Greece. Took part in numerous exhibitions of abstract art;

289

has also published art criticism. Lives in Munich.

WIEGAND Charmion von (b. Chicago, 1900). The daughter of the journalist Karl H. von Wiegand, then the senior American correspondent in Europe. She took an active part in journalism and art criticism. Knew intimately the avant-garde milieu in New York from 1920 on. Met Hartley, Max Weber, Stella, Stuart Davis, etc. Began to paint in 1926, at first in a primitive and fanciful manner. Became a friend of Piet Mondrian when the latter came to New York (1940), and under his direct influence, she launched into geometrical abstraction, after having dropped painting for about a year. One-man shows at the Rose Fried Gallery, New York (1947 and 1948); at the Saidenberg Gallery, New York (1952). A number of other one-man shows in the United States. Since 1947, she took part in the exhibitions of the 'American Abstract Artists' group of which she was elected president in 1951. Travelled in Europe and in Mexico. Lives in New York. — *Bibl.* Seuphor: *La Peinture aux États-Unis,* "Art d'Aujourd'hui" (Paris, June 1951); *The world of Abstract Art,* Wittenborn (New York, 1957).

WINTER Bryan (b. London, 1915). Studied at the Slade School, London. A number of exhibitions in London; exhibited also in Germany, in France, and in New York. A professor at the Bath Academy of Art. Lives in London.

WINTER Fritz (b. Altenbögge, Germany, 1905). Attended the Dessau Bauhaus from 1927 to 1930. Studied under Schlemmer, Kandinsky, and Klee. While he was staying in Berlin, he met and made friends with the constructivist sculptor Gabo. Travelled extensively in Switzer-

land and in France. Friendship with Kirchner. Gave lectures at the Halle-Saale academy. Was under a Nazi ban while Hitler was in power: his works, classed as 'degenerate art', were taken from the German museums and sold in Zurich (1934) and in London (1938). Made a prisoner in Russia in 1945. When he returned to Germany, he retreated to Diessen-am-Ammersee where he now lives. "We are working on objects and pictures the beginning of which goes back thousands of years. And our present action is addressed to the future. Like obedient servants, we link the beginnings of time to the millenia of the future according to the law of an order directly superior to ours. In painting, form and colour are the expression of consciousness. A new art demands a knowledge and a continuity which the artist must be able to guarantee. He must broaden his inner range. The compass of knowledge makes the grandeur of the style." (Winter). — *Bibl.* Domnick: *Abstrakte Malerei* (Stuttgart 1947).

WOLFF Robert Jay (b. Chicago, 1905). Attended Yale University. Worked as a painter and a sculptor in London (1927), in Paris (1929-1931), then in New York and Chicago (1932-1942). Since 1935, has devoted himself entirely to painting. Numerous one-man or group-shows in New York, Chicago, San Francisco, etc. Took part also in exhibitions in Paris, Munich, Rome, and other European cities. Moholy-Nagy's collaborator in the foundation of the Chicago School of Design (now Institute of Design). Drafted during the Second World War. Then appointed a professor of drawing at Brooklyn College. Now spends half his time in Brooklyn and half in Ridgefield (Connecticut) where he has a studio. Lyrical composition in brief multicoloured touches, a sort of fireworks assembled by an optimistic and sensitive mind.

WOLS. PAINTING. 1946.
Jean Paulhan Collection, Paris.

WOLS (b. Berlin, 1913; d. Paris, 1951). His real name was Otto Alfred Schulze Battman. Took the name of Wols in 1937. Spent some time at the Bauhaus, in Dessau, and went to Paris (1932) where he met Miro, Max Ernst, Tzara and Calder (whom he tutored in German). In Spain (1933) he made photographs to earn a living. Returned to France, had an exhibition of photographs and was appointed official photographer for the Exposition Universelle, Paris. At the beginning of the Second World War, was imprisoned for about a year as a German citizen. Once liberated, he kept on painting in the South of France. Became a close friend of Pierre-Henri Roché in Dieulefit. Back in Paris, he met Sartre and Simone de Beauvoir who encouraged him. One-man show at the Galerie Drouin, in 1947. Took part in numerous group-shows in Paris and in Italy. One-man show at the Hugo Gallery New York, in 1950.

When Wols goes beyond literary allusions (the *Villes* series) and lasciviousness (drawings with suggestions of expressionism and surrealism) and attains pure abstraction, his work may sometimes show a great density of nervous energy and exude an extraordinary magnetism. The large paintings composed of an incalculable number of little touches forming one single mass, both changing and homogeneous, are probably among the most powerful and rare works of abstract art. Organized deliriums, states of intellectual ecstasy which seem to have consumed the painter, for he falls back after that into a woolly indecision. Wols also wrote poems: his natural anarchy found a favorable climate in Chinese mysticism. — *Bibl*. Bryen et Roché: *Wols,* Galerie Drouin, (Paris, no date); Guilly: *Wols,* Galerie Drouin (Paris 1947); *I 4 Soli,* n⁰ 5 (Turin, Sept. 1955). Wols also illustrated books by Kafka, Artaud, Paulhan, Sartre, etc.

291

X.Y.Z.

XCERON Jean (b. Isari, Greece, 1890). In the United States, 1904. Attended the Corcoran Art School (Washington) from 1910 to 1916, then various New York art-schools. Was in Paris from 1927 to 1937. During that time, he took part in numerous exhibitions in Paris and in various European countries. First one-man show in New York in 1935, followed by many others in a number of cities throughout the United States. One-man shows at the Sidney Janis Gallery, New York, in 1950, and at the Rose Fried Gallery, New York, in 1955. Lives in New York. Xcéron's style is highly individual. His work is strongly built, yet without excessive rigour; there is always a touch of playfulness in the composition which is pleasing to the eye and the mind.

YOUNGERMAN Jack (b. in the United States, 1925). Came to Paris in 1947. Attended the École des Beaux-Arts for a year. Took part in the Salon de Mai, the Salon des Réalités Nouvelles, and the exhibition 'Les Mains éblouies' at the Galerie Maeght, 1950. One-man show at the Galerie Arnaud, Paris 1951. In 1952, took part in a group-show at the Galerie Denise René. Lives in the United States. Free geometries in discreetly coloured swathes.

YUNKERS Adja (b. in Riga, Latvia, 1900). Studied art in Leningrad, Berlin, Paris, and London. One-man shows in the main European and American cities. Taught at the New School for Social Research, New York (1947-1954) and

ZACK. COMPOSITION. 1954.

ZAO-WOU-KI. EARLY OCTOBER. 1955.

summer sessions at the University of New Mexico in 1948 and 1949. Spent 1954-1955 in Europe (Paris and Rome). Yunkers's works are impressions obtained through superimposing wood-cuts: sometimes a great number of colours are attained. His work is rooted in expressionism, but it blossoms out in a skilful and sometimes subtle abstract organization.

ZACK Leon (b. Nijni-Novgorod, Russia, in 1892). Studied classics at the University of Moscow. Attended at the same time schools of painting and design. Was in Italy from 1920 to 1922. After spending a year in Berlin, where he designed sets and costumes for the Russian Romantic Ballets, he came to Paris and settled there (1923). Exhibited at the Salon d'Automne, the Salon des Indépendants, the Salon des Surindépendants (of which he is a founder), and, after 1952, at the Salon de Mai. One-man shows in various Paris galleries since 1926. He took part in many exhibitions in the main European countries. His art passed through various representational periods before it slowly made its way to abstraction. One-man shows of abstract paintings at the Galerie des Garets, Paris (1949), at the Centre Saint-Jacques (1953), and at the Galerie Kléber (1956). Lives in Paris. Monochromatic compositions of very simple geometrical figures and touches, sometimes isolated in the middle of the canvas. A complete stripping of the spirit which tends sometimes toward Malevitch, and sometimes toward a direct expression of sensibility centred around the disposition of the spots.

ZAO WOU-KI (b. Peiping, 1920), Entered the National School of Fine Arts in Hanchow at the age of fifteen. Taught at the same school from 1941 to 1947. Came to Paris in 1948. One-man shows at the Galerie Pierre, Paris, since 1950, and at the Galerie Cadly-Birch, New York, since 1952. Takes part regularly in the Salon de Mai. Lives in Paris. Zao Wou-Ki's work, at first representational and sometimes marked with a certain preciosity, has progressed in recent years toward pure calligraphy. When abstract, it becomes more transparent to the mind, and henceforth more significant.

ZARITZKY Joseph (b. Borispol. Ukraine, 1891). Until 1914, studied at the Academy of Fine Arts in Kiev. Settled in Israel in 1923 but came to Paris in 1927 in order to complete his studies. Once back in Israel, he organized an Association of painters and sculptors and was a co-founder of the group *New Horizons*. Took part in the Venice Biennale. One-man show at the Municipal Museum in Amsterdam, 1955. Zaritsky's painting is a supple and light improvisation. His work, full of discoveries and shades, testifies with great elegance to an infinitely subtle sensibility. Lives in Israel.

ZEID Fahr-el-Nissa (b. Prinkipo, Turkey, 1903). In 1920, entered the Sénaï-Néfissé Academy. Came to Paris in 1928. Attended the Académie Ranson. Returned to Turkey the following year, and travelled extensively throughout Europe. Was in Berlin in 1937; in Budapest 1939-1940. One-man show in Istanbul in 1941. Back again in Paris in 1948. Launched resolutely into abstraction and exhibited at the Galerie Colette Allendy (1950) and the Galerie de Beaune (1951). Took part in the Salon des Réalités Nouvelles and the Salon de Mai, with large abstract compositions, veritable symphonies with countless bright and sprightly facets. She is the mother of the painter Nejad (cf. that name). Lives in London or in Paris. — Bibl. *Témoignages pour l'Art abstrait* (Paris 1952).

ZIMMERMAN Leo (b. Pennsylvania, U.S.A., 1924). Attended the Kentucky School of Fine Arts. Came to France with the American armed forces (1944-1946). Took part in group-shows in Kentucky in 1948. Came back to Paris the same year. Took part in the Salon des Réalités Nouvelles in 1949 and in an exhibition at the Galerie Denise René in 1952. Returned to the United States in 1953. Lives in Louisville, Kentucky.

Bibliography of Abstract Art

I. General Works.

Willard Huntington Wright: *Modern Painting, Its Tendency and Meaning,* New York, John Lane, 1915.

Willard Huntington Wright: *The Future of Painting,* New York, B. W. Huebsch, 1923.

Herwarth Walden: *Einblick in Kunst,* Berlin, "Der Sturm", 1925.

Katherine S. Dreier: *Modern Art,* Société Anonyme, New York, 1926.

J. Bendien : *Richtingen in de Hedendaagsche Schilderkunst,* Rotterdam, 1935.

Herbert Read: *Art Now,* London, Faber & Faber, 1933. New Edition 1950.

Alfred H. Barr Jr.: *Cubism and Abstract Art,* New York, Museum of Modern Art, 1936.

Christian Zervos: *Histoire de l'Art Contemporain,* Paris, "Cahiers d'Art", 1938.

Art of This Century, Edited by Peggy Guggenheim, New York, 1942.

Sidney Janis: *Abstract and Surrealist Art in America,* New York, 1944.

American Abstract Artists, The Ram Press, New York, 1946. (Albers, Gallatin, Léger, Moholy-Nagy, Knath, Mondrian, Morris).

Ottomar Domnick: *Die Schöpferischen Kräfte in der Abstrakten Malerei,* Müller und Kiepenheuer, Bergen, 1947.

Henry-Russell Hitchcock: *Painting Toward Architecture,* New York, 1948.

Charles Biederman: *Art as the Evolution of Visual Knowledge,* Red Wing, Minn., 1948.

Michel Seuphor: *L'Art Abstrait, Ses Origines, Ses Premiers Maîtres,* Galerie Maeght, Paris, 1949. New Edition 1950.

Collection of the Société Anonyme, Yale University Art Gallery, New Haven, Conn., 1950.

Michel Ragon: *Expression et Non-Figuration,* Paris, 1951.

Andrew Carnduff Ritchie: *Abstract Painting and Sculpture in America,* New York, Museum of Modern Art, 1951.

Thomas B. Hess: *Abstract Painting* (Background and American Phase), The Viking Press, New York, 1951.

Charles Biederman, *Letters on the New Art,* Red Wing, Minn., 1951.

Témoignages pour l'Art Abstrait, Editions Art d'Aujourd'hui, Paris, 1952.

Pierre Courthion: *Peintres d'Aujourd'hui,* Geneva, 1952.

Modern Artists in America, Wittenborn, New York, 1952.

Michel Tapié: *Un Art Autre,* Paris, 1952.

A Dictionary of Modern Painting, Hazan, Paris, 1954; Methuen, London, 1956.

Lawrence Alloway: *Nine Abstract Artists,* London, 1954.

Alfred H. Barr, Jr.: *Masters of Modern Art,* New York, Museum of Modern Art, 1954.

Charles-Pierre Bru: *Esthétique de l'Abstraction,* Privat, Toulouse, 1955.

Michel Ragon: *L'Aventure de l'Art Abstrait,* Laffont, Paris, 1956.

Léon Degand: *Langage et Signification de la Peinture,* Architecture d'Aujourd'hui, Paris, 1956.

H. L. C. Jaffé: *De Stijl, 1917-1931,* Meulenhoff, Amsterdam, 1956.

Marcel Brion and Arnulf Neuwirth: *L'Abstraction,* Gründ, Paris, 1956.

Marcel Brion: *Art Abstrait,* Albin Michel, Paris, 1956.

Alberto Sartoris: *Encyclopédie de l'Architecture Nouvelle,* (3 vol.), Hoepli, Milan, 1957.

The World of Abstract Art, Wittenborn, New York, 1957.

Jean Bouret: *L'Art abstrait,* Club Français du Livre, Paris, 1957.

II. Periodicals Directly Connected With Abstract Art.

Der Sturm, Berlin, 1910-32.   Editor: Walden.

De Stijl, Leyden and Paris, 1917-28.   Editor: Van Doesburg.

Dada, Zurich and Paris, 1917-20.   Editor: Tzara.

Het Overzicht, Antwerp, 1921-25.   Editor: Seuphor (F. Berckelaers).

Ma, Vienna, 1922.   Editor: Kassak.

Manomètre, Lyons, 1922-28.   Editor: Malespine.

Merz, Hanover, 1923-25.   Editor: Schwitters.

G. Zeitschrift für Elementare Gestaltung, Berlin, 1923-25.   Editors: Hans Richter and Lissitzky.

The Next Call, Groningen, 1923-25.   Editor: Werkman.

Vouloir, Lille, 1924-27.   Editor: Del Marle.

Zenith, Belgrade, 1924-26.   Editor: Mitzich.

Bulletin de l'Effort Moderne, Paris, 1924-27.   Editor: Léonce Rosenberg.

Cahiers d'Art, Paris, founded 1926.   Editor: Zervos.

Bauhaus, Vierteljahr-Zeitschrift für Gestaltung, Dessau, 1927-32.

Documents Internationaux de l'Esprit Nouveau, Paris, 1927. One issue only. Editors: Dermée and Seuphor.

Internationale Revue i 10, Amsterdam, 1927-29. Editor: A. Müller-Lehning.

Transition, Paris, The Hague and New York, 1927-38. Editor: Eugène Jolas.

Cercle et Carré, Paris, 1930. Three issues only. Editor: Seuphor.

Art Concret, Paris, 1930. One issue only. Editor: Van Doesburg.

L'Art Contemporain, Paris, 1931-32. Three issues only. Editors: Grabowska and Brzekowski.

Abstraction-Création, Paris, 1932-36. Five albums. Editors: Herbin and Vantongerloo.

Axis, London, 1935-36. Editor: Myfanwy Evans.

Plastique, Paris, 1936-39. Five issues only. Editors: Sophie Taeuber and César Domela.

Réalités Nouvelles, Paris, 1947-56. Album published annually for the Salon des Réalités Nouvelles.

Art d'Aujourd'hui, Paris, 1949-54. Editor: André Bloc.

Numero, Florence, founded 1949. Editors: Vigo and Sartoris.

XXᵉ Siècle, Paris, founded 1951. Editor: San Lazzaro.

Arte Visive, Rome, founded 1952. Editor: Colla.

Cimaise, Paris, founded 1952. Editors: Galerie Arnaud.

Phases, Paris, founded 1954. Editor: Jaguer.

Bokubi, Kyoto, Japan, founded 1951. Editor: Shiryu Morita.

Bokuzin, Kyoto, Japan, founded 1951. Editor: Shiryu Morita.

I 4 Soli, Turin, founded 1954. Editor: Parisot.

Aujourd'hui, Paris, founded 1955.   Editor: André Bloc.

Quadrum, Brussels, founded 1956.   Editors: Palais des Beaux-Arts.

L'Œil, Paris, founded 1955.   Editor: Bernier.

III. Works by Practising Artists.

See under artists' names in the Biographical section—in particular: Kandinsky, Van Doesburg, Mondrian, Malevitch, Moholy-Nagy, Arp and Herbin.

IV. Works Dealing With Artists.

See under artists' names in the Biographical section.

V. Exhibition Catalogues (containing texts or information of interest).

Die Erste Ausstellung der Redaktion der Blaue Reiter, Munich, 1911-12.

Internationale Tentoonstelling van Moderne Kunst, Amsterdam, 1911.

Moderne Kunst Kring.   Catalogue of paintings, Amsterdam, 1912.

L'Art d'Aujourd'hui, Paris, Catalogue, 1925.

Catalogus 2e Tentoonstelling A.S.B., Amsterdam, 1929.

Tentoonstelling Abstracte Kunst, Stedelijk Museum, Amsterdam, 1938.

Almanach Neuer Kunst in der Schweiz, Die Allianz, Zurich, 1940.

Masters of Abstract Art, Helena Rubinstein's New Art Center, New York 1942.

Austellung Moderne Malerei, Gstaad, 1943.

Konkrete Kunst, Kunsthalle, Basle, 1944.

Art Concret, Galerie Drouin, Paris, 1945.

Allianz, Kunsthaus, Zürich, 1947.

Peinture d'Aujourd'hui, Cannes, 1947.

Exposition de Peintures et Sculptures Contemporaines, Avignon, Palais des Papes, 1947.

Albers, Arp, Bill, Herrmann Gallery, Stuttgart, 1948.

Zürcher Konkrete Kunst, Lutz und Meyer Gallery, Stuttgart, 1949.

Antoine Pevsner, Georges Vantongerloo, Max Bill, Kunsthaus, Zürich, 1949.

Der Blaue Reiter, Retrospective Exhibition, Munich, 1949.

Advancing French Art, Louis Carré Gallery, New York, 1950.

Contemporary American Painting, California Palace of the Legion of Honor, San Francisco, 1950-51.

40 American Painters, 1940-1950, University of Minnesota, 1951.

De Stijl, Retrospective Exhibition, Stedelijk Museum, Amsterdam, 1951.

Dynaton 1951, San Francisco Museum of Art, 1951.

Arte Astratta e Concreta in Italia, Roma, 1951.

15 Americans, Museum of Modern Art, New York, 1952.

Art Abstrait Contemporain, Cannes, Toulon, Aix-en-Provence, 1952.

Regards sur la Peinture Américaine, Galerie de France, Paris, 1952.

Grupo de Artistas Modernos de la Argentina, Viau, Buenos Aires, 1952.

12 Peintres et Sculpteurs Américains, Musée d'Art Moderne, Paris, 1953.

Catalogue of the *Espace* Group, Biot, 1954.

Younger European Painters, Sol. R. Guggenheim Museum, New York, 1954.

Younger American Painters, Sol. R. Guggenheim Museum, New York, 1954.

Arte Nuevo, Buenos Aires, 1955.

Artistas Abstractos de la Argentina, International Circle of Art, Buenos Aires, 1955.

Peintures et Sculptures Non-Figuratives en Allemagne d'Aujourd'hui, Cercle Volney, Paris, 1955.

50 Ans d'Art aux États-Unis, Musée d'Art Moderne, Paris, 1955.

Divergences 3, Galerie Arnaud, Paris, 1955.

R. V. Gindertael: *Propos sur la Peinture Actuelle,* Paris, 1955.

Vanguard 1955, Walker Art Center, Minneapolis, 1955.

Divergences 4, Galerie Arnaud, Paris, 1956.

La Calligraphie Japonaise, Musée Cernuschi, Paris, 1956.

L'art abstrait — Les premières générations (1910-1939), Musée de Saint-Étienne, 1957.

50 ans de Peinture Abstraite, Galerie Creuze, Paris, 1957.

The main catalogues of individual exhibitions are listed under artists' names in the Biographical section.

VI. Articles of Importance and Special Numbers of Periodicals.

Buch Neuer Künstler, publ. *Ma,* Vienna, 1922.

Die Neue Welt, publ. *Das Werk,* 1926.

L'Art Abstrait, Galerie Maeght, " Derrière le Miroir", May 1949.

Painting in Paris, Magazine of Art, New York, 1950.

Das Kunstwerk, Baden Baden, Heft 8-9, 1950.

Punto dell'Arte Non Obiettiva, Spazio, Rome, Jan.-Feb., 1951.

Thomas B. Hess: *Introduction to Abstract,* Art News Annual, New York, 1951.

Tendances Actuelles de la Peinture Française, in *XXᵉ Siècle,* New Series, No. 1.

John Begg: *Abstract Art and Typographic Format,* Magazine of Art, New York, Jan. 1952.

Michel Seuphor: *Il n'y a pas de Repos,* "Derrière le Miroir", Oct. 1952.

De Hedendaagse Schilderkunst in België, "Die Meridiaan", 5-6, Brussels, 1954.

Michel Seuphor: *Algèbres et Géométries,* "Cimaise", Paris, May 1954.

Léon Degand: *Défense de l'Art Abstrait,* "Le Point", Mulhouse, 1954.

Michel Seuphor: *Le Style et le Cri en 1955,* "Aujourd'hui", Paris, June 1955.

Michel Seuphor: *Au Temps de l'Avant-Garde (en Russie),* "L'Œil", Paris, Nov. 1955.

Michel Seuphor: *De Stijl,* "L'Œil", Paris, Oct. 1956.

Cimaise, issue on art in the U.S., Paris, Nov.-Dec. 1956.

VII. Museum Catalogues — Miscellaneous.

Collection Internationale d'Art Nouveau, Lodz Museum, 1932.

Gallatin Collection, Philadelphia Museum of Art, 1940.

Art of Tomorrow, Guggenheim Foundation, New York, 1939.

Anatole Jakovski: *Erni, Schiess, Seligmann, Taeuber-Arp, Vulliamy,* Paris, Abstraction-Création, 1934.

Anatole Jakovski: *Arp, Calder, Hélion, Miro, Pevsner, Seligmann,* Paris, undated.

Alexander Dorner : *The Way Beyond Art,* Wittenborn, New York, 1947.

Possibilities I, Wittenborn, New York, 1947-48.

Vrij Beelden, Group of Modern Dutch Artists, Amsterdam, 1948.

What Abstract Art Means to Me, Statements by Morris, de Kooning, Calder, Glarner, Motherwell, Davis. Museum of Modern Art, New York, 1951.

S0-BYP-172

Musical Notations of the Orient

東洋音樂記譜法

BY WALTER KAUFMANN

INDIANA UNIVERSITY PRESS
BLOOMINGTON · LONDON 1967

Musical Notations of the Orient

NOTATIONAL SYSTEMS OF CONTINENTAL
EAST, SOUTH, AND CENTRAL ASIA

MT
35
,K33

AS
36
I 385

4/29/68 Eastern 13, 75

Indiana University Humanities Series Number 60
Indiana University, Bloomington, Indiana

Editor: Edward D. Seeber
Assistant Editor: David H. Dickason
Assistant Editor: Rudolf B. Gottfried

The Indiana University Humanities Series was founded in 1939 for the publication of occasional papers and monographs by members of the faculty.

COPYRIGHT © 1967 BY INDIANA UNIVERSITY PRESS
Library of Congress Catalog Card No. 66-64235

Second Printing, 1967

53698

Eberle

LG

PREFACE

The impact of Western civilization upon Eastern cultures has caused so many changes that it is difficult to point out any Oriental community which does not reflect foreign influences in its diverse social and economic reforms, such as the creation of unions, the introduction of new strategies of expansion, far-reaching changes in industry and education, the effacing disappearance of the autocratic power of the family and of the divine rulers and living Buddhas, and many others. The indigenous arts, particularly music, by imitating and absorbing imported Western elements, often of remarkably mediocre quality, have frequently suffered a deterioration from which there is no recovery.

It is hardly necessary to repeat observations made by numerous authors about the "killing of indigenous music in the interest of poor and second-hand Western trash," about the "hopeless succumbing of native music to a technical age with military service and factory work, with rapid buses, planes, and cars, with phonographs, radios, and television sets" (Sachs).

Similar, perhaps less noticeable but equally severe and incessant changes have occurred in the notational systems of the East as a result of Western influence. Numerous indigenous Oriental notations were, and still are, so diverse, so ingeniously vague, so perfectly suited to denote the improvisational character of native music that,

v

although we may not be able to decipher all of them, we feel profound regret about their being gradually and irresistably superseded by the rigid staff notation of the West or, in some instances, by an unimaginative, international system which employs Western (Arabic) numerals as notational symbols.

It is the aim of this book to collect and preserve these indigenous Oriental notational systems, which face a vulgarization similar to that felt by all other forms of native musical activity. The broad scope of this work necessarily entails shortcomings, probable errors, imbalance, and unusually lengthy explanations and notes, for all of which I beg clemency.

The difficulties in the preparation of this work arise from numerous facts: the sources are not as easily accessible and available as their counterparts in the West; authors, publishers, dates and places of publication are often obscure; copied notational examples are not always correct; the numerous languages and scripts may have subtleties and allusions which could have escaped me; and, finally, as most Oriental notations only serve mnemonic purposes, the symbols offer only vague instructions to the performer and transcriber and can lead to differing interpretations.

This book provides a description and preservation of Oriental notational systems, the study of which makes possible a deeper understanding of Eastern art music and demonstrates its character to the student more meaningfully than does the mere presentation of recordings and musical examples written in Western staff notation. The numerous problems arising from styles and techniques which are based upon improvisation and extramusical concepts are also considered.

The purposes of this study will have been fulfilled if it serves as a stimulus toward further research in this fascinating, but, alas, quickly vanishing field. The presentation of Eastern notations may also provide some aesthetic pleasure from the study of unusual and often complex systems and symbols.

Although I envisage two volumes, this one may be considered as a complete work in itself, as it deals mainly with musical notations used in continental East, South, and Central Asia. A second volume will describe the indigenous notations of Japan, the Ryukyu Islands, Indonesia, and the Islamic world.

In the chapters dealing with Chinese and Korean notations, Chinese characters and Korean letters are employed. The spelling of Chinese words is based upon Mathews' Chinese-English Dictionary (Cambridge, Mass., 1956). The terminology of the chapters dealing with the notations of India and Tibetan chant is presented in romanized letters because, unlike those chapters in which Chinese words are used, misunderstandings are far less likely to occur.

Acknowledgments and thanks are due principally to Professor Willi Apel, the distinguished authority in the field of musical notations and Gregorian chant; to the Graduate School of Indiana University; and to the Ford International Program (Indiana University). For permission to quote copyrighted material and to use notational examples in original and transcribed forms, I am very grateful to Dr. R. H. van Gulik (Tokyo), Dr. Lee, Hye-ku (Seoul), and Dr. Laurence Picken (Cambridge). These three scholars have been extremely kind and generous in various ways with their valuable advice.

I am also deeply indebted to Dr. Fritz Kuttner (New York) for his excellent help; to Mrs. Jeanette Snyder and the Lama Geshe Nor-nang (University of Washington) for translating and transcribing Tibetan texts; to my dear friend Dr. Arnold Bake (London University) for his permission to reprint two of his Tibetan manuscripts; to Professor Charles Kent for his most helpful advice in theoretical matters; and to Professor Pao-ch'en Lee (Monterey, California), who, despite his own heavy schedule, read through the Chinese and Korean chapters, made corrections, and offered excellent suggestions.

Finally, my very sincere thanks to Professors Wu-chi Liu (Indiana University), Tien-yi Li (Yale University), Arthur Corra (Indiana University), Mrs. Miranda Pao and, last but not least, to my untiring friend and assistant, Mr. Byongkon Kim, for his invaluable suggestions and for the help that he gave me with translations, copying, and miscellaneous checking.

Notwithstanding these acknowledgments of assistance, I must, of course, take responsibility for any errors that may occur in this book.

Walter Kaufmann

Indiana University
Bloomington, Indiana

CONTENTS

LIST OF ILLUSTRATIONS

TABLAS

To my Wife

INTRODUCTION

Notation, the craft of expressing music in written form, appears in a multitude of forms both in the Orient and Occident. The elements used in notational systems can be words, syllables, letters, numbers, curves, and other symbols or signs, many of which reflect the function and importance music has in the cultural lives of the various peoples.

Occidental notations, having developed from the use of letters and cheironomic signs to systems showing the increasing need to notate every minute detail of pitch, duration, speed, dynamics, and other features, eventually reached a point where in the staff notation of the present time notated music denotes everything the composer wishes to convey and, excepting the thorough-bass of the Baroque period, contemporary jazz, and some notational experiments of very recent time, allows no improvisational freedom by the performer.

Oriental notations, denoting in most instances monophonic music not bound by precise score-arrangements, often provide only sketchy outlines of the music, which receives its final form not from the composer but from improvising singers and players. The elements employed in Oriental notations occasionally indicate cosmological, metaphysical, or religious connotations. In contrast to Occidental systems which are accessible to all persons of adequate learning, Oriental notations are often guarded jealously by a few masters and may be kept vague purposely in order to avoid their use by un-initiated persons.

Before turning to the consideration of Oriental notational sys-tems a brief description of Oriental art music in general will be of importance. We shall view this music from a time a few decenniums ago before Western music, not always of a high level, began to infil-trate into Oriental musical life, mainly through the mediums of radio, films, and, later, television. This Oriental art music is the music of civilized man in the following four cultural areas:

a) East Asia (China, Korea, and Japan)

b) Southeast Asia (Indonesia, the region of Indochina, Thailand, Malaya, and Burma)

c) South Asia (India)

d) West Asia and North Africa (Iran, Iraq, Arabia, Syria, Egypt, Libya, Algeria, and Morocco).

Music of these areas has two features in common: it is per-formed either by professional musicians or by members of special castes; and it is distinguished from primitive tribal music as well as from music of the Occident by its musical systems, theories, and notations. Although the various systems in Oriental art music differ considerably from one another, most are based upon or incorporated into wider philosophical, historical, or scientific concepts.

Many authors of the past — for example, Lü Pu-wei,[1] Ssŭ-ma Ch'ien,[2] Al-Fārābī,[3] and Al-Kindī,[4] in the Eastern world; and Plato,[5] Aristotle,[6] Euclid,[7] and Plutarch,[8] and many others in the West — did not deal with music separately but embedded their musical ideas in philosophical or scientific frameworks. This inclusion of music in a larger concept can also be observed in medieval European education where, in the Oriental manner, music was grouped together with the mathematical branches of arithmetic, geometry, and astronomy under the Quadrivium.[9]

Another feature common to all Oriental art music is that its practices, theories, systems, and notations, and even the shapes of musical instruments, have remained remarkably static, with very little, if any, development during the past, quite in contrast to the amazing changes which occurred in the same aspects of Western music. The reason for this unusual tenacity is the strong relationship of Oriental art music with the cosmos, magic, religion, philosophy, and other extramusical concepts.

It is important to note that to the Oriental mind, melodic patterns and scales, and even single notes and instruments, may have extra-musical (e.g., magical) properties, and, only secondarily, esthetic ones. The Orient abounds in beliefs and legends that music can influence the cosmos, nature, and fate. For instance, in China the five basic notes are supposed to be closely related to the cardinal points, the elements, the seasons, the planets, colors, materials, numbers, parts of the human body, and to many other things. It is believed that several rāgas of India possess magical properties and are tied in with certain periods of the day or night or, in some cases, the seasons of the year. Thus, the performance of rāga Dipak is supposed to create fire and that of rāga Kedar to melt stones and cure diseases. The Mallār rāgas are reputed to have an influence on the rainy season; it is considered a grave mistake productive of disastrous consequences if morning rāgas are performed in the evening, or vice versa. Similar convictions flourish throughout the Orient.

Except for some ritual and ceremonial pieces, music of the Oriental cultural areas makes extensive use of improvisation. No performer will play or sing a piece for the second time exactly as he did the first. There is unusual latitude in elaborating and embellishing a skeletal melody, and an Oriental performer places greater emphasis upon his virtuosity and his ability to improvise than upon giving an exact and literal reproduction of the musical notations. Significantly, the program of one of the first concerts of Western music in Japan omitted the names of composers but listed those of all performing musicians.[10]

As mentioned before, Western musical notations developed from letters and other signs which served as a mnemonic aid to the performers, who already knew the melodies, toward symbols which denote both pitches and rhythms in an increasingly precise manner. The East, with only a few exceptions, used and retained in its notational systems the ancient symbols — syllables, letters, and neumatic signs — without ever aiming at greater precision and efficiency.

Besides its improvisational character, a reason for the remarkable tenacity of Oriental music is the typically Oriental manner of oral-aural teaching. The student seated in front of his master is even now required, as he has always been, to repeat over and over again what is shown to him, so that notational symbols rarely become more than a mnemonic help. Still another reason why the Oriental notational systems have remained static is that they were frequently kept secret. Among all those who performed music only a few of the most learned would master the symbols, and they would rarely impart their knowledge to all their students. Occasionally different schools would evolve their own notations, so that the same symbol might be given various interpretations by different masters.

Following a line of thought similar to that prevailing in the medieval West, where secular music was considered unworthy of being notated, the East employed notation mainly to preserve the melodies of ritual and ceremonial music. It was only gradually that there appeared tablatures and other notational systems for use in secular music as well. Even more than in the West, where manuscripts were rescued from oblivion by repeated copying, Oriental copyists often made mistakes in calligraphy, which were rarely corrected throughout the centuries, because sometimes the scribes could not read the notation.

Oriental notations can be grouped into systems according to whether or not they indicate rhythmic features, and, based on the notational elements employed, four categories can be distinguished:

a) phonetic systems which use words, syllables, or their abbreviations;

b) ideographic and diastematic systems which use notational curves, neumatic and ekphonetic signs;

c) tablatures;

d) systems which use Western devices such as meter signatures, Arabic numerals, bar lines, repeat signs, and others.

I

Chinese Lü and Related Notations

CHINESE NOTATIONS

An art catalogue of the Eastern Han period (25-220), written by the historian Pan Ku in A. D. 92,[1] is probably the earliest extant Chinese document to offer indirect information on notated music, although it contains no musical notations. This catalogue lists, in succession, four books: (a) Songs of the Chou period (1027-256) of Honan — seven poems; (b) "Tone-movements" of the Honan texts of the Chou period — seven items; (c) Texts of 75 folk songs of the Chou period — 75 items; (d) Tone-movements of 75 folk-song texts of the Chou period — 75 items. The term "tone-movements" seems to indicate some form of notation, and we can assume that items (b) and (d) were the notations of the texts contained in (a) and (c). These tone-movements could have been the p'ing-tsê (平反),[2] signs which prescribe the tonal inflections of Chinese words. The earliest reference to these inflections is made in the Yüeh-chi (樂記) chapter on music, in the Li Chi (禮記), the "Book of Rites," one of the Chinese Classics.[3] The texts of the Li Chi seem to date back to a period from the late Chou to the early Han dynasties, and Pan Ku's tonal movements which were mentioned in A. D. 92 could have originated that early. The difficulty of combining these tone-movements with the p'ing-tsê is that the tonal inflections were not classified until the fifth century A. D., and that only since then, particularly during the T'ang and Sung periods (618-1279), did Chinese literati become fully aware of them and create an

9

art of preset tonal patterns for poems and songs, about 500 years after Pan Ku wrote the catalogue.

The question as to whether notational systems existed in pre-Confucian periods cannot be answered with any certainty at the present time. Until the 23,000 (or more) bone, tortoise-shell, and bronze inscriptions have been examined in their entirety and definite assessments have been reached by sinologists and musicologists, we shall have to confine ourselves to assumptions and hypotheses.

Both "oracle bones," as the inscribed bones and shells are called, and some inscribed bronzes date back to early periods. The inscriptions are written in ideographic and pictographic ancient Chinese comprising a vocabulary of about 3,000 characters, of which roughly half have been deciphered.[4] These inscriptions show no literary efforts and are, in the main, brief statements dealing with divination; there are such questions as, how will the harvest be, when can rain be expected, when will winter come, what date will be auspicious for a sacrificial ceremony, what is the best time to go hunting, and so forth. Occasionally the inscriptions show also the date of the oracle consultation together with a brief statement indicating whether the oracle was fulfilled. "Among the thousands of these records, there is yet to be found a single poem, a single story, or anything that arouses our esthetic or emotional response. All entries are factual and brief."[5]

The inscriptions on Chou bronzes, however, are longer, and show literary efforts in the form of a refined style of language and some florid rhymes.[6] The written characters either agree with or resemble those incised in the oracle bones. We have to admit that it is possible that a few of these inscriptions may refer to music, musical instruments, or ritual. The question of whether any of the earliest inscriptions contain notational symbols remains hypothetical at the present time. A search in this direction was made by Fritz A. Kuttner several years ago. It met with no success. Yet (quoting from a letter by Dr. Kuttner sent to this author) we find that since the known early names of the twelve lü and the various scale degrees were represented by characters that simultaneously denote their names and functions in music, we may have had in early China a system of musical terms which begs overpoweringly for some sort of notation. Although the physical and documentary evidence is missing, it would be astonishing if such a system of pitches together with notational characters did not exist. "It seems probable that .... there must have been beautiful songs sung, touching prayers said .... [but] might these not have been committed in writing on some material more perishable than bones, shells, and bronzes and therefore irrevocably lost to posterity?"[7]

Probably the earliest extant musical notation can be observed in a manuscript[8] discovered by Sir Aurel Stein at the beginning of this century in the Caves of the Thousand Buddhas at Tun Huang, the westernmost Chinese city in Kansu. Several excavations brought to light valuable silks and other objects of the Han period (202 B.C.-A.D. 220) and numerous bundles and scrolls of Chinese and Tibetan writings. Among these scrolls were manuscripts containing ballads in various forms, passages of rhymed and plain prose, Buddhist stories, and song texts. The music is lost.[9] "Some manuscripts have musical indications above the verses; but these have not been satisfactorily explained. Only one piece of formal musical notation was found at Tun Huang (Pelliot 3808), and this gives the string accompaniment to lyric songs (ch'ü-tzu) and has no relevance to the ballad tunes. We also have two specimens of dance-script (Pelliot 3501 and Stein 5643, No.

5). The latter is wrongly called musical notation in the British Museum Catalogue."[10]

The music scroll (Pelliot 3808) is believed to date back to the T'ang period (618-907) or to a period several centuries earlier. A carbon 14 dating of this valuable manuscript would, once and for all, remove the doubts which are uttered occasionally concerning its age.

The Japanese scholar Hayashi Kenzo made an interesting attempt to decipher the notational symbols of this manuscript. He published a Study on the Explication of an Ancient Musical P'i-pa Score Discovered at Tun Huang, China in the Bulletin of Nara Gakugei University, Nara, Japan (V, No. 1, 1955). The author transcribed the notational symbols into Western notation without attempting any rhythmic interpretation. By comparing gaku biwa notation with that on a T'ang shō (Japanese mouth organ; the Chinese term is shêng) preserved in the Shōsōin, on which the pipes are marked with notational symbols that in some cases differ from the present shō notation, he is able to make plausible suggestions for all the signs. However, a final, undisputed assessment of the Tun Huang notation is still to be awaited.

We abstain from discussing this interesting manuscript any further at this time, because our concern is, first of all, to present the basic notational systems. It is planned to offer a detailed discussion of the Tun Huang notation and its ramifications in a later volume.

THE LÜ-LÜ (律呂)

The thought of omitting speculations about theoretical and cosmological matters has come to mind but, after careful consideration, has been discarded, because the sources abound with extramusical connotations and may offer the reader a clearer picture of the cultural back-

ground of early Chinese musical matters than would be possible otherwise. This necessitates some recapitulating of already often-related
facts. Furthermore modern research (Kuttner) points to the view that
some of these admittedly vague and mysterious connotations may possess factual, down-to-earth foundations, facts that still require careful
investigation.

The fundamentals on which Chinese serious music of the past,
i.e., the ritual music of the Confucian temple and the ceremonial music of the imperial court, is based are the pentatonic scale and the
huang-chung (黃鐘). The pentatonic scale, although it has been
frequently expanded into heptatonic and other scale-forms, appears
constantly throughout the long history of Chinese music. The more
remarkable feature, however, is the huang-chung ("Yellow Bell"), a
more or less fixed pitch resembling the "Kammerton" of Western
music. The widespread belief that musical sounds possess magical
powers demanded a fixed pitch of this kind, from which all other pitches
could be derived. In China it was believed that appropriate musical
sounds could regulate the harmony between heaven and earth, darkness
and brightness, peace and unrest, and that the balance created by the
correct music was expressed in harmonious government, happiness of
the people, and so forth. The first duty of every emperor upon his
accession was to establish the correct pitch of the huang-chung. If
the preceding government had been unsatisfactory in any manner, or
if there had been epidemics, wars, earthquakes, floods, droughts, or
other disasters, it was the duty of the new emperor and his yüeh-fu
(樂府), the imperial music office (a section of the imperial office
of weights and measures), to improve matters by revising the basic
musical sounds in fixing the pitch of the huang-chung.

The book Lü-shih ch'un-ch'iu (呂氏春秋), "The Spring and Autumn of Lü Pu-wei,"[11] which was written in the third century B.C., relates how the huang-chung and the pitches derived from it were established. We read about twelve pitch-pipes, the lü-lü (律呂),[12] made of bamboo, whose origin is ascribed to the legendary emperor Huang Ti (c. 2700 B.C.); and we learn that in later periods the pipes were replaced by pitch bells. The first of this series of pitches, the huang-chung, possessed enormous importance not only in music but also in measures and weights. The size of the pipe determined the measure of one Chinese foot, and its volume had to be such that it would hold exactly 1,200 grains of wheat.

Various authors have attempted to reconstruct this Chinese "Kammerton." Van Aalst[13] places it at the pitch which corresponds to our note D. Courant[14] and Mahillon[15] place it at E; Amiot[16] at F, and others at Eb and F#, but the range of possibilities is even greater, for in China

the foot measure itself was anything but constant; it varied between a minimum of twenty centimeters in the Chou period and a maximum of thirty-four centimeters under the Ming. The ratio of these extremes, 3:5, forcibly resulted in a musical variation within a minor sixth: if the pitch tone was C under the Chou, it was E below under the Ming![17]

Recent research has shown that the changes of the pitch of the huang-chung may have been much less than those indicated by Sachs.

The Princes-of-Han litophones at the Royal Ontario Museum of Archaeology in Toronto, excavated in Lo-Yang (Honan) have the precise standard pitches of 261 cps (C) and 440 cps (A) respectively, according to verbal information received from F.A. Kuttner.

Since it is impossible to reconstruct the exact pitch of the huang-chung, we shall arbitrarily represent it by the note C. Once the pitch of the huang-chung had been established, eleven other pitch-pipes were fashioned and their pitches derived from it. They were tuned in a succession of pure fifths, for Chinese theorists considered that the number 3 was the symbol of heaven and the number 2 the symbol of earth. Thus, the ratio 3:2 represented the harmony between heaven and earth.[18]

The excerpt, on page 16, from the Lü-shih ch'un-ch'iu (Book V) relates the story of how the huang-chung was created.

The characters denoting the huang-chung in the Lü-shih ch'un-ch'iu and in several other works are 鐘, not, as generally employed 鐘

A rough translation of this excerpt reads as follows:

In olden times Huang-ti ("Yellow Emperor") ordered Ling Lun to establish the lü. Ling Lun travelled from the western to the shady northern side of Mount Yuan Yü. He selected bamboo grown in the Chieh Ch'i valley. He chose only a piece which was hollow and of even thickness. He cut off its knots and used the hollow section between the two joints, the length of which was 3.9 ts'un (inches). And he blew the pipe and produced the sound kung (the basic tone) of huang-chung. He then brought twelve other pipes of different lengths down from the mountain and he listened to the sounds of the male and female Phoenix birds. He grouped their sounds into the twelve lü. There were six sounds of the male bird, and another six of the female. He related them to the kung of the huang-chung and found that the huang-chung was the foundation of the lü-lü.

This story has been repeated over and over again in numerous works

昔黃帝令伶倫作為律伶倫自大夏之西乃之阮隃

之陰取竹於嶰谿之谷以生空竅厚鈞者斷兩節間

其長三寸九分而吹之以為黃鍾之宮吹曰含少次

制十二筒以之阮隃之下聽鳳皇之鳴以別十二律

其雄鳴為六雌鳴亦六以比黃鍾之宮適合黃鍾之

宮皆可以生之故曰黃鍾之宮律呂之本

on Chinese music. It is a typical example how Chinese writers of later periods invented pretty little stories which made the readers search for deeper meanings. We have to admit that it is difficult to free oneself from the assumption that there is more to these stories than what the text offers.

Ssŭ-ma Ch'ien (163-85), who completed the Shih Chi, "Records of the Historian," begun by his father Ssŭ-ma T'an (who died in 110 B.C.), offers a frequently quoted explanation of how the pipes were to be tuned by stating the well-known formula san-fen-sun-i-fa (三分損益法): "Subtract and add one third." The lengths of the bamboo pipes, all of the same diameter, were calculated in such a manner that the second pipe was one third shorter than the first, the third pipe one third longer than the second, and so forth. The ratio of the length of the second pipe to that of the first was 3:2, making the pitch of the second tone a perfect fifth above that of the first, while the ratio of the length of the third pipe to that of the second, being 4:3, made the third tone a perfect fourth below that of the second. By continuing this process (san-fen-sun-i-fa) of ascending fifths and descending fourths in an alternating manner, the following system resulted:

```
        G       A       B       C#      D#      E#
   C        D       E       F#      G#      A#      B#
```

The notes of the upper progression were called lü (律), "rules"; the notes of the lower progression were originally called t'ung (同), "companions." Gradually, however, all twelve tones came to be called lü.

A system such as the one above, which can be thought of as formed by a succession of pure fifths and octave transpositions, is

not a circle of fifths but a spiral, for it can never close. The b#,
twelve fifths above C, is not quite the same as the c seven octaves
above C. There are two methods of "overcoming" the spiral. One
is to continue the succession of pure fifths until a point is reached
when all tones of the spiral can be projected into the range of one octave by octave-transposition so that a more or less satisfactory group
of sounds can be found among them. The second method is to alter
deliberately the natural pitches and create a tempered system which
will form a closed circle.

Although it has no direct bearing upon notation, we shall continue the consideration of the lü in order to offer a comprehensive
view of the complex problem. Both methods mentioned above were
explored by Chinese music theorists. The first was used by several
scholars, among them Chiao Yen-shou (c. 70 B. C.), who extended
the spiral to 60 fifths, and Ching Fang (43 B. C.), whose system included 60 fifths, but perhaps also 53. The latter system, which actually divided the octave into 53 commas, proved more satisfactory
than the former, for it permitted transposition of the pentatonic scale
onto each of the 53 tones. Ching Fang called the 53 tones the "Inner
Circle" and the basic twelve lü the "Outer Circle." Among other experiments of his was a spiral of 60 fifths, which resulted in a system
of great complexity,[19] and another system of 84 seven-tone scales
formed by transposing the seven basic scales onto each of the twelve
lü. This latter system was further developed by several theorists,
one of whom was Wang Fo, who died A. D. 959.

The theorist Ch'ien Lo-chih (425-453) in a treatise called Lü-
lü sin-p'u (律呂新譜), "New Treatise on the Lü"), ex-

tended the spiral to 360 tones; and, during the Sung period (960-1279),
another, Ts'ai Yüan-ting, explored the possibility of adding six additional tones to the twelve basic lü, thus creating a system of eighteen
lü. However, no extension of the spiral of pure fifths could ever lead
to a true closing of the spiral, for no power of 3 ever equals a power
of 2.

Possibilities of creating tempered systems were also explored.
Van Aalst[20] assumes the existence of a tempered system before the
disastrous Great Burning of Books (ordered by Ch'in Shih-huang-ti,
the "First Exalted Emperor of the Ch'in," in-213 B.C.); but, since
none of the stone or metal chimes of this period reveal any form of
tempered tuning, the matter remains entirely hypothetical; it is true,
however, that a scholar by the name of Ho Ch'eng-t'ien (370-447) was
accused of "having done violence to figures."[21]

The pure fifth (3:2) contains 702 (actually 701.955) cents. The
interval formed by adding twelve fifths (702 x 12) contains, therefore,
8424 cents, and seven octaves cover a span of 8,400 cents (1,200 x 7).
The difference between these intervals (i.e., between B# and c) is
approximately 24 cents, the Pythagorean comma.

Kurt Reinhard,[22] whose report we quote below, includes a statement about an author named Huai-nan-dsi that requires a few remarks:
Huai-Nan-Tzu (淮南子) is actually the title of a work consisting of
twenty-one parts written by Liu An (劉安), the Prince of Huai-Nan,
who died in 122 B.C. Reinhard's statement is not incorrect because
Liu An was also known as Huai-Nan-Tzu. Liu An calculated the twelve
lü in a manner which makes us think of the remarkable mixture of number mysticism with scholarly observation of ancient Greek music theory:

Note	Number	relationship	Cents
B	43	43,000	1,096
A#	45	45,000	1,017
A	48	48,000	906
G#	51	51,000	801
G	54	54,000	702
F#	57	57,000	602
E#	60	60,000	519
E	64	32,000	408
D#	68	34,000	303
D	72	36,000	204
C#	76	38,000	110
C	81	40,500	0

The lower five numbers (we read the list from bottom to top) in the first "Number relationship" column are to be multiplied by 500, the upper seven by 1,000. The starting point (C) is 81. Thus:

$$81 \times 500 = 40,500.$$

Another number, 749, is now used to divide the result:

$$40,500/749 = 54 \text{ plus a remainder of } 54.$$

54 now becomes the numerical representation of the G, a perfect fifth above the original C. Since this is one of the upper seven tones, 1,000 is the multiplying factor:

$$54 \times 1,000/749 = 72 \text{ plus a remainder of } 72.$$

This represents the D below the G.

$$72 \times 500/749 = 48 \text{ plus a remainder of } 48.$$

This represents A above the D, and so forth.

The number representing E# is 60. The number for B# is computed thus:

$60 \times 1,000/749 = 80$ plus a remainder of 80.

The ratio of the interval C-B# is, therefore, 81:80, the syntonic comma (the comma of Didymos).

The ingenious, though devious, arithmetic employed to produce this system results in eight pure fifths and four tempered fifths. Thus it is in no sense an equal-tempered system. The four tempered fifths are of unequal sizes; their decimal ratios are shown below:

E - B	1.4883721
B - F#	1.3255813
C# - G#	1.4901960
D# - A#	1.5111111

Why 81 has been used as numerical starting point has been a puzzle to numerous authors. One can assume that 81, being $3 \times 3^2 \times 3$, shows already a certain refinement in the calculation of pitches and may represent the first cautious step in the direction toward a tempered system. It may be of importance to point out that the numbers 81 (for C), 54 (for G), 72 (for D), 48 (for A) and 64 (for E) appear in the Shih Chi (c. 90 B. C.), where the lengths of the standard pipes are described. The actual Chinese text appears on page 22 and is a quotation translated in the legend below the text.

Two further endeavours to reach a satisfactory temperament were made by Prince Chu Tsai-yü (朱載堉) in 1584 and 1596. He calculated numbers to the ninth decimal point in order to define more exactly the tempered pitches. It is interesting to note that in his work, Lü-lü ching-i (律呂精義 , "The Exact Meaning of the Lü''), Chu Tsai-yü established a usable temperament 100 years before Andreas Werckmeister. This system was not put into practice in the lifetime of Chu Tsai-yü.

First column (right side): 9 x 9, 81 as <u>kung</u>

Second column: Of three parts, adding one, as <u>shang</u>

Third column: Of three parts, adding one, as <u>chiao</u>

Fourth column: Of three parts, taking off one, as <u>chih</u>

Fifth column: Of three parts, taking off one, as <u>yü</u>.

(The names <u>kung</u>, <u>shang</u>, <u>chiao</u>, <u>chih</u>, <u>yü</u> will be discussed on page 53.)

In 1664, the beginning of the Ch'ing period (1644-1911), the trend toward equal-temperament was forcibly halted by the imperial music office, and the ancient spiral of the twelve <u>lü</u> was again adopted — at least in theory. Practice, however, was by now subject to increasing influences from Europe and inclined more and more toward tempered tunings based upon those of the West.

It is important to note that the twelve <u>lü</u> were never thought of as forming a chromatic scale. True scales were derived only from melodies and never from "rows," such as those formed by the twelve pitch-pipes. The <u>lü</u> were, however, grouped into basic and auxiliary and into <u>yang</u> (male) and <u>yin</u> (female) tones.

Before we present the characters which serve as notational symbols representing the lü, we have to point out that their written forms
have changed since the early sources were first written. At the Great
Burning of Books in 213 B.C. most of the primary sources were destroyed with the exception of the Shih Ching, the Book of Odes, and
some works on divination, medicine, and agriculture. We can assume
that these early works contained chapters on music together with notational symbols written in the "old script."[23] The characters shown
below represent the "modern script," a manner of writing which came
into use during the Han period — that is, several centuries after the
original works had been written.

The Five Basic Lü

Names:			Pitches (assuming C as the first lü):
Huang-chung	黄鐘	, "Yellow Bell"	C
Lin-chung	林鐘	, "Forest Bell"	G
T'ai-ts'u	太簇	, "Great Frame"	D
Nan-lü	南呂	, "Southern Tube"	A
Ku-hsi	姑洗	, "Old, purified"	E

The Seven Auxiliary Lü

Ying-chung	應鐘	, "Answering Bell"	B
Jui-pin	蕤賓	, "Luxuriant Vegetation"	F#
Ta-lü	大呂	, "Greatest Tube"	C#
I-tse	夷則	, "Equalizing Rule"	G#

The Seven Auxiliary Lü (cont.)

Names: Pitches (assuming
                                                               C as the first lü):

Chia-chung   夾鐘 , "Pressed Bell"   D#

Wu-i   無射 , "Not Determined"   A#

Chung-lü   仲呂 , "Mean Tube"   E#

Besides the division into basic and auxiliary tones, the lü were also grouped into yang and yin. In addition, the lü were linked to the months of the year. With every month the key of the hymns performed in the Confucian temple was changed so that one lü after the other served as the basic note.

Yang ("The light side of the mountain"), the male, the positive, and the moist principle:

A# appropriate for September

G# appropriate for July

F# appropriate for May

E appropriate for March

D appropriate for January

C appropriate for November

Yin ("The dark side of the mountain"), the female, the negative, and the dry principle:

B appropriate for October

A appropriate for August

G appropriate for June

E# appropriate for April

D# appropriate for February

C# appropriate for December

The two rows of yang and yin, the only whole-tone "scales" outside of Europe, had little practical value in Chinese music and were based upon philosophical speculation.[24] The only practiced exception occurred in the grouping of stone and metal chimes.

The names of the twelve pitch-pipes have been used, in an abbreviated form, as a unique system for denoting absolute pitches. It was mainly employed in ritual music where absolute pitches had important extramusical connotations. The age of this unusual notation cannot be stated clearly, but we know that the names of the pitch-pipes had already appeared in the Chou Li,[25] which was written about the first century B.C. If used as a notation, only the first words of each of the twelve lü names are used. Instead of huang-chung only huang, or instead of lin-chung only lin is employed, and so forth.

The twelve abbreviated lü names, if used as notational symbols, are (in modern script):

Huang 黄 , C

Ta 大 , C#

T'ai 太 , D

Chia 夾 , D#; alternative symbols: 圂 or 員

Ku 姑 , E

Chung 仲 , E# (F); alternative symbols: 中(呂) or 小(呂)

Jui 蕤 , F#

Twelve Abbreviated Lü Names (cont.)

Lin 林 , G; alternative symbol: 函

I 夷 , G#

Nan 南 , A

Wu 無 , A#; alternative symbol: 𠃊

Ying 應 , B

Chinese music theory is similar to that of India, which groups all musical sounds into a lower octave (mandra saptaka), a middle octave (madhya saptaka), and an upper octave (tar saptaka). The Chinese theorists do the same: the lü are grouped into pei-lü (倍呂 , "double pitch-pipes"), the lowest; the chêng-lü (正呂 , "principal pipes"), the middle; and the pan lü (半呂 , "half pipes"), the upper octave. These three octaves are also called cho shêng (濁聲 , "muddy sound") for the lowest; chung shêng (中聲 , "middle sound") for the middle; and ch'ing shêng (清聲 , "clear sound") for the upper octave.

Of the lowest octave only the following four notes below the 黄 are used:

Huang   黄 , C
_____

Pei-ying   倍應 , B

Pei-wu   倍無 , Bb (A#)

Pei-nan   倍南 , A

Pei-i   倍夷 , Ab (G#)

These four symbols have been in use only since the Manchu period
(1644-1911). They represent sounds which are derived from the spiral
of perfect fifths. This implies that there will be a difference in pitch
when the octave has been reached or passed. Hence pei-wu, for instance, is not a pure octave duplication of wu. The same concerns
the upper octave, which is indicated by the affix ch'ing (清 , "clear"),
placed either to the left or the right of the lü character. Thus, a sound
an octave higher than 黃 (of the middle octave) would be notated
清黃 or 黃清.

This notational system made up of the first characters of the
twelve lü names served to notate important melodies of the Confucian
temple and the imperial palace and, occasionally, to notate "lute"-
songs, such as the songs by Chiang K'uei.[26] Although this notation
lacked all rhythmic indications, it was an important tool in the hands
of the learned musicians because it enabled them to prescribe absolute
pitches.

Lü symbols can also be found in pieces notated in systems not
denoting absolute pitches. In such cases, at the beginning of a piece,
a complete lü symbol indicates the required pitch of the basic or initial note of the melody. For instance, at the beginning of the hsiao[27]
part of the "Spring Hymn to Confucius," which is notated in kung-ch'ê,[28]
we find the following annotation:

chia	夾	The lü chia-chung, which stands for D#
chung	鐘	
wei	為	acts [here as]

kung 宫   kung, the basic note — expressed

by means of solmization syllables

of the Chinese five-tone notation.

Kung has the same significance as

the Western (movable) ''do.''[29]

The abbreviated lü characters (e. g., chia) are employed only in notating entire melodies. Whenever a single absolute pitch is prescribed,
as in the present case, the complete lü name is used.

The following example, Figure 1, represents a score written
much later, and shows the first eleven measures of the first ode of the
Shih Ching.[30] In order to offer as full an explanation as possible we
shall transcribe every character and symbol, irrespective of whether
or not they are lü, although this may cause some deviation from our
consideration of the lü notation. We begin reading from the top right-
hand corner of page 29:

The first four characters are:

樂   yüeh (music)

正   chēng (principal, chief)

倡   ch'ang (to lead, to direct)

贊   tsan (to assist, to help).

The next characters, written in a frame below, are:

合   ho (joined, together)

樂   yüeh (music)

關   kuan (''kuan,'' onomatopoetical, the sound of ...)

雎   chü (the osprey, a kind of fish-hawk).

Figure 1

Figure 1 (<u>cont.</u>)

The whole title column thus reads in full: "The music director leads and assists... (in frame): the accompaniment ('together music') of the Kuan-chü Ode."

The subsequent columns, each of which represents a "measure," are to be read from top to bottom and from right to left. The music begins with the second column; here we observe symbols outside and inside an oblong frame. The ones outside, immediately to the right of the frame, are:

搏 po (lit., "to strike," "to beat with the fist")

and, below it,

拊 fu (lit., "to slap," "to tap")

The two characters indicate "loud and soft," respectively. When 搏 and 拊 are combined, they are the name of a small drum (called po-fu) which is used in the Confucian temple.[31] To the right of po we find only the second of the two characters ch'ung tu (春 牘), "pounding tablet," which, in this instance, stands for "wooden clapper."

The characters po-fu and tu appear throughout columns two, three, and four. The characters placed in the oblong frame offer the following instructions (read from top to bottom):

播 po ("beat," "strike")

鼗 t'ao (abbreviation of t'ao ku[32])

第一. 第二. 第三. "first," "second," "third," in columns two, three, and four, respectively.

通 "stanza"

止 "stop"

These six characters are not to be considered as notational symbols but merely as instructions concerning the use of percussion instruments in the first three stanzas ("measures"). In short, we are dealing here with a brief "instrumental prelude" to the ensuing ode.

The transcription of columns two, three, and four is as follows:

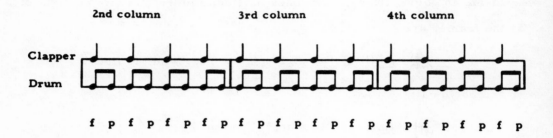

The fifth column begins the melody and its accompaniment. At the top of Figure 1 (pp. 29-30) the large characters in circles represent the text.[33] Each column is headed by one text word which is sung to one note and is held for the whole measure. Below the text, in small circles and squares in the center of each column, are the lü symbols indicating a quick-moving accompaniment performed by the pien-ch'ing.[34] The music for this instrument is always notated with lü symbols. At the top of the fifth column, to the right, immediately below the textual character, we observe in a square the character which means ch'ing (abbreviation of t'ê ch'ing[35]). The small signs below ch'ing indicate drum beats, soft and loud, as has already been explained. Of considerable interest are the characters to the left of the lü symbols. They read: fei li wu shih; fei li wu t'ing; fei li wu yen; fei li wu tung. This sixteen-syllable sequence appears unaltered in each subsequent column. A rough translation of one column reads as follows: "Do not see anything improper; do not hear anything

improper; do not speak anything improper; do not do anything improper."
These words are not sung but are used merely as a mnemonic formula
for the accompanists. The words "fei" and "wu," notated with the
same lü symbol, represent the melody note. The word "li" represents
the interval of a fourth or fifth above the melody note; and "shih,"
"t'ing," "yen," and "tung" correspond again with the respective
melody note or its higher octave, as shown in Figure 2 on page 34.

The lü notation does not show any duration of the sounds; the
symbols indicate only pitches and nothing else. Yet, Chinese musicians were able to convey in this notation a certain pulse by placing
the evenly flowing words fei li wu shih, etc., side by side with
the pien-ch'ing notes and, furthermore, by placing the lü symbols in
small circles and squares. The regular succession of circle-square-
circle-square conveys the idea of a uniform, regular pulse:

Figure 2, following (pp. 34-36), is a transcription of columns
two to eight.

Occasionally the yang-yin principle can be observed in some
lü notations of Confucian hymns. Figure 3, following (p. 37), is the
pien-ch'ing part of the first strophe of the Hymn to Confucius.[36]

53698

Figure 2

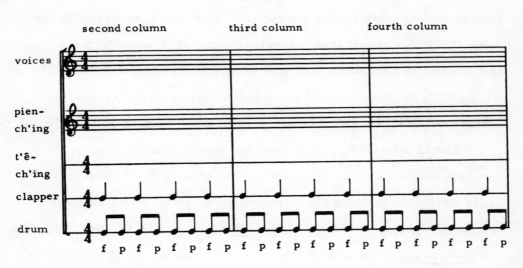

Figure 2 (cont.)

sixth column

seventh column

Figure 2 (cont.)

eighth column

In the excerpt on page 37 (Fig. 3), all notational symbols indicate the sounds of the yang row. It is obvious that by using only one of the two rows of slabs of the pien-ch'ing an anhemitonic pentatonic scale cannot be performed. If, however, custom ruled that only yang notes were to be used on the pien-ch'ing in this hymn, the missing sounds of the pentatonic scale had to be replaced by others that approximated the intended sounds and yet were degrees of the yang row.

Let us assume that the melody would have to begin with the low note A. As A belonged to the yin,[37] the female row, the nearest tone in the yang row, the pei-i (Ab), had to be substituted. As the slabs of the pien-ch'ing were tuned to the spiral of pure fifths, Ab (or G#) being the ninth fifth, the sounds were somewhat "out of tune." This, however, was of no consequence, for the aim was to use yang notes exclusively. A literal transcription of the hymn would read as follows, (Fig. 4, p. 37):

倍夷黃太姑倍夷夷姑
太黃太夷姑倍夷夷姑
姑姑夷黃太黃夷倍夷
夷黃太倍夷姑黃太黃
倍夷

Figure 3

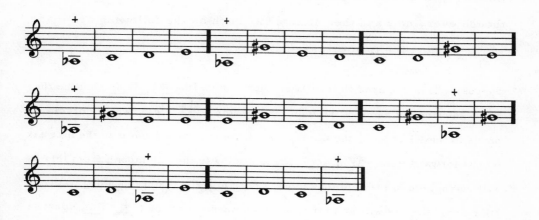

Figure 4

The Aufführungspraxis of these particular hymns was such that the pien-ch'ing part used only the yang lü while the vocal part was performed in its proper pentatonic shape, beginning with the note D, a pure fourth above the intended initial note A.[38] In other words, the vocal part did not consist exclusively of yin notes but employed the entire gamut of tones in an anhemitonic pentatonic melody. It is most probable that other accompaning instruments, in addition to the pien-ch'ing, also did not use yang notes exclusively and, as with the vocal line, played the melody in its proper shape.[39] There must have been severe dissonant clashes during such a performance, which is remarkable considering the acute hearing of the Chinese. This strange custom can also be observed in Korea. Andreas Eckardt[40] has observed that when two slabs of a set of chimes were hung in the wrong order, the leading musician refused to have this obvious mistake corrected. The argument was that the slabs had always hung in this way and that no change could be made on such a revered instrument. This, it is assumed, shows how strongly extramusical considerations influenced musical practice. One cannot help but severely doubt this view although every now and then statements such as the following are made which support the former assumption:

Supposing it is required to form a gamut of which [the lü] jui-pin shall be the base: knowing the name of the tonic or key note (㽔 賓 , which corresponds to the 5th moon), the Chinese musician will pass from it to the note six moons forward (thus, 黃 huang, corresponding to the 11th moon); from this he will retrograde to the note four months back (夷 i, corresponding to the 7th moon); then he will go to the sound six moons forward (太 t'ai, corresponding to the 1st moon); then four moons back again (無 wu, 9th moon). He will thus create a scale of five sounds to which he will give the names kung,

shang, chiao, etc.[41] If we put this pentatonic gamut in apposition to the corresponding western notes, we shall have

and it will be readily perceived that the C and D are nearly half a tone too
flat; but to the Chinese this is no objection, their aim being to prove the irrefutable connection of their music with astronomy and nature . . . .[42]

Although the Chinese musical past deals mainly with two
scale-forms, the anhemitonic pentatonic and the heptatonic, at
various times China may have used more complex scales, compelling scholars to enlarge the number of their notational symbols.
Symbols for microtonal alterations can be found in the notations
of Chiang K'uei (1155-1229),[43] in which appear a slightly sharpened
E and B, both notated with the same symbol: 折字 . This
symbol always occurs either between two 姑 (E) or between two
應 (B). If written in Western notation it would appear in the
following manner:

The Chinese term for microtonal alterations is chê-tzŭ (折字),

"bent letters (notes)." These two sharpened notes seem to function merely as ornaments of E and B respectively.

Following is an example (Fig. 5) containing such microtonal alterations and their notational symbols. This example, a composition of the above-mentioned Sung composer, Chiang K'uei, is followed (Fig. 6) by a transcription in Western notation[44] in which the note $\overset{+}{\rho}$ indicates the microtonal sharpening of the notes E and B.

In Figure 5 the lü notation appears to the right side of the textual columns. We find that Chiang K'uei's melody uses the material D E (É) F# G A B (B̈) d. We observe that there is a resemblance between this scale and that of the North Indian rāga Khamaj (Khammaja).[45]

It may be of interest to deviate here from the discussion of the chê-tzŭ in lü notation in order to trace briefly some influences from India and Central Asia on the music of China, especially during the Sung period, the time when Chiang K'uei composed his pieces. For many centuries there had been a strong link between China, Central Asia, and India. Pantomimes, a rich variety of dances, and other theatrical shows gained such popularity in China that this imported foreign music (Hu-yüeh, 胡 樂)[46] threatened to obliterate the indigenous ritual and ceremonial music. The imperial music offices of the various emperors had to create special music departments in order to deal with these imported musical styles. There were seven "departments" (with their own orchestras) during the brief Sui dynasty (590-618), and ten during the T'ang period (618-907); and later, especially during the Sung period (960-1279), the introduction of impressive theatrical performances of Islamic origin could be observed. These had come to China via Central Asia. The Confucian philosopher Chu Hsi (朱熹) 1130-

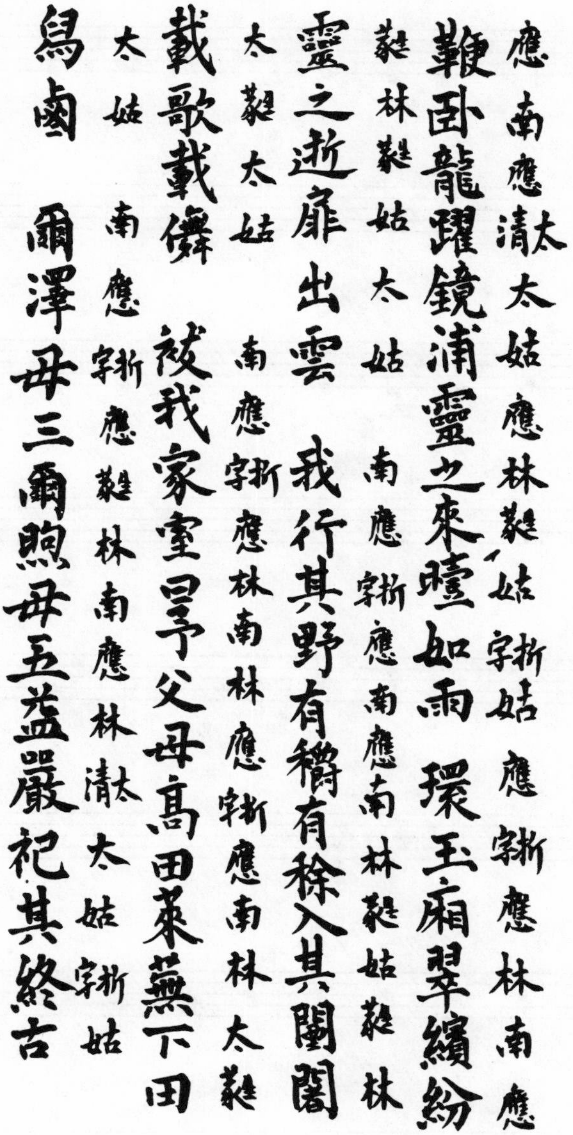
應南應清太太姑應林蕤姑字析姑應字析應林南應
鞭卧龍躍鏡浦靈之來曀如雨環玉珮翠繽紛
蕤林蕤姑太姑南應字析應南應南林蕤姑蕤林
靈之逝靡出雲我行其野有穧有稌入其闉闍
太蕤太姑南應字析應林南林應字析應南林太蕤
載歌載儛祓我家室曰予父母高田萊蕪下田
太姑南應字析應蕤林南應林清太太姑字析姑
烏虖爾澤毋三爾煦毋五益嚴祀其終古

Figure 5

Transcription of the melody notated in Figure 5:

Figure 6

1200) composed twelve melodies to texts of the Book of Odes. To illustrate this, here is the first of these melodies:[47]

Figure 7

If we replace A# with Bb and D# with Eb we get the scale F G
A Bb C D Eb f (or, transposed, C D E F G A Bb c), which
also corresponds to the North Indian rāga Khamaj. Although
Khamaj is a rāga of Hindu origin, it is not too fantastic to assume
that with the Muslim invasion of Northern India, which began
during the Ghaznavid (Yamin) dynasty in the tenth century,
Mohammedan singers imported Khamaj and other popular rāgas
as far as China. It is to be expected that the original Indian
acales underwent some modifications before that time or when
they were used in China. Further evidence in support of this
assumption can be found in another song by Chiang K'uei, "The
Spirit of the Billows,"[48] as shown in Figure 8 below.

Figure 8

Figure 8 (cont.)

If we read Bb instead of A#, Eb for D#, and Ab for G#, we get the scale F G Ab Bb C D Eb f corresponding to the ancient and popular North Indian rāga Kafi, which even today is a favorite of Muslim musicians in North India.

YUL-CHA-PO (律字譜)

YUL-CHA-PO, which means "principal letter notation," is the Korean name of the Chinese lü notation. Yul-cha-po can be found in the famous Ak-hak-koe-pŭm (樂 學 軌 範 , Music Study Guide Model), a handbook on music in nine volumes. This important work was written by order of the King, Sung-chong, in 1493.[49] In collaboration with other scholars of the Hong-mun-kwan College, the author, Sŭng Hyŭn (成 俔 , 1439-1504), describes general musical matters, the history of Chinese music,[50] dance and popular music, accessories used in dancing, and the prescribed costumes to be worn by musicians and dancers. Sŭng Hyŭn emphasizes in his work the most important features of ancient serious Korean music, the Ah-ak (雅 樂 , "pure music").

Before we continue, a brief description of Ah-ak, which denotes the ancient (pure) music of temple and palace, may be of interest. The term appears first in a Chinese work, the Confucian Analects

(論語), where we read that "the bad music of the territory of Chĕng spoils the pure music."[51]   Gradually the term Ah-ak was applied to all music performed at festive gatherings of the nobility.

The beliefs in the divine origin of music, in its divine message to all, and in its divine powers of influencing fate, guiding education, and maintaining prosperity are still noticeable in Ah-ak. From the remote past, China had supposedly been under the guidance of the twelve heavenly and human legendary emperors, more or less symbolical figures of great ancestral importance, to whom were ascribed the invention of music, the arts, sciences, and crafts. Each of these legendary emperors had his own music which was called by a special name. Although today these ancient types of music have disappeared, Korean Ah-ak still reverently retains some of the old names. Korean court musicians of the recent past distinguished six kinds of Ah-ak, each differing from the others in the use of specific instruments and in its functions at the various ceremonies:

a) Un-mun-ak (雲門樂 , lit. "cloud-gate music"), music in honor of the spirits of heaven. Un-mun-ak represents the music and dances of the legendary Chinese emperor Huang Ti (黃帝).

b) Ham-chi-ak (咸池樂 , lit. "entire influence of King's virtue music"), music in honor of the spirits of the earth. Ham-chi-ak represents the music of the legendary emperor Yao (堯) of China.

c) Tae-kwŭn-ak (大卷樂 , lit. "big turn music"), dance music appeasing and honoring the spirits of the four directions (cardinal points); the "four directions" (sa mang, 四望) can also be interpreted with the "four views" — sun, moon, stars, and ocean.

d) Tae-ha-ak (大夏樂 , lit. "big summer music"), music in honor of the mountain and river spirits. Tae-ha-ak represents the music of the Chinese legendary emperor Yu (禹); the character 夏 (in Korean: ha) stands for the Chinese Hsia dynasty, which was founded by Yu.

e) Tae-ho-ak (大護樂 , lit. "great protection music"), music in honor of the (female) ancestors. Tae-ho-ak represents the music of the Chinese legendary emperor Shēng T'ang (成湯), the founder of the Shang (商) dynasty (1523-1027).

f) Tae-mu-ak (大武樂 , lit. "great Mu [military] music"), music in honor of the rulers Mun and Mu. The character 文王 represents the Chinese ruler Wēn (Korean: Mun), the ancestor of the Chinese emperor Wu (武 , Korean: Mu), the founder of the Chou dynasty (1027-256).

A seventh kind, not included in the official six types, was Tae-so-ak (大韶樂 , lit. "great beauty music"), music in remembrance of the virtues of emperor Shun (舜), also described as music for the "four views" and "five mountains." This music was highly praised by Confucius: "When Confucius heard the Tae-so of the Chē country he lost his appetite for three months — he was so deeply impressed by it."[52] According to Shimonaka Yasaburo (下中彌三郎),[53] the six kinds of Ah-ak in China were listed in a slightly different manner: Un-mun-ak and Tae-kwǔn-ak were grouped together, and Tae-so-ak was listed as the third of the six kinds of Ah-ak.

Today Korean Ah-ak can be heard in the ceremony in honor of Confucius (Mun-myo, 文廟), where it is called Che-chǔn-ak 祭典樂 , lit. "ceremony-law music"). This ceremony is performed twice a year, in spring and in fall. Ah-ak of recent and present times includes not only ritual and ceremonial melodies of T'ang and Sung China, but has added to its repertoire some popular Chinese melodies and a few original Korean tunes and melodies of Buddhist origin; the latter music is called Hyang-ak (鄕 樂 , "indigenous Korean music"). It appears that Hyang-ak melodies are based upon six-tone scales, contrary to the strictly pentatonic character of real Ah-ak.

Continuing now our consideration of yul-cha-po, we observe that this notation can be found in the Sae-chong shillok (世 宗 實 錄), a famous historical document dealing with the events which occurred during the reign of King Sae-chong (fifteenth century A.D.). This work contains thirteen pieces of court music compiled by the Korean imperial music office.[54] During the second half of the fifteenth century, yul-cha-po was less frequently used. Occasionally, some learned court musicians of later periods would revert to this notational system, as for instance in the book Sok-ak won-po (俗 樂 源 譜), "Original Source of Popular Music."[55] This collection of songs, probably compiled during the eighteenth century by the imperial music office, contains only one piece still notated in yul-cha-po. Lee reports[56] that court musicians were not always able to read the yul-cha-po symbols correctly and that manuscripts copied by them showed numerous mistakes. Gradually yul-cha-po disappeared and became replaced by the simpler O-ŭm-yak-po (五 音 略 譜), "Abbreviated Notation of the Five Sounds."[57] This new notational system, which appeared sporadically during the reign of King Sae-cho, quickly gained in popularity during the following centuries.

The symbols of yul-cha-po are identical to those of the abbreviated Chinese lü names but, of course, are pronounced in Korean:

Hwang	黄	(e.g.,)	C
Tae	大		C#
Thae	太		D
Hyŭp	夾		D#
Ko	姑		E
Chung	仲		F
Yu	蕤		F#
Im	林		G
I	夷		G#
Nam	南		A
Mu	無		A#
Ŭng	應		B

The following is an example[58] of yul-cha-po as quoted from the Ak-hak koe-pŭm, Vol II ("Shi-yong-a-bu-jae-ak," 時 用 雅 部 祭 樂):

南 應 太 黃
林 南 姑 南
黃 蕤 南 林
太 姑 林 姑

If we transcribe this example into Western notation, we see that the resulting melody probably represents a part of the Chinese "Hymn to Confucius."[59]

This Korean version of the famous hymn now employs heptatonic tone-material: C D E F# G A B.

Japanese imperial court music (gagaku), too, established a system of absolute pitches. Unlike the Korean usage of Chinese lü characters, Japanese musical practice employed different characters and names for the twelve pitches, maintaining only one of the Chinese lü, the huang-(chung). This tone, which is called ōshiki in Japan, does not represent the first note of the twelve sounds as it did in China and Korea. The basic tone of the Japanese system of twelve semitones corresponds to the Western note D. Its name is ichikotsu (壹越 or 一越). The tone ōshiki (黄鐘), the Chinese huang-chung, is here represented by the Western note A. The following are the Japanese names of the twelve sounds within the octave and their Western equivalents:

Character and name		Western equivalent	popular designation by numbers	
盤渉,	Banshiki	B	三	(3)
鸞鏡,	Rankei	A#	二	(2)
黄鐘 (黄鐘),	Ōshiki	A	一	(1)
烏鐘 (烏鐘),	Husho	G#	十二	(12)

Character	and	name	Western equivalent	popular designation by numbers
双調，		Sōjō	G	十一 (11)
下無，		Shimomu	F#	十 (10)
勝絶，		Shōsetsu	F	九 (9)
平調，		Hyōjō	E	八 (8)
斷金，		Tangin	D#	七 (7)
壹越，		Ichikotsu	D	六 (6)
上無，		Kamimu	C#	五 (5)
神仙，		Shinsen	C	四 (4)

Besides the three notational systems of more or less absolute pitches
thus far discussed, we must mention the Japanese shakuhachi tablature[60]
and some endeavors to utilize — partially or wholly — Western staff notation.[61]

In order to complete our review of absolute-pitch notations, we
digress here from our consideration of the lü and symbols derived
from the lü and describe two unusual attempts made by Indian musicians to establish absolute pitches. Indian music theory of the past
derived the pitches of its seven-tone scale from the cries of various
animals. The argument was that animal cries remain unchanged and
thus could serve, to some degree, to establish pitches. The lowest
pitch was derived from the cry of the peacock, the next higher from
that of the chataka, the fever-bird of the rainy season, the third from
the bleat of the goat, the fourth from the call of the crane, the fifth

from the sound of the koil bird, the sixth from the croak of the frog, and the seventh from the trumpeting of the elephant. It is obvious that this method could not have led to satisfactory results. During the nineteenth century missionaries from Europe had taken into India a small portable harmonium which quickly gained great popularity and which, up to the middle of the present century, could be found in the homes of many music-loving Indians. The keys of this harmonium served to determine absolute pitches: "white one" (safed ek), the first white key, indicated the note C; "white two" (safed do), indicated D; "black one" (kali ek), stood for Db or C#; and so forth. These pitch definitions were never used in Indian notations. At the beginning of a concert, however, the Tanbura[62] player and the drummer and any other accompanists would consult the soloist concerning his basic note. This basic note, the Indian SA (the Chinese kung) would then be defined by reference to the keys of the European harmonium.

THE OLD CHINESE FIVE-TONE NOTATION

This notation uses five characters which represent the five degrees of a pentatonic scale. The five-tone scale was, and still is, the main feature of Chinese music. Although many other scales appeared in the course of China's long history, eventually there was always a return to the basic pentatonic anhemitonic scale. This five-tone notation is the favorite medium of Chinese, Korean, and, to a certain degree, Japanese[63] music theorists who employ the five characters not only in their descriptions of scales and modes, but add them to other, more complex notational systems as a technique of clarification.

The earliest source that mentions the names of the degrees of the ancient five-tone scale of China is the Tso Chuan (左傳), a commentary to the Ch'un-ch'iu (春秋 – Annals of Spring and Autumn), one of the Confucian classics.[64]   The Tso Chuan was written in the fourth century B. C. by Tso Shih Ch'iu-ming (左 史 丘 明), the so-called "father of Chinese prose." In this and numerous other works the five degrees of the scale are:

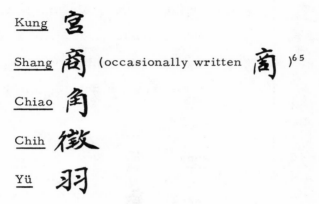

Kung 宮

Shang 商 (occasionally written 啇)[65]

Chiao 角

Chih 徵

Yü 羽

These names are comparable to the solmization syllables of the West. Kung can represent any of the twelve lü and, in the same manner as the European "movable do," denotes the first degree of any pentatonic (or heptatonic) scale.

The excerpt on page 54 (Fig. 9) is taken from a copy of the Chou Li (Book 21), where the notational symbols are recorded in modern script.

Roughly translated the passage reads: ... these are represented by the following five tones: kung, shang, chiao, chih, and yü. All these tones can be produced by the "eight sounds" [the eight materials from which musical instruments are constructed]: metal, stone, earth (clay), skin, silk, wood, gourd, and bamboo.

Of interest is the writing of chih in the following passage: the

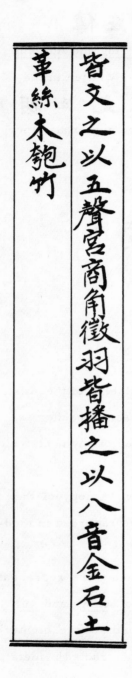

Figure 9

tenth character of the first column is written 徵 while in all other instances we find 徵.

Although these five degrees do not signify absolute pitches, they were considered to be part of the yang and yin "rows," similar to the male and female lü, and were arranged into three male and two female degrees. Assuming that kung corresponds to the Western note C, the grouping is:

	Yang			Yin	
kung	宮	(C)	chih	徵	(G)
shang	商	(D)	yü	羽	(A)
chiao	角	(E)			

Kung has been described as the man who takes a wife, chih; their son, shang, marries yü; but their offspring, chiao, cannot marry, for the next fifth (B), would lie a semitone from C and would thus mar the peaceful effect of the pentatonic (family) group.[66] These five notes are included in the Chinese philosophical concept of the "Five Agents." Within this concept numerous connotations are ascribed to the five degrees of the scale on page 55.[67]

Kung	Chih	Shang	Yü	Chiao
Earth	Fire	Metal	Water	Wood
"5"	"7"	"9"	"6"	"8"
Saturn	Mars	Venus	Mercury	Jupiter
Center	South	West	North	East
	Summer	Autumn	Winter	Spring
Wind	Heat	Cold	Rain	Sunshine
Ox	Chicken	Dog	Pig	Sheep
Naked	Feathered	Hairy	Shell-covered	Scaly
Millet	Beans	Hemp	Chinese sugar-cane	Wheat
Emperor	Works	Official	Things	People
Fragrant	Burnt	Rancid	Rotten	Goat-smell
Sweet	Bitter	Sharp	Salty	Sour
Yellow	Red	White	Black	Green
Desire	Cheerfulness	Anger	Grief	Joy

The excerpt on page 56 (Fig. 10), taken from a copy of the Shih Chi, XXIV (Yüeh-shu, 2), illustrates this concept.

Roughly translated the excerpt reads:

Kung symbolizes the emperor, shang the government officials, chiao the people, chih the national affairs (actions), and yü the harvest (material things).

If the five (tones) are not disturbed then there is no disorder. If kung is wrongly intoned, suffering follows, because the emperor is arrogant and proud. If shang is wrongly intoned, depravity follows, because the officials are idle and corrupt. If chiao is wrongly intoned, sadness arises, because the people are disturbed and harbour resentment. If chih is wrongly intoned, pain follows, because the affairs (actions) will be wearisome. If yü is wrongly intoned, danger arises, because the wealth is exhausted. If all five tones are wrongly intoned, everything deteriorates, and the country will face destruction in the near future.

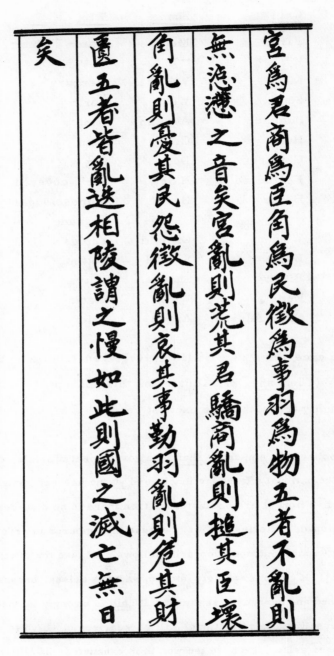

Figure 10

This passage from the Shih Chi is nearly identical with one in the Li Chi (Yüeh-chi, V). In the Shih Chi excerpt the seventeenth and nineteenth characters of the second column are 搥 ("throw," "beat") and 臣 ("subject"), while in the corresponding places in the Li Chi the characters 陂 ("uneven") and 官 ("official") are used.

The foregoing passage is another of the frequently quoted ones. It cannot be dismissed as easily as the phoenix-and-pitch-pipes story because it aims at a description of the relationship of the five basic notes and grades them according to their importance. The second part of the passage which threatens the performer with various punishments if the tones are incorrectly presented deserves to be considered because we observe similar phenomena in the music of medieval India. There are numerous authors who threaten the performer and listener with poverty and a reduced span of life if the rāgas are not correctly sung or played (e. g., Nārada, Sangīta-Makaranda, written some time between the seventh and eleventh centuries).

As already mentioned, these five characters appear in Chinese, Korean, and Japanese works; their forms remain unaltered, but, of course, the pronunciations vary in the three countries:

China	Korea	Japan
Kung	Kung	Kyū
Shang	Sang	Shō
Chiao	Kak	Kaku
Chih	Chih	Cho (Chi)
Yü	U	U

The notes represented by the third and fifth characters (chiao and yü) vary in their relationship to kung, as can be seen in the following chart:

宫　商　角　徵　羽

China:

Early five-tone scale:	C	D	E	G	A
Ming scale:	C	D	F	G	A

Korea:

Kung scale:	C	D	E	G	A
Chih scale:	C	D	F	G	A
Sang scale:	C	D	F	G	Bb

Japan:

Ryo mode:	C	D	E	G	A
Ritsu mode:	C	D	F	G	A

An example in which the five characters are used to clarify other notational systems can be seen in Figure 11. This example, taken from the Ak-hak koe-pŭm,[68] is notated in Korean yul-cha-po with the additional Chinese five-tone symbols.

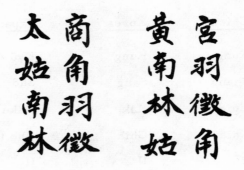

Figure 11

THE OLD CHINESE SEVEN-TONE NOTATION

This notational system adds two symbols to the Five-Tone Notation and is, therefore, only an enlarged form of it. Neither indicates
any absolute pitches, and the notational symbols signify only the relative positions of the tones within the octave.

The Tso Chuan[69] states that the seven-tone scale had been adopted
in ritual music as early as the Chou period (1027-256). At this time
two auxiliary tones were added to the basic five degrees of the scale:
the pien-kung and the pien-chih (B and F# respectively, provided kung
is transcribed as C). These two tones were not considered as basic
scale-degrees and were of lesser importance than the other five sounds.
The word pien (變), meaning "to change," "to alter," or "to
lead up to," indicates the dependence of these two tones upon the basic
notes of kung and chih. Thus, the ancient heptatonic scale was C D
E (F#) G A (B) c.

During the Chou period the two pien tones were also called ho
(和 , "harmony") for pien-kung (B); and miu (繆 , "misleading")
for pien-chih (F#).[70] During the T'ang dynasty (618-906) the same
two pien tones were called chun (準 , "regulating," "equalizing")
and pien. In the late sixteenth century Prince Chu Tsai-yü refers to
pien-kung (B) again as ho, and pien-chih (F#) as chung (中 , "middle").[71] During the Yüan dynasty (1260-1368) the Mongols introduced
an eight-tone scale: C D E F F# G A B c. Unlike the earlier
scale, the Mongolian scale made no distinction between basic and auxiliary tones; all were considered equally important.[72] The endeavors
during the Ming period (1368-1644) to revive national consciousness
and to remove all foreign influences from music are reflected in the
official Ming scale. All semitones were deleted, and, although the

resulting pentatonic scale did not duplicate its predecessor, it definitely helped to restore the dignity and simplicity of Ming music. This new scale was: C D F G A c.

Toward the end of the Ming period and during the Ch'ing dynasty (1644-1911) a new heptatonic scale consisting of the Ming scale and two additional tones was established. This scale, similar to but not identical with the corresponding tempered major scale of the West, was approximately C D E F G A B c. Eventually the official Ch'ing scale consisted of fourteen degrees within the octave, and its notes did not coincide with the spiral of pure fifths.[73] The degrees of this impractical and purely theoretical scale were not notated with the symbols of the ancient Seven-Tone Notation, but with the symbols of the simple and flexible kung-ch'ê-p'u system,[74] which had become increasingly popular with musicians and theorists since the Yüan and Ming dynasties.

During more recent times, Western influence became so strong that both the pentatonic and the heptatonic forms of the Chinese scales moved toward equal temperament.[75]

Assuming that kung represents the Western note C, the ancient heptatonic scale was notated as follows:

宮	kung	C
商	shang	D
角	chiao	E
變 徵	pien-chih	F#
徵	chih	G
羽	yü	A
變 宮	pien-kung	B

Instead of the complicated pien symbol (變), abbreviations in the form of ◯ or ⌐ were used. Thus, pien-chih could be notated by 徵 or 徵 ; pien-kung by 宫 or 宫 .[76]

The higher octave was indicated by adding the character 少 (shao, "little") to the notational symbol. Thus if 宫 denotes C, 宫少 (the "little kung") would be c.

The use of the Old Five and Seven-Tone Notations diminished considerably during the late Sung (Southern Sung) and Yüan dynasties (1127-1368) because another notational system, the kung-ch'ê-p'u[77] was rapidly gaining in popularity.

In the Ming period (1368-1644), which followed the Yüan dynasty, the ancient symbols again came into use, although kung-chê-p'u continued to be the most frequently employed notation. The Ming scale, as mentioned before, differed from the ancient pentatonic form in the interpretation of the chiao (角):

Old Scale:						Ming Scale:				
C	D	E	G	A		C	D	F	G	A
宫	商	角	徵	羽		宫	商	角	徵	羽

During the Ch'ing period (1644-1911), which followed the Ming, Chinese musicians and theorists — undoubtedly influenced by Western musical practice — employed the seven-tone symbols together with some affixes to notate all twelve degrees of the chromatic scale. We remind the reader that none of these symbols represent absolute pitches but are merely "solmization characters." Assuming that kung represents the Western note C, the chromatic scale was notated as follows:

宮	kung	C
滆	ch'ing-kung[78]	C#
商	shang	D
滴	ch'ing-shang	D#
角	chiao	E
涌	ch'ing-chiao	E# (F)
變徵	pien-chih	F# (Gb)
徵	chih	G
澂	ch'ing-chih	G#
羽	yü	A
翊	ch'ing-yü	A# (Bb)
變宮	pien-kung	B (Cb)

The symbols of the Old Chinese Five and Seven-Tone Notations occasionally appeared also in Japan. There they were used in some notations of the imperial court music (gagaku), in the music books of the Buddhist chant (shōmyō),[79] and in theoretical works.

While the symbols for the various scale-degrees were the same as in China, in Japan one additional symbol was employed: it denoted the raising of certain notes, particularly the notes 商 and 羽 , by a semitone; this symbol, called ei, is 嬰 , or in its abbreviated form, 妥 .

In the foregoing scale-forms[81] the symbols of hen-chi and hen-kyu should be transcribed with Ab and db, respectively, and those of ei-shō and ei-u with E# and B#, because hen indicates an alteration by a lower semitone and ei an alteration by a higher semitone. We use the enharmonic alternatives of G#, c#, and F, c, respectively, because they are more plausible in Western notation and because neither Chinese nor Japanese performing musicians make any distinction between enharmonic degrees.

The piece shown in Figure 12[82] on page 64 is a short excerpt from a Japanese saibara (催馬樂), a song accompanied by a small instrumental ensemble, usually without drums and patterned after folk music, which had become fashionable in gagaku during the Heian period (794-1185). The saibara imitated or utilized the materials of horsemen's songs, Tibetan love songs, devotional songs, and others. The melodies of saibara were written in the two official modes

Figure 12

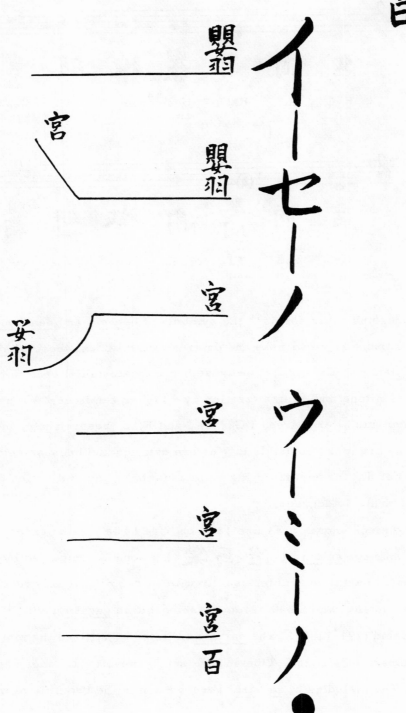

of imperial court music: ryo and ritsu.[83]   The adaptation of these melodies into the prescribed musical limitations of gagaku made them acceptable to the imperial household.[84]

The horizontal lines and curves of Figure 12 are read from right to left and top to bottom. They show the movement of the melody. The second curve rises from ei-u to kyū (c to d), the third descends from ei-u to kyū (d to c); here ei-u is notated in its abbreviated form. The straight lines represent held notes:: the first ei-u, the fourth, fifth, and sixth kyū. The large letters on the right side represent the text: Ise no umi no..., "Ise of the sea of...."[85]   The symbols 百 (hyaku, lit. "hundred") indicate percussive features.[86]   Transcribed into Western notation the excerpt would read:

In works dealing with music theory, scales can be described by placing the symbols of the old Five-Tone Notation in a system of twelve horizontal staves which represent the twelve semitones in the octave. In such cases it becomes unnecessary for the writer to elaborate the description of the notes by adding ei or hen, because any alterations of the basic degrees (kyū, shō, kaku, etc.) are demonstrated by their positions in the twelve staves as shown in Figure 13, page 66. In Figure 13 a rising and descending scale is notated in which shō (商) represents Eb (D#) in ascent and Db (C#) in descent. U (羽) stands here for Bb (A#) in ascent and descent.

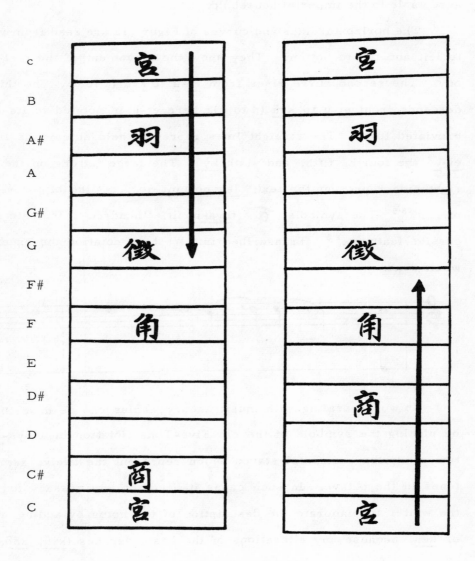

Figure 13

II

The Chinese Kung-Ch'e-P'u and Related Notations; Indian Notations and North Indian Drumming

KUNG-CH'Ê-P'U (工 尺 譜)[1]

The kung-ch'ê-p'u is often described as the notational system of the Yüan (元) dynasty (1260-1368), the period of Mongol rule over China. Although it is true that kung-ch'ê-p'u became widely popular during this period, it originated earlier — probably in the Sung (宋) dynasty (960-1279), or perhaps in the restless times of the Five Dynasties (五代 , 906-959), or even, as Courant assumes,[2] in the late T'ang (唐) dynasty (618-906).

The most likely period of origin was the Sung dynasty. Although as a rule less glorious than the T'ang, the Sung dynasty was a time of political relaxation which tolerated flourishing antimilitary theories and esteemed literati, philosophers, and dilettanti. It was then that books were first printed with movable type, so that for the first time a large portion of the population had access to the Confucian Classics; and it was a period when growing political stability fostered increased artistic activities. Thus, one can imagine that a simpler, more flexible system of notation might have come into use — one that was no longer the exclusive property of learned scholars but available to everyone interested in music.

Political stability was short-lived for, after the death of Genghis Khan in 1227, the savage and pitiless Mongols turned against China, and the Sung empire began to disintegrate; but the comparatively sim-

69

ple kung-ch'ê-p'u endured and was used by both invaders and invaded.
It was adequate for notating the newly imported Mongol scale[3] as well
as the established scales of the Sung and T'ang dynasties and those of
earlier periods. Indeed, it became the most popular notational system and has held its ground down to the present time. Chinese operatic music was notated almost exclusively with kung-ch'ê symbols,
and the operas, produced not only in large cities but taken by traveling
companies to the most remote villages, helped to spread the use of
this system of notation. Moreover, the provincial audiences who
watched these dramas became informed about Chinese legends and
heroes, history, literature, and music. One can assume that both
city-dwellers and villagers who were interested in music adopted this
notation because it was available and comparatively easy to learn.

The earliest source containing a description of the kung-ch'ê-p'u
symbols is a work called Mêng-ch'i-pi-t'an (夢 溪 筆 談),
"Brush Talks from the Dream Book," written A. D. 1093 by the North
Sung author Shên Kua (沈 括).[4] The work consists of twenty-six
volumes and two appendices (later a twenty-seventh volume was added),
and deals with history, fine arts, tools, medicine, dialectics, divination, government, miracles, and, in the fifth and sixth volumes, music.
In volume six the author explains the notational symbols of the kung-
ch'ê system by comparing them with the symbols of the older Chinese
notations. Of particular interest is his comparison with the lü. In the
page cited in Figure 14 (which bears no number in the Chinese text)
Shên Kua writes that the gamut of the twelve lü (十二律) spread
over sixteen semitones from C (宮) beyond its octave (清宮)
to the note e, a range which he describes as that of ancient music.
According to Shên Kua, this range has changed to fifteen semitones

十二律并清宮當有十六聲今之燕樂止有十
五聲蓋今樂高於古樂二律以下故無正
黃鐘聲只以合字當大呂猶差高當在大
呂太蔟之間下四字近太蔟之高四字近
大鐘下一字近姑洗高一字近中呂上字近
蕤賓勾字近林鐘尺字近夷則工字近南
呂高工字近無射六字近應鐘下凡字爲
黃鐘清高凡字爲大呂清下五字爲太蔟
清高五字爲夾鐘清法雖如此然諸調殺
聲不能盡歸本律故有偏殺側殺寄殺元
殺之類雖與古法不同推之亦皆有理知
聲者皆能言之此不備載也

Figure 14

(C - d#), the range of the Yen-yüeh (燕 樂 , "banquet music").[5] He also states that the absolute pitch of the huang-chung (黃 鐘) has "ceased to exist" (無 正 黃 鐘 聲), which implies that now the huang-chung represents an arbitrary pitch. In his comparison of kung-ch'ê-p'u with the ancient lü notation Shēn Kua states that ho (合), the first kung-ch'ê symbol, only approximates ta-lü (大呂), that hsia-ssŭ (下 四), the next kung-ch'ê symbol, indicating a note a semitone higher than the former, only approximates t'ai-ts'u (太 簇), and so forth. The reason why these tones are only approximate is that he does not relate them to any absolute pitches, but uses the lü only to demonstrate the equidistant semitone intervals between the notes indicated by the kung-ch'ê symbols. The following list represents an extract of Shēn Kua's explanation.

Kung-ch'ê-p'u: Lü:

合   (ho)   approximates   大   (ta)

西   (hsia-ssŭ, "low ssŭ")   approximates   太   (t'ai)

四   (ssŭ)   approximates   夾   (chia)

上   (hsia-yi, "low yi")   approximates   姑   (ku)

高   (kao-yi, "high yi")   approximates   仲   (chung)

上   (shang)   approximates   蕤   (jui)

勾   (kou)   approximates   林   (ling)

尺   (ch'ê)   approximates   夷   (i)

工   (kung)   approximates   南   (nan)

Kung-ch'ê-pu: Lü:

高壹   (kao-kung, "high kung")   approximates   無   (wu)

六   (liu) [sic]   approximates   應   (yin)

下凡   (hsia-fan, "low fan")   approximates   黃清 (huang,
                                                                              ch'ing)

高凡   (kao-fan, "high fan")   approximates   大清 (ta,
                                                                              ch'ing)

下五   (hsia-wu, "low wu")   approximates   太清 (t'ai,
                                                                              ch'ing)

高五   (kao-wu, "high wu")   approximates   夾清 (chia,
                                                                              ch'ing)

The order of Shên Kua's kung-ch'ê symbols differs from that of all subsequent kung-ch'ê systems. In Shên Kua's explanation kao-kung is followed by liu, while in all later forms kao-kung, or its equivalent, is
followed by hsia-fan and kao-fan, which in turn are followed by liu,
hsia-wu and kao-wu.[6]

The symbols of kung-ch'ê-p'u represent solmization syllables
written in simple, sometimes abbreviated, Chinese characters. In
the South it had become habitual to transcribe ho (合), the first
symbol, as the western note C, while the North seemed to incline toward transcribing ho as the note D. We shall transcribe ho as C, in
the same manner as we transcribe the huang-chung and the kung of the
older notations.

The kung-ch'ê symbols after Shên Kua's time are devoid of all
kao signs. Chromatic alterations, with the exception of kou (勾 , F#),
are only indicated by the affix hsia (下 , "flat"); C#, D#, G#, and
A# become Db, Eb, Ab, and Bb (hsia-ssŭ, hsia-yi, hsia-kung, and

hsia-fan), respectively. The accepted and correct[7] sequence of the
kung-ch'ê symbols (and some of their variants) used in North China,
where this system was first adopted, is as follows:

Name:	Symbol:	Variants:	Western equivalent:
Ho	合		C (e. g.)
Hsia-ssǔ	盂四	四	Db
Ssǔ	四	(宮四)	D
Hsia-yi	乞	一	Eb
Yi	乙	一 (宮一)	E
Shang	上		F
Kou	勾		F#
Ch'ê	尺		G
Hsia-kung	玉	丁	Ab
Kung	工	(宮工)	A
Hsia-fan	尬	几	Bb
Fan	凡	凡 (宮凡)	B
Liu	六		c
Hsia-wu	盂	歹	db
Wu	五		d
Hsia-yi	仁		eb

Name	Symbol:	Variants:	Western equivalent:
Yi	亿		e
Shang	仕		f
Kou	佝		f#
Ch'ê	伬		g

The variants representing hsia-ssǔ, hsia-yi, hsia-kung, and hsia-fan are incomplete in that one horizontal stroke is omitted in each symbol.

In theory the kung-ch'ê symbols cover a gamut of three octaves;[8] in practice, however, the entire range is never used. The three octaves are called:

cho-shêng (濁聲), ''muddy,'' lowest notes,

chung-shêng (中聲), middle notes,

ch'ing-shêng (清聲), ''clear,'' highest notes.

The symbols denoting tones of the upper octave beyond 五 are usually notated with the affix 亻 :

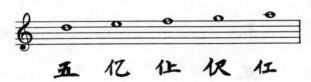

五 亿 仕 伬 仜

Symbols denoting tones below 合 are marked with a small comma:

合 凡 工 尺 上 乙

Occasionally we notice some inconsistency in the use of affixes indicating notes of the highest and lowest octaves. In some instances the affix 亻 denotes the lowest, and 彳 the highest notes of the gamut. Thus, while 亿 may read e (a tenth above middle C) in one manuscript, it may denote E (a sixth below middle C) in another. The latter version is easily discernible because its notes above 五 have the affix 彳 .

In South China (Canton) only nine kung-chê symbols are used, eight of which are the same as those of the North. The one which differs is shih (士), another reading of the northern ssǔ (四):

Ho	合	C (e. g.)
Shih	士	D
Yi	乙	E
Shang	上	F
Ch'ê	尺	G
Kung	工	A
Fan	凡	B
Liu	六	c
Wu	五	d

The system which prevails in the South uses neither kao nor hsia signs for sharpening and flattening notes. Chromatic alterations are made by transposition. If Bb is required, 合 is considered to be F, whereupon 上 , being a fourth higher than 合 , can become Bb. The

shifting of ho (合), comparable to the "movable do" of the West,
led to the creation of a number of scales, some with a pure fourth,
others with an augmented fourth, which facilitated transpositions and
changes of mode. This method was employed in various ways in the
diverse musical categories of China,[9] especially in the operatic styles,
where stringed instruments such as the êrh-hsien (二 絃 , lit.,
"two strings")[10] or the hu-ch'in (胡 琴 , "foreign ch'in")[11] play
an important role. As a detailed discussion of these systems would
lead far beyond the scope of this book,[12] we shall confine ourselves
to one example: the two strings of the êrh-hsien are tuned to 合 and
尺 (C and G, the mu-hsien 母 絃 , "mother string," and tzŭ-
hsien 子 絃 ,"son string," respectively). An êrh-hsien player,
who as a rule knows little about kao and hsia notes, is able to master
the various modes required in operatic music by memorizing a few
transposing scales without even altering the tuning of his two strings.
If the two strings are called by different tone names, a number of
scales (comparable to the western do-mode, re-mode, etc.) are created in the following manner:[13]

Lower (mu) string: Upper (tzŭ) string:

C (ho)   D E F ⟶   G (ch'ê)   A B c

D (shih)   E F G ⟶   A (kung)   B c d

E (yi)   F G A ⟶   B (fan)   c d e

F (shang)   G A B ⟶   c (liu)   d e f

G (ch'ê   A B c ⟶   d (wu)   e f g

                         and others.

The player would thus name the various scales according to the tone
names given to his two strings: ho-chê-t'iao (合 尺 調 , ho-chê

scale), shih-kung-t'iao (士工調 , shih-kung scale), yi-fan-t'iao (乙 凡 調 , yi-fan scale), and so forth.[14] As the tuning of the two strings remains unaltered (C and G), all scales have to begin with C:

	Mu:				Tzǔ:			
Ho-ch'ê-t'iao	C	D	E	F	G	A	B	c
Shih-kung-t'iao	C	D	Eb	F	G	Ab	Bb	c
Yi-fan-t'iao	C	Db	Eb	F	G	Ab	Bb	c
Shang-liu-t'iao	C	D	E	F#	G	A	B	c
Ch'ê-wu-t'iao	C	D	E	F	G	A	Bb	c

and others.[15]

In addition to the scales mentioned above, there are others which can be compared to the "fixed do" system.[16] Among them are scales used in the operatic styles of êrh-huang (二 黃)[17] and pang-tzǔ (梆 子).[18] For instance, the basic êrh-huang scale is

尺　工　凡　六　五　一　生　伬
G　　A　　Bb　　c　　d　　e　　f#[19]　g.

In this scale 凡 invariably stands a minor third above 尺 . Such practices in this and other scales may have been the reason for the eventual appearance of additional symbols in the kung-ch'ê-p'u of the South. We observe occasionally two symbols for fan, two for shang, and two for yi. While in the kung-ch'ê-p'u of the North similar pairs of symbols were in common use and each symbol had its specific signif-icance, in the South (Canton) they were employed indiscriminately; each member of a pair could be used for notating either the basic tone or its alteration.

However, the fact that the notation of the South possessed two symbols for the degrees mentioned — even if the symbols were used carelessly — seems to indicate that originally each symbol may have had a specific significance. One could assume that originally 凡 may have denoted Bb; 反 , another symbol for fan may have denoted B; 乙 may have stood for Eb; 一 for E; 上 for F; and 生 (shēng) for F#. The last symbol (shēng) in particular was and is often used to represent a tone a pure fourth above ho as well.

A similar method of transposition is applied in the notations of music for the hsiao [20] and the ti. [21] While in ti notation ho is transcribed with the note c, [22] in hsiao notation ho represents a tone a fourth lower: G. [23]

	Ti		Hsiao
合	c	合	G
四	d	四	A
乙	e	乙	B

Occasionally the tones of the ti and the hsiao are notated as they sound:

Ti: 六 五 乙 上 尺 工 凡 伬 伍 亿 仩 伖
c d e f g a b c' d' e' f' g'

Hsiao: 尺 工 凡 六 五 乙 上 伬 仜 伬 伬 伍
G A B c d e f g a b c' d'

Similarly the tones produced on the yüeh-ch'in (月琴) [24] and san-hsien (三絃) [25] are notated as follows:

Yüeh-ch'in		San-hsien		
Inner string:	Outer string:	Low string:	Middle string:	High string:
上	六	四	尺	五
尺工凡六五乙仜伬仜	伍乙仜伬仈伬伍亿仜伬仜	乙上尺工凡六五乙仜伬仜伬仈	工凡六五乙仜伬仈伬伍亿	乙仜伬仈伬伍亿

The foregoing ti, hsiao, yüeh-ch'in, and san-hsien scales illustrate the use of the affix 亻. If a scale begins with high notes, such as 六 and 五, the affix 亻 is frequently omitted in the notation of either the next higher note 乙 (六 五乙仜, etc.), or of all subsequent notes up to 伬 .

In recent times Chinese musicians, with the exception of those who use Western staff notation or the highly popular chien-p'u (簡 譜), an abridged notation employing Arabic numerals,[26] have, mainly in the North (Peiping), ceased using signs for flat and sharp notes in kung-ch'ê-p'u. North China confines itself to the use of three scales, similar to the transposing scales of the South: a "major," a "minor," and the hsi-p'i (西 皮)[27] scale, which is a "Dorian mode." In all these instances simple kung-ch'ê symbols are used without any kao or hsia indications.

Kung-ch'ê-p'u was used to notate both ritual and secular music; the many styles of secular music led to a number of methods of notating rhythmic features. The prevailing syllabic style of ritual music required few, if any, rhythmic signs because the monosyllabic words of Chinese sacred texts were set mainly to chains of long notes of equal length. These uniform beats were organized into groups (measures) of four or eight, and the end of each group was often indicated by the sound of a percussion instrument. Accompanying instruments could be used to sub-divide each beat into halves or quarters,[28] but the meter, the strict succession of four or eight uniform beats, remained unchanged.

The following represents the Hymn in Honor of Confucius performed

according to a decree issued in the eighth year of Ch'ien Lung (A. D. 1743). The same words and the same music are always used, the only difference being the change of lü or key-note. The hymn is always sung in the lü corresponding to the moon during which the ceremony takes place; for instance, during the second moon chia-chung is assumed as lü, and during the eighth moon the keynote is nan-lü. The hymn is divided into six stanzas:

1. Ying shên, receiving the approaching spirit.

2. Ch'u hsien, first presentation of offerings.

3. Ya hsien, second presentation.

4. Chung hsien, third and last presentation.

5. Ch'ê chuan, removal of the viands.

6. Sung shên, escorting the spirit back.[29]

The notational symbols are placed to the left of the textual characters of the six strophes of the hymn shown on pages 82 and 83. Each strophe is read from top to bottom and from right to left.

Figure 15

迎神

工大合哉四孔乙子
工先尺覺乙先四知
合與四天尺地乙參
工萬尺世乙之乙師
乙祥尺徵合麟四紱
合韻尺荅四金尺絲
合日四月工既乙揭
合乾四坤合清工怡

初獻

工予合懷四明乙德
尺玉合振工金尺聲
四生合民尺未乙有
合展四也乙大四成
乙俎合豆工千乙古
四春四秋尺上四丁
工清尺酒合既工載
合其四香合始工升

亞獻

工式合禮四莫乙愆
尺升乙堂合再乙獻
尺響乙協合鼓四鏞
乙誠尺孚乙罍工獻
乙肅乙肅四雍四雍
合譽工髦尺斯工彥
尺禮乙陶合樂四淑
乙相四觀合而工善

Figure 15 (cont.)

We have already observed that occasionally writers take liberties with the use of the affix 亻. In the fifth and sixth strophes of Figure 15 we notice 亻工 appearing several times in conjunction with notes of the middle octave. Let us consider the last sixteen notes of the sixth stanza:

Of the three transcriptions shown above, (a) represents a literal reading with unusually large intervals, (b) shows transpositions of notes belonging to the middle octave into the high range of 亻工 (for the purpose of avoiding these improbable intervals), and (c) shows a reading in which the affix 亻 is ignored, suggesting that the writer may have employed it for other than musical purposes. The third version seems to be more acceptable than the other two because 亻工 is not used throughout the hymn; in the first four stanzas the writer uses 工 exclusively; only in the last two stanzas does he use the affix, and even then not constantly.

Another interpretation of 亻工, less plausible than the previous one, could be that occasionally the sign 亻 was used for denoting the

high-alteration of a note by a semitone.[30] In such instances 仁
could be transcribed as A#. This reading is highly improbable
here because the melody has a purely anhemitonic pentatonic character in its first four stanzas, and the sporadic use of 仁 in the
last two stanzas cannot possibly mean a sudden change from A to
A#, which would thus destroy the pentatonic character, particularly
in ritual music.

Figure 16 (pp. 86-87) is the score of the Confucian heptatonic
hymn Ssŭ-wên (思文), "Contemplation of refined writing":[31]

The score has to be read horizontally from right to left across
pages 86 and 87. The characters at the top of both pages read:

Chin	tzŭ	ching	êrh - shih - ssŭ	pai
(Golden	words	classic (books)	twenty-four	strikes

ku	pan	chieh	tsou	p'u
drum	wooden block		rhythm	score).

Below the heading we find three annotations in oval frames on page 86
and three others on page 87. Further down on both pages we find
another three horizontal rows of such annotations. These inform us
about "measure one," "measure two," and so forth, up to "measure
twenty-four" (第廿). Each annotation, placed at the first beat of
each measure, is marked with a black dot representing a percussive
beat. In all there are twenty-four strokes (measures), a fact which
is also indicated in the heading. Below these annotations we observe
the melody notated in kung-ch'ê symbols, each of which is placed in a
small circle.

The meter of the hymn is clearly indicated by the fact that there

Figure 16

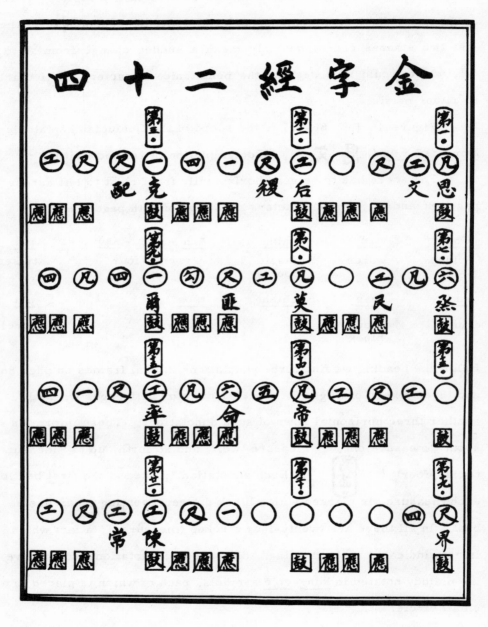

Figure 16 (cont.)

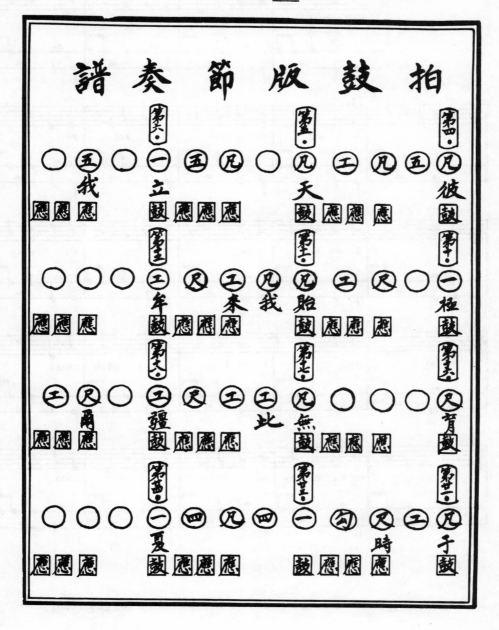

Figure 17

1. Signifies a small drum; 2. Signifies a large drum.

are four circles in each measure. Whenever a rest (or held note)
occurs, an empty circle is used. The text[32] appears below the circles
in small characters. In this hymn the rigid syllabic style of ritual music is not strictly observed because some of the words are held over
more than one note (and beat). Below the text we find characters
placed in square frames which denote the percussion part; these characters are:

 Ku, the general term for drum,

 Ying (ying-ku), "corresponding drum."[33]

A transcription of the hymn is shown on page 88.

In various instrumental parts of ritual, and in many notations of
secular music where there are neither textual characters nor such
clearly organized scores as that of the hymn Ssŭ-wên to guide the
reader, several methods of notating rhythmical features are employed.

The simplest was to write notes of long duration in large characters and notes of shorter duration in small ones. Writing music by
means of large and small notational symbols occurred only sporadically and did not become a popular method because it was indistinct
and showed no marked endeavor to notate rhythm clearly. Another
device used to indicate notes of long duration was to leave one or more
spaces open immediately after (below) the note to be prolonged. An
example of an instrumental part of the Tao-yin (導引), "The
Imperial Guiding March,"[34] on page 90 will illustrate this. The march
is to be performed by two mouth organs (shêng, 笙),[35] two ti,[36]
two hsiao,[37] two gong chimes (yün-lo, 雲鑼),[38] two drums, and
wooden clappers.[39]

導引樂譜

四四、工合。四　　四、合。

工六。五六。工　尺。上四

合、工。　四合。工六、五六。、

工　尺。上、四合。、工。　四、

合。、工六。、五六。工、　尺。上、

四。　　合、工。、合四。、合工。、

尺。

Figure 18

As already stated, the gaps after (below) the symbols indicate prolongations of the preceding notes. Each gap corresponding to the size
of one notational symbol represents one beat — in the transcriptions
shown below, a quarter note. Thus, if a wide gap the size of two or
more notational symbols appears, it signifies a correspondingly longer
duration of the preceding note.

Occasionally, however, the gaps are not clearly spaced — they
may be too large or too small and thus cause some ambiguity in transcription.

The first column of Figure 18 shows a gap large enough to contain
two notational symbols. We therefore assume that the note preceding
the gap has to be held for three beats, one beat being represented by
the notational symbol (ssŭ) itself, the other two by the gap. A similar
gap appears in the sixth column. The other gaps, being smaller, denote the prolongation of the preceding notes by one beat only.

The drumbeats are notated by small circles and the beats to be
performed by the wooden clapper by commas. In ritual and ceremonial
music it was customary to place a drumbeat at the end of a measure, a
habit not strictly observed, as can be seen in the notation of the "Imperial Guiding March." If we adjust our transcription to the exact
sizes of the gaps, we get:

This version, if continued, may cause some doubts as to whether a "literal" transcription is the proper solution and whether the gaps are correctly spaced. If, according to custom, we expect the drumbeat to appear at the end of every four-beat measure, we find that the large gap of the first column has to be reduced to a one-beat duration. In this case the note ss̆u will be held only for two beats:

Continuing the transcription, it becomes obvious that in this particular piece a drumbeat cannot be placed at the end of every measure.

From the preceding discussion we conclude that this method of notating rhythmic features may have served mainly as a mnemonic aid to the performer who already knew the rhythmic shape of the melody and did not require detailed rhythmic information. However, for persons not acquainted with the rhythm of this melody, it can be expected that different transcribers will achieve different results. To show the ambiguity of interpreting the gaps we give two transcriptions (p. 93) of the Tao-yin, one written by Kurt Reinhard,[40] the other by J. A. van Aalst.[41] A comparison of these two transcriptions shows not only rhythmic differences but a number of octave transpositions as well. As stated before in the discussion of flute notations,[42] symbols denoting sounds of the middle octave occasionally were used for sounds of the upper octave, and, in some cases, vice versa.[43] Van Aalst's transcription places the majority of low notes in the higher octave in

(Reinhard)

(Van Aalst)

Figure 19

A. Signifies clapper; B. Signifies drum.

order to achieve a less angular form of the melody than the one by Reinhard, which adheres to the notated symbols.

Another method of notating rhythmic features is shown in Figure 20, a song called "The Fresh Beautiful Flower" (鮮花).[44]

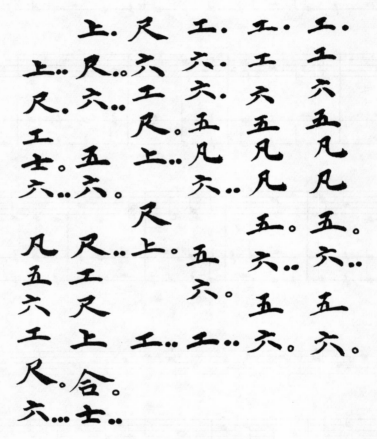

Figure 20

In this method, which is similar to the one just described, the prolongations of notes are indicated by dots placed at the right side of the notational symbols, with each dot prolonging the note by one beat. In addition to the dots, small circles are used (with a few exceptions) to denote the final beats of eight-beat measures. These circles may occur as well on the fifth, sixth, or seventh beats, in which case they indicate a prolongation of the respective note to the end of the measure. Although this method has an advantage over the one that uses gaps, errors can still occur. Thus, an ambiguity can be observed if we consider the last symbol of the fifth and the first four symbols of the sixth columns. The passage allows two different transcriptions which can be seen in the first half of the last line of Figure 21. Conceivably copyists commit errors and, just as in the case of the widening and narrowing of gaps, add or omit dots. The upper stave of the first half of the last system of Figure 21 shows the literal, the lower one a probable and, perhaps, more plausible interpretation of the doubtful passage; that is to say, we assume that the notes concerned may have been 士. 上. 尺. 工 士 。 and not, as written, 士.. 上.. 尺. 工 士 。. Following is the transcription of "The Fresh Beautiful Flower":

"The Fresh Beautiful Flower," (cont.)

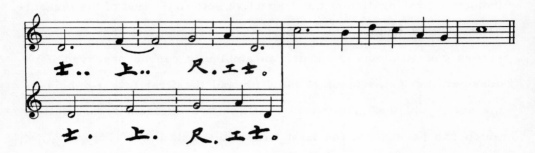

Figure 21

Still another method[45] of notating rhythmical features which aims at greater accuracy uses a considerable number of metrical signs placed, as usual, to the right side of the notational symbols. There are two sets of signs: those which indicate notes which occur on any of the four beats of a measure, and those which denote syncopated or held notes.

The first group consists of the following signs:

> First beat ▼
> Second beat •
> Third beat o
> Fourth beat •

In practice the signs are used in the following manner:

Occasionally the black triangle which represents the first beat can be replaced with ❨ or ✖. Especially in pieces in 2/4 meter[46] the main beat (opening beat) is usually denoted by the sign ❨ , called chêng-pan, (正板), "main beat," or t'ou-pan (頭板), "head beat," or hung-pan (紅板), "red beat."

In pieces with four-beat measures the first beat can also be no-tated with ✖ , called tsêng-pan (贈板), "conferring, bestowing beat," or hêh-pan (黑板), "black beat."

The sign ○ , called chêng-yen (正眼), "main eye," in-dicates the third beat of a measure. The second and fourth beats of this group, if notated, are each marked by a single dot. If two or more notes are to be performed within any of the four beats, they are nota-ted as follows:

A second set of metrical signs is used if notes are held from one into the next beat or beats. Each of the following signs represents not the starting point of a note (♩ ♩), but that part of a note which is held over into the next beat (♩ ♩):

First beat **L** or **凶** or **一**
Second beat **L**
Third beat **△**
Fourth beat **L**

The sign **L** is called t'ou-chih-pan (頭制板), "head restrained beat," and **凶** , hêh-chih-pan (黑制板), "black restrained beat." These two signs denote the metrical main beat applied to notes which are held over from the preceding beat; and, as stated before, they never occur when a note begins with the main beat. The sign **L** , ch'ê-yen (拆眼), "cut-off eye," denotes the second or fourth beats, notes which are held over from the preceding beats. These signs are used in the following manner:

Figure 22

Figure 23

In the foregoing example (Fig. 23) we note that the sequence

✗ ◬ ㇄   stands for 1 (2) 3 4. It is unnecessary to insert a sign

for the second beat because ✗ ◬ ㇄   suffice to indicate that the

note is to be held from the first to the third and beyond it, to the

subsequent fourth beat.

The metrical sign notated with ➖ , which must not be confused

with the abbreviated yi symbol (➖) of kung-ch'ê-p'u is used in the

following manner:

or:

If notational symbols are placed in the column of metrical signs,

they represent grace notes (short appoggiaturas) which approach the

succeeding note from below:

Grace notes which are higher than their succeeding notes — that is, ornamental notes which approach the main notes from above — are not indicated by specific notational symbols but by the general sign ∪ . This sign usually denotes a grace note which is one tone higher than the preceding note and, of course, higher than the succeeding note:

An exception is made if the grace note occurs, for example, between two main notes the second of which is a tone higher than the first. In such instances the grace note has to be two tones higher than the preceding main note:

Repeated notes are indicated by dots placed below the notational symbols:

We notice that the down beat of a measure in a succession of repeated notes is notated not only with the customary dot but also by the metrical sign ⼳ , an abbreviated h̄eh-chih-pan (⼳). Trills and glissandi are shown by an oblique line in the notational column:

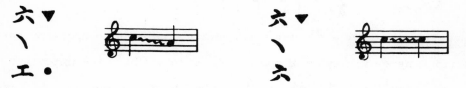

The end of a phrase is indicated by a ⌐ framing the last notational symbol in the following manner:

All Chinese dramas use music, most of which is written and arranged by professional musicians of a much lower social level than the distinguished literati. Many operas use the same standard melodies, "song labels" (ch'ü-p'ai, 曲牌), "leitmotifs" (ya-ti, 雅笛), and "leit-rhythms" which are the common property of the Chinese operatic repertoire.[47] They refer to certain situations, and when performed are immediately recognized by Chinese audiences.

Before considering Chinese operatic melodies, it is important to discuss briefly some of these features, particularly the rhythms characteristic of certain operatic styles. A typical êrh-huang[48] rhythm is:

$$\frac{4}{4} \quad \text{(musical notation)} \quad \text{etc.,}$$

called i-pan san-yen (一板三眼), one accented, three light beats ("eyes"); another êrh-huang rhythm is:

$$\frac{2}{4} \quad \text{(musical notation)} \quad \text{etc.,}$$

called i-pan i-yen (一板一眼), one accented, one light beat. In hsi-p'i (西皮)[49] style the characteristic rhythms are also i-pan san-yen and i-pan i-yen, but both have to begin with up-beats:

$$\frac{4}{4} \quad \text{(musical notation)} \quad \text{etc.,}$$

and

$$\frac{2}{4} \quad \text{(musical notation)} \quad \text{etc.}$$

Occasionally these and other rhythms are mentioned in operatic manuscripts; hence it may be of some interest to list here the important ones: Chêng-pan (正板), "principal beat," refers to a succession of main beats:

$$\frac{4}{4} \quad \text{(musical notation)}$$

or

$$\frac{2}{4} \quad \text{(musical notation)}$$

San-pan (散板), "scattered beat," or Yao-pan (摇板), "rocking beat," refer to free rhythms; K'uai-pan (快板), "fast beat," consists of a series of quick, accented (drum) beats without any yen; Man-pan (慢板), "slow beat," is, as the term implies, a succession of slow beats, usually performed in a free manner; Yüan-pan (原板), "original beat," consists of the sequence i-pan i-yen and refers to a return to the original rhythm after an arioso, recitative, or spoken dialogue.

The next two terms, although they use the word pan, have no relation to rhythmical features. They are: Fan-pan (反板), "turned back pan," which refers to the reversed tuning of the strings of the hu-ch'in in hsi-p'i operas; and Tao-pan (倒板), "falling back pan," which denotes a brief introductory melody sung by the actor behind the curtain before his appearance on the stage.

In order to round out the list, it is necessary to mention the tzŭ-pai (自白), "self-introduction," performed by the actor, either in the form of a recitative or as a spoken monologue.

We now turn to an operatic example which shows to what extent the foregoing symbols, signs, and annotations are used. Figure 24 represents a brief excerpt from Lao-yüan (老圓), "The Old Buddhist Priest," a drama by Yü Yüeh (俞越), who lived during the late Ch'ing (清) period. Yü Yüeh, a former admiral, who in later years turned to the study of ancient Chinese literature, wrote approximately 500 volumes dealing with various literary subjects.[50] As the author of this drama, which deals with the story of an old Buddhist priest, a general, and a prostitute, Yü-Yüeh probably had little to do with the music, for as stated before, operatic music was provided by professional musicians who drew their material from the common pool of motives, melodies, and rhythms and adjusted it to the text.

Following (Fig. 24, p. 105) is the excerpt from the drama Lao-yüan. This figure shows two broad vertical columns both containing at their left sides the text[51] and, to the right of each textual character, kung-ch'ê symbols written in slanting rows. The reading of the two broad columns is from top right to bottom right, then from top left to bottom left. The slanting rows of kung-ch'ê symbols, each headed by a textual character, are to be read from left to right because it was impossible for the copyist to place them vertically. The fact that each slanting row of the left column appears to be joined to one in the broad column at the right is of no consequence.

Some of the notational symbols are variants created by the copyist: the symbol ho (合) becomes 全 , and ssŭ (四) becomes の . This alternative writing of ssŭ is derived from the common (commercial) writing (碼 字 , ma-tzŭ) of the number 四 (four): ㄨ .[52] If written carelessly ㄨ becomes の. It is of interest to note that the same ㄨ was also an ancient form of the number 五 (five).[53] In su-tzŭ-p'u, symbols such as の and の can represent both 四 (D) and 五 (d), the higher octave and their alterations. We also find that the main beats are not only indicated by ㄨ and Ⅸ , but also by ヽ , the sign of the main beat in 2/4 meter.

Following (Fig. 25, p. 106) is a transcription of the Lao-yüan excerpt. It does not claim to be the only possible one because, as we have noticed before, there are still certain ambiguities in the notation, and furthermore, we must take into account traditional motives and rhythms which, although not indicated in the manuscript, were known to performers and listeners of the late Ch'ing dynasty.

Figure 24

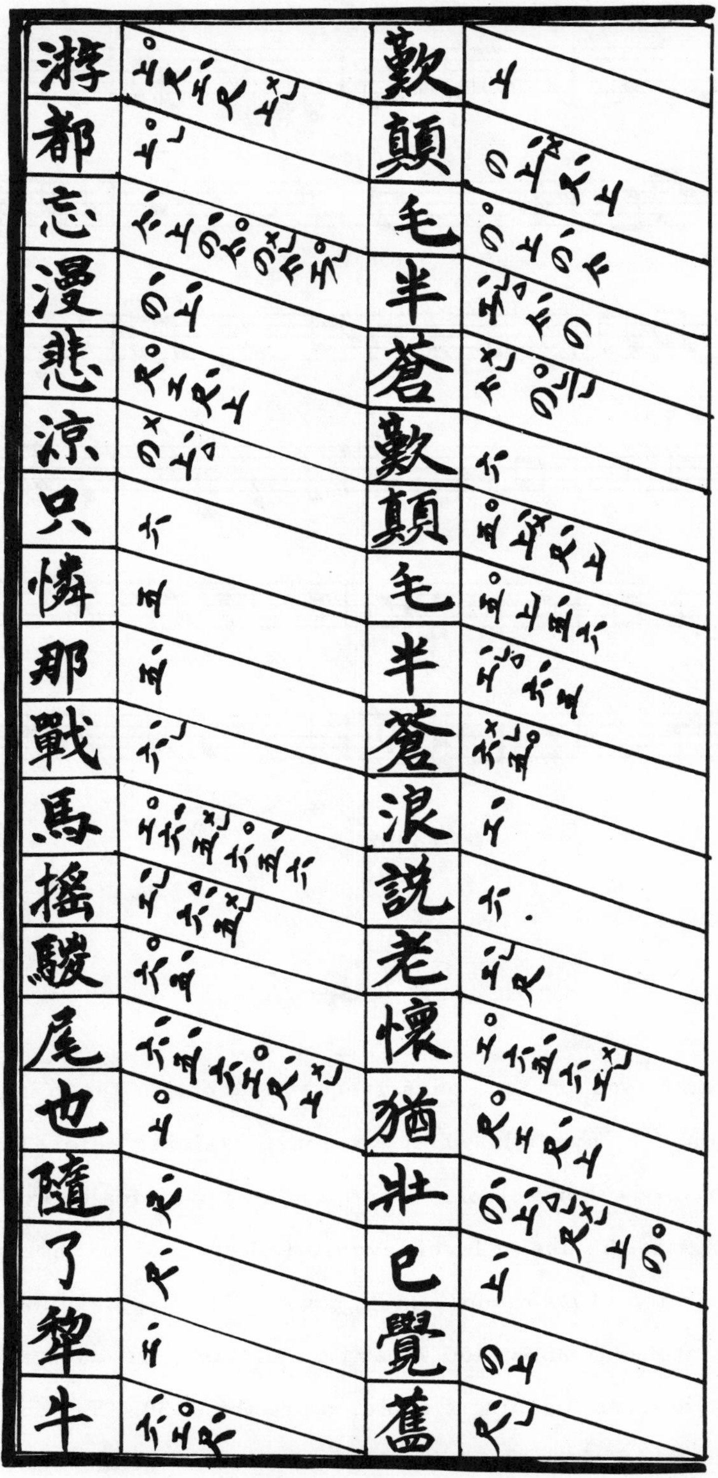

Figure 25

P'ING-TSÊ (平仄)

The notations of art songs frequently contain the p'ing-tsê ("level-oblique"), symbols which we must examine before discussing the song notations themselves. A most remarkable feature of the Chinese language is the use of level (even), falling, and rising tones in the pronunciation of its monosyllabic words. The basic Chinese vocabulary consists of only about 400 separate syllables, but each syllable may have numerous meanings; some, more than 150. For instance, the word fu when uttered with a high even tone means "a sage"

(夫), with a lower even tone, "a raft" (桴), a rising tone alters its meaning to "dried meat" (脯), and a falling tone changes it to "pot" (釜), and so forth. In writing, however, every meaning of a word is expressed by a different character.

In dictionaries these tones are indicated by the numbers 1-4. According to the introduction of Mathews' Chinese English Dictionary, [54] they are listed in the following manner:

1 (陰平(聲))   yin-p'ing Upper Even (Tone) — High level

2 (陽平(聲))   yang-p'ing Lower Even (Tone) — High rising

3 (上(聲))   shang Rising (Tone) — Low rising

4 (去(聲))   ch'ü Falling or Going (Tone) — High falling

An excellent description of these tones is offered by Professor Teng Ssu-yü:[55]

First tone   — Slight surprise — oh?

Second tone —   question   — oh?

Third tone   —   doubt   — o-oh?

Fourth tone —   emphasis   — oh!

If we notate the four tones above and below one stave, we get:

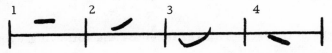

In their relationship to music the four tones[56] are generally called:

Upper even (shang p'ing, 上平)

Lower even (hsia p'ing, 下平)

Rising   (shang, 上)

Falling   (ch'ü, 去)

During the T'ang and Sung periods (618-1279) the linguistic tones of poetic song texts were correlated with the tonal movements of the vocal lines and thus had considerable influence upon the shape of the melody.

These tones, called shēng (聲), probably reach back into the early history of the Chinese language. There is vague reference to them in the Yüeh-chi, the music chapter of the Li Chi, the "Book of Rites."[57] In the fifth century A.D., Shēn Yüeh [Shēn Yo] (沈約), 441-513, classified these tones,[58] and roughly a hundred years later, T'ang poets began creating poetry (lü-shih, 律 詩 , "regulated poetry") by making conscious use of them. A new style of poetry called hsin-t'i (新 體) was devised in which preset tonal patterns provided strict rules for the writing of poems.

A Chinese poem is at best a hard nut to crack, expressed as it usually is in lines of five or seven monosyllabic root-ideas, without inflection, agglutination, or grammatical indication of any kind, the connection between which has to be inferred by the reader from the logic, from the context, and least perhaps of all from the syntactical arrangement of the words. Then, again, the poet is hampered not only by rhyme but also by tone.... the natural order of words is often entirely sacrificed to the exigencies of tone, thus making it more difficult than ever for the reader to grasp the sense.... [59]

In writing, these tones were expressed by the following symbols:

1. 平 { p'ing, "even tone" { 陰平 yin p'ing (high level)
2. 　　　　　　　　　　　　　　 陽平 yang p'ing (high rising)

3. 上 shang, "rising tone," (low rising)

4. 去 ch'u, "falling tone," (high falling)

A fifth symbol, often employed in the writing of the dialects of the South, does not denote a type of inflection but represents the shortening of a syllable:

入 ju.

This latter symbol, frequently described as "entering tone," has been abolished in the Mandarin dialect (national language) and combined with the other tones.

A comparison of the shêng with the medieval neumes of the West shows that p'ing corresponds to the punctum and virga, shang to the podatus or pes, and ch'ü to the clivis. The neumes, like the shêng,

indicated not so much accentuation in the modern sense of the word, but rather an inflection of the voice, the acutus (a), a raising, the gravis (b), a lowering of the pitch. The former became the virga (which, as a rule, is used for a higher note), the latter, the punctum (which usually indicates a lower tone).[60]

Linguistic tones were related to the yang and yin principle in the same manner as musical tones. High tones (high and low could be applied to even, rising, and falling inflections) would be ascribed to the yin and low tones to the yang principle. Another classification placed both high and low even tones into the yin, and all oblique forms, rising, falling, and "entering," into the opposite, yang. This remarkable technique of creating poems (and, subsequently song melodies) to preset tonal patterns reached its greatest refinement during the Sung period (960-1279). We refer particularly to the tz'ŭ (詞), an important form of poetry of the late T'ang and Sung dynasties in which this art can be studied.[61] Numerous Chinese authors discuss the relationship between the shêng and the tonal movement of melodies.

In the history of the Southern Sung period (A. D. 420-478)[62] there is a biography of a certain Lu Chüeh (陸厥) (A. D. 472-499), author of a History of the Four Neumes. The following passages from this biography, quoted by Ku Yen-wu (顧 炎 武) are significant: "At the end of Yün Ming (A. D. 483-493) various scholars, including Shên Yüeh, wrote poems and compositions using kung shang [the tones of the scale — J. H. L.] with p'ing, shang, ch'ü and ju... using these as the basis for arranging the rhymes and rules according to the eight rules of Shên Yüeh." ... and Chiang K'uei (姜 夔) in the music section of the official history of the Sung dynasty (宋史樂志.) only repeats...: "It is inherent in their very nature, that the seven musical tones [of the scale — J. H. L.] should be matched in harmony with the four linguistic neumes" (七音之協四聲各有自然之理).[63]

After the Sung dynasty this art of writing poetry and music to pre-set tonal patterns[64] became neglected, and it happened not infrequently that a linguistic even tone would be linked to an oblique musical tonal movement, or vice versa.

We now turn to the consideration of the kung-ch'ê notation of an untitled song (p. 111).[65] The large characters in the middle of each of the four columns are the text. To their right we notice the kung-ch'ê symbols and to their left the p'ing-tsê annotations. Although the notation shows no rhythmic signs, the placing of one or more notational symbols against each textual character shows how many notes are to be performed with each word (and beat).

The basic movement form, which includes the distribution of themes and metres, is by an unknown composer, but preceded the writing of the words of the poem.

The words were by Ts'ao Kuan (曹 冠) during the Sung dynasty. The tonal superstructure [the melody] was composed in 1848 by Hsieh Yüan-huai (謝 元 淮) in the Ch'ing dynasty, and follows the musical character of the words of Ts'ao Kuan and the preconceived movement,

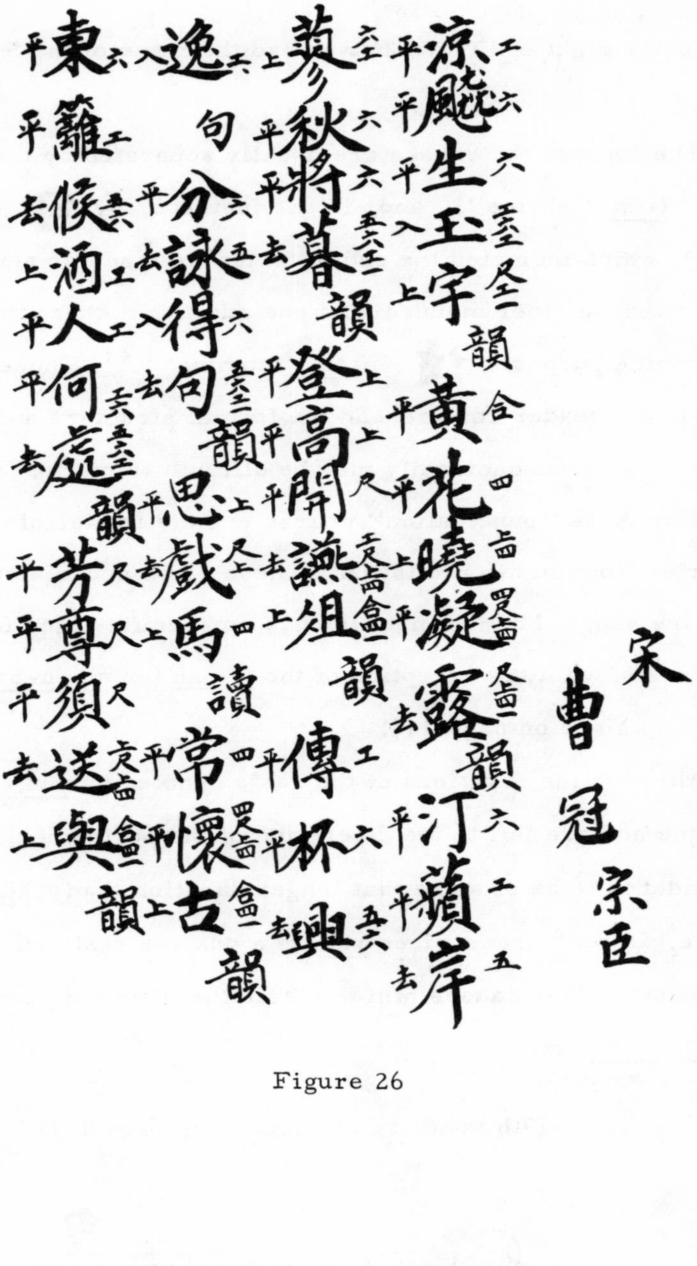
宋 曹冠 宗臣
涼颸生玉宇 韻 黃花曉凝露 韻 汀蘋岸
蓼秋將暮 韻 登高開讌俎 韻 傳杯興
逸句 分詠得句 韻 思戲馬 讀 常懷古 韻
東籬候酒人何處 韻 芳尊須送與 韻

Figure 26

thematic and metric form of the unknown original composer. This music-poem is taken from the Sui Chin Tz'u P'u (碎 金 詞 譜), Vol. 5, p. 2.[66]

At the outer right of Figure 26 we read the name of the Sung poet Ts'ao Kuan.

The lines of the verses are usually separated by the character 韻 (yün, "rhyme"), and, in one instance, by 句 (chü, "sentence"), which indicates the end of textual phrases or sentences. We may add that in other manuscripts one additional character can be used for the same purpose, 讀 (tou, "comma").[67] These three characters help the reader comprehend the formal structure and meaning of the poem, which occasionally may be difficult to grasp. At spots indicated by these "punctuation" characters the reader of the poem allows brief stops in his recitation. These stops occur also in the vocal line of the song. Musical notation has no specific signs for the indication of rests, with the exception of the ti-pan (or chieh-pan), which will be explained on page 114.

Although the durations of the rests denoted by yün, chü, and tou are vague and are left to the discretion of the performer, yün usually is considered to be of somewhat longer duration than chü and tou. For instance, Levis[68] transcribes yün as a quarter rest and chü and tou as eighth rests. This causes him to notate the meter of certain phrases as $4\frac{1}{2}{\over 4}$, $7\frac{1}{2}{\over 4}$, etc.:

(9th measure of Figure 26, page 111)

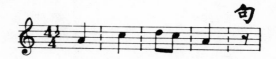

(11th and 12th measures of Figure 26, page 111)

The indefinite durations of the rests allow us to simplify the matter by interpreting the various rests so that they always complete a measure:

Each textual character will be transcribed with one beat of the duration of a quarter note. For instance, if three notational symbols are placed against one textual character, they will be transcribed as triplets. The three notes could also be considered as one eighth and two sixteenths, or two sixteenths and one eighth; such rhythmic subtleties are not notated in kung-ch'ê-p'u and are left to the discretion of the performer.

The kung-ch'ê symbols next to the fifth textual character of the first column (right-hand side) are: 全一 The third symbol, a short horizontal line, can easily be confused with the abbreviated yi symbol (━). The reasons why it cannot be yi are: (1) the melody is purely anhemitonic pentatonic; and (2) immediately below this short line appears yün (韻), the indication of a rest. This short horizontal line in the notational column indicates the end of a phrase, a short rest. It is called ti-pan (底 板), "end beat" or chieh-pan (截 板), "cut-off beat." Other ti-pan can be noticed next to the tenth, seventeenth, twenty-second, thirtieth, thirty-sixth, forty-third, and forty-eighth characters of Figure 26.

The following transcription of Figure 26 is provided with (a) the original text written in Chinese characters, (b) transliteration and translation (literal),[69] (c) a general translation, and (d) the original shēng (and the modern tones of each word), in order to enable the reader to compare linguistic with musical tonal movements.

Figure 27

涼 飆 生 玉 宇   韻

Liang   piao   sheng   yü   yü

Cool   wind   arises   jade   vault
Cool   wind   blows   in the   firmament

平   平   平   入   上
2   1   1   4   3

黄 花 曉 凝 露   韻

Huang   hua   hsiao   ning   lu

Yellow flowers morning congealed dew
In the morning the yellow chrysanthemum is heavy with dew

平 平   上   平   去
2   1   3   2.4   4

Figure 27 (cont.)

汀　蘋　岸　蓼　秋　將　　暮　　韻

Ting　p'ing　an　liao　ch'iu　chiang　mu

Beach　duck-　bank　smart-　autumn　toward　late
　　　weeds　　　weeds

Duckweeds and smartweeds on the beaches and banks herald
the approach of late autumn

平　平　去　上　平　平　去
1　　2　　4　　3　　1　　1　　4

登　高　開　讌　　俎　　韻

Teng　kao　k'ai　yen　tsu

Ascending heights open　feast　　dishes
Ascending the heights we give a banquet

平　平　平　去　上
1　　1　　1　　4　　3

傳　杯　興　逸　句

Ch'uan　pei　hsing　i

Pass　cups　spirit　wanders
A round of drinks — and our spirits wander joyfully

平　平　去　入
2　　1　　1　　4.5

Figure 27 (cont.)

分 詠 得 句 韻
Fen yung te chü

Divide sing obtain lines
We take turns to compose poems and to obtain beautiful lines

平 去 入 去
1 3 2.5 4

思 戲 馬 讀 常 懷 古 韻
Ssu hsi ma ch'ang huai ku

Thinking playing horse often meditate ancient
Thinking of the Hsi-ma terrace, we often meditate of the ancient

平 去 上 平 平 上
1 4 3 2 2 3

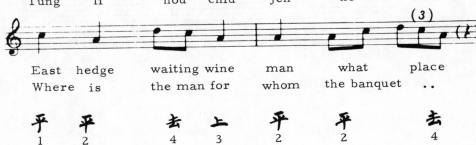

東 籬 候 酒 人 何 處 韻
Tung li hou chiu jen ho ch'u

East hedge waiting wine man what place
Where is the man for whom the banquet ..

平 平 去 上 平 平 去
1 2 4 3 2 2 4

Figure 27 (cont.)

If we compare the shêng with the tonal movement of the melody (Figure 27), we find that in several instances the melody does not follow the prescribed rise and fall of linguistic tones. Next to the eighth character of the first column in Figure 26 we find: 上曉上 . Shang (上) indicates a rising linguistic tone, whereas the melody actually descends from 上 to 四 . A similar instance can be observed next to the first character of the second column.

In the year 1713 the Imperial Music Office of the Ch'ing dynasty (1655-1911) established a new official (theoretical) scale with fourteen degrees in the octave.[70] The first twelve of these fourteen degrees were named after the twelve lü (huang, ta, t'ai, etc.), and the last two (the thirteenth and fourteenth degrees) were again called huang and ta; thus, the next higher octave would not begin with huang, but with t'ai:

(C) 1   huang   6   chung   11   wu
     2   ta   7   jui   12   ying
     3   t'ai   8   lin   13   huang
     4   chia   9   i   14   ta
     5   ku   10   nan   1   t'ai   (c)

	Lü name	Ti	Hsiao	Courant's definition
11	I(-tsê)	凡	上	ut# 3
12	Nan	仉	仩	re
13	Wu	合	尺	re
14	Ying	六俗	伬	re#
1	Huang	四	工	mi
2	Ta	五	仜	fa
3	T'ai	乙	凡	fa#
4	Chia	亿	仉	sol
5	Ku	上	侌	sol#
6	Chung	仩	衮	la
7	Jui	尺	罡	la
8	Lin	伬	磊	la#
9	I	工	乙	si
10	Nan	仜	亿	ut
11	Wu	凡	上	ut#
12	Ying	仉	仩	re
13	Huang	六	尺	re
14	Ta	伏	伬	re#
1	T'ai	五	工	mi

This nomenclature shows that the ancient significance of the lü as absolute pitches had disappeared; only the names of the lü were still in use. In notating this scale by means of kung-ch'ê-p'u, additional symbols had to be employed. The chart on page 118 shows the lü names in the left-hand column, the kung-ch'ê symbols as used in ti music in the center, and the kung-ch'ê symbols as used in hsiao music in the right-hand column. A simple calculation shows that the interval between any two of the fourteen degrees consists of $\frac{1200}{14}$ = 85.714 cents. The notation of the fourteen equidistant notes utilizes the affix 亻. This symbol, which formerly indicated the higher octave, now means that the notes are altered. Moreover, we observe a number of combinations of symbols such as 畣, 俟, 罡, 磊, the significance of which has been shown in the foregoing chart.

KONG-CHŬK-PO

Kong-chŭk-po is the Korean pronunciation of 工 尺 譜 (the Chinese kung-ch'ê-p'u), the popular notational system of China which appeared in Korea in the fifteenth century. Unlike China, where kung-ch'ê-p'u was used mainly to notate operatic and other secular music, Korea confined its use to the notation of ritual and ceremonial melodies. Korean musicians had a profound respect for Chinese musical culture and valued melodies, instruments, and notations imported from China as highly as they did the ritual and music of their own temple and imperial palace. This was perhaps one reason why kong-chŭk-po never gained popularity in Korea;

another was the invention of an indigenous Korean notational system, the o-ŭm-yak-po (五音略譜), which will be discussed on pages 124-27.

Kong-chŭk-po is first mentioned and used in the Sae-cho shillok (世祖實錄), a historical document dealing with the events and achievements of the reign of King Sae-cho (1456-1469).[71] The musical pieces in this work are grouped in the following manner:

a) Chong-myo-ak (宗廟樂),"Imperial Temple Music";

b) Hwan-ku-ak (圜丘樂), lit., "Around the Hill Music," a royal ceremony, performed at the winter solstice upon and around a circular platform, the "hill," which represents heaven;

c) Ch'ang-su-chi-kok (創守之曲),"Song of Creation and Protection";

d) Kyong-kŭn-chi-kok (敬勤之曲),"Song of Respect and Diligence."

Another fifteenth-century work which contains kong-chŭk notations is the seventh volume of the Ak-hak-koe-pŭm.[72]

Contrary to Chinese kung-ch'ê-p'u, the symbols of kong-chŭk-po are devoid of all affixes; and 四 , 一 , 工 , 凡 , and 五 can denote both D and Db, E and Eb, A and Ab, B and Bb, and d, db, and d# respectively.   The Korean names of the symbols are:

Hap	合	C
Sa	四	Db and D
Il	一	Eb and E
Sang	上	F
Ku	勾	F#
Chŭk	尺	G
Kong	工	Ab and A
Pŭm	几	Bb and B
Yuk	六	c
O	五	db, d, and d#.

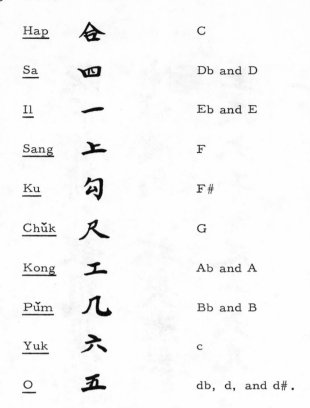

Following is an example from the Sae-cho shillok, a hymn of
Chong-myo-ak (宗廟樂).[73] It is notated in kong-chŭk-po
and yul-cha-po:

Figure 28

Figure 28 (<u>cont</u>.)

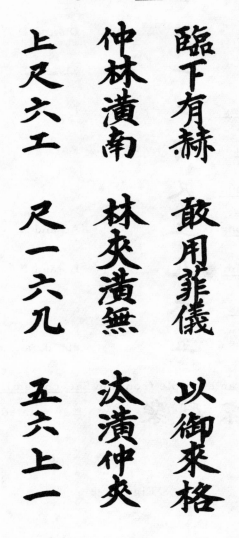

The text of the hymn, written in Chinese characters but pronounced in Korean, reads as follows: "Yu hwang ho chŭn; im ha yu hyŭk; kam yong bi ui; ui u re kyuk." Its meaning is: "Only you, my heavenly, imperial emperor, to us, your subjects, you appear in divine majesty, how should I dare to offer you my trifling presents and approach [invoke] you?"

The eighth and thirteenth symbols of the center and left-hand

columns of Figure 28 are somewhat surprising. Although it is possible
that in addition to Eb, F, G, Bb, c, the hymn uses the "pien" notes A
(南) and d (汰), one should expect at first hearing to find anhemitonic pentatonic tone material and assume that the copyist made
some mistakes. The symbol 五 , as we know, could be interpreted
as d# (eb), but its transcription into 汰 clearly shows that the note
d was intended. The symbol 工 , too, allows no other interpretation,
as it is transcribed with 南 .[74] Such doubtful instances, probably
caused by the widespread illiteracy among court musicians who were
expected to read and write the notational systems, necessitated the
adoption in the fifteenth century of a simple system which employed
mainly numbers and the signs 上 (up) and 下 (down), a notation
called o-ŭm-yak-po,[75] which caused increasing neglect of the older
notational systems.

As in Korea, kong-chŭk-po did not gain widespread popularity in
Japan. There are only two instances of this system's coming into use:
in the notations of imported Ming and, later, Ch'ing compositions from
China. Since 1877 Ming and Ch'ing music have usually been mentioned
together in Japan as Minshin-gaku (明 清 樂). Chinese
Ming music became known in Japan in 1629 in the form of vocal pieces
with instrumental accompaniment.[76] Although imported Ming music
contains some heptatonic and hexatonic melodies, the majority are
anhemitonic pentatonic. About 200 pieces are extant, and these are
notated in kong-chŭk-po. Music of the Ch'ing period appeared in Japan in 1804.[77] This too consists of vocal pieces with instrumental
accompaniment, also notated in kong-chŭk-po. However, when denoting the next higher octave, their symbols are provided with the affix
亻(伵 , 亿 , 仩 , etc.), and the octave above that with 彳

(佪, 仡, 𠆢 , etc.).   In Japan the notational symbols
in Minshin-gaku are called:

symbol	Japanese name
乙	i (イ)
上	shang (シャン)
尺	chieh (チェ)
工	kong (コン)
几	hang (ハン)
六	liu (リウ)
[合	hō (ホー)]
五	u (ウ)
四	sui (スイ)

In the Japanese language the characters 乙 , 上 , 尺 , 工 , and so
forth, are pronounced quite differently from the manner in which they
are pronounced in musical notation. In the latter the symbols are
spoken in imitation of their Chinese (or Korean) names.

O-ŬM-YAK-PO (五音略譜)

During the reign of King Sae-cho (1456-1469) yul-cha-po became
obsolete, and a much simpler system, the o-ŭm-yak-po, "Five-Sound
Abbreviated Notation," became established in Korea.   The earliest
mention of this system is made in the Sae-cho shillok.   Extensive use
of o-ŭm-yak-po is made in the important Tae-ak-hu-po (大樂

後 譜, lit., "Great Music Later Notation"),[78] a collection of twenty-seven pieces dating from the period of King Sae-cho and compiled in 1759 under the auspices of King Yong-cho. The music contained in the Tae-ak-hu-po is cho-ak (朝 樂 , imperial court music), notated in several systems: yul-cha-po, o-ŭm-yak-po, and chŭng-kan-po.[79] Items 3 to 7 in the Tae-ak-hu-po represent several versions of an important piece of ah-ak, called Chung-tae-yŭp (中 大 葉), that has been notated in different modes.[80] Another source is Shi-yong-hyang-ak-po (時 用 鄉 樂 譜), a collection of twenty-six pieces. The date of its origin is unknown; it was reprinted in 1945 by the Institute of Oriental Literature, Yŭn-sae (延 世) College (Christian College), at Seoul.

O-ŭm-yak-po, like kong-chŭk-po, does not indicate any absolute pitches. With the exception of the first (basic) note of the scale, which is represented by kung (宮), o-ŭm-yak-po uses the numbers 1 to 5 (一 , il; 二 , i; 三 , sam; 四 , sa; and 五 , o) instead of solmization syllables. The system encompasses a gamut of two octaves the center of which is kung, which we shall transcribe as the note C, although any other tone could be used as well. Notes above kung use the affix 上 (sang, "upper"), below kung, 下 (ha, "lower").

O-ŭm-yak-po, which denotes the anhemitonic pentatonic scale, was (and still is) the popular Korean counterpart of the Old Chinese Five-tone Notation (宮 , 商 , 角 , 徵 , 羽); its notational symbols are:

上 五   or   㐀 (or 宮)   sang o   c'
上 四   or   㐀   sang sa   a
上 三   or   㐀   sang sam   g

Five-tone Notation (cont.)

上二 or 上二	sang i	e
上一 or 上一	sang il	d
宮	kung	c
下一 or 下一	ha il	A
下二 or 下二	ha i	G
下三 or 下三	ha sam	E
下四 or 下四	ha sa	D
下五 or 下五 (or 宮)	ha o	C

These symbols were applied to the four modes of Korean music,[81] particularly to pyong-cho (平調) and u-cho (羽調), and less frequently to their respective kae-myon-cho (界面調) forms:[82]

Symbol	Old Chinese notes	Pyong-cho	Pyong-cho kae-myon-cho	U-cho	U-cho kae-myon-cho
上五	c	c	c	f	f
上四	A	A	Bb	d	eb
上三	G	G	G	c	c
上二	E	F	F	Bb	Bb
上一	D	D	Eb	G	Ab
宮	C	C	C	F	F
下一	A	A	Bb	D	Eb
下二	G	G	G	C	C
下三	E	F	F	Bb	Bb
下四	D	D	Eb	G	Ab
下五	C	C	C	F	F

As in Chinese custom, Korean musicians would define the required pitch of kung by stating a yul-cha-po symbol at the head of the notated piece. For instance, we find formulas such as: kung is hwang-chong: 宮 is 黃 = C; or: kung is hyŭp chong (the Chinese chia-chung): 宮 is 夾 = Eb, and so forth.

Although o-ŭm-yak-po denotes only the degrees of a pentatonic scale, some efforts were made to indicate the pyŭn (變 ; Chinese: pien) tones in two pieces of the Sae-cho shillok.[83] In these two instances in which o-ŭm-yak-po is used to notate "T'ang music"[84] we find the symbols 一 (il) and 凡 (pŭm). Both are borrowed from kong-chŭk-po and are used without the affixes sang or ha in order to avoid confusion. The symbol 一 corresponds to the Chinese pien chih (F#), and 凡, of course, to the Chinese pien kung (B).

As o-ŭm-yak-po appears frequently in conjunction with another system, the chŭng-kan-po (井 間 譜), we shall delay presenting notational specimens until that system has been discussed.

CHŬNG-KAN-PO (井 間 譜)

Chŭng-kan-po (井 間 譜)[85] is one of the earliest systems which permits notating the duration of notes. According to the Sae-cho shillok, its invention was ascribed to King Sae-cho (1456-1469). However, chŭng-kan-po is already mentioned and used in the Sae-chong shillok (世宗實錄),[86] the historical document of King Sae-chong (1450-1452), who ruled before Sae-cho.

From the time of its appearance[87] chŭng-kan-po was combined with most Korean musical notations with the exception of some tablatures and the neumatic system of yŭn-ŭm-pyo (連 音 標).[88] Chŭng-kan-po is notated in the form of a chart in which each of the smallest rectangles represents one metrical unit (chŭng-kan). These chŭng-kan (which we shall notate with quarter notes) are usually organized into six groups (kang, 綱) of 3, 2, 3, 3, 2, 3 chŭng-kan, respectively, amounting to a total of sixteen metrical units. These sixteen chŭng-kan — or six kang — constitute one haeng (行). Thus, a composition consists of several haeng, each haeng contains six kang, and each kang consists of two or three chŭng-kan:

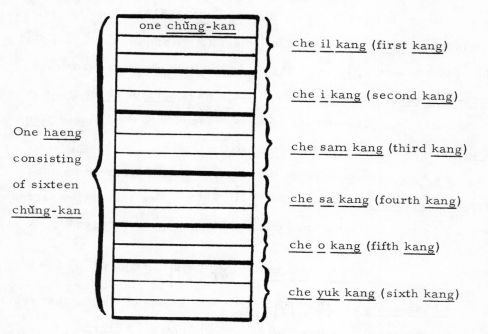

The six kang are often called yuk tae kang (六 大 綱 , "six great principles"). As stated before, there are generally sixteen chŭng-kan in one haeng, but in some rare instances twenty chŭng-kan may be used.[89] In the Yang-kŭm shin-po,[90] a famous zither book of 1610, only two large kang are indicated in each haeng, and the subdivision into chŭng-kan is omitted.

Not every piece begins with the first chŭng-kan; some begin with the second or third, in a way similar to upbeats in Western music.[91] The following excerpt (Fig. 29) illustrates the combination of chŭng-

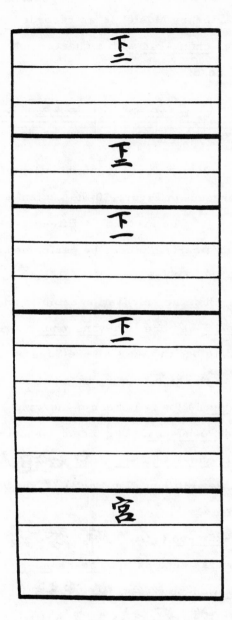

Figure 29

kan-po with o-ŭm-yak-po; the piece is called Himun-ak-po (熙文 樂譜 ,"Bright Literary Music"), as recorded in the Sae-cho shillok. If we represent each chŭng-kan with a quarter note, the transcription of Figure 29 would read:

As a further illustration of the combination of o-ŭm-yak-po with chŭng-kan-po we present in Figure 30 the ancient song Po-hŭ-cha (步虛子). The protocol of fifteenth-century Korean court music prescribed that certain pieces be performed when the king entered the throne hall,[92] others when the subjects paid their homage,[93] and one Po-hŭ-cha when the celebration came to an end and the king left the hall.[94] Po-hŭ-cha and Nak-yang-chun[95] are the only two melodies extant which date back to the Chinese Sung period,[96] and Po-hŭ-cha is the only piece of which both music and text are preserved; the text of Nak-yang-chun is lost. Korean manuscripts of varying ages contain notations of Po-hŭ-cha. The oldest manuscript, pronounced in Korean Paek-sŭk-to-yin-ka-kok-po (白石道人歌曲譜 , lit., "White Stone Hermit Song Notation"),[97] shows Po-hŭ-cha notated without any ornaments.

The An-sang-kŭm-po (安瑺琴譜), a zither book of 1572,[98] and later works such as the Tae-ak-hu-po (大樂後譜) of 1759, the Sok-ak-won-po (俗樂源譜),[99] written before 1776, and the Yu-yae-ji (遊藝誌),[100] written after 1776, notate the same melody with an increasing amount of ornamentation.[101]

Po-hŭ-cha differs in a few details from other, similar compositions, and it is these differences which make it difficult to determine whether the melody is of Chinese or Korean origin. In order to explain

these points a brief digression on the formal structure of Po-hŭ-cha
is necessary:

First verse:	1st line		2nd line	3rd line	4th line
	7 words		5 words	10 words	6 words
	Different melody in first and second verses		Same melody in first and second verses		
Second verse:	7 words		6 words	10 words	6 words

Or, briefly expressed:

First verse: A | B C D
Second verse: E | B C D.

This rare song form is characterized by the two opening phrases (A
and E), called hwan-tu (換頭 , ''exchanged heads'') and the
longer recurrent sections in both verses (B, C, D), are called to-tŭ-ri
도 드 리 , ''coming again''). The to-tŭ-ri sections usually
show a quickening of tempo and a characteristic 6/8 meter that is not
common to related Chinese forms.

Po-hŭ-cha is performed vocally with instrumental accompaniment,
but unlike other important pieces such as Man-tae-yŭp (慢大
葉),[102] Chung-tae-yŭp (中大葉), and Sak-tae-yŭp (數
大葉), which have instrumental interludes and postludes, Po-hŭ-
cha has none.[103]

In the Tae-ak-hu-po version every fourth word of the text is
marked by a percussive beat — a style called sa-kyun-pak (四均
拍 , ''Four Even Beats'') — whereas in Chinese ritual music percussive beats would occasionally appear with every word.

Po-hŭ-cha differs from related Chinese pieces in form and
Aufführungspraxis. We have to repeat that it is impossible to deter-
mine whether these differences were added to a piece imported from
China or whether the song was created in this manner in Korea.

Figure 30 (pp. 132-40) is the Tae-ak-hu-po version of this ancient melody.[104]

Figure 30

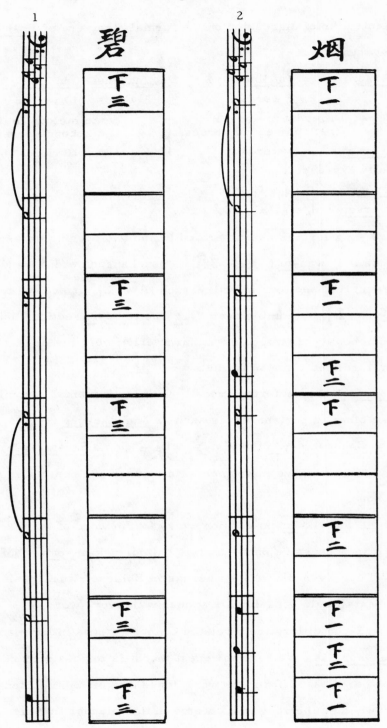

Figure 30 (cont.)

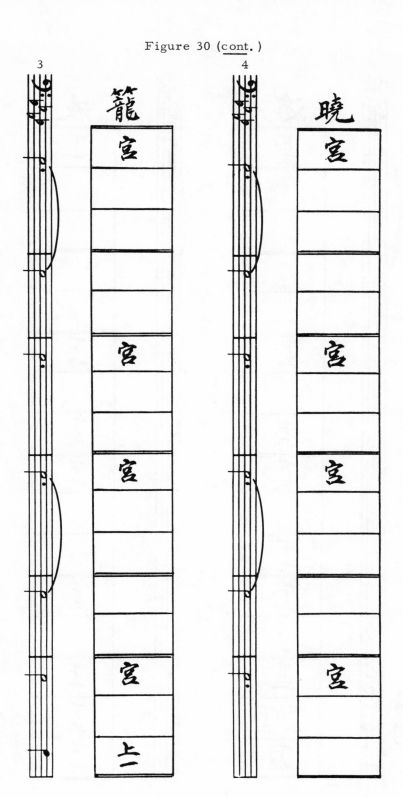

133

Figure 30 (cont.)

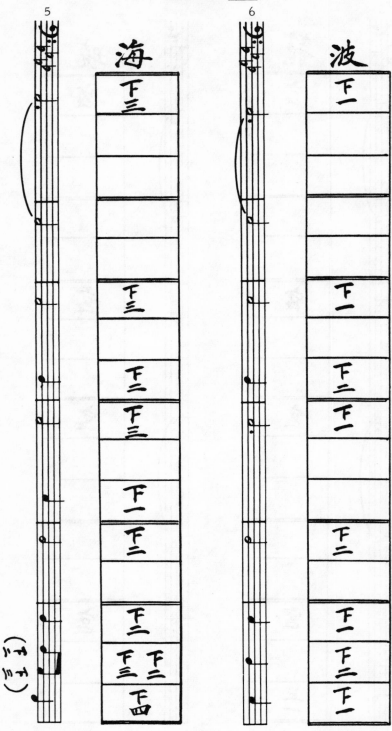

Figure 30 (cont.)

Figure 30 (<u>cont.</u>)

136

Figure 30 (cont.)

17	18	19	20	21	22
珮	環	聲	裡	異	
下二	下一	宮	宮	下一	下三
	下一		下一		
下二	下一	宮	宮	下一	下三
			下一		
			宮	下二	下二
下二	下一	宮	上一	下一	下三
			上三		下一
下一	下二			下一	下二
下二	下一	宮	宮	下二	下三
	宮		上一	下一	下三 下二
下三	上一	上一	宮	下二	下四

Figure 30 (<u>cont.</u>)

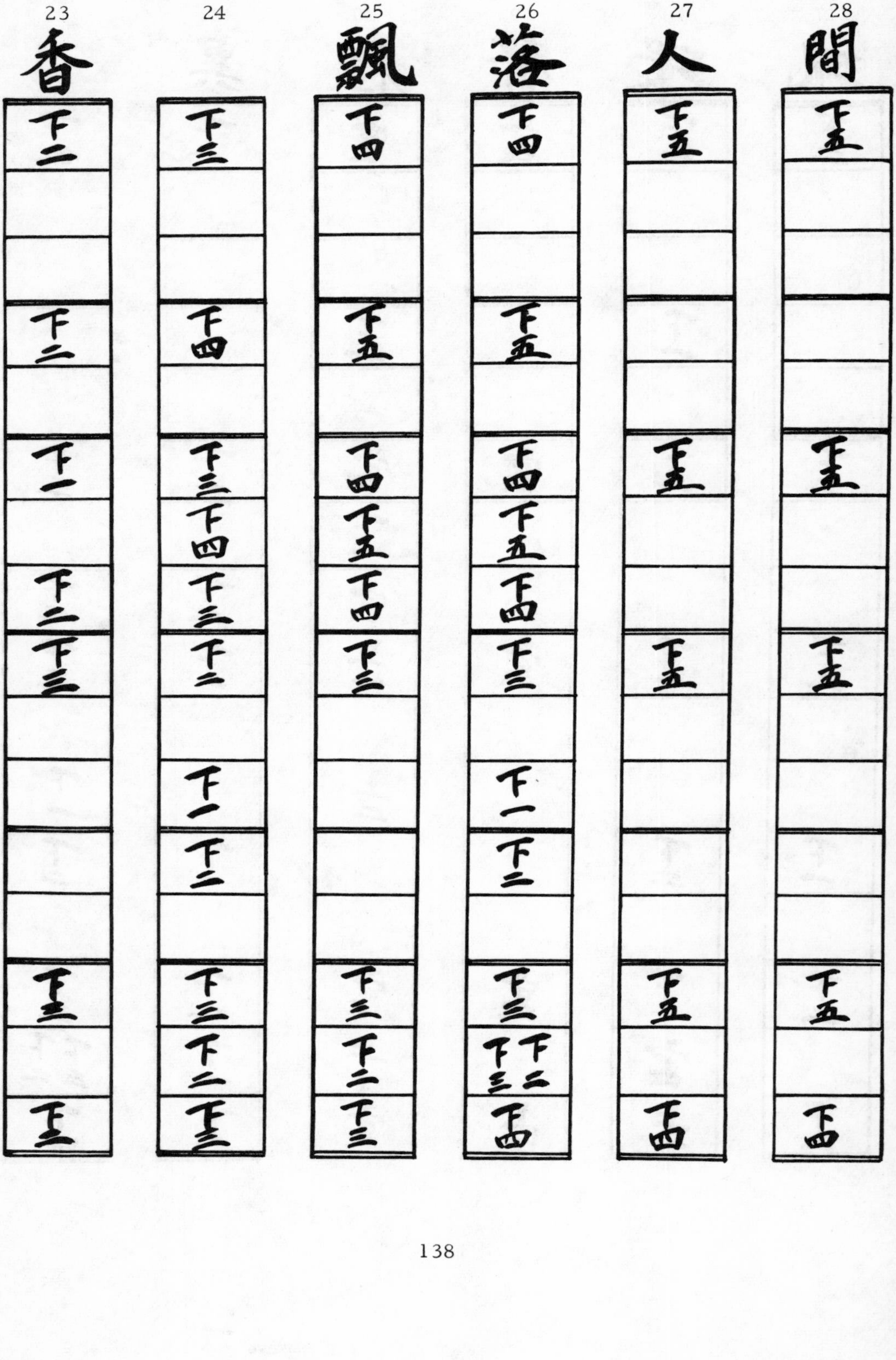

138

Figure 30 (cont.)

29   30   31   32   33   34

139

Figure 30 (<u>cont.</u>)

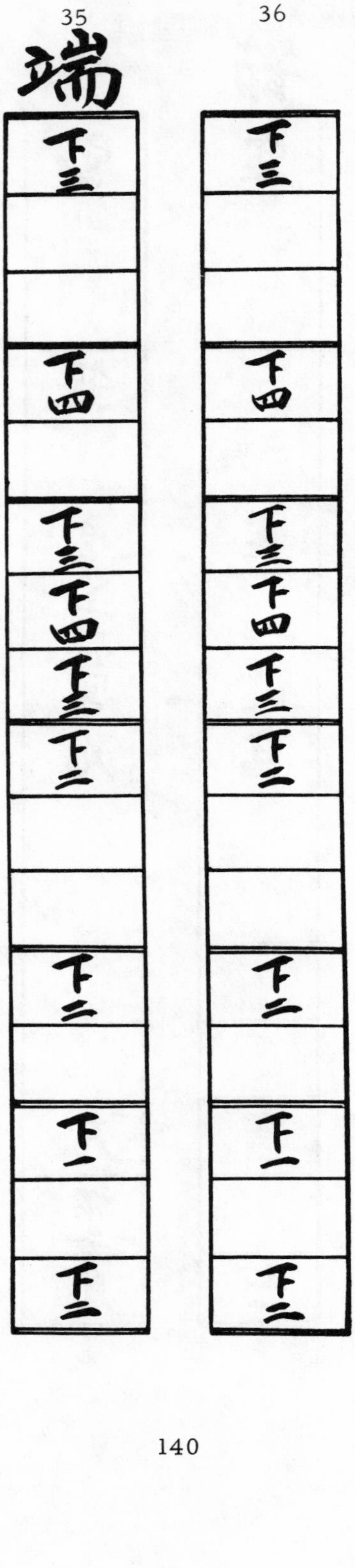

35　　　　　36

140

The text of Po-hŭ-cha, written in Chinese, pronounced in Korean, follows below, together with a general translation:

碧　Pyŭk　　　The blue mist
　　　　　　　covers the sea in
烟　In　　　　the haziness of dawn;

籠　Nong

曉　Hyo

海　Hae

波　Pa　　　　The moving waves encircle the
　　　　　　　numerous hills which protrude
閑　Han　　　out of the water, as a cool,
　　　　　　　ornamental bracelet of precious
江　Kang　　　stones clings around one's wrist.

上　Sang

數　Su

峰　Pong

寒　Han

珮　Pae

環　Hwan

聲　Sŭng　　　The rare beauty of music
　　　　　　　flutters in the wind;
裡　Ri

異　I

香　Hyang

Text of <u>Po-hu-cha</u> (<u>cont.</u>)

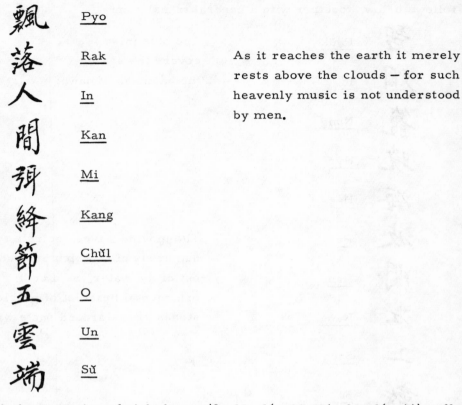

Pyo

Rak   As it reaches the earth it merely
             rests above the clouds — for such
In   heavenly music is not understood
             by men.
Kan

Mi

Kang

Chŭl

O

Un

Sŭ

With the exception of eight <u>haeng</u> (8, 12, 16, 22, 24, 32, 36, 44), all
other <u>haeng</u> show at their heads textual characters. Each word has
to be held throughout the duration of its <u>haeng</u>, or, if there is no text
at the head of the following <u>haeng</u>, the preceding text has to be held
over.[105] We have transcribed only the first six <u>haeng</u> of the song, but
the reader will have little difficulty in completing the transcription.
Two unusual features may be observed in <u>haeng</u> 32; first, the use of
無 (<u>mu</u>, Chinese: <u>wu</u>), a symbol borrowed from <u>yul-cha-po</u>. Originally <u>mu</u> represented the "absolute" pitch of Bb (A#), a tone which is
untenable in <u>o-ŭm-yak-po</u> because its <u>kung</u> is variable and, with it, all
degrees above and below. <u>Mu</u>, being a minor seventh above the <u>hwang-
chong</u> (Chinese: <u>huang chung</u>), therefore, has to be treated as a rela-

tive pitch, representing a note which stands a minor seventh above
kung of o-ŭm-yak-po. Since kung is Eb in the present instance, mu
will be Db. The use of the symbol mu is justified because there is no
specific symbol in o-ŭm-yak-po for notating the minor seventh above
kung.

Second, similar considerations apply to the use of 凡 (pŭm),
borrowed from kong-chŭk-po. Since kung is Eb, pŭm must be transcribed as D.

Figure 31 on page 144 represents Nak-yang-chun (the second
extant melody of the Chinese Sung period), as notated in the Sok-
ak-won-po.[106] In this instance chŭng-kan-po and yul-cha-po are combined. The reader will have no difficulty in transcribing this famous piece.

In Figure 32 (p. 148) we present another important melody of
Korean court music, called Yŭ-min-ak (與 民 樂 , lit., "Grant
People Music").[107] Originally it was vocal music accompanied by a
chang-ko,[108] but it gradually became an instrumental piece. According
to the Ak-hak-koe-pŭm[109] it was used as opening and closing music
for court celebrations in the fifteenth century.[110]

The text of Yŭ-min-ak was derived from 龍 飛 御 天
歌 (Korean: Yong-pi-ŭ-chŭn-ka, lit., "Dragon Flying Royal Heaven
Song"), a sequence of poems in 125 strophes, selected by Chŭng-in-
ch'i (鄭 麟 趾) by order of King Sae-chong in 1446. The words
were written in Chinese characters and in the newly created Korean
script.[111] The Chinese poem, together with the melody to which it was
sung, is called Yŭ-min-ak. The text consists of two versions, one of
five verses, the other of ten. The first five (Chinese) characters of
the text are to be found at the top of p. 145.

Figure 31

洛陽春

	林	太	林	無	潢	黃
太	仲	潢	仲	林	潢	
仲						黃
太	仲	汰	南	林	南	
黃		汰	潢			太
	太	潢	南	林	潢	
還		南	林	林	潢	太
入	黃	潢	仲	仲	南	太
	太	潢	仲	汰	林	
南	太					黃
潢		汰	太	潢	林	
潢	仲	潢	仲	潢	林	太
	姑	南	太	南	仲	太
	太		太	林		黃
		林			南	
	黃	南	仲	林	南	南

pronounced in
Korean:

海　Hae　　　　　Sea
東　Tong　　　　East　}（meaning: Korea）
六　Yuk　　　　　Six
龍　Yong　　　　Dragons[112]
飛　Pi　　　　　　Flying

There were four types of Yŭ-min-ak:

1) Yŭ-min-ak-man (與民樂　慢),

2) Yŭ-min-ak-yŭng (與民樂　令),

which were ascribed to T'ang-ak,[113]

3) Yŭ-min-ak-man, and

4) Yŭ-min-ak-yŭng,

the latter two ascribed to Hyang-ak.[114]

Yŭ-min-ak-man of T'ang-ak is notated in the Sae-chong shillok (ten verses), in the Sok-ak-won-po (five verses), and is also preserved in the archives of the former Royal Band of Seoul (originally five verses; later, verses 6-10 of the Sae-chong shillok were added to it). Yŭ-min-ak-yŭng of T'ang-ak is preserved in the Sok-ak-won-po, and in two versions, pon-ryŭng (本令) and hae-ryŭng (解令), in the archives of the former Royal Band. Yŭ-min-ak of Hyang-ak is notated in the An-sang-kŭm-po; and Yŭ-min-ak-yŭng of Hyang-ak in the Sok-ak-won-po (hyŭn-po, "string-notation"), in the Shin-sŭng-kŭm-po (申晟琴譜), and preserved by the former Royal Band. The T'ang-ak forms of Yŭ-min-ak preserved by the for-

mer Royal Band are often simply called man-po (man-notation), and
the Hyang-ak forms preserved by the Royal Band are called yŭ-min-ak,
without the additional words man and yŭng.

The term man (慢) means "slow" and denotes the original
form performed at a slow speed. Yŭng (令), "special," denotes
a variation of man — the variation is made by adding rhythmic embel-
lishments to the melody and performing it in a lively tempo.

Lee contradicts this by stating that one verse of yŭng was performed in seven minutes, while ten (all) verses of man were performed
in twenty minutes.[115] The explanations concerning man and yŭng
forms[116] are so contradictory that it seems impossible to arrive at
an intelligible definition. The Ak-hak-koe-pŭm states that if Yŭ-min-
ak-man of T'ang-ak (as notated in the Sae-chong shillok) is used as
dance music, it is called Yŭ-min-ak-yŭng. The Sae-chong shillok, however, describes the same piece (used with or without dancing) as Yŭ-
min-ak-man.

The only distinct difference between the various types can be
noted in the instrumentation of the T'ang and hyang forms of Yŭ-min-ak:
the T'ang forms, both man and yŭng, are performed by the T'ang-p'iri
(唐觱篥), a type of oboe with seven holes, played by the leader
of the ensemble; the pang-hyang (方響), metal chimes (which
consisted of two rows of eight iron slabs each and which appeared in
Korea in A.D. 1115); the T'ang-chŭk (唐笛), the Chinese ti, a
cross flute with seven holes; the t'ong-so (洞簫), the Japanese
shakuhachi, a vertical flute with five holes and one side hole (one hole
near the mouthpiece is covered with paper); the T'ang-p'i-pa (唐琵
琶), the Chinese p'i-pa, a lute with four strings; and the a-jěng
牙箏), a bowed zither with seven strings. The basic note of all

these instruments has to be the hwang-chong (Chinese: huan-chung).

The hyang-ak forms of Yǔ-min-ak are performed by the hyang-p'iri (鄉觱篥), the hyang-oboe, a little larger than the T'ang-p'iri, played by the leader of the ensemble; the tae-kǔm (大笒), a flute with six holes; the hae-kǔm (奚琴), related to the Chinese hu-ch'in, a fiddle with two silken strings; the kaya-kǔm (伽倻琴), a zither with twelve strings;[117] and the chang-ko. The basic note of all these hyang-ak instruments has to be hyǔp (the Chinese chia-[chung]).

All types of Yǔ-min-ak were required material in the national examinations for court musicians.

Following (p. 148) is the beginning of Yǔ-min-ak-man as notated in the Sae-chong shillok (Vol. CXL).

The score specimen (Fig. 32) shows thirty-two chǔng-kan in each of the three vertical columns. Although the chǔng-kan are not grouped into kang, they can be read without difficulty. Each of the three columns contains: at the right-hand side, the yul-cha-po (Chinese: lü) symbols; in the middle, annotations for the chang-ko player; and, at the left, textual characters.

The chang-ko words are:

鼓   ko, "drum-side" (left side)

鞭   pyǔn, "whip-side" (right side)

搖   yo, "roll"

雙   ssang, a beat performed by both hands on
      both sides simultaneously.

The text is already known to us[118] except for the fourth character, 拍 . This character pak, literally meaning "to clap," signifies

Figure 32

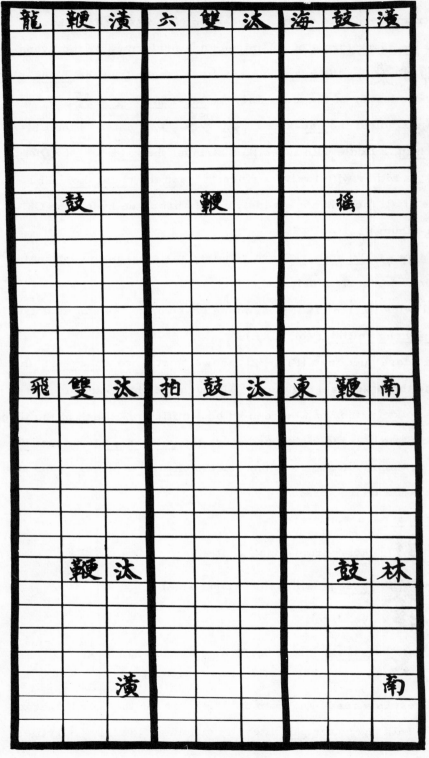

與民樂

to the performer that the word yuk (六) is to be held over into the second half of the thirty-two chŭng-kan of the second column.

As we are dealing with thirty-two chŭng-kan in each column, we reduce the metrical unit from a quarter note to an eighth note. Transcribed, the excerpt will read:[119]

Figure 33 (p. 150) represents Yŭ-min-ak-yŭng as notated in the Sok-ak-won-po.[120]

The title of Figure 33 informs us that we are dealing with hyŭn-po (絃譜), "string notation." There is some doubt as to whether this piece was performed solely by string instruments, as the notational symbols show no differences from those of other scores cited previously.

The man version of Yŭ-min-ak as notated in the Sok-ak-won-po begins as follows (Fig. 34, p. 151).[121]

Figure 33

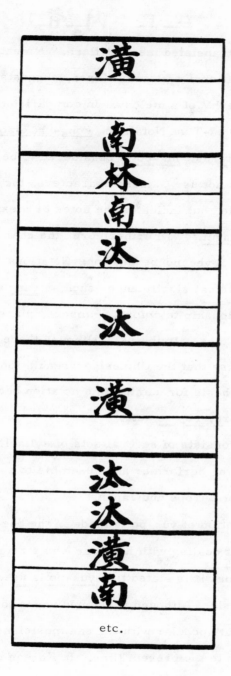

Figure 34

YUK-PO (肉譜)

Yuk literally translated means "flesh," "meat," or "body"; thus, yuk-po, a notational system of Korea, suggests a manner of notating the "mere flesh" of a melody. In comparison to yul-cha-po, the old Five and Seven-Tone Notations, kong-chŭk-po, o-ŭm-yak-po, and the zither tablatures, yuk-po is considered to be an inferior system because it does not use Chinese characters, the medium of writing of learned people, but indicates the notes by means of Korean syllables written in hangŭl.[122] Furthermore, the characters used in yul-cha-po and the old Five and Seven-Tone Notations have connotations far beyond their musical significance, such as yang and yin characteristics and the relationship to colors, numbers, planets, and so forth.[123] Yuk-po has none of these attributes. Although there is no proof, one is tempted to surmise that the Chinese pronunciation of 肉 , rou, may have served as the basis for naming this notation because it often employs the syllables rŭ, ru, ro, etc.

The system consists of several sets of syllables which serve as a mnemonic aid to the performer and resemble to some extent the solmization systems of Europe and Japan.

The first mention of yuk-po is made in the Sae-cho shillok, the historical document dealing with King Sae-cho's reign in the fifteenth century. In this work it is stated that yuk-po is used only in notations of instrumental music. Although it seemed vague to the uninformed, yuk-po became highly popular with Korean musicians and amateurs and has remained so up to the present time. In Korean music books it is frequently combined with other more "learned" notational systems, particularly with hap-cha-po.[124] Extensive yuk-po notations can be found in the An-sang-kŭm-po (1572),[125] the Yang-kŭm shin-po (1610),[126]

the Hong-kee-hu-po (洪基厚譜 , n.d.),[127] and the Cho-
sŭng kŭm-po (趙晟琴譜 , after 1759),[128] as well as in
other works of lesser importance.

The yuk-po syllables vary with every instrument. In notations
of the hyŭn-kŭm (玄琴)[129] and occasionally, in kaya-kŭm
(伽倻琴)[130] music, the following five syllables are used:

Tŭng 덩

Tung 둥

Tang 당

Tong 동

Ting 딩

When used in notating music of the p'il-lyul (觱篥),[131]
a variant of the p'iri (篥), a type of oboe, the yuk-po syllables
are changed to:

Rŭ 러

Ru 루

Ra 라

Ro 로

Ri 리

which, for the sake of easier pronunciation, are usually read: Nŭ, Nu,
Na, No, Ni. In tae-kŭm (大笒)[132] music the syllables begin
with a strong T, e.g., Tta (따). As already stated, in kaya-kŭm
music the yuk-po syllables can begin either with the letter T, or, in
some instances, with K. When representing high notes the syllables
begin with J, JJ, or CH. When two successive sounds are slurred,

combinations of two syllables occur; for instance: Tang and Tong become Tarong (다롱); Tang and Jing become Taring (다링).
Similarly, we find combinations such as Sareng (솅), Sŭreng
(슁), and occasionally others.

In the famous Korean hyǔn-kǔm book — the Yang-kǔm shin-po —
the yuk-po syllables begin, of course, with the letter T. In this work
where symbols of hap-cha-po are placed side by side with yuk-po
syllables, we find that the note Bb, performed on the fifth fret of the
"big string" (大絃),[133] and the note Eb, a fourth higher, performed on the fourth fret of the "play string" (方絃), are both
notated with the syllable Tang. The same syllable is also applied to
the note F performed on the fifth fret of the "play string," and to Ab,
performed on the seventh fret of the same string, if the fourth finger
is used to stop the string in all four instances. The syllable Tong is
used if the index finger stops the "play string," or if the middle finger stops the "big string." Jing is used if the thumb stops the "play
string." Tung occurs when the index finger or the thumb stops the
"big string."

Although these features do not occur invariably, they appear
frequently enough to create the impression that the playing technique
rather than the representation of notes is being referred to.

If we investigate the yuk-po (notation) of a whole piece and
count the frequently occurring yuk-po syllables, we find, for instance,
that in Chung-tae-yǔp (中大葉),[134] the note produced by the
index finger on the sixth fret of the "play string" is notated ten times
with Tong and twenty times with Ting. In the same piece, the note produced by the index finger on the seventh fret of the "big string" is notated nine times with Tung and twice with Ting.

Before trying to reach a conclusion regarding the significance
of yuk-po syllables, let us consider a prescript concerning the tuning
of two Korean zithers in terms of yuk-po and afterwards investigate
the use of these syllables in p'iri notations.

According to Lee,[135] the tuning procedure of the kaya-kŭm is as
follows: the fourth string is to be tuned to Tang, the fifth to Tong; the
third string is to be tuned to Tung, and the second to Hŭng. The intervals between Tang and Tong, Tung and Hŭng have to be "little weak"
seconds,[136] while the interval between Tŭng and Tang has to be a pure
fourth. If the tuning is correct, the interval between Tang (also called
An-tang, (안 당) and Pat-tang (밧 당), that is, the interval
between the open fourth and seventh strings, has to produce a perfect
fifth, and the interval between Tŭng and Pat-tang, that is, between the
open third and seventh strings, an octave. The remaining twelve
strings[137] are to be tuned in octaves to the strings already tuned. The
only exception to the octave-tuning method is the eighth string, which
has to be tuned to Ji (지), a note usually a major second or,
in some instances, a minor third higher than Pat-tang. Thus, the
following strings would be tuned in octaves: 2 and 6, 3 and 7, 4 and
9, 5 and 10, 6 and 11, and 7 and 12. The tuning of the first string is
not yet known to us, but, we may suppose that as far as the tuning of
the octave-pairs is concerned, the change from four strings (2-6,
3-7) to five (4-9, 5-10, etc.) is caused by the tuning of the eighth
string (Ji), which does not fit into the octave pattern. At present
all of this is still doubtful on account of the indefinite instructions,
which offer no help as to definite pitches. Nevertheless, we may
risk drawing a tentative chart containing the few points we have
elucidated:

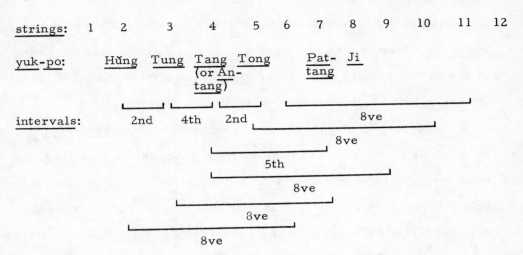

strings: 1 2 3 4 5 6 7 8 9 10 11 12

yuk-po: Hŭng Tung Tang Tong Pat- Ji
(or An- tang
tang)

intervals: 2nd 4th 2nd 8ve
8ve
5th
8ve
8ve
8ve

Eckardt relates[138] that in early ages there were two tunings, but he offers no definite information as to how they were arrived at. The sole intelligible tuning given, which dates back to only 1927, is:

D E G A* d e g a c* d' e' g'.

At A* and c* the bridges can be moved in order to achieve an occasional alteration by a semitone, e. g., Bb and b respectively. A comparison of the notes we have established with the modern tuning stated by Eckardt shows that the two coincide if we shift the modern tuning one step to the left:

(Lee) 1 2 3 4 5 6 7 8 9 10 11 12
Hŭng Tung Tang Tong Pat- Ji
tang

(Eckardt) (D E G A d e g a c d' e')
D E G A d e g a c' d' e' g' ?

In the Han-kuk-ŭm-ak-yon-gu (after p. 82) Lee presents the following tuning of the kaya-ko (kŭm):

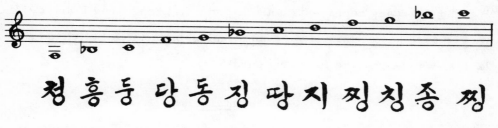

청 흥 등 당 동 징 땅 지 찡 칭 종 찡

Chŭng   Tung   Tong   Ttang   Jjing Ching Jong Jjing
 Hŭng   Tang   Jing   Ji

The strings most frequently used are F, G, and Bb (Tang, Tong, and Jing). The eighth string, tuned to d (Ji), is called the "lonely widower's string" because it is not used in an octave pair.

We notice that again the intervals Hŭng and Tung, Tang and Tong, Ttang (or Pat-tang) and Ji, are seconds, that the interval Tung and Tang is a fourth, that Tung and Ttang (Pat-tang) form an octave, and that strings 1-4, 2-6, 3-7, 4-9, 5-10, 6-11, and 7-12, are tuned in octaves.

The yuk-po syllables in notations of yang-kŭm (洋琴)[139] music are applied to the thirteen (or fourteen) strings of the instrument. In this instance we are able to lay them out at once in scale form without any preliminary investigation:

홍 둥 등 당 동 지 징 당 동 디 딩 팅 쫑
(밧당)(밧동)

Ab	Bb	C	Eb	F	Gb	ab	bb	c	db	eb	f	ab'
Hŭng	Tung	Tŭng	Tang	Tong	Ji	Jing	Tang	Tong	Ti	Ting	T'ing	Jjong
							or	or				
							Pat-	Pat-				
							tang	tong				

We find that Tang represents both Eb and b flat, and Tong F and c. If we compare kaya-kŭm and yang-kŭm tunings as notated by yuk-po syllables, we observe the following parallels:

Intervals:

	second	fourth	octave
Kaya-kŭm	Hŭng-Tung Tang-Tong	Tung-Tang	Tung-Pat-tang
Yang-kŭm	Hŭng-Tang Tung-Tŭng Tang-Tong, etc.	Tung-Tang etc.	Tung-Pat-tang, etc.

Continuing our investigation, we now consider the first page of a piece called Man-tae-yŭp (慢大葉)[140] as it is notated in the Yang-kŭm-shin-po of 1610.[141] In this work three notational systems are used side by side: the old Chinese Five Tone Notation, hap-cha-po,[142] and yuk-po. Hap-cha-po and the old Five Tone Notation enable us to interpret the yuk-po syllables with comparative certainty. For the present, we can disregard the hap-cha-po symbols and confine ourselves to the other two notations.[143] They read as follows:

商	딩	Ting
商	솅	Sŭreng
宮	당	Tang

宮　　　쇵　　Sareng

商　　　딩　　Ting

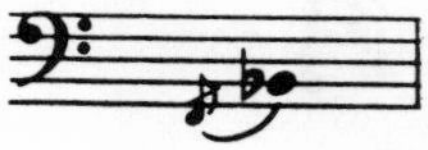

宮　　　나　　Ta . .
(calligraphic mistake
for 당 , Tang).

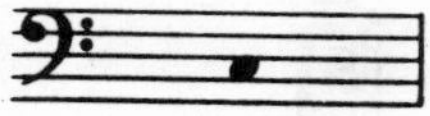

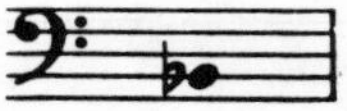

羽　　　등　　Tŭng

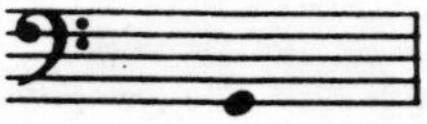

徵　　　덩　　Tŭng

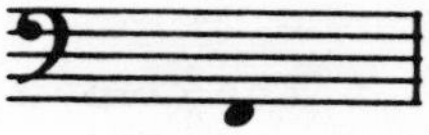

徵　　　슝　　Sŭreng

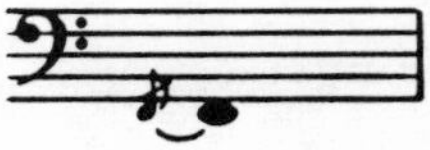

宮　　　쳥　　Chŭng

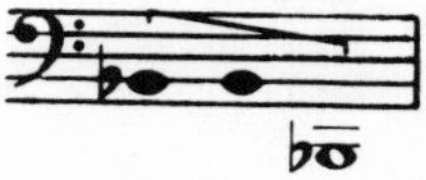

角　　　딩　　Ting

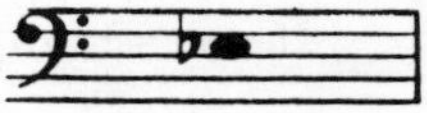

商　　　둥　　Tong

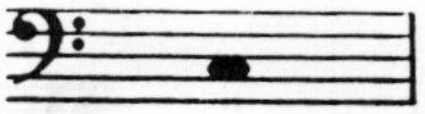

宮　　　쇵　　Sareng

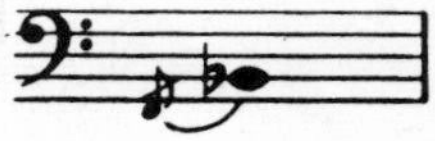

徵　　　딩　　Ting

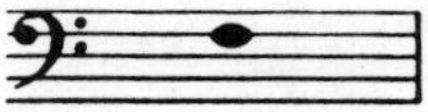

角　　　슝　　Sareng

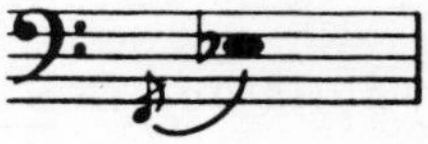

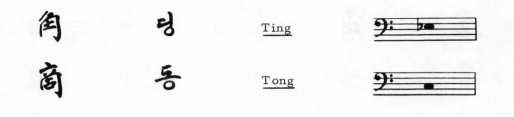

角   딩   Ting

商   둥   Tong

In somewhat the same way as do the yuk-po syllables of kaya-kŭm and yang-kŭm music, hyŭn-kŭm syllables denote the following intervals:

Second:	Fourth:	Octave:
Tŭng — Tung	Tŭng — Tang	Tŭng — Ting
Tang — Tong		

The combinations Sŭreng and Sareng do not indicate specific notes but only imitate the sounds of appoggiaturas. The syllable Chŭng is employed to represent a slow arpeggio across the three "chong" strings:

If we arrange these syllables (excepting the combinations) in an ascending order we get:

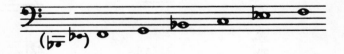

Tŭng Tung Tang Ting Ting Ting
Ta . . Tong

The following four examples (Fig. 35)[145] show the use of yuk-po syllables in p'iri[146] and chang-ko[147] notations:

Figure 35

Item (a) of Figure 35 is called Yŭm-pul, "Buddhist Meditation."
The yuk-po syllables of the p'iri part (upper line) read:

First measure:

느 Nŭ

니 Ni

루 Ru (♪)

로 Ro

느 Nŭ

나 Na

히 Hi (♪)

레 Re

나 Na

레 Re

Second measure:

노 No

니 Ni (♪)

레 Re

나 Na

시 Shi (♪)

루 Ru

루 Ru (♪)

나 Na

시 Shi

루 Ru

니 Ni

로 Ro

The yuk-po syllables denoting the chang-ko rhythm (lower line)
are:

First measure:

떵 Ttŭng

떵 Ttŭng

기 Ki (♪)

Second measure:

쿵 K'ung

기 Ki (♪)

덕 Tŭk

First measure (cont.)   Second measure (cont.)

덕   Tŭk   쿵   K'ung

덩   Tŭng   더   Tŭ

더   Tŭ   러   Rŭ

러   Rŭ   러   Rŭ

러   Rŭ   떡   Ttŭk

Lee transcribes both drum rolls with ♪ ,[148] although the yuk-po syllables indicate a difference between the roll of the first and that of the second measure: the first roll is denoted by Tŭng-Tŭ-Rŭ-Rŭ, showing that the beginning of the roll is an "appoggiatura" (Tŭng) to the subsequent roll (Tŭ-Rŭ-Rŭ). The second roll (Tŭ-Rŭ-Rŭ), however, is performed without the initial Tŭng.

The second item (b) of Figure 35 is a version of Tha-ryŭng (lit., "Hit the Bell"), a popular court dance melody which is supposed to have had its origin in the music imported from T'ang China.[149] Its meter is 12/8 or 6/8.[150] According to Mr. Won Kyung Cho, of Seoul, the dancer has to wear a green costume with rainbow-colored sleeves and a crown when performing Tha-ryŭng. The yuk-po syllables of the p'iri part are:

First measure:

루   Ru

로   Ro

느   Nŭ

나   Na

네   Ne

Second measure: Third measure:

네 Ne   네 Ne
레 Re   니 Ni
레 Re   레 Re
네 Ne   라 Ra
니 Ni   레 Re
레 Re   노 No
라 Ra   느 Nŭ
레 Re   루 Ru
노 No   로 Ro
느 Nŭ   느 Nŭ
                             나 Na

The chang-ko part is not provided with yuk-po syllables.

The third item (c) of Figure 35 is a section of a piece called to-tŭ-ri.[151] The yuk-po syllables of the p'iri part[152] are:

First measure: Second measure:

렌 Ren   시 Shi (♪)
띠 Tti   레 Re
시 Shi (♪)   니 Ni
렌 Ren   레 Re
띠 Tti   나 Na
                             레 Re
                             노 No

Second measure ($\underline{\text{cont.}}$)　　느　　$N\breve{u}$

로　　$\underline{Ro}$

나　　$\underline{Na}$

The fourth item (d) of Figure 35 is called $\underline{\text{kut-k}\breve{\text{u}}\text{-ri}}$ ("Ritual Things"). The $\underline{\text{yuk-po}}$ syllables of the $\underline{\text{p'iri}}$ part[153] are:

First measure:　　　　　　　　　　　　Second measure:

노　　$\underline{No}$　　　　　　　　　　　　란　　$\underline{Nan}$

나　　$\underline{Na}$　　　　　　　　　　　　시　　$\underline{Shi}$

니　　$\underline{Ni}$　　　　　　　　　　　　로　　$\underline{Ro}$

레　　$\underline{Re}$　　　　　　　　　　　　니　　$\underline{Ni}$

나　　$\underline{Na}$　　　　　　　　　　　　노　　$\underline{No}$

　　　　　　　　　　　　　　　　　　　　베　　$\underline{Ne}$

　　　　　　　　　　　　　　　　　　　　라　　$\underline{Ra}$

The $\underline{\text{yuk-po}}$ syllables of the $\underline{\text{chang-ko}}$ part are:

First measure:　　　　　　　　　　　　Second measure:

덩　　$\underline{T\breve{u}ng}$　　　　　　　　　　덩　　$\underline{T\breve{u}ng}$

기　　$\underline{Ki}$　$(\flat)$　　　　　　　기　　$\underline{Ki}$　$(\flat)$

덕　　$\underline{T\breve{u}k}$　　　　　　　　　　덕　　$\underline{T\breve{u}k}$

쿵　　$\underline{K'ung}$　　　　　　　　쿵　　$\underline{K'ung}$

덩　　$\underline{T\breve{u}ng}$　　　　　　　　덩　　$\underline{T\breve{u}ng}$

더　　$\underline{T\breve{u}}$　　　　　　　　　　더　　$\underline{T\breve{u}}$

러　　$\underline{R\breve{u}}$　　　　　　　　　　러　　$\underline{R\breve{u}}$

Third measure (<u>Kut</u>-<u>kŭ</u>-<u>ri</u>,
rhythm of the South):

덩		Tŭng		덩	Tŭng
기	Ki	(♪)		드	Tŭ
떡	Tŭk			르	Rŭ
기	Ki	(♪)		르	Rŭ

The frequently occurring <u>yuk</u>-<u>po</u> syllables of the four <u>p'iri</u> pieces
represent the following long and short notes:

Piece: ↓									
(a)	long note			Ro, No Ru	Nŭ	Na			
	short note	Ru		Nŭ, Ru	Re, Shi Ni	Ni, Na	Re	Hi, Ni	
(b)	long note			Ro, No	Nŭ		Ne, Re		
	short note	Ru		Ro	Re	Ra	Na, Re Ne	Ni	
(c)	long note			No	Re	Na	Ren		Tti
	short note			Ro	Re, Nŭ		Shi, Re	Ni	
(d)	long note			No		Na			
	short note	Ra	Ne	No, Ro	Na, Shi Ni	Nan	Re	Ni	

Although Lee maintains that yuk-po cannot be considered as a solmization system because the syllables are used without order and purpose,[154] we notice that the foregoing chart does show a certain deliberate intent: syllables with dark vowels, such as u or o, represent lower sounds, with brighter vowels, a, e, or i, representing higher sounds; and, although there are a few exceptions, the general method of correlating vowel and pitch cannot be disregarded. This method is applicable to both p'iri and zither music. The highest sounds are denoted by syllables with the vowel i and by an intensified opening consonant as, for instance, in Jjing (찡), Tti (띠), and so forth.

The syllable Ttŭl (뜰 or 쓸) indicates the repetition of a note, for instance, in:

155

| Sal | Ttŭl | | Ttŭl | Kaeng | | Hŭng | Ch'ŭng | Ttŭl | Ch'ŭng |
| Kaeng | | Tong | | Ssal | | Tong | | | |

As already mentioned, in zither music appoggiaturas are denoted by combinations of syllables such as Sureng, Sareng, Sal Kaeng (Ssal Kaeng), and other similar ones. In p'iri music appoggiaturas are indicated by syllables such as Ru Ro, Hi Re, Ni Re, Shi Ru, Shi Ren, and so forth. With the exception of Shi Ru (   ), we find that the syllables containing bright vowels such as Hi, Ni, and occasionally Shi represent grace notes which are higher in pitch than the succeeding

main notes, while syllables with dark vowels (Ru, Ro, etc.) denote
grace notes lower in pitch than the succeeding main notes.

The yuk-po syllables of the chang-ko parts imitate the sounds
produced on the drum and use the vowel ŭ. Only when the drummer
performs a brief, dry-sounding appoggiatura-like initial stroke (succeeded by a stroke of longer duration) is the syllable Ki employed. If,
after the stroke, the skin is allowed to reverberate, the syllable Tŭng
is used; if the sound is stopped abruptly, Tŭk is applied. The quality
of drum sounds is discernible by the syllables used: Tŭng, Ttŭng,
K'ŭng, for dark, reverberating beats; Tŭ, Rŭ, for strokes which constitute drum rolls; Tŭk, Ttŭk, for dry-sounding beats.

Items (a) and (d) of Figure 35 show how the right and left hands
strike the drum: the upper notes of the chang-ko line indicate the
strokes performed by the right hand, the lower notes those by the left.
Strokes performed by both hands simultaneously — with one exception
in item (d) — are denoted by the syllable Tŭng, and, if emphasized, by
Ttŭng. Strokes performed by the left hand alone are notated with
K'ŭng. Tŭk (Ki-Tŭk) and Ttŭk represent dry sounds performed by the
right hand.

Features related to yuk-po can be found in Japan in Shakuhachi
and, to some degree, in Samisen notations.[156] Another similar system can be noticed in Bali in the notations of Kidung[157] songs. The
symbols are:

Ding	Dong gedé	Dang gedé	Deng	Dung	Dang tjenik	Dong tjenik
E	F	G	A	B	c	d

Dong and Dang can be either gedé ("big," "loud") or tjenik ("small,"
"high"). As can be noted, neither Dong gedé and Dong tjenik, nor
Dang gedé and Dang tjenik have octave relationships. This notation is
more vague than the Korean yuk-po, and the date of its origin is unknown. It served as a mnemonic aid in vocal music, although occasionally the symbols were employed also in instrumental music, as,
for instance, in the music of the ritual Wayang Kulit (Shadow Plays),
which is performed by the Gendér Wayang orchestra, a gamelan consisting of four gendér.[158] The tones of the Gendér Wayang are called
Ding, Dong, Déng, Dung, and Dang, roughly corresponding to E, F#,
G#, B, and c#. These notations were scratched into palm leaves.[159]
Schlager reports[160] that the vowel of each text syllable was the key for
the note to be used with it. For instance, the syllables madu, containing the vowels a and u, were set to music to the tones Dang and Dung.
This "literal" setting to music of the text receives little attention
today.

KU-ŬM (口音 , lit., "Mouth Sound")

This unusual Korean notational system uses the full lü names[161]
written in Korean letters and employs these words merely for mnemonic
purposes. The original significance of the lü, the indicating of absolute pitches, is completely ignored.

The origin of ku-ŭm is unknown. One can assume that the habit
of using lü names freely dates back to the fifteenth century, when yul-
cha-po became neglected and less cumbersome notational systems were
adopted. Figure 36, following, represents a part of a Confucian hymn,
Mun-myo-ak (文廟樂) notated by Cho-sŭng,[162] as preserved
by the National Institute of Music at Seoul:[163]

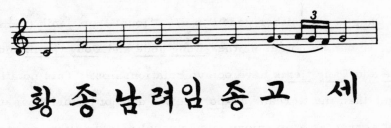

황 종 남 려 임 종 고   세

Hwang-chong Nam-ryǔ Im - chong Ko -   sae

태 주 고 세 남 려 임 종

T'ae - cho   Ko -   sae Nam-ryǔ Im - chong.

Figure 36

It will be noticed that the lü names and the notes of the melody do not
tally. The actual pitches of the lü stated above should be:

Hwang-chong	C
Nam-ryǔ	A
Im-chong	G
Ko-sae	E
T'ae-cho	D

This habit of using pitch names in an indiscriminate manner shows
how even musicians of the imperial court and the Confucian temple
had become ignorant of the ancient significance of the lü. In addition
to having a mnemonic function, these words sounded impressive to the
listeners and gave a certain nimbus of learnedness to the performers.

YŬN-ŬM-PYO (連音標,
"Continued Sound Symbols")

Yŭn-ŭm-pyo is the only real ekphonetic notation of Korea. Its symbols do not indicate specific pitches but the rising and falling of two or more sounds in succession.

The history of yŭn-ŭm-pyo is unknown, and the available material is exceedingly scarce. The symbols of this system appear to be related to the Japanese Heike-biwa notation.[164] The symbols of yŭn-ŭm-pyo are:

＼ , called nu-rŭ-nŭn-pyo (누르는표 , lit., "press down symbol"), indicating a falling of two or more notes.

／ , called tŭ-nŭn-pyo (드 는표 , lit., "lift up symbol"), indicating a rising.

∨ , called nul-lŭ-se-nŭn-pyo (눌러세는표 , lit., "press down and rise symbol"), indicating a progression of notes from a lower to a higher level.

✓ , called tŭn-hŭl-lim-pyo (든 흘림표, lit., "float, shake symbol"), indicating a progression from high to low and a return to high, performed legato.

口 , called mak-nae-nŭn-pyo (막 내는표 , lit., "random produce symbol"), denoting even, level sounds.

乙 , is called chŭp-ŭ-tŭ-nŭn-pyo (접 어드는표, lit., "fold, lift sound symbol"). The interpretation of this symbol is somewhat vague; the common reading is a slight descent followed by an ascent, generally at the end of a phrase.

) , called <u>yŭn-ŭm-pyo</u> (연 음표 , lit., "continued sound symbol"), from which the name of this notational system is derived. It denotes the slurring of two or more successive notes.

⋮ , called <u>pan-kak-pyo</u> (반 각표 , lit., "add another eight-beats symbol"). This symbol appears only once — in the fifth verse of the song <u>pyŭk-sa-ch'ang</u> (碧 紗 窓 , lit., "sapphire-blue lace window").[165]

The <u>yŭn-ŭm-pyo</u> symbols are placed at the right-hand side of the text and are used only by singers who are already acquainted with the melody. They cannot be deciphered by uninformed persons.

Figure 37, following (p. 173), represents the song <u>Pyŭk-sa-ch'ang</u>.[166]

The Korean text of <u>Pyŭk-sa-ch'ang</u> reads as follows:

Pyŭk-sa-ch'ang-i ŭ-run kŭ-nŭl nim-man-yŭk-yŭ. Pŭl-ttŭk ttwi-ŭ ttuk na-sŭ po-ni nim-ŭn a-ni o-ko. Myŭng-wŭl-i man-chŭng hŭn-tui pyŭk-o-tong chŭ-chŭn-nip-hoe pong-huang-i wa-sŭ kin-mok-ŭl hwi-ŭ-ta-ka chit-ta ta-tŭm-ŭn. Kŭ-rim chae-ro-ta. Mat-ch'o-a pam-il saet-mang-chŭng haeng-yŭ nat-i rŭn-tŭl nam u-hil pŭn-ha-yŭ-ra.

Roughly translated, the words mean:

As the sapphire-blue lace curtain at her window trembles

碧 紗 窓

碧紗窓이、어룬커늘
(ㅁ)
님만여겨 펄떡뛰어 뚝나서보니、
님은아니오고 明月이滿庭헌듸、(ㅁ)

碧梧桐져즌닙헤
鳳凰이와서 긴목을(ㄴ)
짓다듬은 그림지로다。

맛초아 밤일셋망졍
헹여、낫이런들 남 우힐번하여라。

Figure 37

> She rises quickly and leaves the room to see
>
> whether the beloved has arrived.
>
> But only the silver of the full moon floods
>
> the garden.
>
> A phoenix settles upon the glistening leaves
>
> of the sultan's parasol tree and
>
> Bending his slim neck to smooth his ruffled
>
> wings carelessly
>
> His shadow makes the curtains tremble.
>
> Fortunately it is night; had it been daytime
>
> people would have smiled.

SU-TZŬ-P'U (俗 字 譜)

Su-tzŭ-p'u, "common notation," is a term that has been applied to Chinese notational systems in use mainly outside the Confucian temple and the imperial court. In particular the term refers to a notation which came into use at the same time that kung-ch'ê-p'u appeared — probably during the Sung period (960-1279). For this reason su-tzŭ-p'u is also called "Sung-notation."

Su-tzŭ-p'u never became as popular as kung-ch'ê-p'u, the reasons being that a "common notation" was ignored by many of the learned scholars and that many literary and musical works which probably contained su-tzŭ notations were lost during the political upheavals which occurred with the change from the Sung to the Mongol-dominated Yüan period.

Courant[167] believes that the Sung-notation was employed by the Ch'itan (契 丹),[168] originally a nomadic Tungus tribe which had settled in northeastern China (Liao, 遼) between 907 and 1125. The bellicose Ch'itan gradually acquired civilization, adopted Chinese customs, and became devoted students of Chinese literature. In the year 1124 the Ch'itan were driven into western Turkestan, where they were called Kara Kitan or Kitay, and, by European writers, Cathayans. These people, who had become completely assimilated by the Chinese, preserved Chinese literary works and, probably, also possessed and used one or the other form of su-tzǔ-p'u.

The symbols of su-tzǔ-p'u were subject to more variations in writing than those of any other of the Chinese notational systems. Courant assumes that the symbols were abbreviations of the lü characters; but since the graphic resemblance between the two notations is very vague, no definite conclusion as to the origin of su-tzǔ symbols can be made.

The first information concerning su-tzǔ-p'u appears in the works of the Sung philosopher Chu Hsi (朱熹 , 1130-1200),[169] who compares su-tzǔ symbols with those of the (abbreviated) lü and kung-ch'ê notations.

We extend in the following table (p. 176) Chu Hsi's comparison by presenting the symbols of several su-tzǔ systems together with those of the lü and kung-ch'ê notations.

Columns 1 and 2 represent the lü and kung-ch'ê symbols respectively. Columns 3 and 8 contain su-tzǔ symbols as used by Chu-Hsi: column 3 shows the symbols as quoted by Courant,[170] column 8 shows them according to the Ch'in-lü-shuo (琴律説).[171] Columns 4 and 7 represent su-tzǔ symbols as used in the second volume of the Tz'ǔ-yüan (詞源 , "Source of Poetry"), a work written in 1248 by Chang Yen (張炎).[172] Column 5 contains su-tzǔ symbols as used in the eighth volume (p. 10) of T'ien-wên-ko-ch'in-p'u-chi-ch'êng (天聞閣琴譜集成).

		1	2	3	4	5	6	7	8	9	10
黄	鐘	合	厶	△	厶	厶	△	厶	④	厶
大	呂	下四	マ	③マ	マ	マ	マ	マ	⊕	マ
太	簇	高四	マ	ヌマ	ヲ	マ	マ	マ	⊝	マ
夾	鐘	下一	二	⊝	T	一	⊖	=	◉	一
姑	洗	高一	二	一幺	亠	一	一	=	◉	幺幺
仲	呂	上	マ	ケワ	亠	幺幺幺ケ	マ	④	幺幺幺
蕤	賓	勾	厶	しワ	し	厶	L	厶	④	厶
林	鐘	尺	厶	八	八	八	八	八	⑧	八
夷	則	下工	フ	⑦	T	フ	⑦	フ	⑦	フ
南	呂	高工	フ	ケフフ	亠	フ	フ	フ	⑦	フリ
無	射	下凡	刂	⊘	几	リ	⑩	リ	⑪	リ
應	鐘	高凡	刂	八	刂	リ	リ	リ	⑪	リ
黄	清	六	六	幺	六	叁	幺	六	⊜	
大	清	下五	刀	す	⊒	ㇹ	⑤	刀	⑤	
太	清	高五	刀	⑤	⊒	ㇹ	す	刀	⑤	
夾	清	緊五	⑤	⊐	ㇹ	ㇷ		刀		
姑	清	尖一		⺊ゆ		⺊	⺊ゆ		⺊ゆ	
仲	清	尖上		幼		幺幼	幼		幼	
蕤	清	尖勾				◎			⺊ゆ	
林	清	尖尺(冰)		⺊ゆ		⺊ゆ	⺊ゆ			
南	清	尖工				⺊			⺊ゆ	
無	清	尖凡				⺊			⺊ゆ	
應	清	大凡(冰)	[ゆ]?				吶	吶		
黄	清	小	住				力	力		

a collection of zither pieces in sixteen volumes, by T'ang I-ming (唐彝銘), published in 1876.[173] Column 6 shows the su-tzŭ symbols of Chiang K'uei (姜夔), a famous author and composer of the South Sung period (1127-1279); the symbols appear as they were in the third volume of his Pê (pai)-shih-tao-jên-ko-ch'ü (白石道人歌曲).[174] Along with other song cycles this work contains the Yüeh-chiu-ko (越九歌), (Nine) Songs of Yüeh,[175] which are notated in lü notation. Another group of songs in the same work (Vol. IV), called Tzŭ-tu-ch'ü (自度曲),[176] "Personally thought-out Songs," however, are notated in su-tzŭ-p'u, a system which no one has been able to satisfactorily decipher since the Yüan and Ming dynasties (Hsia Ch'êng-ch'ou).[177]

Column 9 represents su-tzŭ symbols of the Sung encyclopedia Shih-lin-kuang-chi (事林廣記), by Ch'ên Yüan Ching (陳元靚).[178] Column 10 shows the su-tzŭ symbols as stated by Levis.[179]

It may be of interest to quote here in free translation, together with our comments, some of the remarks of Hsia Ch'êng-ch'ou[180] concerning the origin, interpretation, and ambiguities of some of the su-tzŭ symbols:

ム, △, ㋰, (黄): according to Chang Wên Hu (張文虎),[181] this symbol is derived from the upper half of 合.

一, ㊀, 二, (丶), (夾): according to the collected works of Chu Wên Kung (朱文公),[182] of the Ming period, 二 and 下一 are the same as 夷. However, 二 and 二 are mistaken for each other, as are 夷 and 夾.

茲 , 么 , マ , ㊂ , (仲): Chiang K'uei notates this tone with ㇈ ; the same symbol is used in the Tz'ǔ-yüan. It is possible that this symbol was derived from 匕 , the common script form of 上 . In a commentary on 律呂 (lü-lü) it is stated that ㇀ and 姑 represent the same tone. Hsia Ch'êng-ch'ou adds: "I really do not know which of these is the correct one."[183]

厶 , 乚 , ㊄ , (㲎): there are various symbols to denote this tone. The music theorist Hsü Hao[184] writes that the kung-ch'ê symbol 勾 is the combination of the Sung notation symbols ㇈ and 乚 . In the notations of Chiang K'uei 勾 is used in only two songs;[185] in other instances the symbols 乚 , ㇈ , 𠃌 , and マ , are employed.

ㅅ , ㊁ , (林): Chu Hsi states that this tone was notated with 厶 ; according to Hsia Ch'êng-ch'ou, this is erroneous.

夂 , 厶 , 六 , ㊅ , (潢): Chang Wên Hu, a music theorist of the nineteenth century and an authority on Chiang K'uei's songs, believes that this note was notated with 又 , which is the script form of 六 .

勹 , ㋿ , 兀 , (大清): in a commentary to the Tz'ǔ-yüan this tone is notated with 司 ; T'ang Lan[186] believes that it has the same meaning as 尖五 , which, according to Hsia Ch'êng-ch'ou, is erroneous.

勹 , 丂 , 兀 , ㋿ , (太清): in a commentary to the Tz'ǔ-yüan this tone is notated with ⓓ .

丂 , 丂 , 丂 , (夾清): in the Tz'ǔ-yüan this tone is notated with 高五 (d#). In music books of the Sung period[187] this note is called "tight d" (緊五), a term derived from p'i-pa playing. [188] The Ch'in-lü-shuo does not use this symbol. Occasionally the symbol 刁 is used, but no supporting reference can be found. T'ang Lan states that with the exception of the symbols used by Chiang K'uei, all others are unreliable or incorrect.

⺄ , 𠃌 , (尖一 , being the higher octave of 姑): T'ang Lan argues that this tone is incorrectly notated in the Tz'ǔ-yüan with 𠃌 ; it should be ⺄ ; Chiang K'uei uses ⺄ . Nevertheless, both 𠃌 and 𠃌 (radicals) are in use. Occasionally 𠃌 has been considered as a rhythmic sign, which is incorrect. Only in the Pê-shih-tao-jên-ko-ch'ü of Chiang K'uei, [189] is the symbol ⺄ interpreted as 一 , together with 折 (chê), "possibly a rhythmic sign" (Hsia Ch'êng-ch'ou). [190] Hsia Ch'êng-ch'ou writes: "I thought that 𠃌 and 𠃌 were equivalent. Looking them up in several music books I find that 尖一 , 尖上 , 尖凡 , 尖尺 , 尖工 , and 尖凡 are identical with the notations in the 'Kuang Book'." [191] The question whether 𠃌 may have had some rhythmic significance in notations other than the one mentioned above remains unanswered.

纠 , 幼 , 幼 , (尖上 , being the higher octave of 仲): T'ang Lan believes that the notation of this tone, 幼 , as used in the Tz'ǔ-yüan, is erroneous; it should be 幼 . T'ang states that Chen Wên Chüeh[192] corrected this symbol to 幼 .

◎ , 𠃌 , (尖勺 , being the higher octave of 㽞): this is wrongly notated with 尖人 in the "Kuang Book"[193] —

it should be 尖勾 .

个 , 仙 , (尖尺, being the higher octave of 林): in the Kuang Book this tone is notated with 尖八 because 八 is the common script form of 尺 . Chang Yen in his Tz'ŭ-yüan wrongly notates this tone with 个刁 or 仙 .

状 , (大凡, being the higher octave of 應.): in the Tz'ŭ-yüan this tone is notated with 大住 .[194] (反): this symbol occurs in neither the Tz'ŭ-yüan nor the Kuang Book. It seems that 反 is used only when the rhythm is agitated. It is possible that 丁 is an abbreviation of 反 .

And so forth. We have noticed some of the numerous discrepancies and doubtful features which first have to be clarified before this remarkable notational system can be fully deciphered. Figure 38 (p. 181), is a song by Chiang K'uei.[195] It contains a number of unknown and several composite symbols, many of which cannot be transcribed.

Although su-tzŭ-p'u never gained popularity, it had survived during the six centuries since the Sung period and occasionally still comes into use. The symbols of nineteenth-century su-tzŭ-p'u are:[196]

Symbol	Name		Pitch
㇄	Ho	(e. g.)	C
⊘	Hsia Ssŭ		Db
>	Ssŭ		D
⊖	Hsia Yi		Eb
一	Yi		E
㣺 or 丩	Shang		F

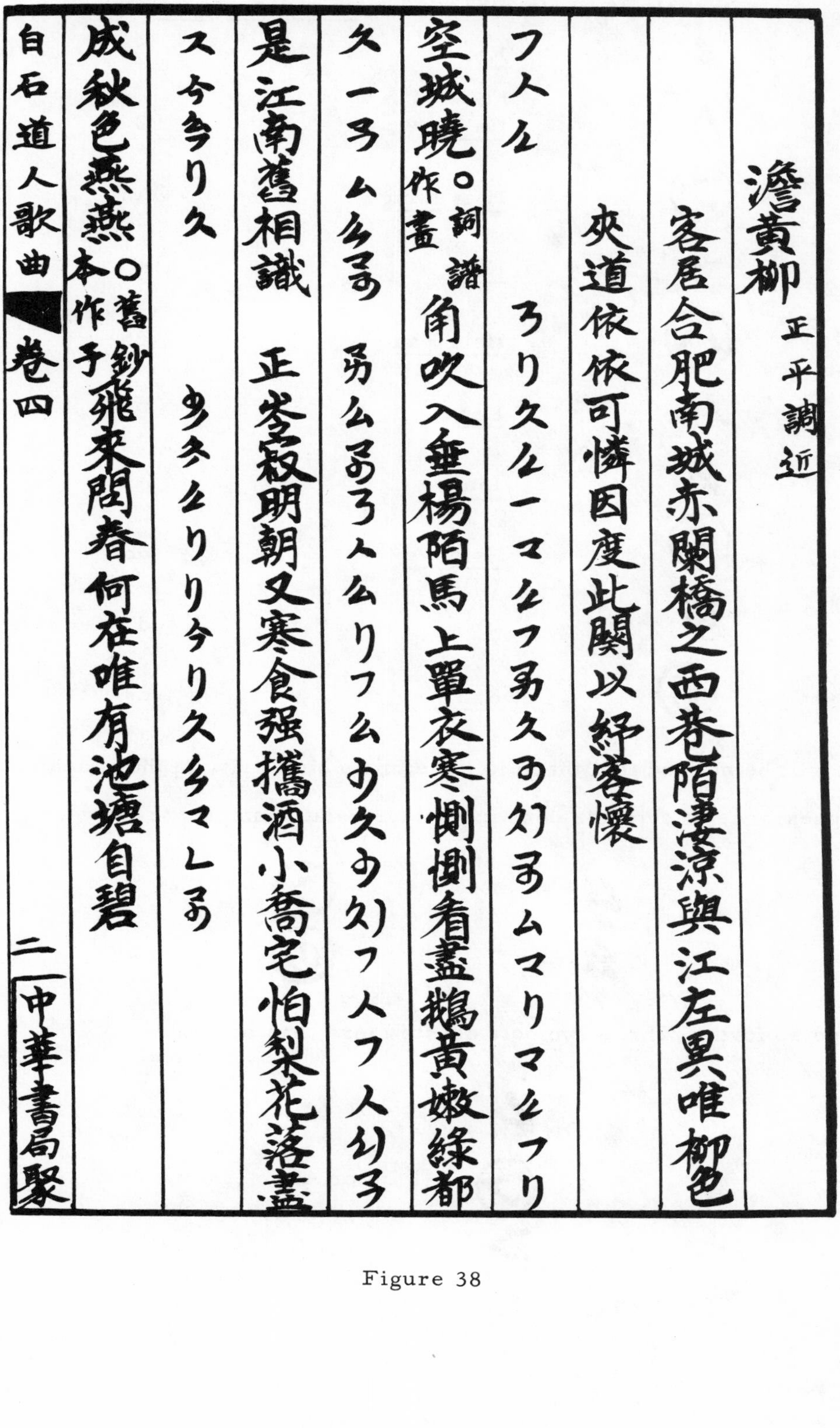

澹黃柳　正平調近

客居合肥南城赤闌橋之西巷陌淒涼與江左異唯柳色

夾道依依可憐因度此闋以紓客懷

フ人厶　ろり久厶一マ厶フ另久ろ刃ろ厶マり　マ厶フり

空城曉。詞譜 作畫　角吹入垂楊陌馬上單衣寒惻惻看盡鵝黃嫩綠都

久一ろ厶ろ　另厶ろ人厶り　フ厶　あ久ろ刃フ人フ人幻ろ

是江南舊相識　正岑寂明朝又寒食強攜酒小喬宅怕梨花落盡

ス今今り久　　多久厶り　り今り久タマしろ

成秋色燕燕。舊鈔本本作于　飛來問春何在唯有池塘自碧

白石道人歌曲　卷四　　二 中華書局聚

Figure 38

Symbols of nineteenth-century su-tzǔ-p'u (cont.)

 ム	Kou	F#
∧	Ch'ih	G
 ⊘	Hsia Kung	Ab
 ∨	Kung	A
 ⊗	Hsia Fan	Bb
 八	Fan	B
 幺	Liu	c
 ⊘	Hsia Wu	db
 万	Wu	d
 ⊛	Kao Wu	d#

It will be noticed that there is little or no similarity in the graphic appearance of symbols denoting octave relationships:

$$ム - C \qquad\qquad ⊘ - Db$$
$$幺 - c \qquad\qquad ⊘ - db,$$

and so forth.   Three symbols denote more than one note:

$$ム - C \text{ or } F\#$$
$$⊘ - Db \text{ or } Ab$$
$$∨ - D \text{ or } A$$

THE NOTATIONS OF INDIA

In India, as in many other Oriental countries, music teaching is done by rote. The teacher presents a musical phrase and the student repeats it until, after it is mastered, another phrase can be proffered. This method of instruction has its advantages because the Indian musician, before performing a rāga, has to be acquainted not only with the tone material, but with the characteristic intonations, ornaments, "strong and weak" notes and other, often minute, but highly essential details, most of which cannot be notated and have to be learned by frequent listening and imitating.

As Indian music is basically an art of improvisation, it is of little importance to the musician whether the first and the subsequent performances of a piece are literally the same. What matters is his observing all the rules and regulations of the rāga, a tightly knit framework of more or less important notes and phrases, within which the performer is expected to demonstrate his artistry by skillful improvisation. Notation which "freezes" a melody into a rigid form would not assist but hinder a performance based upon the spontaneity of improvisation.

With the exception of tone words or tone syllables used in theoretical treatises, musical notation in India did not come into widespread use until the late nineteenth century, and even then it was employed mainly for didactic, analytical, and referential purposes. At the end of the nineteenth, and particularly in the first third of the twentieth century, when the eminent Pandit V. N. Bhatkhande of Bombay successfully endeavored to unify different interpretations of rāgas into more or less standardized forms and created a satisfactory classification of the northern rāgas, the use of tone syllables developed into a notational system, a valuable tool in the hands of numerous Indian authors. As a result, the tone syllables have been more recently employed to notate not only scales and characteristic phrases, but extended pieces as well.

Like the West at the present time, India possesses only one notation, which, with a number of modifications, is used by musicians of both North and South. In the North the tone syllables are written in the Nagari script, in the South either in Nagari or in Tamil script. Muslims occasionally write the syllables in Urdu script, but the pronunciation of these syllables is basically the same throughout India.

Although Indian art music occasionally employs microtonal alterations,[197] musical notation has created no specific symbols for them. While the contemporary northern notation clearly indicates the chromatic alterations of the seven basic degrees within the octave, southern notation, as a rule, does not; it confines itself to the notation of the seven basic notes.[198] The performer who consults a notated melody before his recital already knows the tone material, the chromatic alterations, ornaments, and all the other essential details of the rāgam.[199] In order to read South Indian notation, irrespective of the fact that it may be written in Nagari or Tamil script, the knowledge of the elaborate system of the 72 Melakartas[200] of Karnatic music is essential [201]

The aim of Indian music theorists of the past was to establish workable basic scales and derive from them definitions and classifications of the multitude of other subordinate scales. At the present time North Indian musicians use as their basic scale the notes of rāga Bilaval, which is very similar to the Western major scale. South

India's basic scale, ragam Kanakangi, expressed in Western terms, is C Db Ebb F G Ab Bbb c. The degrees of this scale are the shuddha svaras, the pure (i.e., "natural") notes.

In the past India used various basic scales, the notes of which served to define the degrees of other scales with chromatic alterations. Since theorists often were vague in defining both basic and derivative scales, misunderstandings arose. For instance, a most famous theoretical work in Indian music, the Sangitaratnakara by Sarngadeva, written in the second half of the thirteenth century, offers no clear definition of the basic scale; therefore, every scale description derived from this basic scale is vague. [202] If we consider that almost every Indian author after Sarngadeva used to quote from the Sangitaratnakara and that the Indian musician Kallinatha (fifteenth century) wrote a frequently quoted commentary (the Sangitaratnakaratika) on it and — furthermore — that hundreds of authors referred to different basic scales, the confusion in theoretical matters becomes apparent. [203]

While the South Indian system of the 72 Melakarta ragams is comparatively distinct, North Indian music, subject to numerous foreign influences, particularly the Islamic invasions, suffered considerably from this confusion until a solution was introduced first by Mohammed Rezza in 1813 (Naqmat-e-Asaphi) and finally perfected by Pandit V. N. Bhatkhande, whose works Lakshya Sangitam (in Sanskrit) and Hindusthani Sangit Paddhati [204] employed the notes of raga Bilaval as a basic scale and presented an efficient classification of North Indian ragas.

NORTH INDIA: TONE SYLLABLES

If we transcribe the first note of the scale with the Western note

C, the notes of Bilaval are indicated as follows:

Tone syllable	Tone name	Western equivalent
SA (सा)	Sadja (Shadja)	C
RI (or RE) (री or रे)	Rsabha (Rishabha)	D
GA (ग)	Gāndhāra	E
MA (म)	Madhyama	F
PA (प)	Pañcama (Panchama)	G
DHA (ध)	Dhaivata	A
NI (नि)	Nisāda (Nishāda)	B

These tone syllables do not represent absolute pitches; they constitute a solmization system with a "movable do."

The notes SA and PA are never sharped or flatted. The notes RI, GA, DHA, and NI can be flatted only by a semitone and cannot be sharped as is done to their corresponding degrees in the West. The flat is indicated by a horizontal line below the syllable:

री   RI komal denotes Db (if we assume that SA is C),

ग   GA komal denotes Eb,

ध   DHA komal denotes Ab, and

नि   NI komal denotes Bb.

The only note which can be sharped by a semitone (but not flatted) is MA. The high alteration is indicated by a short vertical line above the syllable: म॑ , MA tīvra (F#).

The practice of placing a line below the syllable to indicate a low alteration and a vertical line above it to indicate a high alteration exists in the notations of the vedic chant. For instance, the hymns of the oldest veda, the Rig Veda, were recited on three tones within the gamut of a third. The middle tone was called udātta (raised tone), the one below, anudātta (not a raised tone), and the upper one svarita (a resounding tone). These three tones were applied according to the meaning of the words and thus represent the ancient melody of spoken Sanskrit based upon three accents of high, medium, and low, similar to the accents of classical languages of European antiquity. The melodies were not of an independent character; each of these three tones depended upon the correct recitation of the sacred text.

Anudātta and svarita were denoted by a short horizontal line below the textual syllable and by a vertical dash above it, respectively. The udātta used for the pracaya, the "multitude" of unaccented syllables, was not marked.

In some treatises we can find terms such as MA komal, or GA tīvra, which mean nothing but MA shuddha ("pure," natural MA) and GA shuddha, the notes F and E respectively, in contrast to any altered forms that may have occurred before. Indian music theory uses terms such as atikomal, "very flat," and tīvratar, "very sharp," but musical notation has no symbols for these terms. The gamut of notes is divided into three octaves:[205] mandra saptaka, the lowest, madhya saptaka, the middle, and tāra saptaka, the highest octave.[206] Recent authors,[207] particularly in South India, have enlarged the range to five octaves, adding a very low and a very high one which are called anu mandra sthāyī and ati tāra sthāyī, respectively. The adoption of a range of five octaves seems to be the result of influences from the West. As Indian music is basically vocal, a gamut of three octaves is fully adequate. Notes of the lower octave are marked with a dot below the syllable, those of the upper octave with a dot above the syllable.

If we again transcribe SA as the note C, the Western chromatic scale can be notated as follows:

THE RHYTHMIC MODES OF NORTH
AND SOUTH INDIAN MUSIC

Before discussing the notation of durational values, we must survey briefly the rhythmic modes (tālas). The modes and melody patterns of Indian rāgas find their counterparts in the rhythmic modes which, although more complex, resemble somewhat the rhythmic modes of thirteenth-century music in Europe.

Although there are numerous rhythmic modes, a perusal of notated Indian songs of the North and the South shows that only a comparatively small number of them is in frequent use. The simplicity of North Indian notation permits transcriptions into Western notation without an intimate knowledge of the rhythmic modes because the vibhāgas ("divisions," "bars") are clearly indicated by short vertical lines which correspond to the Western bar lines. South Indian notations do not always use dividing marks between the vibhāgas. Occasionally commas are used which can be interpreted as bar lines, but since commas are also used to indicate prolongations of notes, this method can create misunderstandings. However, the use of specific signs indicating the durations of shortened and extended notes facilitates the reading even if there are no bar lines; moreover, South Indian notations always state at the head of a piece the name of the rhythmic mode (tālam), a practice which serves the reader and transcriber as a reliable guide.

Indian tāla proceeds in groups of bars (āvartas) in which each bar may contain a different number of beats. For instance, the āvarta of the North Indian Dhamār Tāl has the following structure:

The āvarta of northern Jhaptāl is:

It is important to note that each vibhāga (bar) in an āvarta has a distinct significance. If we compare the simple 4/4 meter of a Western march with the similar Tintāl (or Tritāl) of North Indian music, we find that both metrical schemes consist of successive bars each containing four beats. In Tintāl, however, the four vibhāgas within an āvarta differ from each other in character and require specific drum beats. North Indian notation marks the beginning of each vibhāga in

the following manner:

x   2   o   3

One vibhāga — in our example it is the first of the āvarta — has as its

first beat the sam (lit., "complete," "total"), the musical accent of

the āvarta, which is marked with an x placed below the first tone syl-

lable. The sam shows no dynamic stress; it is the point at which solo-

ist and accompanying drummer are expected to meet, where melody and

rhythm of singer and drummer coincide. The soloist, when reaching

the sam will usually perform either the basic note (SA), or the highly

important vādī (amsa), the predominant note of the rāga.[208] The

drummer, when reaching the sam, has to perform a special beat,

usually executed on both heads of the tabla pair [209] or the mridanga.[210]

If the performers, particularly after intricate elaborations both

melodically and rhythmically, achieve a precise and musically satis-

factory coincidence, it is acknowledged by nods and smiles from

performers and audience.

The vibhāga marked with the number 2 has no particular signifi-

cance; in it and in the fourth vibhāga, marked 3, the performers are

free in their improvisations. The first beat of the third vibhāga is

generally marked with an o. This beat is called khāli, the "empty"

beat. It too is produced by a special sound on the drums and serves

as a warning to the soloist that after a certain number of beats (in our

example, eight), the sām will return and with it a new āvarta will

begin. The khāli is most useful, particularly in complicated tānas

(fiorituras and melodic variations), in which the soloist is apt to stray

from the metric pattern. In short, the vibhāgas of an āvarta are frequently marked with X 2 o 3 (for instance in the northern Tintāl or

Tritāl), or, if there are more than four vibhāgas in the āvarta, with

X o 2 o 3 4 (for instance in the northern Ektāl and Chautāl), or

with X 2 o 3 o 4 o (in northern Ādachautāl), or with X o 2 3 o

(in the northern Sultāl), and so forth. Occasionally it may happen that

the drummer becomes so enthusiastic in his performance of complex

syncopations that the khāli is produced in an indistinct manner. This

can mislead the soloist and the sām may not come off as clearly as

intended with the result that angry arguments between soloist and

drummer may ensue when the performance is over.

For the purpose of transcribing Indian melodies into Western

notation a knowledge of the general structure of the āvarta will be

helpful because, in order to present a clear picture of both melody

and rhythm, the transcriber should write each āvarta on a separate

line.

The following table shows the frequently used tālas of North

Indian music:

Ādachautāl:

1	2	3	4	5	6	7	8	9	10	11	12	13	14
X		2		o		3		o		4		o	

Brāhmtāl:

1	2	3	4	5	6	7	8	9	10	11	12	13	14
X		o		2		3		o		4		5	

15	16	17	18	19	20	21	22	23	24	25	26
6		o		7		8		9		10	

27	28
o	

Chautāl:

1	2	3	4	5	6	7	8	9	10	11	12
X		o		2		o		3		4	

Dādra:

1	2	3	4	5	6
X			o		

Dhamārtāl: | 1 2 3 4 5 | 6 7 | 8 9 10 | 11 12 13 14 |
            | X | 2 | o | 3 |

Dipchandi: | 1 2 3 | 4 5 6 7 | 8 9 10 | 11 12 13 14 |
           | X | 2 | o | 3 |

Ektāl: | 1 2 | 3 4 | 5 6 | 7 8 | 9 10 | 11 12 |
           | X | o | 2 | o | 3 | 4 |

Jhampa: | 1 2 | 3 4 5 | 6 7 | 8 9 10 |
           | X | 2 | o | 3 |

Jhaptāl: | 1 2 | 3 4 5 | 6 7 | 8 9 10 |
           | X | 2 | o | 3 |

Jhumra: | 1 2 3 | 4 5 6 7 | 8 9 10 | 11 12 13 14 |
           | X | 2 | o | 3 |

Panjabi: (same as Tritāl)

Rūpak: | 1 2 3 | 4 5 | 6 7 |
           | X | 2 | 3 |

Shikar: | 1 2 3 4 5 6 | 7 8 9 10 11 12 | 13 14 |
           | X | o | 3 |

           | 15 16 17 | (The second vibhāga is usually not
           | 4 | indicated by a number)

Sultāl: | 1 2 | 3 4 | 5 6 | 7 8 | 9 10 |
           | X | o | 2 | 3 | o |

Tilvada: | 1 2 3 4 | 5 6 7 8 | 9 10 11 12 | 13 14 15 16 |
           | X | 2 | o | 3 |

Tivra: | 1 2 3 | 4 5 | 6 7 |
           | X | 2 | 3 |

Tritāl (Tintāl) | 1 2 3 4 | 5 6 7 8 | 9 10 11 12 | 13 14 15 16 |
                | X | 2 | o | 3 |

The tālas Chautāl and Ektāl, Dipchandi and Jhumra, Tilvada, Tritāl, and Panjabi, and others, are structurally the same. They differ, however, in the types of drum beats used. For instance the basic drum beats, expressed by specific drum words, of Tilvada and Trital are:

	1	2	3	4	5	6	7	8
	X				2			
Tilvada:	DHA	TUKA	DHAN	DHAN	DHA	DHA	TI	TI
Trital:	TA	DHAN	DHAN	DHA	TA	DHAN	DHAN	DHA

	9	10	11	12	13	14	15	16
	0				3			
Tilvada:	TA	TUKA	DHAN	DHAN	DHA	DHA	DHAN	DHAN
Trital:	DHA	TIN	TIN	TA	TA	DHAN	DHAN	DHA

South Indian music, too, possesses a considerable wealth of rhythmical modes, many of which resemble those of the North. In contrast to the northern modes, Karnatic talas are organized into five groups (jatis). This tendency to group rhythms and scales is characteristic of the Indian South, where the absence of foreign influences allowed the systems of ragas and talas to become astonishingly orderly.

Karnatic notation does not, as a rule, indicate the sam and khali features. The performers are expected to know the various significances of the vibhagas within the avarta. The following chart shows the grouping of rhythmic units into jatis and talas:

Tala   Jati

	Trisra	Chatusra	Khanda	Mísra	Sankirna
Eka	3	4	5	7	9
Rūpaka	2 + 3	2 + 4	2 + 5	2 + 7	2 + 9
Jhampa	3 + 1 + 2	4 + 1 + 2	5 + 1 + 2	7 + 1 + 2	9 + 1 + 2
Triputa	3 + 2 + 2	4 + 2 + 2	5 + 2 + 2	7 + 2 + 2	9 + 2 + 2
Matya	3 + 2 + 3	4 + 2 + 4	5 + 2 + 5	7 + 2 + 7	9 + 2 + 9
Dhruva	3 + 2 + 3 + 3	4 + 2 + 4 + 4	5 + 2 + 5 + 5	7 + 2 + 2 + 7	9 + 9 + 2 + 2
Āta	3 + 3 + 2 + 2	4 + 4 + 2 + 2	5 + 5 + 2 + 2	7 + 7 + 2 + 2	9 + 9 + 2 + 2

The indications trisra, chatusra, etc., refer to the number of metrical units contained in the first vibhāga: trisra, three; chatusra, four; khanda, five; misra, seven; and saṅkīrna, nine.

The āvarta of Eka tāla possesses only one anga ("member") or vibhāga; Rūpaka tāla consists of two angas; Jhampa, Triputa and Matya tālas consist of three angas; and Dhruva and Ata tālas of four.

In notated songs we observe that in certain instances the jāti of the tāla is not indicated. This method refers to specific jātis: Triputa tāla, without any jāti indication, signifies only its Trisra jāti form. Eka, Rūpaka, Matya, and Dhruva tālas, without jāti indications, refer always to their Chatusra jāti forms. Ata tāla, without jāti indication, refers only to its Khanda jāti form; and Jhampa tāla, without jāti indication, denotes only its Misra jāti form.

One of the most popular Karnatic rhythmic modes is Ādi tāla, which is nothing else but Triputa tāla in its Chatusra jāti form (4 + 2 + 2). In addition, there exist several irregular tālas, such as Chapu tāla ("Trisra jāti," 1 + 2), Chapu tāla ("Misra jāti," 1 + 2 + 2 + 2), both frequently employed in folk and popular music. One rather complex tāla is Simhanandana tāla, which contains seventeen angas with a total of 100 rhythmic units in the following order: 8 + 8 + 4 + 8 + 4 + 8 + 2 + 2 + 8 + 8 + 4 + 8 + 4 + 8 + 8 + 4 + 4.

Nomenclature of Durational Values

The durations of notes are measured by fractions or multiples of the mātrā ("unit," "instant") in the North and of the laghu ("short") in the South. If we represent the mātrā (or laghu) with a quarter note the other note values are:

	North	South
♪	Anumātrā ("under-mātrā")	Anudrutam ("under-quick")
♪	Ardhamātrā ("half-mātrā")	Drutam (Durut) ("quick")
♩	Mātrā (or Hrasva, "short")	Laghu ("short")
♩.	Adhyardha (1 1/2 mātrā)	Laghu druta(m)
♩	Dirgha ("long")	Guru ("heavy")
♩♪	Ardhatisra (2 1/2 mātrās)	Guru druta(m)
♩.	Pluta (or Vrddha, "augmented")	Pluta(m)
𝅝		Kākapāda(m) ("crow's foot")

Occasionally the following symbols are employed to denote the various note values of South Indian music:

∪	Anudruta(m)
○	Drutam
∣	Laghu
8	Guru
∣̊	Plutam
✝	Kākapādam

According to Sambamoorthy,[211] the signs ✝ and ▬ are used together with fractions (written in Arabic numerals): ▬ $\frac{3}{4}$, for instance, indicates that the melody begins after $\frac{3}{4}$ of an anudrutam has passed once an āvarta (♪· ♪ in our interpretation) has begun. Similarly ✝ shows that the melody starts with an upbeat of half of an anudrutam before the first beat of the āvarta (♪ in our interpretation).

These signs appear only in a few contemporary treatises and cannot be considered to be part of the generally accepted notational system of the South.

As already stated both northern and southern notations can use short vertical "bar" lines after each vibhāga. The older South Indian manuscripts, particularly those notated in Nagari script, omit bar lines altogether.

The Northern Notation of Durational Values

Each tone syllable, if not otherwise indicated, has the duration of one rhythmic unit, a mātrā. A short horizontal line placed at the right side of the syllable prolongs the note by one mātrā; two horizontal lines, one after the other, by two mātrās; and so forth:

Subdivisions of a mātrā are notated by slurs placed below the tone syllables:

Dotted and syncopated notes are denoted by means of a comma, usually in combination with the lower slur which brackets together all notes that comprise one mātrā. For instance, can read

or . With the exception of rests

at the beginning or end of an āvarta, North Indian notation makes no distinction between dotted notes and rests which would occur instead of the extension of the note. Occasionally the writer makes sure that the note is to be held by using a very short and thinly written horizontal line:

Appoggiaturas are indicated by placing the ornamenting note (written as a small letter) above and slightly to the left of the main note. For instance, [Devanagari notation] will read: [music notation]

A mīnd (glide) is notated by a slur placed above the notes involved: [Devanagari notation] is [music notation] ; [Devanagari notation] is [music notation] . If a tone syllable is placed in parentheses, it means that a particular ornament is to be performed on it. For instance, (सा) will read: [music notation] or (प) ,

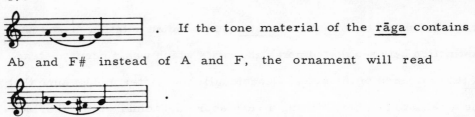

. If the tone material of the rāga contains

Ab and F# instead of A and F, the ornament will read

The text is placed below the notes. If a textual syllable is to be held for two or more notes, the sign S is used in the textual line in the following manner:

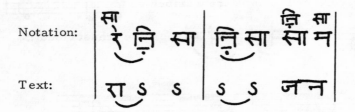

Notation:

Text:

which reads:

Text: Ra — — — — ja – n

The sign S (avagraha, lit., "separation," the mark of an interval) occasionally appears also at the beginning of an āvarta when the melody does not start with the first beat or beats. While in the notational line there is no indication of rests at the beginning of a section (sections such as sthāyī [asthayi], antara, and others),[212] the textual line shows them:

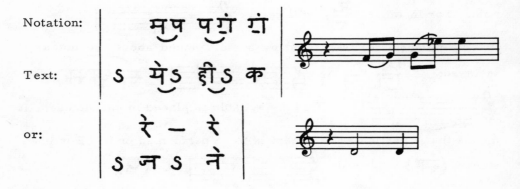

Notation:

Text:

or:

If the melody begins late in the āvarta, for instance
with the last vibhāga, or with only one or two beats at the
end of the āvarta, the space preceding the actual start is left
blank both in the notational and textual lines, and the bar line
indicating the beginning of the last vibhāga is omitted. For
instance:

Figure 39, following (p. 200), is the first section (sthāyī)[213]
of a song in rāga Bhairav (Dhamārtāl). The notes of Bhairav are
C Db E F G Ab B c, both ascending and descending. The vādī
is Ab, the less important samvādī, Db. On both notes heavy
vibratos have to be performed.

The melody begins with the khāli bar which appears at the
end of the line. The sequence of bars is not X 2 o 3, but
3 X 2 o, which is permissible.

The sam in this particular song coincides first with the first
note of the scale, C, and, at its second occurrence, with Db,
the samvādī. As the vādī is Ab, belonging to the upper half of
the scale, it will appear in the second section of the song, the
antara (which is not shown here), in which the notes of the upper
half of the scale predominate.[214]

Figure 39

SOUTH INDIA: MELAS AND NOTATIONS

Although related to the northern notational system, the southern notation differs from the former in avoiding signs denoting chromatic alterations of the seven basic (shuddha) notes within the octave, by almost never indicating sam and khāli features, by frequently omitting "bar lines," and by notating durational values in a different manner.

We shall turn first to a brief consideration of the southern system of the 72 melakarta rāgams,[215] because as already stated, without this information it is impossible to read South Indian notations.

In contrast to the music of the northern half of the peninsula which, in the past, was frequently exposed to foreign influences, the system of South Indian scales has remained comparatively undisturbed and shows considerable orderliness. The word melakarta, meaning "group maker," represents a primary scale, the notes of which are the same as, or related to, the notes of a number of subordinate and derivatory scales (janya rāgams). The melakartas (melas) represent 72 straight (in contrast to certain vakra, "zig-zag" types), heptatonic (sampurna) scales which are grouped into twelve chakras ("wheels") of six melas each. The first and fifth notes (SA and PA) remain unaltered in all 72 scales. The first 36 use the pure fourth, shudda MA (F), the other 36 the augmented fourth, prati MA (F#). The first three notes, identical in the six scales of each chakra, change from the first to the sixth chakra in the following manner: C Db Ebb, C Db Eb, C Db E, C D Eb, C D E, to C D# E, respectively. The seventh to the twelfth chakras use the same notes as the first six chakras but, as stated before, change the note F to F#.

The upper three notes of the six scales of each of the twelve chakras change from Ab Bbb c, via Ab Bb c, Ab B c, A Bb c,

A B c, to A# B c, respectively. We simplify this information in
the form of two charts, the first showing the notes of the lower tetrachord, the second those of the upper:

Chart I

Chakra	1:	C	Db	Ebb	F
Chakra	2:	C	Db	Eb	F
Chakra	3:	C	Db	E	F
Chakra	4:	C	D	Eb	F
Chakra	5:	C	D	E	F
Chakra	6:	C	D#	E	F
Chakra	7:	C	Db	Ebb	F#
Chakra	8:	C	Db	Eb	F#
Chakra	9:	C	Db	E	F#
Chakra	10:	C	D	Eb	F#
Chakra	11:	C	D	E	F#
Chakra	12:	C	D#	E	F#

Chart II

Chakra:

1	2	3	4	5	6	7	8	9	10	11	12				
Rāgam															
1	7	13	19	25	31	37	43	49	55	61	67	G	Ab	Bbb	c
2	8	14	20	26	32	38	44	50	56	62	68	G	Ab	Bb	c
3	9	15	21	27	33	39	45	51	57	63	69	G	Ab	B	c
4	10	16	22	28	34	40	46	52	58	64	70	G	A	Bb	c
5	11	17	23	29	35	41	47	53	59	65	71	G	A	B	c
6	12	18	24	30	36	42	48	54	60	66	72	G	A#	B	c

If we wish to determine the notes of a certain mela we have to
consult the two charts in the following way: suppose we wish to ascertain the notes of mela 48; Chart II informs us that it belongs to chakra
8. Chart I shows that the lower notes of chakra 8 are C Db Eb F#;
the note G remains unaltered, and the upper four notes can be found

in Chart II to the right of number 48; they are G A# B c. Thus
melakarta 48 consists of the notes C Db Eb F# G A# B c.

Following is the list containing the names of the 72 melakartas
and showing their organization into twelve chakras:

I. Indu Chakra   II. Netra Chakra
    1. Kanakāngi   7. Senāvati
    2. Ratnāngi   8. Hanumattodi
    3. Gānamūrti   9. Dhenuka
    4. Vanaspati   10. Nātakapriya
    5. Mānavati   11. Kokilapriya
    6. Tanarupi   12. Rūpavati

III. Agni Chakra   IV. Veda Chakra
    13. Gāyakapriya   19. Jhankāradhvani
    14. Vakulābharanam   20. Natabhairavi
    15. Māyāmālavagaula   21. Kiravāni
    16. Chakravākam   22. Kharaharapriya
    17. Suryakāntam   23. Gaurimanohari
    18. Hātakāmbari   24. Varunapriya

V. Bhana Chakra   VI. Rutu Chakra
    25. Nāraranjani   31. Yāgapriya
    26. Chārukeshi   32. Rāgavardhani
    27. Sarasāngi   33. Gāngeyabhushani
    28. Harikāmbhoji   34. Vāgadhishvari
    29. Dhirashankarābharanam   35. Sulini
    30. Nāganāndi   36. Chalanāta

VII. Rishi Chakra   VIII. Vasu Chakra
    37. Sālagam   43. Gavāmbhodi
    38. Jalārnavam   44. Bhavapriya
    39. Jhālavarāli   45. Subhapantuvarāli
    40. Navanitam   46. Shadvidhamārgini
    41. Pāvani   47. Suvarnāngi
    42. Raghupriya   48. Divyamani

IX. Brahma Chakra   X.   Disi Chakra
        49. Dhavalāmbari   55. Śyāmalāngi
        50. Nāmanārāyni   56. Shanmukhapriya
        51. Kāmavardhani   57. Simhendramadhyama
        52. Rāmapriya   58. Hemavati
        53. Gamanashrama   59. Dharmavati
        54. Viśvambari   60. Nitimati

XI. Rudra Chakra   XII. Aditya Chakra
        61. Kāntāmani   67. Sucharitra
        62. Rishabhapriya   68. Jyotisvarūpini
        63. Latāngi   69. Dhātuvardhani
        64. Vāchaspati   70. Nāsikabhūshani
        65. Mechakalyani   71. Kosalam
        66. Chitrāmbari   72. Rasikapriya

South Indian musicians can state almost at once the number of any particular mela (abbr. for melakarta) if they are given its name or state the name if they are given the number. This surprising feat of memorizing 72 names and their numbers is based upon a comparatively simple method which can be learned by anyone acquainted with the Sanskrit alphabet (practically all Indian languages use its sequence of letters). Its consonants are grouped into the kātapayādi system — four categories, the first consisting of letters related to ka (the kādinava category), the second referring to ta (tādinava), the third to pa (padinava), and the fourth to ya (yādyashta):

I.	Kādinava:	K	Kh	G	Gh	Ng	Ch	Chh	J	Jh	Jn
		1	2	3	4	5	6	7	8	9	0
II.	Tādinava:	T	Th	D	Dh	N	T	Th	D	Dh	N
		1	2	3	4	5	6	7	8	9	0
III.	Pādipancha:	P	Ph	B	Bh	M					
		1	2	3	4	5					
IV.	Yādyashta:	Y	R	L	V	Ś	Sh	S	H		
		1	2	3	4	5	6	7	8		

Most people in the South who can read and write know these four groups of letters. Even a child who has learned in school the correct sequence of the letters can find out their numbers within each group by counting the letters on his fingers. We notice that there are ten in the kādinava and tādinava groups, five in the pādipancha, and eight in the yādyashta. In the first two groups, Jn and N — the tenth letters — are not numbered with 10 but with 0.

Knowing these four groups of letters and their numbers, we are fully equipped to determine the numbers of the 72 melas. Suppose we wish to find out the number of mela Rūpavati; we take the first two consonants of the name, R and P, and note their numbers: R is 2 of the yādyashta, P is 1 of the pādipancha groups. This gives us two digits, 2 and 1; if we reverse the two numbers to 1 and 2, we have the correct number of Rūpavati (12).

It is of no consequence which of the four groups of letters is referred to when the number of a mela is being determined. A few more examples will illustrate this:

Melakarta rāgam:

Kosala(m)	K is	1	of I	1 7, reversed: 71,
	S is	7	of IV	
Dhenuka	Dh is	9	of II	9 0, reversed: 09,
	N is	0	of II	
Simhendramadhyama	S is	7	of IV	7 5, reversed: 57,
	M is	5	of III	
Sūlini	S is	5	of IV	5 3, reversed: 35.
	L is	3	of IV	

In several instances care has to be taken about the correct spelling of a name such as Sūlini where the first letter is a S.

Some other difficulties arise when conjunct consonants are employed. For instance, in Ratnāngi the letters R (2 of IV) and N (0 of II) have to be considered. The rule is that when two conjunct consonants occur, the second letter which precedes the second vowel has to be used for counting. However, in Chakravāka, Divyamani, Visvambhari, Simhendramadhyama, and Chitrāmbari, not the second but the first of the conjunct consonants has to be used.

To describe the origin of this remarkable system of melas, names, numbers, and letters, would require a lengthy chapter dealing with the history of South Indian music, a history which has not yet been written in its entirety.

Briefly and incompletely stated, we can assume that by the middle of the seventeenth century South Indian music had evolved most of its characteristics. We know that then the center of musical activity was Tanjore and that a musician-author of great fame, Veṅkaṭamakhin, wrote under the auspices of the court, his Caturdandīprakāsikā (1637 or 1660), a treatise in which a system of 72 melakartas is mentioned.[216]

The views about Veṅkaṭamakhin's merit of having introduced the system of the 72 melakartas differ considerably. T. R. Srinivāsa Ayyaṅgār, in his introduction to the Samgraha-Cūdā-Mani[217] by Govinda (eighteenth century), states that Veṅkaṭamakhin's names for the 72 melas were based upon the katapayādi system, that is, upon the system which derives melạ numbers from the first two consonants of the names.

P. Sambamoorthy in his South Indian Music[218] is of the opinion that Veṅkaṭamakhin's melas are not related to the katapayādi sankhyā. We fully agree because numerous mela and janya names of Veṅkaṭamakhin differ from those of Govinda and from those of later systems.

During the last two centuries two systems evolved: the Kana-kambari-Phenadyuti, partly different from, partly related to the list of Veṅkaṭamakhin, and another, employing mostly new mela names established by Govinda in his Samgraha-Cūḍa-Maṇi, the Kanakangi-Ratnangi system. The latter represents, excepting a few minor modifications, the modern system. It contains 72 krama sampurna (straight heptatonic) scales,the names of which conform with the katapayadi sankhyā (katapayādi numeration).

Numerous musicians and theorists have endeavored to adjust the names in order to make them conform to the numbers, an effort that has been in progress throughout the last two centuries. Today the system is well established if we take into consideration the exceptions mentioned before. The various conferences, particularly those of the Madras Music Academy, the All India Music Congresses, and the activities of the Music Department of the University of Madras have contributed considerably toward a final clarification of the complex system.

As we have mentioned before, South Indian music can be notated either in Nagari or in Tamil scripts. The Nagari script does not contain any rhythmic indications. Occasionally commas are employed at the ends of groups consisting of five to seven tone syllables which can be sung within one breath. The rhythm of the melody is indicated by an annotation at the head of the piece which states the tālam. The relationship between tone syllables and beats is regulated by the text.

The following is the beginning of a song in the first mela Kanakāngi and, according to the title annotation, should be performed in Triputa rhythm (3 + 2 + 2):

Melody: सा, निधनिसारिगारि, मगारिगारिसस, . . .

Text: चा णू र म ल यु ड़ॆ . . .

We notice that a long SA is written सा, a short one स, that a long

RI is written री , a short one रि , and so forth. The tone sylla-

bles are not provided with dots which indicate the use of mandra and

tara saptakas. As we already know, the tone material of Kanakangi

is C Db Ebb F G Ab Bbb c. The melody fragment stated above

can be transcribed as follows:

The only doubtful spot is the second SA (सा) which we transcribe as

a quarter note, in order to fit it into Triputa tāla. It is, of course,

possible, to lengthen the SA and shorten some of the following notes

accordingly; for instance

because the notational syllables allow several interpretations as far

as the rhythmic elaboration of the tāla is concerned.

The question of whether the second note (Bbb) is to be read a

seventh above the first C or a second below is answered by the fact

that Indian melodies, with very few exceptions, tend to use small in-

tervallic steps.

The notational system which uses Tamil syllables is more effi-

cient than the South Indian Nagari notation because the rhythmical

features can be denoted with greater clarity. The Tamil tone syllables

are:

SA ௶ [219]

RI ரி

GA	க
MA	ம
PA	ப
DHA	த
NI	நி

In addition to the frequently used tone syllables a system of Telugu letters is occasionally employed. It is weak in notating rhythmical features although it uses specific letters for short and long notes. The letters of this second system are:

	Short notes (♪)	Long notes (♩)
s(a)	స	సా
r(i)	రి	రీ
g(a)	గ	గా
m(a)	మ	మా
p(a)	ప	పా
dh(a)	ధ	ధా
n(i)	ని	నీ

We shall confine our discussion to the system which employs Tamil script. Tone syllables of this system representing notes of the lowest and highest octave registers are marked with dots below or above the syllables as is done in the notational system of North India.

Although the northern mātrā and the southern laghu denote the duration of a Western quarter note, there is a difference in the concept of rhythmic unit in northern and southern music. In the North a tone syllable notated without any additional signs represents the duration of one mātrā. In the South, however, a tone syllable without any additional signs represents the duration of a "durut," a drutam, which we interpret as an eighth note. Longer note values than this rhythmic unit of a drutam have to be indicated by additional signs as shown in the following chart:

	♪	♩	♩.	𝅗𝅥	𝅗𝅥‿♪	𝅗𝅥.	𝅗𝅥.‿♪	𝅝
SA	ஸ	ஸா	ஸா,	ஸா;	ஸா;,	ஸா;;	ஸா;;,	ஸா;;;
RI	ரி	ரீ	ரீ,	ரீ;	ரீ;,	ரீ;;	ரீ;;,	ரீ;;;
GA	க	கா	கா,	கா;	கா;,	கா;;	கா;;,	கா;;;
MA	ம	மா	மா,	மா;	மா;,	மா;;	ம;;,	மா;;;
PA	ப	பா	பா,	பா;	பா;,	பா;;	பா;;,	பா;;;
DHA	த	தா	தா,	தா;	தா;,	தா;;	தா;;,	தா;;;
NI	நி	நீ	நீ,	நீ;	நீ;,	நீ;;	நீ;;,	நீ;;;

Shorter note values than an ♪ are indicated by placing short horizontal lines below the tone syllables: ♫ (♪), ♫ (♪), and so forth, or, in recent notations, by placing one or more horizontal lines above the syllables; for instance, in Mela Dhirashankarabharanam (29):

, which reads:

Rests are notated by commas and semicolons:

	Western equivalent	
,	𝄿	(1/8)
;	𝄾	(1/4)
; ,	𝄾.	(3/8)
; ;	𝄾 𝄾	(2/4)
	and	
,	𝄿	(1/16)
,	𝄿	(1/32)

The notation of dotted notes uses commas:

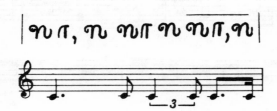

The notation of syncopations can be observed in the following:

and

Figure 40, following, is the first section (pallavi) of a song in Hanumattodi, the eighth mela. Its notes are C Db Eb F G Ab Bb c, the rhythm is Āditālam, 4 + 2 + 2 (laghus), or 8 + 4 + 4 ("duruts"):

Figure 40

We know that the horizontal line above a group of notes, for instance, in 𑀦𑁄 𑀢𑀭 , reduces the time values of the notes to half their durations. Although this group of notes could be notated as 𑀦𑁄 𑀢 (♫♩), South Indian musicians prefer to include the longer note in the group placed below the horizontal line by doubling its duration (𑀢𑀭). This method facilitates reading and avoids the risk of distorting, by misprinting, the length of the horizontal line.

If, in a subordinate rāgam, a melody uses F in descending and F# in ascending, it is notated simply as மமகரிகமபா. The notated tone syllables show no distinction between shuddha and prati MA (F#), both are indicated by ம (MA). The performer, however, knowing the required alterations, will interpret the notes in the correct manner. (In the following transcription we assume that க and ரி can be represented as E and D, respectively.)

In order to illustrate the diverse interpretations of South Indian tone syllables we show below a simple melody notated both in Nagari script (in the southern manner, without "komal" and "tīvra" indications), and in Tamil script, together with transcriptions referring to the melas Kanakāngi, Māyāmalavagaula, Hanumattodi, Harikambhoji, Kharaharapriya, Varunapriya, DhirashankarābhaBharanam, and Rāmapriya:

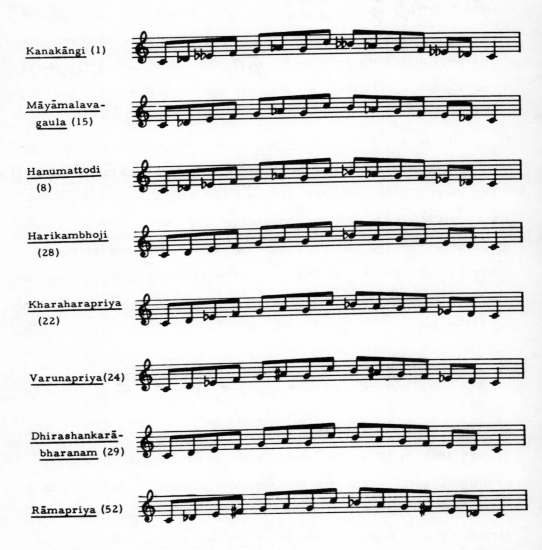

Figure 41, following, is the beginning of the first part (pallavi) of a Kirtanam, an art song, comparable to the northern Khyāl.[220] The rāgam is Mānavati (5) and the rhythm is Āditālam. The notes of Mānavati are C Db Ebb F G A B c:

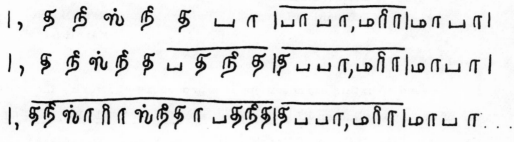

Figure 41

South Indian music theory uses separate names for three alterations of RI, GA, DHA, and NI, respectively, and two for shuddha and
prati MA:

C		SA
Db	Shuddha RI	
D, Ebb	Chatuśruti RI	or Shuddha GA
D#, Eb	Shatśruti RI	Sādhāraṇa GA
E		Antara GA
F	Shuddha MA	
F#	Prati MA	
G	PA	
Ab	Shuddha DHA	

A, Bbb	Chatusruti DHA	or	Shuddha NI
A#, Bb	Shatsruti DHA	or	Kaishiki NI
B			Kākali NI [2 21]
c		SA	

Based upon this arrangement is a procedure of altering the vowels of the tone syllables RI, GA, DHA, and NI to RA, RI, RU; GA GI, GU; DHA, DHI, DHU; and NA, NI, NU, respectively. The two MA, shuddha and prati, are denoted by MA and MI. This system is said to have had its origin with the seventeenth-century musician Govinda Dīkṣita of Tanjore. It may be of interest to note that a similar changing of the vowels was already in use in the seventh century A. D. It was found in an inscription discovered at Kuḍumiyamālai in the province of Pudukottai of the Madras Presidency. [222]

The following list demonstrates the written form of these vowel changes:

SA				C
RA				Db
RI		GA		D (Ebb)
RU		GI		Eb
		GU		E
MA				F
MI				F#
PA				G
DHA				Ab
DHI		NA		A (Bbb)
DHU		NI		Bb
		NU		B

In treatises which use Roman letters the twelve chromatic degrees have been expressed in the following manner:

s	C
r_1	Db
r_2	D
g_1	Eb
g_2	E
m_1	F
m_2	F#

and so forth.

A note which is extended to twice the value of a tone syllable is written as a capital letter. For instance:

$$s \quad r_1 \quad G_1 \quad m_2 \quad r_2 \quad S.$$

This would be transcribed as:

Another recent method of notating uses capital letters for the indication of the notes of mela Dhirashankarābharanam (29), which for all practical purposes is the same as the Western major scale. In this case the older basic scale of Kanakāngi is ignored and the notes of the Western major are adopted as "naturals." Chromatic alterations are shown by small letters. In this system the twelve chromatic notes are:

S	C
r	Db
R	D

Twelve Chromatic Notes (cont.)

g	Eb
G	E
M	F
m	F#
P	G
d	Ab
A	A
n	Bb
N	B

THE DRUM WORDS AND DRUM PHRASES OF NORTH INDIAN MUSIC

If we consider the term notation in its broadest sense the drum words (bols) and drum phrases (thekas) of Indian music, although not written down, may be added to the list of musical notations because the words and phrases represent a spoken and memorized system of fixed symbols which denote the various types and sequences of strokes performed by the drummers.

The drum in Indian art music has a different function from that of the drum in the West and is of infinitely greater importance. In the West the drum is used to emphasize accents or to intensify dynamic changes, or, as in Baroque music, to supply the bass part for the brass instruments. The Indian drum, however, is the "king among instruments." It accompanies the soloist (not on a subordinate level) throughout most of his performance and articulates the tāla with an amazing variety of strokes, occasionally even of great intricacy. The various drum strokes differ from each other not so much in pitch and intensity, as in quality and timbre.

Although India has produced an enormous number of drums (according to Curt Sachs, India has evolved more drums than the entire African continent), only two drum types occur in its art music: the older, the mridanga, and a type of more recent origin, the tabla pair.

The mridanga is mentioned in Sanskrit literature as early as 400 B.C. Its name means "earthen-" or "clay-drum" (Sanskrit: mrdānga; Hindi: mridanga; Tamil: mritangam; Prakrit: muinga; Pali: mutingo). Legend ascribes its invention to Brahma. Ganesha, the god with an elephant head, was supposed to have played it first when Mahadeva danced to celebrate his victory over the demon Tripurasura, the heretofore invincible one.

We find the drum depicted in Buddhist sculptures in Sanchi (first century A.D.) as well as in the paintings of the Ajanta Caves (A.D. 700). The mridanga of recent and present times has a wooden corpus.[223] Tanjore in South India is the center of the mridanga makers, who use the wood of the breadfruit tree (artocarpus integrifolia) or that of the Acacia Catechu, of the pterocarpus marsupinum, and of the pterocarpus santalinum. The body of the drum has the shape of two frusta of cones linked together with their broader bases. We must add here that in most cases the profile of the mridanga is not angular but gently curved. The drum heads on both sides, of slightly unequal sizes, are held and stretched by a crisscross of leather straps. The bigger skin is tuned to SA, the basic note of the rāga to be performed, and the smaller skin may be tuned either to the upper fourth or fifth, or even to the upper octave of SA. In modern practice we often observe that the smaller skin is tuned to SA while the bigger one produces a note that has a lower pitch and is not always distinct. The tuning of the smaller (right hand) drum head

is achieved by tightening the knots of the leather straps and by applying a paste consisting of flour and water [224] (āta) to the center of the
skin, which lowers the sound to the required pitch. The larger (left
hand) drum head is usually left bare; some players have the habit of
occasionally applying to it a paste consisting of boiled rice, ashes,
and water.

Some mridangas are provided with small, cylindrical wooden
tuning blocks which are wedged between corpus and straps. By shifting the blocks up and down the pitch of the drum head can be lowered
or raised, respectively.

The following, Figure 42, shows an average sized mridanga.

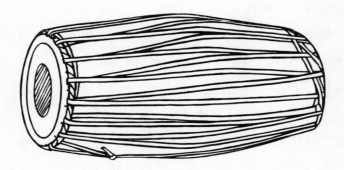

Figure 42

Today mridangas are used only in the performance of certain
tālas such as Tivratāl, Sultāl, Chautāl, Dhamār Tāl, and Jhaptāl. [225]
The latter tāla may be performed on the tabla pair (two small kettle
drums) as well. Dhrupad [226] songs must be accompanied invariably
on the mridanga, while khyāls [227] and music of lighter nature require
the popular tabla pair, two small kettle drums. Both mridanga [228]
and the tablas have practically the same playing technique except that
the mridanga is placed horizontally in front of the drummer while the
tablas stand vertically before him.

The tablas came to India with the Islamic invaders and gradually gained widespread popularity. Today they represent the most popular drum-type of India, with the exception of the southernmost districts of the peninsula, where the mridanga predominates. The prevalence of tablas, even in the South, is the reason that northern bols and thekas have found acceptance in the music of the South as well. One of the two drums, specifically called tabla[229] (Fig. 43), is played with the right hand while the other drum, called bayan ("left") or banya, is struck by the left. The corpus of the tabla is made of wood and is similar in shape to the mridanga, but smaller and shorter as shown in Figure 43.

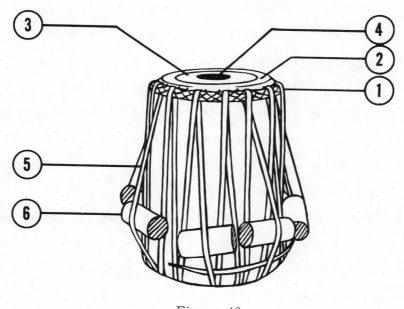

Figure 43

The drum head is called girwa or puri. The gajra (1) is a strip of leather that is twisted like a rope and holds together the tuning straps and the girwa. The got (2) is the thick leather border which covers the rim of the drum head. The rim itself is called chanti. The maidan (3) is the "open space" of the drum head, the space between the rim and the black center. The siyahi (4), which means "blackness" or "ink" is the circular patch of dried paste, more or less in the center of the drum head. The leather tuning straps (5) are the badh. The addu are six or eight small, wooden, cylindrical blocks wedged between corpus and badh. As already mentioned, the addu can be moved up and down with a hammer (usually a special hammer made of brass) in order to decrease or increase the tension of badh and drum head. (This moving of the addu is similar to the shifting of the wooden tuning blocks on some types of the mridanga.) If the addu are hammered upward, toward the drum head, the pitch of the drum is lowered and, conversely, if they are hammered downward, the pitch is raised. The ring-shaped cushions upon which both drums rest are called indhvi.

The tabla (dayan) is tuned invariably to SA. The tuning of the drum is done in the following manner: first the addus are hammered into their appropriate places (if necessary, the hammer is also applied to the gajra); then the right hand, held flat (with the fingers straight) and horizontal or slightly slanted toward the little finger, strikes the drum head; after the stroke, the fifth finger remains with its tip on the left half of the siyahi. This procedure creates a "harmonic" which tells the player whether the tuning is correct. Then the drum is turned horizontally about 90 degrees and the same testing is repeated until each quadrant of the drum head produces the correct pitch.

The corpus of the second drum of the tabla pair (bayan) has the shape of a kettle (Fig. 44). Originally it was made of clay; at the present time copper or brass is used.

If the bayan has a siyahi, the drummers place the paste (gila ata,

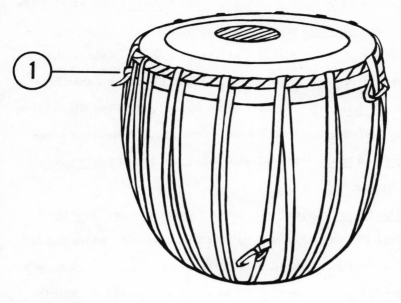

Figure 44

"wet flour") not in the center of the drum head, but slightly to one side of it. Musicians believe that the application of a small siyahi on the drum head of the bayan helps to achieve the gunj dar, the "echo effect." The bayan is tuned lower than the tabla; usually its sound is dull and indefinite in pitch. The bayan has no tuning blocks, and the tuning, if any, is done by tightening or loosening the knots in the badh. See (1) in Figure 44.

The tone of the two tablas is softer and more flexible than that of the mridanga. The tālas performed on the tabla pair are Tintāl (Tritāl), Tilvada, Dadra, and other popular rhythms.

As already indicated, Indian drums, with the exception of those used in primitive and folk music, are struck with one or more fingers. Some fingers may dampen the sound or create harmonics, and, in some strokes, the flat part or the heel of the hand is employed. Each drum stroke has its own name, a bol, and each tāla has its more or less fixed sequence of bols,[230] a theka. These thekas can be elaborated into numerous parands (variations).

Before describing the thekas, we shall have to consider the technique of drumming and present the various bols, the constituent elements of the thekas. We shall confine ourselves to the discussion of tabla playing because there are only a few minor differences between mridanga and tabla strokes, and today the art of tabla playing predominates by far.

The tablaji (tabla player) sits on the floor in a cross-legged fashion; the right knee is supposed to touch the ground, while the left leg (from foot to knee) is placed in a vertical or slightly oblique position. The tabla (dayan) rests in front of the right shinbone, and the bayan stands in front of the left knee of the drummer.

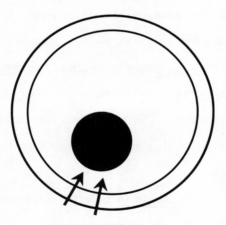

Figure 45

Two important strokes — one a version of the other — are performed on the bayan. GHE (KHE) is the bol for the so-called khula (khola) bayan, the "open bayan." It is performed by the left hand either by the second, or third finger, or by the second and third fingers held close together, striking the maidan at a spot between siyahi and chanti where the maidan is at its narrowest.

The finger (or both fingers) strikes the maidan in such a manner that the finger tip performs a movement toward the palm of the hand. The drum head is struck for a fraction of a second and then is allowed to vibrate freely. The heel of the striking (left) hand rests either on the rim of the drum, or, in a second version of GHE, it slides toward the vibrating center of the drum head and presses the maidan for a brief moment. This pressure raises the pitch of the vibrating skin. As soon as the pressure is relaxed the pitch falls. This second type of GHE is generally combined with a simultaneous stroke on the tabla.

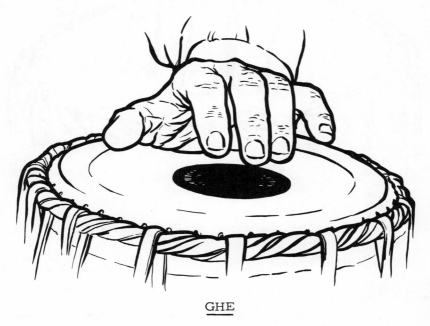

GHE

Figure 46

GE (KE), is the bol for the band bayan, the "closed bayan." The spot struck is again between siyahi and chanti (see Figure 45). When playing GE, the performer allows the heel of his left hand to remain on the rim of the drum while with his second, third, fourth, and fifth fingers slightly curved and held closely together, he strikes the maidan. All four fingers remain on the drum head after the stroke.

The thumb is bent toward the palm and thus fingers and thumb obstruct any vibrating of the drum head. The sound created is dull, dry, and "closed."

Figure 47: GE

Basic Strokes on the Tabla (Right Hand)

An important simple stroke on the Tabla (Dayan) is DIN (TIN, DIN, TIN, DI, TI). These bols all represent the same stroke. The second finger held stiffly above the drum head is thrown against the maidan and strikes it with its tip and immediately snaps back to its original position. At the same time the third finger, slightly bent, strikes the space between siyahi and maidan and remains on the drum head. The fourth and fifth fingers together with the third finger, with lesser force, fall upon the maidan and rim, respectively, and remain there. The thumb and the heel of the hand do not touch the drum.

Figure 48: DIN

TA: the tip of the second finger strikes the border line between chanti and maidan with greater force than in DIN and remains on the drum head. The third finger stays slightly lifted while the fourth and fifth fingers are set down on the maidan and rim, respectively. The heel of the hand does not touch the drum.

Figure 49: TA

NA is produced in the same manner as TA, but the striking force of the second finger is less marked. The tip of the straight, stiff second finger strikes only the chanti and stays there. NA is more popular with the tablajis than TA and is frequently confused with it.

NA

Figure 50

TIT (TID) is produced by the second, third, and fourth fingers jointly, all striking the center of the siyahi. These three fingers remain on the drum head, creating a "closed" (dull) sound. The thumb, fifth finger, and the heel of the hand do not touch the drum (See Fig. 51).

LA is produced by the tip of the fourth finger, which gently strikes the border of the siyahi. After the stroke, the finger remains on the drum head, thus creating a "closed" sound. Some musicians, particularly those belonging to the Delhi school, do not recognize this stroke, which is favored by drummers of the Lucknow school.

TIT

Figure 51

LA

Figure 52

DI: the flat hand is slightly curved, the fingers and the palm of the hand creating an angle of about 120 to 150 degrees. The whole hand moves in such a manner that the part of the chanti which is nearest to the player is struck by the fleshy bases of the second, third, fourth, and fifth fingers — or in some instances only by the second and third fingers. The finger tips do not touch the drum at all. The sound created is "open."

A second version of DI, performed in and around Bombay, is often called DUN (TUN) or DU (TU). It is performed in the same manner as DI except that in this version the tips of the stiffly held fingers strike the siyahi for a fraction of a second. After the stroke the drum head vibrates freely and creates a gentle, "open" sound. The bol DUN, or DU, imitates the sound very adequately.

DI

Figure 53

Simple, combined strokes on the tabla and bayan are used to

produce DHIN (DHIN, or DHI). In each of these the sound is produced by a simultaneous striking of DIN on the tabla and GHE on the bayan.

DHA is produced by a simultaneous performance of TA on the tabla and GHE on the bayan.

DHIT (DHID) is produced by a simultaneous performance of TIT on the tabla and GHE on the bayan.

Special complex strokes on the tabla alone are used to produce the sound of TE-TE. Two strokes, each having the duration of half a

Figure 54: TE

mātrā (a durut) (♪♩) are required. TE (or T, त) is performed by striking the center of the siyahi with the tip of the third finger, which remains on the drum head for the duration of half a mātrā. This stroke is followed by TE (or T, ट), which is executed by turning the hand to the left around an imaginary horizontal axis which runs from the elbow to the tip of the third finger. While the hand turns from right to left the second finger strikes the siyahi with its tip. This stroke, too, has the duration of half a mātrā. Thumb and other fingers do not touch the drum.

$\underline{TE}$

Figure 55

Figures 54 and 55 exaggerate the rotating movement of the hand, which is slanted to the right in $\underline{TE}$ and to the left in $\underline{TE}$. In reality the turning is usually only a slight twist, just enough to enable the player to perform both strokes smoothly in an even tempo.

There are two other methods of performing $\underline{TE}$-$\underline{TE}$. One is to hold the fingers straight and rigid and roll the hand from right to left, thus allowing first the right side of the tip of the third finger, then, after the roll, the left side of the tip of the second finger to strike the center of the siyahi. The other method which must not be applied in a dugan (the fast "stretta" of a song[231]) involves rolling the hand with the rigidly held fingers from right to left, as in the previously described method, but striking the siyahi at $\underline{TE}$ with the thumb.

TE

Figure 56

TE

Figure 57

In the following bols T (तं) must be performed on the siyahi:

TIT: tabla

bayan

KAT: tabla

bayan

In the following set of strokes the use of both hands on both drums is shown. Although we are still considering the strokes on the tabla, we add the bayan strokes in order to present as complete a picture as possible.

TAKAT: tabla

bayan

TAK: tabla

bayan

TAKA: tabla

bayan

TIRIK: tabla

bayan

TIRIKIT: tabla

bayan

KITTIK: tabla

bayan

TITKAT: tabla

bayan

KITIR: tabla

bayan

DHIT: tabla

                  bayan

TADHIN: tabla

                  bayan

TADHINNA: tabla

                  bayan

TADHA: tabla

                  bayan

In the following bols, T (त) is to be struck on the chanti:

TIT (with two त) : the first
T is to be struck on the chanti,
the second on the siyahi: tabla

                  bayan

TĀ: tabla

                  bayan

DHADHIN: tabla

                  bayan

TAG: tabla   (TA+ GE)

                  bayan

TIGAN: tabla

                  bayan

GITA   tabla

                  bayan

TAT: in this bol the first T
is struck on the chanti, the
second on the bayan: tabla

                  bayan

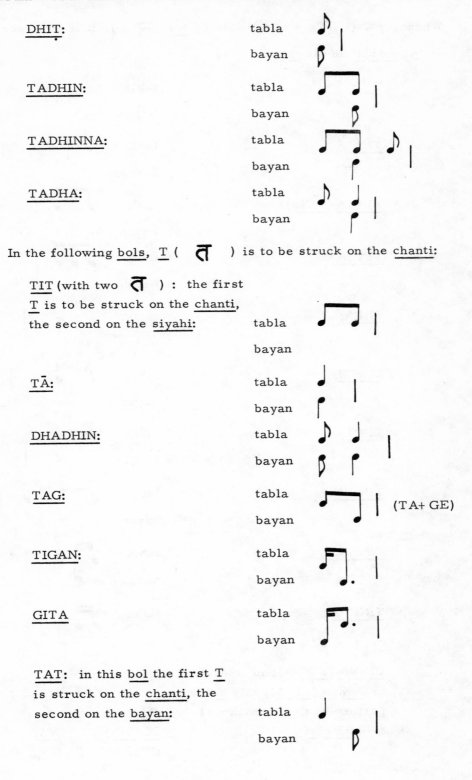

Whenever $\underline{T}$ (तं) is followed by $\underline{N}$ (न), it is to be performed on the maidan of the tabla:

TIN: tabla
                               bayan

TĪN: tabla
                               bayan

TĪNNA (TĪNA):   tabla
                               bayan

TINNAN: tabla
                               bayan

TININ̄:   tabla
                               bayan

TINEH: tabla
                               bayan

TING: tabla
                               bayan

TINGIN: tabla
                               bayan

TĪNGAN: tabla
                               bayan

TINING: tabla
                               bayan

DINNA (TINNA): in contrast
to TĪNNA (TĪNA), this bol is
performed to the rhythm of
two mātrās:

DI (DIN)   NA
(Fig. 48)   (Fig. 50)

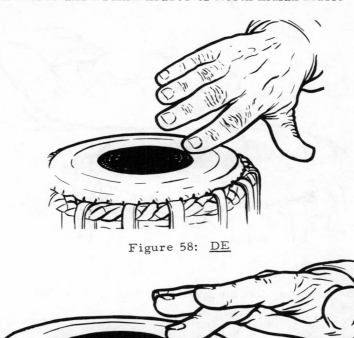

Figure 58: <u>DE</u>

Figure 59: <u>NA</u>

<u>DENA</u> is performed to the rhythm of two <u>durut</u> (♪♪) in the following manner. First the tip of the straight second finger hits the <u>maidan</u> of the <u>tabla</u> on a spot nearest to the player in such a way that the hand, during the stroke, tilts to the left. Thus when the second finger strikes, the third, fourth, and fifth fingers are raised. As soon as the tip of the second finger has struck the maidan, it glides on the drum head to the left; then the hand tilts to the right and allows the tip of the third finger to strike the <u>maidan</u> on the same spot where the second finger had struck before. Thereby the second finger is removed from the drum head. Both phases of <u>DENA</u> are performed in a smooth, rolling movement (See above, Figs. 58 and 59).

Figure 60: TA

In the following list the first N of bols 2, 3, 4, 10, 11 and the last N of bols 1, 5, 6, 7, 8, 9, 12 are to be performed on the chanti while the other N, in the bols which have two N, is to be performed on the maidan:

1.	DINA (DENA)	7.	DHAGHIN
2.	DIHIN	8.	GIDGIN
3.	DINGIN	9.	DHINA
4.	TINGIN	10.	DHININ
5.	TAGIN	11.	DHINGHIN
6.	TAGHIN	12.	GHIDGHIN

DENENA is performed to the rhythm of three durut: DENA ♫, and NA ♪ . DENA is produced on the maidan as already illustrated, the subsequent NA on the chanti (Figs. 58, 59, and 50).

TALE is performed to the rhythm of three durut (♫ ♪) by the fifth, fourth, and second fingers in succession. First the fifth finger strikes with its tip the left side of the siyahi, then the fourth finger tip gently touches the maidan while the fifth finger is raised; after these two motions the hand rotates to the left and the tip of the second finger strikes the left side of the siyahi.

LE

Figure 61

NARE is performed to the rhythm of one mātrā and on one durut:

♩ ♪ .
NA RE

NA is produced with the tip of the second finger (Fig. 50); then RE (or RA=LA) is produced with the tip of the third finger on the edge of the siyahi (Fig. 52). The player has to keep in mind, however, that in this particular instance the third finger is to be used.

TĪĪ is a variation of TIN (Fig. 48). In this bol the stroke lasts only one durut and has to be followed by a rest of one mātrā: ♪ 𝄾 |.

TIE is performed in the same manner as TĪĪ but has half the duration of the former bol: ♪ 𝄾 (Fig. 48).

TATE requires two durut: TA (Fig. 49) and TE (Fig. 54).

TATA requires two durut: TA (Fig. 49) occurs twice in succession (♫).

TATETE requires three durut: TA (Fig. 54) and TE (same as TA, Fig. 55).

DIDI requires two durut: two DI (Fig. 48) are performed in succession.

DIDINA requires three durut: DIDI (Fig. 48, twice) and NA (Fig. 50) (♩♩ ♪).

NANA requires two durut: NA (Fig. 50) performed twice in succession.

TADIN requires one durut and one mātrā: TA (♪ , Fig. 49) and DIN (♩ , Fig. 48).

DINANA requires three durut: DI (♪ , Fig. 48) is followed by NANA (♩♩ , Fig. 50, twice).

Common Combined Strokes on Tabla and Bayan

In order to simplify our explanations we place the numbers of the illustrations shown previously below the corresponding syllables of the bols:

KE NA (GE NA)		tabla	
47 50		bayan	
TA GE		tabla	
49 47		bayan	
NA GE		tabla	
50 47		bayan	
KA TA		tabla	
47 54		bayan	

(TA, the same as TE, Fig. 54, is performed without turning the hand; KA is the same as KE.)

KE TA		tabla	
47 49		bayan	
TIN GE (DIN GE)		tabla	
48 47		bayan	
TA GE NA		tabla	
49 47 59		bayan	

NA GE NA   tabla
50 47 59   bayan

TA KE TE   tabla
55 47 54   bayan

NA KE TE   tabla
50 47 54   bayan

TA KU   tabla
54 47   bayan

(TA, being TE, Fig. 54, is usually performed by the
third and fourth fingers jointly striking the center of
the siyahi; the turning of the wrist is not required. The
bol KU, the same as KE, or GE, indicates the "closed
bayan," Fig. 47.)

DI GE NA (TI GE NA)   tabla
48 47 50   bayan
        (or 59)

DI GE NA   tabla
48 47 50 (or 59)   bayan

DE NA GE NA   tabla
58 59 47 50   bayan

TI NA GE   tabla
48 50 47   bayan

GE DI   tabla
47 53   bayan

GE DE   tabla
47 53   bayan

DI GE (TI GE)   tabla
48 47   bayan

DI NA GE NA (TI NA GE NA)   tabla
48 50 47 50   bayan

KE LE DIN   tabla
47 52 48   bayan

KE	LE	DI		tabla
47	52	48		bayan

KE	LE	TĀ	NA	tabla
47	52	49	50	bayan

GE	GE	NA	GE	tabla
47	47	50	47	bayan

KE	LE			tabla
47	52			bayan

KE	LE	NA	KE (GE LE NA GE)	tabla
47	52	50	47	bayan

TE	RE	KA		tabla
54	61	47		bayan

(TE and RE, the same as LE, are to be performed without the rolling movement of the hand.)

TE	RE	KA	TA	tabla
54	62	47	54	bayan

(In this bol RE is to be performed as indicated in Fig. 62: the second finger strikes the boundary line between the siyahi and the maidan):

Figure 62: RE

KE	TE	tabla
47	55	bayan

KE TE TA KA   tabla
47 55 54 47   bayan

TE TE KA TA   tabla
54 55 47 54   bayan

TA KA   tabla
54 47   bayan

(TA can be substituted for TE, Fig. 55.)

TA GE   tabla
60 47   bayan

GE TA   tabla
47 49   bayan

GE DE GE NA   tabla
47 53 47 59   bayan

(NA can also be performed with the fourth finger in a
straight movement instead of as shown in Fig. 59, where
the third finger is employed.)

GE DI NA   tabla
47 48 50   bayan

KA DHE TE   tabla
47 54   55   bayan
    46

KE LĀ NA   tabla
47 52 50   bayan

KE LE DHĀ   tabla
47 52 49   bayan
        46

KE LE DHA   tabla
47 52 49   bayan
        46

KE LE DHĀ NA   tabla
47 52 49   50   bayan
        46

KE LE DHIT   tabla
47 52 51   bayan
        46

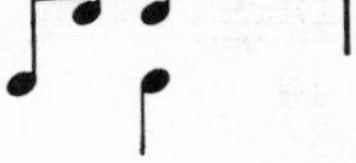

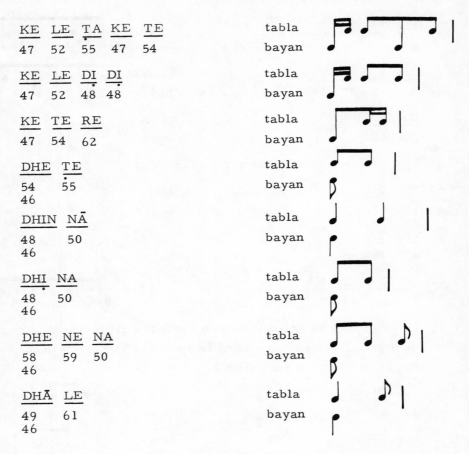

KE	LE	TA	KE	TE	tabla	
47	52	55	47	54	bayan	

KE	LE	DI	DI	tabla	
47	52	48	48	bayan	

KE	TE	RE	tabla	
47	54	62	bayan	

DHE TE — tabla / bayan
54 55
46

DHIN NĀ — tabla / bayan
48 50
46

DHI NA — tabla / bayan
48 50
46

DHE NE NA — tabla / bayan
58 59 50
46

DHĀ LE — tabla / bayan
49 61
46

(If DHĀLE is followed by DHITETE or TATETE, LE, Fig. 61, can be replaced by LA, Fig. 52, in order to facilitate the smooth succession of DHĀ and LA.)

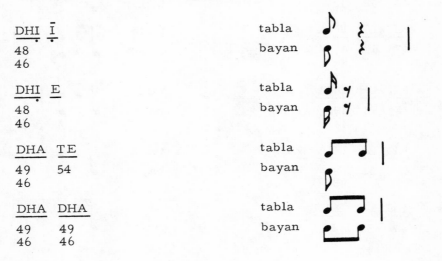

DHI Ī — tabla / bayan
48
46

DHI E — tabla / bayan
48
46

DHA TE — tabla / bayan
49 54
46

DHA DHA — tabla / bayan
49 49
46 46

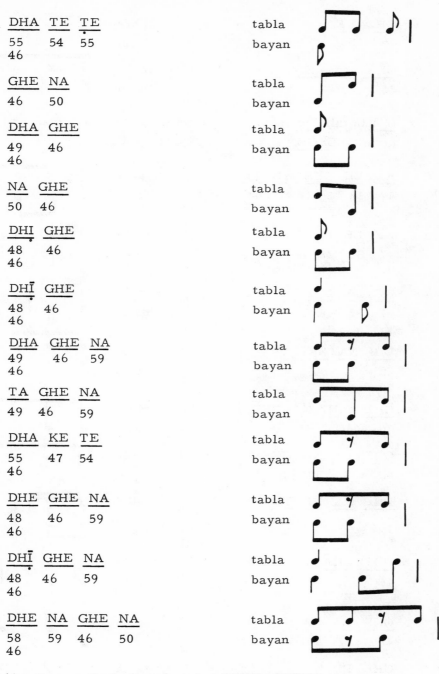

DHA	TE	TE		tabla
55	54	55		bayan
46				

GHE	NA		tabla
46	50		bayan

DHA	GHE		tabla
49	46		bayan
46			

NA	GHE		tabla
50	46		bayan

DHI	GHE		tabla
48	46		bayan
46			

DHĪ	GHE		tabla
48	46		bayan
46			

DHA	GHE	NA		tabla
49	46	59		bayan
46				

TA	GHE	NA		tabla
49	46	59		bayan

DHA	KE	TE		tabla
55	47	54		bayan
46				

DHE	GHE	NA		tabla
48	46	59		bayan
46				

DHĪ	GHE	NA		tabla
48	46	59		bayan
46				

DHE	NA	GHE	NA		tabla
58	59	46	50		bayan
46					

(Another method of performing DHENAGHENA is:
48 50 46 50.)
46

DHE	NA	GHE		tabla
48	50	46		bayan
46				

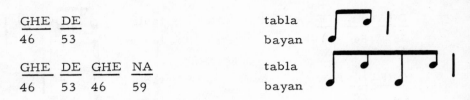

GHE	DE			tabla
46	53			bayan

GHE	DE	GHE	NA	tabla
46	53	46	59	bayan

(NA in this bol should be performed in the same manner as in GEDEGENA; see page 243.)

KE	LE	DHA	KE	TE	tabla
47	52	55	47	54	bayan
		46			

KE	LE	DHIN	tabla
47	52	48	bayan
		46	

KE	LE	DHI	tabla
47	52	48	bayan
		46	

DHI	NA	NA	tabla
48	50	50	bayan
46			

GHE	GHE	NA	GHE	tabla
46	46	50	46	bayan

GHE	LE	NA	GHE	tabla
46	52	50	46	bayan

DHE	RE	KE	TE	tabla
54	62	47	54	bayan
46				

GHE	DHĀ	tabla
46	49	bayan
	46	

GHE	LA	NA	tabla
46	52	50	bayan

GHE	DĪ	tabla
46	48	bayan

GHE	NA	GHE	tabla
46	50	46	bayan

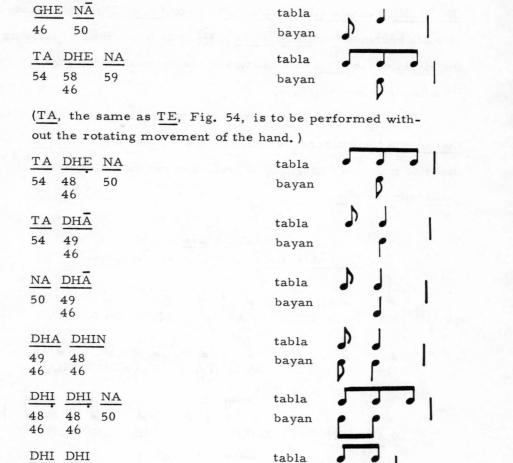

GHE NĀ		tabla	
46	50	bayan	

TA	DHE	NA	tabla
54	58	59	bayan
	46		

(TA, the same as TE, Fig. 54, is to be performed without the rotating movement of the hand.)

TA	DHE	NA	tabla
54	48	50	bayan
	46		

TA	DHĀ		tabla
54	49		bayan
	46		

NA	DHĀ		tabla
50	49		bayan
	46		

DHA	DHIN		tabla
49	48		bayan
46	46		

DHI	DHI	NA	tabla
48	48	50	bayan
46	46		

DHI	DHI		tabla
48	48		bayan
46	46		

GHE	NA	LA	NA (GHINALANA)	tabla
46	50	52	50	bayan

We may add that musicians often use the bols NA (Fig. 50) and TA (Fig. 49) in strokes which have the duration of one mātrā. TA (Fig. 60) is generally used to indicate the sām. The bols NA (Fig. 59) and TA (Figs. 54, 55, and 57) frequently occur in strokes which have the duration of one durut.

Occasionally the spellings of certain bols cause confusion: DIN may become TU+GHE, or TU alone; GA may become KA, KI, KE, and

GHE. DDHI can be GHE+TA ($\overline{c}$), or GHE+TIN; and DHA occasionally becomes NA+GHE. TTI (हि) is performed by striking the siyahi of the tabla with the tips of the second, third, fourth, and fifth fingers close together.

After these introductory remarks we are ready to consider the thekas, the "drum phrases" or chains of bols within an āvarta. In order to maintain uniformity of presentation, we shall begin each theka with the sām.

The Thekas
TINTĀL (TRITĀL, TETĀLA), on tablas:

The third of these three versions, (c), is an amateurish way of drumming Tintāl. Musicians, if they wish to have a joke, order the tablaji to play his "famous" Tintāl theka of NA DHIN DHIN NA. The drummer will, of course, begin with DHA DHIN DHIN DHA.

Qaidas[232] in Tintāl (Tritāl)

A qaida is a fixed elaboration of a tāla which provides the basic material for complex variations. A very simple qaida in Tritāl is:

| DHA | GHE | NA | GHE | DI | NA | KE | NA | | DHA | GHE | NA | GHE | DI | NA | KE | NA |
| X | | | | • | | | | | 2 | | | | • | | | |

| TA | GE | NA | GE | DI | NA | KE | NA | | DHA | GHE | NA | GHE | DI | NA | KE | NA |
| o | | | | • | | | | | 3 | | | | • | | | |

After having performed this qaida, the drummer returns to the original theka DHA DHIN DHIN DHA.

Occasionally two qaidas are performed in succession. The term for this procedure is dohra.[233] Thus a dohra always extends for two āvartas. The bols and rhythmic structure remain unaltered except that if the first āvarta begins with an open DHA, the second āvarta will begin with a closed TA.

A palta[234] is a variation of a dohra. It usually shows different bols only in one vibhāga, while the rest of the āvarta remains the same as in the dohra. Sometimes one can observe a palta of a palta, that is, a palta which is altered either in one or two vibhāgas.

A qaida (in Tritāl), its dohra and palta, and a palta of the palta are shown in the following examples:

QAIDA

| DHA | TETEKATA | DHA | KATA | GHENA | KATA | GHENA | DINA | KENA |
| X | • | | | | | | • | |

| TA | TETEKATA | TA | KATA | GHENA | KATA | GHENA | DINA | KENA | (DHA) |
| o | | | | | | • | | | X |

DOHRA

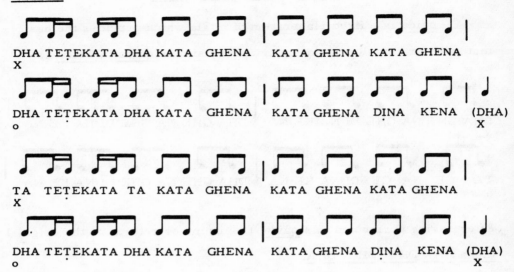

DHA TEṬEKATA DHA KATA GHENA KATA GHENA KATA GHENA
X

DHA TEṬEKATA DHA KATA GHENA KATA GHENA DINA KENA (DHA)
o   X

TA TEṬEKATA TA KATA GHENA KATA GHENA KATA GHENA
X

DHA TEṬEKATA DHA KATA GHENA KATA GHENA DINA KENA (DHA)
o   X

PALTA

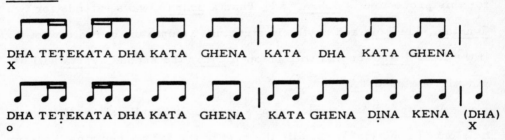

DHA TEṬEKATA DHA KATA GHENA KATA DHA KATA GHENA
X

DHA TEṬEKATA DHA KATA GHENA KATA GHENA DINA KENA (DHA)
o   X

PALTA OF PALTA

DHA TEṬEKATA DHA KATA GHENA DINA KENA DHA TEṬEKATA DHA
X

KATA GHENA DINA KENA KATA GHENA DINA KENA
o

TA TEṬEKATA TA KATA GENA DINA KENA DHA TEṬEKATA DHA
X

KATA GHENA DINA KENA KATA GHENA DINA KENA (DHA)
o   X

In addition to the numerous qaidas and their modifications we have to mention the gat and gat paran. The gat is a variation performed at twice the original speed, and the gat paran is four times faster than the original. Examples of two gat and one gat paran are shown below:

GAT (in Tritāl)

Another gat in Tritāl is:

GAT

KATA   GHEGHE   NAGHE   DHENA   DHAGHE   TEREKA   DINA   KENA
X

DHAGHE   TEREKA   DHINA   GHENA   DHAGHE   TEREKA   DINA   KENA
o

DIN   TA   KELE   TA   TAGE   TEREKA   DINA   KENA
X

TENA   GENA   DHENAGHENA   NAGENA   DHAGHE   TEREKA   DINA   KENA
o

KATA   GHEGHE   NA GHE   DHENA   DHAGHE   TEREKA   DINA   KENA
X

DHAGHE   TEREKA   DHINA   GHENA·   DHAGHE   TEREKA   DINA   KENA   (DH
o   X

GAT PARAN

DHA DHETE TETEGHELE NAGHETA KETE   DHA DHETE TETEGHELE NAGHETA KETE
X

DHA DHETE TETEGHELE NAGHETA KETE   DHATA   KETE   DHA
o

DHETETETE GHELENAGE TAKE TEDHA   GE   DI   KAT   TA   DHA
X

TETE   KATA   GHEDHE   GHENA   DHADHETE TETEGHELE NAGHETA KETE
o

DHA DHETE TETEGHELE NAGHETA KETE   DHA DHETE TETEGHELE NAGHETA KETE
X

DHA   DHETETETE GHELENAGHE TAKE   TEDHA
o

GHE   DI   KAT   TA DHA   TETE   KATA   GHEDHE   GHENA
X

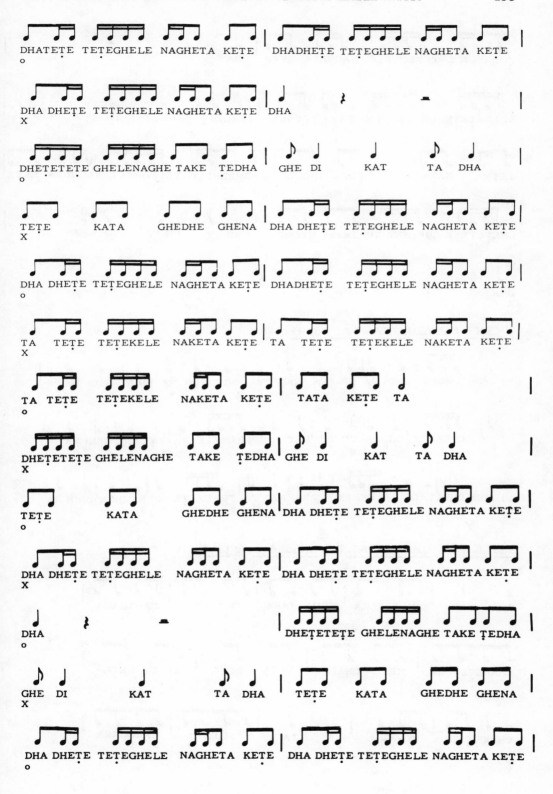

DHATETE TETEGHELE NAGHETA KETE   DHADHETE TETEGHELE NAGHETA KETE

DHA DHETE TETEGHELE NAGHETA KETE DHA

DHETETETE GHELENAGHE TAKE TEDHA   GHE DI   KAT   TA DHA

TETE   KATA   GHEDHE GHENA   DHA DHETE TETEGHELE NAGHETA KETE

DHA DHETE TETEGHELE NAGHETA KETE   DHADHETE   TETEGHELE NAGHETA KETE

TA   TETE   TETEKELE NAKETA KETE   TA   TETE   TETEKELE NAKETA KETE

TA TETE   TETEKELE   NAKETA KETE   TATA   KETE   TA

DHETETETE GHELENAGHE   TAKE   TEDHA GHE DI   KAT   TA DHA

TETE   KATA   GHEDHE GHENA DHA DHETE TETEGHELE NAGHETA KETE

DHA DHETE TETEGHELE   NAGHETA KETE   DHA DHETE TETEGHELE NAGHETA KETE

DHA   DHETETETE GHELENAGHE TAKE TEDHA

GHE DI   KAT   TA DHA   TETE   KATA   GHEDHE GHENA

DHA DHETE TETEGHELE   NAGHETA KETE   DHA DHETE TETEGHELE NAGHETA KETE

DHA DHEṬE TEṬEGHELE NAGHETA KEṬE DHA
X

DHEṬETEṬE GHELENAGHE TAKE ṬEDHA GHE DI KAT TA DHA
o

TEṬE KATA GHEDHA GHENA DHADHEṬE TEṬEGHELE NAGHETA KEṬE
X

DHEṬETEṬE GHELENAGHE TAKE ṬEDHA GHE DI KAT TA DHA
o

DHA
X

THEKA OF ADACHAUTĀL (on tablas):

a) DHI TEREKA DHIN NA DIN NA KAT TA DHIN DHIN NA DHIN DHIN NA
X   2   o   3   o   4   o

b) DHI TEREKETE DHI NA TU NA KAT TA TEREKETE DHI NA DHIN DHIN NA
X   2   o   3   o   4   o

c) DHIN DHIN TAGE TEREKEṬE TU NA KAT TA TEREKEṬE DHI NA DHIN DHIN NA
X   2   o   3   o   4   o

THEKA OF BRĀHMTĀL (on mridanga or tablas):

DHA TAT DHINA NAKA DHINA NAKA TITIKATA GADEGANA
X   o   2   3   o

DHAKEṬE DHA KEṬE DHADHA KEṬE KEṬE KEṬE KEṬE
4   5   6   o

DHAKE TEDHA NA DHA DIN TA TITIKATA GADEGENA
7   8   9   10   o

THEKA OF CHAUTĀL (mainly on mridanga or pakhawaj):

DHA DHA DIN TA KAT DHA DIN TA TEṬEKAṬA GHEDEGHENA
X   o   2   o   3 ·   4

or:

DHA DHA DIN TA KEṬA DHA DIN TA TEṬEKAṬA GADEGANA
X   o   2   o   3 ·   4

(1) DIN in this theka is generally performed as TU+GHE.

(2) DE is performed as TU or TIN.

(3) GA is performed as GHE.

THEKA OF DADRA TĀL (on tablas):

a) DHA DHIN NA DHA TU NA
   X   o

b) DHIN DHIN DHA DHA TIN NA
   X   o

c) DHIN TI DHA DHA TI NA
   X ·   o   ·

Version (a) is the one most commonly used.

THEKA OF DHAMĀR TĀL is performed mainly on mridanga and pakhawaj, although at the present time tablas are occasionally used.

a) KA DDHI TA DHI TA TA TA KI TA KI TA TA
  X   2 o   · 3 ·

b) KA DDHI TA DHI TA DHA GA TTI TA TA ṬA TA
  X   2 o   · 3 ·

DDHI is performed as GHE+ṬA (or ṬE, ट).

Occasionally musicians hold the view that Dhamār Tāl has only seven

mātrās (fourteen duruts). The effect is nearly the same because the

theka will contain the same number of bols as in the version with four-

teen mātrās; the only difference is that in the seven-mātrā theka the

bols are slightly altered to:

THEKA OF DIPCHANDI TĀL (on tablas):

Dipchandi Tāl is very popular and occurs frequently in light songs in

conjunction with various rāgas — Kafi, Sindhura, Khamaj, Pilu, and

others.

THEKA OF EKTĀL (on tablas)

The theka of this popular tāla can be represented in two different ways:

(a) as shown on page 191, and (b) with four mātrās in each of the

three vibhāgas, without a khali beat. The omission of khali indicates

that the theka is used in light music where sām and khali are of little

importance. Below follow three thekas of Ektāl in their common,

popular forms (type b):

a) DHA DHIN DHA DHA   DI NA KAT TA ⁻DHA DHA TI NA
   X   2   3

b) DHIN DHIN DHAGE TRAKA TU NA KAT TA ⁻DHIN TRAKA DHIN NA
   X   2   3

c) DHIN DHIN TAGE TEREKETE TU NA KAT TA DHA GE TEREKETE
   X   2   3

KAT is performed on the bayan by striking the rim opposite the player
with the tips of the second, third, fourth, and fifth fingers joined.
TRAKA (actually TEREKA) is performed on the tabla by striking the
siyahi first with the fourth, then the third, and lastly with the second
finger tip. The heel of the hand does not touch the drum:

TE RE KA

THEKA OF JHAMPA TĀLA (JHAPTĀL) (tabla version):

DHI NA DHI DHI NA TI NA DHI DHI NA
X   2   o   3

The mridanga (or pakhawaj) theka of this tāla differs considerably
from the tabla theka. It is:

DHA – DHA GI KI TA KADA DHA KI TA
X   2   o   3

GI, KI, and KA denote the same "closed" stroke on the larger drum
head; DHA and TA are performed in the same manner as on the tablas.

THEKA OF JHUMRA (on tablas):

a) DHIN NA TEREKA DHIN NA DHIN NA KAT TA TEREKA DHIN NA DHIN NA
   X   2   o   3

b) DHI   DHA TRAKA DHI DHI DHAGI TRAKA TI   TA TRAKA DHI DHI DHAGI TRAKA
   X   2   o   3

c) DHIN DHA TEREKETE DHIN DHIN DHAGE TEREKETE TIN TA   TEREKETE
   X   2   o

DHIN DHIN DHAGE. TEREKETE
3

THEKA OF PANJABI TĀLA (on tablas):

This tāla is a fast variant of Tintāl (Tritāl); it is generally used in light music. The difference between Panjabi and Tintāl can be observed in the bols:

a) DHA DHI GHE DHA DHA TI GE TA TA TI GHE DHA DHA DHI GHE DHA
   X   2   o   3

b) DHA DHA DHIN TRAKA DHIN   DHA DHA DHIN TRAKA DHIN
   X   2

TA TA TIN TRAKA DHIN   DHA DHA DHIN TRAKA DHIN
o   3

THEKA OF RŪPAK (RŪPAKA TĀLA) (on tablas):

a) TIN NA   TEREKA DHIN NA   DHIN NA
   X   2   3

b) TIN   TAKU DHI Ī GHE DHA DHA
   X   2   3

c) TIN TIN NA   DHI NA   DHI NA
   X   2   3

d) DHI DHA TRAKA DHI DHI   DHA TRAKA
   X   2   3

THEKA OF SHIKAR TĀLA (on pakhawaj or mridanga):

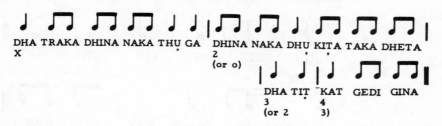

THU AND DHU are performed as TU+GHE; DHE is DHI, and GI is GE.

THEKA OF SULTĀL (on pakhawaj or mridanga):

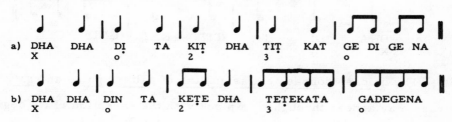

THEKA OF TILVADA TĀLA (TIRAMBA TĀLA) (on tablas):

THEKA OF TIVRA TĀLA (on tablas):

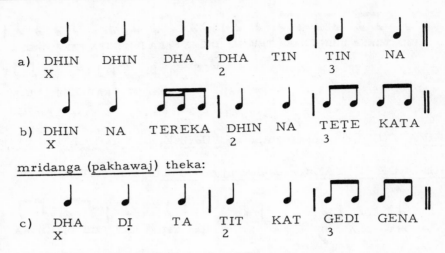

The qaidas, dohras, paltas, paltas of paltas, gats, and gat parans may appear throughout a piece with the exception of its beginning and its end. The opening drum phrase, called peshkar, is a particular qaida (or half a qaida) which can begin with the sām or the khāli. The khāli requires a "closed" sound while the sām has to be indicated by an "open" sound. If the peshkar begins with the khāli, the drummer has to be sure that the following sām is provided with a DHA. A typical peshkar is:

DHI GHE NA DHA GHE DI NA NA   TI GE NA DHA GHE DI NA NA

The last āvarta of a piece, called mohra (or mukhra), may contain a variety of bols and is of interest for its rhythmic structure: a brief rhythmic phrase has to appear three times in succession in such a manner that its final stroke coincides with the concluding sām. This repeated phrase is called tia and is applied in all tālas.

A tia (in the mohra) of Tintāl is shown in the following:

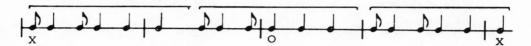

A tia may also occur within only the last two vibhāgas of an āvarta.
Examples (of Tintāl) are:

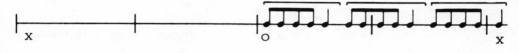

or:

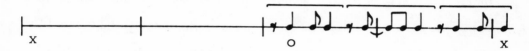

A tia in the mohra of dadra tāl would be:

or:

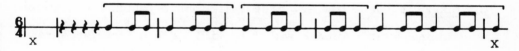

Occasionally musicians make a distinction between the terms
mohra and mukhra. A mohra invariably contains a tia while a mukhra
may be a qaida which concludes a piece but does not include a tia.

The closing section of many Indian art songs consists of a fast
stretta, the so-called dugan, often in a different tāla than that of the
preceding melody. For instance, if the song is in Dipchandi Tāl, the
dugan may begin in Tritāl and close in Keherwa Tāl, a tāla consisting
of eight mātrās, without a khāli beat, and having a theka such as

DHA DHIN NA TIN, TA TA DHIN NA; or DHA DHIN NA TIN, NA KA DHIN — .
X   2   X   2

If at the end of the dugan every note is shortened to one third of its original value, the diminution is called ad. The ad usually contains a tia. In the following example (p. 263), which shows a part of a song in Trital, the dugan is in Keherwa Tāl. This is followed by eight vibhāgas of Trital and the ad again in Keherwa Tāl. The song ends on the note G, the sām.

The example on page 263, shows that dugan and ad with the tia resemble the device of the color of the isorhythmic motet of Western fourteenth-century music. They repeat the notes of the song melody, but in the form of diminutions. The last note of the tia (D) should coincide with the sām; in our example the tia ends immediately before the sām, a deviation from the rule which would not be acceptable to orthodox musicians.

Another term in North Indian drumming is the tukhra. This denotes a variable number of vibhāgas in succession in which the bols differ considerably from the other bols of the theka. In short, the tukhra is one of the few free variations in which the drummer may impress his audience with his skill. These free measures may (but need not) contain a tia.

Laggi denotes the repetition of one vibhāga; it is used only in popular music where sām and khāli are of no importance.

Some of the rhythmic phrases are given picturesque names. For instance, ♩ ♪♩ is called palankha (palanquin); ♪♩ ♪ is called mridanga because the phrase has a shape similar to that of the mridanga; ♪ ♪ ♪ is called gaupuchha (cow's tail), and so forth.

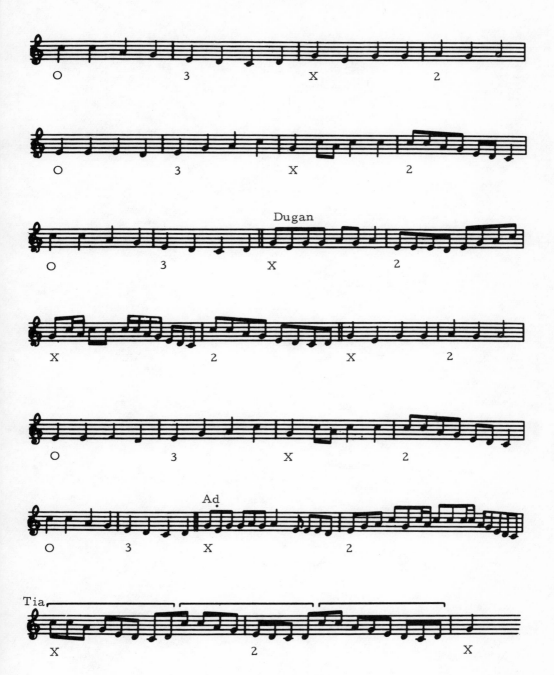

III

Zither Tablatures

ZITHER TABLATURES

The distinctive and popular European lute of the sixteenth and seventeenth centuries has as its Eastern counterpart not the Asiatic lute but the zither. Similar to the three main types of European lute tablatures — those of Italy, France, and Germany — we can distinguish the three types of zither tablatures of China, Korea, and Japan.

The tablatures are more complex than pitch notations and inform the player directly about the technical procedure of playing. Thus, they offer a convenient detour around the less concrete symbols of pitch notations and their theoretical ramifications, such as scales, intervals, and so forth. Although the information given to the player by means of tablature symbols is comparatively distinct, one must remember that Oriental notations, tablatures, and other systems indicate only the skeleton of the melody, serving as a reminder to the player who already knows the melody. In short, the elaboration of music is left to the performer; and each of several performances of the same piece, by the same player, based upon the same notated music, may differ considerable in interpretation.

CH'IN TABLATURE (减 字 , CHIEN TZǓ)

The ch'in (琴), often poetically translated by Western writers as "lute," is the classical zither of China, the instrument of

267

the poets, philosophers, and scholars. At the present time there are very few who still master the intricate technique of this distinguished instrument, and it is not surprising that the ch'in notation, a tablature of considerable complexity, reflects many of the subtleties that are characteristics of ch'in music.

In the distant past the ch'in was used in the ensemble music of the imperial court and in the ritual of the Confucian temple. At that time the strings were most often plucked with a plectrum. Gradually, with the growing refinement of solo-ch'in music, which required a great variety of shadings in the tone production, the plectrum was abandoned, and the strings were plucked with the fingers, thus producing a sound that was more intimate and more flexible.

The origin of the ch'in is not known to us. We have some vague information that the instrument was invented by one of the legendary emperors.[1] The ch'in-tsao (琴 操), the oldest known catalogue of ch'in melodies (written without musical notations in the second or third century A. D.), states that "Fu-hsi, in addition to his interests in writing, fishing, and other arts and crafts, made the 'lute'." This emperor is supposed to have invented musical instruments, especially the two ancient zithers, the ch'in and sê (瑟). According to tradition he may have lived in the third millenium B.C.

Literary sources — for instance the Chinese Classics[2]— contain numerous references to music and musical instruments, particularly to the ch'in:

> .. when Shun was emperor...,
> he played the five stringed ch'in.... [3]
>
> .. here long, there short, is the duckweed;
> on the left, on the right, we gather it.

The modest, retiring, virtuous young lady: —
with lutes, small and large, let us give her
    friendly welcome. [4]

And I will hope to grow old with you.
Your lute in your hands
will emit its quiet pleasant tones. [5]

Legge remarks that, ''The superior man, according to the rules of antiquity, was never, without some urgent reasons, to be without his lute by his side.... The quiet harmony of the lute was a common image for conjugal affection. ''[6]

.. why not daily play your lute,
both to give a zest to your joy
and to prolong the day?[7]

.. when we have seen our prince,
we sit together with him, and
they play on their lutes.... [8]

.. I have here admirable guests
for whom are struck the lutes,
large and small.... [9]

Loving union with wife and children
is like the music of the lutes.... [10]

The oldest known Chinese manuscript dealing with ch'in playing is the Yu-lan-p'u (幽 蘭 譜 , ''The Refined Orchid Book'')[11] which originated during the T'ang period (618-906).[12] Its extant fifth part is preserved in the Shinko-in (神光院) at Kyoto. The manuscript was copied repeatedly, principally in Japan. One of the recent publications was made in 1936 by the Commercial Press of Shanghai.

In examining the photostatic copy of the manuscript, we find that no musical notation is used. The melody, known as the ''yu-lan, '' is indicated by means of detailed instructions which indicate which finger to use, which fret and string to stop, whether to move the finger slowly or quickly, when to make a short rest, and so forth.

Following (Fig. 63, p. 271) is a copy of the first page of this remarkable manuscript which, according to Lee, may be the earliest music book of the Orient. Below is an approximate translation of this page:

Chieh Shih Melody Introduction to Elegant Orchids:

Ch'iu Kung, known as Ming, originally came from K'uai-chi. At the end of the Liang dynasty [A. D. 502-557] he was a hermit living on the Chiu-yi hill. His work exhausted the beauty of the Ch'u tune. And in the Elegant Orchids it was especially refined and brilliant. The tune was so subtle, the theme so profound, that no one could learn and master it. In the third year of Ch'ĕn-ming, of the Ch'ĕn dynasty [A. D. 590], he taught the piece to Wang Shu-ming of Yi-tu. Ch'iu Kung died in Tan-yang canton, in the tenth year of Kai-huang of the Sui dynasty, at the age of ninety-seven. He had no son to hand down his music. Therefore the tune was abridged here.

(The fifth section of the Elegant Orchids):

Put the middle finger about half an inch on the tenth hui and produce the shang tone. The second and the middle fingers jointly handle kung and shang. Hide the middle finger, and afterwards press it on the thirteenth hui, about an inch [down], in the form of a hook. Then stop shang. Lift the second finger slowly. Maintain the tone of kung and shang in the half way. The second finger carries the shang tone. Again maintain kung and shang in the half way. Let the third finger go downward, about one inch beyond the thirteenth hui. Produce shang and chiao. At this juncture separate it into two halves. Maintain it, clasp it, lift it, and emphasize it. Make a lift then....

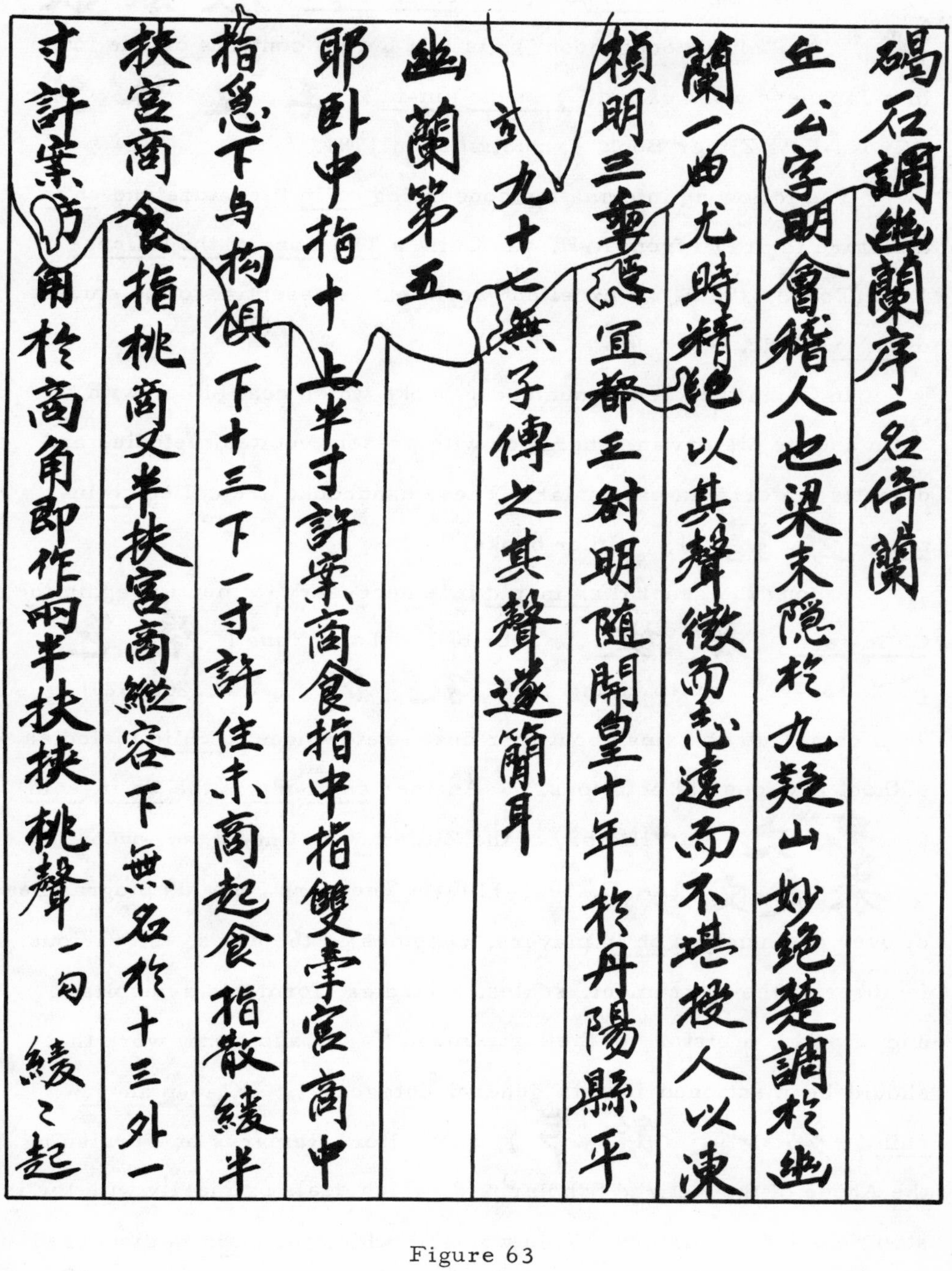
碣石調幽蘭序一名倚蘭
丘公字明會稽人也梁末隱於九疑山妙絶楚調於幽
蘭一曲尤時精絶以其聲微而志遠而不堪授人以陳
禎明三年授宜都王叔明隨開皇十年於丹陽縣卒
年九十七無子傳之其聲遂簡耳
幽蘭第五
耶卧中指十上半寸許案商食指中指雙牽宮商中
指急下與搆俱下十三下一寸許住末商起食指散緩半
扶宮商食指挑商又半扶宮商縱容下無名於十三外一
寸許案商角於商角即作兩半扶挾挑聲一句 緩々起

Figure 63

Another early ch'in book, Hui-ch'in ko-p'u (徽琴歌 譜 , "Hui Zither Song Book"), is lost but its contents can be found in a Japanese work called Gyoku-do kin-fu (玉堂琴譜 , "Gyoku-do's Zither Book"), published in 1781.[13]

The following information concerning ch'in literature and ch'in tablature is drawn from R. H. van Gulik's The Lore of the Chinese Lute (Tokyo, 1940), an excellent work that is essential to the student of ch'in music.

In China there exist numerous books which deal either with the ch'in and its history in general or with present notated melodies and didactic material in particular. These handbooks are called ch'in- p'u (琴譜), "zither books."

Among the general ch'in-p'u it is necessary to mention again the Ch'in-tsao (琴操), ascribed to Ts'ai Yung (蔡邕 , A. D. 133-92), or to K'ung Yen (孔衍 , A. D. 268-320). This catalogue contains about four dozen references to ch'in melodies without any musical notations.[14] Another ch'in-p'u is the Ch'in-shih (琴史), "History of the Zither," by Chu Ch'ang-wĕn (朱長文 , A. D. 1041-1100). The work contains biographies of over one hundred ch'in players, chapters on the notes, the various features of the instrument, scales, melodies, form and symbolism, and, finally, a history of the instrument.[15] An additional work that should be mentioned in this general category is: K'ao-p'an-yü- shih (考盤餘事), "Desultory Remarks on Furnishing the Abode of the Retired Scholar,"[16] which deals primarily with the in- strument and its history. This work, in which the ch'in is discussed at the end of the second chapter, was compiled by T'u Lung (屠 隆) in the sixteenth century. Other works dealing with the same

subject are: Ch'in-ching (琴經), "Classical Book on the
Ch'in" by Chang Ta-ming (張大命) of Fukien in the early
seventeenth century that discusses the structure of the instrument and
quotes a number of older ch'in works; Ch'ing-lien-fang-ch'in-ya
(青蓮舫琴雅), "Elegance of the Ch'in, from the
Blue Lotus Boat," compiled by Lin Yu-lin (林有麟) in
the early seventeenth century; Ch'in-hsüeh-ts'ung-shu (琴學
叢書), "Collected Writings on the Study of the Ch'in," a valuable series of treatises compiled by Yang Tsung-chi (楊宗
稷) in 1911.[17] Of particular importance is its sixth part called
Ch'in-ching, a collection of ch'in melodies notated in a system invented
by the author. Ch'in-shu-ts'un-mu (琴書存目), a sys-
tematic catalogue dealing with the available ch'in literature, was published by Chou Ch'ing-yün (周慶雲) in 1914. He pub-
lished a second Ch'in-shih in 1919, which was meant to serve as a
supplement to Chu Ch'ang-wên's work.

The didactic ch'in-p'u were usually published in limited numbers
by the ch'in masters; the quantity was just sufficient to serve the small
groups of selected disciples. These books were printed on cheap
paper, and only a few have survived in complete form. Generally a
ch'in-p'u consists of an introductory chapter dealing with the name and
history of the instrument, a theoretical section which explains the
tones and their significance, and, finally, a chapter which discusses
the finger technique and describes the tablature symbols. In many
cases this last chapter has been separated from the booklet, or the
ch'in-p'u omits it altogether. The reason for withholding this important chapter was that ch'in masters were reluctant to impart the knowledge of how to read the chien-tzŭ to unqualified people.

The oldest known of these specific ch'in-p'u is the Shēn-ch'i-mi-p'u (神奇祕譜) by Chu Ch'üan (朱權), the Prince of Ning, who died in 1448. The literary name of Chu Ch'üan was Ch'ü-hsien (臞仙), "Emaciated Immortal" (lit. "crane"), hence the work was also known as Ch'ü-hsien-ch'in-p'u. Its preface is dated 1425. "The author has not been consequent in his system of notation, and...the chien-tzŭ therefore have become unnecessarily complicated. One gets the impression that the compiler purposely made the notation obscure, so that only expert players could use it... In his preface he says that properly only high officials should be allowed to occupy themselves with the lute."[18] The specific ch'in-p'u are represented by the following works: Pu-hsü-t'ang-ch'in-p'u (步虛堂琴譜), a ch'in handbook compiled by Ku I-chiang (顧艷江) in the sixteenth century, and a work that shows Taoist influences; dating from the same period is the Ch'in-p'u-ho-pi-ta-ch'üan (琴譜合璧大全), compiled by Yang Piao-chēng (楊表正); the T'ai-ku-i-yin (太古遺音), compiled by Yang Lun (楊倫), belongs in the early seventeenth century; the Wu-chih-chai-ch'in-p'u (五知齋琴譜), a very popular and easily obtainable work by the famous Hsü Ch'i (徐祺), originated in the eighteenth century; the Ch'ēng-i-t'ang-ch'in-p'u (誠一堂琴譜) by Ch'ēng Yün-chi (程允基) dates from the early eighteenth century;[19] the Tzŭ-yüan-t'ang-ch'in-p'u (自遠堂琴譜) by Wu Hung (吳灴), from the early nineteenth century; and, finally, the Ch'in-hsüeh-ju-mēn (琴學入門) by Chang Ho (張鶴) of the same period. This latter work is a popular treatise and has been reprinted a number of times.[20]

The body of the ch'in consists of two narrow wooden boards,
one placed above the other. The upper board, curved slightly convex,
is made of t'ung wood (paulownia imperialis). The lower board, flat
at the bottom and made of tzŭ wood (tecoma radicanus), has two rectangular or oval resonance holes. Each part of the instrument has
symbolic significance. To mention only a few: the ancient ch'in had
a length of $\frac{366}{10}$ inches (its width was 6.6 inches) because the year had
a maximum of 366 days. The upper board, representing heaven, is
frequently inscribed or engraved with the name of the zither, its
owner, and the period when the instrument was built. The lower board
represents earth. The names of the two resonance holes are "Dragon
Pond" and "Phoenix Pool," respectively. The left side of the zither
is called "Scorched Tail," and the bridge upon which the strings are
attached is the "Yo Mountain," a symbol of detachedness and sturdi-
ness. Thus, the symbolism of the various parts is expressed even
to the smallest detail.

The five strings of the ancient ch'in correspond to the five elements;[21] the thickest and lowest string, the one farthest from the
player, must consist of 240 silken threads; it represents the emperor.
The second and fourth strings consist of 206 threads each, and the
third and fifth consist of 172 threads. The seven strings of the later
instrument were supposed to represent the seven days of the week.

The ancient five- and seven-tone scales of China determined the
tuning of the pre-Ming (seven string) ch'in which was C D E G A
c d, assuming that the lowest string was tuned to C. When the Yüan
dynasty (1260-1368) came to an end and the Ming dynasty (1368-1644)
was established, Chinese art, in every realm, experienced a renaissance of national sentiment. It was then that musicians and theorists

endeavored to re-establish the ancient anhemitonic pentatonic scale; as stated before, all semitones were abolished as foreign, and the Ming scale, although not quite the same as the scale of ancient China, became C D F G A (or, transposed, G A C D E). Although the official scale of the imperial court underwent some modifications in subsequent periods, since the Ming period the ch'in tuning has remained essentially unaltered (G A C D E G A).

Occasionally, in addition to these main patterns of tuning, other tunings could occur. For instance:

C D E G A B d

mentioned in the Korean work Shih-ak hwa-sŭng (詩 樂 和 聲 , lit. "Poem Music Harmonized"), written by order of Chŭng-cho (正祖 , 1777-1800), twenty-second king of the (Korean) Yi dynasty;

C D F G Bb c d
C Eb F G Bb c eb
C Eb F Ab Bb c eb

used by Sung composers such as Ch'iang K'uei, (Lee);

G Bb C D F G Bb
G Bb C Eb F G Bb
Ab Bb C Eb F Ab Bb

mentioned by Prince Chu Tsai-yü (sixteenth century);

C D E F# G A B

particularly in recent times.

The instrument is placed horizontally in front of the player in such a manner that the highest (seventh) string is nearest to him. Although the ch'in has no frets, we find instead thirteen small inlaid or painted studs below the outermost (lowest) string. The studs, called hui (徽),[22] serve a purpose similar to the frets on other instruments. We shall discuss their positions and use after we have explained the numbering of the strings.

The complexity of the ch'in tablature prevented its use by the common people and thus confined the elaborate ch'in playing to the learned musicians, poets, and philosophers.[23] The tablature system, consisting of symbols called chien-tzǔ (減字), "abbreviated characters," had its origin in the first centuries A. D. (according to van Gulik). Literary reports are vague about the time of its first appearance.

In order to read the tablature it is essential to be acquainted with the Chinese numerals from one to thirteen: 一 (1), 二 (2), 三 (3), 四 (4), 五 (5), 六 (6), 七 (7), 八 (8), 九 (9), 十 (10), 土 (11, 圭 (12), 圭 (13). The seven strings of the ch'in in both pre-Ming and Ming (and post-Ming) periods use the same numbers but denote different pitches:

Pre-Ming:

一 二 三 四 五 六 七

or:

Ming and post-Ming:

一 二 三 四 五 六 七   一 二 三 四 五 六 七

In the symbols of ch'in tablature there appears another set of numbers (1-13), which indicates the thirteen hui. These hui are arranged in such a manner that the distances between them in both directions (to the left and to the right), beginning from a central stud (七),

become — with one or two minor exceptions — increasingly smaller. The hui are numbered from right to left; that is, the highest stopped note on each string is indicated by the first hui and the lowest stopped note (not the open string) by the thirteenth.

The following two charts illustrate the sounds produced by the open and stopped strings in both the old (pre-Ming) and the new (Ming and post-Ming) tunings:

Pre-Ming Tuning

String	Hui:	13	12	11	10	9	8	7	6	5	4	3	2	1
I		C	D	Eb	E	F	G	A	c	e	g	c'	e'	g'	c''
II		D	E	F	F#	G	A	B	d	f#	a	d'	f#'	a'	d''
III		E	F#	G	G#	A	B	c#	e	g#	b	e'	g#'	b'	e''
IV		G	A	Bb	B	c	d	e	g	b	d'	g'	b'	d''	g''
V		A	B	c	c#	d	e	f#	a	c#'	e'	a'	c#''	e''	a''
VI		c	d	eb	e	f	g	a	c'	e'	g'	c''	e''	g''	c'''
VII		d	e	f	f#	g	a	b	d'	f#'	a'	d''	f#''	a''	d'''
Ratio of string division	1		$\frac{7}{8}$	$\frac{5}{6}$	$\frac{4}{5}$	$\frac{3}{4}$	$\frac{2}{3}$	$\frac{3}{5}$	$\frac{1}{2}$	$\frac{2}{5}$	$\frac{1}{3}$	$\frac{1}{4}$	$\frac{1}{5}$	$\frac{1}{6}$	$\frac{1}{8}$

Ming and Post-Ming Tuning

String	Hui:	13	12	11	10	9	8	7	6	5	4	3	2	1
I		G	A	Bb	B	C	D	E	G	B	d	g	b	d'	g'
II		A	B	C	C#	D	E	F#	A	c#	e	a	c#'	e'	a'
III		C	D	Eb	E	F	G	A	c	e	g	c'	e'	g'	c''
IV		D	E	F	F#	G	A	B	d	f#	a	d'	f#'	a'	d''
V		E	F#	G	G#	A	B	c#	e	g#	b	e'	g#'	b'	e''
VI		G	A	Bb	B	c	d	e	g	b	d'	g'	b'	d''	g''
VII		A	B	c	c#	d	e	f#	a	c#'	e'	a'	c#''	e''	a''

A third set of numbers (1-10) is occasionally used to indicate the fên (分): imaginary, small subdivisions between any two adjoining hui. As shown before, the distances between any two successive hui vary — for instance (in pre-Ming tuning) the interval between hui 6 and 7 is a major third, while the interval between hui 12 and 13 is only a semitone — therefore the distances between the ten assumed fên in each of these intervals also vary proportionally. The interval between any two successive fên, for instance between fên 6 and 7, will be one tenth of a major third, while the interval between two successive fên between hui 12 and 13 will be only one tenth of a semitone, an unlikely interval to be used in ch'in playing. In practice only such fên are employed which divide the intervals between successive hui into sections which generally are not smaller than semitones.

The fên are not marked on the instrument and have to be learned by the player. They, too, are counted from right to left, a procedure which may cause some confusion when transcriptions of ch'in tablatures are made. 上 ("up") means, of course, a rise in pitch (on the string, a movement of the depressing hand from left to right), while rising numbers, both for hui and fên, indicate descending pitches. Thus, for instance, the fourth hui plus the fourth fên will be lower in pitch than the fourth hui plus the second fên, and so forth.

In addition to the three sets of numbers there exists a wealth of notational symbols that denote technical details of playing. Of about 200 chien-tzǔ, we quote here only a few: [24]

Chien-tzǔ: Name:

屮   San (散)   Only the right hand is used for plucking the string.

毛   T'o (托)   The string is pulled in an outward

Chien-tzǔ:	Name:	
		direction (away from the player) by the right thumb.
尸	Po (擘)	The string is pulled in an inward direction (toward the player) by the right thumb (nail).
木	Mo (抹)	The string is pulled in an inward direction by the right index finger.
ㄑ	T'iao (挑)	The string is pulled in an outward direction by the right index finger.
ㄅ	Kou (勾)	The string is pulled in an inward direction by the right middle finger.
丁	T'i (剔)	The string is pulled in an outward direction by the right middle finger.
ㄅ	Ta (打)	The string is pulled in an inward direction by the right ring finger.
仐	Chê (摘)	The string is pulled in an outward direction by the right ring finger.
厂	Ch'üan fu (全扶)	Three strings are pulled simultaneously: one is pulled by the right index finger; the second by the right middle finger; and the third by the right ring finger.
	Li (歷)	Two or three strings are pulled in quick succession in an outward direction by the right index finger. This movement is also called Tu (度).
省	Shao hsi (少息)	A pause of short duration.
夋	Ju man (入慢)	Slowing down.

Chien-tzu: Name:

Chih (至)   "Up to"; for instance it can be used in 滾六至一 , meaning k'un from the VI up to the I string.

Lien (連)   Smooth; legato.

Ch'ing (輕)   Soft.

Chung (重)   Loud.

Huan (緩)   Slow.

Chi (急)   Very fast.

Ta chih (大指)   The left thumb is to be used.

Shih chih (食指)   The left index finger is to be used.

Chung chih (中指)   The left middle finger is to be used.

Ming chih (名指)   The left ring finger is to be used.

Ch'o (綽)   A short range glissando which starts slightly below the written note and glides up to it; it is performed by a finger of the left hand.

Chu (注)   A short range glissando which starts slightly above the written note and glides down to it; it is performed by a finger of the left hand.

Yin (吟) — Vibrato. According to van Gulik there are numerous varieties of vibrato; the important ones are: ch'ang-yin (長吟), a wide vibrato; hsi-yin (細吟), a thin vibrato; yu-yin (遊吟), a swinging vibrato; and the ting-yin (定吟), a fine vibrato in which the finger hardly moves, and only the pulsation in the finger tip is supposed to influence the sound.

Jou (猱) — A broad vibrato which is more accentuated than the yin. Ch'in players pronounce this character jou, although it should be read nao — "monkey."

Chuang (撞) — "To strike against": immediately after the string is plucked by the right hand, the left moves quickly up and down the string to the right (above) of the indicated note.

Hu (滸) — The left thumb, which stops the string, glides on the vibrating string to the right to the next hui in a slow motion.

Kuei (跪) — "To kneel": the string is depressed with the back of the first joint of the left ring finger instead of its tip, especially in t'ao-ch'i when it is difficult to press the string with the finger tip.

Fan ch'i (泛起) — "Here the floating sounds begin": this is a symbol that indicates where the player has to begin using harmonics.

In addition to the manifold plucking and stopping instructions the ch'in-p'u occasionally contain indications concerning the various touches (timbres) of ch'in playing. [25] The ch'in masters write about light, loose, crisp, lofty, rare, and many other touches which can be ignored here because they have very little to do with the actual tablature symbols.

Each tablature symbol contains specific signs for the depressing and plucking fingers, the number of the string to be plucked, the number of the hui and, in some instances, the number of the fēn. The general organization of the tablature symbols is illustrated in the following two examples:

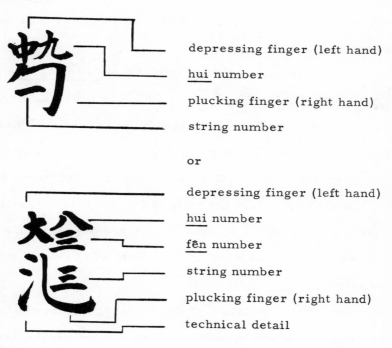

depressing finger (left hand)

hui number

plucking finger (right hand)

string number

or

depressing finger (left hand)

hui number

fēn number

string number

plucking finger (right hand)

technical detail

Occasionally ch'in tablatures use the character 上 (shang), "above," "up," to indicate a high alteration of a note without referring to the next higher sounding hui and its fēn. For instance, if we assume that hui 7 produces the note G, hui 7 plus fēn 7 will indicate a note lower than G, approximately the note F. But if hui 7 is provided with shang it will indicate a note becoming or being higher than G and, if not otherwise indicated, a note between hui 7 (G) and hui 6 (B). Shang may denote both a rising or a raised sound. We shall transcribe shang by a raised sound although the interpretation of rising sound is equally acceptable.

Shang is notated on top of the plucking finger symbol either in a detached form, 亐 , or in combination with the finger symbol, 亐

If in certain symbols the signs for the depressing finger and the hui and fên numbers are omitted, the player is expected to apply the last notated instructions (concerning depressing finger, hui, fên, etc.) to all subsequent symbols which are without these signs until new instructions are given.

Figure 64 represents the first page of the Ch'êng-i-t'ang ch'in-p'u (誠一堂琴譜).[26] This work, as already mentioned, was compiled by Ch'êng Yün-chi in the early eighteenth century. The title columns inform us that Ch'êng Yün-chi came from Hsin-an, that the book was revised by his younger brother Ch'êng Yün-p'ei, that the music is in the style of Lu, the home of Confucius, and that there are fourteen strophes. As we are dealing with an eighteenth-century work we know that the ch'in will be tuned in the post-Ming manner, G A C D E G A.

Below follows a discussion of the symbols. These symbols provide information regarding only the notes and technical details about their production on the instrument. Meter and rhythm are practically ignored; the few signs which offer some guidance are a small circle — for instance near the fifth symbol of the first notational column — which denotes the end of a phrase, and rare instructions to perform certain passages in a slow or fast tempo. Like most ch'in

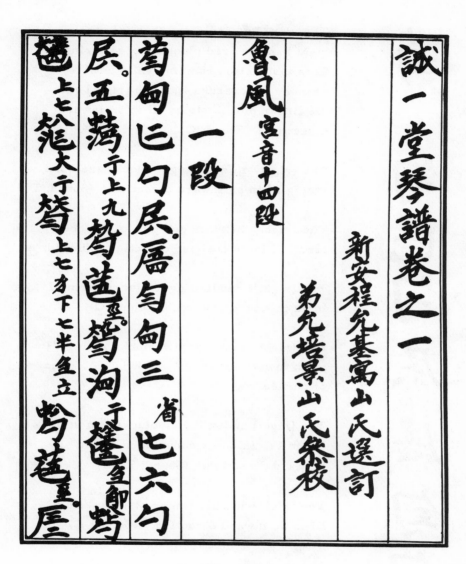

Figure 64

masters, the brothers Ch'êng expected the performer to be acquainted
with the rhythmical shape of the piece before he used the notation.

The sign ⇥ indicates that only the
right hand is used plucking open strings.
This instruction remains valid until a
new one supersedes it. The (right) middle finger plucks string III in an inward
direction. (Sound: C)

The (right) middle finger plucks the open
string IV in an inward direction. (Sound: D)

The (right) index finger plucks the open
string II in an outward direction. (Sound: A)

The (right) middle finger plucks string I
in an inward direction. (Sound: G)

The (right) thumb (nail) plucks string VI
in an inward direction. (Sound: G). End
of phrase.

The (right) index finger plucks two strings,
V and IV, in quick succession and in an
outward direction. (Sound: E, D)

The (right) middle finger plucks string
III in an inward direction. (Sound: C)

The (right) middle finger plucks string
IV in an inward direction. (Sound: D)

Here the plucking finger sign is not given.
In such instances the previous instruction
remains valid; the (right) middle finger plucks
string III in an inward direction (Sound: C)

"Shao hsi," a short pause (少息).

The (right) index finger plucks string VII in an outward direction. (Sound: A)

The previous finger sign (⌐) remains valid; the (right) index finger plucks string VI in an outward direction. (Sound: G)

The (right) middle finger plucks string I in an inward direction. (Sound: G) (End of first notational column.)

The (right) thumb (nail) plucks string VI in an inward direction. (Sound: G)

The previous plucking finger sign remains valid; the right thumb plucks string V in an inward direction. (Sound: E)

This complex symbol instructs the player that the right middle finger (ㄱ) plucks string I in an outward direction (刃); the left middle finger (中), starting with a short glissando from above (㇁), depresses the string on hui 10. (Sound: C)

("right") Annotations such as this one are inserted into Chinese, Korean, and Japanese zither ("up") tablatures. This annotation instructs the player to move the depressing finger ("9") (中) up to the right to hui 9.

The (right) middle finger plucks string II in an inward direction; the left thumb (大) depresses the string at hui 9. (Sound: E)

The sign ✋ indicates that only the right
hand is to be used. The index finger plucks
(the open) string V in an outward direction.
(Sound: E)

Ch'ing, "softly." The lowest horizontal
bar of this character is missing in the manuscript. End of phrase.

The (right) middle finger plucks string III
in an inward direction; the left thumb depresses the string above hui 9. The sign
⤴ (below 九) is shang (上),
its lowest horizontal line being combined
with the right middle finger sign. Instead
of stating an exact fên number, the writer
indicates that the spot where the string is
to be depressed is above hui 9 (and below
hui 8). (Sound: approximately G#)

Since we find no detailed instructions regarding hui or fên, and since no open string
is prescribed, the hand position of the preceding symbol (楚) remains valid.
This note is to be start ed with a short
glissando from above on string IV, hui
9, plus shang. (Sound: approximately A#
or B)

The (depressing) hand moves to the right.

The (right) index finger plucks string V
in an outward direction. At this instant the
left thumb still depresses the string at hui
9 plus shang. Then, as indicated by 丁
("right") of the preceding sign, the left
thumb glides to the right to the next (8th)

hui (午), and the string is plucked again by the (right) index finger in an inward direction (木). The hui number 八 (8) appears to be combined with 午 into 牟 . (Sound: B-c#)

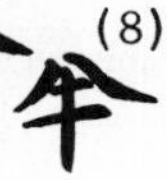

"very fast"

"joining" (the following note 仝).

The (right) middle finger plucks string I in an inward direction; the left middle finger depresses the string above (上) hui 八 (8). (Sound: approximately F#) (End of second notational column.)

The (right) index finger plucks string IV in an outward direction. The left thumb depresses the string below hui 7 at fên 7. (Sound: between d and B)

The (left) thumb moves up to hui 7.

The (right) index finger plucks string III in an outward direction. The left thumb begins a short glide from above and ends at hui 8. (Sound: A)

The left thumb moves to the right.

The (right) middle finger plucks string II in an inward direction. The left thumb depresses the string below hui 7 at fên 8. (Sound: between A and F#)

"Up to"

(hui) 7

jou, a broad vibrato,

"down" (toward hui 8)

the left thumb glides to the right to the next hui (7)

"very fast"

After the string is plucked by the right hand, the left moves quickly up and down string II to the right of hui 7, fên 8. (Sound: a fluctuation between A and F#)

The (right) middle finger plucks string I in an inward direction. The left thumb depresses the string at hui 8. (Sound: E)

The (right) thumb plucks string V in an outward direction. The sign instructs the player that the open string is used. (Sound: E)

"Softly." End of phrase.

Although this symbol stands at the end of the third notational column, it is the beginning of a new phrase. The (right) index finger plucks in quick succession strings III and II in an outward direction. (Sound: C, A) (End of third notational column.) [27]

The following ch'in piece (Fig. 65), called "The Three Intoxications of Yo Yang,"[28] is notated by means of chien-tzŭ and kung-ch'ê symbols. As mentioned before, during the last two centuries it has become common to facilitate reading of difficult ch'in tablatures by combining them with a popular notation, a practice not unlike that in

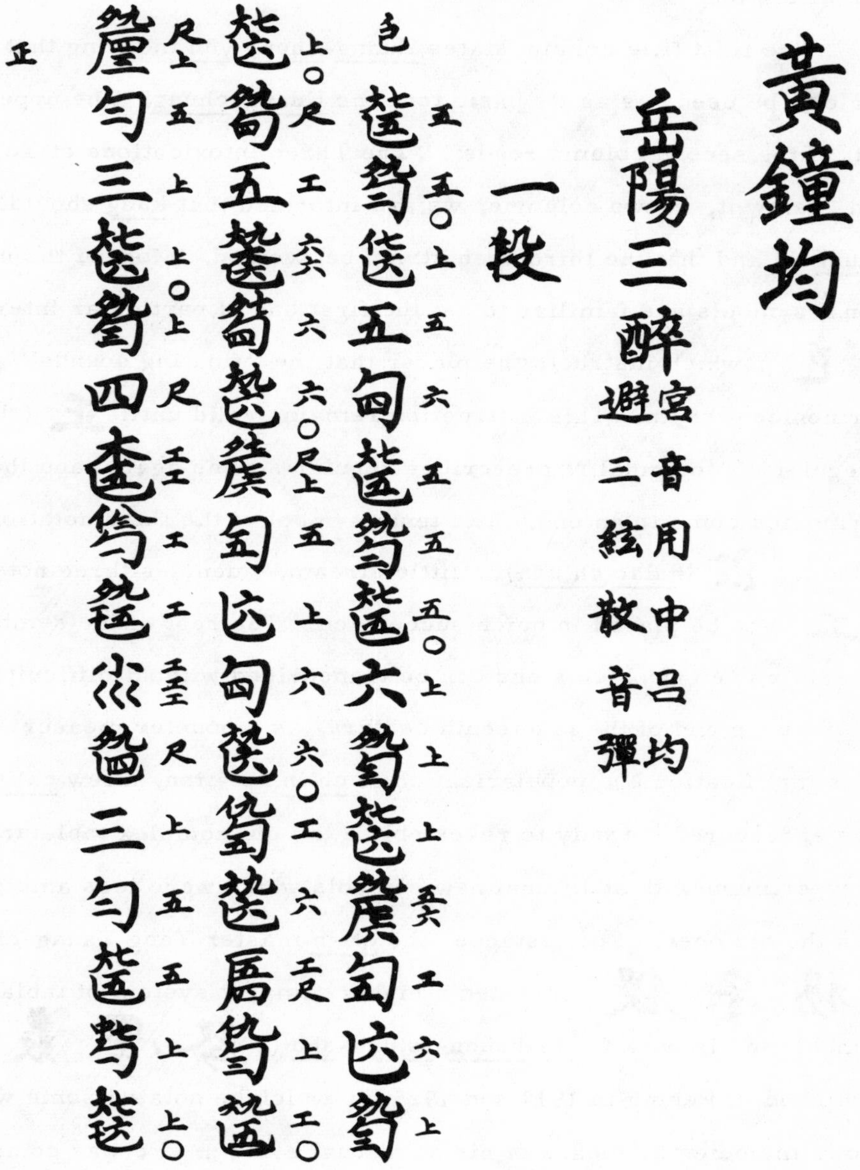

黃鐘均

岳陽三醉

Figure 65

which European lute tablatures underwent modifications aimed at simplification.

The first title column states Huang-chung yün, meaning that the scale to be used has as its basic tone the Huang-chung. The upper half of the second column reads: "The Three Intoxications of Yo Yang," and, below it, in two columns, we are informed that kung should sound Chung-lü and that the third open string be avoided. Most of the notational symbols are familiar to us; the first one of particular interest is 乇 , which instructs the player that the "floating sounds" — harmonics — begin. This instruction remains valid until 正 (chêng), "regular," "original," prescribes regular sounds again, and the harmonics come to an end. The tenth symbol of the third notational column, 泬 (hsiao ch'uan), "little stream," denotes three notes (工) to be played in quick succession. The rest of the symbols present no new problems and can be transcribed without difficulty. [29]

At the end of the nineteenth century, as a counter measure against the simplification and popularization of ch'in notation, a few ch'in masters endeavored not only to re-establish the old complex tablature but to experiment with additional new symbols which were less ambiguous than the old ones. For instance, the ch'in master Yang Tsung-chi (楊宗稷) created a highly complex system of tablature symbols in his book Ch'in-hsüeh-ts'ung-shu (琴學叢書), published in Peking in 1911 and 1925, in which he notated some well known melodies by means of his notational system. He was compelled to print a multitude of explanations together with his symbols and, although Yang's instructions are comparatively clear, the reading of his notation required a considerable amount of additional study by ch'in players. For this reason the new system did not achieve any appreciable recognition.

Another experiment concerning ch'in notation was made by Wang Kuang-ch'i (王光祈) in his Fan-i-ch'in-p'u-chih-yen-chiu (翻譯琴譜之研究), published in Shanghai in 1931. Influenced by Western notation, Wang tried using notes and staves plus a number of complex special signs. None of these experiments — simplification, invention of new symbols, introduction of Western notational elements — achieved any lasting success.

Ch'in notation of ritual and ceremonial ensemble music is comparatively simple. With a few rare exceptions it avoids technical subtleties, fên, and rhythmic freedom, and limits its symbols to denoting open strings plucked either by the right index or middle fingers. This simplified ch'in tablature is combined with other Chinese notational systems, each of which denotes the music of a specific instrument. For instance, Figure 66 (p. 294) is the beginning of the middle part of the Confucian ancestral hymn,[30] a score in which four notations are used: lü, the old Five-Tone, kung-ch'ê, and simple chien-tzŭ.

The large characters at the top of the page, written in circular fields, represent the sacred text. Immediately below each textual character, written horizontally (from right to left), we find indications for the note to which each word is to be sung: below the first textual character we read, ''Huang-chung acts as kung''; below the second textual character, ''T'ai-ts'u acts as shang''; and so forth.[31] Below these annotations we find (in the second horizontal line) the notes prescribed for the shêng (笙) notated in kung-ch'ê symbols. The first one reads: ''the shêng blows ho''; the second one, ''the shêng blows ssŭ''; and so forth. The vertical notational columns, below the vocal and shêng notes and grouped into pairs, each of which belongs to one textual word, represent the accompaniment. The right hand top

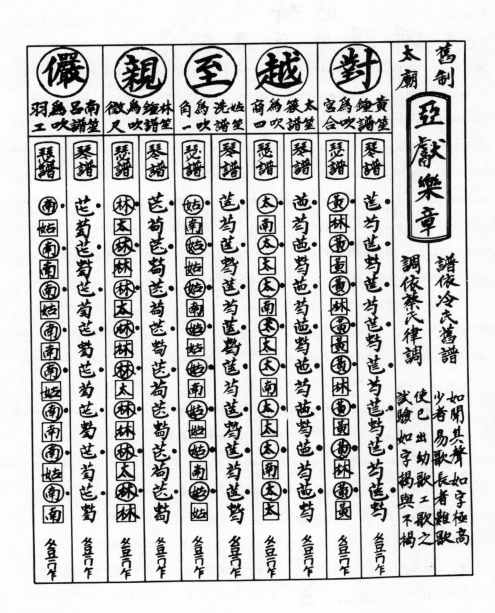

Figure 66

(written in a rectangular frame) reads: "ch'in notation," the left hand top, "sê notation."[3][2] The sê part is notated in lü symbols placed in small circles and squares. The circles indicate principal beats, the squares secondary beats. The principal beats are further marked with dots placed to the right of the sê and ch'in symbols.

The ch'in symbols can be read without difficulty; a sequence of four symbols is repeated throughout each column. In the first one we find:

芷	open string III	C
芍	open string I	G
芷	open string III	C
芐	string I, hui 10	C

If we compare ch'in and sê notes we find that both instruments perform in unison. The annotations at the bottom of each column indicate repetitions.

SÊ TABLATURE

Ensemble sê music is notated with lü and occasionally with kung-ch'ê symbols. Solo sê music, besides using the aforementioned systems, is sometimes notated in a simple form of tablature which is derived from the chien-tzǔ.

Before we consider this tablature, a few remarks about the sê are indicated.

The sê (瑟), like the ch'in, is a Chinese zither, the origin

of which has been ascribed to the mythical emperor Fu Hsi. Since
both ch'in and sê are frequently mentioned together in the Confucian
Classics[33] we may assume that they date from approximately the
same era. The sê is larger than the ch'in and consists of a long board
(the sizes vary — the longest measures 81 inches) which is more curved
than the upper board of the ch'in. It resembles the upper half of a
wooden cylinder. Along the curved surface 25 strings are strung,
tuned most often in an anhemitonic pentatonic, less frequently in a
heptatonic order.

According to legend the instrument originally had 50 strings, but
this number had been reduced to 25 at the time of the legendary emperor Huang Ti. The Êrh Ya[34] reports that one day a Miss Su played
the sê, and the emperor was so overwhelmed by the mournful sound of
the instrument that he issued an order to reduce the number of strings
from 50 to 25 in order to reduce the saddening effect. The number of
strings varied from one instrument to another. The so-called ''Great
Sê'' used to have 27, the ''Elegant Sê'' 23 (or 19), and the ''Praise Sê''
23 strings.

In contrast to the ch'in the sê has no hui but uses movable bridges.
Each string has its own bridge and each group of five bridges is painted
in a different color: blue, red, yellow, white, and black. The instrument is always played in octaves; that is, two open strings are plucked
simultaneously.

During the later Chou period the sê disappeared as a solo instrument,[35] and only in the nineteenth century, after more than a millen-
nium of neglect, did it become popular again. Several factors may have
contributed to this revival: the movable bridges allow a number of differing tunings, the sê is relatively easy to play since only open strings

are used, and its tablature is remarkably simple.

In order to read this tablature we list below the Chinese numbers from 1 to 25 which represent the 25 strings together with their pentatonic tuning:

In sê tablature each number is placed in an abbreviated kou (勹), and two strings tuned an octave apart are always plucked simultaneously. The following pairs are in use:

The number of the right represents the lower note of the octave; the one on the left, the upper note. The following (Fig. 67, p. 299) is the sê part of the Hymn to Confucius.[36] This form of sê tablature was also applied to the notation of music of other Chinese zithers (e. g., the Chêng).

Following (Fig. 68, p. 300) is one page of a Sê-p'u (瑟 譜)[37] by Hsiung P'êng Lai (熊 朋 來), a composer who lived during the Yüan period. The title column at the right reads: ''sê-p'u, second book.'' The second column informs us that it is a poem with old notation; the third column is the title of the poem, ''Deer Calling, III.'' .The text which follows, in columns four and five, is one of three stanzas of a famous ode of the Shih Ching. The English translation of this stanza,[38] as far as it is shown in Figure 68, is as follows:

> Yu, yu, cry the deer
>
> Nibbling the black southernwood in the fields.
>
> I have a lucky guest.
>
> Let me play my zithern, blow my reed-organ,
>
> Blow my reed-organ, trill their tongues,
>
> Take up the baskets of offerings.
>
> Here is that man that loves me
>
> And will teach me the ways of Chou... .

The notation of the melody appears twice: lü symbols in column six, kung-ch'ê symbols in column seven. The reading of both notations causes no difficulties. We observe that the tone material is C D E F# G A B c d, which shows the sê tunings were not always pentatonic.

Figure 67

Figure 68

瑟譜卷二

詩舊譜

鹿鳴之三

呦呦鹿鳴食野之苹我有嘉賓鼓瑟吹笙吹笙鼓簧承

筐是將人之好我示我周行

黃南蕤姑南姑太黃蕤林應南林南黃林蕤林南姑應

黃姑南林南黃姑林南太黃

六工勾一工一四合勾尺凡工尺工六尺勾尺工一凡

六一工尺工合一尺工五六

300

KOREAN ZITHER TABLATURE
(HAP-CHA-PO, 合字譜)

All East Asiatic zithers have their origin in China; some have retained the features of their Chinese prototypes while others have developed along individual lines.   Korea possesses a number of zithers,[39] but only one approximates the nobility and distinction of the Chinese ch'in.   This instrument is the hyŭn-kŭm (玄琴), a zither often freely and poetically translated as ''black lute.'' Eckardt writes[40] that it is possible that the Korean general term for zither, kŭmunko (usually pronounced komunko, 거문고), is derived from the ''black zither,'' because kŭmunko or komunko means ''black ko.'' The syllable ko may have been the ancient Sino-Korean kŭm, a sound that is still recognizable in the Chinese ch'in and the Japanese koto.[41]

Although legend relates[42] that the kŭm was invented in the fifth century A. D. in Kokuryo, [43] and that the description ''black'' is explained by a story in which a group of black storks danced around the inventor after he had completed the zither, there is no doubt that the kŭm had its origin in China.   In contrast to the Chinese ch'in, which has seven strings and no frets, the hyŭn-kŭm has six strings and is fretted.   A further difference is that the strings of the Chinese ch'in are usually plucked with the fingers while the strings of the hyŭn-kŭm are generally plucked with a small rod called suttae (숫대), which the player holds in his right hand.

The hyŭn-kŭm has approximately the same shape as the Chinese ch'in.   The chief characteristics of the Korean zither are its sixteen frets and six strings, of which the first, fourth, fifth, and sixth remain open while the second and third are strung across frets.   It must be noted that although the frets extend below the fourth string, this string is never depressed against the frets but always remains open. Contrary to the hui of the Chinese ch'in, the frets of the hyŭn-kŭm are numbered from left to right.

The first information about the appearance of a kŭm type in Korea can be found in the oldest Korean historical document, the Samkuk-saki (三國史記),[44] the "History of the Three Kingdoms,"[45] written by Kim Pu-shik (金富軾) at the order of In-chong, King of Korea, about 1145. In the ak-chi (樂志), the chapter on music in the Samkuk-saki, one reads that a man brought an instrument with seven strings from Tsin (晋) China (265-420) to Kokuryo, but that no one was able to play it. The Samkuk-saki contains no musical notations but mentions the titles of a number of pieces[46] written by a musician called Ok Po-ko (玉寶高), who lived in the kingdom of Silla. The information given in the Samkuk-saki that a zither had been imported from China which could not be played by Korean musicians is repeated in a Japanese work called Tai-ho ryō (大寶令) — its full name is Tai-ho ritsu-ryō — written in A.D. 701 under the auspices of Emperor Mommu Tennō (697-707). It states that although students were studying the kŭm, they were unable to perform music on it.[47]

In 1370 the first ruler of the Chinese Ming dynasty, Tai Ts'ou (太祖), sent a number of instruments to Korea. Among them were stone chimes (with sixteen stone slabs), bell chimes (with sixteen bells), a Chinese shēng (Korean: saeng), a kŭm, a sŭl (the Chinese sê), and others. A year later, in 1371, several Korean students went to Ming China to study the art of kŭm playing. In the fifteenth century, too, instruments were sent from China to Korea and treated with great respect. According to the Ak-hak-koe-pŭm[48] these imported instruments were used only by court musicians who had learned how to master them. The kŭm and sŭl were used in the ritual of the ancestral temple (Chong-myo, 宗 廟) and, according to the ceremonial order of this period,[49] six kŭm were used in the temple and another six in the orchestra of the imperial court.

It is not known when the specifically Korean form of the hyŭn-kŭm (six strings and frets) evolved and when solo kŭm music became popular in Korea. We can assume that this evolution occurred after the fifth and before the tenth centuries A. D.

The hyŭn-kŭm tablature is called hap-cha-po (合字譜), "combined letter notation." Indications concerning its first appearance can be found in the Ak-hak-koe-pŭm. This work relates that hap-cha-po was used for notating music of the various zithers (hyŭn-kŭm, kaya-kŭm, etc.) and lutes (T'ang- and Hyang p'i-pa). Sŭng Hyŭn, the author of the Ak-hak-koe-pŭm and of a second work, the O-chu-yŭn-mun (五 洲 行文 , "Five States Travel Report"),[50] was given the honorary title "Inventor of Hap-cha-po." It is more likely, however, that hap-cha-po was already in use in the fifteenth century, and that Sŭng Hyŭn's contribution was more one of recording than of inventing. If he had been the inventor of hap-cha-po, one would expect to find some notational examples of hap-cha-po in his work, but neither the Ak-hak-koe-pŭm nor the O-chu-yŭn-mun contain any.

Figure 69 (p. 304) illustrates how the first kŭm tuning was notated in the Ak-hak-koe-pŭm. The work discusses five tunings, of which only the first was in use. We observe the old Chinese Five Tone Notation[51] in the left column, the definition of pitches expressed by lü symbols[52] in the middle column, and the numbering of the seven strings in the right column.

Figure 69

The lü symbols in Figure 69 inform us explicitly that the seven strings are to be tuned to $C^{5\,3}$ D E G A c d. This tuning refers to the Chinese ch'in at the time when it was imported into Korea and musicians began to use the instrument. The Korean kŭm tunings eventually underwent changes which make them differ considerably from the Chinese types.[54]

The earliest zither books came from China. It is probable that manuscripts such as the Yu-lan-p'u,[55] with detailed playing instructions, were favored by Korean musicians because they enabled them to learn zither playing without any detours to study notational symbols. We know (Lee) that the original Hui-ch'in ko-p'u[56] (in Korean: Hwi-kŭm ka-po) had been preserved in Korea by the late Dr. Yun Yong-ku until it was lost recently during the Korean War.

There are numerous zither books which represent the Korean art of kŭm playing; particularly important are two works from the sixteenth and seventeenth centuries respectively: the An-sang kŭm-po (安 瑞 琴 譜), the "Kŭm Book of An-sang," written in 1572, and the Yang-kŭm shin-po (梁 琴 新 譜), "Yang's New Kŭm Book," written in 1610. The name in this title must not be confused with the name of the (Korean) zither with fourteen strings, called yang-kŭm (洋 琴). Both books are collections of zither pieces, some of which are original and some of which are songs arranged for the instrument.

The An-sang kŭm-po[57] contains eleven pieces, among which we find the famous Man-tae-yŭp (慢 大 葉), Yŭ-min-ak (與 民 樂), Po-hŭ-cha (步 虛 子), and Sa-mo-kok (思 母 曲), which will be discussed later in this chapter. The author and compiler of the Yang-kŭm shin-po[58] was Yang Tŭk-soo (梁

德 壽), a Korean court musician of the seventeenth century.
As a result of the Japanese invasion (Hideyoshi) Yang fled to Namwon
and was ordered by Kim Tu-nam, the ruler of the province of Im-sil,
to compile a book of zither music in order to preserve the important
melodies of his time. For this work Yang Tŭk-soo has been referred
to as the inventor of hap-cha-po, an ascription which is, as we know,
erroneous because hap-cha-po had been mentioned one hundred years
earlier in the O-chu-yŭn-mun. The Yang-kŭm shin-po contains nine
pieces, all notated in hap-cha-po and none of which is an original composition of Yang's. They all are Sok-ak (俗 樂), "popular
music," which usually is not performed officially at the royal court.
If we consider that sok-ak pieces were collected by Yang, a court musician, they must indeed have been well known to be deemed worthy of
being recorded by him. The titles of all nine pieces are: a) Man-tae-
yŭp (慢 大 葉), lit. "Wandering Big Leaf"; b) Puk-chŭn
(北 殿), lit. "North Palace"; c, d, e, f, g) Chung-tae-yŭp
(中 大 葉), lit. "Middle Big Leaf"; h) Cho-ŭm (調
音), a tuning piece; i) Kam-kun-ŭn (感 君 恩), lit.
"Appreciating the King's Favor."

Chung-tae-yŭp (pieces c, d, e, f, g), written in several modes
which will be discussed later, has been described as the oldest-known
Korean melody. These five versions are notated for the first time in
the Yang-kŭm shin-po; the other four items can be found in other
collections as well.

The importance of Chung-tae-yŭp is evidenced by the fact that
it is included in another collection which contains only ceremonial
music, the Tae-ak hu-po (大 樂 後 譜), lit. "Great Music,
Later Book," published in 1759.⁵⁹ The pieces of this collection are

called Cho-ak (朝 樂), "Palace (Morning) Music," which were performed at the Cho-hoe (朝 會), the official morning audience at the royal palace.[60]

Following a Chinese custom similar to one of medieval Europe, the writers of the An-sang kŭm-po and the Yang-kŭm shin-po placed the symbols of hap-cha-po side by side with those of one or more other notations. The most frequent combination is hap-cha-po and yuk-po (肉 譜)[61] in parallel columns. This particular combination gradually led to a modification of hap-cha-po which will be discussed below. At the present time hap-cha-po is used only for notating music of the hyŭn-kŭm.

The Tuning of the Hyŭn-kŭm

The tunings of the imported Chinese ch'in[62] underwent changes in Korea, especially between the time of the Ak-hak koe-pŭm and the time of the great zither books, the An-sang kŭm-po and Yang-kŭm shin-po. Instead of using all strings for performing the melody, the hyŭn-kŭm usually confines the playing of the melody to two strings while the other four remain open. This practice necessarily led to changes in tuning which we shall endeavor to describe.

The six silken strings of the hyŭn-kŭm are numbered in such a manner that the first is nearest the player and the sixth is farthest from him. The first, fourth, fifth, and sixth strings are always open, while the second and third are depressed against the sixteen frets of the instrument. The following chart (Fig. 70) illustrates the board, strings, and frets (in our subsequent descriptions of hap-cha-po we shall again number the strings with Roman numerals, the sixteen frets with Arabic numerals):

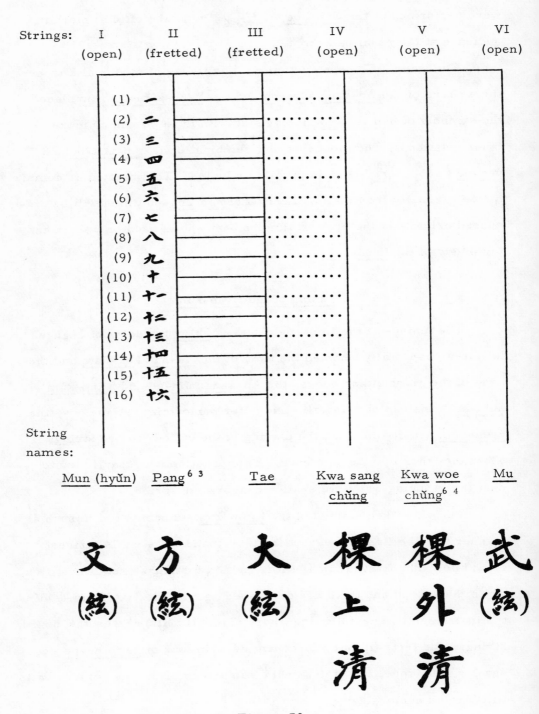

Figure 70

It is remarkable that the open second and third strings are indicated by "fret one," that is, the strings are not depressed if fret one is notated. The strings have names: I is called the Mun (hyŭn), the "civil" (string); II, the Pang (hyŭn), "play" (string); III, the Tae (hyŭn), the "big" (string); IV, the Kwa sang chŭng, the "clear one above the frets"; V, the Kwa woe chŭng, the "clear one outside the frets"; and VI, the Mu (hyŭn), the "military" (string). Strings IV, V, and VI are often played in quick succession with a sweeping arpeggio stroke. The word chŭng, "clear," "high," used in the names of strings IV and V indicates that they are tuned an octave higher than string VI.

Before turning to the tuning of the instrument we have to consider the four modes (cho) of Korean Ah-ak; all four are anhemitonic pentatonic. There is no adherence to absolute pitches; the instruments are tuned either to accommodate the requirements of the singer or, if used in ensembles, according to stone or bell chimes, in which instances pitches are fixed. The chimes, however, are not always in tune and vary in pitch from one set to another. The lowest string is usually tuned to the note Bb (or Eb), a procedure which we shall adopt. The four modes of Ah-ak are:

a) Pyong-cho (平 調):[6][5]
    Bb   C   Eb   F   G   Bb

b) U-cho (羽 調):
    Eb   F Ab   Bb   c   eb

c) Pyong-cho-kae-myon-cho (平 調 界 面 調):
    Bb Db Eb   F Ab   Bb

d) U-cho-kae-myon-cho (羽 調 界 面 調):
    Eb Gb Ab   Bb db   eb.

Both pyong modes begin with the note Bb, and both U-cho modes, beginning with Eb, are transpositions a fourth higher than the pyong forms. Pyong-cho is believed to represent the tranquil and peaceful voice of justice and wisdom; U-cho, the open, virile moods; and the kae-myon modes represent the peacefully pathetic and the virile pathetic moods, respectively.

The introductory chapter of the Yang-kŭm shin-po, which explains the tuning of the instrument, offers the following instructions: the strings IV and V are to be tuned to kung (宫)[66] in the pyong modes. String VI has to be tuned to chok kung (蜀宫), also called tak kung (濁宫), "cloudy kung," both terms indicating a note an octave below that of strings IV and V:

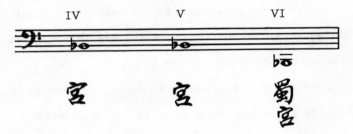

In the U-cho forms, where the kung is a fourth higher (Eb), the tuning of strings IV, V, and VI is:

Even though the instructions concerning the tunings of the hyŭn-kŭm, as we find them in the Yang-kŭm shin-po, are somewhat involved, we shall discuss them because they provide an interesting view of how Korean kŭm masters of the seventeenth century dealt with the problems.

Before we consider these instructions we have to remember that "fret
one" always indicates the pitch of the open string. Thus "fret two"
will be the first one to alter the pitch of the string. Another unusual
feature is the instruction "lightly depressed." If, for instance, the
string is to be "lightly depressed" on the third fret, the finger touches
the string in such a manner that it is stopped not by the third but by
the next taller fret — the second one. In short, the pitch will be lower
than if it were produced by the third fret, yet it is notated by means of
the third fret symbol. If we read that a string is to be "lightly depressed" on fret two it means that fret one (the open string) is intended.
The reason for this practice is that it can suggest a change of hand
position on the instrument and, in certain cases, may facilitate (or
confuse) notation.

Pyong-cho Tuning:

The pitch of string III is indicated by an indirect instruction: fret six
of string III when "lightly depressed" should produce the same note as
that of the open string IV. Fret two of string II, if "lightly depressed,"
should again produce the same pitch as that of the open string IV, and
the open string I should be tuned to the pitch produced by fret two of
string III.

U-cho Tuning:

Strings II and III retain the same tuning as in Pyong-cho. String II on
fret one or on fret two, "lightly depressed," has to have the same
pitch as string IV; string III on fret six, "lightly depressed," has to
produce the same pitch as string IV. In contrast to the Pyong-cho
tuning, string I has to produce the same pitch as string III on fret two
"lightly depressed" (which means open string), and which is also the
pitch of string VI.

Yang's involved tuning method can be reduced into two short formulas:

Pyong-cho: (宮 is Bb)

I, 1 = III, 2   (徵 is F)

II, 2 (lightly depressed) = IV, V (宮 , Bb)

III, 6 (lightly depressed) = IV, V

IV ⎫
    ⎬ = 宮 (Bb)
V ⎭

VI = 宮 (lower Bb)

U-cho: (宮 is Eb)

I, 1 = III, 2

II, 2 (lightly depressed) = IV, V (徵 , Bb)

III, 6 (lightly depressed) = IV, V (Bb)

IV ⎫
    ⎬ = 徵 (Bb)
V ⎭

VI = III, 2 = I (宮 , Eb)

We must add that several notes on both strings are never performed but may occasionally be used as bases for alterations. In practice, III, 3 is never used. It represents the note G (natural), which does not occur (in that position) in any of the four modes. However, it can become important as a low alteration of III, 3.

Below is a list of the notations of the pitches commonly produced on strings II and III, irrespective of the alterations in the kae-myon modes. The notes on string II are notated with "pang" (方), on string III with tae (大). The fret numbers are written below the pang and tae symbols.

String II

String III

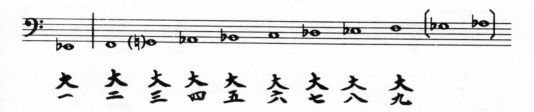

The "big string" (III) is never played higher than the ninth fret. The open "play string" (II), invariably tuned a fifth higher than the "big string," corresponds to the pitch of III, 5. Since the kae-myon-cho forms require alterations of notes, notes which in Pyong-cho and U-cho can be produced by merely stopping the strings on the rigid frets, the player has to apply pressure against the string with his left hand in order to modify the sounds. For instance, in U-cho, II, 5 produces the note F; U-cho kae-myon-cho, however, requires Gb (and omits F), and here the player has to apply pressure to the string in order to change F to Gb. This procedure is notated with the symbol 力 , which is placed below the fret number, e.g. 𠀀 , and will produce the required Gb in U-cho kae-myon-cho. The symbol 力 is called yok ("strength") in Korea.[6] [7]

The following chart shows the commonly-used notes of all four modes notated with basic hap-cha-po symbols:

Pyong-cho	Pyong-cho kae-myon-cho	U-cho	U-cho kae-myon-cho
Bb	(亥)	eb	(室)
	Ab 方六刀		db 方九刀
G 方六		c 方九	
F 方五	F 方五	Bb 方八	Bb 方八
Eb 方四	Eb 方四	Ab 方七	Ab 方七
	Db 大六刀		Gb 方五刀
C 大六		F 方五	
Bb 大五	Bb 大五	Eb 方四	Eb 方四

In Pyong-cho kae-myon-cho the notes Db and Ab, and in U-cho kae-myon-cho the notes Gb and db, are notated with yok. These four notes are produced by applying pressure to the notes C and G of Pyong-cho and F and c of U-cho.

The opposite effect of yok is created by the "lightly depressed" sign, 又 .[68] As already mentioned this sign instructs the player to touch the string on the prescribed fret so lightly that the next lower sound is produced. For instance, in U-cho, we may find 大五 大五又 , which will sound [musical notation] ; it could be notated in a less complex manner by 大五 大四 . Or, in Pyong-cho kae-myon-cho, the following could be written: 大四 大三又 which will sound [musical notation] ; 大三 , denotes that the note G (natural) cannot be used in this mode. We could, however, notate 大四 大三又 as 大四 大二 .

In the introductory part of the Yang-kŭm shin-po[69] we read that fret six of string III when "lightly depressed" should produce the same pitch as the (open) string IV. We know that successive frets produce a diatonic sequence of notes; thus, if we assume that fret six of string III produces Bb (the same as the open string IV), all we have to do is count in reverse, or better, down the scale until we reach fret one. Before we do this we have to keep in mind that the "lightly depressed" fret six produces the same pitch as fret five, hence counting down the scale must start from Bb. If fret five produces Bb, fret one (the open string) will produce Eb.[70] Similarly, if we endeavor to ascertain the pitch of string II we again have to remember that the "lightly depressed" fret two of string II produces the same pitch as the open string (fret one). This has to produce the same pitch as the open string IV (Bb). String I should be tuned to the pitch produced when depressing fret two of string III. The open string III produces Eb, hence fret two will produce F, one diatonic degree higher.

The Yang-kŭm shin-po still refers to movable bridges placed below the open strings (I, IV, V, VI). These bridges are no longer in use; when they were they served only as tuning devices. The famous kŭm-po states that in the tuning of Pyong modes the bridge of the Mun string (I) should be moved in such a manner that the pitch of the string (I) becomes the same as that produced by string III when "lightly depressed" on fret three. We read further that in the tunings of the U modes the "big string" (III) and strings IV and V should be tuned in the same way as in the Pyong modes, but that the Mu string (VI) should be raised to Eb and the bridge of the Mun string (I) should be moved in such a manner that the pitch becomes a whole-tone lower than that in the Pyong mode tunings, namely Eb.

Figures 71 and 72 (pp. 317-18), taken from the Yang-kŭm shin-po, illustrate the tuning of the old hyŭn-kŭm in both Pyong and U modes. Both charts shown in these figures are provided with the symbols of the old (Chinese) Five-Tone Notation, which are applicable to any specific five-tone tuning.

The first chart informs us (outer right column) that we are dealing with the hyŭn-kŭm; the second column from the right mentions that this is the Pyong-cho sang-hyong ("scattered form") tuning. Below it we read that the mode is a five-tone form in which the notes kak (角) and chih (徵) are used. In the second chart, which deals with the U-cho tuning, the corresponding annotation states that the notes U (羽), kung (宮), and sang (商) are used. These two annotations refer to the Eb - F location in both modes: in Pyong-cho (Bb C Eb F G), with the appropriate Bb as kung, the

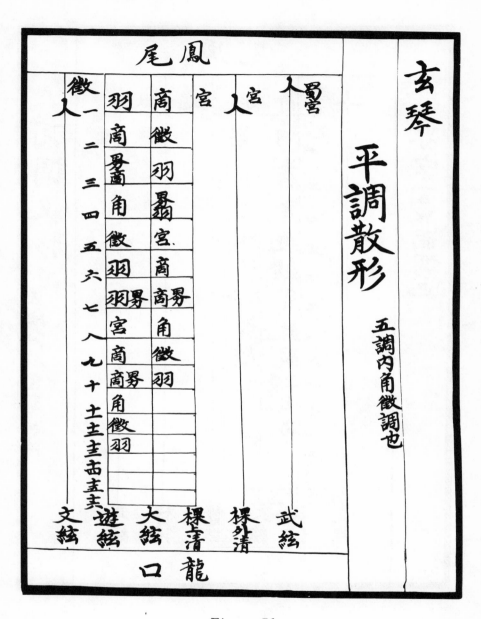

Figure 71

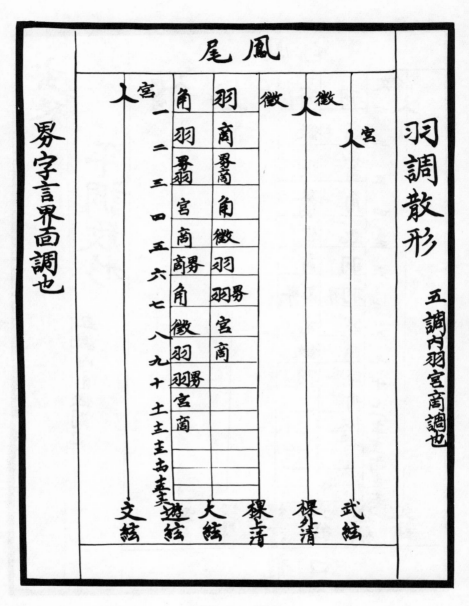

Figure 72

notes Eb and F are kak and ch'ih; in U-cho (Eb F Ab Bb c), with
the required Eb as kung, the notes Eb and F are kung and sang, and,
furthermore, the preceding U is given. This is helpful because in
both modes the upper three notes progress by whole-tone steps. Hence
the position of U, kung, and sang is a determining factor; the interval
between sang and kak becomes that of a minor third.[71]

At the top of both charts stands "Phoenix Tail" and at the bottom
"Dragon Mouth" — terms for the two ends of the board of the hyŭn-kŭm.
At the outer left side of the U-cho chart (Fig. 72) is an indication
that the symbols provided with 畏 appear only in the kae-myon-cho
forms where sang and U have to be raised by a semitone (to 商畏
and 羽畏). This remark applies also to the Pyong-cho chart.

Somewhat puzzling are the relative pitch indications for strings
II and III. The charts show that the two strings, when open (fret one),
are supposed to produce the pitches U and sang respectively, each of
which is a fourth lower than the pitches produced when the strings are
depressed at fret two. Instruments built during the last two centuries
show that the interval between open string and fret two has become
that of a major second.

Upon examining the prescribed relative pitches on strings II and
III, beginning with fret two, we find that the charts are in accordance
with our previous statements except that fret three would produce a
note which is a semitone higher than sang (fret two) on string II and
would also produce the note U, which is a whole tone higher than the
preceding chih on string III. This is technically impossible because
the frets are rigid, and the distance between frets two and three cannot produce an interval of a semitone on string II and one of a whole
tone on string III. The charts show these unequal intervals because

string II is never used below fret four, hence the carefree approach to notation found in the two charts, though most puzzling to a person who tries to study the subject without the help of a kŭm master, is of no consequence to the initiated. In short, a certain amount of secrecy, perhaps even purposeful misleading of the uninitiated, can be detected in these charts.

We shall now leave the charts of Yang and turn to basic string and fret signs, assuming that the distance between fret one and two creates the interval of a major second. In order to save the reader the bother of checking the four modes as notated in the charts, we list the notes once more:

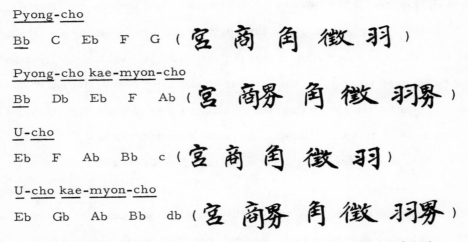

Pyong-cho

Bb   C   Eb   F   G

Pyong-cho kae-myon-cho

Bb   Db   Eb   F   Ab

U-cho

Eb   F   Ab   Bb   c

U-cho kae-myon-cho

Eb   Gb   Ab   Bb   db

The following illustrates the notes of the four modes notated in hap-cha-po. As some notes can be performed either on strings II or III, the common alternatives are shown:

Pyong-cho

Pyong-cho kae-myon-cho

U-cho

U-cho kae-myon-cho

Occasionally writers omit the yok sign and notate only the string symbol and the number of the fret. If the note produced by this particular
fret does not appear in the mode prescribed (this can happen only in
one of the two kae-myon-cho forms), the fret number will then represent the note as if it were raised by a yok sign. For instance, if a

writer wishes to notate Db in U-cho kae-myon-cho, he may do this by writing 杳 or by omitting the yok sign and writing only 夲 . In Pyong-cho and U-cho 夲 represents the note C, but since the piece is in U-cho kae-myon-cho the writer assumes that the player knows that the symbol cannot possibly denote C and expects him to perform Db, the correct note appropriate for the kae-myon-cho forms.

The organization of hap-cha-po symbols differs from that of the Chinese chien-tzŭ. The Korean symbol places the fret number below the string sign and any other instructions regarding the plucking finger, direction of plucking, arpeggio, and others are placed to the left or right of the string-fret combination. The Korean symbols do not number the strings because only two strings are employed for melody playing (大 and 方). In Chinese chien-tzŭ the plucking finger sign is the central feature of the complex symbol; in hap-cha-po the central feature is the string-fret combination:

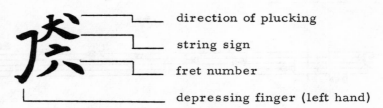

direction of plucking
string sign
fret number
depressing finger (left hand)

In contrast to the Chinese ch'in tablature Korean hap-cha-po does not use any signs for the plucking of strings because, as mentioned before, a small rod is employed. However, the Ak-hak koe-pŭm of the fifteenth century reports that two kinds of (finger) plucking were in use: 勺 (ku), the right middle finger plucking in an inward direction, and 挑 (cho), the right middle finger plucking in an outward direction. Since the great zither masters of Korea used the small rod (suttae), no plucking finger instructions are given in their books except the two

comma-shaped signs placed to the right and left of the notational symbol, which denote the direction of the plucking movement. Technical
details are indicated by:

ㄱ

the left thumb depresses the string; the
sign is an abbreviation of 母 ("thumb").

人 (イ)

the left index finger depresses the string;
it is an abbreviation of 食 ("index finger").

レ

the left middle finger depresses the string;
it is an abbreviation of 長 ("middle finger").

夕

the left ring finger depresses the string; it
is an abbreviation of 名 ("ring finger").

丨

denotes an appoggiatura; the ornamental
note has to be performed by the rod on the
open Mun string (I) and can be followed by a
note on string II or III. The succeeding note
is notated in the symbol while the ornamenting
note is indicated by the vertical line; for instance, 陸 is transcribed as

at the left side of the notational symbol;
indicates that the string is to be plucked in
an outward direction away from the player.

at the right side of the notational symbol;
indicates that the string is to be plucked in
an inward direction toward the player.

Some of the foregoing signs may be combined:

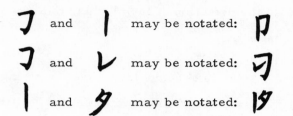

Frequently we find annotations such as 肖 (or 仝), "the same as above," which mean that the preceding note is to be repeated and performed in the same manner as before. We may also find 肖又 which indicates that 又 is to be applied when the preceding note is being repeated. For instance,

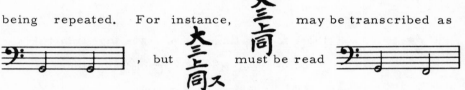

may be transcribed as

, but   must be read   .

The sign ㄴ indicates an arpeggio across the open strings. It usually begins with string I and, avoiding strings II and III, extends to one of the strings IV, V, or VI. Avoiding strings II and III is not difficult because the open strings are strung slightly higher than are the two fretted strings.

The following shows two typical annotations in which the use of ㄴ is illustrated:

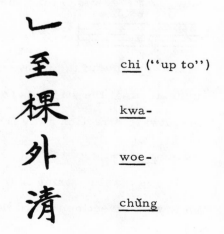

chi ("up to")

kwa-

woe-

chŭng

This means that an arpeggio, which always begins with string I, is
performed up to the kwa-woe-chŭng string (V).

nae (namely'')

chi (''up to'')

mu-

hyŭn

The second annotation indicates an arpeggio beginning with the Mun
string (I) and ending with the Mu string (VI).

Occasionally the symbol ㄴ , and particularly the words kae
chŭng (皆 清), ''all chŭng, '' indicate the succession of
strings IV, V, and VI without string I.   This generally occurs when
the arpeggio becomes the concluding feature of a phrase or a piece.[72]

The rarely-used sign ○ indicates a full arpeggio across all
six strings. The sign ⧻ indicates a shake or a vibrato. ㄙ denotes a lateral push of the string after it has been plucked — the left
hand depresses the string at a prescribed spot, the right hand plucks,
and then the left hand pushes the vibrating string laterally whereby the
pitch is raised. For instance:

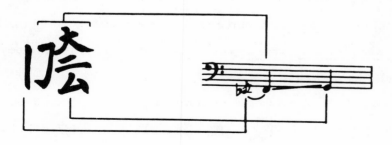

The left ring finger depresses only the pang string (II), the middle finger the tae string (III), and the left index finger and thumb can thus be used on both strings II and III. If the symbol does not contain any signs for the depressing finger and if the note is to be produced on an open string, the plucking can be done by either the middle finger, the index finger, or the thumb of the left hand.

Hap-cha-po is frequently combined with the (Chinese) Five Tone Notation, the two being written in parallel columns side by side. In such instances the Five Tone Notation shows a "new" symbol (畀) which is added to represent the raised sang and U (the hap-cha-po combinations with yok) in the modes of Pyong-cho kae-myon-cho and U-cho kae-myon-cho. For instance, if Bb is kung, C is sang in Pyong-cho. In Pyong-cho kae-myon-cho, where sang becomes Db, the symbol is denoted by 畀商 (or 商畀). The same applies to the note Ab, the raised U in the two kae-myon-cho forms: 畀羽 (or 羽畀).[73]

While ch'in tablatures show very little rhythmic organization, leaving most of it to the player's memory and invention, we find that hyŭn-kŭm tablatures show some clarity in rhythmic matters by using the chŭng-kan-po.[74] The division of a "measure" (haeng) into six kang and each kang into two or three chŭng-kan may be observed in many kŭm books.

The piece shown in Figure 73 (p. 327) has two haeng in each column without showing a detailed organization of the required eight beats within each haeng. Another piece, shown in Figure 75 (p. 347), utilizes chŭng-kan-po, whereby the rhythmic shape of the melody becomes fully explicit.

We shall turn first to the rhythmically less-distinct piece, the famous Man-tae-yŭp (慢 大 葉)[75] (pp. 327-34) by

Figure 73

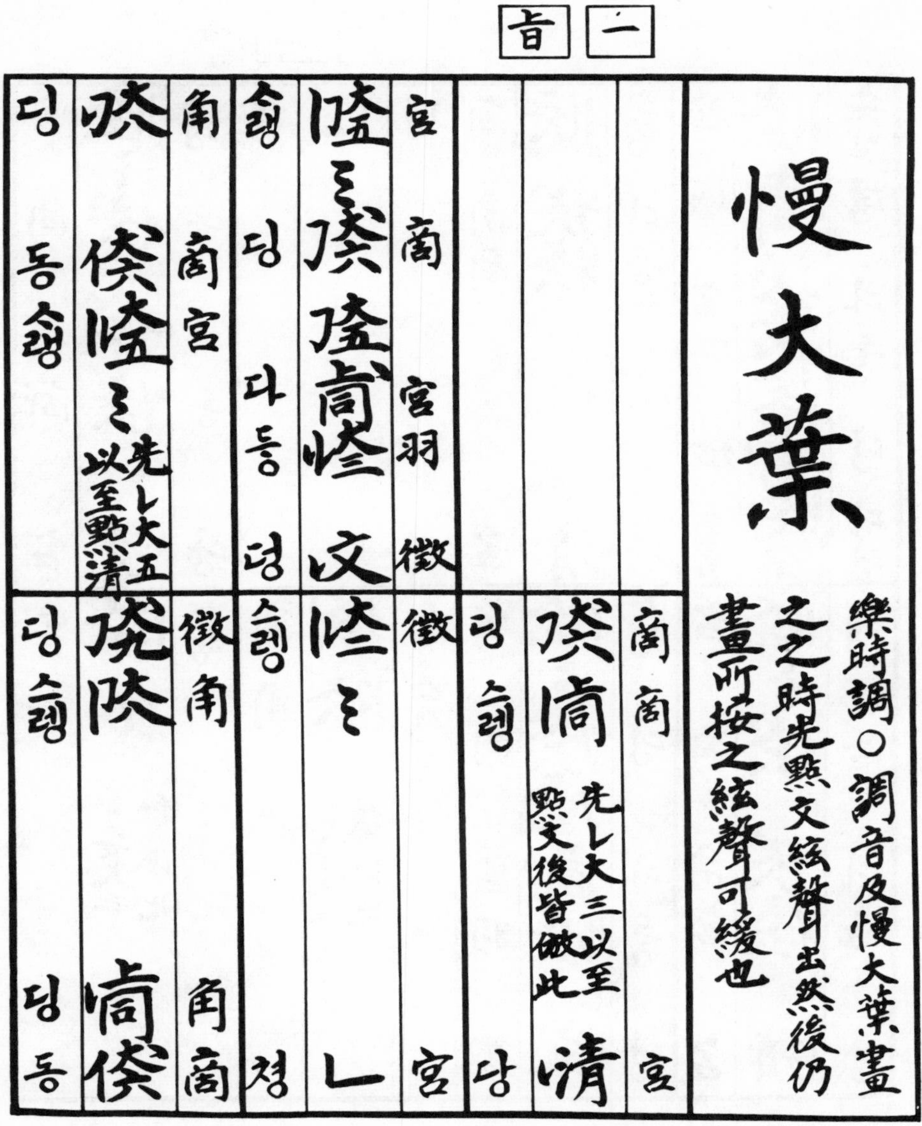

Figure 73 (<u>cont.</u>)

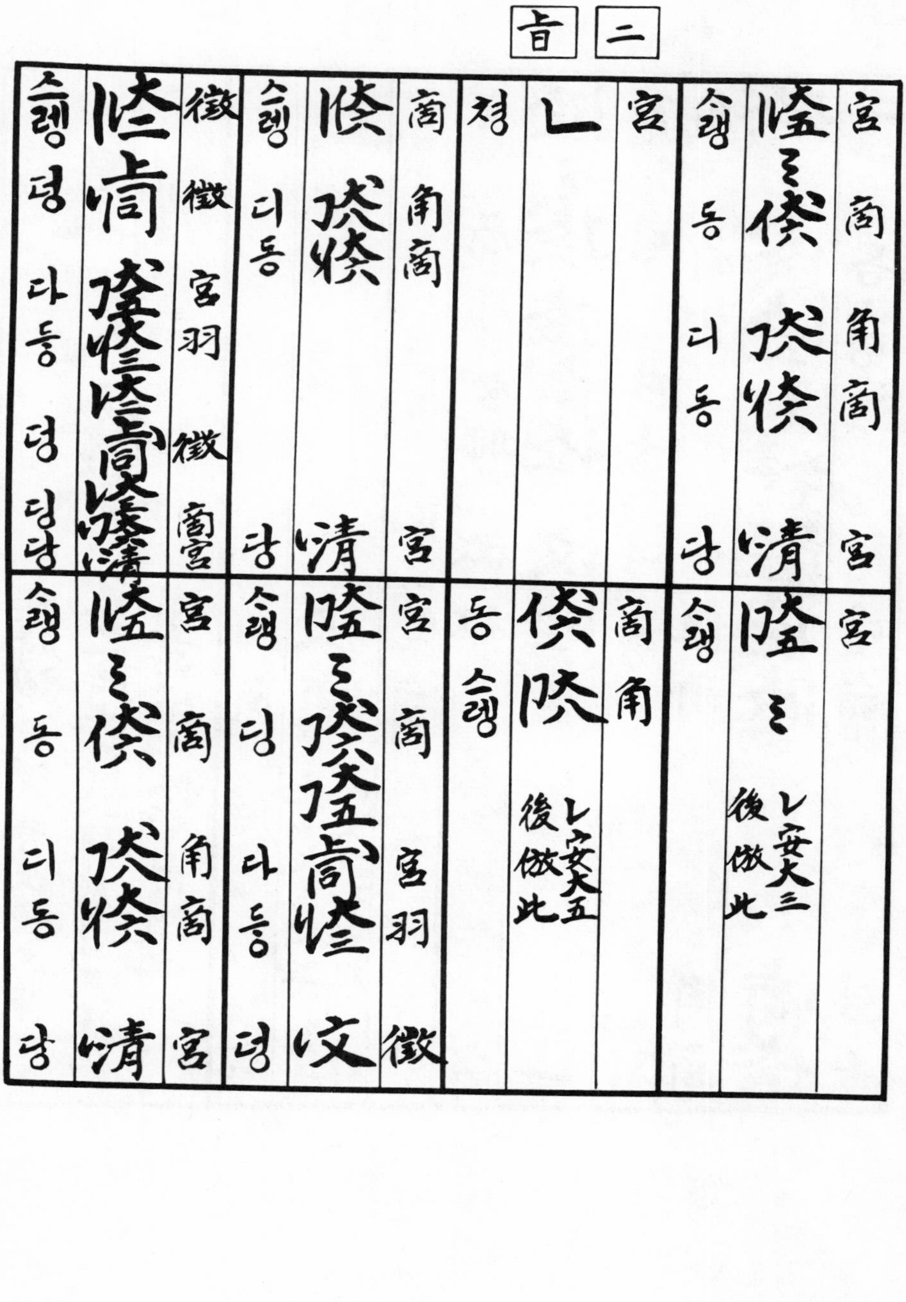

Figure 73 (cont.)

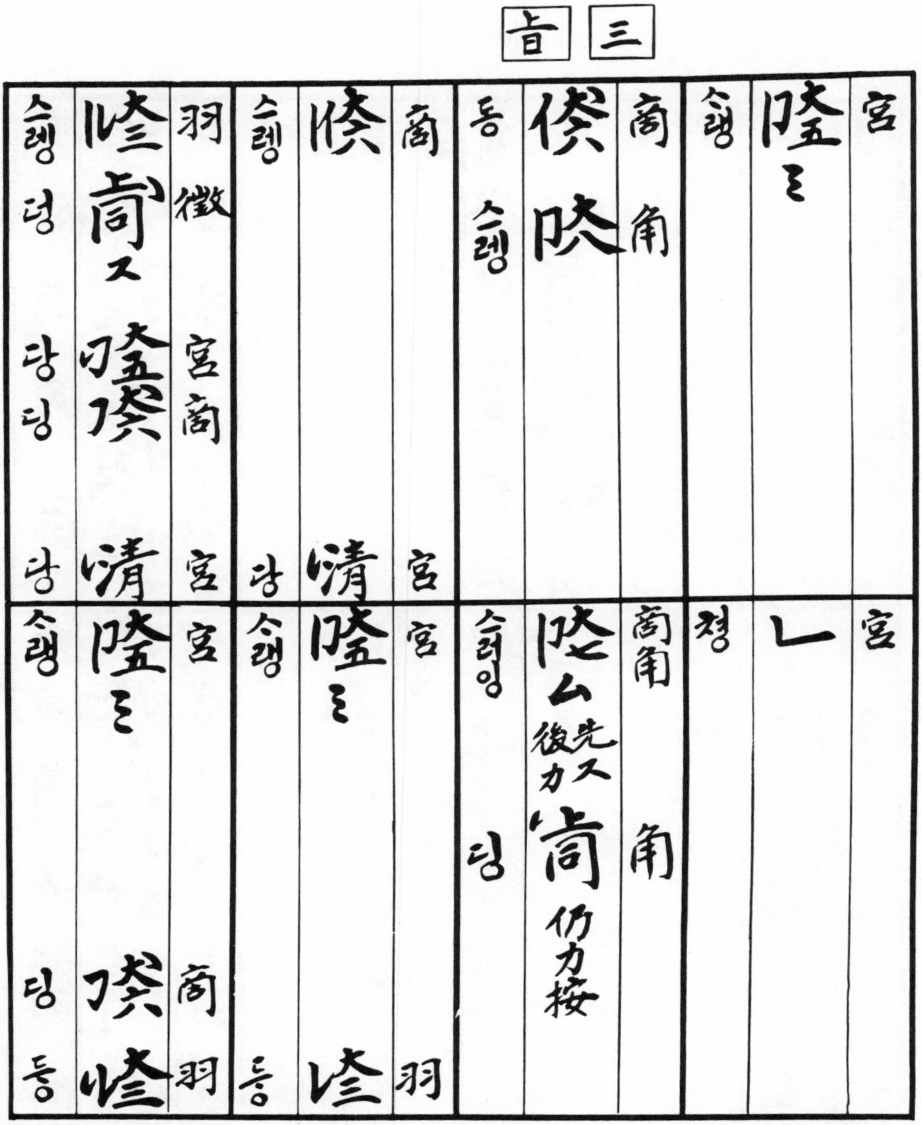

Figure 73 (<u>cont.</u>)

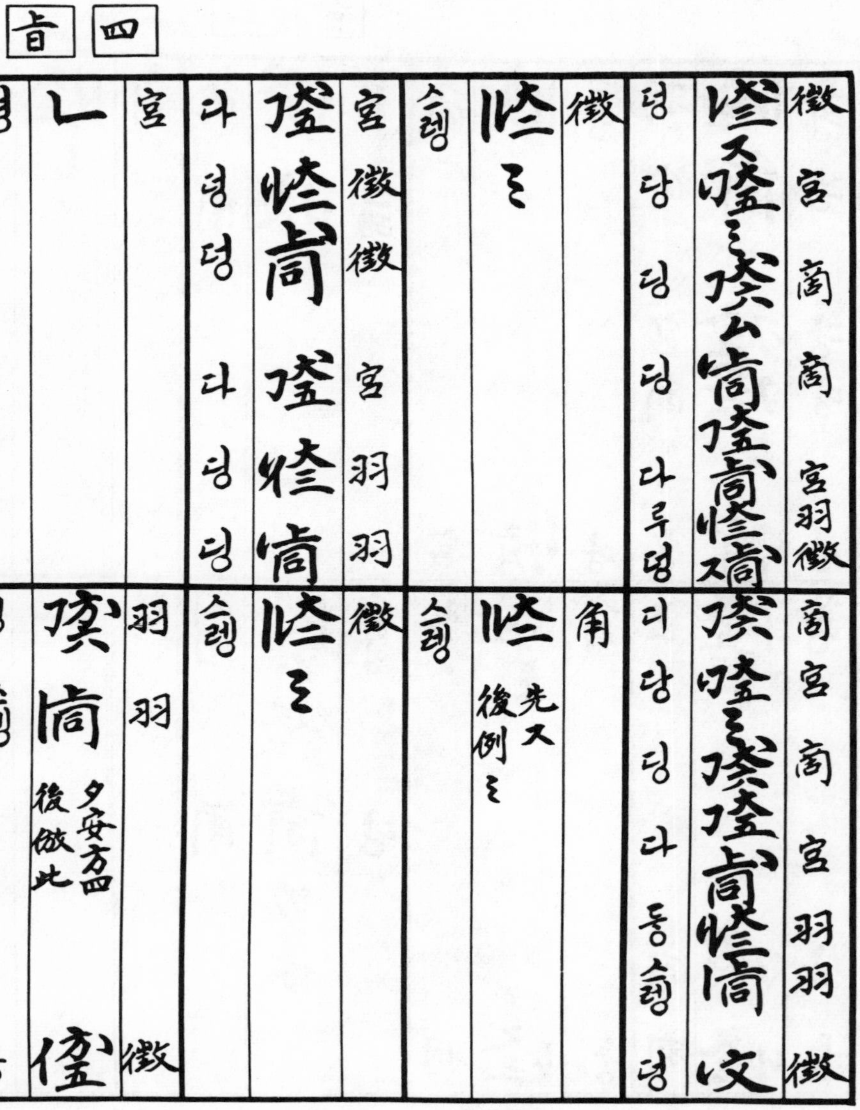

Figure 73 (<u>cont.</u>)

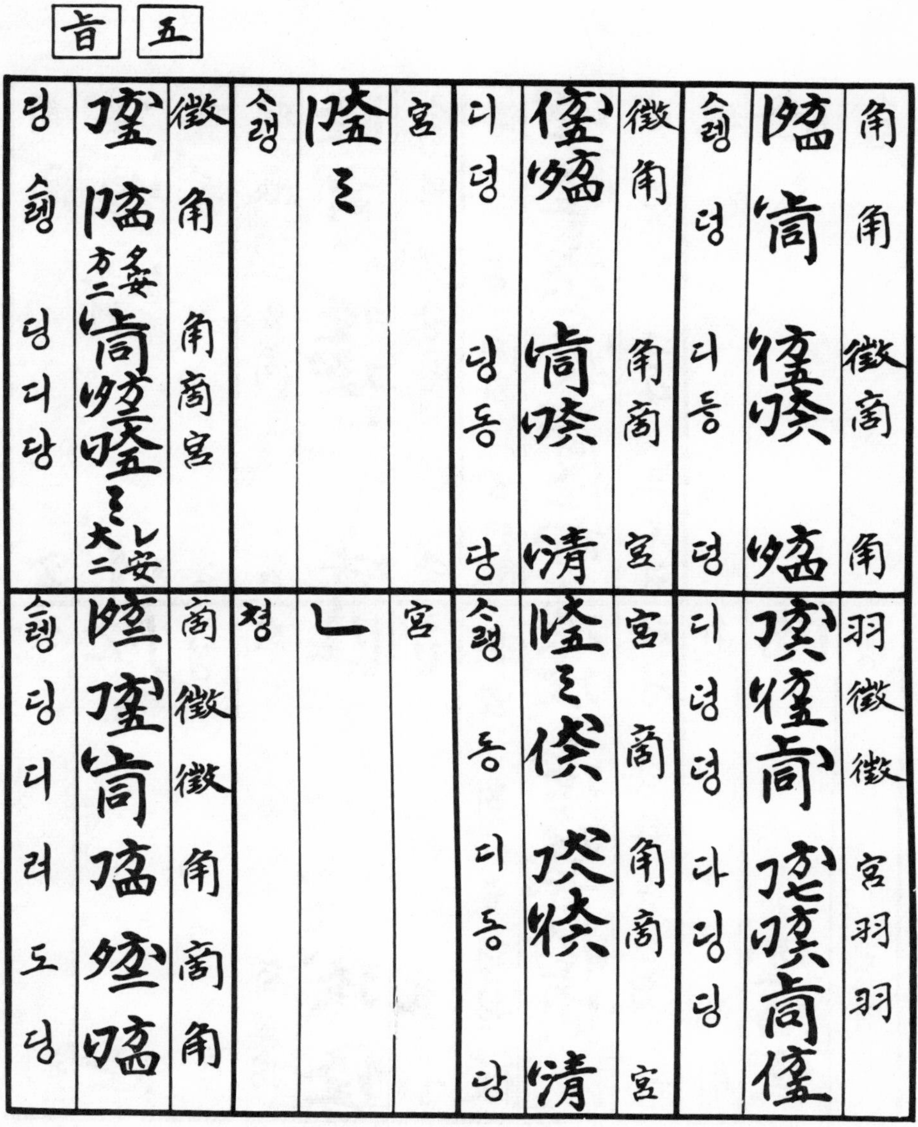

Figure 73 (<u>cont.</u>)

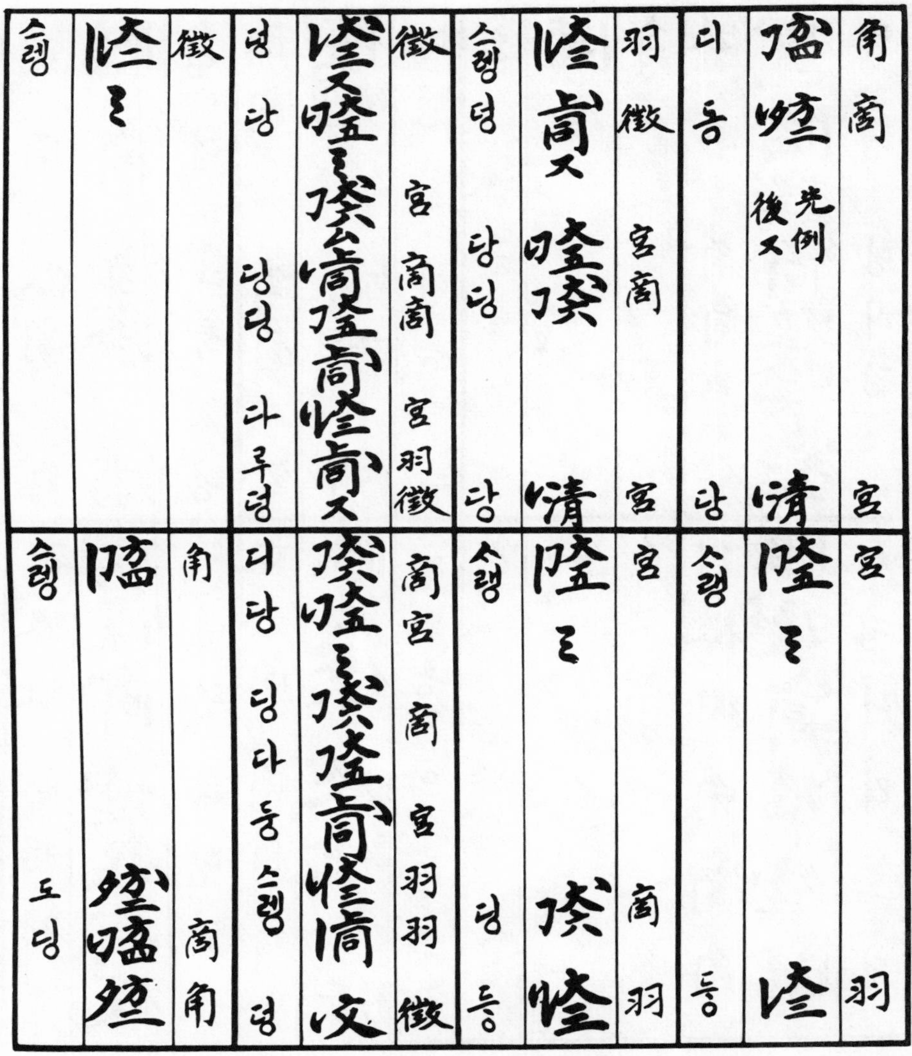

Figure 73 (cont.)

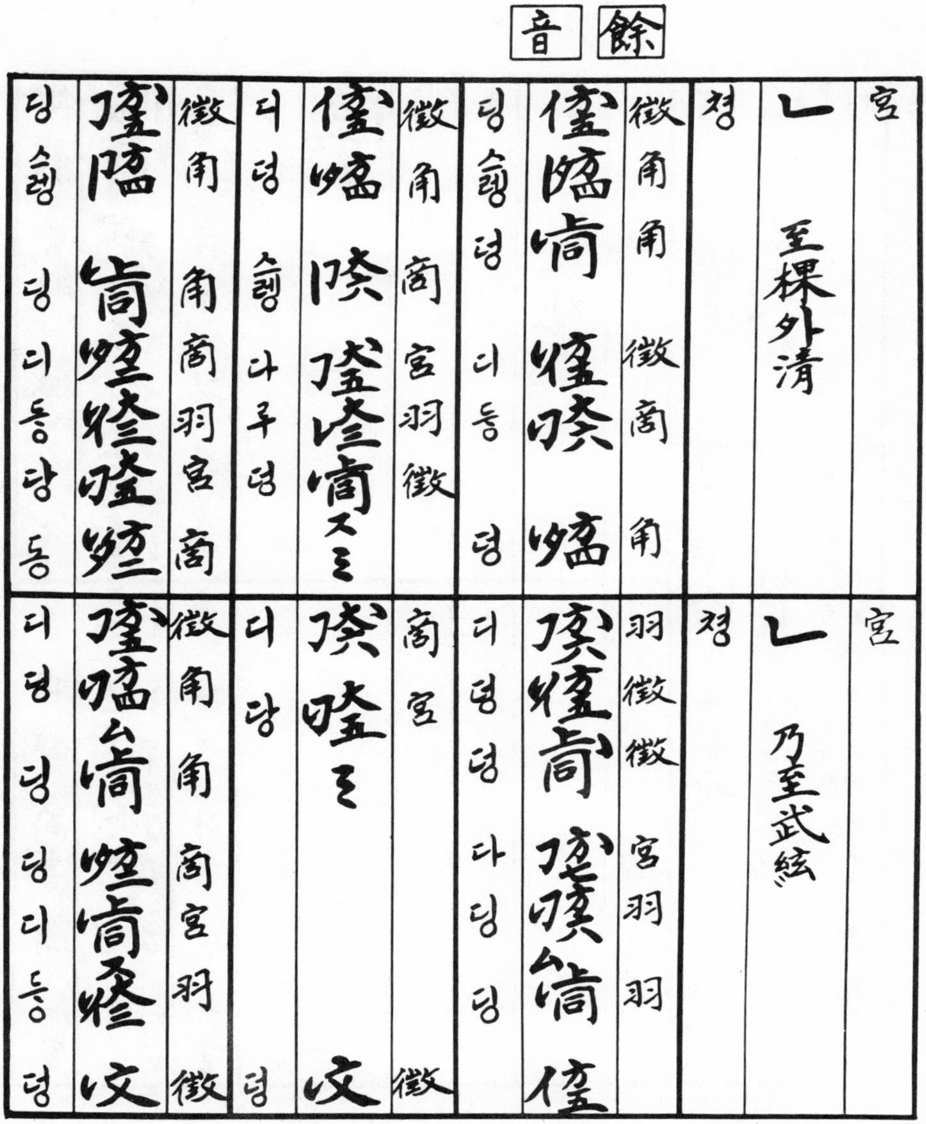

Figure 73 (cont.)

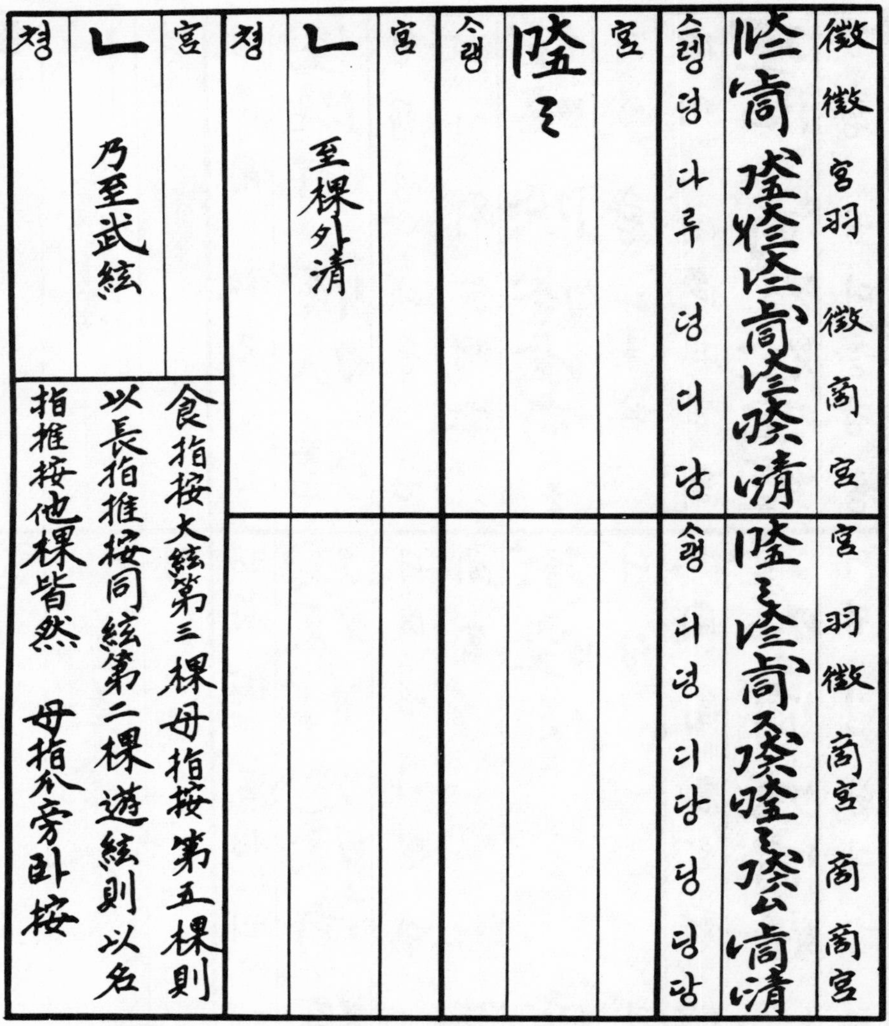

Cho-sŭng (趙晟) of the fifteenth century, as notated in the Yang-kŭm shin-po. For easier reading the pages of this copy are arranged in the Western manner — in a left to right sequence. However, each page is to be read in the Korean way, that is, each (big) column from top to bottom and the columns on each page from right to left. The title Man-tae-yŭp appears in large characters in the outer right column of page 327. The annotation below the title informs us that the melody is in Ak-shi-cho[76] (樂時調), which is another term for Pyong-cho. The rest of the annotation offers advice in tuning, a procedure we have discussed before in detail.

The hap-cha-po symbols begin with the second column. We observe that each column is divided into two haeng. As in Chinese solo ch'in music the player has considerable freedom concerning the duration of the notes. However, in hap-cha-po he must observe the basic eight (or sixteen) beats within each haeng, and, whenever possible, he must endeavor to maintain the $\frac{3+2+3}{4}$ meter.

The example shows the combination of three notational systems: the center column contains hap-cha-po symbols, the left side shows the melody notated in yuk-po, [77] and to the right are the symbols of the Chinese Five-Tone Notation. At present we shall confine our attention to the hap-cha-po and the Chinese Five-Tone symbols.

First measure (second column from the right, lower half):

String III is depressed on fret 6 by the left thumb; the string is plucked (scooped) in an outward direction. As we have transcribed kung as Bb, the Chinese Five-Tone symbol substantiates our finding: III, 6 and 商(商) denote C.

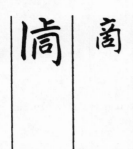

The second character in the <u>hap-cha-po</u> column is 商 , meaning "the same as above." Included in the symbol is 〡 , which means that the note must be preceded by an appoggiatura beginning with the <u>Mun</u> string (I):

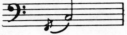

What follows now is characteristic of numerous East Asiatic tablatures: the musical notation is interrupted and an annotation is interpolated instructing the player about technical details — mainly about the required position of his left hand.

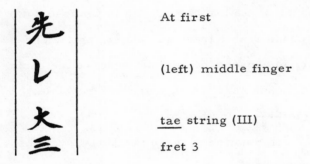

At first

(left) middle finger

<u>tae</u> string (III)

fret 3

The meaning of this portion of the annotation is "at first the left middle finger depresses fret 3 of string III." This implies a basic hand position on the <u>hyŭn-kŭm</u> in which the left index finger and thumb are ready to depress the string on frets 5 and 6.

with (stay "with" former position)

come to, until

strike

<u>Mun</u> (string I)

This portion of the annotation means "maintain the hand position (described in the previous paragraph) until string I (Mun) is struck." In order to understand this we must consider briefly the hap-cha-po symbols in the second measure (the upper rectangle of column three). There we find that frets 5, 6, and, again, fret 5 of string III are to be depressed by the left thumb (丁), and, below, fret 3 is to be depressed by the middle finger (ㄴ). This fingering cannot be executed unless the previously indicated hand position is maintained. A change from this position is shown by the first symbol of the second rectangle of the third column (㐱), where the middle finger has shifted from fret 3 to fret 2. In short, up to 㐱 the original hand position remains unaltered. The rest of the annotation is:

後	afterwards
皆	all
倣	imitate
此	this

These last four characters of the (first) annotation instruct the player that "after the plucking of string I at the end of the first rectangle of the third column, all other symbols of the tablature refer to the new hand position assumed at 㐱 at the beginning of the lower rectangle of the third column."

We now return to the lower rectangle of the second column. The symbol below the (first) annotation at the end of the lower rectangle is

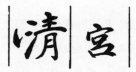, meaning that strings IV and V are to be scooped in succession in an outward direction.

The rhythmic shape of the first measure remains vague except that we know that the total number of beats in each rectangle must be eight. The basic grouping of the beats should be 3+2+3, but the position of the annotation after the second symbol seems to indicate that this is the note of longest duration. We may transcribe this measure as:

or as:

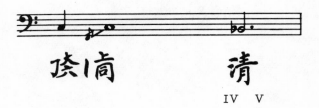

Second measure (top of third column):

III, 5 depressed by left thumb; appoggiatura from string I:

The wavy line indicates that the note is to be held — its duration is determined by the total of durations of the other notes in this measure.

III, 6 depressed by left thumb:

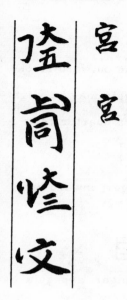

III, 5 depressed by left thumb:

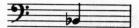

Same as above. Plucking motion inward.

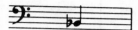

III, 3 depressed by left middle finger:

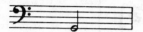

I, plucking motion outward:

As we are aiming at the basic 3+2+3 rhythm we extend  to the duration of a half note in order to get

Third measure (bottom of third column):

II, 2 appoggiatura from I

The wavy line again indicates that the note is to be held. This is the point at which the position of the left hand is changed.

This is a "cadential" arpeggio in which the open strings IV, V, and VI are played in succession:

Fourth measure (top of fourth column):

III, 8 depressed by left thumb; the outward stroke which follows the cadential arpeggio may be slightly delayed, hence we interpolate a quarter rest:

III, 6 depressed by left index finger; inward motion of plucking:

III, 5 depressed by left middle finger; appoggiatura from string I:

The annotation that follows again deals with the position of the left hand; the right hand column of the annotation reads:

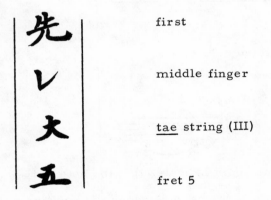

first

middle finger

tae string (III)

fret 5

This means that the (left) middle finger moves to fret 5 of string III. The left hand column of the annotation reads:

herewith

continue

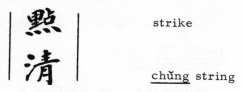

strike

chŭng string

This means that the middle finger of the left hand maintains its position on fret 5 of string III until the chŭng string is struck (at the end of the sixth measure — second page of the manuscript, first column, top).

Fifth measure:

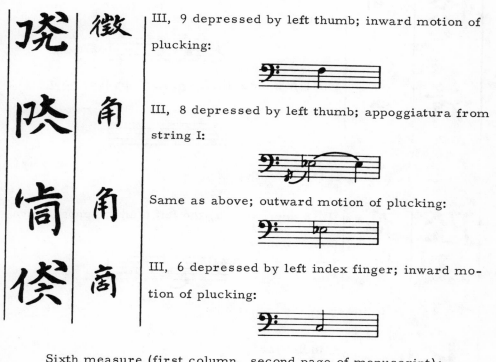

III, 9 depressed by left thumb; inward motion of plucking:

III, 8 depressed by left thumb; appoggiatura from string I:

Same as above; outward motion of plucking:

III, 6 depressed by left index finger; inward motion of plucking:

Sixth measure (first column, second page of manuscript):

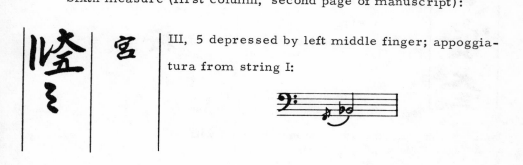

III, 5 depressed by left middle finger; appoggiatura from string I:

III, 6 depressed by left index finger:

III, 8 depressed by left thumb; inward plucking motion. The quick succession of Eb and C (next symbol) results from the inward-outward strokes (➘ ➚).

III, 6 depressed by left index finger; outward plucking motion:

The left middle finger plucks the open chŭng string:

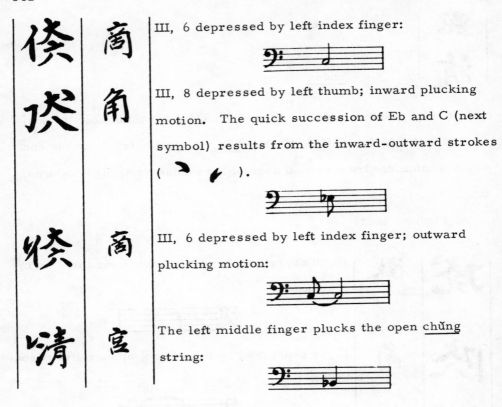

The beginning of the seventh measure is:

III, 5 depressed by the left thumb; appoggiatura from string I:

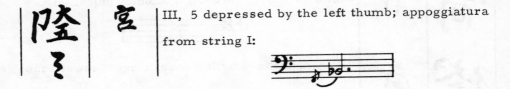

This is followed by the annotation:

middle finger

stops (an abbreviation of 按)

tae string (III), fret 3

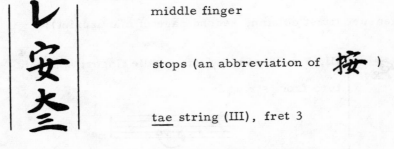

and, at the left, the annotation continues with:

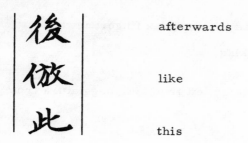

afterwards

like

this

which means that the following remains unchanged. The complete
seventh measure reads:

Eighth measure (second column, top, second page of manuscript):

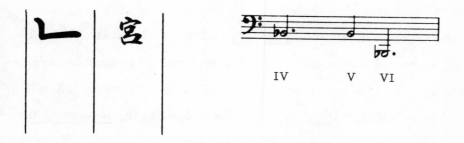

The arpeggio has to fill the whole measure, hence the characteristic
3+2+3 grouping of beats.

The ninth measure begins with:

 III, 6 depressed by left index finger; inward motion of plucking.

 III, 8 depressed by left thumb; appoggiatura from string I.

The following annotation has the same meaning as the one found in the seventh measure except that the middle finger (⌄) has to move up to fret 5 of string III.

There is no necessity for us to continue this analysis. The transcription of the melody is comparatively easy because most of the symbols discussed before occur over and over again. Moreover, we have mentioned previously that occasional annotations including the lengthy one at the end of the piece deal with technical details (mainly hand positions) which have no direct bearing upon the notation and transription of the melody.

The following, Figure 74 (pp. 345-46) shows the transcription of Man-tae-yŭp in its entirety.[78] The reader is advised to transcribe the entire piece and to compare his result with Lee's transcription. This comparison will show that in terms of rhythm, several interpretations are possible.[79]

In ensemble music the hyŭn-kŭm tablature, like that of the Chinese ch'in, becomes simplified, and the rhythmic organization becomes more explicit than in solo pieces. The following, Figure 75 (p. 347) represents an excerpt of Yŭ-min-ak[80] as notated in the An-sang-kŭm-po.[81] At the right side the melody is notated in o-ŭm-yak-po,[82] the column next to it is hap-cha-po, the third column contains the text, and the outer left column the symbols for the chang-ko (drum) part. The use of chŭng-kan-po[83] enables the performer to get a clear rhythmical

Figure 74

Figure 74 (<u>cont.</u>)

Figure 75

347

outline. There are two haeng in each column. Each haeng shows the characteristic division into 3+2+3 chŭng-kan. Our excerpt contains only three textual characters. They are: 海 , hae, "ocean"; 東 , tong, "east"; and 六 , yuk, "six." The chang-ko signs are: 鼓 , ko "drum," which indicates that the hand-beaten skin of the drum is to be used; 摇 , yo, "roll"; 鞭 , pyŭn, "whip," the stick-beaten side of the drum is to be used; and 双 , sang, "both," both sides are to be beaten simultaneously.

The transcription of the four haeng of Yŭ-min-ak is shown below in Figure 76:

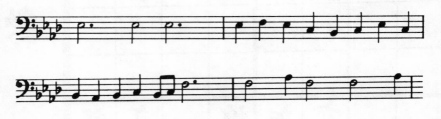

Figure 76

The following, (Fig. 77, p. 349), is Yŭ-min-ak as notated in the Shin-sŭng kŭm-po (申 晟 琴 譜), "Shin-sŭng's Zither Book." [84] The example shows the combination of hap-cha-po and yuk-po. Three textual characters are written near the first and penultimate symbols of the first column and near the fourth last symbols of the second column of hap-cha-po. The second textual character is placed to the left of the notational symbol while the other two are written to the right.

It is remarkable that this specimen shows no rhythmic indications. Nevertheless, the reading of this version of yŭ-min-ak causes no difficulties. Following (Fig. 78, p. 350) is Lee's transcription[85] together with the hap-cha-po symbols.

Figure 77

申晟琴譜 所載 與民樂

당스랭당스랭 스랭 딩 스랭동 당 스랭 동 당 스랭 당

海方四上同上同 大六方五 方五大六方四己 方七方五方四己 大東六 清

스렝딩 당 동 스렝 동 덩 스랭딩 덩 동 스렝 당 스랭 동 딩

大六方五方四大六 大五大四大五 大七大六大五大四 大二力 清六 大二上同力 大四

註 方四（潢）。 大六（南）。 方五（汰）。

方七（沖）。 大五（林）。 大四（仲）。 大二（太）。

Figure 78

Beyond the left edge of Figure 77 we find an annotation (註) which informs the performer about the pitches in relation to hap-cha-po symbols. 畜(潢) means that II, 4 should produce the Huang-chung, here notated as 潢 , with the ch'ing sign denoting the higher octave.

In our discussion of the lü (Part I) we transcribed this symbol as the note C. Lee, however, uses the note Eb, as may be observed in his transcription. The entire annotation reads (left to right):

II, 7	(Ab)	II, 4	(Eb)
III, 5	(Bb)	III, 6	(C)
III, 4	(Ab)	II, 5	(F)
III, 2	(F)		

In the introductory pages of the Anthology of Korean Traditional Music (민 속 악 보)[86] are given a few symbols that

are variants of the ones shown above. In addition, the work presents a
few symbols which concern notations of the kaya-kŭm (kaya-ko)[8 7] and
hae-kŭm (奚琴)[8 8] music. As they may be of some interest,
we present a few of them here.

丁	pluck string I of the komunko
乌	strike or pluck a string of the komunko with the left hand
冫	strike or pluck a string of the komunko or the kaya-ko with a small stick
上	pluck string IV of the komunko
下	pluck string V of the komunko
大	pluck string VI of the komunko
○	"putting the nail of the fore-finger on the inside of the thumb, forming a circle, strike the string of the . . . kaya-ko"
8	"in the same way, strike the strings of the . . . kaya-ko successively with the nails of small finger, ring finger and middle finger"
天	move the left forefinger down to the place of the middle finger (hae-kŭm)
ㅎ	move the left forefinger down to the place of the small finger (hae-kŭm)
上	return the left index finger to where it had started moving (hae-kŭm)

IV

The Notations of the Buddhist Chant (Tibet)

THE NOTATIONS OF THE BUDDHIST CHANT (TIBET)

With the exception of the Japanese shōmyō, which we shall discuss in a second volume, information about musical notations of Buddhist chant of the continent of Asia is meager and vague; and information particularly relating to Indian Buddhist chant is practically non-existent. Buddhism in India came more or less to an end when the Muslims invaded the land, particularly Bihar and Bengal at the close of the twelfth century. At that time the monks were expelled or killed and monasteries and libraries were destroyed. Today there exist only some very small scattered Buddhist communities, and they possess no notational system of their own.

In China, where Buddhism flourished, and a multitude of sects, schools, and a wealth of translations of Indian Buddhist scriptures appeared, there exists to our knowledge no characteristic Buddhist notational system. Notations used were mainly the lü, the Five Tone, and kung-ch'ê systems.

Of some interest may be the notation or notations of Tibetan liturgical chant. Buddhism made its first appearance in Tibet during the reign of King Srong-tsan gam-po in the sixth century A.D., but it was not until the year 750 that the saintly Indian Padma-Sambhava widely propagated the new religion and incorporated into it numerous rites of the ancient Bön religion. These ancient rites, dealing with

355

magic, demon cult, and devil dances, made Buddhism appear more formidable as well as more enticing to the Tibetan people. During Padma-Sambhava's lifetime monasteries were built and the various orders of monks established. Sacred Buddhist texts, which had been imported from India across the Himalayas, were gradually translated into Tibetan, and there is little doubt that with the texts sacred images and Buddhist melodies came into Tibet.

Most of the Tibetan melodies are anhemitonic pentatonic and in strict meter. This can be noticed in indigenous folk songs, in secular music — influenced by Chinese stylistic elements, particularly Chinese opera — and in the liturgical chant of monasteries.[1] In order to illustrate this pentatonic character we show Figure 79, a short, religious song performed by school children at the monastery school in Ghoom near Darjeeling.[2] Part A of the song is repeated several times. In Part B a feature appears that resembles the organum of the medieval West. That is, the lower voice in the second part, which uses the material G A B D E, runs strictly parallel with the upper voice, which uses C D E G A. Similar phenomena appear in China and, occasionally, in the Buddhist chant of Japan.

Tibetan Buddhist prayer-songs, hymns, presentations of offerings to the Buddha and other deities, mystery play songs, and so on, like the plainsong of the West, are generally performed by monks in the lowest attainable register in unison, but, unlike the chant of the Roman Catholic Church, Tibetan chant is metrical and is accompanied by a drone produced by two, long, telescope-shaped copper trumpets (rag-dung)[3] and one or more drums. The use of these instruments is illustrated in the following example, Figure 80 (p. 358), which represents a fragment of a liturgical melody as performed in the monastery

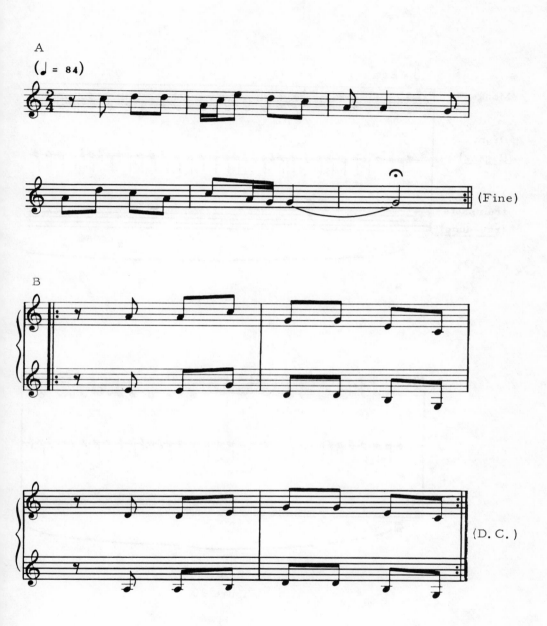

Figure 79

Monks

Drum
(lag-na)

Long
trumphets
(rag-dung)

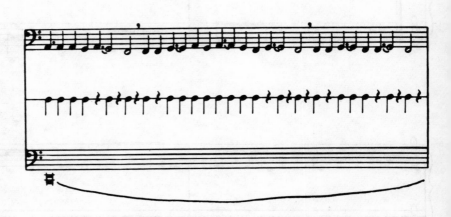

Figure 80

of Gyantse. The latter melody (Fig. 80) also shows pentatonic character.[4]

Recordings of some Tibetan melodies convey the impression that semitones and, occasionally, microtonal intervals are in use. While we have to agree that the sounds produced do show complex intervallic steps, we must point out that the basic tone-material of these melodies is predominantly anhemitonic pentatonic. This writer, who had numerous opportunities to listen to these chants performed in Ladakh and in eastern Tibet, came to the following conclusion: the liturgical melodies have to be chanted by the monks in as low a range as possible, and the massed bass voices produce a sound that indeed becomes tremendously impressive and unforgettable to the Western listener. However, only a few of the choir usually are able to sing the very low notes correctly. The majority of the choir, who cannot perform these low notes, incline to intone them a little higher; the difference between the intended note and that actually produced by the "baritone" voices being a semitone, or even a whole tone. Often the majority of the voices are somewhat out of tune, hence unusual intervals result. For instance, if the actual melody is to be F G A C C A G, we hear the majority of the monks chanting F# G# A C C A G#, or similar alterations generally affecting the lowest notes. Occasionally singers having intoned the lowest notes somewhat higher remain in that higher "key" until the rest of the voices either join them in the higher key or until some powerful voices pull them back into the original key. These differences do not occur only in liturgical chant where they are clearly noticeable but also in folk music. In folk melodies, occasionally, Indian influences (semitones, different intervals in the rising and descending scale) become apparent, and the same may happen in liturgical chants when a choir master, who is acquainted with Indian music, introduces some complex intervals; but, as a rule, folk music and liturgical chant of Tibet have predominantly pentatonic character. The range of the liturgical melodies rarely exceeds the interval of a fifth except at syllables such as PHAT, when nga ("strong voice") is to be performed. [5]

It is not known when the notational system (or systems) of Buddhist Chant in Tibet was first used. This writer was informed by Tibetan monks that the song books, called yang-yig, are "very old and have been copied over and over again for a long time." [6] The available manuscripts show two related types of neumatic notation; one with short, simple hooks and curves, the other with large, florid symbols. Both forms are written from left to right, and each curve is placed to the right or above the textual syllable.

Although we have no proof, we may conjecture three possible sources of these neumes: it is possible that they are an indigenous Tibetan product; there is some slight possibility that the neumes originated in the mysterious hand positions and patterns of small wooden sticks of Vedic India; but a much more plausible assumption is that the use of neumes for notating important melodies was imported by the Nestorians and by other Christian missions in their remarkable eastward movement.

Although Mazdaism was the state religion in Persia, Christianity under Constantine (306-337) had become the official religion of the Roman Empire and had found its way into Mesopotamia and Persia. However, Christians were so severely persecuted by the Persians that they finally broke their relationship with the church of Antiochia and eventually established a center in Edessa (the modern Urfa) which joined with the followers of Nestorius. Under the reign of the great Persian warrior king and patron of the arts, Khosru I (531-579), this Nestorian church began to flourish and expand. Its missions spread the gospel not only in Syria, Armenia, and Persia but moved to the East into India, Central Asia, and parts of China.

In the year 1625 Jesuit priests discovered a marble slab at Sin-ganfu on the Yellow River. The inscription of the tablet in Syriac and Chinese reports the events of a Syrian mission and gives the name of a missionary called Olopan who had come from Judaea to China in the year 636. The tablet also tells of how the emperor ordered a church to be built; how, after great favors were bestowed upon the mission, persecution of the Christians began in 699; and how, later, Christianity was tolerated again, and so forth.[7]

The Syrian church, which had been carried by the Nestorians into Persia, India, Central Asia, and China, had also spread between the fourth and seventh centuries to the West as far as Verona and Ravenna; to some extent its influence could be felt even in Germany and England. In short, members of the Syrian church had ample op-portunities for learning the numerous types of musical notations not only of Asia Minor but of Europe as well. A comparison between the neumes of Tibetan liturgy and those used in the fragments of the New Testament and in the Manichaean hymns with texts written in Syriac characters[8] in Soghdic — a middle Persian dialect — shows no appar-ent similarities. The Nestorian notation consists of dots, the Tibetan of hooks and curves.

We do know that the Soghdic dialect[9] was used by Buddhists, Manichaeans,[10] and Nestorians for the propagation of their respective religions in Central Asia. The notational dots, although not directly related to the Tibetan signs, deserve our attention: they are placed above or below the textual line and occasionally they appear in pairs, triplets, and quadruplets. According to Wellesz[11] the meaning of some of these dots is as follows:

(dot above the line), the voice rises;

(dot below the line), the voice falls;

rise and fall of the voice.

The doubling of dots intensifies the rise or fall; similarly a tripling partially indicates further intensification. Of interest is the grouping of four (or more) dots to form the sign ●·●, which denotes the end of a section. According to Wellesz the sign which has the function of the teleia (+) in Greek evangelistaria often appears after headings such as: ''Jesus said,'' ''Thus He spoke,'' ''Jesus spoke to the disciples.'' Later, when we examine the Tibetan manuscript, this sign can be found again in the form of [symbol] (and other, corresponding ones), where it has a similar function. Similarly we may find Tibetan parallels to the oxeia, bareia, and the syrmatike, and, probably, to other neumes not necessarily of West Asian origin.

Tibetan neumes show no Chinese features at all. If we consider that in the Yüan period the Chinese kung-ch'ê system became widely popular and that the Confucian temples still adhered to the Lü and the old Five and Seven-Tone Notations, it is remarkable that neither during the Yüan period nor in the subsequent dynasties of their culturally-productive neighbor, nothing concerning musical notation came into Tibet.

Notational influences seem to have been confined to the West and, perhaps, to some degree, to the South. We know that at the time of Marco Polo there existed considerable cultural exchange between West and East, and there is not the slightest doubt that caravans brought to the East missionaries and manuscripts, and not necessarily only those of the Syrian church.[12] We can assume that several notational systems from the West may have found their way into Tibet and, perhaps, even into Chinese Buddhist monasteries. The monks may not have retained the original significance of the neumatic symbols which they found in the imported manuscripts but may have imitated the symbols and adapted them to their own requirements. For instance, a quilisma of the West may have had a different meaning than its corresponding symbol in the Tibetan neumes. The wriggly part of the symbol would possibly represent some form of vibrato in both notations, but the intervallic characteristic of the symbol, which concerns a minor third in the West, may be interpreted quite differently in Tibet.

Without taking into consideration their musical significance, we list below a number of neumatic symbols.[13] By merely viewing their shapes we find that ╱, ⌐, ✓, ⌐, ⌐, ⌣ and ⌐, ⌐, ⌐, ⌐ in Syriac, Byzantine, and Armenian notations, or ╱, ⌐, ⌐, ⌐, ⌐, ⌐, ⌐ of St. Gall, appear in one form or another in the Tibetan system.

Throughout the centuries leading up to recent times, a great deal of music was used in Tibetan monasteries. The chanting was accompanied or interrupted by the sound of conch shells, trumpets, cymbals, drums, and other instruments. The yang-yig, used by the choir leaders,[14] contains neumes and instructions as to the use of the various instruments.

The following, Figure 81 (pp. 365-80), is a part of such a yang-yig, showing a photographic reproduction of a manuscript fragment from the monastery at Phyang. The pages shown below represent the beginning of an old text common to all sects of Tibetan Buddhism, an invocation of Shri He-ru-ka, Lord Heruka, the patron saint of Sikkim. Heruka, "unclad," is the title given to Lha-tsün ch'en-po, "The Great Reverend God," who was born in 1595 in southeastern Tibet. In the middle of the seventeenth century Lha-tsün appeared in Lhasa where he became famous and gained the high esteem of the Grand Lama. The latter part of his life was spent in Sikkim where he founded the monastery of Dub-de. The building of the monasteries of Tashiding, Pemiongchi, Sa-nga-ch'öling, and others is ascribed to him, although not proven. The date of his death is not known. Lha-tsün supposedly had many miraculous powers, particularly the power of being able to fly. He is depicted almost naked (hence: Heruka), with a dark blue complexion, and seated on a leopard skin. He is adorned with human skulls, his left hand holding a skull cup filled with blood, his right hand performing a teaching gesture. His personal belong-ings became sacred relics and were preserved and worshipped in the monastery of Pemiongchi; later the relics were removed to the monastery of To-lung.[15]

Although we do not know where the manuscript was written, we can assume that it originated in Sikkim. Described as "very old," it may date back to the end of the seventeenth century, the period following the death of Lha-tsün, which was a time of intense religious activity in Sikkim.

MANUSCRIPT I

Figure 81

Sheet 1a

365

Figure 81 (cont.)

Sheet 1b

366

Figure 81 (cont.)

Sheet 2a

367

Figure 81 (cont.)

Sheet 2b

Figure 81 (cont.)

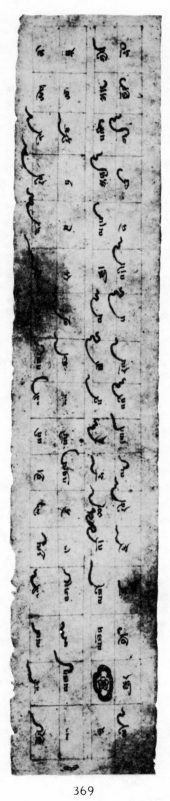

Sheet 3a

369

Figure 81 (cont.)

Sheet 3b

370

Figure 81 (cont.)

Sheet 4a

371

Figure 81 (cont.)

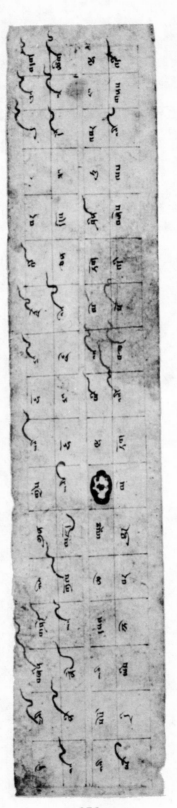

Sheet 4b

Figure 81 (cont.)

Sheet 5a

373

Figure 81 (cont.)

Sheet 5b

Figure 81 (cont.)

Sheet 6a

375

Figure 81 (cont.)

Sheet 6b

Figure 81 (cont.)

Sheet 7a

377

Figure 81 (cont.)

Sheet 7b

378

Figure 81 (cont.)

Sheet 8a

379

Figure 81 (cont.)

Sheet 8b

Before turning to a consideration of the notational symbols and annotations, we shall present the text both transliterated[16] and translated, together with a few explanatory remarks. Each sheet consists of four horizontal lines (read from left to right) which will be identified with Roman numerals (I-IV). The small subdivisions appearing in each of these four lines will be identified with Arabic numerals (1-15, 16, etc.) In the transliteration the textual words are printed in capital letters. Between them, in small letters, appear Tibetan "phonetics" which are used to continue preceding words (and notes) or to join them to the following words. Below the text, and extending and joining the phonetics, we find at a few specific points instructions for the singer, which are shown in italics. The text is interspersed with Sanskrit syllables which are rendered in Tibetan phonetics. These have not been translated because to bring these phonetics back into their original Sanskrit form would require lengthy considerations which would unnecessarily delay our already extended presentation. Moreover, these phonetics are prayer formulae which have no direct bearing on our subject.

Sheet 1a (title sheet):

'KHOR   LO   SDOM   PA'I   DKYIL   MCHOG   MCHOD   GAR   DANG
Wheel   of binding   to   cycle   ritual   dance together

BCAS   PA'I   GLU   DBYANGS   KYI   DRA   YIG   MEI NA KA'I
       with   sacred   song   of diagram   lettered   Mei-na-ka's

ZLOS   GAR   BZHUGS   SO   BKRIS.
dance   this book   contains —   Blessings.

Sheet 1b:

I.   1   2   3   4   5   6   7   8
     ◯   OM   mo'o   ĀH   'a'a   BA   DZRA   WI
            yid tsam bteg   cung shod

     9   10   11   12   13   14   15
     NI   HŪM   ngo'o   HŪM   PHAT   ta'a   ◯
            nab myur   nga

II. 1   2   3   4   5   6   7   8
     OM   mo'o   SHRI   ri'ri   HE   RU   KA   a'a

     9   10   11   12   13   14   15
     PRA   WAR   SAT   KA   RA   MA   HĀ
                                                 cung bteg

III. 1   2   3   4   5   6   7   8
     AR   ra'a   GHAM   ma'a   PRA   TITS   'a'i   TSHA
                                                 cung bnan

     9   10   11   12   13   14   15   16
     HŪM·   nga'a SWA   HĀ   OM   mo'o   SHRI   ri'ri
                            bcad

IV. 1   2   3   4   5   6   7   8
     HE   RU   KA   'a'a   MA   HĀ   SĀ   wa'a
                                          cung shod

     9   10   11   12   13   14   15
     DYAM   ma'a   MA   LA   TAT   TWAM   GHRI
            bcad

Sheet 2a:

I. | 1 | 2 | 3 | 4 | 5 | 6 | 7 | 8 | 9 |
|---|---|---|---|---|---|---|---|---|
| HA | NA | SI | DHI | ME | PRA | YATSTSHA | HŪM | nga'a |

bteg cham

10	11	12	13	14	15	16	17
SWA	HĀ	◯	DKYIL	le'e	'KHOR	'or	KUN
			mandala				all

II. | 1 | 2 | 3 | 4 | 5 | 6 | 7 | 8 | 9 |
|---|---|---|---|---|---|---|---|---|
| 'o'o | TU | 'u'a | RGYAL | la'i | BA | 'a'a | MNYES | 'a'i |
| "over" | | | victorious | | | | veneration | |

10	11	12	13	14	15	16	17
BYED	'e'e	CING	nga'a	GZUGS	MDZES	ya'i	DKAR
to		and		form	beautiful		white

III. | 1 | 2 | 3 | 4 | 5 | 6 | 7 | 8 | 9 |
|---|---|---|---|---|---|---|---|---|
| ra'a | PO | wo | RDO | ro'o | RJE | ya'i | DRIL | 'a'i |
| | | | thunderbolt | | | | bell | |

10	11	12	13	14	15	16	17
BU	'u'a	DANG	nga'a	ME	'e'e	TOG	SPUNGS
		and		flowers			heaped

IV. | 1 | 2 | 3 | 4 | 5 | 6 | 7 | 8 | 9 |
|---|---|---|---|---|---|---|---|---|
| ngu'a | PA'I | 'a'i | RIN | ne'a | CHEN | SNOD | yo'o | 'DZIN |
| | of | | jewelled | | | receptacle | | |

10	11	12	13	14	15	16	17
'en	MA	wa'a	NAM	ma'a	MKHA'	GANG	nga'a
			heavens			fills	

Sheet 2b:

I.   1   2   3   4   5   6   7   8
      BA'I   'a'i   DKYIL   le'e   'KHOR   'or   LHA   wa'a
      which   mandala   gods

      9   10   11   12   13   14   15   16   17
      TSHOGS   swa'a   MCHOD   do'o   OM   mo   ĀH   'a'a   BA
      assembly   veneration   to

                                      bcad

II.   1   2   3   4   5   6   7   8   9
      DZA   PUSH   wu'i   PE   'e'e   HŪM   ngo'o   HŪM   PHAT

      10   11   12   13   14   15   16   17
      ta'a   ◯   'DZAM   ma'a   BU'I   'u'a   GSER   ra'a
              world   of   gold

III. 1   2   3   4   5   6   7   8
      LAS   ya'i   RANG   nga'a   BYUNG   ngwa'a   LTE   ya'i
      from   emerging   middle

      9   10   11   12   13   14   15   16   17
      BA   ZLUM   ma'a   RTSIBS   ba'i   STONG   ngo'o   MU   wu'a
      axle   circle   spokes   1000   rim

IV.   1   2   3   4   5   6   7   8
      KHYUD   MCHOG   ga'a   TU   'u'a   RNAM   ma'a   'PHRUL
               great   parts   divided into

      9   10   11   12   13   14   15   16   17
      wa   MKHA'   wa'a   LA   'a'a   RAB   ba'a   'PHAGS   ga'a
            heavens   in   most   exalted

Sheet 3a:

I.

1	2	3	4	5	6	7	8
PHYOGS	'o'o	LAS	'a'i	RGYAL	le'e	BYED	PA'I
over all		directions		victorious		is	which

9	10	11	12	13	14	15	16	17
'a'i	'KHOR	'or	LO	'o'o	RIN	ne'e	CHEN	NAM
	wheel				precious			heavens

II.

1	2	3	4	5	6	7	8
ma'a	MKHA'	wa'a	BGANG	nga'a	TE	'BUL	OM
			honor			offer to	

9	10	11	12	13	14	15	16	17
mo'o	TSAG	KRA	RAT	NA	PRA	TITS	TSHA	SWA

III.

1	2	3	4	5	6	7	8
HĀ	◯	MTHON	MTHING	'OD	CHAGS	RDO	RJE
		high	blue	light	producing	thunderbolt	

9	10	11	12	13	14
PI	WAM	MA	RGYUD	MANGS	SNYAN
p'i-pa				("harp", "zither")	sweet (sounding).

15	16	17
PA'I	SKAD	KYIS
of	voice	by

IV.

1	2	3	4	5	6	7	8
YID	SGYUR	BYED	RDO	RJE	RIG	MA	DGA'
mind	diverted	be	thunderbolt		mudra		joy

9	10	11	12	13	14	15	16	17
BA'I	ROL	PA	'DIS	HE	RU	KA	KHOD	RDO
of	dance		by this	He-ru-ka			your	adamantine

Sheet 3b:

I.
1	2	3	4	5	6	7	8
RJE	YID	DGYES	MDZOD	OM	mo'o	$\bar{A}$H	BA
	mind	pleased	made				

9	10	11	12	13	14	15	16	17
DZRA	WI	NI	H$\bar{U}$M	nga'i	H$\bar{U}$M	PHAT	◯	H$\bar{U}$M

II.
1	2	3	4	5	6	7	8	9
nga'i	GANG	nga'a	GIS	ya'i	DRIN	na'i	GYIS	ya'i
	"your"				grace		by	

10	11	12	13	14	15	16	17
BDE	ya'i	CHEN	NYID	ya'i	SKAD	da'i	CIG
happiness		great	itself		word		one
							(in one instant)

III.
1	2	3	4	5	6	7	8	9
ga'i	NYID	ya'i	LA	'a'a	'CHAR	ra'a	BA	GANG
	itself				realized			"all things"

10	11	12	13	14	15	16	17
nga'a	◯	OM	mo'o	HE	ya'i	RU	'u'a

IV.
1	2	3	4	5	6	7	8
KA	wa'a	DPAL	ya'i	DAM	ma'a	TSHIG	RJES
		great		vows			follow

9	10	11	12	13	14	15	16	17
ya'i	SU	SKYONGS	ngo'o	HE	ya'i	RU	'u'a	KA
		one who protects						

Sheet 4a:

I.

1	2	3	4	5	6	7	8	9
ya	DPAL	ya'i	NYID	da'i	KYI	LTE	'a'i	BAR
	magnificence		itself			center		

10	11	12	13	14	15	16	17	18
GNAS	ya'i	BDAG	ga'a	LA	wa'a	BRTAN	na'i	RGYAS
abides		Lord		to		attachment		expansive

II.

1	2	3	4	5	6	7
CHAGS	ga'i	SHING	DGYES	ya'i	PAR	MDZOD
produce		and	joyfulness			"let there be"

8	9	10	11	12	13
da'a	DNGOS	swa'a	GRUB	bo'o	THAMS
	siddhi (perfections)				all

14	15	16	17	18
ma'a	CAD	da'i	BDAG	ga'a
			me	

III.

1	2	3	4	5	6	7	8	9
LA	RAB	ba'a	TU	STSOL	lo'o	LAS	ya'i	KUN
on	generously			bestow		deeds		all

10	11	12	13	14	15	16	17	18
na	LA	YANG	nga'a	BDAG	ga	SEMS	NGES	ya'i
	in	also		my		mind	true	

IV.

1	2	3	4	5	6	7	8	9	10
LEGS	MDZOD	HŪM	nga'i	HA	HA	HA	HA	HO	wa'i
do	be								

11	12	13	14	15	16	17	18
BCOM	ma'i	LDAN	na'i	KHYOD	ya'a	DANG	nga'a
victorious		one		you		and	

Sheet 4b:

I.   1   2   3   4   5   6   7   8
      DE   ya'i   BZHIN   GSHEGS   ge'e   KUN   GYIS   ya'i
      Tathagatas   all   by

      9   10   11   12   13   14   15   16   17
      RDO   rwa'a   RJE   'I   BAR   ra   DU   'u'a   BDAG
      adamantine   space   me

II.   1   2   3   4   5   6   7
      ga'a   NI   RNAM   ma'a   GROL   MDZOD   ya'i
             "as for"   deliver   from   circle   of existence

      8   9   10   11   12   13   14   15
      RDO   rwa'a   RJE   e'e   CAN   DNGOS   swa'a   DAM
      thunder - bolt   like   true   vow

      16   17
      ma   TSHIG

III. 1   2   3   4   5   6   7   8   9
      ga'i   SEMS   ma'i   DPA'   CHE   AH   ◯   LHA   YI
             mind   brave   great   gods   of

      10   11   12   13   14   15   16   17
      'a'a   ME   TOG   SHIN   TU   'BAR   ra'a   LHA
             flowers   most   radiant   gods

IV.   1   2   3   4   5   6   7   8   9
      YI   DRI   YIS   LTE   BAR   BYUGS   ME   TOG   'a'i
      of fragrance by   center   anointed   flowers

      10   11   12   13   14   15   16   17
      BZANG   PO   'DI   BZHES   LAS   'a'i   GNAS   'DI
                       these   accept   "and"   this

Sheet 5a:

I.   1   2   3   4   5   6   7   8   9
     NYID   DU   BZHUGS   SU   GSOL   OM   ma'i   ĀH   BA
     itself "in" remain   to beseech

          10   11   12   13   14   15   16
         DZRA   PUSH   PE   PRA   TITSTSHA   HŪM   ngo'o

II.   1   2   3   4   5   6   7   8   9
     SWA   HA   ◯   E   MA   'a'a   BDE   MCHOG   ga'a
                       Listen   happiness great

          10   11   12   13   14   15   16
         SGYU   MA'I   yi'i   LONGS   SPYOD   dwa'a   RDZOGS
        illusion of   use   perfected

III.   1   2   3   4   5   6   7   8
     PA'I   'PHRUL   'la   E   MA   PI   WAM   nga'i
     who   emanation   listen   p'i - pa,

          9   10   11   12   13   14   15   16
        GLING   BU   wu'a   RNGA   ZLAM   mo   DZA   RNGA
        (flute)   (drum)   (drum)

IV.   1   2   3   4   5   6   7   8
      MA   wa'i   ◯   HŪM   nga'a   BCOM   mo   LDAN
                                     victorious   one

          9   10   11   12   13   14   15   16
        MGON   PO   DPA'   BO'I   DBANG   PHYUG   NI   ya'i
        protector   heroic   might   "as far"

Sheet 5b:

I.

1	2	3	4	5	6	7	8
BSKAL	PA'I	ME	CHEN	LTA	wa'i	BUR	RAB
world destruction	of	fire	great	like			greatly

9	10	11	12	13	14	15	16
wa'i	TU	BAR	◯	OM	ma'i	BA	DZRA
		radiate					

II.

1	2	3	4	5	6	7	8	9
LĀ	'a'a	SYĀ	MĀ	'a'i	LI	GIR	TI	'i

10	11	12	13	14	15	16
NRI	TE	HŪM	nga'a	PHAT	ta	OM

III.

1	2	3	4	5	6	7	8
ma'i	BDZRA	LA	'a'a	SYA	MA	'a'i	LI

9	10	11	12	13	14	15	16	17
GIR	TI	'i	NRI	TI	HUM	nga'a	PHAT	ta

IV.

1	2	3	4	5	6	7	8	9
◯	MTHON	MTHING	'OD	CHAGS	RDO	RJE	PI	WAM
	high	blue	light	producing	thunderbolt		p'i-pa	

10	11	12	13	14	15	16
MA	RGYUD	MANGS	SNYAN	PA'I	SKAD	KYIS
	("harp")		sweet sounding	of	voice	by

Sheet 6a:

I.

1	2	3	4	5	6	7
YID	SGYUR	BYED	RDO	RJE	RIG	MA
mind	diverted	be	thunderbolt		mudra	

8	9	10	11	12	13	14	15	16
DGA'	BA'I	ROL	PA	'DIS	HE	RU	KA	KHYOD
joy	of	dance		by this	He-ru-ka			your

II.

1	2	3	4	5	6	7
RDO	RJE	YID	DGYES	MDZOD	OM	ma'i
adamantine		mind	pleased	made		

8	9	10	11	12	13	14	15	16
AH	BDZRA	WI	NI	SU	DZA	ME	GHA	SA

III.

1	2	3	4	5	6	7	8	9
MU	DRA	SA	YA	RA	NA	SA	MA	YE

10	11	12	13	14	15	16
HŪM	TE	NA	TE	NA	'a'e	'a'a

IV.

1	2	3	4	5	6	7	8
'a'a	TE	NA	HŪM	◯	DNGOS	ya'a	'a'i
					samsara		

9	10	11	12	13	14	15	16
ya'i	KUN	na'a	SRID	ya'i	'a'i	yas	DANG
							and

Sheet 6b:

I.

1	2	3	4	5	6	7	8
nga'a	ZHI	ya'a	BA	'I	DPAL	la'a	a'i
	nirvana				exalted one		

9	10	11	12	13	14	15	16
ya'a	wa'i	MCHOG	wa'a	a'i	wa'a	GI	ya'i
		most excellent				of	

II.

1	2	3	4	5	6	7	8
BDE	ya'a	a'i	ya'i	BA	wa	CHER	ra'a
happiness						greatly	

9	10	11	12	13	14	15	16
SDOM	mo'o	PA	wa'a	'a'i	ya'a	wa'i	BRTAN
binds							moving

III.

1	2	3	4	5	6	7	8
na'a	'a'i	na'i	G. YO	wa'a	KUN	na'a	'o'o
			things		all		

9	10	11	12	13	14	15	16
no'o	LA	wa'a	KHYAB	wa'a	PA	'I	BDAG
			embraces		who		master

IV.

1	2	3	4	5	6	7	8
ga'a	'a'i	ya'a	wa'i	RDO	ra'a	'a'i	ra'i
				thunderbolt			

9	10	11	12	13	14	15	16
RJE	ye'e	SEMS	me'e	a'i	me'e	DPA'	wa'a

Sheet 7a:

I.

1	2	3	4	5	6	7
PHYAG	ga'a	'TSHAL	la'i	BSTOD	ya'a	'a'i
make		obeisance				

8	9	10	11	12	13	14	15	16
ya'a	wa'i	◯	$H\bar{U}M$	nga'i	$H\bar{U}M$	nga'i	$H\bar{U}M$	nga'i

II.

1	2	3	4	5	6	7	8
DE	HA	WA	TU	'u'a	SAN	$P\bar{A}$	'a'a

9	10	11	12	13	14	15	16
RA	$T\bar{A}$	TU	DWAN	DWA	LING	KA	NA

III.

1	2	3	4	5	6	7	8	9
YO	A	WA	TU	'u'a	$SHR\bar{I}$	ri'i	HE	RU

10	11	12	13	14	15	16
KA	$H\bar{U}M$	TE	NA	$H\bar{U}M$	TE	NA

IV.

1	2	3	4	5	6	7	8
TE	NA	TE	TE	$H\bar{U}M$	SU	RA	NA

9	10	11	12	13	14	15	16
RA	BAN	TI	TA	TSA	RA	NA	WA

Sheet 7b:

I. | 1 | 2 | 3 | 4 | 5 | 6 | 7 | 8 | 9 |
|---|---|---|---|---|---|---|---|---|
| TU | KU | SU | MA | BI | NIR | $\overline{MA}$ | YA | RO |

10	11	12	13	14	15	16	17	18
WA	KA	RU	SHRI	ri'i	HE	RU	$\overline{KA}$	HŪM

II. | 1 | 2 | 3 | 4 | 5 | 6 | 7 | 8 | 9 |
|---|---|---|---|---|---|---|---|---|
| TE | NA | TE | NA | TE | TE | HŪM | BHA | WA |

10	11	12	13	14	15	16	17	18
PI	MUG	TI	BE	SHE	KA	GU	NA	KU

III. | 1 | 2 | 3 | 4 | 5 | 6 | 7 | 8 | 9 |
|---|---|---|---|---|---|---|---|---|
| TI | A | I | NA | MA | MI | NA | MA | MI |

10	11	12	13	14	15	16	17	18
SHRĪ	ri'i	HE	RU	KA	HŪM	GU	NA	SI

IV. | 1 | 2 | 3 | 4 | 5 | 6 | 7 | 8 | 9 |
|---|---|---|---|---|---|---|---|---|
| TAM | A | I | | OM | ma'i | BA | DZRA | STWA |

10	11	12	13	14	15	16	17	18
TWA	?	?	HŪM	nga'a	PHAT	ta'a	◯	HŪM

Sheet 8a:

I.

1	2	3	4	5	6	7	8	9
nga'i	YE	SHES	BSKAL	PA	ME	LTAR	'BAR	ra'a
	divine	wisdom	universe		fire	like	blazes	

10	11	12	13	14	15	16	17	18
BA	'I	'OD	ya'a	'a'i	ya'a	MA	RIG	'DOD
which		light				ignorant		desire

II.

1	2	3	4	5	6	7	8
PA'I	MUN	KHAMS	THAMS	ma'a	CAD	ya'a	BSGREGS
of	dark	regions	all				consume

9	10	11	12	13	14	15	16	17	18
'a'a	'a'i	ya'a	◯̣	OM	ma'i	GZI	BRJID	ya'a	CHEN
						great	splendid		one

III.

1	2	3	4	5	6	7	8	9
na'a	'a'i	wa'i	PO	wa	ME	YI	'a'i	wa'i
					fire	of		

10	11	12	13	14	15	16	17	18
wa'i	'a'i	LHA	wa'i	wa'a	LAS	KYI	ya'a	DON
		god			activity	of		objects

IV.

1	2	3	4	5	6	7	8	9	10
na'a	'a'i	wa'i	KUN	na'a	BSGRUB	PA	'a'i	wa'i	wa'i
			all		fulfills	one			

11	12	13	14	15	16	17	18
'a'i	PO	wa'i	wa'a	SNYING	RJES	ya'a	SEMS
who				compassion	(through)		mind

Sheet 8b:

I.   1   2   3   4   5   6   7   8
      'a'a   'a'i   wa'i   CAN   na'a   DON   MDZAD   'a'i

             creatures   for the benefit of   act

       9   10   11   12   13 14   15   16   17   18
      wa'i   wa'i   'a'i   PHYIR   ri 'a   'DI   NYID   ya'a   DU

             because   to this very place

II.   1   2   3   4   5   6   7   8   9
      wa'a   'a'i   wa'i   NI   ya   NYE   BAR   'a'i   wa'i

             "as for"   close

       10   11   12   13   14   15
      wa'i   'a'i   MDZOD   ya'i   ya'a   ◯ ◯ ◯ ◯

             remain

The general translation of the text is as follows:

Sheet 1a: This book contains the dance of the Mei-na-ka, the lettered
    diagram of sacred song together with the ritual dance cycle of
    'KHOR LO SDOM PA — blessings.

Sheet 1b: contains only Tibetan phonetics of Sanskrit syllables.

Sheet 2a: I, 1-12: Tibetan phonetics of Sanskrit syllables.

2a, I, 13 to 2b, I, 12: Veneration to DKYIL 'KHOR KUN TU RGYAL
    BA and veneration to the assembly of gods, the mandala[17] which
    fills the heavens, the jewelled receptacle of heaped flowers, the
    bell, the thunderbolt,[18] and the white beautiful form.

The first mantra[19] ends with the syllable PHAT (1b, I, 13; see also
5b, III, 16 and 7b, IV, 15), a sound full of mystic power. Other

mantras often end with SWA HĀ, "I offer" (for instance: 1b, III, 11

and 13; 2a, I, 10-11; 3a, II, 17 to 3a, III, 18; 5a, II, 1-2). The syl-

lables OM and HŪM are the first and last of the sacred opening salu-

tation OM MANI PADME HŪM, "OM, the jewel in the lotus, HŪM."

OM corresponds to the Indian AUM, the representation of the triad:

Creator, Preserver, and Destroyer. These four words have exceed-

ingly involved significances; for instance OM may represent the world

of gods, HŪM that of the purgatory, and even the form of the letters

which are employed to write these sacred words receive manifoldly

profound interpretations.

2b, I, 13 to 2b, II, 10: Tibetan phonetics of Sanskrit syllables.

2b, II, 12 to 3a, II, 7: Offer to and honor the heavens, the precious

    wheel which is victorious over all regions, most exalted in the

    heavens, divided into parts, the great rim, the thousand spokes,

    the axle, self-emerging from the gold of the world.

3a, II, 8 to 3a, III, 2: Tibetan phonetics of Sanskrit syllables.

3a, III, 3 to 3b, I, 4: MTHON MTHING 'OD CHAGS RDO RJE, let

    your mind be diverted by the voice of the sweet sounding pi-wa-

    ma, the rgyud mangs.[20] May your adamantine mind, Heruka,

    be pleased by the joyful dance of the RDO RJE RIG MA.

3b, I, 5 to 16: Tibetan phonetics.

3b, I, 17 to 4a, IV, 2: HŪM. Through your grace all things are rea-

    lized in an instant of great happiness. OM, Heruka. DPAL

    DAM TSHIG RJES SU SKYONGS, let there be joyfulness and

    expansive attachment to Heruka, the Lord who abides in the

    center of magnificence itself. Bestow generously on me all

    siddhi (perfections). Let my heart beat true in all deeds.

4a, IV, 3 to 10: Tibetan phonetics.

4a, IV, 11 to 5a, I, 5: BCOM LDAN, you and all the Thatagatas, deliver me from the circle of existence unto the adamantine space. RDO RJE CAN DNGOS DAM TSHIG SEMS DPA' CHE ĀH. I beseech you to remain in this very place and to accept these good flowers which are the most radiantly divine flowers anointed by the fragrance of the gods.

5a, I, 6 to 5a, II, 3: Tibetan phonetics.

5a, II, 4 to 5b, I, 11: Listen! You who are an emanation who has perfected the use of illusion, listen! The pi-wa, gling-bu, rnga-zlam, dza rnga²¹ HUM BCOM LDAN MGON PO DPA'A BO'I DBANG PHYUG, radiate greatly like the great conflagration of the universe.

5b, I, 12 to 5b, III, 16: Tibetan phonetics.

5b, IV, 1 to 6a, II, 5: MTHON MTHING 'OD CHAGS RDO RJE, let your mind be diverted by the voice of the sweet sounding pi-wa-ma rgyud mangs. May your adamantine mind, Heruka, be pleased by the joyful dance of the RDO RJE RIG MA.

6a, II, 6 to 6a, IV, 4: Tibetan phonetics.

6a, IV, 6 to 7a, I, 5: I make obeisance to RDO RJE SEMS DPA', master who embraces all moving things, he who binds himself greatly to the most excellent happiness, he who is the exalted one of samsara and nirvana.

7a I, 6 to 7b, IV, 17: Tibetan phonetics.

7b, IV, 18 to 8b, II, 15: HŪM. The light of divine wisdom which blazes like the conflagration of the universe, consumes all the dark regions of ignorant desire. OM. GZI BRJID CHEN PO, ME YI LHA, he who fulfills all objects of activity, through com-passion for the benefit of sentient creatures, remain close to this very place.

The text at the bottom of <u>sheet 8b</u> is difficult to read — many words
are faded, hence no satisfactory transcription and translation can be
offered. The readable parts contain sentences such as:

> I make obeisance to RDO RJE SEMS DPA', master who em-
> braces all moving things, he who binds himself greatly to the
> most excellent happiness, he who is the exalted one of samsara
> and nirvana.

and:

> Having seen creatures oppressed by the five poisons, abolish
> all misery.

The last sentence is:

> Obeisance to the leader of the circle of the assembly of DPA'
> 'O NA RO MA, . . . great happiness arising from the Five
> Buddhas.

Some of the neumes of the manuscript are provided with the following annotations:

BEBS, ("falling")

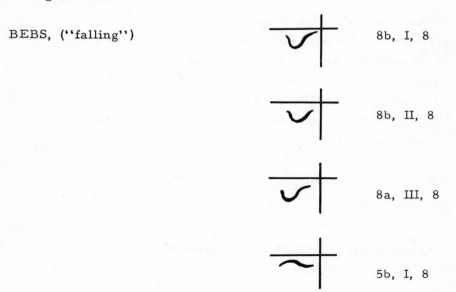

8b, I, 8

8b, II, 8

8a, III, 8

5b, I, 8

BCAD, ("cut")²²   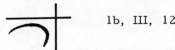   1b, III, 12

                                                         1b, IV, 10

BTEG CHAM ("short rise")   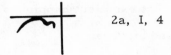   2a, I, 4

BTEG TSAM ("raised voice")   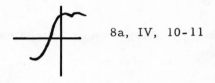   8a, IV, 10-11

    This neume seems to be the
same as NAM BTEG TSAM
(8a, III, 10-11).

CUNG BNAM ("tighten voice")   1b, III, 8

    This neume may have the same
significance as BCAD (1b, III,
12 and 1b, IV, 10).

CUNG BTEG ("raise voice a little")   8b, I, 2

    There is no noticeable difference
between the shapes of this neume   8b, II, 2
and the one denoting BEBS. The
reason why we interpret BEBS as   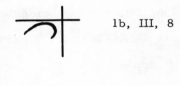 8a, III, 2
"falling" and CUNG BTEG as
"raising the voice a little" is due   8a, IV, 2
to the Tibetan annotations.

            but also (?):   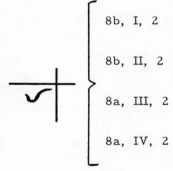   1b, II, 15

CUNG SHOD ("little louder"?)   1b, I, 7

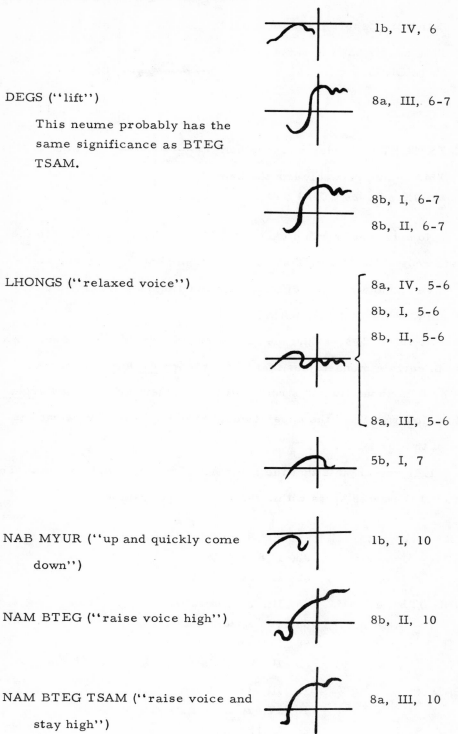

1b, IV, 6

DEGS ("lift")

    This neume probably has the
same significance as BTEG
TSAM.

8a, III, 6-7

8b, I, 6-7

8b, II, 6-7

LHONGS ("relaxed voice")

8a, IV, 5-6

8b, I, 5-6

8b, II, 5-6

8a, III, 5-6

5b, I, 7

NAB MYUR ("up and quickly come
    down")

1b, I, 10

NAM BTEG ("raise voice high")

8b, II, 10

NAM BTEG TSAM ("raise voice and
    stay high")

8a, III, 10

NYER 'BEBS ("short rise, then fall")

This neume has the same shape
as LHONGS.

YID TSAM BTEG ("rise and lengthen")

This neume probably has the same
significance as CUNG BTEG.

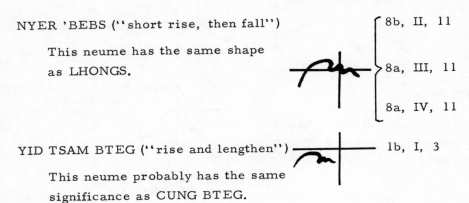

8b, II, 11

8a, III, 11

8a, IV, 11

1b, I, 3

No notational symbol except the annotation nga is added to the
mysterious syllable PHAT at 1b, I, 11 (nga meaning "strong voice").

The annotation in a different handwriting at 5b, IV, 9 means
the same as the text: PI WAM MA.

At 1b, I, 1-3 we find the text word AR-GHAM. There exists a
rule in certain monasteries that "at the word Argham the cymbals
are held horizontally and struck with mid-finger erect. On Pargham,
held below waist and the upper cymbal is made to revolve along the
rim of the lowest . . . . ."23

It is remarkable that the same notational symbols now and then
recur at the same spots within the lines. For instance,

BEBS occurs at   8a, III, 8 with 'a'i
                        8b, I, 8 with 'a'i
                        8b, II, 8 with 'a'i

CUNG BTEG at   8a, III, 2 with wa'i
                        8a, IV, 2 with 'a'i
                        8b, I, 2 with 'a'i
                        8b, II, 2 with 'a'i

BCAD at   1b, III, 12 with HA
                        1b, IV, 10 with ma'a
                        2a, I, 11 with HA

2a, II, 13 with nga'a

2a, III, 13 with nga'a

2a, IV, 12 with wa'a

2b, I, 12 with do'o

(2b, II, 11 [symbol])

2b, III, 11 with ma'a

2b, IV, 9 with wa

MYER BEBS at

8a, III, 11 with 'a'i

8a, IV, 11 with 'a'i

8b, II, 11 with 'a'i

LHONGS at

8a, III, 5 with wa

8a, IV, 5 with na'a

8b, I, 5 with na'a

8b, II, 5 with ya

The recurrence of the same symbol at approximately the same spot in nearly every line of a page of the manuscript occurs mainly in conjunction with the extension sounds 'a'i, wa'i, nga'a, and others. Only occasionally is the recurrence of a symbol combined with a proper textual word such as:

DEGS at

8a, III, 6-7 with ME YI

8b, I, 6-7 with DON MDZAD

8b, II, 6-7 with NYE BAR

or, as already shown:

1b, III, 12 with HA

2a, I, 11 with HA

and so forth.

The meaning of these frequent recurrences is not known to us. We cannot speak of some endeavor to create rhymes by this procedure because the four lines of each manuscript page do not necessarily represent four separate "verses" or sections so that, for instance, spot

8 in a line would rhyme or otherwise correspond to spot 8 in another line. The literal translation shows that sentences can be shorter or longer than a line of the manuscript pages and generally do not fit into the 15, 16, 17, or 18 syllables allotted to each line.

The recurrent syllables, mainly of a "liquescent" nature and linking textual syllables or words, are performed to the same or similar melismas as shown by the corresponding neumes. For instance, the syllable 'a'i is notated mainly by the neumes BEBS, CUNG BTEG, and NYER BEBS, curves which indicate a short melodic movement: a small descent, a small ascent, and a short rise and fall, respectively.

The syllables ma'a, nga'a, wa are notated mainly by BCAD and LHONGS, symbols which indicate "cut," a vaguely delineated cadential descent, and "relaxed voice," either a held note or a slight descent, both with a cadential character.

This feature can also be observed in instances when there are no recurrences of neumes at specific spots. For instance: YID TSAM BTEG, CUNG BTEG, and NAB MYUR are combined with the linking syllables mo'o, ngo'o, ro'o, and wo; CUNG BTEG, BCAD, BEBS, and NAB MYUR with ra'a, ma'a, nga'a, ngwa'a, and wa'a. We notice that there is some ordering principle in the use of Tibetan neumes and their textual syllables. A complete clarification of this principle will be possible only when more material becomes available for analysis.

The following two sheets (Fig. 82), although not directly related to the first manuscript are, however, a part of the same group of seven or eight volumes of which the entire text (including the first manuscript) supposedly consists.[24] The two sheets contain chants used during offering ceremonies and neumes written by a different person than those of the first manuscript.

MANUSCRIPT II

Figure 82

Sheet 1

Sheet 2

405

The first offering chant (sheet 1) is complete; the longer, second one (sheet 2) is not — one or two pages are probably missing. According to the Lama Geshe Nornang this text, when chanted, is accompanied by a dance performed by two monks.

The text is as follows:

Sheet 1:

'o OM o AH 'a'a'a $H\bar{U}M$ 'o LUS sa NGAG ga SEMS

OM AH $H\bar{U}M$; body speech mind.

Below the $H\bar{U}M$ neume we read rnga, "drum." A general translation of the text is the same as the literal translation.

Sheet 2:

ME 'e'e'e LA 'o ya ya 'a'a'a GNAS 'a'a'a PA'I

Fire "in" reside "who"

'o BGEGS ga KYI 'a'a'a TSHOGS KUN no NGA ba

demons of assembly all me

LA ba 'a'a'a NYON

to listen.

The general translation of this text reads: Listen to me, assembly of demons who reside in the fire.

Not shown in the photographic reproduction of this manuscript is the fact that it is written in three colors: the text (in our presentation shown in capital letters) is written in black, as are the notational curves; the extensions of, or links between, the text syllables or words ('a'a'a, and others — in our presentation shown in small print) and the curves $\int$ (first and fifth of sheet 1, third of the first line and first of the second line of sheet 2) are in blue; and the word rnga ("drum") in red.[25] The colors are used to facilitate the reading. Whether or not they have any symbolic or mystic significance is uncertain and subject to differing opinions. The word rnga appears below LA and GNAS in the first line and below TSHOGS in the second line of sheet 2.

We shall now consider the neumes, starting from the beginning of sheet 1. The first small curve (∫), written in blue, represents a brief introductory sound on 'o before the first regular text word OM is intoned. This habit of chanting, occasionally humming, an introductory note to the sound of a following sacred syllable can also be observed in the manuscripts and performances of Japanese shōmyō.

The notational curve of the word OM, written in black, consists of two parts: the first, immediately above the word OM, and the second, continuing the first, above the letter 'o (written in blue), which extends and, following the outline of the curve, raises the sound:

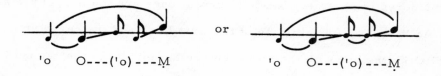

'o   O---('o) ---M   or   'o   O---('o) ---M

This is followed by ĀH (black) — 'a'a'a (blue). The "quilisma" at the end of the first half of the curve is performed to the three 'a'a'a extensions of ĀH; the second half of the curve raises the sound:

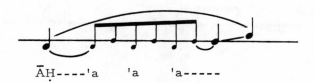

ĀH----'a   'a   'a-----

The following curve written above HŪM (black) represents the end of the formula OM ĀH HŪM. With this temporary halt we can expect a descent of the voice which seems to be indicated by the wriggly right-hand side of the curve. Below the word HŪM stands rnga (drum) written in red ink:

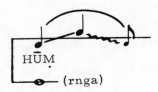

The next curve (blue) again denotes an introductory or a linking sound, chanted to 'o, aiming at the next word LUS. LUS has the same notational curve as ŌM; the upper part of the curve is chanted to sa (blue), forming the extension of LUS. NGAG-ga, too, is performed in the same manner as ŌM and LUS. The last curve on sheet 1, above SEMS, is comparatively simple. It resembles the virga of the West (as in the several St. Gall manuscripts) and the oxeia of Byzantine neumes, and may have had a similar function.

Sheet 2 contains two rows of neumes, most of which have been considered in sheet 1. The two unusual ones are the long curve above GNAS 'a'a - 'a, (penultimate of the first line) and the curve above TSHOGS (the one with the spiral before the middle of the second line).

The GNAS curve consists of 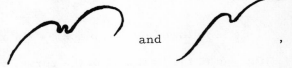 and   ,

both of which are more or less "known" to us:

At the beginning of GNAS, below the text word, stands rnga (in red).

The TSHOGS curve resembles in shape the Western cephalicus or ancus without having the function of a liquescent neume. As mentioned before, TSHOGS too is annotated with rnga.

Each of the notational curves of manuscript II, with the exception of and the sign for the introductory sound ( ),

consists of two parts. The first part usually indicates the note or notes of the text word, while the second part assumes a function which resembles that of Western liquescent neumes. For instance, in sheet 1 we find

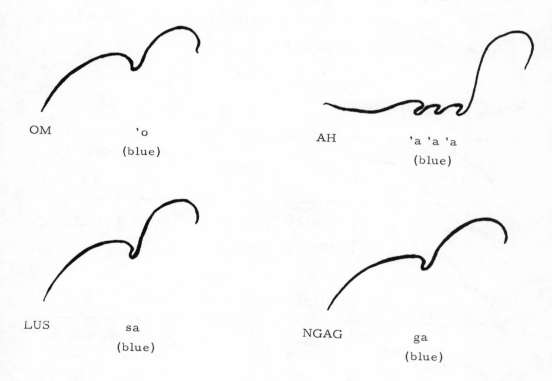

OM	'o	AH	'a 'a 'a
	(blue)		(blue)
LUS	sa	NGAG	ga
	(blue)		(blue)

and so forth.

Sheet 2 contains two unusual sequences of neumes. The first one beginning with LA (first line, second curve) is:

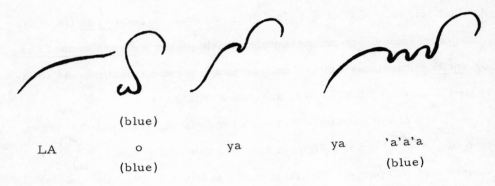

(blue)

LA   o   ya   ya   'a'a'a
(blue)   (blue)

Below are listed the neumes which occur most frequently in
these manuscripts and also commented upon are their similarities to
other neumatic signs that possibly had found their way at one time or
the other into Tibet. The names of Byzantine, Syrian, and related
neumes[26] are shown in brackets:

MS. I:	MS. II:	Similarities:
╱ ╱		virga (Ban. tav. I); [oxeia, •]
(rising curve) (S-curve)	CUNG SHOD "little louder" indication to inten- sify the sound	[oxeia, ⫽ ; ••]
(rise-fall curves)	(curves + signs) NYER 'BEBS "short rise and fall" (curves + signs)	virga and clivis

MS. I:	MS. II:	Similarities:
		Scandicus (?)
		(Scandicus, Ban. tav. IV)
	CUNG BNAN "tighten voice"	Clivis; (Flexa, Ban. IV) [bareia; apostrophos, elaphron?; ——.]
	BTEG CHAM "short rise"	(Pes flexus, Ban. tav. III)
		(Pes flexus, Ban. tav. III)
	BCAD "cut"	Clivis; (flexa, Ban. tav. IV; cephalicus ?)
	NAB MYUR "(up) and quickly down"	Clivis, (flexa, Ban. IV) [apostrophos ?]
	YID TSAM BTEG ("raise and lengthen")	(Pes, Ban. tav. II) combination of and LHONGS.

MS. I:	MS. II:	Similarities:
	LHONGS ("relaxed")	(Punctum, Ban. tav. I) [oligon]
		Porrectus (?) (Flexa resupina, Ban. tav. V) Torculus resupinus (?)
	BTEG TSAM ("raise voice")	Podatus (Pes, Ban. tav. II)
	NAM BTEG ("raise voice high")	Podatus (Pes, Ban.)
	CUNG BTEG ("raise a little")	Podatus (Pes, Ban.) [Petaste; pelaston]
	BEBS ("falling")	(Flexa resupina, Ban. tav. V, exs. e, f, g) [synemba (?)]
	BEBS (?)	[syrmatike;]
		Torculus, (Pes flexus, Ban. tav. III)
	NAM BTEG TSAM ("raise voice and stay high")	Podatus, (Pes, Ban. tav. II) [oxeia; pelaston (2)]

MS. I: MS. II: Similarities:

	DEGS ("lift") see YID TSAM BTEG	Podatus
		Cephalicus (?) Ancus (?) (Climacus liqu., Ban. tav. X)
		(Climacus, Ban. tav. VII, ex. A 12)
		(Introduce sound)

Another fragment of a manuscript can be found in Waddell's
The Buddhism of Tibet,[27] which shows the same or similar symbols
as the ones presented in Figures 81 and 82. The reproduction of Waddell's score is not distinct enough to enable us to read the important
annotations. The example consists of three sheets printed on one page.
The upper one contains triple curves such as   , probably
choir neumes; the middle and lower ones show curves similar to the
ones we have observed in Figures 81 and 82. The lowest notation, perhaps an instrumental part, contains in its lower right corner the drawing of a conch shell, indicating the use of the tun, the conch-shell horn.
This instrument produces an unusually deep sound which is generally

combined with that of the si-nen (written: sil-smyan), a pair of large cymbals.

In summing up we may say that Tibetan neumes serve only as mnemonic aids to the music masters and choir leaders who know the melody. This writer was informed that the same notation may receive different interpretations in different monasteries. Thus, even if we had notations and recordings from one particular place we would still be in doubt as to how the same notations were read in other places.

It is possible for us to reconstruct a vague outline of the notated melody by depending upon the few instructions we have found in manuscript I and by following the rise and fall indicated by the shapes of the neumatic curves, but the limited information we have does not suffice to enable us to make a clear transcription.[28]

As already mentioned we know nothing about a musical notation of Buddhist chant in China. There is no doubt that the learned monks used one or more notational systems because the complexity of Buddhist service, the singing of the office, the chanting of hymns and responses, the strictly prescribed use of drums, bells, gongs, cymbals, "wooden fish," and other instruments, are unthinkable without some form of musical score.[29]

Buddhism began to appear in China in the first century A. D., during the reign of Han Ming Ti, an emperor of the Eastern Han period who ruled during the latter part of the Han dynasty (25-220). Tradition relates[30] that the emperor had a dream about a mighty deity in the West. He sent ambassadors to India who returned with sacred texts and images and probably also with melodies of Indian Buddhist chant. The texts were translated into Chinese and chanted in the Chinese manner; that is, the chanting was based upon the anhemitonic

pentatonic scale with the occasional use of the two less important pien[31]
notes. Any Indian characteristics, such as complex scales and ornaments, were completely ignored. By the year A. D. 500, after several
comparatively mild persecutions instigated mostly by the Taoists, Buddhism prevailed over the whole of China.[32] During the T'ang period
(618-906) Buddhism became fully adjusted and modified to the various
Chinese beliefs and customs and, although it never gained any political
power, it attained a permanent place in Chinese culture.

Although no information exists regarding a definite Buddhist
chant notation in China, we must assume that some type of notational
system was employed.[33] If a melody was notated, non-Buddhist notations
borrowed from the imperial court or from secular music[34] were used.
Even in Japan, where definite Buddhist notations can be found, we occasionally discover the use of koto, biwa, and flute tablature signs, a
habit that may very well have had its origin in China. We may, however, assume that one or more definite Buddhist notations must have
existed in China — and in Korea, too — because, we are informed,
eleventh-century Japan saw the "invention" of meyasu-hakase,[35] a
notational system based upon the medium of curves similar to the one
used in the Lāmaist liturgy of Tibet. It is unlikely that the notational
curves of Tibet, although modified, would appear in Japan without
ever having appeared in China, whose culture was the most important
of East Asia. Moreover, scales, melodies, formulae, and instruments which had come from the West always appeared in China before
they found their way into Japan.

The following, Figure 83,[36] shows a typical Chinese Buddhist
melody. With one exception (measure 15) it is purely pentatonic. It
is sung at the Incense Offering ceremony.

Figure 83

The melody shown in the foregoing example strongly resembles a
popular Chinese operatic aria. The light-hearted quality of this piece,
characteristic of most Chinese Buddhist melodies, stands in noticeable contrast to the heavy dignity of Tibetan Buddhist chant melodies.

Notes
Bibliography
Index

NOTES*

Introduction

1. A Chinese chancellor and chronicler of the third century B. C.

2. A famous Chinese historian who lived between 163 and 85 B. C. His monumental work, the Shih Chi (史記), deals with history, geography, literature, astrology, divination, the calendar, biographies of important persons, and music. See Burton Watson, Records of the Grand Historian of China (New York, 1961), II, 55, 397.

3. Abū Naṣr Muhammed b. Muhammed b. Tarkhan b. Uzalāgh al-Fārābī (870-950); famous for his works on ethics, politics, philosophy, mathematics, and music. See MGG, I, 315.

4. Abū Yūsuf Ya'qūb b. Isḥāq al-Kindī (790-874), the "Philosopher among the Arabs," was famous for his works on music and its relation to other fields.

5. 429-347 B. C. See, e. g., H. Albert, Die Lehre vom Ethos in der griechischen Musik (Leipzig, 1899).

6. 384-322 B. C. See MGG, I, 631. See also W. Vetter, "Die antike Musik in der Beleuchtung durch Aristoteles," AfMW, I (1936), 2-41.

7. 305-285 B. C. See MGG, III, 1614-15. See also H. Menge, Euclidies Opera Omnia (Leipzig, 1916), Vol. VIII.

8. A. D. 46?-120? See Plutarchi De Musica, ed. Ricardus Volkmann (Leipzig, 1856).

9. Concerning the Quadrivium see H. Abert, "Die Stellung der Musik in der antiken Kultur," Die Antike, II (1926), 136-54.

---

* Throughout the Notes the running heads refer to corresponding pages of text. Wherever a note is expanded by a following full-page example of Chinese text, the reader is referred by a subheading at the top of the example to the note that is being commented on.

10. See Eta Harich-Schneider, "Japanische Impressionen," Musica, IV (1949), 129 ff.

Part One

1. See Wang Guang Ki (also written Wang Kuang-ch'i), "Ueber die chinesischen Notenhandschriften," Sinica, III (1928), 110 ff.

2. See p. 106.

3. Since the earliest times, Chinese authors have left a wealth of information about music. Among these works are the Chinese Classics (or Confucian Classics) which, although not necessarily confined to the actual teachings of Confucius (551-479), were written and preserved by Confucian scholars. The first, the Shu Ching, is a book of historical documents which dates back to to the Chou period (1050-221). The work which was known to Confucius is simply called Shu in the Analects, and 400 years after the death of Confucius the compilation of the Shu Ching was ascribed to him. In later times the book was severely altered, especially during the Han period (206 B.C.-A.D. 220). The original text, supposedly discovered in a wall of the house of Confucius, is called the "Old Text," while the changed work is called the "Modern Text." Most of this text is in prose, with a small part in verse. In addition to valuable historical facts, the Shu Ching offers information regarding music. In Part II, Book I ("The Canon of Shun") we are informed about the standard pitch pipes and the "five instruments of gem"; in the same book, paragraph 13, we read that "all within the four seas, the eight instruments [these are the eight materials producing the eight sounds: instruments made of metal, stone, silk, bamboo, gourd, earth, leather, and wood] were stopped and hushed." In Book IV, paragraph 4, we read about the songs of the period; in paragraphs 9 and 10 indirect reference is made to the "lutes" (the famous Chinese zithers); and so forth.

The second of the Classics is the Shih Ching, the "Book of Odes." It must not be confused with the Shih Chi, an important historical work by the Han historian Ssŭ-ma Ch'ien (145-86). The Shih Ching, also called "The Three-hundred," contains 305 rhymed ballads — poems that originated in a pre-Confucian era. Although Confucius expressed admiration for them and later writers credited him with compiling the poems, doubts concerning this have arisen. A passage in the Li Chi (another of the Chinese Classics) exists which suggests the true origin of the poems (see J. Legge, trans., The Chinese Classics [London, 1871], IV, i [Prolegomena]; II, 23-24): "Every fifth year, the son of Heaven made a progress through the kingdom, when the grand music-master was commanded to lay before him the poems collected in the States of the several quarters, as an exhibition of the manners of the people." This means that according to the quality of the poems the emperor would judge how the princes had ruled the various states and would then reward or punish them accordingly. Although none of the melodies to which the poems were sung have survived, the rare and simple beauty of these odes shows how impressive the songs must have been.

The third Chinese Classic is the I Ching, the "Book of Changes." This pre-Confucian work, probably the oldest of the Classics, consists of two texts which in later periods were joined to make one book. The first of these consists of omen-texts in rhyme dealing with the pa-kua, the eight mysterious trigrams (hexagrams), used for divination. The I Ching has been ascribed to Wên Wang, the father of Wu Wang, who was the first emperor of the Chou dynasty (1027-256).

The fourth Chinese Classic, the Li Chi ("Book of Rites"), is a collection of tractates of varying dates written sometime between the fourth and second centuries B.C. Some parts of the work, especially chapters three and four, are perhaps older than the rest and may go back to the time of Confucius. The Li Chi was compiled by an uncle and his nephew named Tai during the first and second centuries B.C. The uncle, Tai Teh (or Ta Tai), shaped the work into 85 sections, and his nephew, Tai Shêng (or Hsiao Tai), shortened it to 46. Although the Li Chi was not written by Confucius, it reflects Confucian thinking and in A.D. 175 became an official part of the Confucian Classics. Section 27, Yüeh-chi, "Record of Music," is of considerable importance to the musicologist. See J. Legge, trans., Sacred Books of China (Oxford, 1885), Vol. XXVIII; also Richard Wilhelm, trans., "Das Buch der Sitte," Li-Gi (Jena, 1930), chap. "Yo-ki."

Another Chinese Classic, the Chou Li, "The Rites of the Chou Period," was added to the Li Chi during the Han dynasty (202 B. C. -A. D. 220). It was written during the first century B. C. and deals mostly with ritual and constitutional matters of the Chou period. It contains information about the pitch-pipes (lü), the stone-chimes, and the kau-ku — a twelve-foot-long drum used at imperial hunting parties — but offers no remarks about the famous Chinese zither, the ch'in.

The Ch'un-ch'iu, "The Annals of Spring and Autumn," another Classic (not to be confused with the Lü-shih-ch'un-ch'iu, "Spring and Autumn of Lü Pu Wei"), is a history of the state of Lu from 722 to 481 B. C. It contains brief entries about victories, murders, treaties, and natural phenomena and, as was the custom, adds to the date of each entry the season when the event occurred — hence the title, "Spring and Autumn." According to Mencius (372-289? B. C.) this was a work which Confucius believed would make him known in the future. As with the Shih Ching, later writers tried to read hidden meanings into its text. Linked with the Ch'un-ch'iu is the important Tso Chuan, Tso Ch'iu-ming's Commentary on the Ch'un-ch'iu, which was written about 300 B. C. Both works contain numerous references to music and musical instruments, and in the Tso Chuan we note that a clear distinction has already been made between the musical styles of North and South China.

A work that does not belong to the Chinese Classics (certain doubts have been raised about its importance and value) is the Lü-shih ch'un-ch'iu, the "Spring and Autumn of Lü Pu Wei" (third century B. C.), which offers some information about the early periods of Chinese history and music.

The monumental collection of the Confucian Classics has been translated into English by James Legge under the title of The Chinese Classics: Li Ki (Li Chi) (Oxford, 1885); She King (Shih Ching) (London, 1871); Shoo King (Shu Ching) (Hongkong, 1865); Yi King (I Ching) (Oxford, 1882). See also Sacred Books of the East, ed. Max Müller (Oxford, 1897-1927). Of considerable importance is Notes of Chinese Literature by A. Wylie, published in Shanghai in 1867. This work contains information about 2000 Chinese works, including the Classics, history, philosophy, and other fields.

4. Yin-hsü wên-tzǔ chui-ho (殷虛文字綴合), publ. by Chung-kuo k'o-hsüeh-yüan k'ao-ku-yen-chiu-so (中國科學院考古研究所) (Peking, 1955).

5. Ch'ên Shou-yi, Chinese Literature (New York, 1961), p. 5.

6. For further information on bronzes see Kuo Mo-jo (郭沫若), Liang-chou chin-wen tz'ǔ ta hsi t'u-lu k'ao-shih (両周金文辭大系圖錄考釋) (Peking, 1956).

7. Ch'ên Shou-yi, op. cit., p. 6.

8. The manuscript is preserved in the Bibliothèque nationale, Collection Pelliot, No. 3808.

9. See Arthur Waley, Ballads and Stories from Tun-Huang (London, 1960).

10. Ibid., p. 242.

11. See Richard Wilhelm, Fruehling und Herbst des Lü Bu We (Jena, 1928), esp. book five, chap. two; see also above, n. 10. (Chinese editions: Ssu-pu ts'ung-k'an, first series, Shanghai, 1920-1922; third series, 1935).

12. The twelve pitches were grouped into six male (律 , "laws") and six female (呂 , "pipes"); both words are pronounced lü, but the former is pronounced in the high-falling tone, and the latter in the low-rising tone and, of course, are written differently.

13. J. van Aalst, Chinese Music (Shanghai, 1884; repr. Peking, 1933).

14. Maurice Courant, "Essai sur la musique classique des Chinois avec un appendice relatif a la musique Coreenne," in Encyclopédie de la musique, ed. A. Lavignac (Paris, 1913), Vol. I.

15. V. Ch. Mahillon, Annuaire du Conservatoire de Bruxelles (Ghent, 1886, 1890).

16. Père Amiot, Mémoire sur la musique des Chinois tant anciens que modernes (Paris, 1779).

17. Curt Sachs, The Rise of Music in the Ancient World (New York, 1943), pp. 116-17. See also Georges Soulié, La Musique en Chine (Paris, 1911). Soulié transcribes the Huang-chung with A# below the middle C.

18. See Li Ki (Li Chi), "Book of Rites," chapter on music; trans. J. Legge in The Sacred Books of China, ed. F.M. Müller (Oxford, 1885), Vol. XXVII.

19. Cf. A. Daniélou, Introduction to the Study of Musical Scales (London, 1943), pp. 75-82.

20. "Exposé de la musique des Chinois," in L'Echo musical (Brussels), October 12, 1890.

21. Cf. E. Faber, "The Chinese Theory of Music," China Review (1873), p. 388. See also Laurence Picken, "Chinese Music" in Grove's Dictionary of Music and Musicians, 5th ed. (New York, 1959), II, 230.

22. Chinesische Musik (Kassel, 1956), pp. 79-82.

23. A dictionary showing the characters of the ancient script is Shuo-wên chiai-tzŭ chên-pên (說文解字真本) by the Han author Hsü Shên (許慎) (Shanghai, n.d.).

24. The thought underlying the organization of the lü is the principle of the union of the male and female in procreation. Similar doctrines can be found throughout the Orient, especially in the Jewish Cabbalah. According to the Cabbalists, God the Infinite Being, far removed and beyond all mundane existence, and God the Active Being, who influences creation and life, represented a paradox which the Cabbalists resolved in the Sefirot, the ten spheres of divine manifestation — luminous rays in which God emerges from the concealed Infinite and Incomprehensible. The Sefirot, described as male and female, arose from the first Sefirah, the Keter (Crown), an absolute primeval unity from which the two other male and female Sefirot emerged — a male called Chochmah (Wisdom), and a female called Binah (Intellect); together these formed the "Father and Mother." The remaining seven Sefirot were the result of the union of Chochmah and Binah.

25. The excerpt on page 427 is taken from a copy of the Chou Li, Book 37 of the Ssŭ-pu-pei-yao edition (Shanghai, n.d.). A rough translation of this excerpt reads as follows:

Ta Shih (the name of a musical official) is in charge of the six lü and their six companions. The former represent the sounds of yang,

(Refers to Note 25)

大師掌六律六同以合陰陽之聲陽聲黃鐘大簇姑

洗蕤賓夷則無射陰聲大呂應鐘南呂函鐘小呂夾鐘

consisting of Huang-chung, T'ai-ts'u, Ku-hsi, Jui-pin, I-tsê, and Wu-i, and the latter (the six companions) represent the sounds of yin, consisting of Ta-lü, Ying-chung, Nan-lü, Han-chung (丞鍾), Hsiao-lü (小呂), and Chia-chung.

Remarkable are the names Han-chung and Hsiao-lü, which are used here instead of the usual Lin-chung and Chung-lü.

Another excerpt (p. 429), taken from a copy of the Kuo Yü (國語 , "Episodes of State"), Vol. III, is a work attributed to Tso Ch'iu-ming, the author of the Tso Chuan, who adds four principles to the yang and yin and elaborates the extramusical connotations of the lü. Roughly translated this excerpt reads:

In ancient times a learned blind musician (Shên Ku) examined the central tone and established it as the basis of a system of tones. Rules (to this effect) were postulated which were used by numerous government officials. He (Shên Ku) established three tones (representing heaven, earth, and men), then he divided (split) them into six and then, from six into twelve (which included the yang and yin tones). Six is the central number between heaven and earth. Yellow is the central color among all colors, hence the first tone was called Huang-chung ("Yellow Bell") and was employed to harmonize with the six principles (yin, yang, wind, rain, cloudiness, and clearness) and the nine te (water, fire, metal, wood, earth, grain, virtue, resources, and industry). The second tone (after the Huang-chung) is T'ai-ts'u, which fosters growth and does away with all tardiness. The third tone, Ku-hsi, assists in the cleansing of all objects under the sun, honors the gods and welcomes guests. The fourth tone, Jui-pin, pacifies both people and spirits and encourages friendship. The fifth tone, I-tsê, praises the harvest and calms the people. The sixth tone, Wu-i, announces the virtues of the sages in order to guide the people in the correct ceremonies.

There are also six chien ["spaces," "intervals"] which harmonize with the former six lü: Ta-lü assists the Huang-chung in the completion of its task. Chia-chung harmonizes the weather of all seasons. Chung-lü presents the universal law. Lin-chung supervises deeds and prevents fraud. Nan-lü assists the yang lü in order to make the world prosperous. Yin-chung maintains the most effective functioning of both officials and objects.

26. See p. 39.

(Refers to Note 25)

古之神瞽考中聲而量之以制度律均鍾百官軌儀

紀之以三平之以六成於十二天之道也夫六中之

色也故名之曰黃鍾所以宣養六氣九德也由是第

之二曰太簇所以金奏贊陽出滯也三曰姑洗所以

修潔百物考神納賓也四曰蕤賓所以安靖神人獻

酬交酢也五曰夷則所以詠歌九則平民無貳也六

曰無射所以宣布哲人之令德示民軌儀也為之六

間以揚沈伏而黜散越也元間大呂助宣物也二間

夾鍾出四隙之細也三間仲呂宣中氣也四間林鍾

和展百事俾莫不任肅純恪也五間南呂贊陽秀也

六間應鍾均利器用俾應復也

27. The ancient Chinese vertical flute was made of bamboo and had five holes above and one below. It was used in the music of the Confucian temple.

28. See p. 69.

29. See van Aalst, Chinese Music, p. 20.

30. Maurice Courant, "Chine et Corée," in Encyclopédie de la musique, ed. A. Lavignac (Paris, 1913), I, 126. It may be of interest to study the following example (p. 431); it represents another setting of the first ode in lü notation and is quoted from Wang Kuang-ch'i (王 光 祈), Chung-kuo yin-yüeh-shih (中 國 音 樂 史 , "History of Chinese Music"), published in Taipei in 1956.

Below follows the transcription of the heptatonic melody:

31. Although not prescribed in the score of this ode music, the po-fu player can perform three different beats:

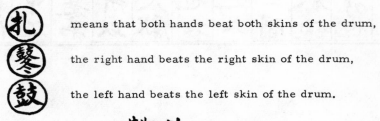

means that both hands beat both skins of the drum,

the right hand beats the right skin of the drum,

the left hand beats the left skin of the drum.

32. The t'ao-ku (鞀 鼓) is a small barrel-shaped drum (or two or more drums tied together), the corpus of which is pierced by a wooden handle.

(Refers to Note 30)

關雎

參差荇菜左右芼之窈窕淑女鐘鼓樂之

參差荇菜左右采之窈窕淑女琴瑟友之

求之不得寤寐思服悠哉悠哉輾轉反側

參差荇菜左右流之窈窕淑女寤寐求之

關關雎鳩在河之洲窈窕淑女君子好逑

Setting of First Ode in <u>Lü</u> Notation

Strings are attached to the middle of the corpus, on both sides, with freely swinging balls at their ends. When the drum is turned to and fro, the balls strike against the two drum skins. In Confucian temples one t'ao-ku is placed at the east side, the other at the west side. At the present time the instrument is also used by traveling vendors and beggars. An illustration of the t'ao-ku can be found in van Aalst, p. 77.

33. The text, as far as it is shown in Fig. 1 reads: Kuan, kuan, chü chiu tsai ho chih chou; roughly translated the words mean: "Kuan, kuan, cry the fish-hawks from the island in the river . . . ."

34. The pien-ch'ing (編磬), a stone-chime, consists of sixteen L-shaped stone slabs hung in two rows of eight slabs each, from a wooden frame. All slabs are equally long but differ in thickness. The slabs are tuned to the twelve lü in the following manner:

Upper row (yang lü):

wu   i   jui   ku   t'ai   huang   pei-wu   pei-i

Lower row (yin lü):

ying   nan   lin   chung   chia   ta   pei-ying   pei-nan

The ancient instrument had sixteen slabs; in the Han period (202 B.C.-A.D. 200), nineteen; in the Liang period (502-556), twenty-one; in the Wei (220-581), fourteen; and in the Ming period (1368-1644), twenty-four. The instrument was used only in ritual and ceremonial music of the temple and imperial court. In the Confucian temple the pien-ch'ing corresponds to the t'ê-ching (see below, n. 35). The latter stands at the east side and the former at the west side of the Moon Terrace.

35. The t'ê-ch'ing (特磬 , "single musical stone") is a single L-shaped slab made of black calcareous stone or jade (hence it is often de-

scribed as the "gem") which is hung on a wooden frame. It is placed at the left side of the Moon Terrace of the Confucian temple. Usually at the end of every verse of a hymn the longer part of the slab is struck once with the cushioned end of a wooden mallet. The t'ê-ch'ing produces a clear deep sound which intones the kung, the basic note of the melody. We read in the Analects (XIV, 42) that Confucius frequently uttered his approval of this instrument because its sound was not influenced by climatic changes. Occasionally the instrument is called li-ch'ing (離磬), "separate (distant) ch'ing." (W. E. Soothill, The Analects of the Conversations of Confucius . . . [London, 1937]).

36. See van Aalst, p. 50.

37. This is only an assumption. In reality the Huang-chung was considered to be a yin sound; hence the note A would be a degree of the yang row.

38. Cf. Yüeh-lü ch'uan-shu (樂律全書), a work in nineteen volumes by Prince Chu Tsai-yü (朱載堉); Imperial Catalogue, ch'üan 38, p. 5. The work was written during the last decennium of the sixteenth century.

39. The sounds of the vocal part and of the pien-ch'ing would be as follows:

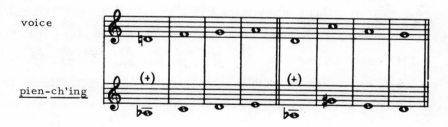

The instruments other than the pien-ch'ing would perform the lower part and "double" it in an anhemitonic pentatonic manner using the notes A and G.

40. Koreanische Musik (Tokyo, 1930), p. 30.

41. See p. 53.

42. Van Aalst, p. 23.

43. The notations of Chiang K'uei (姜夔) are extant in the Pê Shih Tao Jen Ko Ch'ü (白石道人歌曲), Official History of the Sung Dynasty (Shanghai, 1936), Vol. 2037, p. 6. See also p. 177 and p. 456 (n. 174).

44. John Hazedel Levis, Foundations of Chinese Musical Art (Peiping, 1936), pp. 174-75.

45. Also called Kambhojika, Kambhoja, or Kambhoji is a popular rāga of North India. Its tone-material is C E F G A Bb c in the rising, and c Bb A G F E D C in the descending scale.

46. The word hu (胡 , "irregular") was used to denote foreigners, especially Mongol and Tartar tribes.

47. Transcribed by Laurence Picken in New Oxford History of Music (New York, 1957), I, 109.

48. Ibid., p. 110.

49. The Ak-hak-koe-pŭm was reprinted several times, e.g., in 1610 by Rhee Chung-koo of the Ak-su-chŭng (樂書廳), and again during the reign of King Yung-cho (1724-1776). A photographic reproduction of this important work was published in 1933 in Seoul by the Ko-chŭn kan-haeng hoe (古典刊行會), or, as the company's name is often pronounced in Japanese, by the Koten kanko kai of Keijo (Seoul). See also Courant, "Chine et Coreé," in Encyclopédie de la musique, I, 212.

50. Korean musicians called imported music from China T'ang-ak (唐樂), "Music of the T'ang Period." The Korean term T'ang-ak was also applied to music of the imperial courts of Chinese pre-T'ang periods.

51. Chap. 17, sec. 18: 惡鄭聲之亂雅樂也 For English translation see Soothill, The Analects of the Conversations of Confucius. Soothill's translation of the above sentence is: "I hate the way the airs of Chêng pervert correct music."

52. Ibid., chap. 7, sec. 13:

子在齊聞韶。三月不知肉味。日不圖爲樂之至於斯也。

The literal translation by Soothill is: "When the master was in Ch'i [Chê] he heard the Shao music and for three months was unconscious of the taste of meat.

'I did not imagine,' said he, 'that music had reached such perfection as this' '' (pp. 62-63). The character 韶 , pronounced Shao in Chinese (in Korean it is So), is the name of the music of the legendary emperor Shun (舞 , in Korean pronounced Sun), who supposedly ruled from 2255-2205. In addition shao also means ''harmonious,'' ''excellent,'' ''beautiful.''

53. Tōyō-rekishi-dai-jiten (東洋歷史大辭典) (''Dictionary of Oriental History'') (Tokyo, 1937), V. 432.

54. The titles of the musical items (ak-po) contained in the Sae-chong shillok are:

a) Ah-ak-po (雅樂譜)

b) I-yae kyŭng-chŭn t'ong-hae (儀禮經傳通解)

c) Won-cho im-u tae-song ak-po (元朝林宇大成樂譜)

d) Chŭng-tae-ŭp ch'i mu-ak-po (定大業之舞樂譜)

e) Po-tae-pyong ch'i mu-ak-po (保太平之舞樂譜)

f) Pal-sang ch'i mu-ak-po (發詳之舞樂譜)

g) Chŭn-in-cha (前引子)

h) Yŭ-min-ak-po (與民樂譜)

i) Ch'i-hwa-pyong po (致和平譜)

j) Chwi-pung-hyong po (醉豐亨譜)

k) Hu-in-cha (後引子)

l) Pong-hwang-ŭm (鳳凰吟)

m) Man-chŭn chun (滿殿春)

55. The work contains the following twelve pieces notated in yul-cha-po and chŭng-kan-po:

a) Po tae-pyŭng po (保太平譜)

b) Jŭng-tae-ŭp po (in) (定大業譜一仁)

c) Mu-an wang myo-che ak po (武安王廟祭樂譜)

d) Kyŭng-mo-kung che-ak kae-hi-un-po (景慕宮祭樂啓熙運譜)

e) Po-ryung-ŭn po (報隆恩譜)

f) Yŭ-min-ak (man) (與民樂一慢)

g) Nak-yang-chun (ye) (洛陽春一禮)

h) Yŭ-min-ak (kwan-po) (與民樂一管譜)

i) Po-hŭ-cha (步虛子)

j) Yŭng-san hwae-sang (靈山會相)

k) Yŭ-min-ak (hyŭn-po) (與民樂一絃譜)

l) Po-hŭ-cha (ji) (步虛子一智) .

The original of this work is preserved in the former Imperial Library of Seoul.

56. Lee Hye-ku, Han-kuk ŭm-ak yon-gu (韓國音樂研究)
(Seoul, 1957).

57. See p. 124.

58. There are several Confucian hymns (and strophes) which have identical
beginnings. Compare this example, for instance, with the one shown on p. 58.

59. See "Hymne pour le sacrifice à Confucius," in Courant's article
"Chine et Corée," in Encyclopédie de la musique, I, 103 ff.

60. To be discussed in Volume II.

61. To be discussed in Volume II.

62. See Walter Kaufmann, "The Forms of the Dhrupad and Khyal in
Indian Art Music," The Canadian Music Journal, Vol. III, No. 2, (1959), p. 26.

63. To be discussed in Volume II.

64. See Part I, n. 3 (p. 424).

65. The correct writing of shang is 商 ; Korean authors and occasionally a few Chinese musicians use instead the character 商 (which actually reads ti).

66. Four other pentatonic scales were derived from the linear permutations of the kung scale:

Kung Scale

kung	(C)
shang	(D)
chiao	(E)
chih	(G)
yü	(A)

Shang Scale		Chiao Scale		Chih Scale		Yü Scale	
shang	(D)	chiao	(E)	chih	(G)	yü	(A)
chiao	(E)	chih	(G)	yü	(A)	kung	(c)
chih	(G)	yü	(A)	kung	(c)	shang	(d)
yü	(A)	kung	(c)	shang	(d)	chiao	(e)
kung	(c)	shang	(d)	chiao	(e)	chih	(g)

The five basic notes (kung, shang, chiao, chih, and yü) were called chêng (正 , "principal"); additional notes, which will be discussed later, were called huo (or ho, 和 , "to harmonize").

67. For further information see Wm. Theodore de Bary, ed., Sources of Chinese Tradition (New York, 1960), pp. 214 ff.

68. See p. 45.

69. See Part I, n. 3 (p. 424).

70. See Liu Chin Tsao, Yüeh-kao ch'ing-chao hsu-wên-hsien-tung-kao (Shanghai, 1936), CXC, 201.

71. According to the Yüeh-lü ch'uan-shu, V, 191 (See Part I, n. 38 [p. 433]).

72. Ibid.

73. Courant, "Chine et Corée," I, 156.

74. See p. 69.

75. For further details about Chinese scales see Koh Nie Kuh, "A Musicological Study of the Important Tonal Systems of the T'ang Dynasty" (dissertation, School of Education, New York University, 1942).

76. In Korea the pien notes were called pyon-chih and pyon-kung. The notational symbols were the same as in China.

77. See p. 69.

78. 氵 is an abbreviation of 清 (ch'ing) and actually means "clear"; in this context however, 氵 means "higher." Correctly written C# should be expressed with 清宮 .

79. To be discussed in Volume II.

80. Occasionally an alternative for hen (the Chinese pien 變) is used; it is the symbol 变 . Thus 譬 means the same as 譬 . The same applies to hen-chi.

81. According to Japanese custom we interpret kyū (宮) as the Western note D.

82. Ongaku Jiten (音樂事典), "Music Dictionary," ed. Shimonaka Yasaburo (下中彌三郎), 12 vols. (Tokyo: Heibon-sha, 1955-57). Article on notation, III, 87, fig. 2-13.

83. See p. 63.

84. For saibara examples transcribed into Western notation see Shiba Sukehiro (芝 裕恭), Gagaku (雅樂) (Tokyo, 1955-56), II, 23.

85. Ise, near the southern coast of central Japan on the Bay of Ise (Ise Wan), is famous for its ancient shrines, which are frequently visited by pilgrims.

86. See Volume II.

Part Two

1. The characters kung (工) and ch'ê (尺) are not to be confused with kung (宮) and chih (徵) of the old Chinese Five and Seven-Tone Notations. The "ancient" kung (宮) always represents the starting note, the basic tone of the scale, while the "new" kung (工) denotes the sixth diatonic degree of a heptatonic scale.

2. A. Lavignac, ed., Encyclopédie de la musique (Paris, 1913), Vol. I.

3. See p. 59.

4. Shên Kua lived from A. D. 1030-1096. A recent edition of this work (2 vols.) was published by the Chunghwa Bookstore (Shanghai, 1960). See also Donald Holzman, "Shên Kua and his Meng-ch'i pi-t'an," T'oung Pao, XLVI (1958), pp. 260-92.

5. A musical system based upon four basic scales. It is discussed by the T'ang scholar Tu Yu (735-812) in his work T'ung Tien (VII, 766), a rich source of information on economy, examinations, rites, music, etc. There are several publications of this work, the most recent by the Commercial Press (n.d.). The scales are also mentioned by the Sung scholar Chang Yen in the Tz'u Yüan (I, 3). The Tz'u Yüan is the earliest dictionary dealing with Chinese phrases, etc. The work was compiled by Lu Erh-k'uei and published by the Commercial Press in 1915. See also Koh-Nie-Kuh, "A Musicological Study of the Important Tonal Systems of the T'ang Dynasty," (dissertation, School of Education, New York University, 1942).

6. The correct names of the ascending chromatic scale degrees of kung-ch'ê-p'u after the time of Shên Kua are discussed below.

7. There are hundreds of works in which the kung-ch'ê symbols, their proper sequence, and affixes are discussed. One of the early sources is a work called Sê-p'u (瑟譜 , "Sê [zither] – notation") by Hsiung P'eng-lai (熊朋來), an author of the Yüan dynasty (1260-1368). The work, which consists of six parts and was reprinted by the Commercial Press, Shanghai, in 1936 (edited by Wang Yün-wu 王雲五), offers the following comparison (p. 440) between lü and kung-ch'ê symbols. The right hand column states Ya lü t'ung su p'u li (lit. "Refined lü comparison with common notation usage"). The reader will have no difficulties recognizing in the other three columns the lü characters (abbreviated) in large size; below them, in smaller size, are the complete names; and to the left of the lü names are the corresponding kung-ch'ê symbols. Wang Yün-wu transcribes the huang with ho, (黄=合), a method which we adopt in subsequent pages.

8. As already mentioned, the range of three octaves can also be observed in Indian music and Japanese shōmyō.

(Refers to Note 7)

9. E.g., ya-yüeh (雅樂), "classical category"; sung-yüeh (頌樂), "hymn category"; su-yüeh (俗樂), "vulgar category"; yen-yüeh (燕樂), "banquet category"; ch'ing-yüeh (清樂), "pure [Chinese] category"; and others.

10. A popular fiddle with two strings tuned to a fifth. The corpus can be made of coconut, bamboo, etc. The hair of the bow passes between the two strings.

11. A two-stringed fiddle, built and tuned like the êrh-hsien, with a cylindrical corpus covered on one side with snakeskin.

12. For further information see Koh-Nie-Kuh, "A Musicological Study of the Important Tonal Systems of the T'ang Dynasty."

13. We present only five of a larger number of scales.

14. The literary names of the transposing scales are:

chêng-t'iao (正調), "principal scale," for yi-fan-t'iao;

chi-liang-t'iao (寂凉調?), "plaintive scale," for shih-kung-t'iao;

hsien-so-t'iao (絃緣調?) "string instrument scale," for ho-ch'ê-t'iao;

p'ing-t'iao (平調) "even scale," for fan-shang-t'iao;

pei-kung-t'iao (倍宮調), "reversed kung scale," for kung-yi-t'iao;

mei-hua-t'iao (梅花調), "plum blossom scale," for ch'ê-wu-t'iao;

tzǔ-mu-t'iao (子母調), "son and mother scale."

15. For further information see Ch'iu Hao-ch'ou, Kuo-yüeh-hsin-shêng (國樂新聲).

16. See also above, Part II, n. 12.

17. Generally êrh-huang is written 二簧 ; the character 簧 de-

notes the "reed" tongues (made of metal) of the shêng (笙), the Chinese mouth organ. (The top of the character 竹, indicates "bamboo"). However, there are some Chinese scholars who object to the use of 簧 and insist that the character 黃 (huang, "yellow") be used. Their argument is that êrh-huang supposedly has originated in certain districts of China which are called "yellow slope," and "yellow mound," and that the operatic style is named after these places and has to be written 二 黃 . See Liu Ch'eng-fu (劉 誠 甫) in Yin-yüeh-tz'ŭ-tien (音 樂 辭 典 , "Music Dictionary") (Shanghai: Commercial Press, 1936). See also Wang Kuang ch'i (王 光 祈), Chung-kuo-yin-yüeh-shih (中 國 音 樂 史 , "History of Chinese Music") (Taiwan, 1956).

18. See below, n. 27 (p. 443).

19. See p. 79 (shêng).

20. Hsiao (簫), a vertical flute with five holes on the top and one at the bottom, originated during the Han period (202 B.C.-220 A.D.). It was made of bamboo, occasionally also of jade, marble, or copper, and was admitted into the Confucian temple music during the Yüan period (1260-1368). J.A. van Aalst, (Chinese Music [Shanghai, 1884; repr. Peking, 1933], p. 70), states that "at Confucian ceremonies there are six hsiao, placed immediately outside the hall, on the 'Moon Terrace.' The music which they perform is exactly the same as that of the other instruments, but it is noted in a different manner."

21. Ti (笛) is the Chinese transverse flute with six fingerholes and another hole covered with a fine reedy membrane. The tube is wrapped in waxed silk and ornamented with tassels. Contrary to the hsiao, the ti is not a "transposing" instrument.

22. The 合 of ti notation actually sounds or approximates e; in our simplified version the note c is used.

23. According to van Aalst in Chinese Music, 尺 of the hsiao actually sounds d, and 六 of the ti sounds a' (902 vibrations per second).

24. "Moon-ch'in," a guitar with a circular, flat corpus and a short neck with five to ten frets. The instrument has four silken strings tuned in pairs; strings 1 and 2 are tuned a fifth higher than strings 3 and 4. Modern

tunings differ from the tuning in pairs; one tuning in frequent use is: e a d' g'. The strings are plucked with the fingers or a plectrum.

25. "Three-strings," a guitar with a small, flat, cylindrical corpus and a long neck with three lateral pegs. The top and bottom of the body are covered with snakeskin. Most of the san-hsien have no frets, but there are a few exceptions. The three strings are of silk (occasionally of metal) and are tuned to 1 4 8, or 1 5 8, or 1 2 6.

26. See Volume II.

27. Lit. "Western drum (skin)" — one of the important Chinese operatic styles. Hsi-p'i dramas deal with events of civilian middle-class life and are of a quieter nature than those of the related êrh-huang style. In the latter, rhythms begin with down beats, while hsi-p'i rhythms begin with up beats. Both êrh-huang and hsi-p'i evolved from the pang-tzŭ (梆 子) style which came into existance during the reign of Emperor Kang Hsi (1662-1722). Pang-tzŭ indicates "drum sticks" (wood-block) and illustrates the prevalence of percussion instruments. The roots of pang-tzŭ reach back into the Yüan period when it became customary to set great heroic plots to music in a crude and noisy manner. This type of theater with its grandiose pantomimic battle scenes was performed only outdoors because of the overwhelming noise. The êrh-huang style appeared during the reign of Emperor Yung Cheng (1732-1735) as a welcome relief after the noisy pang-tzŭ. Êrh-huang and hsi-p'i employ string instruments, especially the hu-ch'in (See Part II, n. 11 [p. 441]). In hsi-p'i the two strings of the hu-ch'in are tuned a whole tone higher than in êrh-huang. For further information see Xia Ye, "Zur Entwicklung der chinesischen Opernstile," in Beiträge zur Musikwissenschaft, Vol. III (Berlin, 1961).

28. See pp. 31 ff.

29. Van Aalst, p. 27. For translation of the text, pp. 34-35.

30. See p. 119.

31. Maurice Courant, "Chine et Corée," in Encyclopédie de la musique, ed. A. Lavignac (Paris, 1913), I, 133.

32. The transliteration of the text can be seen in the transcription of the hymn, Figure 15, p. 82; a general translation may be found in Courant, "Chine et Corée," I, 135 n.

33. The real ying-ku is larger, but its name is frequently applied to the smaller tsu-ku, a drum which is placed upon a wooden stand on the west side of the "Moon Terrace" of the Confucian temple, and beaten in response to the larger drum. In our transcription ku represents the large and ying the small drum.

34. Van Aalst, p. 26, describes the March as follows: "the way from the first gate to the centre of the temple is left open for the passage of the emperor or his deputy, with his suite of princes, dignitaries, and attendants. At the second gate the emperor leaves his sedan and walks to the temple at a slow, stately pace; a band of fourteen musicians and eleven ensign and umbrella bearers precedes him, while . . . the Guiding March is played."

35. The Chinese mouth organ (the Japanese shô) symbolizes the Fêng-huang, the wonderful bird Phoenix. Supposedly invented in the third millenium B.C., it came into use about 1100 B.C. Its body, the wind chest, was made originally of gourd, but later wood was used. It has seventeen thin cane pipes, mounted into the top of the wind chest, which are arranged in such manner as to depict the tail of the bird Phoenix. Each sound-producing pipe (pipes 1, 9, 16, and 17 are silent) has at its lower end a small brass tongue and a ventage outside which must be stopped by the player's finger in order to produce a sound. The pipes are tuned diatonically. See also Alex. J. Ellis, "Ueber die Tonleitern verschiedener Voelker," in Sammelbaende fuer vergleichende Musikwissenschaft, I (Munich, 1922), 58.

36. See Part II, n. 21 (p. 442).

37. See Part II, n. 20 (p. 442).

38. A set of ten little brass gongs suspended in a wooden frame. All the gongs have the same diameter but vary in thickness; they are tuned diatonically. For tuning see A. Ellis, op. cit., pp. 58-59.

39. See p. 31.

40. Chinesische Musik (Kassel, 1956), p. 184.

41. Chinese Music, p. 26.

42. See p. 79.

43. See p. 104.

44. Van Aalst, p. 19.

45. See Wang Kuang-ch'i, ''Ueber die chinesischen Notenhandschriften'' in Sinica, III (1928), 110-23.

46. E. g., in hsi-p'i style; see Part II, n. 27 (p. 443).

47. See Laurence Picken, ''The Music of China,'' in The New Oxford History of Music (London, 1957) I, 115-17. See also Reinhard, op. cit., p. 211, examples 22 and 23 (a rhythm which symbolizes ''night'').

48. See Part II, n. 17 (p. 441).

49. See Part II, n. 27 (p. 443).

50. Lao yüan, one of the few preserved works, has been reprinted in Ch'ing-jên-tsa-chü (清 人 雜 劇 , ''Dramatic plays of the Ch'ing people''), a work consisting of twelve volumes, published by Chêng Chên-to (鄭 振 鐸) in 1934. A copy of this work is preserved in the library of Indiana University.

51. The general translation of the text is:

Ah, my hair has turned half gray,
Look, my frosted temples.
Though I would still hold that I am strong and vigorous,
Yet age is creeping in and my feeling tells me so.
Roaming through the big cities amidst laughter and excitement,
I try to lessen my growing melancholy.
But as I look at my battle horse, pitiful animal;
Swaying his tail which is bare of all tender and soft hair,
He toddles along like a brindled ox.
Yes, he is only fit to plough now until dusk comes.

52. See R. H. Mathews, Chinese-English Dictionary (Cambridge, Mass., 1956), p. 1178.

53. Ibid., p. 1070, character 7187.

54. Ibid., p. xiv.

55. Conversational Chinese (Chicago, 1947), p. 2.

56. See John Hazedel Levis, Foundations of Chinese Musical Art (Peiping, 1936), pp. 11 ff.

57. See Part I, n. 3 (p. 422).

58. ''In his autobiography he [Shên Yüeh] writes, 'The poets of old,

during the past thousands years, never hit upon this plan [of classifying the four tones]. I alone discovered its advantages.' The Emperor Wu Ti of the Liang dynasty one day said to him, 'Come, tell me, what are these famous four tones?' 'They are whatever your Majesty pleases to make them,' replied Shēn Yo, skillfully selecting for his answer four characters which illustrated, and in the usual order, the four tones in question'' (Herbert A. Giles, A History of Chinese Literature [New York, 1923], pp. 138-39).

59. Ibid., p. 144.

60. Willi Apel, Harvard Dictionary of Music (Cambridge, 1955), p. 487.

61. The tz'ŭ usually consisted of strophes of from four to eight or ten lines, each line having from two to seven syllables. During the T'ang and Sung periods (618-1279) these poems became highly artificial and were filled with learned quotations and allusions which gradually became so complex that only a few educated people could understand them. With the growing complexity of the texts, the song melodies also became increasingly intricate. Soon they no longer corresponded with the prescribed tonal inflecti ns of the text. From this stilted and confused style eventually evolved a new song form which used common language or dialects as texts. These new songs, in contrast to their complicated forerunners, were simple, and, as a result, everybody could understand and perform them. This caused objections raised by the literati of the older generations of the Sung period who condescendingly called these simple songs ch'ü (曲), or ch'ü-tz'ŭ (曲詞) — ch'ü meaning ''wrong,'' ''opposed to straight.'' We have to add here a word of doubt whether or not we can speak of a condescending attitude of the literati. Whenever ch'ü means ''wrong,'' it is pronounced in the high level tone. Ch'ü in its musical sense, however, is pronounced in the low rising tone and has been in use in this form since the period of the Warring States (403-221). These simple songs with simple texts gradually evolved again into more complex forms where intricate verses were joined with melodies spiced with foreign microtones and ornaments (see Chiang K'uei songs, p. 39). In spite of their growing complexity these songs remained popular. Their texts usually dealt with heroic events of the past. The ch'ü were grouped into the pei-ch'ü (北曲), the northern ch'ü, and the nan-ch'ü

(南 曲), the southern ch'ü. In the pei-ch'ü (northern ch'ü) the text was of greater importance than the melody; these songs were usually accompanied by a stringed instrument. In the nan-ch'ü (southern ch'ü) the melody predominated. The accompaniment of the latter was provided by the sound of percussion instruments. Chinese musicians also distinguished between ch'ü sung at the imperial court — songs that were suitable to entertain the highest nobility; ch'ü performed in cycles — often as many as 40 songs used in succession; and ch'ü performed by scholars — artful, sometimes amusing music, which could also be performed in conjunction with dancing. The popular ch'ü appeared also in theatrical performances called tsa-ch'ü (雜 曲) and contributed considerably to the development of Chinese opera.

62. This period must not be confused with the Sung dynasty (960-1279); it belongs to the so-called Southern and Northern Dynasties (420-588), about 400 years before the art of hsin-t'i reached its climax.

63. Levis, Foundations of Chinese Musical Art, p. 38.

64. For detailed information see Ibid., pp. 10 ff.

65. Ibid., p. 104.

66. Ibid., p. 105.

67. This character is pronounced tou here; when it is pronounced tu, it means "to read."

68. Levis, op. cit., pp. 106 ff.

69. Ibid., pp. 105 ff.

70. See Courant, "Chine et Corée," pp. 112 ff.

71. See Lee Hye-ku, Han-kuk ŭm-ak yon-gu (Seoul, 1957), p. 4. The Sae-cho shillok must not be confused with the Sae-chong shillok.

72. See Part I, n. 49 (p. 434).

73. See p. 120; Chong-myo-ak is the ritual music in honor of the royal ancestors. A second type, mun-myo-ak (文 廟 樂), is the ritual music in honor of Confucius.

74. In addition to the modes of pyong-cho, u-cho, pyong-cho kae-myon-cho, and u-cho kae-myon-cho (which are discussed on p. 309), Korean musicians distinguish two basic scales: hap-cho (合 調) using 合 , 四 ,

一 ，勺 ，尺 ，工 ，几 ，and sang-cho (上調), using
上，尺，工，几，合，四，一 . Both scales have the
interval of an augmented fourth and differ only in their first notes, C and F
respectively.

75. See p. 124.

76. Ongaku Jiten, (Tokyo, 1950), V, 3068 ff.

77. Ibid.

78. The only copy of this work is preserved by the National Court Music
Association (Ku-wang kung ah-ak-pu, 旧王宮雅樂部); in addition
to this "later" collection, there existed an earlier one, called Tae-ak chŭn-po
(大樂前譜 , "Great Music Former Notation"), edited in 1653
and/or 1759. The melodies contained in the Tae-ak chŭn-po were originally
collected by order of King Sae-cho; the first editor was Pak Yŭn (朴堧),
1378-1453. The work contained:

雅樂樂歌	步虛子管
定大業	桓桓曲
醉豊亨	水龍吟
致和平	億吹簫
鳳凰吟	夏雲峰
與民樂慢	小拋毬樂
步虛子	五雲開端朝
洛陽春	會入仙
前引子	千年萬歲
後引子	折花
與民樂絃	衆仙會
與民樂管	

The Tae-ak chŭn-po, which had been preserved by the Royal Music Department
(chang ak-won, 掌樂院), at Seoul, is lost. The texts of five pieces

are preserved in Koryo-sa ak-chi (高麗史 樂志 , "Music Chapter of the History of the Koryo Dynasty"). See also Naito Konan (内藤 湖南), Sogaku to Cho-sen gaku (宋樂と朝 鮮樂 , "Sung Music and Korean Music"), in Shina gaku (支那學), "Study of Chinese Music"), in Japanese.

79. See p. 127.

80. See section on hap-cha-po, beginning on p. 301; Chung-tae-yŭp can be found in the Yang-kŭm shin-po, a famous zither book of 1610 (See p. 305).

81. See section of hap-cha-po, beginning on p. 301.

82. Pyong-cho and u-cho are sol-modes; pyong-cho kae-myon-cho and u-cho kae-myon-cho are la-modes.

83. The two pieces are: Chong-myo chae-ak (宗廟祭樂, "Imperial Temple Music") and Pung-an chi-ak (豊安之樂 , "Music of Abundant Ease").

84. Serious music imported from China.

85. Lit., "Well-between Notation" — the name refers to the openings of water wells which are surrounded by four tree trunks placed horizontally in the form of a ♯ . Metrical and rhythmic features in chŭng-kan-po are indicated by means of a chart which consists of horizontal and vertical lines.

86. See Part I, n. 54 (p.435).

87. In addition to the Sae-chong and Sae-cho shillok, chŭng-kan-po is referred to and used in numerous works: for instance in the collection Yŭng-sŭng-so-mu-po (靈星小舞譜 , "Small Dance Notation of Yŭng Sŭng") of the sixteenth century; in the eighteenth-century collection of Ku-kung-tae-sŭng-po (九宮大成譜 , lit., "Nine Palaces Great Achievement Notation"); in Nap-sŭ-yŭng-kok-po (納書楹曲譜 , "Song notation of Nap-sŭ-yŭng"); in Pan-mok-pu-ho (板眼符號 , "Heavy and Light Beats Notation"); in the Japanese works Kin-kyoku shi-hu (琴曲指譜 , "Zither Music Didactic Notation"), of 1764 (using thirty-two chŭng-kan in each haeng); and in Kin-kyoku tai-i-sho (琴曲大意抄 , "Zither Music Summarizing Selection") of 1779 (using the rhythmic signs ◉ and ◯).

88. See p. 171.

89. Such exceptions can be found in the Sae-cho shillok and in the An-sang kŭm-po (安瑺琴譜), a zither book of 1572, preserved as a national treasure in Seoul in the care of Mr. Sŭng Kyŭng Lin.

90. See section on hap-cha-po, beginning on p. 301.

91. Most modern Korean song melodies begin with the third chŭng-kan.

92. Yŭ-min-ak (與 民 樂 , lit., "Grant People Music").

93. Nak-yang-chun (洛陽春 , "Spring of the Royal City").

94. See also A. Eckardt, Koreanische Musik, (Tokyo, 1930), pp. 55-58.

95. See p. 144.

96. Opinions are divided — Po-hŭ-cha may have been of Korean origin.

97. By Chiang K'uei (the "White stone priest"); see section on Sung notation, beginning on p. 174. See also below, p. 456 (n. 174).

98. See Part III, n. 57 (p. 475).

99. See Part I, n. 55 (p. 435).

100. See Lee, pp. 16, 94.

101. A later version of Po-hŭ-cha was published by the National Court Music Association of Seoul; date of publication is unknown.

102. See Eckardt, p. 59.

103. Po-hŭ-cha when performed as an instrumental piece — with or without dancing — is called Chang-chun pul lo chi-kok (長春不老 之曲, "Never Ageing Song").

104. Lee, pp. 101-4.

105. There are different settings of the text of Po-hŭ-cha: in the An-sang-kŭm-po textual characters appear at comparatively regular intervals of about ten chŭng-kan. The first word is extended over eleven chŭng-kan, the second over ten chŭng-kan, and so forth. In the Tae-ak hu-po a character appears with nearly every haeng of sixteen chŭng-kan; while in the Sok-ak won-po each word is held for about twenty chŭng-kan.

106. Lee, p. 105.

107. The character 與 , "to grant," could, perhaps, have been 興 , "to prosper"; however, Lee uses exclusively 與 , hence we are following his manner of writing.

108. The chang-ko (杖鼓) is a drum used mainly for the accompaniment of vocal music. It has the shape of an hour glass and a corpus made of metal, the left side of which is covered with skin. The left hand beats this skin, producing a low, gentle sound ("drum-side"), while the right hand, using the "whip," a small stick, beats against the other end of the corpus. The skin can be tuned to some extent by manipulating the leather straps which encircle the drum in a criss-cross pattern. The chang-ko is probably of Chinese origin. We find its characteristic hour-glass shape depicted in a seventh-century (A.D.) tomb (number 17 of Chipan-Koguryo-kobun, 輯安高句麗古噴, in Manchuria) and in an engraved bell of the Silla period (57 or 37 B.C.-A.D. 935). The bell is now preserved in the shrine Usa-hachiman-goo (宇佐八 幡宮) in the Oita district of Japan.

The drum-side beats are basic beats which occur at the beginning of any kang. The whip-side beats, however, can be performed on any chǔng-kan. In addition to the old Korean drum words (ko, pyǔn, yo, sang) "modern" symbols are used, always in conjunction with chǔng-kan-po. These symbols are: ⟨symbol⟩ , or ⟨symbol⟩ — the latter symbol appears also in notations for kalko (羯鼓, the Chinese chieh-ku, or the Japanese kakko), a chang-ko with two drum skins. This symbol, called hap-chang-tan (합장탄 , "both hands together"), is performed by both drum hand and whip hand simultaneously. The hap-chang-tan always indicates the beginning of a rhythm with the basic sequence of 3, 2, 3, 3, 2, 3 chǔng-kan in one haeng. Modifications, beyond the scope of this discussion, occur if the piece does not begin with the first chǔng-kan. The ancient Korean symbol for hap-chang-tan is 雙 (ssang). Other symbols are: ○ , puk-pyǔn (북편 , "drum-side"), with the drum hand beating the drum (this is also notated with the ancient character 鼓 , ko); | , chae-pyǔn (채편 , "whip-side"), commonly called ki-tǔk, with the whip hand beating the drum (ancient symbol: 鞭 , pyǔn). Occasionally we find the symbol 𝍩 , particularly in kalko parts, indicating that the whip hand beats twice in succession.

109. See p. 120.

110. See p. 130

111. In 1443 by order of King Sae-chong, the Korean phonetic alphabet (hangŭl) was devised; see below, n. 122.

112. The six flying dragons imply six royal ancestors of King Sae-chong.

113. See Part II, n. 84 (p. 449).

114. See p. 48.

115. Lee, p. 123

116. Man and yŭng types appear in only three pieces: Yŭ-min-ak; a song called Yŭng-san-hoe-sang (靈山會相); and supposedly Po-hŭ-cha (Lee).

117. See Eckardt, p. 42.

118. See p. 145.

119. Lee, facing p. 128.

120. Ibid., p. 126.

121. Lee, after p. 124, examples 7/1-5. If the reader wishes to compare the three Yŭ-min-ak types shown above with others he may consult the notations of the An-sang-kŭm-po and Shin-sang-kŭm-po in the section on hap-cha-po, on pp. 347, 349.

122. Hangŭl, originally called Hun-min chŭng-ŭm (訓民正音), the indigenous Korean alphabet invented by order of King Sae-chong in the fifteenth century, enables the less educated Korean to put in writing any form of colloquial speech. In contrast to Chinese characters, the letters of hangŭl can be learned without much effort, and their shapes supposedly represent the human organs of speech. The alphabet is indeed the world's most complete system of phonetic letters. Several scholars endeavored to derive the letters of hangŭl from foreign systems, but with no success. Hangŭl is an original creation of King Sae-chong and his learned helpers. The letters of hangŭl never displaced the Chinese characters, which remained the scholarly medium of writing. Even today learned treatises in Korea (and Japan) are still written in Chinese characters, while common matters are written in hangŭl.

123. See pp. 24, 54; see also Part I, n. 24 (p. 426).

124. See p. 301.

125. See pp. 305 f.

126. Ibid.

127. See Lee, p. 15.

128. Ibid., p. 8; occasionally yuk-po has been called Cho-sŭng-po (趙晟譜) after the zither book of Cho-sŭng.

129. See p. 301.

130. A long Korean zither with twelve strings and twelve movable bridges.

131. Generally it is the T'ang p'il-lyul (唐觱篥), a heterophonic double-reed instrument with seven holes; it is related to the Japanese hichiriki.

132. The largest Korean flute; it has six finger holes, one covered with a membrane.

133. For string names, tunings, frets, etc., of the hyŭn-kŭm see pp. 307 ff.

134. In u-cho kae-myon-cho (mode) see p. 309; for Man-tae-yŭp, Chung-tae-yŭp, Sak-tae-yŭp see Part II, n. 140 (p. 454).

135. Han-kuk ŭm-ak yon-gu.

136. 二度弱

137. A few kaya-kŭm have only ten strings.

138. Eckardt, Koreanische Musik, p. 42. We implement Eckardt's information with the following kaya-kŭm tunings as stated in the Ak-hak-koe-pŭm, VII, 25 ff. Written in the old Five-Tone Notation and in yul-cha-po, read horizontally from left to right:

139. The word yang (洋) in yang-kŭm, which means "foreign," must not be confused with the name Yang (梁) of the famous seventeenth-century zither book, the Yang-kŭm shin-po.

140. Man-tae-yŭp (慢大葉), lit., "Slow big leaf," Chung-tae yŭp (中大葉), lit., "Middle big leaf," and Sak-tae-yŭp (數大葉), lit., "Fast big leaf," originally were song types (kagok, 歌曲 , "vocal music") which, similar to the canzon francese of sixteenth- and seventeenth-century European music, were performed by instrumental ensembles or solo instruments. Of the three types mentioned only Sak-tae-yŭp (also called chad-ŭn-han-ip 잦은한닙 , lit., "Frequent big leaf," or Kŭ-sang-ak, 擧床樂 , lit., "Awakening music,") is used at the present time. Real kagok pieces use short lyrical poems usually consisting of five verses as text. Each piece contains a prelude played by an ensemble (hyŭn-kŭm, kaya-kŭm, hae-kŭm, chŭt-tae, etc.), an interlude (chung-yŭŭm, 中餘音) between the third and fourth verses, and a postlude (tae-yŭŭm, 大餘音) after the fifth verse. The melodies are first performed in the mode of u-cho, then followed by u-cho kae-myon-cho. (These modes are explained on p. 309).

141. See pp. 327 ff.

142. See p. 301.

143. Although the symbols of the Five Tone Notation and yuk-po do not indicate the durations of the notes, we show them — derived from the hap-cha-po symbols (see p. 301) — in staff notation. The reader will be able to examine the whole piece as shown in Figure 74 on pp. 345 f.

144. They are the open strings IV, V, and VI; see p. 308.

145. See Lee, facing p. 82.

146. See p. 147.

147. Ibid.

148. Op. cit., pp. 82 ff.

149. According to Chu Hsi.

150. See Ch. S. Keh, Die Koreanische Musik (Strassburg, 1935), Appendix, example 3.

151. See p. 131; see also Lee, p. 82.

152. Lee, p. 82.

153. Ibid.

154. 肉譜가 音階名을 表示한 것이라고(도) 볼수없다 (Lee, p. 9).

155. This line represents an excerpt of a version of Sak-tae-yŭp as notated by Cho-sŭng.

156. For instance:

Japan:		Korea:	
Tsuru	(ツル)	Ttul	(뜰)
Ten	(テン)	Tŭng	(뎡)
Tsun	(ツン)	Tung	(둥)
Ton	(トン)	Tong	(동)

157. Songs with texts originating in the middle Javanese language period, performed at temple festivals. See E. Schlager, "Bali," MGG, I, 1110.

158. Gendér is a metallophone, consisting of ten (or twelve) metal slabs which are placed horizontally upon a net of cords. Below each slab is a bamboo resonator; both are tuned to the same pitch.

159. See Colin McPhee, "The Balinese Wayang Koelit and Its Music," Djawa, XVI, (1936).

160. MGG, I, 1111.

161. We are using the Chinese term lü instead of the Korean yul.

162. 趙晟 , a Korean court musician under King Myŭng-chong (明宗 , 1546-1567).

163. We quote the example with slight modifications from Lee, p. 3.

164. The notation of the Heike biwa will be discussed in Volume II.

165. See Lee, p. 15. See also below, pp. 172 ff.

166. Ibid.

167. "Chine et Corée," op. cit., pp. 156-57.

168. For further information see C. P. Fitzgerald, China (London, 1954), pp. 427-29.

169. A famous figure of twelfth-century China. He was a commentator on the Confucian canon, a historian of the utmost importance, a prolific writer, and a musician who composed songs using as texts the odes of the Shih Ching.

170. "Chine et Corée," p. 157.

171. "Ch'in Sounds (music) Commentary" is a part of the collected works of Chu Hsi (also called Chu Wên Kung, 朱文公); see also Hsia Ch'êng-ch'ou, "A Study of the Musical Notations of Chiang K'uei's Songs," Yenching Journal of Chinese Studies (Peiping) (December 1932), pp. 2559-89.

172. Column 4, see Courant, loc. cit., column 7, according to Hsia Ch'êng-ch'ou. Liu-ch'êng-fu (劉誠甫) in his Yin-yüeh-tz'ǔ-tien (音樂辞典), a music dictionary published by the Commercial Press (Shanghai, 1936), states that the Tz'ǔ-yüan was reprinted by the Peking University Press (n. d.), edited by Wu Mei (吳梅).

173. Published by Yeh (葉) in Chêng-tu, Szechuan. See also Hsia Ch'êng-ch'ou.

174. Chiang K'uei is often referred to as the "White Stone Hermit." A reprint of the White Stone Songs was made by the Chung-hua-shu-chü (中華書局), Shanghai, 1900.

175. 越 here refers to the old state of Yüeh, which today is the province of Chekiang. 九歌 (chiu-ko, "Nine Songs") was a form of ritual music supposedly used in the time of Emperor Yü of the ancient Hsia dynasty (third millenium B. C.).

176. The second character can also be 製 , chih, "to make," "to construct." This latter version is preferred in Korea and Japan.

177. Other songs composed during the Sung period survived as fragments in Chin-lien-yüeh-chang-tzǔ-yeh (金奩樂章子野), and in P'ien-yü (片玉).

178. According to the Heibon-sha Oriental History Dictionary (Tokyo, 1941), IV, 434, the Shih-lin-kuang-chi was republished several times: (1) in

1325, editor unknown, in four volumes (50 chapters), with one copy preserved in the Cabinet Library in Tokyo; (2) in 1496, editor unknown, in six volumes (6 chapters); (3) a later edition, date of publication and editor unknown, in six volumes (29 chapters); the second part of Appendix II contains musical notations. The work is preserved in the Toyo Library (東洋文庫 , Toyo bunko), Tokyo.

179. Foundations of Chinese Musical Art, p. 91; the symbols are quoted from Hsia Ch'êng-ch'ou.

180. See Bibliography.

181. An author of the Ch'ing dynasty. According to Ts'ao Ch'ou-shêng (曹惆生), Chung-kuo-yin-yüeh, wu-tao Hsi-ch'ü jên-ming tz'ŭ-tien (中國音樂 舞蹈戲曲人名詞典), Dictionary of Chinese Music, Dances, etc., (Peking: Commercial Press, 1959), p. 157.

182. Polite form of referring to Chu Hsi, used in works of the Ming period. For instance in Ch'in-lü-shuo (琴律說).

183. According to T'ang Lan ㇊ can be an abbreviation of 介 . In the Tz'ŭ-yuan 斤 can be used interchangeably with 上 . "This, too, is doubtful" (Hsia Ch'êng-ch'ou).

184. Hsü Hao (徐灝), a scholar of the Ch'ing period. He wrote only one work, called Shêng-lü-k'ao (聲律考 , "Study of Vocal Sounds"); see Ts'ao Ch'ou-shêng, Chung-kuo-yin-yüeh, wu-tao . . ., (Peking, 1959), p. 137.

185. In the songs Yü-mei-ling (玉梅令), lit., "Jade-plum Verse," and Chüeh-chao (角招), lit., "Horn Call."

186. 唐蘭 , T'ang Lan, a music theorist born in 1796, is the author of P'àng-p'u-k'ao (旁譜考), a work which deals with the musical notations of Chiang K'uei.

187. E.g., in Sung-shih-yüeh-chih (宋史樂志).

188. In p'i-pa playing the raising of some notes can be effected by pulling the string; in certain instances by pulling the string across the adjoining string.

189. See p. 39.

190. See Part II. n. 188. Chê is usually not a rhythmic sign but indicates a microtonal alteration. See p. 39.

191. The "Kuang Book" is the Shih-lin-kuang-chi. See Part II, n. 178 (p. 456).

192. Therefore 尖一 is the same as 下一, and 下五 (in the "Kuang Book") is notated with 尖五.

193. Shih-lin-kuang-chi.

194. The character 住 (chu) actually denotes a pause; hence 大住 (ta-chu) means a long (big) pause and 小住 (hsiao chu) a short (small) pause.

T'ang Lan, in an epilogue to Hsia Ch'êng-ch'ou's article, remarks that the following additions may clarify Hsia's text:

Lü	Kung-ch'ê	Pê-shih-tao-jên-ko-ch'u	Shih-lin-kuang-chi		Tz'ǔ-yüan	
清黃	六	久 夊	㊊	六	幺	六
清大	下五		㋾	五	丂	下五
清太	五	夕	㋾	高五	㋐	五
清夾	一五	丂	㋾	尖五	㋾	高五

T'ang Lan summarizes thus: 六 should be 久, as notated by Chiang K'uei; 下五 should be ㋐; both the Tz'ǔ-yüan and the Shih-lin-kuang-chi are wrong; 五 should be 夕, as used by Chiang K'uei; and 一五 should be 丂. Here, too, both Tz'ǔ-yüan and Shih-lin-kuang-chi are incorrect.

195. Pê-shih-tao-jên-ko-ch'ü, IV, 2.

196. See Koh-Nie-Kuh, "A Musical Study of the Important Tonal Systems of the T'ang Dynasty."

197. Śrutis (from Sanskr., śru, "to hear") microtones or microtonal intervals. North and South Indian Music theorists of the past employed these twenty-two (on a few occasions, twenty-four) intervals within the octave in the determination of their various (basic) seven-scale degrees.

198. There are a few exceptions which will be discussed at the end of this part.

199. South Indian term for rāga.

200. Lit. "group maker"; parent-scales.

201. See pp. 203 f.

202. See, e.g., Pandit V.N. Bhatkhande, "A Short Historical Survey of the Music of Upper India," reprint of a speech delivered by Bhatkhande at the First All-India Music Conference, Baroda in 1916; (Bombay, 1934), pp. 16 f.

203. See Walter Kaufmann, "The Classification of Indian Ragas," in Asia and the Humanities, Indiana University: Comparative Literature Committee, 1959, pp. 131-45.

204. Six volumes in Hindi and Marathi (Bombay, 1934-1937).

205. The terms for octave are saptaka ("set of seven"), occasionally also sthāyī ("section"), or sthāna ("register," or "voice").

206. As previously mentioned, the same organization can be found in the notational system of Japanese shōmyō; to be discussed in Volume II.

207. For instance, P. Sambamoorthy, South Indian Music (Madras, 1935), I, 46.

208. Ancient Indian music theory distinguished three important notes in the scale of the rāga: the graha, the starting note; the amśa, the predominant; and the nyāsa, the "finalis," the terminal note. Neither the graha nor nyāsa are in practical use at the present time. The amśa, better known today as vādī, however, still plays an important role. The vādī (and the lesser important samvādī, "consonance," usually a fourth or a fifth apart from each other) is the "king" of the rāga. Musical phrases usually end on it (or on the SA). The position of the vādī is one of the indications of the time when the rāga is to be performed: if the vādī stands in the lower tetrachord of the scale, the rāga is mostly performed in the evening or at night; conversely, if the vādī stands in the upper tetrachord it is usually performed in the morning or during the early part of the day. Indian books on music always state first the tone material of the rāga together with the vādī and samvādī.

209. See W. Kaufmann, "The Forms of the Dhrupad and Khyal in Indian Art Music," The Canadian Music Journal, III, No. 2 (1959), p. 26.

210. Ibid.

211. South Indian Music, I, 33.

212. See Kaufmann, "The Forms of the Dhrupad and Khyal," p. 28.

213. Pandit V.N. Bhatkhande, Hindusthani Sangit Paddhati (Bombay, 1941), II, 223.

214. For further information see Kaufmann, "The Forms of the Dhrupad and Khyal," p. 30.

215. For further information see Kaufmann, "The Classification of Indian Rāgas."

216. As a matter of fact, Veṅkatamakhin lists only 55 rāgams and expresses the opinion that they could be classified under the headings of 19 melakartas, which he describes in detail.

217. Madras, 1938.

218. (Madras, 1953), III, 40.

219. ௮ is not a Tamil but a Malayalam letter derived from the Grantha sign ౨௮ (Sa).

220. See Kaufmann, "The Forms of the Dhrupad and Khyal."

221. Chatuṣruti, "four ṣrutis"

Shatṣruti, "six ṣrutis"

Sādhārana, "twilight"

Antara, "interval"

Prati-, "counter-"

Kaishiki, "hair's breath"

Kākali, "low"

222. See P.R. Bhandarkar, "The Kudimiyāmalai Inscription of Music," Epigraphia Indica, XII (1913-14), 226-37.

223. Occasionally the name khol is used, particularly if the corpus is made of clay.

224. The mixture may contain a number of substances such as iron or manganese dust, boiled rice, tamarind juice (if available), modern factory-made ink, and so forth.

225. Jhaptāl is another name for Jhampa Tāla.

226. See Kaufmann, "The Forms of the Dhrupad and Khyal."

227. Ibid.

228. We must add here the Pakhawaj (pakh, "wing", awaz, "sound"), a comparatively recent member of the mridanga family. It usually is smaller than the mridanga but has the same shape as the ancient drum.

229. Occasionally it is called dayan, "right."

230. The pronunciation of the drum words varies to some extent from one place to the other. We adopt the north Indian forms as used by Hindustani-speaking musicians.

a is pronounced as in the English word lark

e, as in tell

i, as in sing

u, as in root

Long vowels, indicating strokes of extended notes, are indicated by a horizontal line above the vowel, e. g., $\bar{a}$.

t is produced by placing the tip of the tongue between the teeth and roof of the mouth (ट)

n is a nasal sound as in the n in the French name Jean

i, e, u are pronounced with a slight tinge of n

As is customary in Urdu, vowels are not always clearly indicated; GE, GI, KE, KI, GA, KA, may denote the same stroke, and so forth.

231. See p. 261.

232. qaida, "rule," "regulation," "custom."

233. dohra, from dohrana, "to fold," "to double."

234. palta, from palna, "to nourish."

Part Three

1. The origin of Chinese music is ascribed to heavenly and legendary emperors, figures who represent extensive periods of Chinese history. The first of these sovereigns was Fu Hsi (about 2852 B.C.). He was succeeded by Nü-kua and Shen-nung. Ssŭ-ma Ch'ien, the famous Chinese historian (136-85),

ignores these early rulers, and lists as first Huang Ti, the "Yellow Emperor" (about 2697 B.C.).

Dr. R.H. van Gulik in his The Lore of the Chinese Lute (Tokyo, 1940), p. 9, presents an interesting theory for the determination of the age of the ch'in (and the sê) from a paleographic point of view, which deserves careful study by persons who wish to pursue the matter of the history of the ch'in.

2. See Part I, n. 3 (p. 422).

3. James Legge, trans., Sacred Books of China (Oxford, 1885), Vol. XXVIII.

4. Shih Ching, Part I, Book I, ode 1, stanza 3; James Legge, trans. Chinese Classics (London, 1871), IV, Part I. This famous ode originated during the Western Chou period (1122-770).

5. Ibid., Book VII, ode 8, stanza 2.

6. Ibid.

7. Ibid., Book X, ode 2, stanza 3.

8. Ibid., Book XI, ode 1, stanza 2.

9. Ibid., Part II, Book I, ode 1, stanza 3.

10. Ibid., ode 4, stanza 7.

11. The copy in possession of this writer is called Chieh shih tiao yu-lan-p'u (碣 石 調 幽 蘭 譜), the Chieh shih Melody Introduction to Elegant Orchids. Chieh Shih was a piece of music based on the text by Emperor Wu (Wei). The piece consisted of four sections: the first mentioned the emperor's travel eastward to Chieh Shih and the vastness of the ocean from which sun and moon rose and into which sun and moon set; the second mentioned how, after work in the fields was accomplished, the merchants became active; the third explained how the shape and climate of a region influence its inhabitants; the fourth was in praise of the brave man.

12. See Hayashi Kenzo in Tōyō ongaku kenkyu (東洋音樂研究, "Journal of Oriental Music Research") (Tokyo, 1954), II, chap. 4; and Kishibe Shigeo in Tōa ongaku shi kō (東亞音樂史考 , "Thoughts on Oriental Music") (Tokyo). Kishibe believes that the work originated as early as the sixth century.

13. Lee Hye-ku, in Han-kuk ŭm-ak yon-gu (Seoul, 1957), mentions a fourteenth-century work called (in Japanese) Kin-fu dai-jen (琴 譜 大全 , "Zither-book Complete Collection").

14. The work was reprinted in 1799 in Ku Hsiu's collection Tu-hua-chai-ts'ung-shu (讀畫齋叢書), and again, in another collection of texts, compiled by Sun Hsing-yen (孫星衍 , 1753-1808) called P'ing ts'in-kuan-ts'ung shu (平津館叢書). Further reprints appeared in Japan in the nineteenth century. Detailed information about this and subsequent works can be found in van Gulik, op. cit., pp. 167 ff.

15. A recent reprint appeared in the Tung-t'ing-shih-êrh-chung (楝亭十二種) (Shanghai, 1921).

16. A reprint of this popular work appeared in Japan in 1803, edited by Hayashi Jussai (林述齋 , 1768-1841).

17. The work was expanded in 1925.

18. Van Gulik, p. 170.

19. See p. 285, Figure 64, and Part III, n. 27 (p. 464).

20. For additional ch'in-p'u and for further information see van Gulik, op. cit.

21. Earth, metal, wood, fire, and water.

22. The Korean pronunciation of hui is hwi.

23. In the nineteenth century, ch'in-p'u authors endeavoured to simplify the reading of the ch'in tablature by adding to the chien-tzŭ the much less complex kung-ch'ê symbols. The two notations are placed side by side in parallel columns.

24. As already indicated before, we lean heavily upon van Gulik's The Lore of the Chinese Lute, pp. 120 ff., where a larger number of chien-tzŭ is shown.

25. See L. Laloy, La Musique chinoise (Paris, n. d.), p. 71; this concerns the second of the twenty-four articles called Ch'in-k'uang (琴況) by the ch'in master Hsü Hung (徐硤). The Chinese text was first published in the seventeenth century in the Ta-huan-ko-ch'in-p'u (大還閣 琴譜). See also van Gulik, pp. 105 ff, for a translation of the Ch'in-

shḗng-shih-liu-fa (琴聲十六法 , "Sixteen Rules for the Tones of the Ch'in") by Lḗng Hsien (冷仙), fourteenth to fifteenth century.

26. See p. 274.

27. In order to enable the reader to examine a larger part of this ch'in-p'u we present a copy containing strophes 1-14 (pp. 465-73).

28. Georges Soulié, La Musique en Chine (Paris, 1911), p. 36.

29. A detailed explanation of the notational symbols is given by Soulié, pp. 37-41.

30. See Chu Tsai-yü, Yüeh-lü-ch'üan-shu (reprinted Shanghai, 1934), II, 87. See also Maurice Courant, "Essai historique sur la musique classique des Chinois," in Encyclopédie de la musique, ed. Lavignac (Paris, 1913), I, 132; the Chinese text of the hymn can be found in the same work on p. 221 (A, k) and the transliteration and translation of the text on pp. 130-31.

31. Courant transcribes all lü a major third higher than we do.

32. A specific sḗ tablature will be described below.

33. See p. 269; "lutes large and small" indicates the larger sḗ and the smaller ch'in.

34. "Nearing the Standard" (爾雅), a scholarly work which may have been written as early as the twelfth or as late as the fourth century B.C., is a dictionary which deals with the correct use of a variety of terms.

35. See van Gulik, op. cit., p. 7.

36. J.A. van Aalst, Chinese Music (Shanghai, 1884), p. 64.

37. The work was reprinted by the Commercial Press, Shanghai, in 1936.

38. Arthur Waley, The Book of Songs (New York, 1960), p. 192, ode 183.

39. For instance, the tae-cheng (大箏), the "big chḗng," a zither with fifteen strings, derived from the Chinese chḗng and related to the Japanese yamato koto, wagon, (大和琴); the sŭl (瑟), a zither with twenty-five strings, derived from the Chinese sḗ (the Koreans call it the "big komunko"); the yang-kŭm (洋琴), a zither with fourteen wire strings, derived from the Chinese yang-ch'in; the kaya-kŭm, or kaya-ko, (伽倻琴), a zither with seven strings and without frets. It had the name hwi-kŭm (徽琴), the "hui-kŭm" in Korea.

(Refers to Note 27)

Ch'êng-i-t'ang ch'in-p'u

Ch'êng-i-t'ang chin-p'u (cont.)

[Chinese guqin tablature notation — qin jianzi pu characters]

三 段

[Chinese guqin tablature notation — qin jianzi pu characters]

Ch'êng-i-t'ang chin-p'u (cont.)

Ch'êng-i-t'ang ch'in-p'u (cont.)

五 段

六 段

Ch'êng-i-t'ang ch'in-p'u (cont.)

七段

Ch'eng-i-t'ang ch'in-p'u (cont.)

Ch'ēng-i-t'ang ch'in-p'u (cont.)

九段

十段

Ch'êng-i-t'ang ch'in-p'u (cont.)

Ch'êng-i-t'ang ch'in-p'u (cont.)

40. See A. Eckardt, Koreanische Musik (Tokyo, 1930), p. 43.

41. Although the polysyllabic, agglutinative Korean and Japanese languages differ considerably from the monosyllabic Chinese, Chinese ideography has been, and still is, used in the works of the learned Koreans and Japanese, despite the fact that both Korean and Japan have evolved their own indigenous systems of writing.

The older script used in Korea, consisting of Chinese characters, is called han-mun, while the already mentioned "new," indigenous Korean alphabet called han-gŭl, invented by King Sae-cho (A.D. 1443) and his scholars, is far more flexible in representing the Korean language.

At the present time both han-mun and han-gŭl are combined into a modern form, called kuk-han-mun (National Korean and Chinese letters). Persons who wish to emphasize their scholarly prestige still employ the cumbersome han-mun, following a practice which dates back to the introduction of Buddhism in Silla in A.D. 528. The knowledge of Chinese was, and still is, the mark of erudition and sophistication of scholars, poets, and nobility in Korea and Japan.

Even though Chinese characters, pronounced differently in the three countries, retain their common general meaning, subtle differences occasionally appear so that the same character which denotes one particular thing in China means a different, though related one, in Korea, and another, again somewhat different, in Japan. The character 琴 , which denotes "zither," is pronounced ch'in in China, kŭm in Korea, and koto in Japan, and does not imply the very same thing: the zithers ch'in, kŭm, and koto differ in various structural details, especially in the number of strings and the use, type, and number of frets.

42. Lee, op. cit.

43. Kokuryo period, 37 B.C. - A.D. 668. Kokuryo was one of the "Three Kingdoms" of ancient Korea.

44. According to the Japanese Tōyō rekishi dai jiten (東洋歷史 大辞典), "Great Dictionary of Oriental History" (Tokyo), there exist three ancient copies of the work, which can be found in: Tōkyō teidai hong (東京帝大本) Tokyo University; Cho-sen ko-sho kang-kō-kai hong

(朝鮮古書刊行會本), The Korean Old Books Publishing Company, Japan; Cho-sen shi-gak-kai hong (朝鮮史學會本), Academy of Korean Historical Books, Japan. See also Samkuk saki, (reprinted Seoul, 1956) with translation and commentary by Yi Pyongdo (李丙燾).

45. The "Three Kingdoms," Silla, Paekche, and Kokuryo, were formed during the first century B.C.

46. These titles represent the earliest known melodies of Korea; among them is the famous Man-tae-yŭp (慢大葉), which will be shown on pp. 327-34.

47. This book was revised under Emperor Genshō Tennō in A.D. 718 when it was called Yo-rō-rei (養老令); the same work underwent further revision in 833 by the imperial musicians Sugaware Seiko, Ono Takamura, and others, when it was called Ryō-no-gi-ge (令義解); it was republished during the Edo period (1600-1868) and again in the Meiji period (1868-1910). This work, which contains some information about gagaku (imperial court music of Japan), is allegedly preserved in the Imperial Library of Tokyo.

48. See p. 45.

49. Period of King Sae-chong (世宗). A.D. 1429-1450.

50. The exact date of this work is unknown. We can assume that it was written between the late fifteenth and early sixteenth centuries. The author discusses details of tuning and fingering the hyŭn-kŭm in chaps. 8, 10, 17, 19, 23, 24, 31, 34, 37, 43, 55, and 57. See also Lee, op. cit., p. 13.

51. See p. 52.

52. See pp. 25 f.

53. As usual, we transcribe 黃 as the note C.

54. See also Part II, n. 138 (p. 453).

55. See p. 269.

56. See p. 272.

57. The original of the An-sang kŭm-po is preserved by Sŭng Kyŭng-lin (成慶麟), Director of the National Music Institute (國立國樂院) at Seoul. The manuscript was publicly displayed in 1946 at the Seoul Memorial Exhibition.

58. The manuscript is preserved by Mr. Rhee Kyŭm Ro of the Tong Mun K'uan Publishing Co. at Seoul, who published the work in 1959.

59. See Part II, n. 78 (p. 448).

60. The word cho (朝) must not be confused with cho (調), "mode," "scale."

61. See pp. 152 ff.

62. See p. 276.

63. The name of the string is yu hyŭn (遊絃); the middle sign, yu (方) became pang (an abbreviation of yu).

64. There are several terms which denote string V:

Kwa woe chŭng (棵外清), "frets outside clear";

Ki woe chŭng (岐外清), "precipitous outside clear";

Kwa ha chŭng (棵下清), "frets below clear."

65. There are two ways of writing Pyong-(cho): 平 or 平 (調).

66. See p. 58.

67. In Japanese shakuhachi notation the same symbol is employed: ka (kata kana letter); as a word: chikara, -riki, "strength." It prescribes a similar sharpening as in Korean hyŭn-kŭm tablature and has the same significance as the Korean yok.

68. ㅈ actually is a consonant of the Korean alphabet; if read in conjunction with other letters it represents the letter dz; if pronounced separately it is dz'iŭt.

69. See p. 305.

70. This, as we shall see later on, is not always true; the old instruments had a large gap between "fret one" (the open string) and fret two. The open string would sound a fourth lower than the note produced by fret two. It seems that tuning was never done by checking the pitch of the open strings II and III but by stopping certain frets and observing whether these notes were in correct relationship. The open strings (of the old instrument) were tuned, as we stated before, by movable bridges.

71. This structure applies, of course, only to scales in use since the Chinese Ming period (1368-1644). The Yang-kŭm shin-po, a seventeenth-century work, would definitely have been influenced by the Ming scale.

72. See p. 343.

73. See Figure 72 on p. 318.

74. See p. 127.

75. See Part II, n. 140 (p. 454). Man-tae-yŭp has been notated in the Sae-cho shillok and in several zither books, such as the An-sang kŭm-po, the Tae-ak hu-po, and in other works.

76. Ak-shi-cho can also be read Nak-shi-cho (Nak, "pleasure").

77. See pp. 152 ff.

78. Transcribed by Dr. Lee Hye-ku in the introductory part (after p. 16) of the new edition of the Yang-kŭm shin-po (Seoul, 1959). Two other transcriptions of Man-tae-yŭp can be found in Lee Hye-ku, Han-kuk ŭm-ak yon-gu (after p. 47).

79. For further transcriptions of Man-tae-yŭp see Maurice Courant, "Chine et Corée," in Encyclopédie de la Musique, ed. A. Lavignac, (Paris, 1913), I, 215, and in Eckardt, Koreanische Musik, p. 59.

80. See p. 145.

81. See p. 305.

82. See p. 124.

83. See p. 127

84. Originated in 1680; see Lee, Han-kuk ŭm-ak yon-gu, p. 128.

85. Ibid.

86. Edited by the Ministry of Education, Republic of Korea (Seoul, 1959), Vol. II.

87. See Part III, n. .39 (p. 464).

88. The hae-kŭm (or kae-kŭm) is a fiddle with two strings tuned to the same pitch. It is of Mongolian origin and appeared first in Korea during the Silla period (57-935). It is related to the Chinese hu-ch'in and the Japanese kokin and kokyū.

Part Four

1. L. A. Waddell, The Buddhism of Tibet (Lāmaism) (Cambridge, 1939), p. 432.

2. Recorded and transcribed by the author.

3. Rag ("brass"), dung ("tube").

4. Compare this with a strikingly similar example in Peter Crossley-Holland's article "Tibetan Music" in Grove's Dictionary of Music and Musicians, 5th ed. (New York, 1959), VIII, 457.

5. See page 402.

6. Tibetan notation, "a highly decorative system of neumes was most likely introduced at Sakya (perhaps from India) about the twelfth century" (Peter Crossley-Holland in "Tibetan Music," The Pelican History of Music, [London, 1960], I, 72).

7. W. F. Adeney, The Greek and Eastern Churches (New York, 1939), p. 534.

8. See E. Wellesz, "Die Lektionszeichen in den soghdischen Texten," ZfMW, I, (1919), 505 ff.

9. F. W. K. Müller, Die soghdischen Texte, (Berlin, 1913).

10. Manichaeism is a Persian (Zoroastrian) gnosis characterized by the dualism of the kingdoms of light and darkness. It is a mixture of Persian, Hebrew, and Buddhist elements together with some dogmas of the Christian creed. Manichaeism flourished in Asia Minor and Europe during the fourth and fifth centuries, and in Asia for many more centuries. It was opposed by the Roman Church; Manichaeans were persecuted under Diocletian and were considered to be capital offenders under Justinian. (See The Encyclopedia Americana, Canadian edition, 1944, vol. XVIII.)

11. ZfMW, I, (1919), 514. For further details see E. Wellesz, "Syrian Ecphonetic Notation," in The New Oxford History of Music (London, 1955), II, 10-13.

12. See Waddell, p. 422, n. 1.

13. See A. Gastoué, "Les Notations musicales byzantines et orientales,"

Encyclopédie de la musique, ed. A. Lavignac (Paris, 1913), I, 553 ff. See also Henry M. Bannister, Monumenti Vaticani (Leipzig, 1908), Vol. XII; and Willi Apel, Harvard Dictionary of Music (Cambridge, 1955), p. 487.

14. The person who directs the ceremonies and the chant in the temple is called the wu-dze-pa (W. W. Rockhill, The Land of the Lamas [New York, 1891], pp. 88-89).

15. For further details see Waddell, p. 51.

16. Spoken Tibetan sounds quite differently: many of the written consonants are not pronounced nor do they modify the sound of the syllables in which they appear.

17. A mandala is a "magic circle" containing spells and charmed sentences, which cause the gods to assist the devotee in attaining his aim. Mandala, as referred to in our text, denotes the Magic Circle Offering of the Universe. Lamas offer to the Buddhas the whole universe and express it in form of a large circle which represents the Great Continents, the Satellite Continents, the Four Wordly Treasures, the Seven Precious Things, the Eight Matri Goddesses, and the Sun and the Moon.

18. In Lamaist ritual the hand bell (DRIL BU), and the sceptre, the dor-je (RDO RJE), "thunderbolt," are always used together, one being the counterpart of the other. The dor-je corresponds to the Thunderbolt of Indra. Both bell and dor-je must have equal lengths.

19. Mantra, a short prayer, used for casting a spell, "the reciting of which should be accompanied by music and certain distortion of the fingers (mudrā), a state of mental fixity (samādhi) might be reached characterized by neither thought nor annihilation of thoughts, and consisting of sixfold bodily and mental happiness (Yogi), whence would result endowment with supernatural miracle-working power." (Yogicarya-bhūmi Sāstra; quoted by Waddell, op. cit., pp. 141 ff.)

20. The PI WAM MA or PI WANG RGYUD MANG is a lute similar to the Chinese p'i-pa. It has four or more strings. The pi-wang rgyud-gsum (another Tibetan lute) has only three strings. RGYUD MANG(S) means "many strings," hence it can also mean "harp," or "zither."

21. GLIN BU is a vertical flute made of bamboo or other wood. It can appear as a single, double, or triple flute. The instrument has 6-7 finger holes. RDZA RNGA (dza-rnga) means "kettle drum."

22. Compare BCAD with the kiru formula of Japanese shōmyō, which will be discussed in Volume II.

23. Waddell, p. 432.

24. According to the Lama Geshe Nornang.

25. Occasionally green is used also.

26. It may be of interest to extend our comparison to Hebrew ta'amin (accents). We quote the following table from the article on "Jewish Music" in Grove's Dictionary of Music and Musicians, 5th ed. (New York, 1959), IV, 625:

Hebrew Accent	Name	Function	Corresponding Byzantine	Corresponding Latin
	Zarqa	Weak Disjunctive		Podatus
	Munach	Conjunctive		Gravis
	Gershayim	Weak Disjunctive		Strophicus
	Darga	Conjunctive		Oriscus
	Atnach	Strong Disjunctive		Clivis
	Mahpah	Conjunctive		Acutus
	Shalshelet	Weak Disjunctive		Quilisma
	Zaqef qatan	Strong Disjunctive		Climacus
	Segolta	Strong Disjunctive		Triangula
	Tipcha	Weak Disjunctive		Gravis
	Sof pasuq	End of Sentence		Punctum

27. Page 433.

28. A valuable article that came to my attention after having completed this manuscript was W. Graf's "Zur Ausfuehrung der lamaistischen Gesangsnotation," in Studia Musicologica, III fasc. (1962), 1-4.

29. Laurence Picken, New Oxford History of Music (1957), I, 142, assumes that Tibetan notation "may have been brought to China with Mahāyanā Buddhism and borrowed by the Taoists . . . ." He also states that some Taoist

hymns "making use of a notation unlike any other Chinese notation are printed in the Ming Dawtzang [Ming Tao-tsang], 明 道 藏 . . . ." An investigation into these notational symbols may be of great importance.

30. C. P. Fitzgerald, China (London, 1954), pp. 277 ff.

31. See p. 59.

32. In the year 517 the first Tripitaka in Chinese was written by the order of Liang Wu Ti. The second edition, sponsored by Hsiao Wu of the state of Wei, appeared as early as 533.

33. The only contemporary work (no date) which appeared in China and deals with Buddhist songs is: 寺院音樂 ; in Japanese: Ji in ongaku, "Buddhist sacred music." The notation of the melodies utilizes Western (Arabic) numbers, a habit which prevails at the present time in East Asia.

34. Kung-ch'ê-p'u, su-tzǔ-p'u, etc.

35. To be discussed in Volume II.

36. Recording from the monastery Hsüä-gu-si (made by Marie du Bois-Reymond), transcribed by Kurt Reinhard, Chinesische Musik (Kassel, 1956), p. 187.

37. The mu yü, "wooden fish," is a type of wooden slit-drum, shaped like a human skull. It is struck by Buddhist and Taoist priests to beat the time in chanting of prayers and symbolizes "wakeful attention." See Grove's Dictionary of Music and Musicians, 5th ed., II, 233.

BIBLIOGRAPHY

Aalst, J. A. van. Chinese Music. Shanghai, 1884 (1933, 1939).

Abert, H. "Die Stellung der Musik in der antiken Kultur." Die Antike, II (1926), 136-54.

Adeney, W. F. The Greek and Eastern Churches. New York, 1939.

Ak-hak-koe-pŭm. Seoul, 1933.

Albert, H. Die Lehre vom Ethos in der griechischen Musik. Leipzig, 1899.

Amiot, Joseph. Mémoires sur la musique des Chinois tant anciens que modernes. Paris, 1779.

Apel, Willi. Harvard Dictionary of Music. Cambridge, Mass., 1955.

Bake, Arnold. "Indische Musik." Die Musik in Geschichte und Gegenwart, VI, 1150-86. Kassel, 1949——.

——————. "The Music of India." The New Oxford History of Music, Vol. I. London, 1957.

Bandopadhyaya, Shripada. The Music of India. Bombay, 1945.

Bannister, H. M. Monumenti Vaticani di paleografia musicale latina (Tavole). Leipzig, 1913.

Barve, Manohar, G. Manohar Sangitawali (in Hindi). Bombay, 1944.

Bhandarkar, P. R. "The Kudimiyamalai Inscription on Music." Epigraphia Indica, XII (1913-1914), 226-37.

Bharata. Nātyaśāstra (in Sanskrit). Benares: Vidya Vilas Press, 1929.

Bhatkhande, Pandit V. N. Hindusthani Sangit Paddhati. 6 vols. Bombay, 1939 (1941).

"Bukkyo ongaku no kenkyū," in Tōyō ongaku kenkyu. Vols. XII, XIII. Tokyo, 1954.

Chavannes, E. Les Mémoires historiques de Se-ma Ts'ien. 5 vols. Paris, 1895-1905.

Ch'ên Shou-yi. Chinese Literature. New York, 1961.

Childers, R. C. "Khuddaka Patha." Journal of the Royal Asiatic Society (1869).

Chu Tsai-yü. Yüeh-lü ch'üan-shu. Shanghai, 1934 (reprint).

Courant, Maurice. "Chine et Corée." Encyclopédie de la musique, ed. Albert Lavignac, I, 77-241. Paris, 1913.

Crossley-Holland, Peter. "Music of Tibet." The Pelican History of Music, I, 70-75. London, 1960.

_____. "Tibetan Music." Grove's Dictionary of Music and Musicians, 5th ed., VIII, 456-64. New York, 1959.

Daniélou, A. Introduction to the Study of Musical Scales. London, 1943.

Day, C. R. The Music and Musical Instruments of Southern India and the Deccan. London, 1891.

De Körös, C. "Analysis of the Kah-gyur," etc. Asiatic Researches (Calcutta), XX (1820), 41ff.

Deodhar, V. R. Rag Bodh. Bombay, 1944.

Deval, K. B. The Hindu Musical Scale. Poona, 1910.

Durant, W. The Story of Civilization: Our Oriental Heritage. New York, 1954.

Eckardt, A. Koreanische Musik. Tokyo, 1930.

Ellis, A. J. "Ueber die Tonleitern verschiedener Voelker." Sammelbaende fuer vergleichende Musikwissenschaft (Munich), I (1922), 1-75.

Faber, E. "The Chinese Theory of Music." China Review, Vols. I-II (1873).

Fitzgerald, G. P. China. London, 1954.

Fox-Strangways, A. H. The Music of Hindostan. Oxford, 1914.

Giles, H. A. A History of Chinese Literature. New York, 1923.

Gosvami, O. The Story of Indian Music. Bombay, 1961.

Graf, W. "Zur Ausfuehrung der lamaistischen Gesangsnotation." Studia Musicologica, Vol. III, fasc. 1-4 (1962).

Grove's Dictionary of Music and Musicians. 5th ed., 9 vols. New York, 1959.

Gulik, R. H. van. The Lore of the Chinese Lute. Tokyo, 1940.

Ham Wha-jin. Cho-sŭn ŭm-ak tong-ron ("Introduction to Korean Music"). Seoul, 1948.

Hayashi Kenzo. Tōyō ongaku kenkyū ("Oriental Music Research"). Tokyo, 1954.

Hazard, B. N., J. Hoyt, H. T. Kim, and W. W. Smith, Jr. Korean Studies Guide, ed. R. Marcus. Berkeley and Los Angeles, 1954.

Höeg, C. La Notation ekphonétique. Copenhagen, 1935.

Holzman, D. "Shên Kua and his Meng-ch'i-pi-t'an." T'oung Pao, XLVI (1958), 260-92.

Hsia Ch'eng-ch'ou. "A Study of the Musical Notations of Chiang K'uei's Songs" (in Chinese). Yenching Journal of Chinese Studies (Peiping), December, 1932, pp. 2559-88.

Humphreys, C. Buddhism. Harmonsworth, 1954.

Kaufmann, Walter. "The Classification of Indian Ragas." Asia and the Humanities. Bloomington, Ind.: Comparative Literature Committee, 1959.

Kaufmann, Walter. "The Folk Songs of Nepal." Ethnomusicology, VI, No. 2
    (1962), 93-114.
_____. "The Forms of the Dhrupad and Khyal in Indian Art Music." The
    Canadian Music Journal, III, No. 2 (1959), 25-35.
Keh Ch. S. Die Koreanische Musik. Strassburg, 1935.
Kishibe Shigeo. Tōa ongaku shi kō. Tokyo.
Koh-Nie-Kuh. "A Musicological Study of the Important Tonal Systems of the
    T'ang Dynasty." Diss., School of Education, New York University, 1942.
Korea, Her History and Culture. Seoul: Office of Public Information, 1954.
Kunst, Jaap. "Indonesische Musik." Die Musik in Geschichte und Gegenwart,
    VI, 1185ff.

Laloy, L. La Musique chinoise. Paris, n. d.
Lee Hye-ku. Han-kuk ko-chŭn ak-ki hae-sŭl ("Introduction to the Musical In-
    struments of Korea"). Seoul, 1959.
_____. Han-kuk ŭm-ak yon-gu ("Research in Korean Music"). Seoul,
    1957.
Legge, James, trans. The Chinese Classics (Li Ki, Oxford, 1885; Shi King,
    London, 1871; Shu King, Hongkong, 1865; Yi King, Oxford, 1882).
Levis, John Hazedel. Foundations of Chinese Musical Art. Peiping, 1936.
Liu Ch'eng-fu. Yin-yüeh-tz'u-tien (music dictionary). Shanghai, 1936.

McPhee, C. "The Balinese Wayang Koelit and its Music." Djawa, XVI
    (1936), 1 ff.
Mahillon, V. Ch. Annuaire du Conservatoire de Bruxelles. Ghent, 1886, 1890.
Malm, W. P. Japanese Music. Rutland and Tokyo, 1959.
Mathews, R. H. Chinese-English Dictionary. Cambridge, Mass., 1956.
Min-sok ak-po ("Folk Music"). 2 vols. Department of Education, Seoul, 1959.
Müller, F. W. K. Die soghdischen Texte. Berlin, 1913.

Nanamoli (Bhikku). Khuddakapāta, the Minor Readings (Book I). London: Pali
    Text Society, 1961.
New Oxford History of Music, ed. Egon Wellesz. Vol. I. London, 1957.

Ongaku Jiten, ed. Shimonaka Yasaburo. 12 vols. Tokyo, 1955-1957.
Osgood, C. The Koreans and their Culture. New York, 1951.

Paléographie musicale. 17 vols. Solesmes, 1889-1925.
Picken, Laurence. "The Music of China." The New Oxford History of Music,
    I, 83-134. London, 1957.
Plutarchi De Musica, ed. Ricardus Volkmann. Leipzig, 1856.
Popley, H. A. The Music of India. London, 1921.

Ranade, G. H. Hindusthani Music. Sangli, 1939.

Ratanjankar, S. N. Tansangraha (in Hindi). Bombay, 1936.

Reinhard, Kurt. Chinesische Musik. Kassel, 1956.

Robinson, K. and A. Eckardt. "Chinesische Musik." Die Musik in Geschichte und Gegenwart, II, 1195-1216.

Rockhill, W. W. The Land of the Lamas. London, 1891.

Sachs, Curt. The Rise of Music in the Ancient World. New York, 1943.

Sacred Books of the Buddhists, trans. by various oriental scholars. 21 vols. London, 1895-1962.

Sacred Books of the East, ed. Max Müller. 50 vols. London: Oxford University Press, 1897-1927.

Sam-kuk sa-ki, trans. with commentary by Yi Pyongbo. Seoul, 1956.

Sārṅgadeva. Saṅgītaratnākara (in Sanskrit), commentaries and translation by C. Kunhan Raja. Madras, 1945.

Sāstri, Pandit S. S. The Samgraha-Cuda-Mani of Govinda. Madras, 1938.

Schlager, E. "Bali." Die Musik in Geschichte und Gegenwart, I, 1109-15.

Schlagintweit, E. Buddhism in Tibet. London, 1868.

Shirali, V. Hindu Music and Rhythm. Totnes, 1936.

Somanātha. Rāgavibodha, ed. with trans. by M. S. Ramaswami Aiyar. Madras, 1923.

Somervell, T. H. "The Music of Tibet." Musical Times, LXIV, No. 960 (1923), 107-8.

Song Kyong-yin. Cho-sun ui-ah-ak ("Ah-ak of Korea"). Seoul, 1947.

Soothill, W. E. The Analects of the Conversations of Confucius. . . . London, 1937.

Soulié, Georges. La Musique en Chine. Paris, 1911.

Sources of Chinese Tradition, ed. Wm. de Bary. New York, 1960.

Sources of Indian Tradition, ed. Wm. de Bary. New York, 1960.

Sources of Japanese Tradition, ed. Wm. de Bary. New York, 1958.

Teng Ssu-yü. Conversational Chinese. Chicago, 1947.

Tillyard, H. J. W. Handbook of the Middle Byzantine Musical Notation, Vol. I of Monumenta Musicae Byzantinae-Subsidia. Copenhagen, 1935.

Tōyō-rekishi-dai-jiten ("Dictionary of Oriental History"). Tokyo, 1937.

Ts'ao, Ch'ou-sheng. Chung-kuo yin-yüeh wu-tao. . . . ("Dictionary of Chinese Music, Dances," etc.). Peking, 1959.

Vaze, R. N. Sangit Kalaprakash (in Hindi). n. d.

Vetter, W. "Die antike Musik in der Beleuchtung durch Aristoteles." Archiv fuer Musikwissenschaft, I (1936), 2-41.

Vyas, S. G. Sangit Vyaskrit (in Hindi). n. d.

Waddell, L. A. Buddhism of Tibet (Lāmaism). Cambridge, 1939.

Waley, A. The Book of Songs. New York, 1960.

Wang Kuang-ch'i. Chung-kuo-yin-yüeh-shih ("History of Chinese Music").
Taipei, 1956.

_____. "Ueber die chinesischen Notenhandschriften." Sinica, III (1928),
110-23.

Watson, Burton. Records of the Grand Historian of China. 2 vols. New York,
1961.

Wellesz, Egon. "Die byzantinischen Lektionszeichen." Zeitschrift fuer Musikwissenschaft, XI (1929), 513-34.

_____. A History of Byzantine Music and Hymnography. Oxford, 1949.

_____. "Die Lektionszeichen in den soghdischen Texten." Zeitschrift
fuer Musikwissenschaft, I (1919), 505-15.

_____. "Das Problem der byzantischen Notationen und ihrer Entzifferung,"
extract from Byzantion (Brussels), Vol. V, fasc. 2 (1929-1930).

Wilhelm, Richard. Fruehling und Herbst des Lü Bu We. Jena, 1928.

_____. Li Gi. Jena, 1930.

Wylie, A. Notes of Chinese Literature. Shanghai, 1867.

Xia Ye. "Zur Entwicklung der chinesischen Opernstile." Beitraege zur Musikwissenschaft, Vol. III. Berlin, 1961.

Yang, Tuk-soo. Yang-kŭm shin-po ("Yang's Zither Book"). Seoul, 1959 (reprint).

INDEX

Paek-sŭk-to-yin-ka-kok-po (Korean
    pronunciation of Pê-shih-tao-jên-
    ko-ch'u): 130
Pak, 147, 148
Palta, 249
Pañcama (panchama; PA): 186
Pang (hyŭn): 308
Pang-hyang, 146
P'ang-p'u-k'ao, 178n186
Panjabi (tāla): 258
Pan-ku, 9
Pan-lü, 26
Pan-mok-pu-ho, 127n87
Pang-tzŭ, 78
Parand, 224
Pei-, 26
Pei-lü, 26
Pelaston, 412
Pemiongchi monastery, 364
Pes, 109, 412
Pes flexus, 411
Pê-shih-tao-jên-ko-ch'u, 177, 179
Peshkar, 260
Petaste, 412
Picken, Laurence, 19n21, 43, 43n47,
    44n48, 102n47, 414n29
Pien-, 59, 60, 61, 62
Pien-ch'ing, 32
P'il-lyul notation, 153
P'ing, 108
P'ing-tsê: 9, 106-9; and kung-ch'ê-
    p'u, 110-17
P'i-pa: 146; Tibetan name and form
    of, 398-402 passim
P'iri notation, 160-62, 163, 164, 165
Plato, 2
Pluta, 195
Plutarch, 2
Podatus, 109, 412, 413
Po-fu: 26; beats, 31n31
Po-hŭ-cha: 130, 131-43, 305; differ-
    ent versions of, 142n105
Pon-ryŭng, 145

Prati, 201
Pu-hsü-t'ang-ch'in-p'u, 274
Puk-chŭn-yŭp, 306
Pŭm, 121, 127
Punctum, 109, 412
Pyong-cho. See Korean modes
Pyong-cho-kae-myon-cho. See Ko-
    rean modes
Pythagorean comma, 19
Pyŭk-sa-ch'ang, 172, 173, 174
Pyŭn (Chinese: pien): 127

Qaida, 249
Quadrivium, 3
Quilisma, 363

Rāga, 3, 183, 184
Rag-dung, 356
Rankei, 50
Reinhard, K., 19, 92, 93, 94, 102n47,
    415n36
Rezza, Mohammed, 185
Rhythm: Chinese notation of, 32-35,
    85-105 passim; Korean, 127-51
    passim, 326-50 passim; Indian,
    188-200; India (drumming), 248-63
Rhythmic modes, Indian: northern,
    188-93; southern, 193-94
Rig Veda, 187
Rishi chakra. See Chakra
Ritsu mode, 58, 63
Ritual music. See Ceremonial music
Rnga, 408
Rockhill, W. W., 363n14
Rsabha (Rishabha; RI): 186
Rudra chakra. See Chakra
Rūpaka (tāla): 193, 258
Rutu chakra. See Chakra
Ryo mode, 58, 63

Sa, 121
Sachs, C., 14, 17
Sadja (Shadja; SA): 186